Why Access? Why

A database is an incredibly powerful tool. Using one in a business or home environment makes your computer do all the hard work. It can store information and find it again quickly. It can do calculations and produce stylish reports to analyze and pass on that information. However, many people find databases intimidating because on first glance the environment isn't familiar and the terms seem confusing.

This is where The Beginner's Guide to Access 2.0 can help. It has been designed specifically to enable new-comers to both databases and Access to get results. It explains what databases are and how you can use them effectively. It then takes you through each of the stages in Access on a step-by-step basis.

Relax and let this book do the work. The troubleshooting sections will point out potential problems before they occur. The text and page design give you all the information you need, fast, and without unnecessary jargon. The book is a truly visual guide, with each stage fully illustrated to show you exactly what is happening on screen.

Make your information start working for you. This book makes it easy!

What is Wrox Press?

Wrox Press is a computer book publishing company which promotes a brand new concept: clear, non-jargon programming and database tutorials. We publish for the novice through to the Master Class level, keeping communication as the central focus throughout all stages of our book's development. We research the scope of all our titles to make sure they fit the real demands of our readers. From this we carry out continuous improvements on them.

We welcome suggestions and take all of them to heart - your input is paramount in creating the next great Wrox title. Use the reply card inside this book or mail us at:

feedback@wrox.demon.co.uk
or
Compuserve 100063, 2152

Wrox Press Ltd.
2710 W. Touhy
Chicago
IL 60645
USA

Tel: 0101 312 465 3559
Fax: 0101 312 465 4063

The Beginner's Guide to Access 2.0

Wrox Development

Wrox Press Ltd.

The Beginner's Guide to Access 2.0

Published by Wrox Press Ltd. 1334 Warwick Road, Birmingham, B27 6PR UK

ISBN 1-874416-21-4

About Wrox Development

Wrox is an amalgam of industry experts, engineers and communicators. We aim to distill computing knowledge through the unique technical and educational filter established here at Wrox Development.

Wrox Development will continue to issue innovative titles on programming and databases throughout the year.

Trademark Acknowledgements

Credits

Contributing Editor
Gordon Rogers

Managing Editor
John Franklin

Additional Material By
Julian Dobson
Darren Gill

Style Editor
Nina Barnsley

Copy Editors
Wendy Entwistle
Luke Dempsey
Rachel Maclean

Production Manager
Gina Mance

Book Layout
Ewart Liburd
Eddie Fisher
Kenneth Fung
Robert Harrison

Proof Readers
Pam Brand
Sue Thomas

Beta tested By
Mark Holmes

Cover Design
Third Wave

For more information on Third Wave contact Ross Alderson on 44 - 21 456 1400

Thanks to all the Access users whose feedback enabled us to understand how we could help you succeed.

CONTENTS

Summary of Contents

CONTENTS

Contents

Introduction

Introducing Access 2.0

Access 2.0 was introduced onto the market in Spring 1994, to build on the 1,000,000+ sales of the original application. It's a significant upgrade from version 1.1 and places Access at the heart of PC database development. Access 2.0 comes heavily armed with many new features to make it seamless in terms of package integration.

At the core of Access 2.0 is the JET Database Engine, so Access 1.1 users and developers will see a dramatic improvement in performance. Whether you are using this database as a component of Microsoft Office, or as a stand-alone facility, this book will help you put Access to productive work as quickly as possible.

In this section we will cover:

- Installing Access 2.0
- Converting from Access 1.X
- Help and Cue Cards
- Access and Windows
- Mail and Mail Merge
- Overview of Tools and Facilities

Installing Access 2.0

Basic Equipment

When installing Access 2.0 as a single user, make sure you have already installed Windows 3.1/Windows for Workgroups 3.11 (or better) on your computer. You will need a machine that has:

- An 80386/20Mhz microprocessor as minimum (80486 recommended)
- 6 Megabytes of RAM (although we recommend 8MB or more)
- A mouse/pointing device
- A VGA standard display unit (or better)
- MS-DOS version 3.1 (although we recommend version 6.0 or later)
- High-density floppy disk drive (1.44MB 3.5" or 1.2MB 5.25")
- Hard disk with 20MB free (for a typical installation)

Setup for a Single User

Firstly, check that you have the full complement of, normally, eight 3.5" Access disks. Make sure you have no other applications running on your computer before installation begins. Then:

- Ensure Windows is running.
- Place disk No.1 (Installation) in your floppy drive.
- In Windows, switch to or select the **Program Manager** screen.
- Choose File and select Run... from the menu bar.
- In the Command Line of the Run window that then appears, type:

```
a:\ setup
```

If your floppy drive has another descriptive letter substitute that for a: and press *Enter*.

The Setup program will progress automatically and will soon ask you for your name and company name. You will be given the choice of which directory Access should reside in - the installation defaults to a directory called c:\access.

You will then be asked which kind of installation you require: Typical, Laptop or Custom.

- Typical installation is a full installation. It includes Program, Help, Cue Cards, Database Drivers, Microsoft Graph and Sample Databases.
- Laptop load for portables installs just the Access program files (5MB).
- Custom allows you to make individual selections of Help, Cue Cards and so on.

Once a typical installation is complete, your Windows Program Manager Desktop will display the following new Program Group screen.

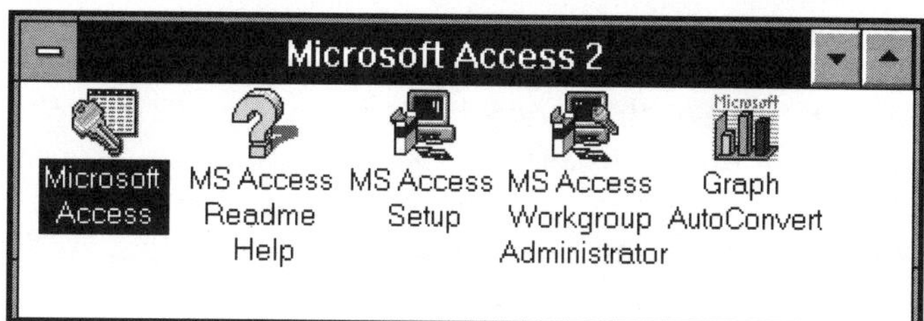

Simply, use a mouse to double-click on the  icon to start Access 2.0.

When Access has started, you will be presented with the normal opening screen:

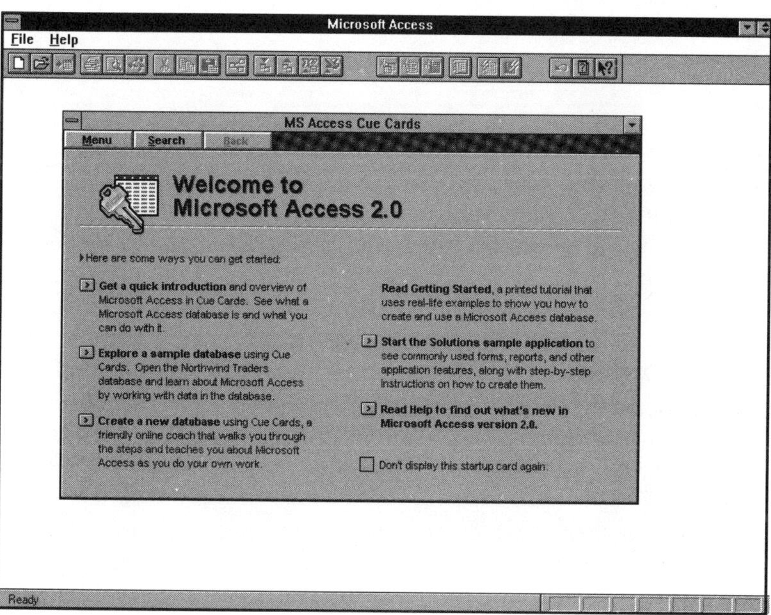

If you are familiar with Access, simply carry on and start building your tables!

Setup for a Network Installation

Access 2.0 comes ready to install on a network as long as the following conditions are met:

- Network server software is present, typically LAN Manager, Novell™ Netware, Windows for Workgoups, Windows NT or Lantastic
- Server has at least 11MB free space
- Microsoft Access License to cover each user

When you are in the directory where the Access 2.0 setup files have been installed Run... the setup.exe from that directory on the network or with a suitable path from your connection. Network Administrators can read the special nework installation information in ACREADME.HLP on Setup disk1 of Access.

SQL servers may require special setups to use their SQL Server system catalog. Your network administrator should decompress the file INSTCATSQ_ on setup disk1 to install on your SQL Server.

You can optimize Access 2.0 on networks by adding a system table called MSysConf. This can hold network traffic controls. You must have already installed ODBC support. See Help files for MSysConf.

Workgroups

When you share data in a multi-user system, you in fact share a workgroup database. This is within the file SYSTEM1X.MDA and holds all the security and setup conditions. If you have been working in workgroups, then you know that your administrator has set up various workgroups for the environment, and that you must have permission to be a user within a group.

If you replace your previous operating files totally with Access 2.0, then your old SYSTEM.MDA will be saved automatically as SYSTEM1X.MDA. By using the Microsoft Access Administrator in your Access program group, you can re-apply previous security and group settings. It would be sensible to start transferring work to Access 2.0, however, to take advantage of its increased security power.

ODBC Connections

ODBC stands for Open DataBase Connectivity and Access 2.0 comes with the correct software for you to take advantage of it. With ODBC you are able to link up with many other SQL database systems that support Open Connectivity. This means that within your Access environment you will be able to interact with other powerful databases with maximum ease.

Remember that ODBC is for connection to SQL servers. Access 2.0 comes already equipped with a Microsoft/Sybase SQL Server Driver (for an Oracle 6 Driver, obtain the Microsoft ODBC Drivers Fulfillment Kit). For simple operations within the same PC or on a plain network, Access comes with many built-in drivers for normal connections to dBase, FoxPro, Btrieve and Paradox.

Before you can use ODBC effectively you must set up:

- The appropriate **ODBC driver** for other database product(s)
- Microsoft ODBC Control Panel Option (with Windows NT use ODBC Administrator)

The Control Panel Option is automatically installed when you have a full installation of Access 2.0.

You will find a new ODBC icon in your Windows Control Panel. Clicking on this will give you choices for ODBC Driver connections and additions, available through a series of dialog screens (see Chapter 8).

When you wish to utilize new sources of data you must setup a logical name for each new server type before adding them to your Access environment - See ODBC Help files and your Network Administrator.

When using Access 2.0 to attach to other data sources, you will use the chosen Data Source Name with each SQL ODBC Server.

Converting from Access 1.X to Access 2.0

You can work with your 1.0/1.1 data while you are in 2.0. You can operate virtually as normal, but you cannot alter or create objects (tables, reports, forms, queries etc.) in 1.0/1.1 by using 2.0.

You may convert the whole 1.0/1.1 database into 2.0 format. Then you may, of course, re-build objects as you please. Once it is converted, then it is essentially a 2.0 database and any users addressing it from 1.0/1.1 environments will not be able to use it. Conversion (explained below) may generate errors. You can study these in the Convert Errors Table that the Conversion utility creates if you encounter a rogue object/property.

Converting your 1.0/1.1 Work

To convert your 1.0 and 1.1 databases:

- Start Access 2.0
- In Access, from the menu bar select File and Convert Database. You will see the screen below:

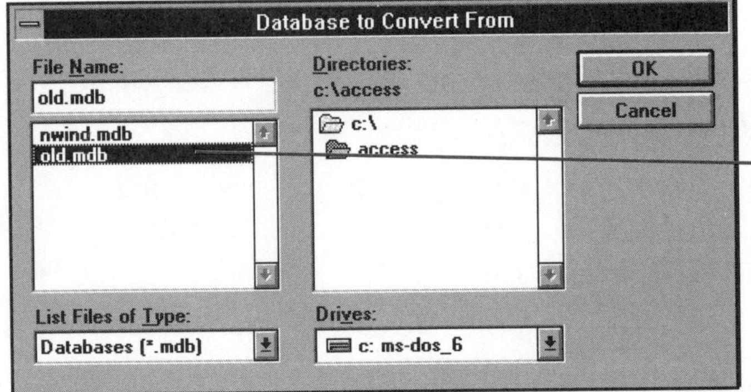

Highlight the database file you want to convert.

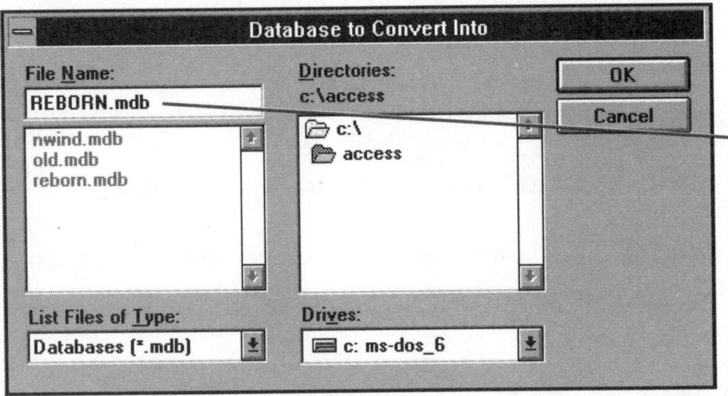

Type in the new database file name - it must be different from the original.

Your database will now be converted into Access 2.0 format, with the database available in the database listing by pressing [icon] or selecting File and Open Database... from the menu bar.

There are various anomalies and improvements made for 1.x Access users. Study the ACREADME.HLP file on your setup disk1 for more detailed information.

Getting Assistance

Access 2.0 comes with its own comprehensive help systems to assist you at every step in using or designing a database. There are several ways for you to call for advice from within the package:

- Using the normal Help screens
- Using the context-sensitive Help icon
- Using the Cue Card tutorials

Normal Help Screen

To use the normal help:

- Click on Help in the Access menu bar.
- Select Contents to see the overview assistance screens.
- Or, select Search... to swiftly track down a subject or generic term.

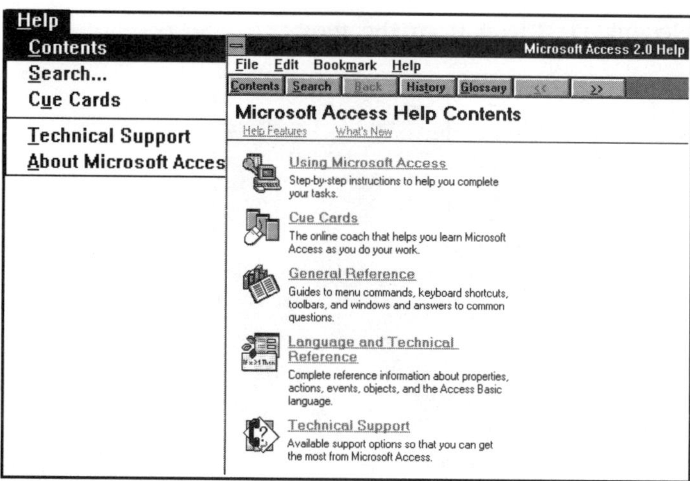

Context Sensitive Help

This is a marvelous new addition to the Access 2.0 armory. You may need swift and immediate help whilst in the middle of a delicate piece of design or, simply need a reminder of an icon's function. To invoke this help simply:

- Click your mouse pointer over the icon.
- Drag your new pointer shape to any object on the screen and you will receive a normal, full help listing on that object.

Cue Cards

Cue Cards are a way for you to get a quick step-by-step tutorial on most common aspects of Access 2.0. Even though you may not have built any real files to work on, Cue Cards can work with the sample database loaded and instruct you as if there were a personal tutor on hand. The cards stay on screen, relating to each stage of a common task. When you have absorbed the information, simply press the Next > button to move to the next stage.

Cue Cards can be invoked:

- From the opening screen in Access.
- By selecting Help and Contents from the menu bar then select the Cue Cards from the help menu.
- By selecting Help and Cue Cards from the menu bar.
- By selecting icon from the toolbar.

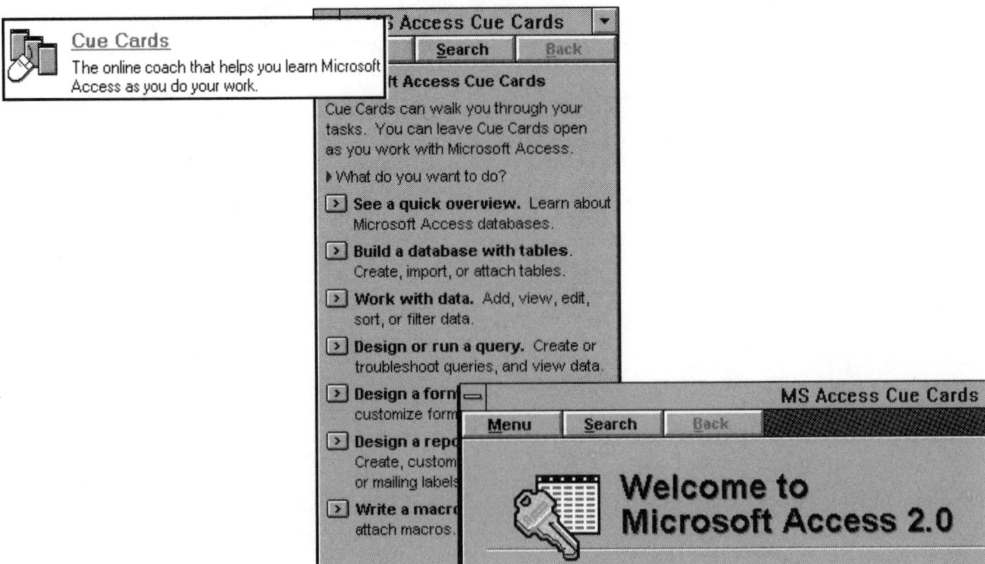

Working With Windows

Access 2.0 is a Windows application and as you would expect uses all the usual Windows-type controls. If you are new to Windows and Access, take a few moments to familiarize yourself with some basic conventions.

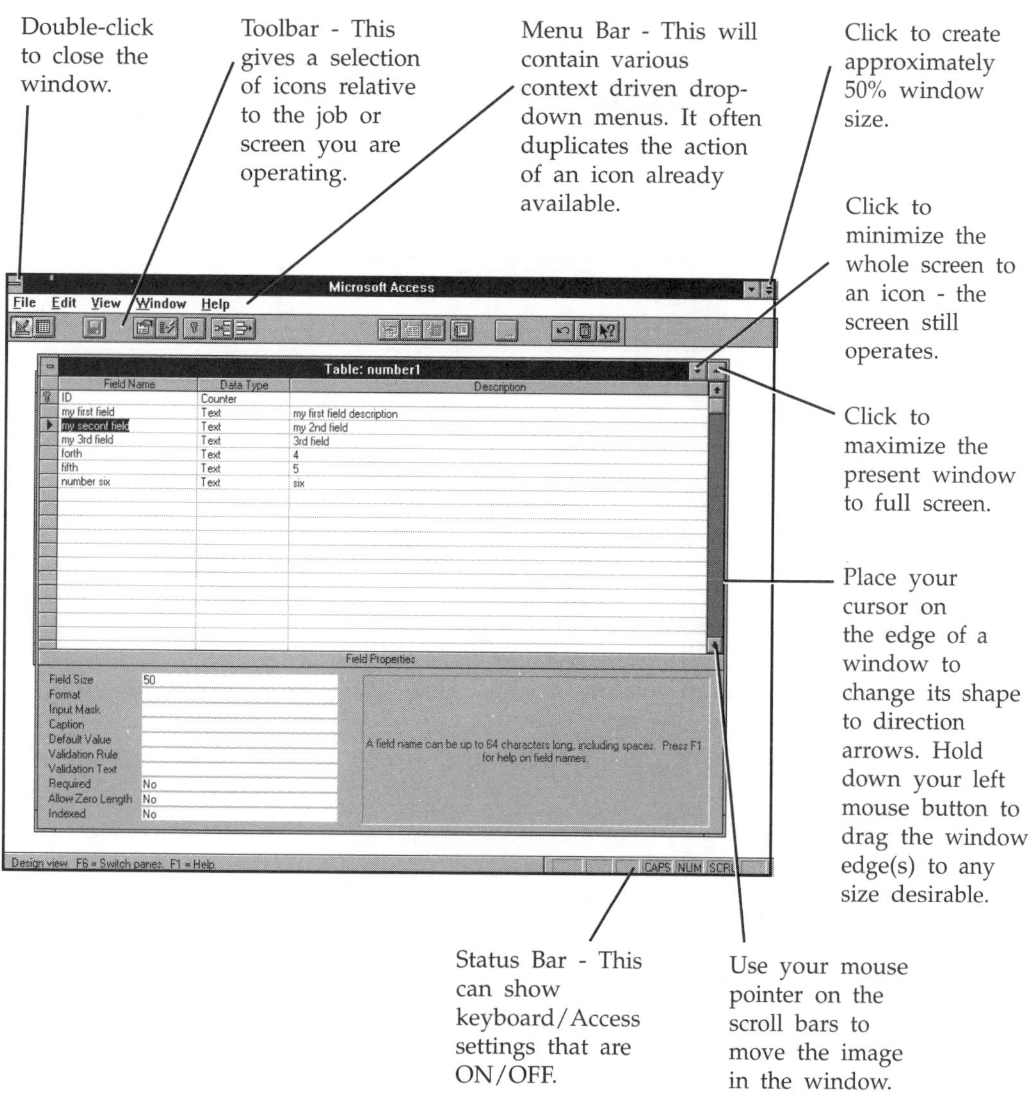

Double-click to close the window.
Toolbar - This gives a selection of icons relative to the job or screen you are operating.
Menu Bar - This will contain various context driven drop-down menus. It often duplicates the action of an icon already available.
Click to create approximately 50% window size.
Click to minimize the whole screen to an icon - the screen still operates.
Click to maximize the present window to full screen.
Place your cursor on the edge of a window to change its shape to direction arrows. Hold down your left mouse button to drag the window edge(s) to any size desirable.
Status Bar - This can show keyboard/Access settings that are ON/OFF.
Use your mouse pointer on the scroll bars to move the image in the window.
Microsoft Access
File Edit View Window Help
Table: number1
Field Name
Data Type
Description
ID
Counter
my first field
Text
my first field description
my seconf field
Text
my 2nd field
my 3rd field
Text
3rd field
forth
Text
4
fifth
Text
5
number six
Text
six
Field Properties
Field Size
50
Format
Input Mask
Caption
Default Value
Validation Rule
Validation Text
Required
No
Allow Zero Length
No
Indexed
No
A field name can be up to 64 characters long, including spaces. Press F1 for help on field names.
Design view. F6 = Switch panes. F1 = Help.
CAPS
NUM
SCRL

Right Mouse Button

Access 2.0 comes with a convenient facility to raise the appropriate menu list for the job in hand. Simply place your cursor on a part of the Access window you wish to carry out a task on. Then, by clicking the right mouse button, a copy of the listings on the menu bar related to the object you are near will appear.

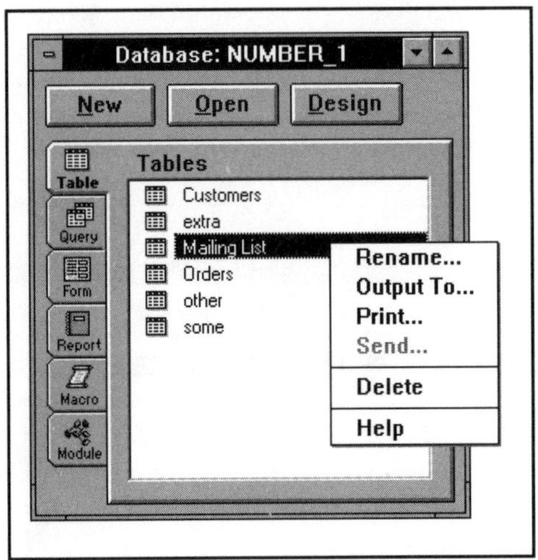

Customizing Access Windows

There are many variations of toolbars and icons that you can customize on your Access workspace. You can:

- Choose different icons: size and type
- Choose custom icons
- Change basic Access options
- Choose custom menus

Changing Icon: Size and Type

On the menu bar choose View and Toolbars...

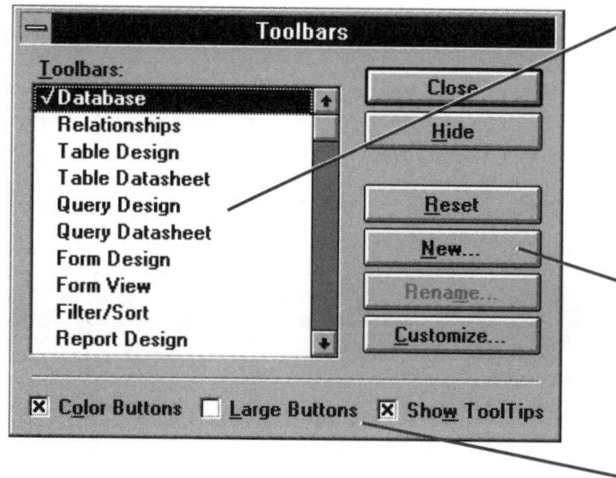

These names represent the default icon selections that will appear at the top of the screen, depending on the job you're doing. You can highlight a name and click Show or Hide to have those icon selections available or not in all screens.

Click the check boxes here to have large/color icons or to get an icon label - this shows the icon's purpose when the cursor is placed on it.

Click on New... to make up a new toolbar name and install your own selection of icons into it.

Customizing Icons

After selecting New... above you can make another toolbar, name it and add the icons you require to it. After a small, empty toolbar has been created, just select the Categories you wish to steal buttons from and a list of the available ones will be shown. Drag icons into your custom toolbar. Clicking on them in the future will activate the requisite action as normal.
Remember you aren't restricted to standard icons. You can have some actions

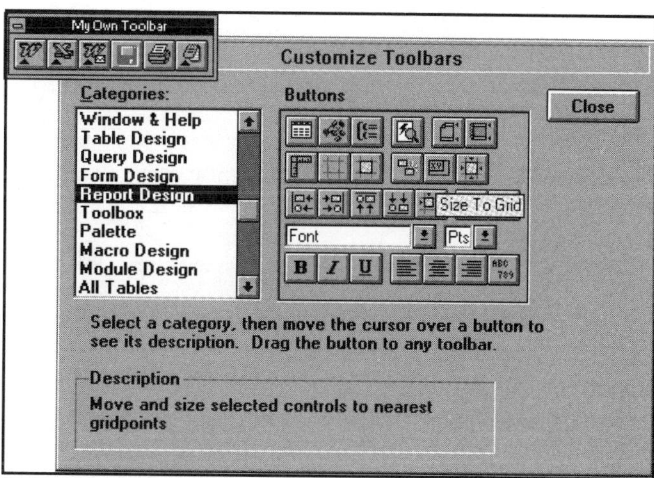

special to your chosen database, like 'open this particular table on this icon selection'. For example, try All Tables at the bottom of the custom list.
You can also set conditions for most of the screens in Access 2.0.

- Select View and Options... from the menu bar to reveal a list of all the variables in the Access system. From various drop-down lists you can set restrictions and enhancements for each element of Access.

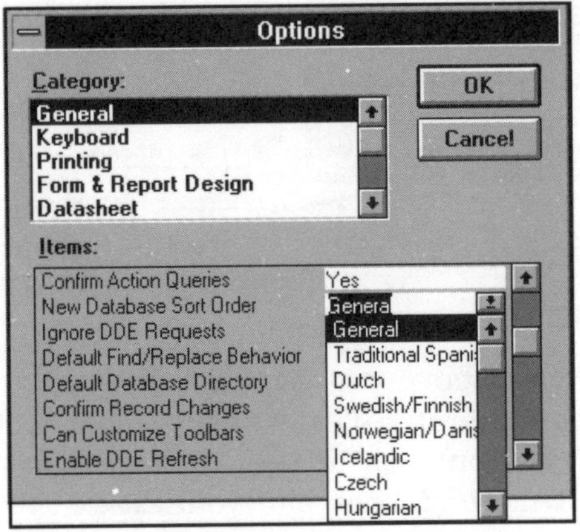

Custom Menu Bars

You can create your own custom menu bars that you can edit to look and behave just like the supplied ones.

- Select File and Add-ins then Menu Builder from the standard toolbar to give you the new menu screen.
- Select New to open the list of command choices that exist already for you to customize, or to add a brand new menu.

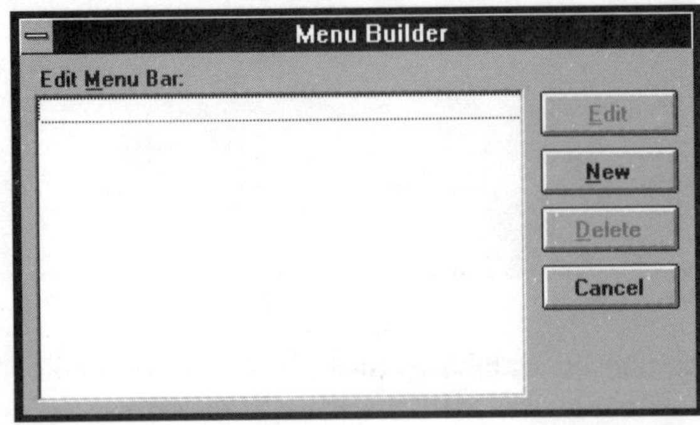

Once you are in the Menu Builder screen, you can choose a new menu or append to existing menus. You can also apply custom key presses to activate your menu. The action of your menu item can be set by a macro or a piece of Access Basic code, and you can also choose from a list of standard actions (DoMenuItem). Whichever way you wish your menu item to behave, you can set appropriate text to appear in the status bar of your window.

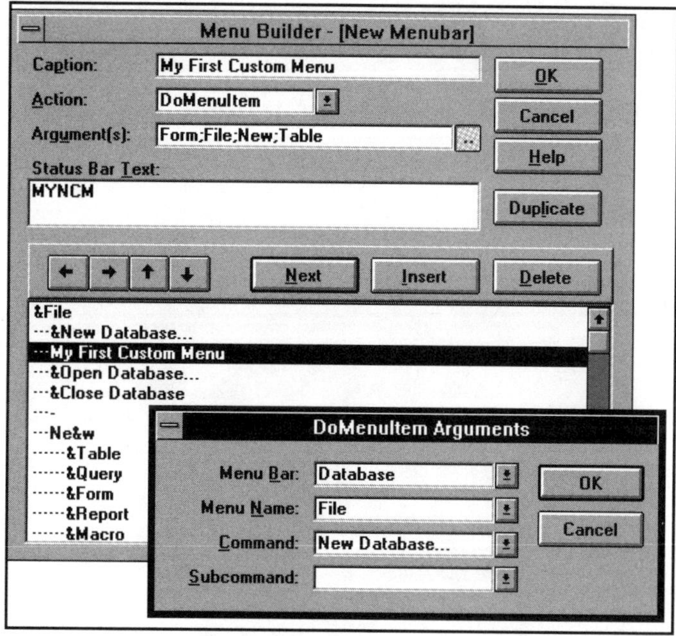

See Menu Builder in the Microsoft Help screens for detailed restrictions on usage.

Mail and Mail Merge

Mail

You can send details of your datasheets, forms, reports and modules across the Microsoft Mail system.

- Select File and then Send... from the menu bar to transmit as a .rtf file.
- Or, click on the Mail icon in the toolbar (select it from custom toolbars if it isn't present normally).

You can also send the data as a Windows for Workgroups mail message.

Mail Merge

You can set up a virtually automatic Mail Merge facility. For example, mailing details that you might keep in your Access database can be setup as letter headers or labels, to be manipulated in Microsoft Word:

- Click the Mail Merge icon to initiate the merge screen selection.

See Chapter 8 for more details.

Overview of Tools and Facilities

Sample Database

Access 2.0 comes with a sample database called NWind.mdb. You can study designs for forms and reports or table design. There are also many sample queries and macros to study. The NWind database is available by:

- Selecting File and Open Database... , and choosing **`c:\access\sampapps\nwind.mdb.`**
- Or, clicking on the open database icon and proceeding through the same screens.

Some of the methods described in this book use the NWind database to illustrate points. Make sure you have the files selected in your Access 2.0 setup, otherwise they will not be available to you. You can add or delete many of Access utilities by clicking on MS Access Setup in your Access program group in Windows Program Manager. This re-enters you into setup and allows you to customize items. Remember to have Access closed before you start altering setup options.

Wizards

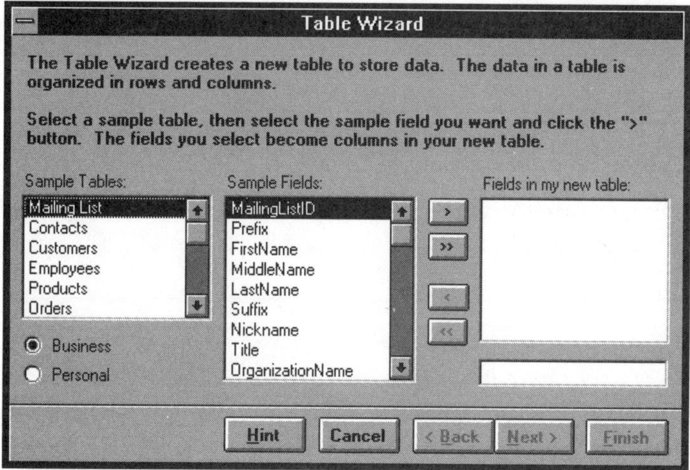

Access 2.0 comes with many new wizards. These help you construct most major elements in Access using friendly multiple-choice screens. They are designed to assist you to master the task of building your database from scratch. Many of the wizards can be used as building assistants, and elements built by using them can be customized afterwards. You can even customize elements of the wizards themselves by using the Add-In Manager. Select File then Add-ins and Add-in Manager to alter basic elements in wizards.

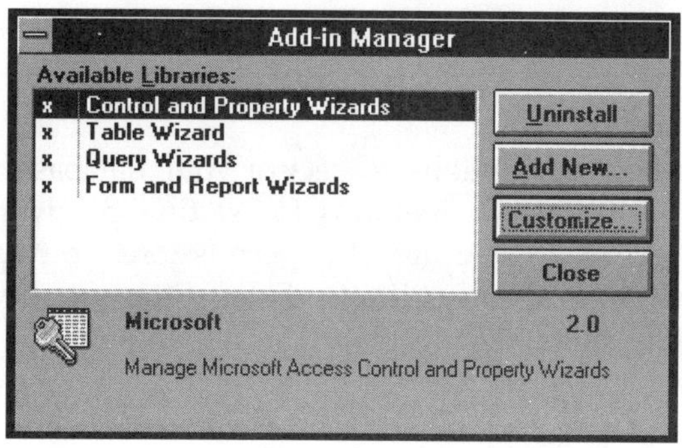

Saving Space

Once you are up and running with your new databases and have used them extensively, you will probably have various fragmented files and leftovers from adding and deleting. You will be able to save considerable space on your hard disk by periodically compacting your databases. When compacting occurs, a copy database is temporarily created, so for the short term, make sure you have the space available to store the original and compacted versions together. When compacting, you can rename the target file.

- Make sure the database is closed.
- Select File and then Compact Database...
- Choose the appropriate database file from the dialog box.
- If you want to, you can choose the same filename from the Database to Compact Into dialog box.
- Choose OK.

Encryption

You can encrypt your database so that, for example, other people can't export your table information to a wordprocessing package to study the data. The database must be closed before encryption, and as with compaction, you must have enough initial space on the hard disk to hold both the unencrypted and the new scrambled database together. If the database remains encrypted, then certain procedures, such as opening a table, may be slowed down proportionally. You can, of course, also decrypt.

- Select File and then Encrypt or Decrypt Database... from the menu bar on the initial Access screen.
- Choose the file of the database in question from the normal dialog boxes.
- Select name, drive etc. for the new encrypted database.
- Choose OK.

Remember to utilize the options to secure your database in Security on the menu bar. There are various methods for setting passwords to the data, and locking out/in records. There are also permissions you can grant to workgroup users and security checks on printing. Follow the security and help screens to engage new safety methods.

Disasters

If the program crashes or shuts down from computer error, some damage may occur to your database. The most recent changes to data that you were carrying out before a save will be lost. However, there's a good chance of recovering everything else.

- Select File/Repair Database... from the bar in the initial Access screen.
- Choose the file of the database in question from the normal dialog boxes.
- Choose OK.

Remember to save your work for safety during a working session or use an automatic back-up from Windows File Manager or MS-DOS. You can also scan the extensive Microsoft Help screens for detail on procedures.

How to Use This Book

There are no awkward conventions to remember when reading this book. We have kept a consistent style for instructions to help you along.

When a piece of text can be seen on the screen, it's shown thus: Report View. All instructions from the Menu Bar have the underscore attached so that they appear exactly as you see them on screen, for example: File. Words of special significance are in bold.

We use two forms of special note:

These are simply for your interest/guidance.

Whereas these are of relative importance.

Reading the Text

You will gain more from the process text (e.g. following the steps of a wizard), if you try to use Access in tandem with the book. The other sections are quite well absorbed away from the computer. We urge you to work with the Tables and Queries chapters to lay a firm grounding for what follows. At all times we have tried to clarify everything that is important in an Access screen action. Fine detail is available from the comprehensive help system that comes with Access - use this to experiment, for example, with various queries before progressing to advanced topics.

Let's Get Started

You should now have installed Access and be ready to set up your database. We hope you enjoy using Access and the rest of the book. If you have any comments, why not fill out the reply card in the back of this book and send it to us? We always try to improve our books and welcome your input. You might even win the prize draw! Thanks for your support.

CHAPTER 1

Fundamentals

Welcome to "The Beginner's Guide To Access 2.0". In this book you will learn all the elements required to produce a database using this software package. It has been written to cater for complete novices to Access and database design and, unlike other books, is written from a novice's point of view. You will be introduced to things such as wizards, the macro builder and referential integrity in an easy-to-understand way, at a pace that suits you.

In this chapter you will cover:

- A description of what Access really is
- The reasons why you would want to use a database
- The difference between a database and other common software packages
- Some basic database terminology
- The advantages of using Access 2.0

What is Access?

This is a really good question! Whether your boss thinks it's a good idea that you use it because you have just bought MS Office, or you're using it stand-alone, you will want the secrets of Access 2.0 revealed as soon as possible. If this is your first time setting up a Windows database, read on - this is the plain-English guide for people who need to nail down the fundamentals and get results fast.

You probably already know that Access is a database, but you may be sitting there wondering what a database is. Before we can get on to the exciting things that Access can do you need to understand a bit about what the package is designed for and the theory behind all databases.

What is a Database?

A database is any predefined structure used to hold a large amount of data. Any data that is contained in the database can be viewed in any manner you require, such as in a list or graph. The data can also be manipulated in a multitude of ways to produce different results. For example, you could sort the data into alphabetical order, you could select specific data based on a given criteria, or you could calculate sums on numerical data.

When you have finished manipulating the data, it's possible for it to be printed in whatever way you require. Mailing labels and boardroom style presentations are all within the scope of Access' output facility.

What is a Relational Database?

To answer this question, you need to take a short look at the history of databases, and the various types of database that are available. This will help you discover where the term originated from, how the theory of databases has blossomed over the years and what the term relational database should mean to anyone using the Access package.

The History of the Database

From the beginning of time, people have been interested in collecting information about their surroundings. This information was first stored on cave walls, but as technology improved the storage medium changed from walls to animal skins, animal skins to paper, and with the silicon revolution, from paper to computer disk.

As our horizons have broadened, both physically and intellectually, the amount of information available for collection has increased exponentially. This has in turn led to an increase in the size of the databases that contain the data. This increase in size has added even more problems to the lot of anyone wanting to make use of the stored information.

Some of these problems are illustrated by one of the best known of early databases - the Doomsday Book. This book was compiled in the eleventh century and contained all the details concerning the peoples and wealth of Britain. However, William the Conqueror, who commissioned this tally, discovered some of the problems that were to haunt all data collection agencies for many years to come.

One of these problems was the creation of an index for information. The amount of data collected by the King's advisors was, for that time, truly amazing. This meant that the time required simply to sort out and categorize the raw information was an eternity, not to mention interrogating the data itself.

Essentially all the information in a database has to be interrogated every time a question is posed, whether the question is simple or complex. This meant that if the King asked a simple question such as: "How many cows belong to the realm?", the guardians would have to spend many days poring over the information dealing with the various parts of the country. They would have to add up the relevant figures for each part when they were identified and then total these figures before the correct answer could be supplied.

Because the amount of data was so large, to produce a result in a reasonable time, the King would have to employ several people as counters to compile the figures. He would then force them to work as quickly as possible under these difficult conditions (does this sound familiar?). This meant that a supposedly correct answer was usually anything but correct, as the counters inevitably made lots of mistakes as they rushed to complete the task.

A combination of the time required, and the inherent human error made the wealth of information practically worthless. The solution to this problem came (much to the pleasure of the IRS) with the invention of computers and the advance of database theory.

With the invention of computers, handling large amounts of data was simplified from days of eye strain and backache, to a few key-presses. Computers are especially suited to working with large amounts of data, as they can perform the same task over and over again and hardly ever misread, forget, or overlook any of the data. They will speed through thousands of data pieces looking for the one you require in double-quick time, saving you a heap of space into the bargain.

Libraries are good examples of real-life databases. They contain many pieces of information grouped together into books. Each of these pieces of information can be located quickly due to an indexing system; the library filing system to locate the books, and the book's index to locate the specific information.

Using computers to organize and control information has necessitated laying down some guide-lines on the make-up of databases. These guidelines are important to you in using Access 2.0, as the designers at Microsoft have used them as a cornerstone for the software's design.

Basic Database Structure

The simplest way to understand databases is to look at a basic database structure and describe what's happening and why.

Do you recognize (and hate) this?

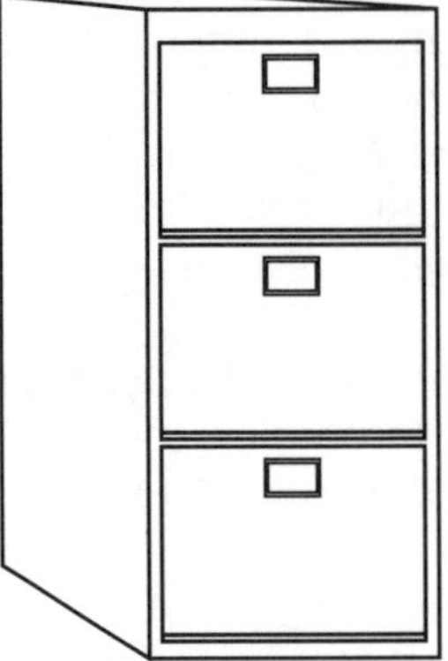

This is a basic database. A filing cabinet contains a number of separate drawers. The drawer contents can be compared to tables within a database.

Table: Invoices

Field Name	Data Type
Invoice number	Counter
Product	Text
Charge	Currency
Payment date	Date/Time
Credit limit	Number
Customer ID	Text

Inside each file, there are a number of sheets. These contain information on a common subject. They can be compared to the records in a database.

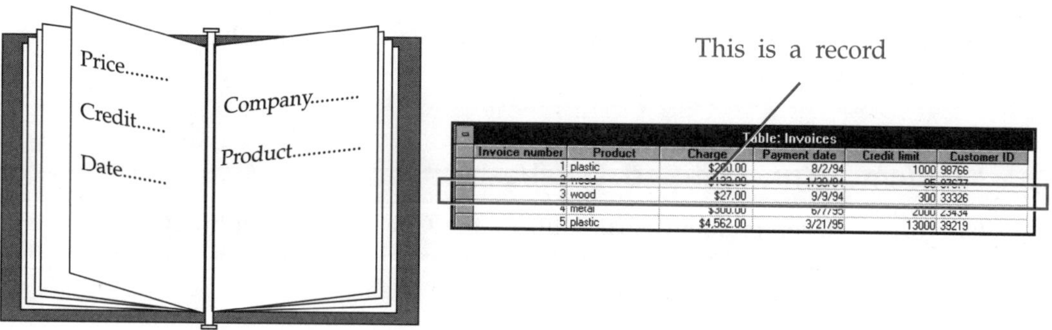

Database Terminology

A **field** is the smallest nugget of information in a database and is the building block for a **record**.

For example, look at the following illustration.

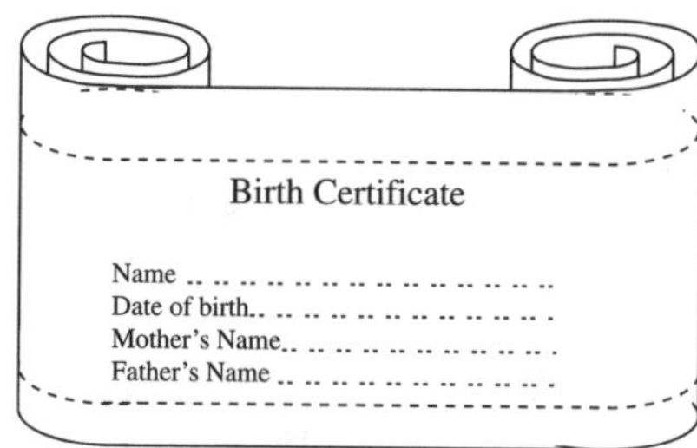

Here, your name and your date of birth are fields and they appear on your birth certificate which is the record.

A **record** is a collection of **fields**. The contents of each of the fields should uniquely identify the subject of the record.

Your entry in a telephone book (record) is made up of your name (field), your address (field), and your telephone number (field). These three fields uniquely identify you and your telephone number.

KING G, 1556 England Rd. HU10 6ET..........**0482 651473**

A **table** is a collection of records. These records will have a common theme, such as the telephone numbers of people living in Long Island, and therefore will naturally be grouped together.

In a telephone directory, for example, the whole book is a table and all the entries are records.

The Problem - The Flat-Bed Database

One of the major problems that William the Conqueror unwittingly faced was embryonic database theory. In the 11th century all databases were based on the same general model - the flat-bed database model.

A flat-bed database is a very simple structure. A classic example would be the card rolodex. Each card rolodex is the database equivalent of a table.

Each of the cards contained in the rolodex is the equivalent of a record in a database.

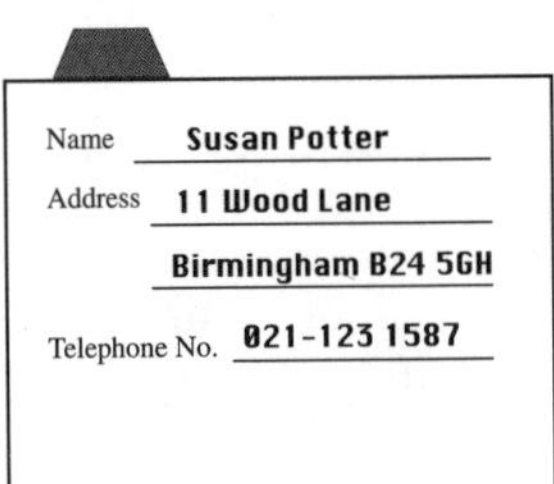

Each of the individual pieces of data on the cards is the equivalent of a field in a database.

Each record is based on the same template of fields. This gives the database its structure. It also means that each field can be given rules as to the type of data that the field can contain. Designers can make sure that the rules for each field are not violated. The rules help when interrogating or querying the data as you should know the type of data that can result from the query.

As you start to think about the various uses that you can put a database to, the flat bed database design inadequacies soon become apparent. There are several tasks that you may wish to use the database for. These include:

- Selecting data by some special criteria
- Rearranging data by a criterion
- Performing calculations on data to produce more meaningful results

All of these tasks are made difficult because the information is spread across a number of cards. Some devious methods have been devised to get around some of these problems, such as placing tabs on the top of some of the cards to denote a characteristic so that selecting data can be speeded up.

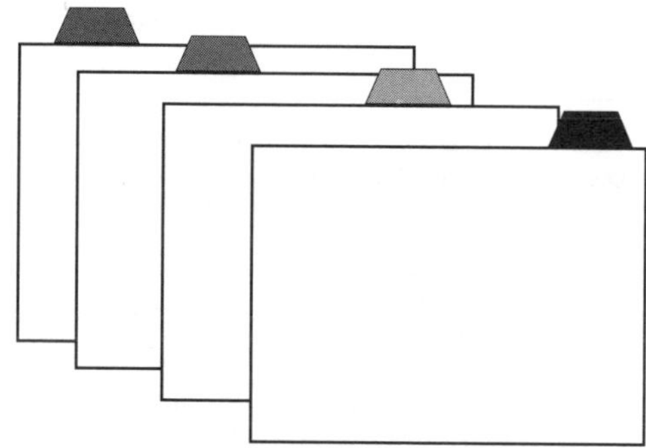

However, there are only a finite number of ways to denote characteristics, so this method can only be used as a stop-gap. It generates too many of its own problems to be called a proper solution. The problem at the core of all these tasks is the time required to extract the data from the database. The solution to this came with the development of computer technology. However, even computers have their limits when very large amounts of data need to be processed, and so the whole problem needed to be looked at again.

The Solution - The Relational Database

The problem of speed was solved as soon as the database structure was looked at in greater detail. At the center of the problem was the structure that computer databases had inherited from their physical flat-bed cousins.

Think about the structure of the individual records in the table. Each record has the same structure based on the same set of fields (for example, name and telephone number in our telephone directory analogy). The information stored in the database will determine the fields that are required on each record.

Take the example of a news stand's flat-bed database. In this database you would store all the information about the customers and the papers that were delivered to them. This would allow the customers' bills to be drawn up automatically at the end of the month.

CUSTOMER	ADDRESS	PAPER	PRICE (c)
SMITH	54, AVERT ST.	USA TODAY	50
JONES	17, ACACIA RD.	N.Y. TIMES	85
CLINTON	1, SMALLHOUSE	NAT. ENQ	90
NIXTONY	3, TAPESVILLE	L.A. TRIBUNE	95
SMITH	54, AVERT ST.	N.Y. TIMES	85
JACKSON	984, CATTLE ST.	NAT. ENQ	90
ROBERTS	1759, LOWCAL	USA TODAY	50
CLINTON	1, SMALLVILLE	SEATTLE SENT.	75

Every time a newspaper is delivered to a customer, a new record showing that delivery has to be entered into the database. The problem with this system is that it is not just the delivery of the paper that needs to be recorded. All the information relating to the customer, as well as all the information about the newspaper, needs to be entered as well. This allows you to retrieve all the records concerning the papers that a customer has had delivered, otherwise you won't know which customer has had which paper.

All this data takes up valuable space in the computer's memory. It also slows down the speed of the computer when you want to do any detailed sorting or selection of the data, due to the sheer amount of unwanted data that it has to plow through.

You will probably have already thought of the solution - only keep the information about the newspaper deliveries in this database, and keep the customer information somewhere else.

Keeping the information outside the computer is clearly fraught with danger. This data could easily be lost, invalidating any possible use of either set of information. Another major problem with holding the data outside the database is the cross-referencing you will have to do manually before the information regains its credibility. As this process can only be done manually, any time gained from using the computer is lost.

Keeping these problems in mind, the only avenue available to the database theorists was to include the data inside the database structure. However, this idea contradicted the very foundation of database theory at the time, as flat-bed databases have only one table to hold the data. Clearly a new model needed to be produced.

The Relational Database Model

In simplistic terms, a relational database is a flat-bed database with more than one table. Let's look at the news stand's database, using a relational database structure.

CUSTOMER	ADDRESS
SMITH	54, AVERT ST.
JONES	17, ACACIA RD.
CLINTON	1, SMALLHOUSE
NIXTONY	3, TAPESVILLE
JACKSON	984, CATTLE ST.
ROBERTS	1759, LOWCAL

PAPER	PRICE (c)
USA TODAY	50
N.Y. TIMES	85
NAT. ENQ	90
L.A. TRIBUNE	95
SEATTLE SENT.	75

As you can see, the same information is included in the database structure as the flat bed version. However, using this relational structure there is less information in each table. This means that the sorts and selections the computer has to do on any one table are automatically speeded up, as it has less data to sift through.

Until then, database theory had only been concerned with information on one table, as that was all there was. Now, the database theorists had a problem. How could they relate the information in several tables? They solved this problem by inventing links that can be placed between the tables. The computer uses these links to understand how the data in the various tables relates together. It is possible to interpret these links as the way the computer would reassemble all the tables into one, as in the flat-bed database structure.

The important point about these links is that they are dynamic. This means the computer only calls them into play when it is necessary to pool information from two or more tables. The computer only has to search through the data relating to the link and not the entire contents of the database. Speed is dramatically increased!

The idea of the relational database model has revolutionized the way that computer databases are designed and has led to faster responses and more complex requests becoming available to the everyday user of any relational database.

What is a Management System?

A management system is simply a way of organizing and managing a structure or process. Examples of management systems in everyday life include a city's traffic control system or the personnel hierarchy in a company.

All of these management systems control some group of elements. In the case of the traffic control system, it is pedestrians and motor vehicles, whereas in the personnel system it is the allocation of the company's work.

In terms of a database, a management system sets the rules for a multitude of tasks involving the data associated with the database. Some of these tasks include: the entry of data into the database, the manipulation of data when in the database and the output of the data once it is in the required format. In short, a database management system structures the way that people using the database work when they are interacting with it.

What is a RDBMS?

Access is a relational database management system (RDBMS). Don't worry about this acronym. It's just a group of technical terms that describe an essentially simple piece of machinery. A relational database management system is simply a set of rules that the computer follows in order to produce a relational database and then allow the user to interact with the relational database to produce the required effects as fast as possible.

Access 2.0 is a very powerful RDBMS including specialized features that allow you to quickly and easily produce a relational database, and then interrogate the data contained in it.

Why Use a Database?

So, this great new way of organizing databases has come about, but what kind of thing should it be used for? And perhaps more importantly, what should it not be used for?

To answer these questions, you need to understand the limitation of the other packages your computer can use. In general, there are three main types of application that are used in the workplace. These are wordprocessors, spreadsheets and databases. If you have the MS Office package you will have all these already. The three types of application overlap to some extent in the way you can use them. For example, you might have arranged MS Word into a kind of database if you set up a file of names and addresses to produce a mailing list. You may also have been used to using your spreadsheet as a form of database for numerical information and realized the limitations when trying to incorporate text based data.

Each of these applications can do some of the things that the other two types can. A database can do basic math on given data and a spreadsheet has a basic wordprocessing capability. However, to obtain the best results, it is important to use the correct application. The ultimate reason for using Access 2.0 is to manipulate mixed data efficiently and effectively. You must always have the right application to retain future flexibility. If an application in any of these areas is of any quality, it will be able to interact with some or all of the other applications. This means that high quality documents containing elements from all three areas can be produced at the end of the day. You have this at your fingertips with OLE, as part of Access 2.0 and MS Office

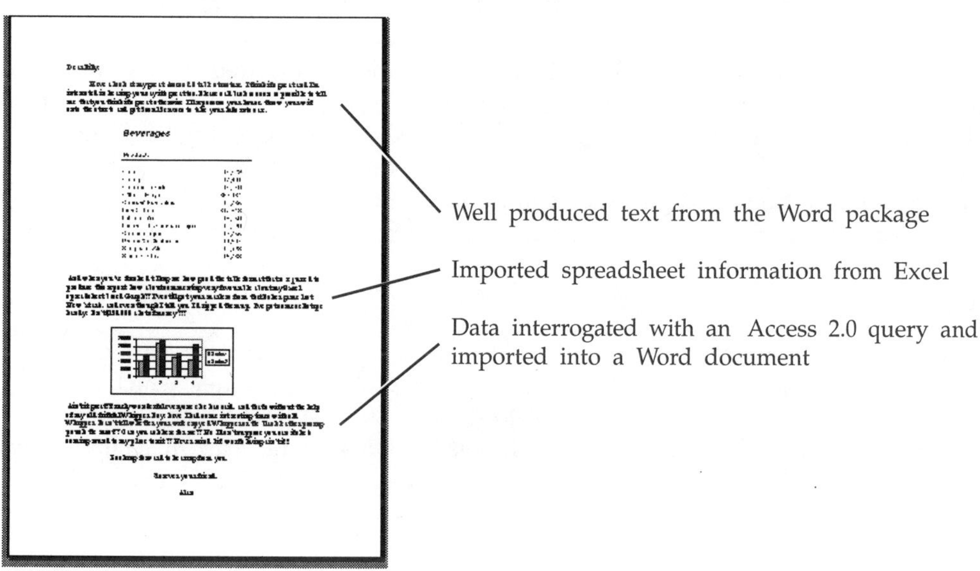

Why Should I Use Access 2.0?

Access 2.0 is the latest version of Microsoft's RDBMS for small to medium sized databases, released in April 1994. This means that Microsoft has been able to include all the leading-edge database technology, allowing both database designers and the end users to enjoy using the product.

Wizards

When Microsoft first considered the idea of producing this kind of package, their major concern was ease-of-use. To that end their project managers included wizards.

These wizards allow all the component parts of a database structure to be created, to a minimum standard, after the database designer has answered a few simple questions. Wizards were designed to cover many common 'build' requirements. This substantially reduces the time required to produce a fully functioning database, and this is one of the reasons why this package is now the fastest selling RDBMS for the PC.

Data Exchange

One of the other issues that Microsoft wished to tackle with this package was that of communication between Access 2.0 and other software packages. Access 2.0 has the ability to exchange information with Paradox, Foxpro, dBase, Btrieve, and any SQL-based databases. It also has the ability to exchange information with non-database software packages including Excel, Lotus 1-2-3 and Word as well as any other software packages that accept text files.

> The term 'file' is the technical name for some computer coded data describing something, for example, a picture or a word processed document. The computer translates anything that is entered into binary numbers, and these binary numbers are stored in a file that can be moved around, both inside the computer and to other computers.

OLE 2.0

Access 2.0 also supports OLE 2.0. This is a way to transpose any part of a project that you are working on into any other project no matter which software package you wish to use (as long as it supports OLE 2.0, see the individual software package manual for details). This is the leap in technology that you demanded, after all those years of struggling with integrated packages that didn't really integrate.

For the professional database designer these facilities are a dream come true, but for a beginner they may be a little overpowering. Fortunately, being able to use these facilities is not a prerequisite for the user of Access 2.0 to produce fully functioning database design. Simply sit back and enjoy Access 2.0 as a database design medium, and use these functions when you are more at home with the whole idea of multi-origin data.

What's Next?

In the following chapter, you will see how to decide on a database design plan from the ground up. We also cover the terminology in Access 2.0 and common database practice.

CHAPTER 2

Planning An Access Database

In this chapter we will discuss some of the techniques we need to produce a good basic plan. In particular, we will look at all the different elements that make up your first relational database. When you decided to enter into electronic information storage, you wanted the speed and reliability that it can offer, as well as the saving in space. You need to take some time to think about the data in your business or project. In doing this you will save yourself a lot of time in the long run. Access 2.0 has a wealth of built-in features to help you construct your database, but even this package cannot discern the absolute requirements of your workplace data. If you are willing to learn the basic rules, then you will never again have to worry about all those customer details, alphabetical organization or conclusive reports.

We will examine the Access building blocks in outline, and look at simple examples to illustrate their purpose. If you're coming from years of using spreadsheets, you will be amazed at the advances made in database flexibility. If you are coming from a DOS based database usage, you will be exchanging sore fingers for simple point-and-click. If you are approaching your first database through this book, we will explain all the fundamentals in plain English. You will quickly get to grips with it and achieve what you want from a software database.

In this chapter you will cover:

- Tables, queries, reports and forms
- Macros and modules
- Interacting outside Access
- A typical approach to planning a database

Why Do I Need a Plan for My Database?

Just like an essay, any database design will benefit from a well-organized and thorough plan, both in terms of the final structure of the database and the ease with which it can be built and used.

If you are a novice, it's much simpler to decide how the screens that make up the database will look before you sit in front of the computer. You don't want a tool that fails in a few months time, so analyze your project on paper first.

Don't be put off; the actual process you are going to work through is a simple one. Once you are confident of your tables, your folders and filing cabinets will soon become redundant.

Before You Begin to Plan

Before you look at the specific techniques that allow you to start designing, you need to have a basic understanding of two topics:

- Some of the major components of an Access database and how you can use them.
- Some of the techniques that Microsoft have provided to make your time as a designer less tedious.

Each of these topics can be broken down into sub-topics. The nuts and bolts of it all are easy to understand once you've been taken through them one step at a time. There are also a variety of Microsoft Wizards to help you along with the major functions.

First of all we will look at each of these sub-topics in more detail. We will then move on to see a working example of a database plan being developed. In this case we will watch Mr. Daily Enquirer produce a plan for his news stand.

The Major Components of an Access Database

There are six major components of an Access 2.0 database including:

1. Tables
2. Queries
3. Forms
4. Reports
5. Macros
6. Modules

We looked at tables a little in the previous chapter. Here you will see what each component looks like, what it does and how to put it to use. All of these major components are listed on the opening screen of your first database.

Tables

Access 2.0 uses tables as the permanent storage place for your data. Each table is comprised of normal rows and columns that create available cells for you to fill in. The heart of a table is made up of rules guiding the type of information that should inhabit the cells. You set these rules by selecting each column heading or field. You should be specific about its content, in other words give the field definitions. You use these definitions to control the kind of information entered, and also to make the whole collection of your tables coherent. The range of information you enter will be constrained by your definitions.

Data Types

You will use a regular menu of data types for your definitions.

Data Types	**Use**
Text	For any alphanumeric characters (that is any letter or number)
Memo	For lengthy text and number entries
Number	For numerical data you intend to perform calculations on
Date/Time	For storing dates and times
Currency	For any figures that make up a currency value
Counter	For automatic numbering - this is the automatic counter that Access can use to keep track of your records
Yes/ No	For use if the answer to a question is Yes or No, True or False
OLE Object	For storing any sound, pictures or video clips

For more information on the different uses of data types for your field definitions, see the Access 2.0 help screens, under data types: field.

Access allows you to set validation rules for these field data types. These act as a filter, which is a way of persuading a user to enter data using data types which have been defined as valid. For example, if we put together a whole supermarket, we must declare that any shape of carton with cookies on it *will* be placed on the cookie aisle!

We can also create indexes for our grid of data and just like any other index, these will aid swift retrieval. All of this takes place in table design. Once completed, data will be entered into a simple table datasheet.

Below is a screen of a typical Access 2.0 table design:

Here is the column that shows which fields have been indexed. The indexes that Access creates are based on some of the field definitions that make up the complete records. Access can take entries in fields and compile an index so that any record can be quickly located no matter where it lives in the database structure.

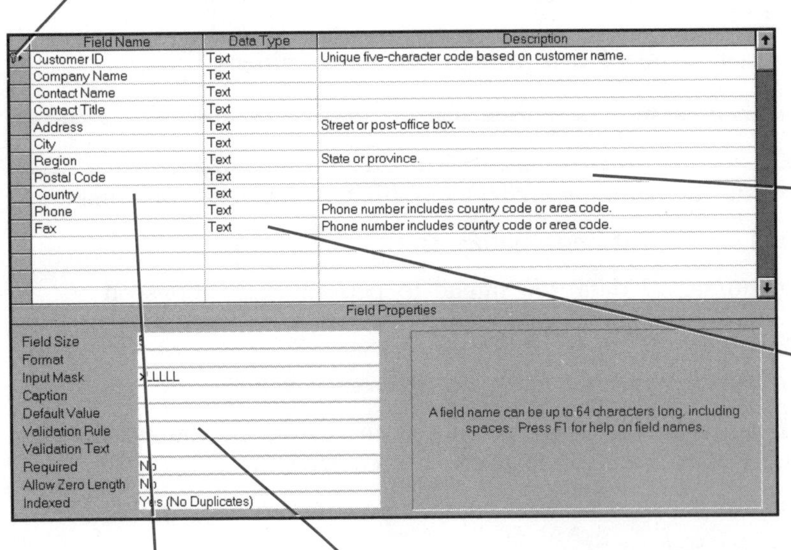

This column contains notes about the field that may be useful when the database is being maintained.

This column defines the type of data that each field can store.

In this column are the names of the various fields that make up your table structure.

This box contains the extra properties (including the validation rule property) and actions that may be assigned to each field. These are used to further refine the type of data which the user must enter.

How to use these features of table design is covered in Chapter 3. In that chapter you will learn about the various aspects of designing a good table by identifying both the number and type of fields you require.

You will also learn how to relate different tables together to produce a truly relational database. The tables in a relational database reduce data duplication whilst speeding up the location of any particular entry by minimizing the size of each entry in a table.

Remember that a table is the permanent store for all of your data.

Now you must learn a little bit about queries, the tools Access provides you with to manipulate the data you have entered into your tables.

Queries

Queries are an Access tool for data manipulation and questioning. Microsoft have provided a query to cope with most eventualities. If there is no specific query for a task, then a combination of some queries on offer will do the job in the short term.

There are many things that you can do to your data. You can **select** a particular grouping that has a common link, **sort** out records with a simple ordering system, and move data from table to table. You can even create new tables for particular sets of data to be copied to. All this at the click of a few buttons.

The queries that will be covered in Chapter 4 of this book include:

Query	**Use**
The Sort Query	This is used to sort out your data, using certain rules.
The Select Query	This is used to obtain a group of records from your database, the records sharing a common link.
The Nest Query	This uses one query to act upon another to produce tailored results.

Query Types

Chapter 9 will introduce queries on multiple tables and how to customize your interrogation to get exact results. In this chapter you will become familiar with all the query types. There are as many queries as there are questions, so queries are available in general headings for you to refine at leisure.

Query	Use
Make-Table	This is used to select records which are then copied into a table that Access creates.
Append	This is used to simply copy records to another table that already exists.
Delete	This is used to delete records that share a common link from a table.
Update	This is used to alter records that share a common link using predefined rules.
Pass-Through	SQL dominated query - This is used to communicate with other databases.
Data Definition	SQL dominated query - This is used to interact with other databases.
Parameter	This is used to ask the user for the common link that will be used when selecting a group of records.
Crosstab	This is used to reorganize the selected data into a tabular format.

There are various other queries that cover archiving and tracking facilities.

In these chapters, you will be introduced to each of these types of query. By looking at examples you will learn which to use and why. You will also become very familiar with what is called the QBE grid. This is a another useful tool provided by Microsoft to help you create queries and looks something like this:

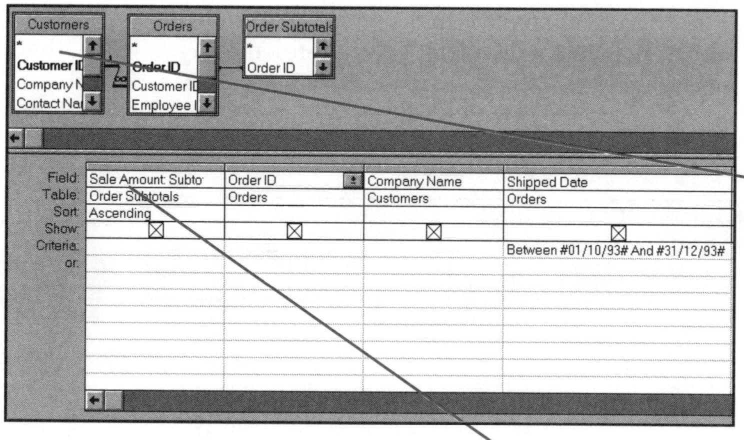

These are tables which you may have created, displayed in miniaturized form. A query can only work upon the data in your tables if you give it express permission to take it from a given table.

These are fields selected from the tables above for use in your query. In this same area, you can set specific rules for the query to adhere to while working with data. For example, you could ask the query to show you all the customers that have ordered an item, and then demand that it only tells you about those that placed their orders between specific dates.

The whole idea of the QBE grid and other methods of querying your data are discussed later in this chapter.

Remember that queries are used to manipulate raw data into an informative conclusion.

Forms

Access 2.0 uses forms in two ways. The first is as a means of entering data into the database. The form appears blank upon the screen, looking very similar to a blank questionnaire. The user moves around the form, by pressing the correct keys, filling in fields that you define.

Data entry validation rules may be created to stop the user from filling in the wrong type of data, and also to provide them with useful messages when they do go wrong. Input masks may be added to prompt the user for a correct type of entry. They can be likened to the set of boxes that appear on governmental forms for you to fill in your social security number.

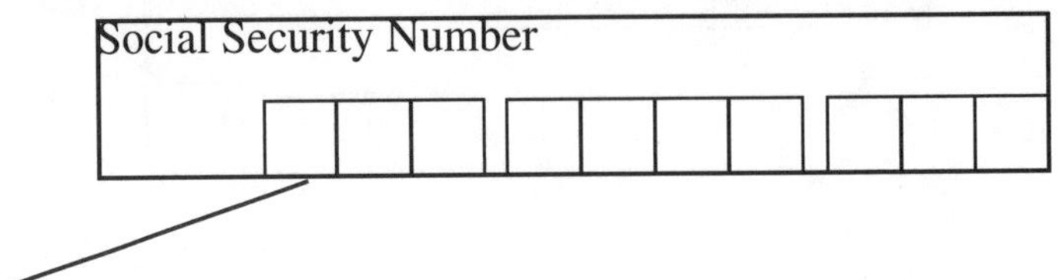

There are ten boxes. This means that the input mask is asking the user for ten individual alpha-numeric entries, one per box. You can also limit the type of characters that the user can enter by using an input mask in conjunction with several other properties. The data type of your underlying field definition also plays a part.

The other use for forms comes into play when a user wants to look at information stored in your database. If a form can be used to enter data into the database, then it must already be in the correct format to display that data, in detail, to the user. Access enables you to provide this facility very quickly with only a few changes to the form design.

You can set up the design of the form so that it can only be used for one of the two jobs. This allows you to restrict the user's freedom within the database. A form gives you the ability to create some sort of flexible security.

Below, you can see a typical form design which is being used as a method for data entry.

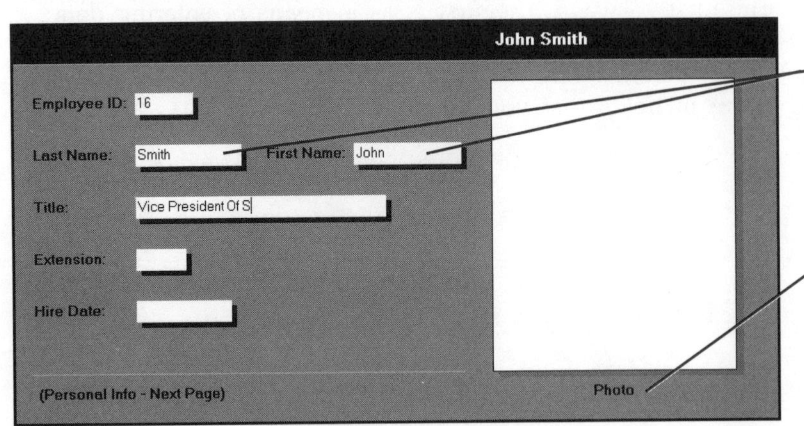

Up until now the user has filled in these fields, and still has more work to do.

You will see that the form is visually attractive and efficiently laid out. This makes the job of data entry much easier than entering data straight into the table structure itself.

> Remember that forms are the most visually helpful way of entering and viewing data in your database. You should always try to use forms as the medium for interacting with the table repositories, especially when you are designing the database for someone who doesn't know much about Access 2.0.

Reports

An Access report is a window into all your hard work. Entering the data into the Access tables, manipulating the data with your queries, and finally altering the format of the data can give you a good boardroom-standard report. You can produce many different kinds of reports, especially when you have learnt how to build them from scratch. You will find that with a bit of practice you will be able to produce stunning reports that incorporate not only data from your database, but also information from wordprocessing packages and spreadsheets.

Below is an example of the type of report you will be able to compile once you have read about basic report design in Chapter 6.

Freight Charges
28-May-94

Company Name:	Order ID:	Freight:	Running Total:
Federal Shipping	10516	$62.78	$62.78
	10519	$91.76	$154.54
Speedy Express	10520	$13.37	$13.37
	10522	$45.33	$58.70
	10527	$41.90	$100.60
United Package	10506	$21.19	$21.19
	10518	$218.15	$239.34
	10521	$17.22	$256.56
	10524	$244.79	$501.35
Grand Total:		$756.49	

Access can also produce graphs from any of the figures contained in your database. You will be able to create a truly magnificent multimedia report, especially if you also add graphics to the report design. All of the more advanced report design techniques are covered in Chapter 11, while designing graphs is covered in Chapter 7.

> The report will probably be the major interaction between Access and the people using it, who are only interested in the conclusions of the stored data. The kinds of reports you will need may influence the way you structure your database.

Macros

You may have come across macros before in other software packages, especially spreadsheets. They are small lists of commands that allow you to automate tasks, simply by the click of a button or a selection from the menu. Very quickly you will be able to use macros to provide message screens and join project elements together.

Macros allow you to take more control of a user's movements around the database. They may help you provide screens which the user must pass through to get at the forms and reports you have created. This set of screens, driven by the power of the underlying macros, is called a **switchboard**. It means you can protect your database structure and the user from getting lost.

As you become confident with the actions of the database structure, you will see more and more opportunities to use macros to automate simple tasks. Think how useful it would be to automatically open the database and bring up the first screen for the user to interact with. By the time you are completely competent with Access, you will wonder how you ever coped without macro assistance.

Below is a typical screen of a macro design.

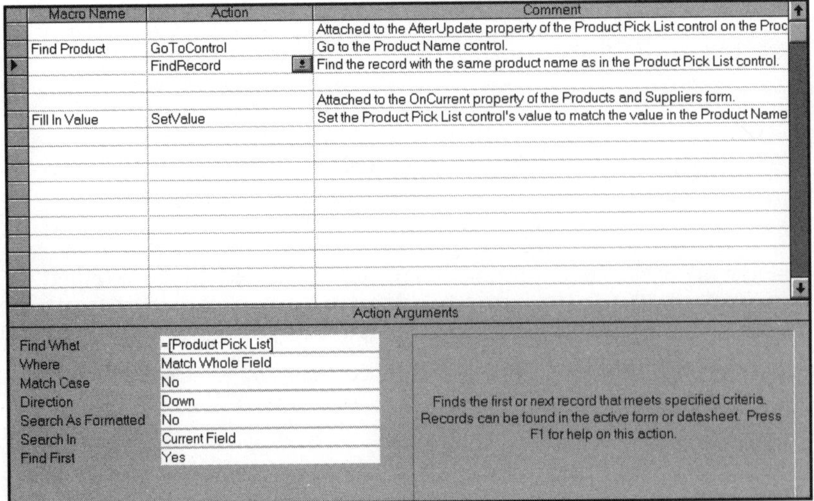

Macros are lists of tasks Access will perform for you when you press a button or when a particular event occurs as you are using your database. Macros can only perform a task that could otherwise be re-created manually through the menus or the icon bar. For example, opening a database is possible, but creating the criteria for a query is not.

Modules

As an Access 2.0 database designer you will be able to tackle more advanced topics like Modules and Access Basic. Modules are the store for any Access Basic programs you may write. When you are running the database, using programs will give you even more control than using macros. Access Basic is the programming language that comes free with Access 2.0 and with it you can control the flow of data around your database, create new parts of the database structure and even produce data manipulations that are beyond powerful queries.

The topic of Access Basic is just on the fringes of this book's scope, and so the coverage given to this subject in Chapter 13 is not comprehensive. It is simply a taster for the language's talents. If you are new to database design and computer controlled databases, we suggest that you forget all about modules and Access Basic until you are confident of Access behavior. Once you are proficient, you may venture into Visual Basic to start building total application environments.

Below you can see a typical screen of some Access Basic code which shows the potential minefield Access Basic can be.

(general) NullToZero

```
Function NullToZero (anyValue As Variant) As Variant
' Accepts: a variant value
' Purpose: converts null values to zeros
' Returns: a zero or non-null value
' From: User's Guide Chapter 17

   If IsNull(anyValue) Then
       NullToZero = 0
   Else
       NullToZero = anyValue
   End If

End Function
```

Access Basic is a programming language. This means that all the problems associated with the use of a programming language come along with it, including complex syntax, lack of readability and the need to study to some degree. However, Access Basic is a more powerful tool than macros, so if you are finding problems creating the exact results with them, you will have to take the plunge and look at programming with Access Basic.

The General Structure of an Access Database

The general structure of an Access database can be illustrated very easily with the following diagram, which shows the interaction of all of the components of an Access database in a fully functional structure.

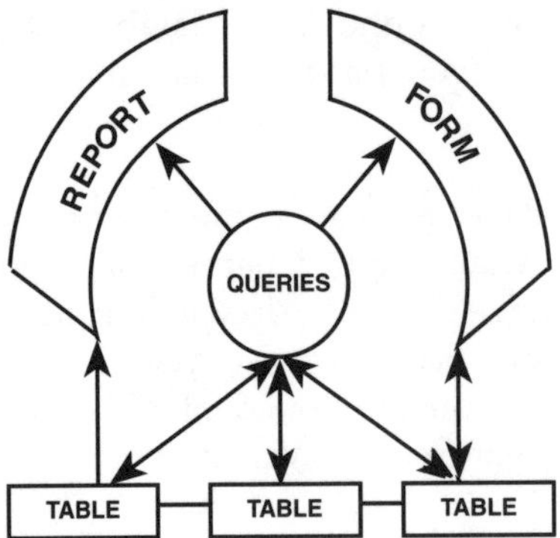

Some of the Tools Microsoft Has Provided With Access 2.0

The tools that Access 2.0 provides to help you both design your database and then keep it running on the correct track include:

- Interrogating the data
- Importing or exporting data using other sources
- Producing graphs from the data in your database
- Using multiple tables
- Using referential integrity

How Does Access Interrogate the Data?

Many other databases are based around or still use Structured Query Language (SQL) to question their data store. Access is no exception, but instead of pushing the new user straight into that kind of industry language, Microsoft has supplied an improved intermediate stage, graphical Query By Example. This is better than the basic Query By Example (QBE) which required some programming knowledge. Graphical QBE was produced to allow a fill-in-the-blanks type of query using graphical techniques. This means you can interrogate your data without having to plunge straight into SQL and you don't need any programming experience.

With the new improved graphical QBE you have all the advantages of the drag and drop windows environment together with the QBE plain text SQL commands. If you are SQL proficient, Access is happy for you to create your queries using this technique. If you are not, you will soon find out how easy query design becomes with graphical QBE. The components of the graphical QBE are elegantly simple; the source window, which is used to inform the QBE grid where the information should be taken from, and the QBE grid itself as discussed below.

The QBE Grid

The entry screen is called the QBE design grid and looks like this:

Field:	Employee ID	Expr1: Format([Order Date]	The Value: Freight	Row Summary: Freight
Total:	Group By	Group By	Sum	Sum
Crosstab:	Row Heading	Column Heading	Value	Row Heading
Sort:				
Criteria:				
or:				

As you can see, the grid is aptly named. To query the data in the database you simply enter the name of the field you wish to query and the type of query you wish to apply - Access does the rest. All the entries into the grid are obvious terms or names you have given to fields in the database.

The QBE Dynaset

The resulting query output is called the **QBE dynaset** and is organized in a similar way to a table:

Product Name	Product ID	English Name	Category ID	Supplier ID	Quantity Pe
Alice Mutton	17	Alice Springs Lamb	6	7	20 - 1 kg tins
Aniseed Syrup	3	Licorice Syrup	2	1	12 - 550 ml bo
Boston Crab Meat	40	Boston Crab Meat	8	19	24 - 4 oz tins
Camembert Pierrot	60	Pierrot Camembert	4	28	15 - 300 g rou
Carnarvon Tigers	18	Carnarvon Tiger Prawns	8	7	16 kg pkg.
Chai	1	Dharamsala Tea	1	1	10 boxes x 20
Chang	2	Tibetan Barley Beer	1	1	24 - 12 oz bot
Chartreuse verte	39	Green Chartreuse (Liqueur)	1	18	750 cc per bo
Chef Anton's Cajun Seasoning	4	Chef Anton's Cajun Seasoning	2	2	48 - 6 oz jars
Chef Anton's Gumbo Mix	5	Chef Anton's Gumbo Mix	2	2	36 boxes
Chocolade	48	Dutch Chocolate	3	22	10 pkgs.
Côte de Blaye	38	Côte de Blaye (Red Bordeaux wine)	1	18	12 - 75 cl bott
Escargots de Bourgogne	58	Escargots from Burgundy	8	27	24 pieces
Filo Mix	52	Mix for Greek Filo Dough	5	24	16 - 2 kg boxe
Fløtemysost	71	Fløtemys Cream Cheese	4	15	10 - 500 g pkg
Geitost	33	Goat Cheese	4	15	500 g
Genen Shouyu	15	Lite Sodium Soy Sauce	2	6	24 - 250 ml bo
Gnocchi di nonna Alice	56	Gramma Alice's Dumplings	5	26	24 - 250 g pkg
Gorgonzola Telino	31	Gorgonzola Telino	4	14	12 - 100 g pkg

Even though this dynaset is organized using a similar method to a table, it cannot be considered to act like a table. The dynaset is just the result of a query. To get at this information the query must itself be referenced, causing Access to re-query the data in the database each time.

To alter any of the results of a query, you need to change the data contained in any tables that the query is based upon, or change the criteria that defined the query.

The method of querying the data (a process you need in any database) must be grasped at an early stage so that the overall plan can take it into account. How you want to interrogate data (the types of query you may want to apply and fields that may be involved in the query) could affect the way the database framework is constructed. For more details on the way to organize your queries and what they can do for you see Chapters 4 and 9.

Importing and Exporting From Other Packages

Another technique you should be aware of is the Access methodology used to communicate with other packages. The packages that make up the Microsoft Office suite (Word, Excel and Access) are prime examples of software that can work together to produce the kind of results shown opposite:

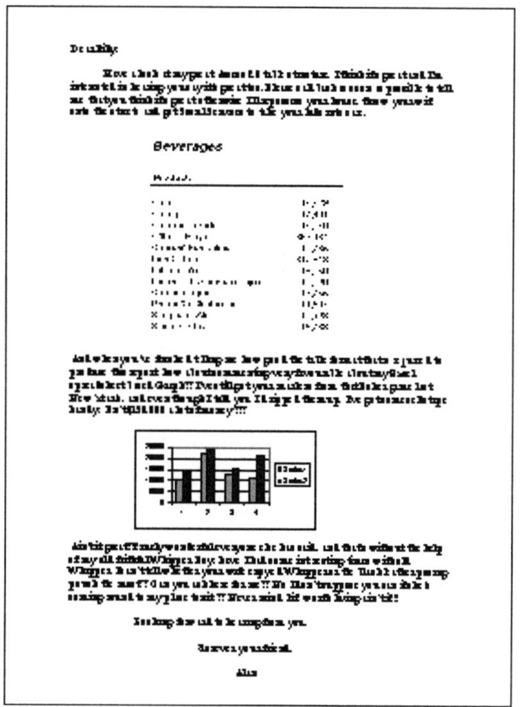

As an example of package integration, suppose you want to produce a written report for an ice-cream company analysis session. In the Access database you create, you would put all the data concerning the various types of ice-cream that the company sells, while the sales and overheads accounts analysis would be in an Excel spreadsheet.

To produce the report you would use the database twice. Firstly, you would use the database and the spreadsheet to get an idea of the position the company was in - you could then decide on important aspects that the report should highlight and the way in which the information should be presented.

Then you could use Access to produce fully integrated reports from the data in the form of tables and graphs, pulling the required information from the spreadsheet files into Access as you wished. You would pass these reports to the wordprocessor, Microsoft Word, to present the conclusions brought by Access and Excel working together.

Access 2.0 also allows you to take advantage of data stored in other databases. Access has the ability to take copies of the tables in other databases and add them to its own store, in its own style. It can also make a link between itself and other packages, so the information you are sharing with them is always up-to-date and kept within the host machine. This is called attaching.

In Chapter 8 we discuss the pros and cons of importing or attaching tables from other databases, and how to achieve it.

Producing Graphs of Your Data

In order to produce any reasonable reports you will have to interrogate the figures in your database and produce graphical displays of those interrogated figures. This will allow you to present meaningful reports that are easily assimilated.

To this end, Microsoft has provided an industrial-strength software package called Microsoft Graph which is devoted to the production of graphical information. This subject is fully covered in Chapter 7, where we discuss using builders to create customized calculations and forming graphs.

Below is an example of the type of graphical output it is possible to produce with Microsoft Graph.

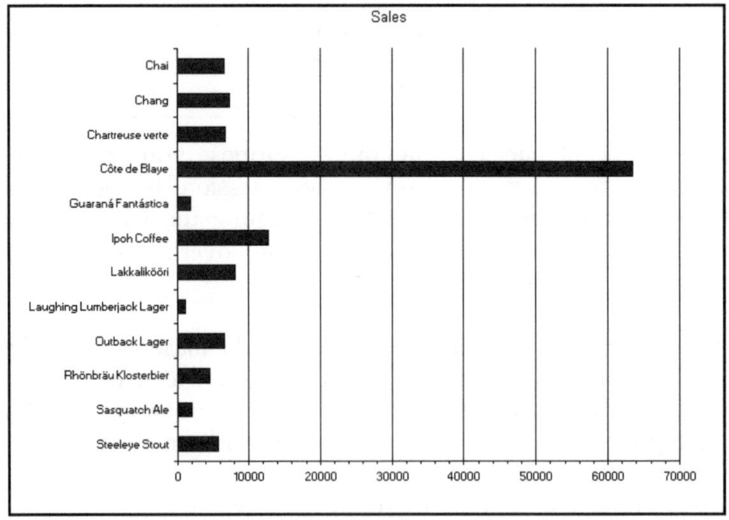

Multiple Tables

As you saw in Chapter 1, the disadvantage of using a flat-bed database is that all the information is stored in one large table. This has several effects on a database, not least that queries are slowed down as the computer plows through all the information in the database in order to complete its task.

The advantage of a relational design is that the amount of repetitive data is dramatically reduced, because all the duplicated data is distilled into another table that only contains unique records. These records are then related to others in the original table. Most of the time, you aren't interested in all the data that makes up a record; therefore with the relational multi-table design you will be able to work with smaller tables and speed up your queries.

Storing unique values in separate tables and then relating the records together means you can reduce spelling errors across records, whilst reducing the amount of data entry that is required. Instead of having to type in the entire record, you can now select the contents of several tables to build up your record.

One of the most useful creations you will make, in conjunction with this task, is a look-up table. This is a table that contains records which are used in the construction of major records. The table contains instances of entries that are made often, and a user may use it as a guide to the correct entry for that field when adding a new record.

One of the most common subjects for a look-up table is your customer names. Instead of typing in the name of a customer when you wish to see information about the orders they have made, simply select the name from a pre-presented list to find the correct customer details every time.

The multiple table design of a relational database makes sense both in terms of the operating speed of the queries you will be running, the organization of the information in your database and the ease with which data entry can be made using look-up tables.

Table Relations

When you create a relational database design, you will naturally produce several table designs. So that Access 2.0 understands the relationship between these essentially distinct objects, you must define how the tables are supposed to interact with each other. You can do this by informing Access of the type and position of each different relation between the tables in your design. There are three basic types of table relationship that you can use; one-to-one, one-to-many, and many-to-many.

One-To-One Relationships

A one-to-one relationship exists between two independent tables, if one record in a table has a relationship to one record in a second table.

An example of this relationship can be illustrated in a business environment combining a customer details table and a confidential customer details table. The customer details table may contain general customer details, including name, address and postal code, whereas the sensitive customer details table may contain information that the customer has given but doesn't want released to all and sundry, for example, their discount rate or their credit limit.

> The ability to set up table security is supplied by Access, allowing you to restrict the use of the information contained in a table.

Therefore, in this example, one customer record relates to one sensitive customer record, producing the need for a one-to-one relationship between these tables. *One* customer has only *one* group of sensitive information.

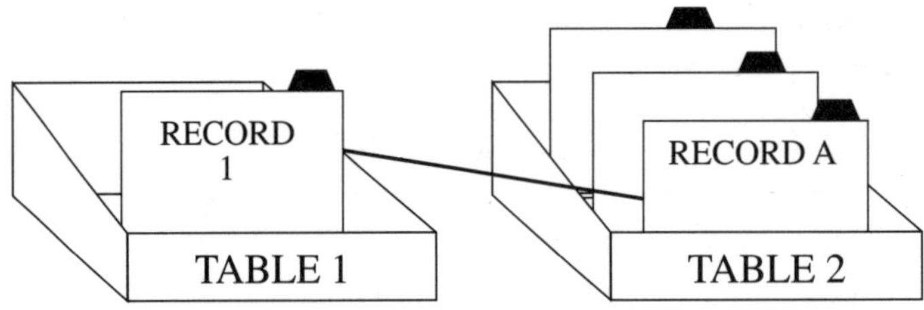

One-To-Many Relationships

A one-to-many relationship exists between two independent tables, if one record in a table has a relationship to many records in a second table.

A good use of this type of relationship occurs between a patient information table that contains details of the patient and a visits table that contains data on the visits that have been made to a surgery by the patients over the last ten years. As each patient may have made more than one visit in the ten year period, a one-to-many relationship exists between the tables. *One* patient will have had *many* visits.

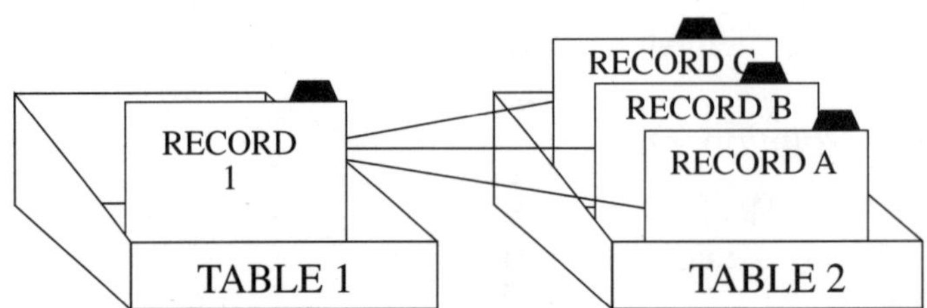

Many-To-Many Relationships

A many-to-many relationship exists between two independent tables, if many records in the first table relate to many records in the second.

A many-to-many relationship is required between a salesman table containing details of each member of the sales force, and a product table that contains details of the products that the sales force may sell. One sales rep may sell many of the products that are manufactured, but one product may also be sold by many sales reps. Hence *many* sales reps sell *many* products.

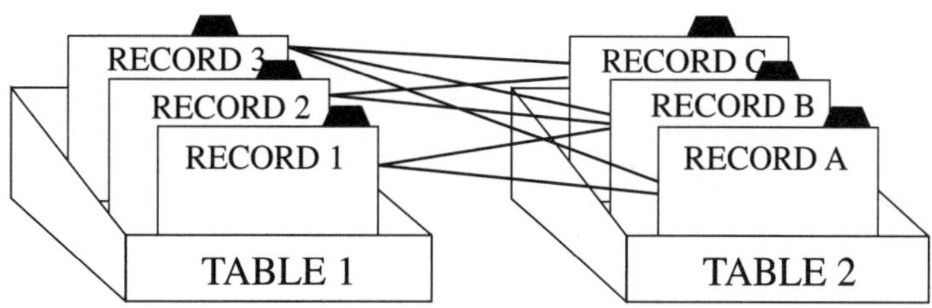

The difference between the one-to-many and the many-to-many relationships is an important one to understand. A many-to-many relationship is really the inter-meshing of the ideas behind two one-to-many relationships, one one way, one the other. This also suggests the way in which Access will handle many-to-many relationships. Each patient can have many visits and each sales rep can sell many products. However, although each product can be sold by many different sales reps, each visit involves only one patient.

The easy way to imagine this many-to-many structure and the way that Access handles the situation is to construct a third table which has a one-to-many relationship from both the first and second tables. This will produce the required structure.

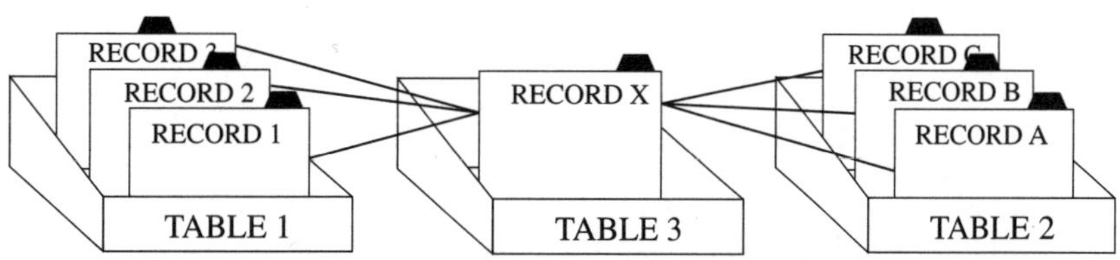

Referring back to our surgery example, suppose we also had a table that contained information on each drug that could be prescribed. Clearly, there would exist a one-to-many relationship between the patients and the drugs. *One* patient can be prescribed *many* drugs.

Now suppose that we wanted to set up the database so that we have a relationship between the drug details and the visits information. Clearly, this is a many-to-many relationship, but we can set this up using the patients table as the third table. We have two one-to-many relationships based on the patients table, and therefore we can link the many end tables together to produce the required many-to-many relationship.

Referential Integrity

One of the problems with having a multiple table structure is that there are groups of related records that must stay related otherwise the entire database structure will come crashing down around your ears.

In an attempt to prevent anything like this happening, a relational database design may incorporate referential integrity. In short, referential integrity will check to make sure that any action you perform on any record in your database won't break this relationship of records.

Whether you are simply altering the contents of a field or you are deleting a whole record, Access can check to see if referential integrity is being maintained, and if it isn't it will stop the action from taking place.

The choice of whether to apply referential integrity to your database is a difficult one. Some designers say that without it the penalties are much heavier, while others say that it cramps the design of the database, restricting what the user can and can't do to too high a degree. We suggest that you experiment with this topic in various situations and come to your own conclusions on when and where you apply this global policeman to any or all of your designs. You may find it wise to apply it just before the real live data is entered, so as to allow you free rein with the design stage. The choice is up to you.

Planning a Database

Now you have an idea of some of the techniques that make Access what it is, you should look at the ideas behind producing a plan. To let the ideas flow freely, follow our example of a manager of the local news stand, Mr. Daily Enquirer.

What is a Database For?

The first thing to do is think about what information you want the database to contain. Make a list of all the different things you will want the database to hold information on. This list will then be worked on to derive tables that will make up your database proper.

Mr. Daily Enquirer runs a news stand, and he also provides a newspaper delivery service for his customers in the local area. He has recently noticed a growth in this side of the business and he's worried about the amount of paper work this is generating. He has therefore decided to move over to a computerized database system.

After thinking about everything he needs in the database, he has prepared the following list:

- The names of the newspapers and magazines I will be selling.
- The cost of those newspapers and magazines.
- How often those newspapers and magazines are printed?
- Who supplies me with the newspapers and magazines?

- The names of the customers I deliver to.
- The addresses of those customers.
- Who delivers to those customers?
- The payments they have made for the newspapers that have been delivered in this month.

- Which newspapers the customer has ordered?
- How many newspapers have been ordered?
- When they want that newspaper or magazine delivered?

- What sales I have made today?
- Sales of which paper and magazine.

As you can see, these requirements fall into natural categories and it's these categories that can be used as the tables in which he will include his field definitions. However, there is one more stage of refinement he must go through to make a true relational database design and that is to check to see if any data will be repeated often in one table, and then separate it into its own table.

The name of the supplier of newspapers and magazines to Mr. Daily Enquirer is a good example of this. One supplier will deliver several different newspapers and magazines, and if this information is stored with the newspaper name information it will be needlessly repeated.

If you take the supplier name and any other information related to this name, such as address, this data can be put into a separate table and referred to there. This will reduce the spelling errors that may crop up from multiple entries of the same information, and also reduce the size of the newspaper information table. If you apply these rules to Daily's list of requirements and think about the type of data you can enter into each of these requirements, you can produce a listing like this:

Newspaper Table

Name	Type	Description
ID	Text	Used to uniquely identify each newspaper or magazine.
Name	Text	
Cost	Currency	
Frequency of supply	Text	
Supplier	Text	Used to identify which supplier supplies these newspapers.

Customer Table

Name	Type	Description
Customer ID	Text	
Name	Text	
Address	Text	
Deliverer ID	Text	Used to label the person who does the delivery.
Payment Week1	Currency	
Payment Week2	Currency	
Payment Week3	Currency	
Payment Week4	Currency	
Payment Week5	Currency	

Deliverer Table

Name	Type	Description
Deliverer ID	Text	
Name	Text	
Address	Text	
Phone Number	Text	Use text because phone numbers aren't always just numbers (you might use hyphens or brackets for the area code) and you don't need to use these figures in calculations.
Start Date	Date/Time	When they began delivering for me.
Date of Birth	Date/Time	

Supplier Table

Name	Type	Description
Supplier ID	Text	
Name	Text	
Address	Text	
Day of usual delivery	Text	

Orders Table

Name	Type	Description
Customer ID	Text	
Order ID	Text	Used to identify each individual component of a customers order.
Newspaper ID	Text	
Number required	Number	
Which day delivery?	Text	

Sales Table

Name	Type	Description
Customer ID	Text	
Order ID	Text	
Newspaper ID	Text	
Number sold	Number	
Date of sale	Date/time	

When you have got to this stage in designing your database you are ready to produce the tables as described in Chapter 3. The relationships between the tables should become obvious as you decide on which data should go in which table. Below is a diagram of Daily's table structure:

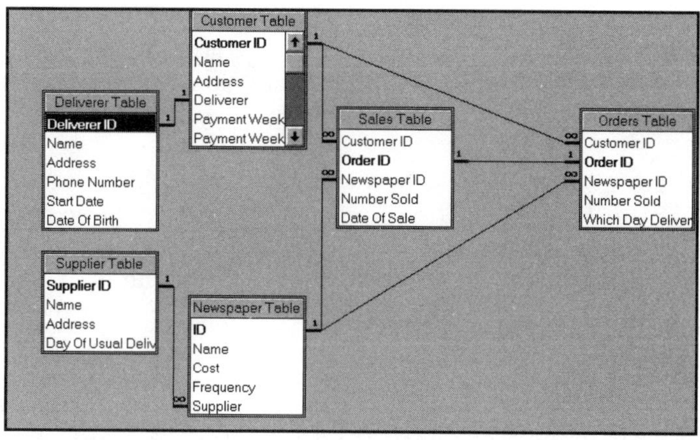

One final point concerns using the fine-tuning properties that you can add to a table design. These include indexing your records to allow the queries to work quicker (but slowing down data entry) or validation rules for what data the users may enter. At the moment you don't need to think about these properties in detail, as you will have to think about them more when actual data is placed into the tables.

Querying the Data

Now we need to begin thinking about what information we are going to need from Daily's database, as well as the movement of the data around the database itself.

In the case of Daily's sales table, the information entered will come from one of three places:

- From the Orders table, automatically at the end of each day.
- From Daily, to rectify any mistakes that occurred in the actual deliveries to customers. For example, a customer went on holiday and so didn't receive that day's delivery.
- From Daily, to record the amount of over-the-counter sales to the general public. This would be attributed to Customer ID 1, standing for A.N.Other (unnamed customers).

To make the data travel from the orders table to the sales table you would use an Append query, adding that day's date to each record as it was added.

The calculation of a customer's bill would need several queries that first isolated all the orders received, then added up how much they had paid so far this month and produced the necessary calculations to provide the resulting, unpaid amount.

For each of the queries, it must be decided which fields hold the information required either to be seen in the completed dynaset or to be included in the criteria for a sort or selection of data. This in turn specifies the tables or queries that are needed to be used as the source of information for your query. The final decision is about which criteria to use to retrieve the necessary records.

For example, to get all the records for the sales table that relate to one customer, the appropriate Customer ID is the criteria, but to get the sales of all the newspapers between two dates, the two dates will make up that criteria.

Use the Like operator to identify text as the criteria and place quotation marks (" ")around the specific text you are searching for.

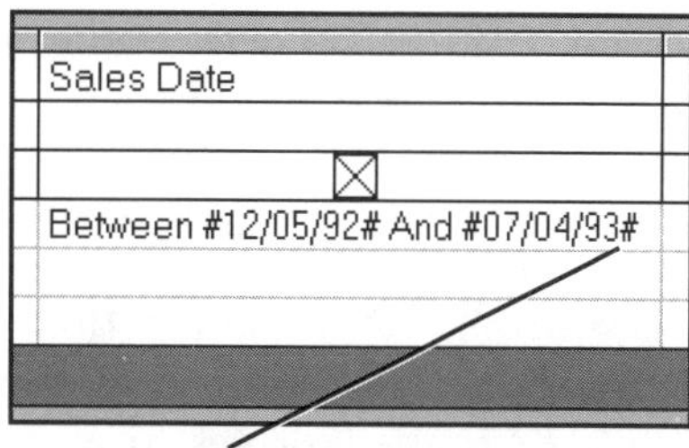

Use the Between...And operator to identify a range of values as the criteria. Place hashes (#) around any dates you include as the criteria. The hash sign is sometimes referred to as the number sign.

Make a list of all the questions you may want to ask of the data in your database, listing all of the tables and fields that will be involved, and any criteria that you think will be appropriate to this query. Remember, you can test out any query as many times as you like without making any serious changes to the data in the database or the database itself.

Some of the questions that Daily has stumbled upon include:

- Which customers have large bills (large being an amount that he must put more thought into defining)?
- Which customers haven't paid their bill for a long period (and what is a long period)?
- Which papers aren't selling well?
- Which papers are selling very well?
- How many new customers has he attracted over a certain period of time?
- How much money has he taken over the past day/week/month/year?

He knows that his list is nowhere near exhaustive and so will return to it at a later date. The design of an Access database is fairly flexible when it comes to adding to the structure at a later date, and so it isn't important to cover all the possible queries that may be needed, just the obvious ones.

To understand the way that a query idea is dissected, follow Daily as he breaks down one of his query ideas and see how easy it is.

Daily's prime concern is the money that his customers owe to him, and so he decides to look at the query that deals with large unpaid bills first. He wants to **select** all the customers who have large unpaid bills; large, he decides, means over ten dollars of unpaid bills. This will give him a listing of all the customers he wants. He then wants to target the customers who have the largest bills over the ten dollar mark, and so he wants to do a **sort** of the records he has obtained, sorting them by the size of the bill to get the largest bills first. We will get to a solution to this demand shortly.

Form Design

You know that Access uses forms to allow user entry or to view data in the database. Therefore, there are two important points you should address in a database plan where forms are concerned:

- Which tables and fields are the forms going to affect?
- How is the form actually going to appear on the screen?

The first of these points can greatly affect the way the database works, and also the number of queries that the database makes use of. If you wish to create a form that uses field definitions from a variety of tables, you will need to base the form on a query that produces the correct dynaset of the fields from those in the underlying tables. You may also wish to base the form on a query if you need to limit the records the user has access to.

The second of these points is where the artist in you can come to the fore. Before you begin to create a form design, it's well worth spending a few moments thinking about where you want all the fields to appear, how you want them to appear, in which colors and with what frilly attachments. Don't forget to think about the switchboards that may control your database and the buttons you will need to control the movement. You can also begin to think about the instructions you will need to execute when these buttons are selected.

Going back to the example, Daily wants lots of forms so that he can view data in many different ways. One particular form he needs will be used to quickly bring up the records of customers who come into the shop to pay their bills. From this form he will be able to see all the customers details, including the amount they owe, and he will be able to enter the amount they pay at this visit. Later he can use this data to update each customer record, and then he can run the query we saw earlier to find the customers who have large bills outstanding.

Printing Out Forms

It is also possible to print out forms with the data included, and so the layout is an important aspect of form design. Daily may use this ability to produce invoices for customers. This means he will want the presentation of the form to look professional. He will make a mental note to look at Chapter 10 for more form presentation techniques.

Reports

The same points should be kept in mind when the reports are being designed (especially the need for a correct query as the source for generating the report).

For more information about the types of report that Access 2.0 has available, see Chapters 6 and 11 which deal with Access reports.

Daily wants to produce a number of reports so he can keep an eye on all parts of his business, including the total amount of monies he has owing, the number of papers he sells, how each paper is selling and any tax he has owing or has paid.

When he looks a little closer at this report on monies owed, he can see that he only wants the name of his serious debtors and the amount they owe, together with a total figure, so he can decide on the action he will take to reduce the amount. This gives him a definite requirement for his report, which he can bring to the design plan.

Macros and Modules

The amount of thought you are able to put towards these components of a database design will be minimal if you are new to this subject. The use of macros in particular can only be successful once you understand the use of all of the other components of the database. The use of Access Basic is also restricted if you are new to database design, simply because the knowledge that you pick up as you learn about Access structure will not help you greatly when you attempt to learn this programming language.

What you can do is begin to consider the opportunities available to you for incorporating these automations into your database.

As an example of a macro, Daily often wants to print out the details of the customers who owe him money. So he produces a macro that first queries the data to find the customers he requires, then prints out the details of these customers in a form he has designed for this purpose.

The Steps Towards Producing a Database Plan

To produce the plan itself you need to think about the following things and answer the following questions. A reasonable basic database plan should then become obvious.

1. Think about why you need the database. Is a database really the correct type of application to use? Are you going to be asking questions of lots of data organized into similar formats? This part of the planning stage will probably spread into the other sections, so make notes of the things as they occur to you.
2. What types of data will you want in the database? Do you want names, addresses, prices etc? These types of data are the fields that go towards making up the database.
3. Do these fields group under any umbrella name, such as customer details or sales? If so, these are the tables you should create and build the field definitions into. Is there any unnecessary data duplication? If so, think about another table for this particular data.
4. What kind of questions are you going to ask of the data? The queries you begin to plan here should have at least the field names required and the type of query that you wish to apply: sort or selection.
5. What kind of data entry screens or data view screens do you want? Do you want some of the fields on the data entry screens to be tied to a specific choice, do you need a look-up table? How do you want the forms to look visually?
6. What kind of connections are going to exist between the tables? What method are you using to connect the tables? For example, the customer details table is connected to the sales table by the customer code in the sales table.
7. What kind of summary print-outs do you want? What fields will have to appear on the various reports to produce the results you want? How do you want the reports to look visually? Should they be bordered, highlighted, colored, shaded?
8. What tasks do you want to automate? Do you want query and print out, or add-to-record and update. These are macros.
9. Do you want to automate the database? Adding switchboards to the database will do this.

Testing the Database

One task that it's important to complete as soon as the creation of the framework to the database is finished is the testing of the framework to destruction. This means you should enter some test data into the database, carry out all the usual jobs upon it and observe the results. If they are unreliable, hold back on entering lots of real data. You can also test the data validation rules by attempting to enter illegal data. This will give you a picture of what will happen if a user enters illegal data (which they will) and you can put in checks to prevent it or design a help system to tell the user what to do.

One Final Word

Finally, this plan should not be set in concrete, especially after the database is created. Access allows the designer to add features to a database fairly freely as long as the basic structure of the database is sound. This is why it is such a good idea to test the database structure with sample data. The results of these tests may mean you decide to make alterations to your database plan and design.

Now you can go on to the next chapter and begin the task of creating a relational database with Microsoft Access.

Tables

This is where you begin to build an Access database, starting with the cornerstone of all databases - **tables**.

From the previous chapters you know that a table is a grid of rows and columns where all your raw data is stored. Each row is a record in your table, and each column is a field. Your raw data now has to be organized so that it will fit into this structure.

You will learn how to transfer your table plan and all your loose information into a concise format that Access can manipulate.

In this chapter you will cover the fundamentals of table creation, how to fill them out and how to edit them. After you have finished this hard work, you will learn how to automate the whole process through the use of wizards.

Chapter 3 contains information on:

- How to create a new database container and your first table
- Aspects of table design
- A guide to table and field properties
- Setting primary keys
- A meeting with the Table Wizard
- Instruction on entering and editing data
- Troubleshooting

Building Your First Database

In all databases, tables are built in a regular grid-like fashion. You can compare this format to a soccer league table, where each country has a record. The fields are represented by the headings at the top of columns, such as games played, goals for/against and points. This grid shape means that each country has a number of 'cells' which you can fill in to reflect the team's performance. The rules for filling in the cells are well known - for instance, a team's points total is calculated from their win/draw/lose performance.

Table: Soccer League Table

Country	Played	Goals For	Goals Against	Total Points
Iceland	4			
Cameroon	4			
Swaziland	3			
Egypt	3			
Iraq	4			

	MATCHES	GOALS	GOALS AGAINST	POINTS
Iceland	4	6	1	10
Cameroon	4	7	4	8
Swaziland	3	5	3	6
Egypt	3	5	3	2
Iraq	4	1	13	0

As you can see, you are already surrounded by table designs in your daily life. The concept of cells within records that are described by fields is how most of the world arranges everyday information.

The process of creating a table in an Access database is very easy, especially if you have completed the planning stage and come up with a good idea of what you require from the database.

Before we build our first Access table, we need to open a brand new database.

Opening a New Database

Run Microsoft Access from the Windows display by either:

- Double clicking on the Microsoft Access icon. 
- Or, choosing the Access icon on your Microsoft Office Suite. 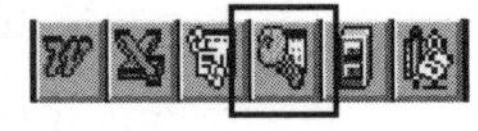

> If the icon is not available on the desktop, see the Installing Access section in the introduction of the book.

- Close the Welcome window by double-clicking in the left-hand corner. 

- Select the New Database icon from the icon bar to give the screen below.

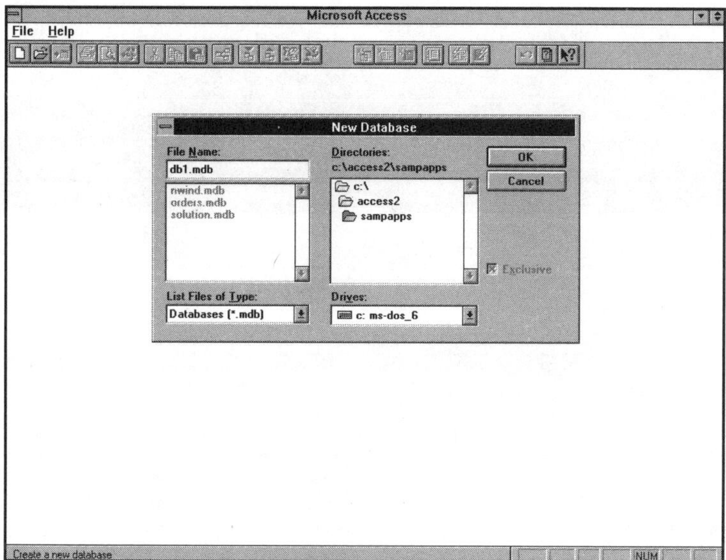

Now you are faced with a complicated window, filled with lots of icons you may not have seen before. Don't worry, most of this is unimportant at the moment.

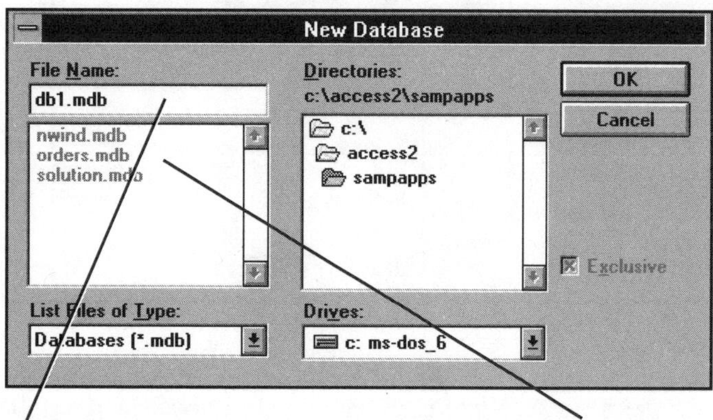

The part that we are interested in is the File Name: box, containing the flashing cursor. This is the box that contains the name of your database, and currently it contains the default database name **db1.mdb**.

These are the databases that already exist in your open **Sampapps** directory. They are demonstration, tutorial and sample applications that come supplied with Access 2.0.

To create a database with a different name, you need to remove db1.mdb using *BkSp* and type in your new database name.

> New database names must conform to the Disk Operating System (DOS) naming conventions. Simply, this means that the name must be in a single case and it shouldn't include mathematical symbols, punctuation marks, spaces or any of the groups of characters that DOS uses as names for other devices. The name of the database can contain up to eight characters - generally any unabbreviated word can be used.

Here are a few example names that are acceptable as the title of a database:

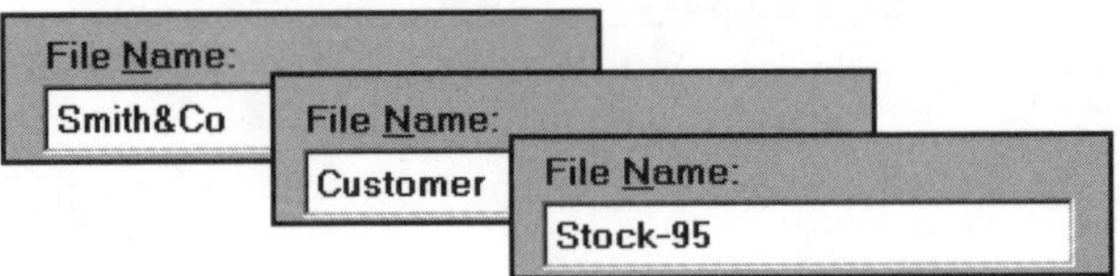

Now, type in your database name and select the OK button. This creates the database with the specified title and leads you to the following screen:

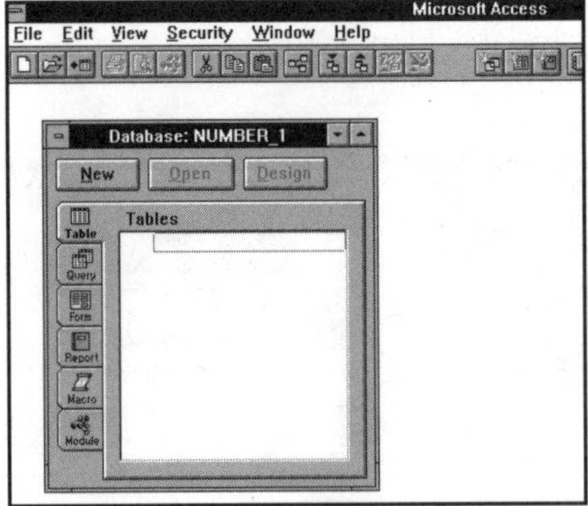

Creating a Table

You can use a Table Wizard, which is described in detail later. Whatever your method, you must have an understanding of table basics, before you can progress with database building.

Here, you will cover those basics while constructing your tables by hand.

To create a table you need to do two things:

- Define a new table.
- Choose fields that define your table.

Defining a Table

To define a table:

- Select the Table tab (if it is not already on top). 
- Select the **New** button.
- Select the New Table button (we'll use wizards later!). 

You should now be looking at your new Table Design window, shown below:

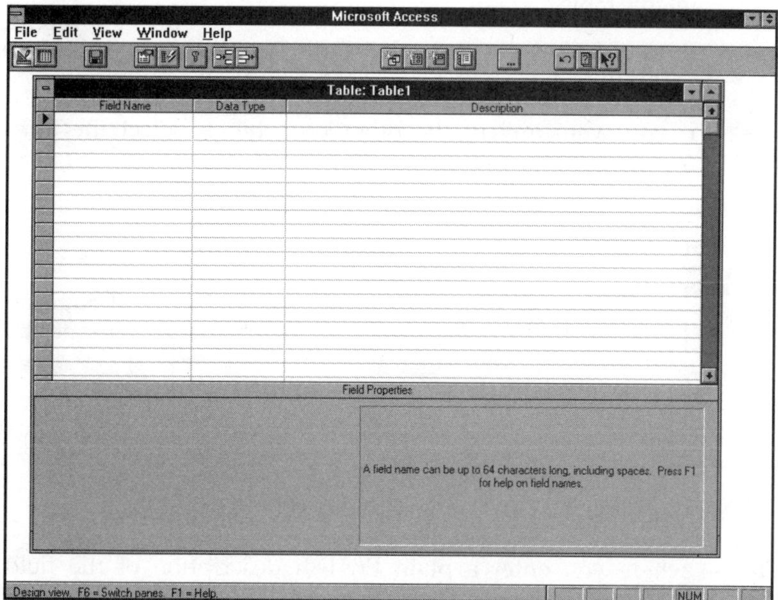

> When your new Table Design window opens, you will notice that the selection of icons on the icon bar changes. The new icons will carry out tasks, relative to table design. Throughout Access 2.0, the menu of icons will change as appropriate.

The Table Design window is used for the actual design of the table structure. This includes the definition of fields, primary keys and other indexes. As we will see, the primary key is used to ensure that there is no record duplication and it also forms the basis for a relational multiple table database.

The table structure will work without primary keys and indexing (if you then decide that more indexing is required, the table can be opened up and altered later).

You have created your basic table shape. You must now proceed to place fields within the table. These fields will be the column headings of your finished table. There must be some restriction on the data that the user will enter into the fields, so that you must set limitations on the kind of data that a field may contain. In other words you are setting a field definition.

Defining Your Fields

To define fields:

- Enter the name of the first field that you want in the table.

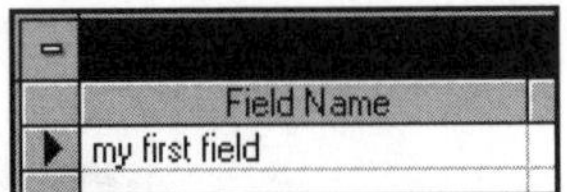

- Press *Tab* to move onto the Data Type column. Access automatically places the default data type (Text) into the cell.
- If you want any of the other data types, select the arrow at the end of the cell.

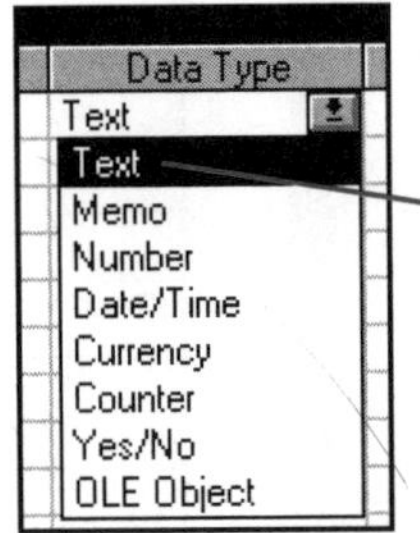

If you highlight your required data type it will automatically be inserted in the cell for you. Remember to choose a data type that is relevant to the entries you will make in this field (as we described in Chapter 2).

- Press *Tab* to move onto the Description column.

This is where you enter a plain English description of the field you are defining. You may enter a lengthy and explanatory sentence of your field, but remember that whatever you write will appear in the status bar in the bottom left of your screen during data entry sessions.

- Press *Tab* to move to the next field name.
- Repeat this process until all the field definitions for this table have been defined.

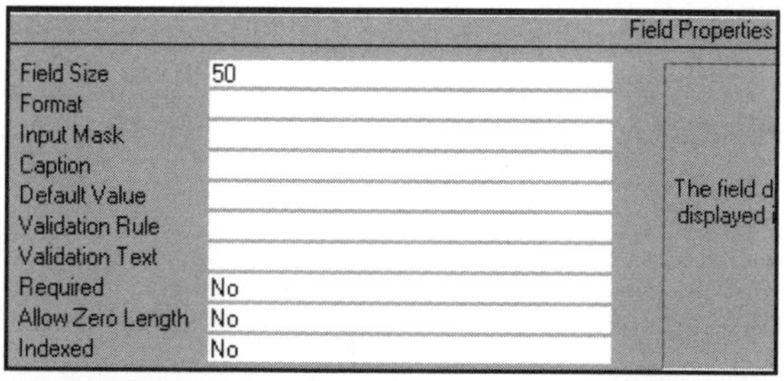

Field Properties	
Field Size	50
Format	
Input Mask	
Caption	
Default Value	
Validation Rule	
Validation Text	
Required	No
Allow Zero Length	No
Indexed	No

The field d
displayed i

This will be covered in depth later in the chapter, so don't worry if some things are still unclear.

Now that we have defined some field definitions that go towards making up our table structure, you may have noticed that movement around the table design screen is limited. There are several ways you can move the cursor around this screen.

Action	Movement
Tab	This moves you along each field definition, one cell at a time.
Shift+Tab	This moves you backwards.
Enter	This moves you onto the next cell.
Mouse	This moves you to the field where the mouse pointer is placed, after depressing the left button.
▶*	Clicking on this moves you to the first field of a new record.

To change any particular cell in the table just click on it, use the *BkSp* key to delete the contents and re-type.

You have now successfully completed the design of your table structure and it may look something like this:

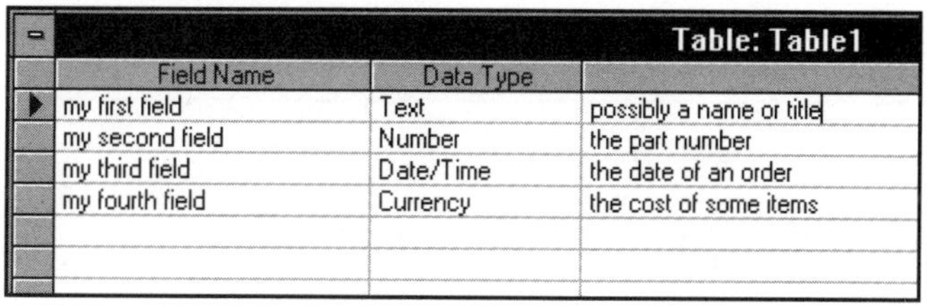

Table: Table1

Field Name	Data Type	
my first field	Text	possibly a name or title
my second field	Number	the part number
my third field	Date/Time	the date of an order
my fourth field	Currency	the cost of some items

Now you can go on to see how it is possible to customize this basic table design, but firstly you want to save your work.

Saving Your Table

To save your table you need to:

- Select File in the top left of the window.
- Select Save As from the drop-down menu.

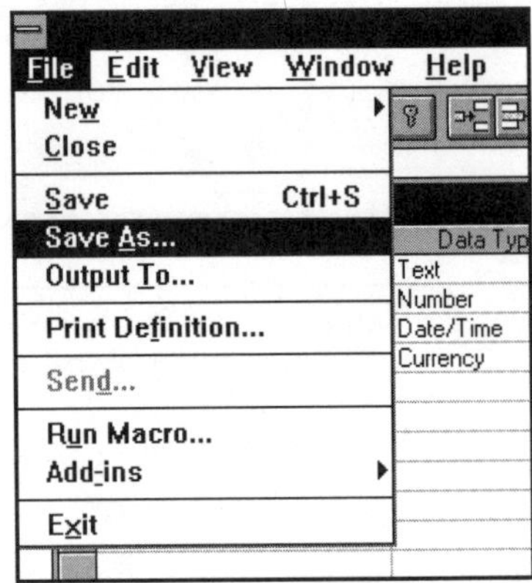

- Enter the title of your table and select OK. This titles your table and saves it.
- Select File and Close from the drop-down menu and the table window will close.

You will be returned to the initial database window, which, when the Table tab is on top, should now show the title of your table. Simply repeat the whole process to produce another table, but remember to use a different name for the new table, otherwise the first table structure will be lost.

> With the exception of the database title, none of the titles in the database (i.e. table titles, form titles) have to conform to the DOS naming conventions, and can be up to 64 characters in length.

Editing Your Table

When you have completed the creation of a table's structure, saved it and closed it down, you may find that you want to alter the structure. To do this you need to be able to get back to the Table Design window.

Re-Opening a Table's Structural Design Window

To re-open your table to change the design:

- Select the Table tab from the database window. You will see the list of tables you have constructed.
- Highlight the table you wish to alter.

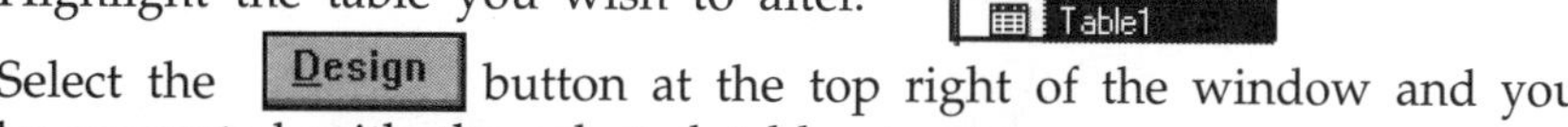

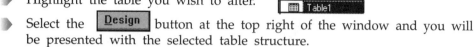

- Select the Design button at the top right of the window and you will be presented with the selected table structure.

Now, we have created some field definitions in our basic table structure, let's go on to look at customising the enviroment by setting the special properties of this table and its fields.

Table Properties

Each part of your database is composed of smaller components, such as a table and its fields. The fields that go into a table define its structure and give the table some uniqueness. Apart from the use of fields to define a table, you can also give the table some properties of its own, which can be used to refine a table's make-up even further. You can assign these properties to a table using the Table Properties box.

Opening the Table Properties Box

When you have opened the table you want to assign table properties to, either:

- Click on the Table Properties icon to open the box.
- Or, select Table Properties... from the View menu on the menu bar.

Whichever method you use, you will see the following window:

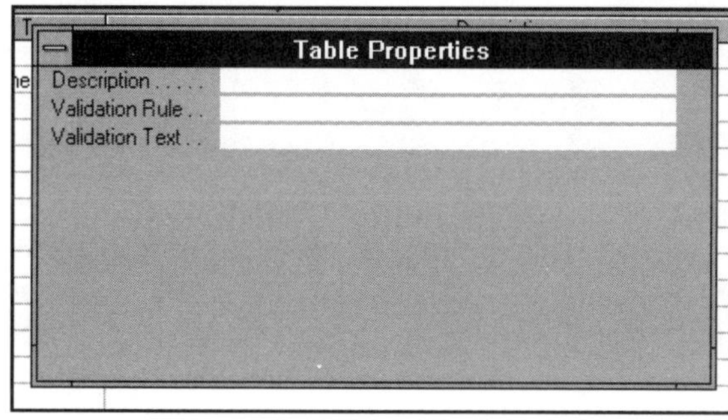

There are three properties that you can attach to the table design itself:

Description, Validation Rule and Validation Text.

Property	Use
Description	This property is used to describe the use of the table. Unlike other description properties, the table version will never appear on the status bar, so it is only used as a way to document your database. This is important for database maintenance, especially if someone other than yourself will be taking on this task.
Validation Rule	This property is used to check the validity of the data contained in a whole record as it is saved. This can be very useful if you want to compare one field entry to another, say Amount Ordered compared to Credit Limit. Note that this property comes equipped with the Build button, allowing you access to the Expression Builder.
Validation Text	This is the text that will appear on the screen when the validation rule is broken. You can use this to inform the user of any rules that they have broken and how to solve the problem.

To set any of these properties, simply move the cursor to the appropriate cell and type in your entry. To close the box, do one of the following:

- Double-click in the top left corner of the box.
- Click once on the box and select Close.
- Click on the Table Properties icon again.
- Select Table Properties... from the View menu on the menu bar.

Note, that when the box is open, Table Properties... in the View menu will have a tick mark next to it that disappears when you close it down.

The Field Pointer

You may have noticed that when you define a field, it is marked on the left by a small pointer. This pointer is used to identify the current field definition that you are working on. This is so that operations such as primary key definition and field deletion can be conducted on a specific field.

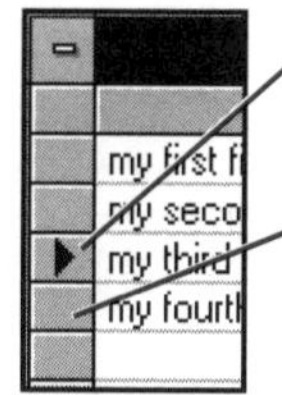

Field pointer.

To move this pointer, click on the small box in the pointers column.

When you use this method to move the pointer you will see that the entire field is highlighted. Highlighted fields can be edited, copied, deleted, etc. If you wanted to apply the same task to several field definitions at one time you could simply highlight them all.

Highlighting Multiple Fields

To highlight multiple fields you need to:

- Hold down the *Ctrl* key.
- Select any other required fields by clicking in their pointer box.
- Release the *Ctrl* key - all the selected fields will be highlighted.

Or:

- Select the first of your required fields.
- Hold down the *Shift* key.
- Select the last of your required fields.
- Release the *Shift* key - all the fields between the first and last will be highlighted.

> This method of selecting several things on the screen at the same time is used throughout Access' various design stages. This allows you to apply the same task to all of your chosen elements.

You've selected some fields, let's look at what you can now do with them.

Editing Fields

As you create a table or even after you have completed it, its structure can still be altered. We can insert or delete a field or change its location.

Insertion

To insert a field:

- Select the field that you wish to follow the new inserted field definition.
- Select the  Insert Row icon from the icon bar.

A new row for field definition should have been inserted and the following fields moved down one row.

Deletion

To delete a field:

- Select the field that you wish to be deleted.
- Select the icon from the icon bar.  Delete Row

The field definition should now be deleted and the field definitions below the removed one will have moved up one row to fill the gap.

Location

To change the location of a field:

- Select the field that is to be moved using the pointer.

Table: Table1

Field Name	Data Type	
my first field	Text	possibly a name or title
my sixth field	Text	paperwork
my second field	Number	the part number
my third field	Date/Time	the date of an order
my fourth field	Currency	the cost of some items
my fifth field	Yes/No	did we send them a letter?

- Place the mouse pointer on the arrow highlighting the field to be moved and hold down the mouse button.
- Drag the field to the place on the table design and release the mouse button. The field definition should now have moved.

We have now completed the process of creating a skeletal table, the basic building block of relational databases. We have gone back and altered some design decisions and we have saved our work. We must now take a moment to study the detailed rules and regulations when creating fields professionally.

Field Properties

You may have noticed when selecting data types earlier, that a smaller box appears under the main design table.

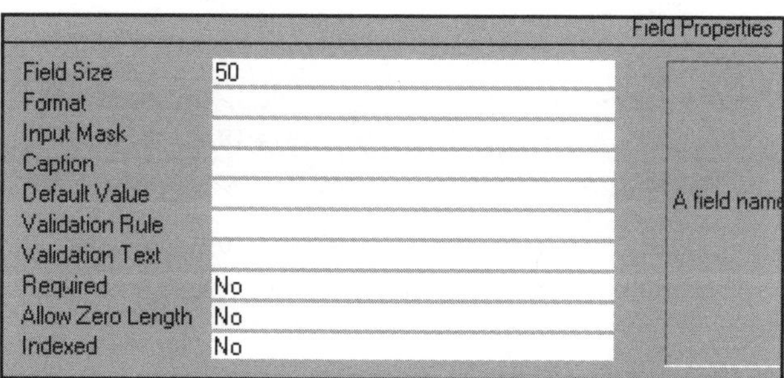

This window is called the Field Properties box and contains more detailed information about a highlighted field. Using the Field Properties box, we can customize the characteristics of each individual field. You may want to limit the number of characters that a text field may contain or you may want to state whether or not a figure is required in a number field. Below is a list of all the field property actions.

> Some data types have more rules attached to them than others. Notice, that the text field can have all 9 properties set, whereas an OLE Object field can only have 2 properties set.

Field Size

This should be set to the maximum length of any entry to be made in the field, but should be as small as possible to conserve memory. Think about the information you will be entering in the future - if you know your longest entry in the field is Antidisestablishmentarianism, then set field size to 28.

Format

This is the way that the data will actually appear on the record, possibly different to the entry format. For example, you may wish to enter a date using short notation: 3/14/94. You can use Format to automatically change the entry to the long notation: 14-Mar-94.

The available formats obviously change depending on the data type in play. For a list of all the alternatives see Appendix I.

Input Mask

This is the format in which you are forced to enter the data into the table. For example, if a phone number is required, you can force the user to enter it using your pre-defined rules. This means you can specify that all the area codes are in brackets before the main number.

Except for Memo, Yes/No and OLE Object fields, all data types can utilize an input mask. There are so many combinations that Access 2.0 supplies an Input Mask Wizard. This accommodates all possible ways you may wish a user to enter information in the future.

The Build Button

From the introduction, you know that the [...] button appears throughout Access 2.0 to help automate various functions. Here you'll see how the Build button helps you to formulate an input mask quickly, by invoking the Input Mask Wizard.

The Input Mask Wizard

When the cursor moves into the Input Mask field property, the Build button appears at the end of the cell:

> Note that the Input Mask Wizard only assists you with Text or Date/Time data types.

Click on this button to invoke the wizard, and after you have saved your table, it will bring with it the following screen:

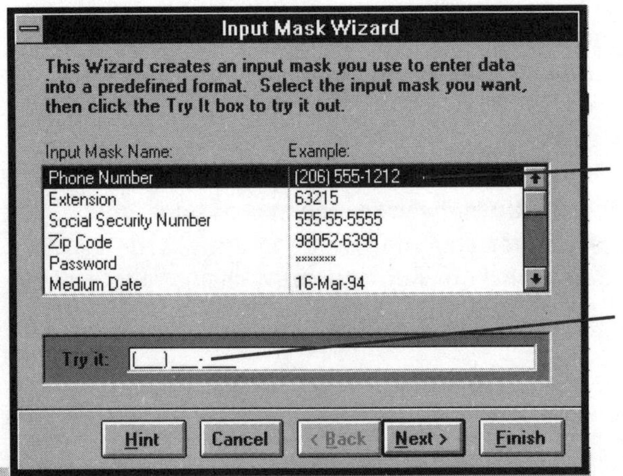

Choose a mask for your field here. The wizard has ten common Text masks or five Date/Time masks on offer.

Once you have highlighted a mask, click in the Try it box and type something to see the effects.

Click on the Next > button to move to the next stage accompanied by the following window:

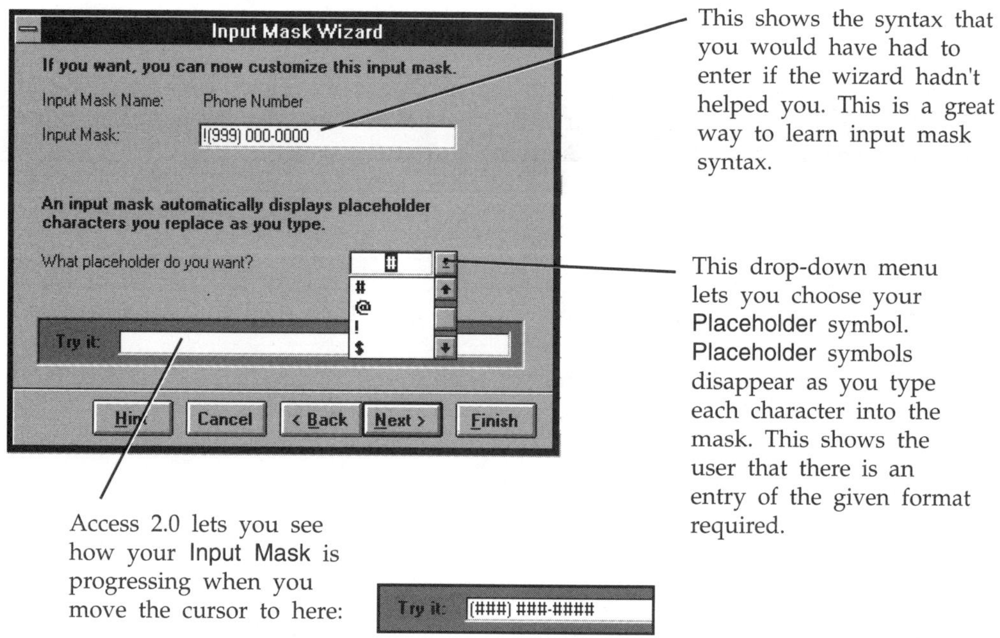

This shows the syntax that you would have had to enter if the wizard hadn't helped you. This is a great way to learn input mask syntax.

This drop-down menu lets you choose your Placeholder symbol. Placeholder symbols disappear as you type each character into the mask. This shows the user that there is an entry of the given format required.

Access 2.0 lets you see how your Input Mask is progressing when you move the cursor to here:

Click on the Next > button to move to the next stage:

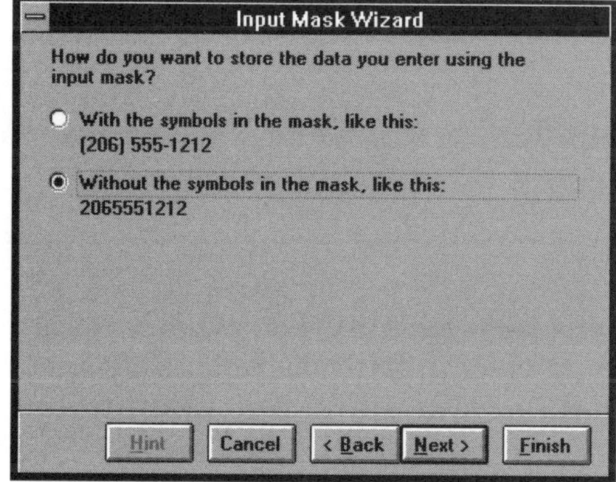

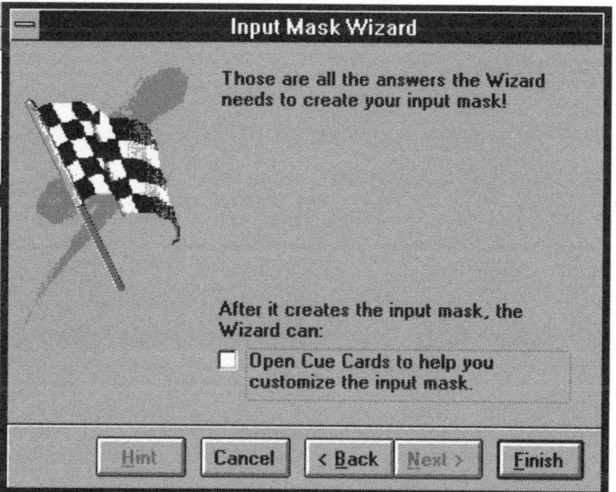

Now, Access 2.0 asks you how you want to store your masked data. This often doesn't affect how you view it in the datasheet. Then with the last window the wizard says "Good-bye".

Caption

This is a full descriptive alternative to the more cursory Field Name (as used in form design). For example, in your form the field name may be Lastname but you could change the caption to Surname Of The Customer.

Default Values

This will appear in the field when a new record is created. It must be of the same type as the field definition, today's date in a Date field for example.

Access 2.0 provides a Builder function to enable you to produce detailed default values easily.

Validation Rule

You can give Access data entry rules. For example, if you define the rule:

"Between #3/3/32# and #10/17/97#"

Access will inform the user if they try to enter a date outside this range.

Access 2.0 provides a Builder function to enable you to produce detailed validation rules easily. This is discussed in Chapter 7: Calculations.

Validation Text

A prompt given to the user if the validation rules are broken, i.e. "Please give a date between 3/3/32 and 17/10/97".

Required

This field property demands that the user makes an entry. For example, in a stock control database you force the user to enter a part number in a Number field.

Allow Zero Length

This field property indicates whether a zero length string is a valid entry. Simply, it could be used to force the user to enter double quotation marks. Why? You may wish the user to state that a field is empty rather than just skipped over.

Indexed

Access 2.0 uses indexes in much the same way as you would use the index in the back of a book, i.e. to find and locate the information you require faster than reading from the first page.

During complex searches, often using a query, Access has to look through a lot of records to settle on those required. The method for searching is linear and in human terms, crude. It has to rely on simple, logical sweeps through all the data to fulfill the most basic request. When databases are mature and contain thousands of records the search and retrieval process starts to slow down. You can help Access along by giving some minimal clues about the kind of data it will be looking for.

These clues are the same as a book index. In Access terms, when indexing is applied an internal table is built. One column has the value of the fields indexed and the other column has the location of the associated records in the table.

Setting a Single Index

Use the NWind sample database Suppliers table in design mode to follow the example:

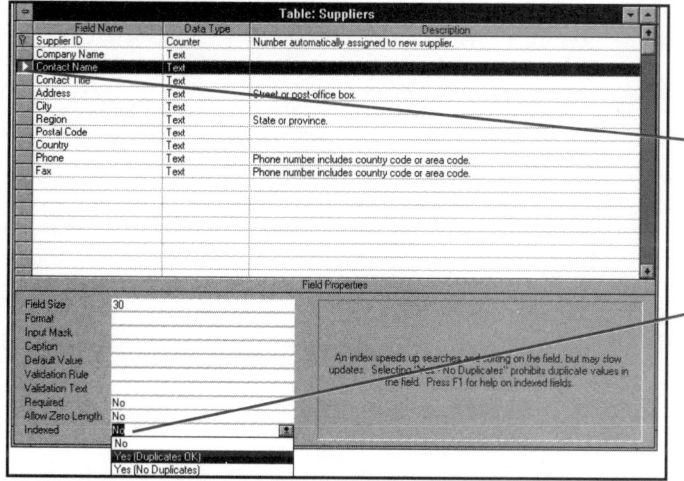

Place the field pointer next to the field you wish to index on (Contact Name is not indexed as yet).

Click in the cell to choose from a drop-down menu. Select either No, Yes (Duplicates OK) or Yes (No Duplicates).

Option	Meaning
No	This is the default setting and means the field is not indexed.
Yes (Duplicates OK)	This means the field is indexed and any duplicates will be allowed by Access. With a postal code, for instance, duplicates will occur. We want Access to let us enter duplicates in the future and tolerate duplicates now.
Yes (No Duplicates)	This means we want to keep the index unique. So, to keep Access operating the index, we must only set this to field entries we know will remain unique. A primary key is a good example as it often uses ID numbers that are only ever used once.

Setting Multiple Index

To help Access even more in its search, we can give several indexes tied together, which refines the clues. For example, we could set two stages of index in the sample table. We could set the first stage of the search to be company name followed by postal code. Our search would be fairly quick and fairly accurate, as the number of companies with the same name, within the same postal code would be minimal. We could of course refine the search further, and add a third stage to the index, for example, contact name. We're close to a solution now, the chances of doing business with two Mr. Mandellas at Dabeards Jewellry Company on Durban Street would be remote.

Let's set a multiple key with NWind, Suppliers table.

- Open the table in Design View.
- Select the Indexes icon, to bring up the Indexes box as shown on the next page.

The Indexes Box

This table already had Company Name set as a single index.

Give your multiple index a name in this cell (avoid using symbols).

List the fields to be indexed either from the drop-down menu, or by typing in. The order you enter the fields will be the order in which the index is carried out.

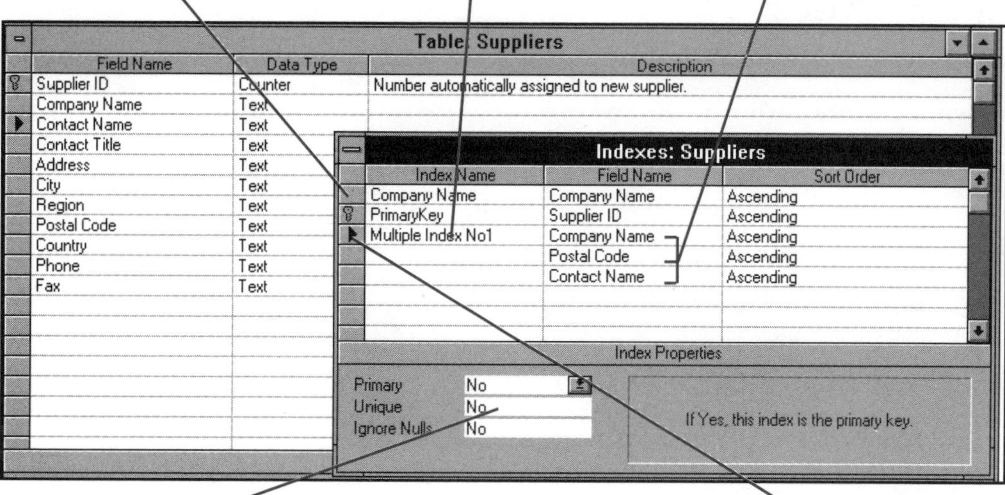

Set some criteria for the index here. Primary keys are often the only ones that are unique. Ignoring Null values may give some speed increase, but what if one of your search records is missing one piece of information? You might skip over a record without a postal code entered, and this may be the very one that had our desired contact name in it.

If you make a mistake, highlight the cell with the pointer and delete as normal.

When you progress to querying your tables, you will use special formulae that tightly define the records that you want. To speed up the search for records, you can utilize single and multiple indexes. Imagine you are looking for a book in the Library of Congress. To quickly focus the search, you would look in the library's catalog, instead of going straight to the shelves. You would only consider browsing, when you had found the correct shelf. Access behaves in a similar way. Rules for the search criteria on the first fields of a multiple index are strict. Only the final field is allowed loose limits. Access says that only the final field in an index may have an inequality in the search criteria. Remember that to take advantage of a multiple index, all the component fields must feature in the QBE grid.

The table can be customized by altering all or some of the above field properties in the Field Properties box. Change them by pressing *BkSp* and re-typing, or selecting from the drop-down menu obtained from the tabs at the end of the cells.

Primary Keys

What Are They For?

Primary keys [key icon] are attached to a field or fields for three main reasons:

1. As an initial indexing to speed up queries
2. To prevent duplication of records
3. To control the order of display of the records in a database

Initial Indexing to Speed Up Queries

As you have seen Access uses indexing to speed up the location of any information that you require. Indexing is a very important concept in the theory of databases.

Preventing Duplication of Records

Preventing the duplication of records is important. Let's take our primary key field to be telephone numbers. This allows many Smiths and Fords to be entered, but if the unique telephone number is duplicated somewhere during data entry Access draws our attention with a warning.

By preventing duplication more than one person can use the database, and Access prevents them both entering in the same information (which would create a corruption of data). An error like this will be caught before it becomes a problem and you won't get the errors associated with multiple copies of the same record.

It is therefore important to be careful not to assign the primary key to a field that will be duplicated as a matter of course, such as street names. If the user attempts to duplicate a primary field Access will simpy lock out the offending record.

Controlling the Order of Display of the Records in a Database

When records are entered into a database, they are normally displayed in *that* order. However, if we have a primary key set, when the table is re-opened the records will be re-ordered (based on which field has the primary key attached).

Ordering is based upon an ascending style, or in other words the list begins with A or 1 and flows alphabetically or numerically from there.

> As an xBase user, you will be used to applying indexes to all fields involved in a multi-table relationship. With Access a primary key is set just once in the primary table - all relationships stem from this. Paradox users will also enjoy the fact that Access does not require the primary key field(s) to appear at the top of the table design.

Adding a Primary Key

Now you have seen some of the uses for a primary key, you need to understand how to use them in your table design.

- Highlight the field that is to be primary keyed.
- Select the [key] icon on the toolbar.

Below is an example table design. This table design has been created for a mailing order company to store the information about their customers.

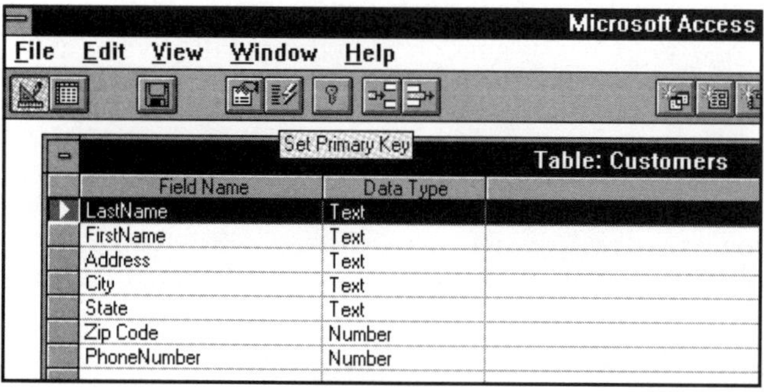

As you can see the LastName field has been highlighted ready for the allocation of the primary key. You *might* choose this field as a natural way to index a list of names and addresses. After all, isn't your phone book organized this way? In reality, though, you will want your primary key to be attached to unique data at all times.

By clicking on Set Primary Key, you have assigned the primary key to your highlighted field. Your table now has its first index. To see all the indexing active upon a table, simply click on the Indexes icon to see the screen below.

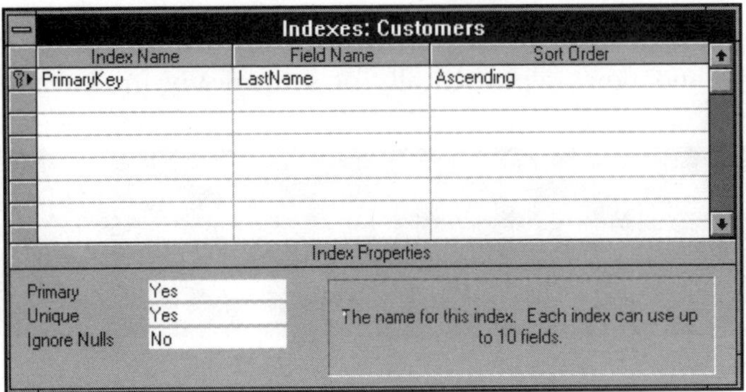

This is your table's Index Properties box. You can use this box to add, edit or delete any of your table's indexes. To perform any of these tasks, use the techniques outlined for the main Table Design window. For example, to delete a primary key, highlight the row by selecting the appropriate part of the pointer column and press *Del*.

Multiple Primary Keys

Access allows you to attach the primary key to more than one field. Why?

Let's take the primary key setting already chosen for the Customers table. Currently this is allocated to one field, LastName. This setting will give you a friendly listing of all of your customers, starting with Mr. Aardvark through to Mr. Zybex.

However, there will be a problem as soon as you want to include two identical last names. For example, when you try to enter two Smiths, Access will disallow the second Smith with the following message:

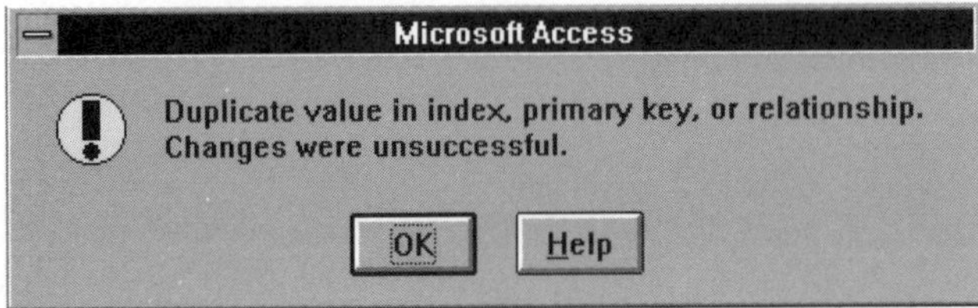

The reason for this is that duplicates are not allowed in primary keyed fields. Does this mean that Access cannot handle the simple task of organizing a phone book when there is more than one Smith?

Of course, the answer is no. Access can use multiple primary keys to solve this problem. For example, two fields may be primary keyed, FirstName and LastName.

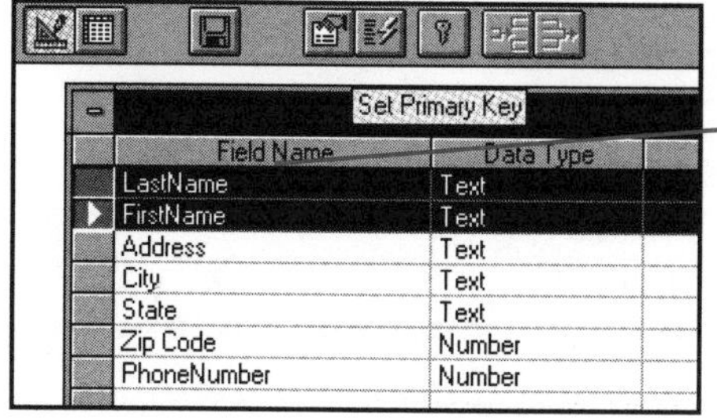

Simply highlight both of the fields, by holding down *Shift* before you select the second field and then click on the Set Primary Key icon.

Now there are a couple of fields within the primary key, Access is happy to allow you to enter more than one Smith, because Access is no longer checking for duplication in just one field - LastName. You could now enter Smith all day long, providing FirstName remains *unique.*

Does this mean that you could enter all of your customer names? The answer is yes, if you are sure you aren't going to have two customers with the same FirstName and LastName.

Why Would You Use a Multiple Primary Key?

You must be confident that several fields will uniquely identify each record. For example, in the world of horticulture a plant's full Latin name may be made up of several unique sections: family, genus, title.

Assigning the primary key to these three fields would mean that a user could enter thousands of Latin plant names, and be sure never to break the duplication rules. The advantage now would be that the table's records are automatically ordered in terms of the primary keyed fields. This means that, by default, you will have a proper alphabetical listing of *all* your records no matter what order they are entered in, and without inventing a code field.

> By default, primary keys carry out their work in the order that they appear in the table design. To alter this, re-order the primary keyed fields in the Index Properties box - the Index Name (PrimaryKey) must be assigned to the first key that is listed.

Code Fields

A code field is a unique identifier that is attached to each record. To use a code field means that you will have to invent a series, most probably using numbers, that marks every entry in the table uniquely. A social security number is a good real-world example of this. Just about everybody in a country is involved in the Social Security database, and so name, address and status duplication would be inevitable. Consequently, during everyday life you will find yourself surrounded by these made up numbers - part numbers, invoice numbers and PIN numbers.

The natural choice for the primary field would be this unique code.

The three main choices for your code field's data type are:

Data Type	Use
Text	If you want your code field to contain any alphanumeric character.
Number	If you want your code field to be made up of numbers.
Counter	If you want Access to automatically assign the code field a value, i.e. the first record is marked 1, the second 2 and so on.

Let's go back to the Customers table design and see it with a code field rather than multiple primary keys.

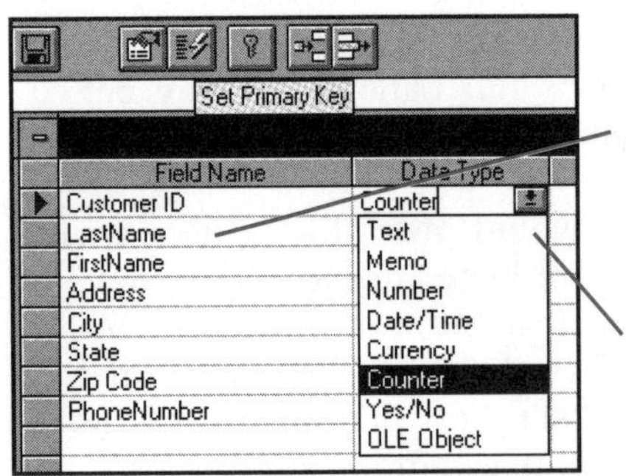

Insert a new row and give your new code field a descriptive name - Customer ID, Personnel ID, Part No. are all good examples - then click on the Set Primary Key icon.

Choose a relevant data type from the drop-down menu.

This method clearly orders the records in terms of the code and not the preferred field(s). This means that the choice between whether to use multiple fields and retain the in-built ordering, or use a code field for your primary key is completely up to the designer, depending on the requirements of the database.

Relating Multiple Tables

From the previous sections of this chapter you have seen how to produce a table design, complete with field definitions and primary keys. However, at the moment, after putting all the work into your plan to produce a fully functional relational database, all you have got is a collection of individual tables. To move from this stage to a relational database structure, you have to understand how to relate each table to the others in the database.

The Relationship Screen

Building the Database Structure

There are two ways to relate a newly created table to your database structure:

1. When you have enlisted the aid of the Table Wizard, you are guided through the relation process. See the following section of this chapter entitled Table Wizard for more details on this method.
2. When you have created the table design by hand and saved it, select the icon from the initial database window.

When you select the Relationships icon (or Relationships from the Edit menu), Access 2.0 presents you with the following screen:

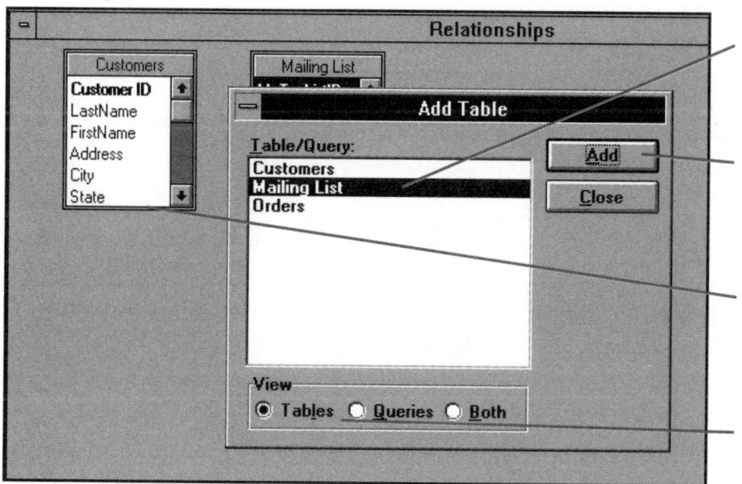

Highlight the table that you want to relate to the database structure.

Click on this button to add the highlighted table to the relating window.

This is the relating window which shows the relationships between the tables and queries that make up your database structure.

Select the appropriate radio button for the listing that you require.

When you have finished adding to the relating window those tables you want to add to the database structure, select the Close button. Now you are ready to define the relationships between the tables or queries in your database structure.

Defining a Relationship

> Remember, that the primary field is the table at the "one" end of the relationship. See Chapter 2: The Types of Table Relations for more details on this.

To define a relationship you need to:

- Select the field in your primary table.
- Keeping the left mouse button down, drag the mouse pointer towards the secondary table (the table that's going to be at the other end of the relationship, see the note above).
- Place the mouse pointer over the field (foreign key) in the secondary table that you wish to join to the primary table.

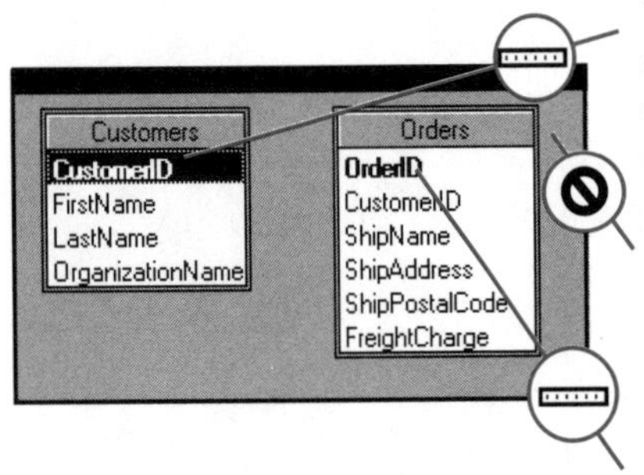

When you begin to move the mouse pointer it changes shape as shown. This indicates that you have successfully chosen the field in the primary table and have started the definition of the relationship.

When the mouse pointer is not over a table or query it changes shape again as shown. This No-Entry sign means that you cannot create a relationship from the selected field to here.

When you arrive at a field that could be related to your selection in the primary table, the mouse pointer changes to this shape.

- To place the relationship between the two tables release the mouse button. You will now have to fine tune the relationship using the following window:

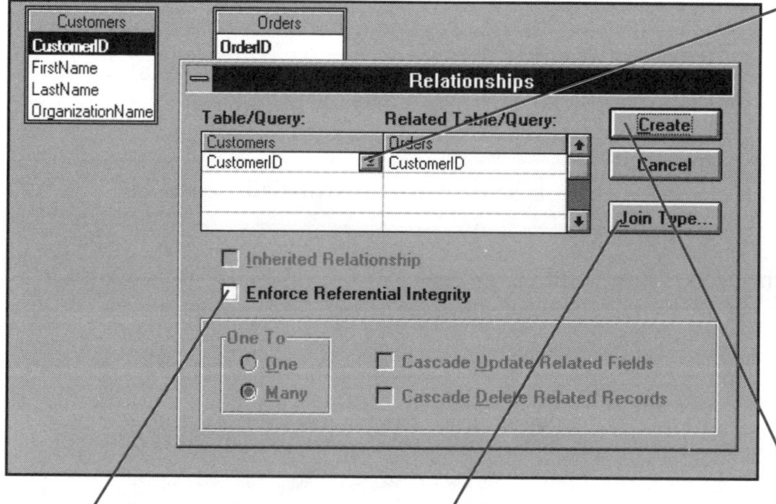

This window shows you the two fields, in the primary and secondary tables respectively, that you have selected. Select the tab at the end of the active cell to change the chosen field to another in that table. Note, that the table names are given at the top of the columns.

Select this check box to Enforce Referential Integrity between the information in the two tables. Making this selection means that you can define the type of relationship you require.

Click on this button to choose the type of join that you want between the tables.

Select this button when you are satisfied with your relation and the fine tuning that you have done.

Referential integrity is a good guardian of your data. Enforcing this guardian allows you to safeguard against orphan records. For example, if your primary table contains information about your sales reps, while a secondary table holds data about the orders that they have created, when a sales rep leaves, you don't want to remove them from the table without first dealing with their related orders. Setting referential integrity forces you to observe this ruling. A user could not alter data, leaving orders drifting around without a sales rep (orphan records).

When the fine tuning of the relationship has been completed and the Create button has been selected, Access 2.0 will place the defined relationship between the two tables, and the database structure will grow by at least one table.

Note that Access 2.0's default relationship is a one-to-one equi-join.

Joins

There are three types of join that you can use when creating the relationship between two tables: the equi-join, the left outer and the right outer.

> Remember that you do not define a self join, you artificially create it.

When you select the Join Type... button, Access 2.0 provides the following window to allow you to make your selection of these three joins:

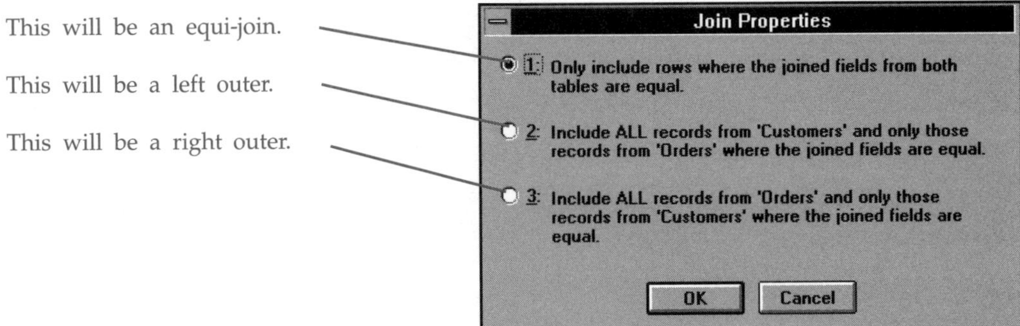

Simply select the appropriate radio button for the type of join that you want and click on the OK button.

Without this tool, Access would not be able to relate together the tables in a database, and therefore wouldn't be a relational database management system. This one tool allows you through the gate that leads to the fertile garden of the relational database.

Dynamically Reviewing the Links

The Relationships screen can also be put to another use. With a complex number of links, your database structure can look like spaghetti. Access 2.0 allows you to focus on sections of your database.

Look at the typically mature and complex database structure in the Microsoft sample database NWind.mdb:

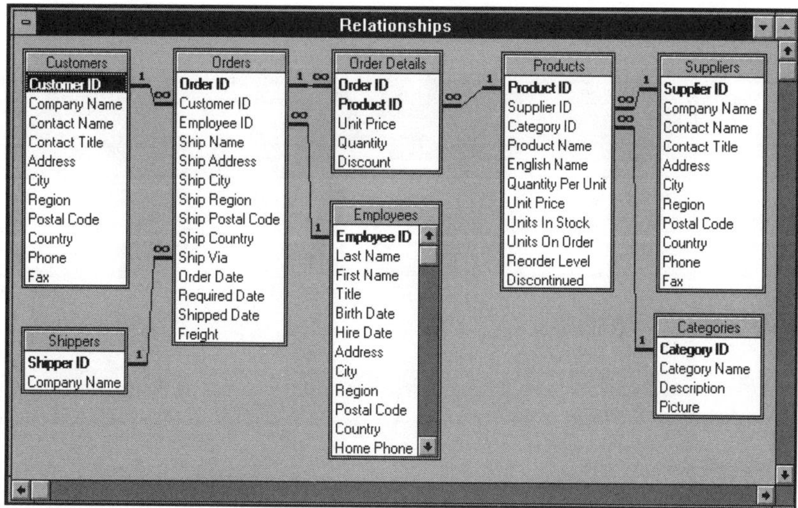

- Clear the Relationships window using Clear Layout from the Edit menu.
- Add the table you wish to focus upon, by clicking on the icon, selecting it from the Add Table window and choosing the Add button. (In this case, try Customers.)

Now, to expand the focus from this table select the icon. This means you can also see the directly related tables.

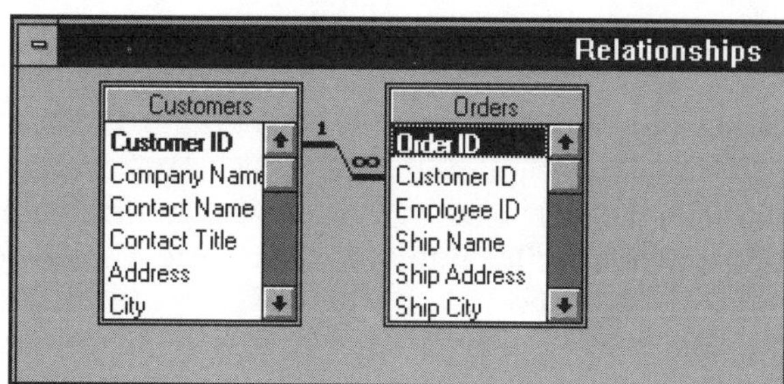

As you can see, Access 2.0 has now added all the tables that have a direct relationship to your focused table. In this case, Access has added the Orders table. The Order ID field is now highlighted in the Orders table. If you select the icon now, Access will repeat the process using the Orders table as the focus, giving the following screen:

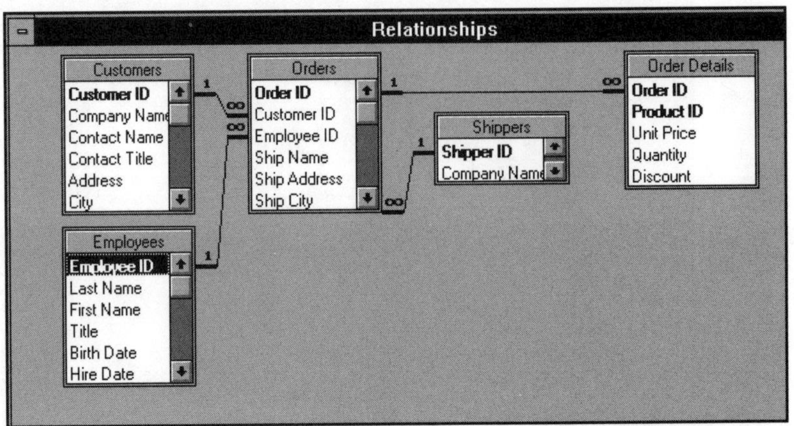

Access has again added all the tables that have a direct relationship to your focused table, in this case the Orders table. The field that is now highlighted is Employee ID in the Employees table. If you select the Show Direct Relationships icon again, nothing will happen. This indicates that all the direct relationships from the Employees table already appear on the diagram.

If you want to see all the tables and queries that make up the *linked* database structure, simply click on the icon. This means that any tables or queries that are *not* linked into your database structure will *not* be shown.

The Table Wizard

By now you've put in some hard work learning the fundamentals of basic table design. If your table design skills are solid, database teething problems are virtually eliminated. With a good structure, queries, forms and reports will naturally fall into place. To automate this basic task, Microsoft have included the Table Wizard into Access 2.0. This takes some of the hard work out of table design. The wizard comes equipped with many pre-built table designs under its hat, all of which you can customize to your own requirements.

Many of the table designs you may need can be created using one of the 45 basic table designs that the wizard has to offer. Whether you are designing for business or pleasure, you can formulate a quick prototype table with the wizard's help.

Calling the Wizard

You can safely mix your own and wizard-designed tables. Firstly, let's take a tour through the basic Table Wizard's actions.

From a new or previously opened database, select the Table tab. Click on the New button to bring up the window shown. To call the wizard, click on the Table Wizard button to open the first table design screen.

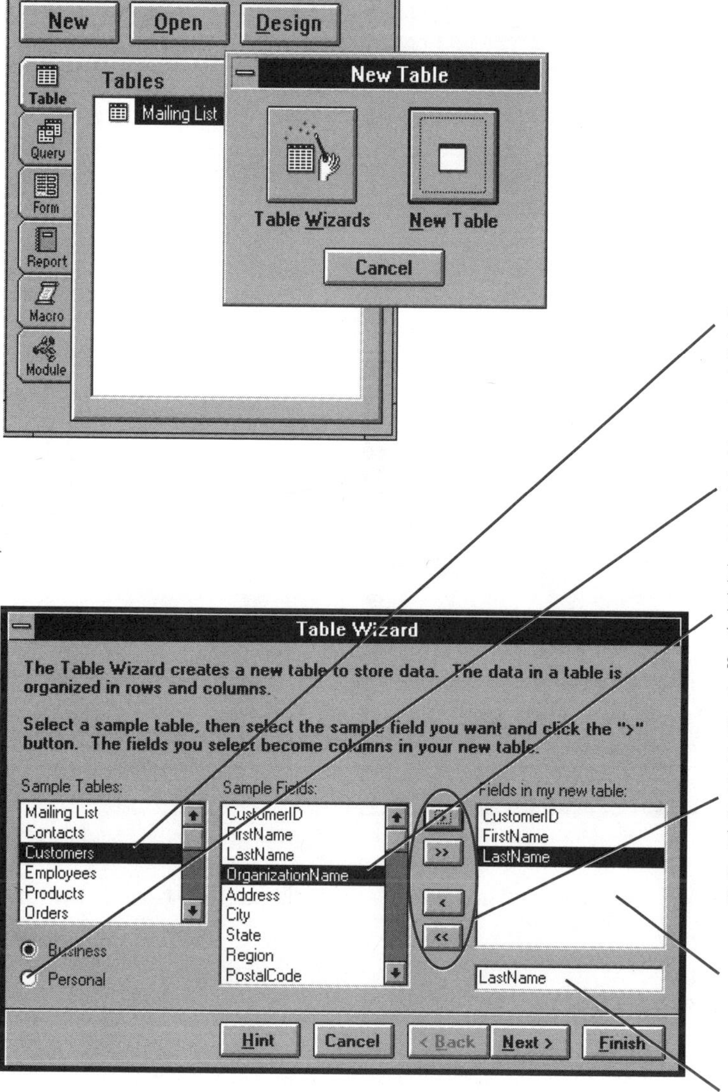

Here is a list of some of the available tables that the wizard has to offer. Highlight the one you want the wizard to base the design upon.

Select this radio button if you want to see the rest of the tables the wizard has to offer.

Here is a comprehensive listing of all the fields the wizard can include in your selected table.

Use these buttons to include or remove the fields that will appear in the finished table. Single arrows move single fields backwards and forwards, double arrows affect all the fields.

Here is where all the fields that you have selected for the table design will appear.

Highlight a field and use this window to change its name.

Select the Next > button to move to the next stage.

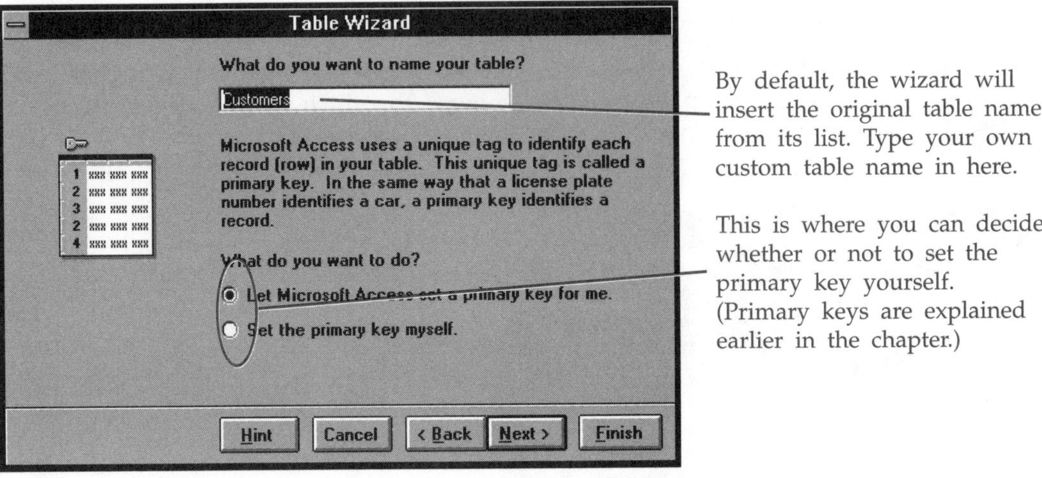

For now, lét Access assign the primary key, select the Next > button and move onto the next stage.

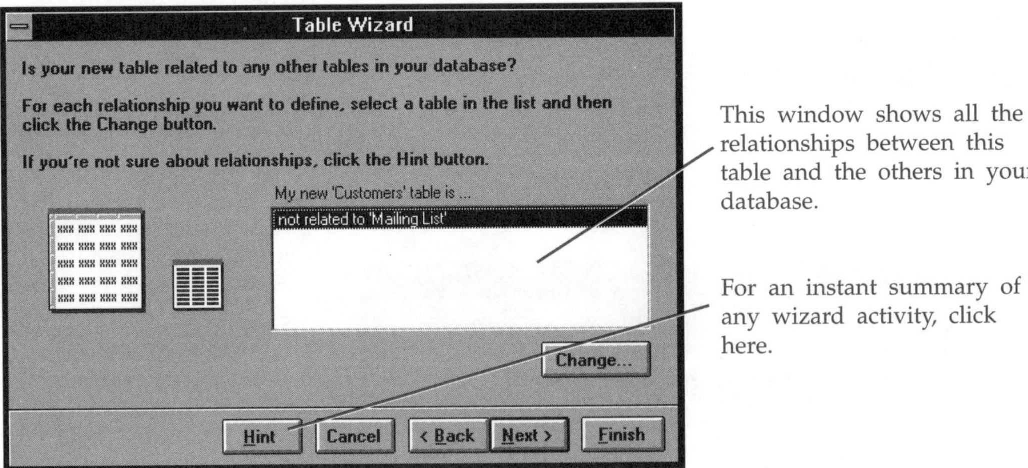

For now, let's assume that this table is unrelated, so click on the Next > button to move to the final stage.

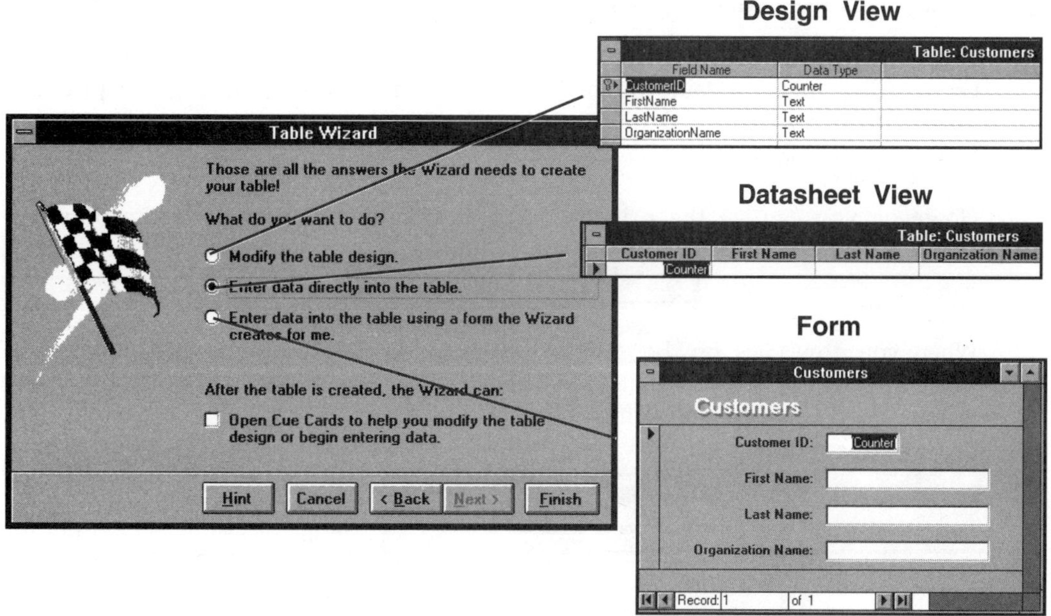

The wizard has now finished the major part of its job. Its final task is to leave you in one of the three views as shown above. Simply select the radio button that corresponds to the view you want. To move to this view and to say good-bye to the wizard, click on the **Finish** button.

Forms

The final radio button produces not only the table design, but also a related form. As you know, a form is the tool Access uses to structure the data entry into its related datasheet. The form is the equivalent of a blank questionnaire. It has its own structure, and so prompts the user for the correct type of response for each question. Usually, each field in your table will have some representative on the form that allows Access to process the entries that the user makes and pass them successfully into the datasheet.

The form can also have friendlier data entry features built onto it than a datasheet. Some of these include friendly messages when the user makes an error, or simply controlling the way the user enters the data in order to make their lives easier. The different types of form and the best times to use them are dealt with in much greater detail in the following chapters.

The Table Wizard and the Primary Key

In the quick tour of the wizard's actions, Access 2.0 was allowed to set the primary key for your table design. Access 2.0 does this by setting the primary key onto the NWormal ID field associated with that table design and adding it to the table design if you haven't already chosen it.

However, you can set the primary key yourself by selecting the radio button.

When you now click on the Next > button to go onto the next stage, Access 2.0 side-tracks you for a moment to get the information it needs about the primary key with the following window.

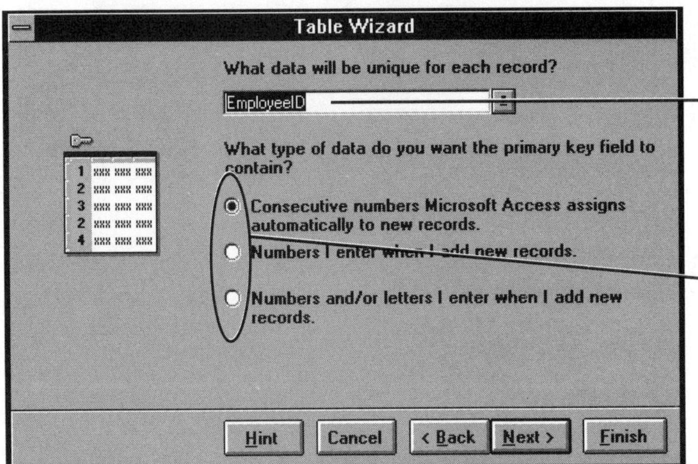

In this window, select the field that you want to assign the primary key to. To see the list of available fields click on the tab at the end of the cell to activate the drop-down menu.

Select the appropriate radio button to assign a data type to your primary key field: Counter, Number or Text respectively.

When you select the Next > button to continue to the next stage, the wizard, having obtained all the information about the primary key field that it requires, carries on with designing the table.

> The wizard must assign a primary key to each of the tables that it helps to create. It cannot assign more than one to each table. To solve this problem you must manually re-design this part of the table's structure in the normal table design view. This option is given to you at the end of the wizard's proffered help.

The Table Wizard and Table Relationships

As you saw in the previous section of this chapter, it is the fact that Access can relate all the information from several tables that makes it such a useful tool. This is the key to relational database design. With Access 2.0 you can use the wizard both to define and customize these relationships.

From this window Access allows you to see the default relationships that it believes are required.

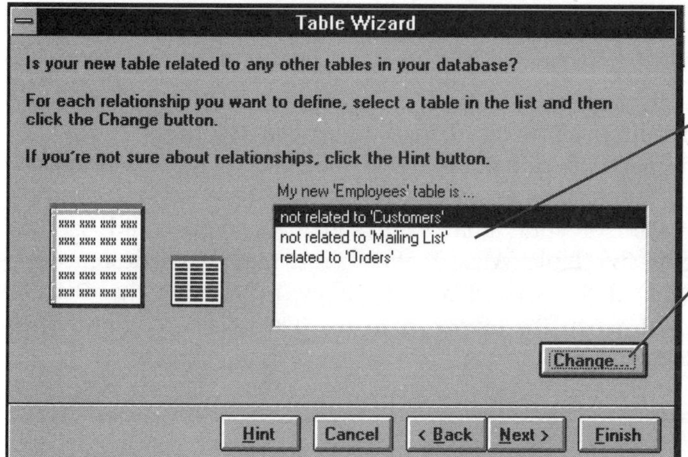

As you can see, Access 2.0 has decided that some of the tables are related and some of them aren't.

To change the relationship between the table currently being designed and the highlighted table in the list, click on this button.

When the Change... button is selected, Access uses the following window to get the necessary information to define your custom relationship.

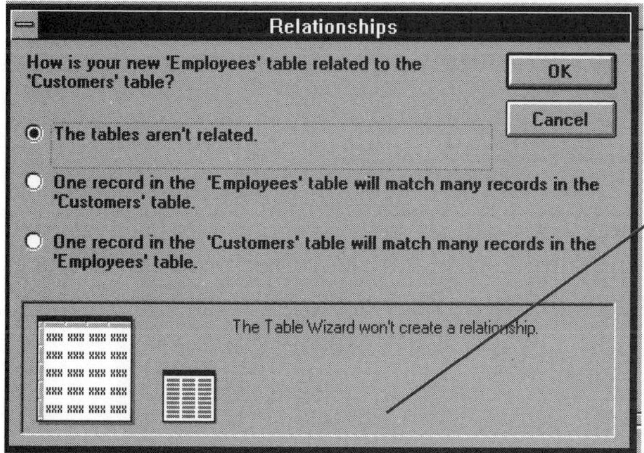

The information in this sunken window changes depending on your selection, both in terms of the graphical way it shows you the type of relationship you have chosen and the effect it has on the two table designs involved.

Select the appropriate radio button for the type of relationship you require between the two tables: no relationship, one-to-many or many-to-one respectively. Now select the OK button to return to see the effects of your customization.

The Table Wizard cannot create a one-to-one relationship between two tables. To produce this effect you should make the two tables unrelated at this point and then add in the one-to-one relationship manually at the end of the wizard's proffered help.

The Build Button

The [...] button appears throughout Access 2.0 to help automate various functions. Here, the Build button allows you to plunder the resources of the Table Wizard, without the need to call it up.

Let's say, while in Design View of your table, you realize that you could use some of the standard fields the Table Wizard offers. You may have designed your table by hand or enlisted the wizard already. Now, by clicking the Build button on the main icon bar when the cursor is in the Field Name column, you will invoke the Field Builder:

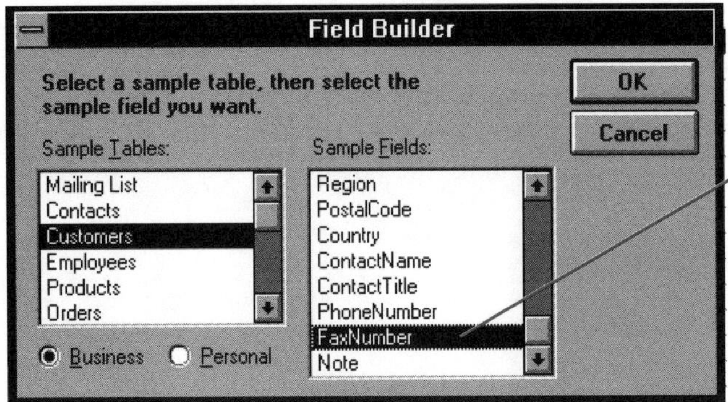

This window is very similar to table selection by the Table Wizard. Highlight the sample table to see its sample fields and select the field you want to add to your design.

When you click on the OK button, you will see your selection has been placed into the table design. It is placed into the table at the cursor position, just as if you had used the Insert Row command and typed it in manually.

Data Entry and Editing

So far you have seen:

- The basic method for designing a table's structure by hand
- How to give each record a unique code
- How to assign the primary key
- Automatic table design using the Table Wizard

Now we can start entering data into your design.

There are three methods for entering data into the database:

1. Using a form
2. Straight into the table Datasheet
3. Using OLE (Object Linking and Embedding)

The first is by using the front-door to the database, the form. Forms are discussed later on in the book, but to explain simply, they are like blank questionnaires. Information can be entered into slots on the form, and if it is well designed the information will be placed into the correct table automatically. You will be designing forms that allow you and other users to enter data safely, through a visually friendly medium.

The second method is by far the simplest one for the designer of the table to organize. You simply open up the datasheet and start typing. Even though this is not the most friendly method of entering data, it will suffice to test your design with a few records.

The third method launches your database into the 21st century by linking the products of other application packages to your information bank. With OLE you are able to include and/or link 'objects' from other packages straight into your database structure.

The Datasheet

All the hard work that you have put into the creation of your table design can now be seen in the datasheet. All the fields that you have defined will now become column headings on the datasheet ready to accept data.

Opening Up the Datasheet

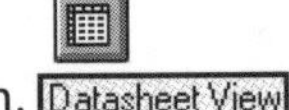

- From your table design simply select the Datasheet View icon.
- From the initial database window highlight your table and select **Open**
- When you open the datasheet, you will see a screen similar to the one below, with the cursor waiting in the first field of the first record ready for you to start entering data. Notice that the table design has set the layout of the datasheet.

Design View

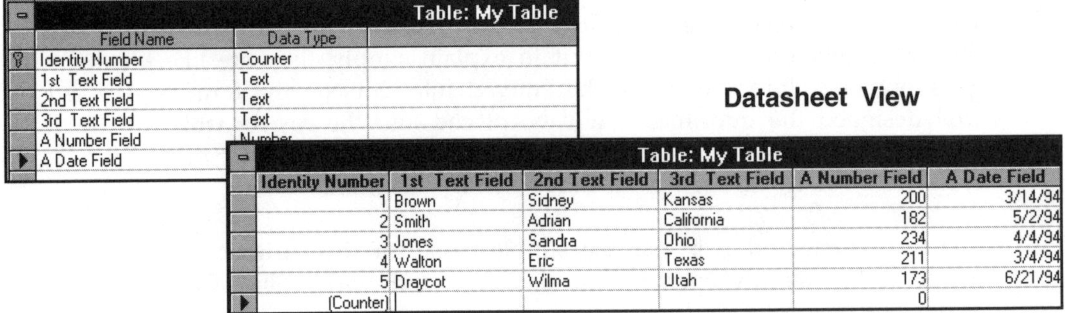

Datasheet View

Identity Number	1st Text Field	2nd Text Field	3rd Text Field	A Number Field	A Date Field
1	Brown	Sidney	Kansas	200	3/14/94
2	Smith	Adrian	California	182	5/2/94
3	Jones	Sandra	Ohio	234	4/4/94
4	Walton	Eric	Texas	211	3/4/94
5	Draycot	Wilma	Utah	173	6/21/94
(Counter)				0	

Entering Data into the Datasheet

When you open the datasheet, the cursor is waiting in the first field of the first record. To enter data into this field, simply type away.

> **Remember, that the type of data you enter here should conform to the data type assigned to this field, otherwise Access will correct or even refuse it.**

You can quickly switch back to the table Design View by selecting the icon. To switch back to the Datasheet View select the icon.

To move around the datasheet, use the same techniques that you would employ to move around the Table Design window:

Action	Movement
Tab	This moves you along each field definition, one cell at a time.
Shift+Tab	This moves you backwards.
Enter	This moves you onto the next cell.
Mouse	This moves you to the field where the mouse pointer is placed after depressing left button.
▶*	This moves you to the first field of a new record.

When you have finished your data entry session, it is good practice to *Tab* onto a new row, before closing the table. This means that Access will save your last record.

When you have completed your data entry session, close down the table using one of the following methods:

- Select File from the menu bar, and click on Close.
- Double-click on the icon.in the corner of the window.
- Click once and select Close from the menu.

Once you have closed down the table, all the data you have entered is safely stored in your database.

OLE to the Table

Object Linking and Embedding means just that, linking or embedding an object (i.e. some sound, pictures, video, wordprocessed documents or spreadsheets) into your application. The only restriction on using OLE is that both applications, the server and the receiver, must support OLE in a Windows environment.

The difference between linking and embedding is subtle:

- When you link objects, Windows creates a dynamic link between Access 2.0 and the source application. This means that when you are using an object from that application any changes made to it are reflected in your database.
- When you embed objects, Access 2.0 simply retains a copy of that object with your database. There is, in fact, still a connection kept between Access and the source application. However, this is not a dynamic link; it just enables you to alter the object using the facilities of the source application.

Linking an Object: An Example

Some of the common uses for *dynamically* linking an object to a table include a graph produced from data in a spreadsheet, or a report produced in a wordprocessor. The dynamic link means that whenever the figures change in the spreadsheet or the text changes in the document, the contents of your object will automatically be updated to reflect these changes. We can look at a graph produced from an Excel spreadsheet as an example, (see below):

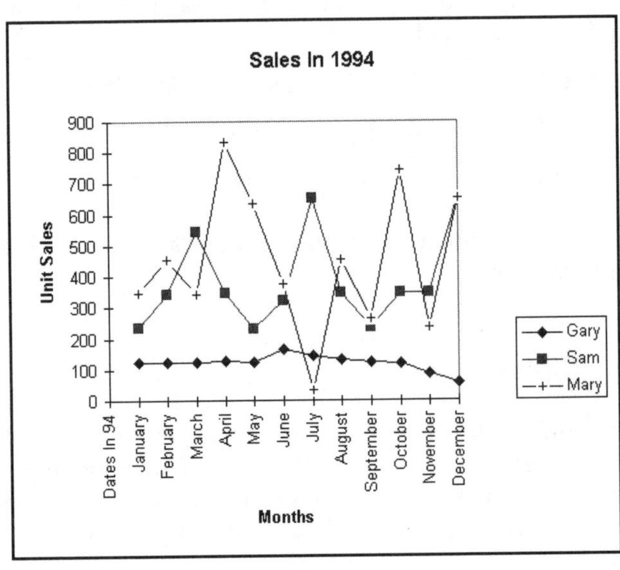

- Highlight the graph and copy it to the clipboard using the usual method of Copy from the Edit menu.
- Go to the relevant cell in your table where you want the image stored. This should be contained in a field that has the OLE Object data type.
- Select Paste Special from the Edit menu to get the following screen:

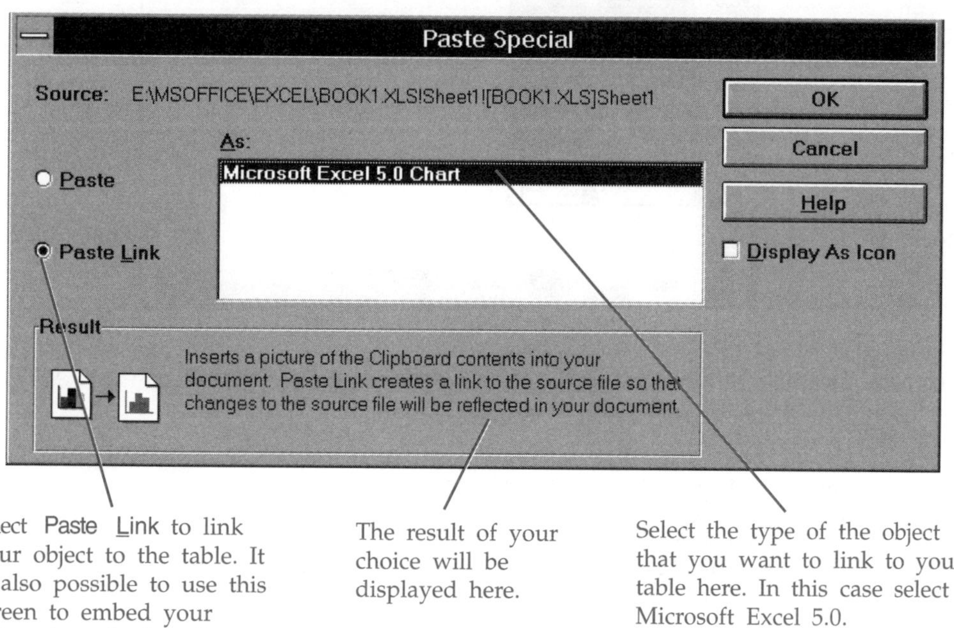

Select Paste Link to link your object to the table. It is also possible to use this screen to embed your objects by selecting Paste here.

The result of your choice will be displayed here.

Select the type of the object that you want to link to your table here. In this case select Microsoft Excel 5.0.

- Select the OK button when you have finished your selection and Access will place the words Microsoft Excel 5.0 into the cell. To see this graph, double click on the cell and Access will boot-up Excel with the correct object displayed.

Embedding an Object: An Example

One of the easiest ways to explain this concept is to work with the Employees table in NWind.mdb. Below you can see your starting point for embedding an object, in this case, a photo of an employee in Paintbrush.

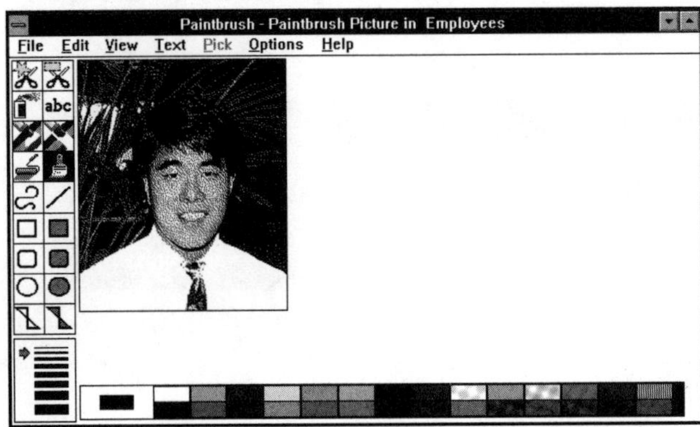

- Using Paintbrush's icon, select the part of the photo you want to embed into your database.
- Select Copy from the Edit menu to copy the selected part of the image as an object to the clipboard.
- Go to the relevant cell in your table where you want the image stored. In this case it is in Employee ID record number 6, under the Photo field (see below):

Table: Employees

ension	Photo	
7	Paintbrush Picture	Education includes a BA in Psych
7	Paintbrush Picture	Andrew received his BTS comme
5	Paintbrush Picture	Janet has a BS degree in Chemis
6	Paintbrush Picture	Margaret holds a BA in English lit
3	Paintbrush Picture	Steven Buchanan graduated fron
		Michael is a graduate of Sussex U
	Paintbrush Picture	Robert King served in the Peace
4	Paintbrush Picture	Laura received a BA in psycholog

Here is a conveniently empty cell for your object to be placed within the Photo field.

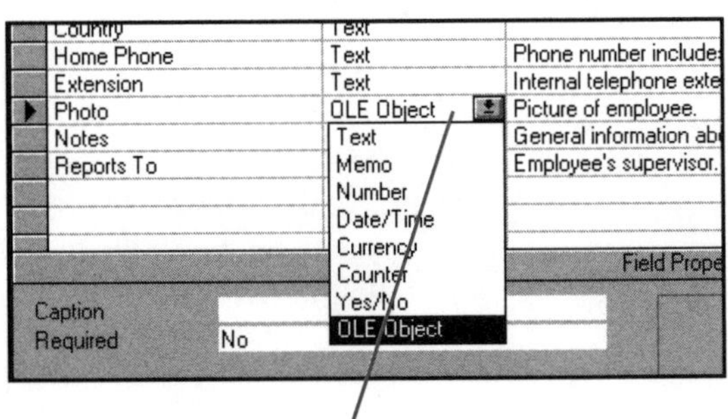

You can see that this field has already been set in the NWind Employee table design to accommodate OLE Objects, specifically pictures of employees.

- To place the photo into the cell, select Paste from the Edit menu on the menu bar. This will put the words Paintbrush Picture into the selected cell. To view the photo, simply double click on the cell and Access will boot-up Paintbrush with the correct object displayed.

You now know enough about OLE and how Access uses it in your database. You can include sound, video clips or any of the other objects that can easily be produced. Now, let's go on to look at re-opening the datasheet and editing the data contained in it.

If you want to edit any of the OLE Objects in your datasheet, double-clicking on them causes Access to boot-up the source application, allowing you to use the facilities of that source application to do any editing you need.

Re-Opening the Table and Editing

On some occasions you may wish to alter the data in the table after you have closed the table down. For example, suppose that you have tested out the table structure by entering in several records and found that there is a problem, not with the table design, but with the data you entered into the table.

There are several different types of editing that you can do, including:

- Cell editing
- Record editing
- Quick sorting

The first step in doing any data editing is to re-open the table. From the Database window select the Table tab and choose the one you wish to look at or edit from the list of tables available. Then, either:

- Select the Open button and the table will be opened showing your first records, or
- Double-click the highlighted table name.

Cell and Record Editing

To edit the records or cells in your table you can do any of the following:

- To alter information in a cell, simply move the cursor to it, press *BkSp* to delete the contents and re-type.

- To delete a record, click the record pointer. Access will highlight your choice. Select Edit and then Delete from the given menu. You will now be asked if this is correct before the deletion takes place.
- To add a record, simply move the cursor to the first cell of the blank record at the end of your table.

> You cannot insert new records between your old entries. They must be tacked onto the end of the table. If you have set a primary key, when you re-open the table, your records will be ordered automatically, as you have seen before.

Access can make use of the Copy and Paste function that Windows provides to allow cells, fields or entire records to be copied between tables (or even between databases). You must highlight the required part of your table and then use the Copy and Paste functions that are supplied in the Edit menu.

Quick Sorting

If you have selected a primary key for your table, then when you open it in Datasheet view the records are automatically sorted. Without a primary key, the records appear in the order that you entered them. To quickly sort the records:

- Highlight the column heading that you wish to sort by.
- Select either the [A↓Z] icon for an ascending sort or the [Z↓A] icon for the descending equivalent.

Display Editing

You can alter the presentation of the records using the usual Windows methods. We will now cover changing the order of the columns, the font, and the width and height of the cells.

Moving Columns

To move a column simply highlight the column heading and then, by holding the left mouse button down, drag the column to its new location and then release the mouse button.

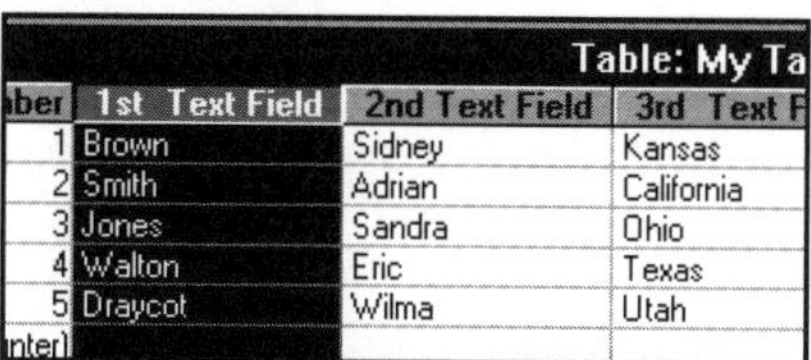

Table: My Ta

ber	1st Text Field	2nd Text Field	3rd Text F
1	Brown	Sidney	Kansas
2	Smith	Adrian	California
3	Jones	Sandra	Ohio
4	Walton	Eric	Texas
5	Draycot	Wilma	Utah
nter)			

Table: My Ta

mber	1st Text Field	2nd Text Field	3rd Text F
1	Brown	Sidney	Kansas
2	Smith	Adrian	California
3	Jones	Sandra	Ohio
4	Walton	Eric	Texas
5	Draycot	Wilma	Utah
unter)			

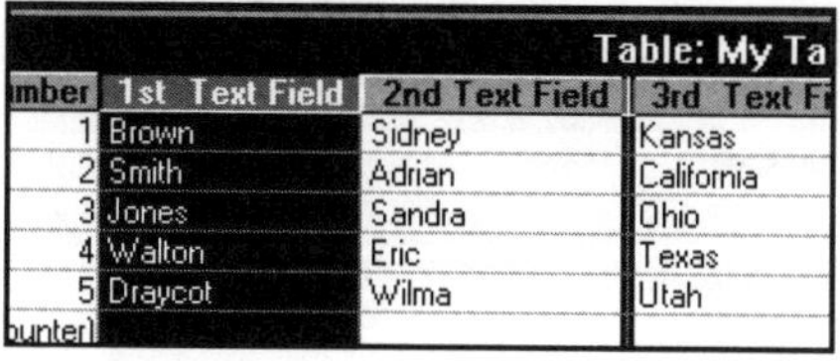

Table: My Ta

mber	1st Text Field	2nd Text Field	3rd Text Fi
1	Brown	Sidney	Kansas
2	Smith	Adrian	California
3	Jones	Sandra	Ohio
4	Walton	Eric	Texas
5	Draycot	Wilma	Utah
ounter)			

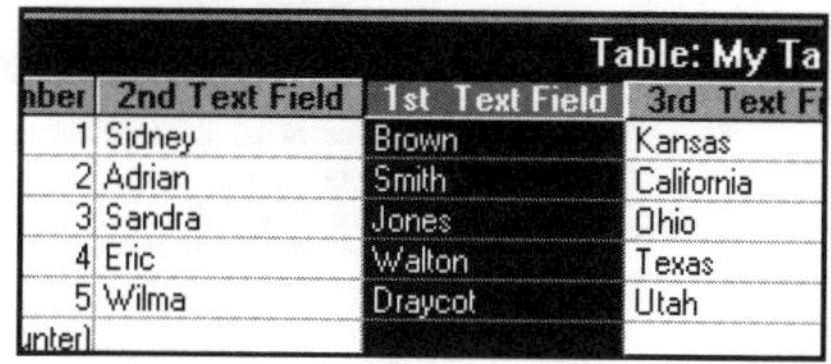

Table: My Ta

nber	2nd Text Field	1st Text Field	3rd Text Fi
1	Sidney	Brown	Kansas
2	Adrian	Smith	California
3	Sandra	Jones	Ohio
4	Eric	Walton	Texas
5	Wilma	Draycot	Utah
nter)			

Sizing Cells

To change the height or width of a cell you must alter the size of the entire row or column that the cell is part of. Simply go to the head of the row or column and place the cursor over the gridline separating the two cells.

Table: My Table

Identity	2nd Text Field	1st Text Field	3rd Text Field	A Num	A Date Field
1	Sidney	Brown	Kansas	200	3/14/94
2	Adrian	Smith	California	182	5/2/94
3	Sandra	Jones	Ohio	234	4/4/94
4	Eric	Walton	Texas	211	3/4/94
5	Wilma	Draycot	Utah	173	6/21/94
(Counter)				0	

The cursor will change shape and, by holding the left mouse button, you can drag the line to the width or height that is required.

Fonts

To alter the font of the text in your datasheet, select Format and then Font from the menu bar. You will be presented with the following window:

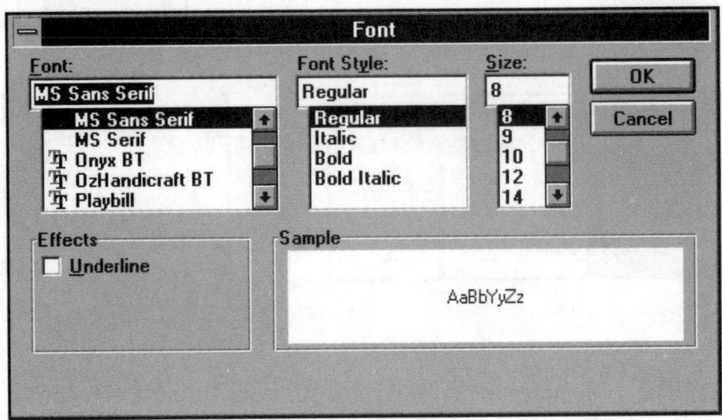

Choose from the selections given, and you will see a sample of the font in terms of type, style and size. Select OK. All the text on the datasheet will be changed to that particular font.

If you wish to change the fonts used in your tables regularly, or you want to allow your user to change the font, say for data entry, add the icon to your toolbar. See Customizing a Toolbar in the Introduction.

Troubleshooting

Q&A When I am moving around the datasheet, the column I want keeps moving off screen. What can I do?

You can freeze a column so that it is visible wherever you move to on the datasheet. Simply click on the heading to highlight the column and select Format and Freeze Columns. The column will now stay permanently on the left-hand side of the datasheet, wherever you scroll to. To unfreeze the frozen columns, select Format and Unfreeze All Columns.

When the frozen columns are thawed, they are not returned to their original positions in the datasheet.

Q&A My table is complex and contains a lot of data. I want to study it at home. Can I print it out?

The simple answer is "yes".

In Datasheet View or highlighted in the initial database window:

- Click on the [printer icon] icon on the tool bar.
- Select File and Print from the menu bar.

There are two other methods to print out table designs:

Either:

- Select File, Add-ins and then Database Documentor from the menu bar.
- Highlight your table from the list given in the Database Documentor and click on the Select button as seen below:

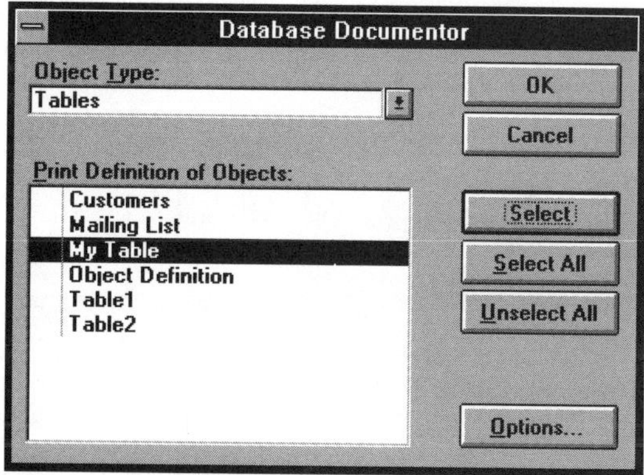

- Select OK, and Access will create an Object Definition. This can now be printed using the methods above.

Or:

- Select Print Definition... from the File menu to get the following window:

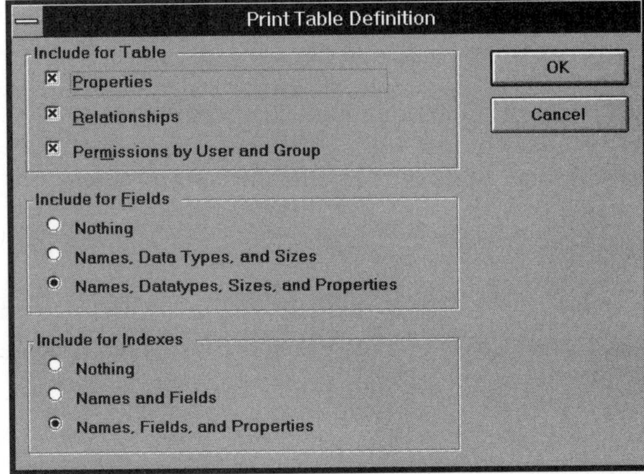

- Select or de-select the elements of the table design you want printed, and then click on the OK button. If you use this method when the table in question is open, Access will ask you to close the table down before it produces the report.
- After a short pause, the report, entitled Object Definition, will document all the components that you selected. It can then be printed out using the methods shown above.

Q&A I don't want to print all of my columns. Can I leave some of them out?

Yes. Use the hide/show column feature.

To hide a column:

- Highlight the column that you wish to hide.
- Select Format and then Hide Columns from the menu bar.

This allows a column to be hidden from view when printing out the table of records.

To restore the column:

- Select Format and then Show Columns from the menu bar.

- Highlight the column you wish to restore.
- Select the Show button.

This restores the hidden column to view.

Q&A How can I quickly find an entry in one of my records?

Use the Find function that Access provides on the Edit menu.

- Select the function using the menu, or by clicking on the icon. Access provides you with the screen given below:

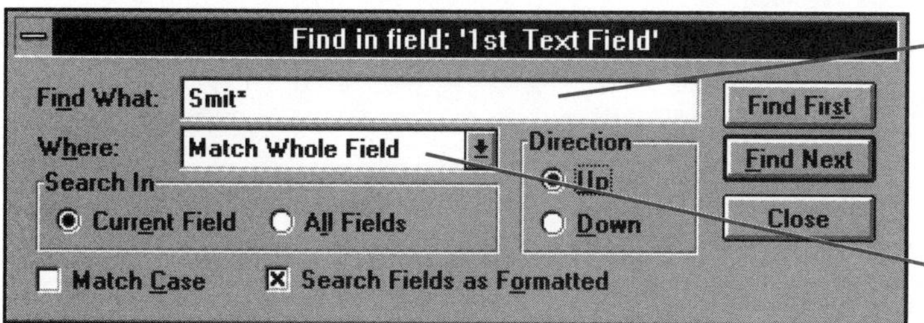

Type in here the entry you want to search for. You can use DOS wildcards just as in a normal Windows search.

Select the part of the field you want searched.

- Select the Find First/Find Next button to continue the search.
- Select the Close button when you have finished the search.

Q&A I've made a few mistakes with some data entries. Is there help?

Yes. You can retrieve your situation:

- In a cell, by using the Undo function before you leave it.
- In a record, by using the Undo Current Field /Record before you leave it.

> Make sure that you undo mistakes in a record before you leave it. Remember that a record is saved when you leave it, and therefore the undo functions won't work.

Q&A What are these icons for?

These icons allow you to place a basic filter over your data. This means that you can select what records are seen or not seen, according to criteria that you set. This is a powerful viewing tool that is essentially an aspect of querying the database. This idea is discussed more fully in the next chapter: Queries.

Q&A I'm opening the same tables every day. Can I get Access 2.0 to open them automatically every time I open the database?

The answer again is yes. Dragging and dropping table names into a new macro can accomplish this. See Chapter 12: Macros for more details.

You have now succeeded in running through the basics of Access tables - now you will want to interrogate these same tables to create useful and meaningful conclusions. We will cover that challenge in Chapter 4: Queries.

CHAPTER 4

Queries

In the last chapter, you learnt how to build a table, the store house for all your data. You then learnt how to flow your data into it. This data is still in a very basic state, just as the files in your filing cabinets are. Before you can do any serious work on them, you need to select all the relevant files, and then extract the useful information from the reams of paper in each file. Fortunately, Access 2.0 allows you to sift through the information in your database very quickly using a set of tools called **queries.**

These tools allow you to sort the data in any way you like, by selecting groups of data from your store house for a more focused study of them. More complex queries allow you to do even more useful things, such as moving selected records from table to table, or even constructing a new table for a selected group of records to be stored in.

In this chapter, you will look at the two more simple types of query: Sort and Selection. These queries take full advantage of the computer's speed, reducing the time required for your data interrogation from perhaps days to seconds. Also in this chapter, you will see how to make use of the Filter function that is available at the datasheet level.

In Chapter 4 you will learn about:

- Basic queries in the QBE grid
- Sort and Selection
- Using operators
- Summary calculations
- Unrelated table query
- Joins and filters
- Troubleshooting

What is a Query?

In a typical relational database, you will have designed several tables and used their structure to organize your information in a way that makes it easy to locate. This basic level of organization is the first step to producing impressive reports with dazzling graphical summaries of your information.

However, as you will see in the following chapters, the forms you design for your data entry and data view, as well as the reports you construct to output the information, can only draw data from one table at a time. This can be a problem in a relational database, where there are normally several tables.

You can use one of the features of a query to solve this problem. This feature allows you to draw the data from several tables into one large temporary table called a **dynaset**. You can then apply the other feature of queries: the ability to sort the data into any order, or choose related groupings for your information.

Using the query tool in this way means that you only have to look at the data that applies to the question you want answered, both in terms of the various tables in your database and the records in your selected tables.

Using Queries in the Real World

To see how this works in practice, let's have a look at the database of a friend's American Football team, the Seattle Surfers. Below you can see the database's relationship diagram, a tool which you learnt how to use in the previous chapter. This is a good way of seeing the tables and queries in a database, as well as looking at the relationships between them.

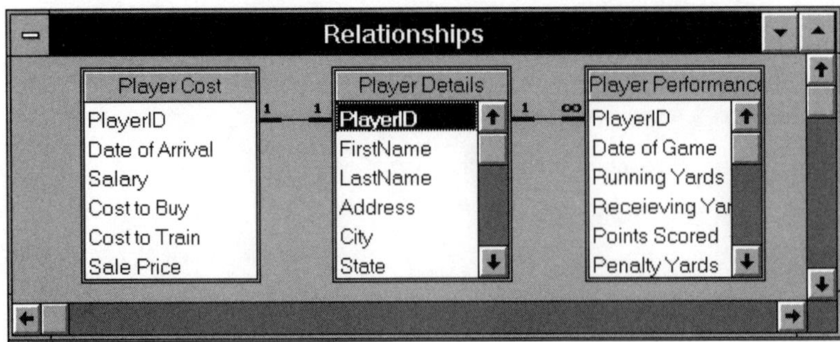

As you can see, the Seattle Surfers' coach uses the database to store information about the players' performance, while the team's accountant uses it to store data about the players' individual costs.

The Surfers' owner, Bill "Bondi" Beach, likes to get the best out of his players, and so he is starting a bonus scheme from the end of the season. The player's performance over the season when compared to a set of required standards will be used as the basis for the amount of money the player receives. The player's performance over the season will be converted to a figure and then plotted against his salary to give his position on the following graph:

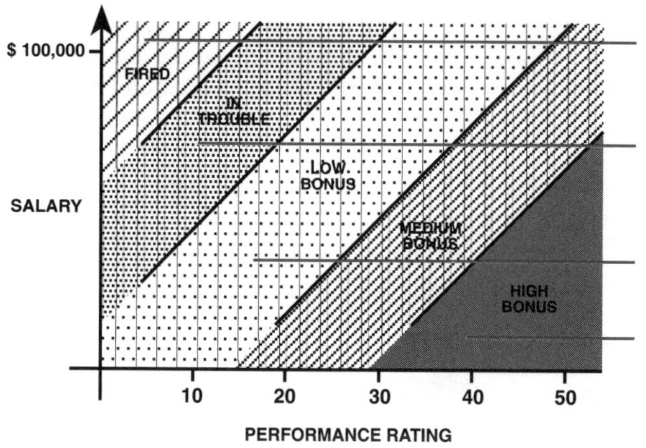

If you fall here you will be playing for another team next season.

If you fall here you will not receive a bonus and you must perform better next season.

If you fall here you get a small bonus.

If you fall here you get a large bonus.

If Bill had wanted to produce this graph before the database existed, it would have involved the accountant sitting down with reams of paper detailing all the players' related information and painstakingly working out where each player fell in the graph. However, now that the information is on the database, with a little bit of hard work designing the correct queries and making use of the graphing facility that Access 2.0 has to offer, all this work can be done very quickly.

One of the queries we will need is used to:

- Produce the figure that represents the player's performance from the relevant data.
- Pull all the information that is required from the tables into one temporary table to pass to the Graph Wizard (See Chapter 7 for a full description of how to use this wizard's help).
- Select the players that have fallen into each area of the graph so that reports of the owner's decisions can be printed out and posted in the locker rooms.

We'll be returning to the Surfers' problems throughout the chapter. In the meantime we will study the various basics you will need to solve any task.

Basic Query Designs

To simplify the design of queries, they are broken into three types:

- To sort data.
- To make selections from data.
- To produce more complex results, such as the automatic production of a new table or the movement of records from table to table.

In this chapter, we will explain the first of these bullet points and give more information concerning queries and the ways to make them work most efficiently for you. The last bullet point is dealt with in Chapter 9: More On Queries. Over the next few pages, you will be looking at what the different types of basic query do and how to create them. We will then go on to see how they can work together. Each query is designed on the same basic template, so before you learn about the specific types of query, let's look at how to get the template ready.

Opening the Basic Query Template

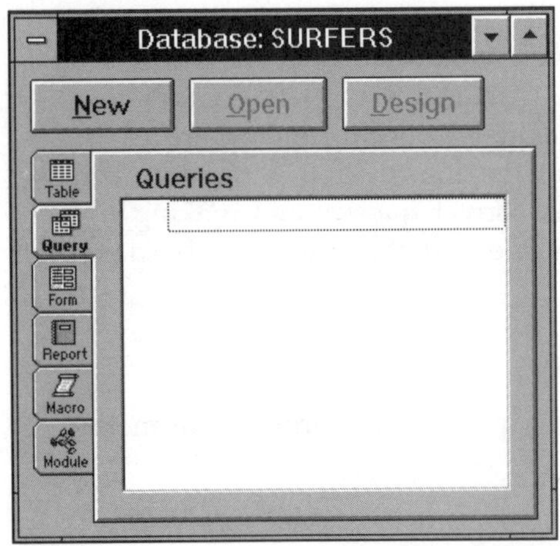

On the initial database window, select the Query tab, and then the New button.

Access 2.0 presents you with the following choice:

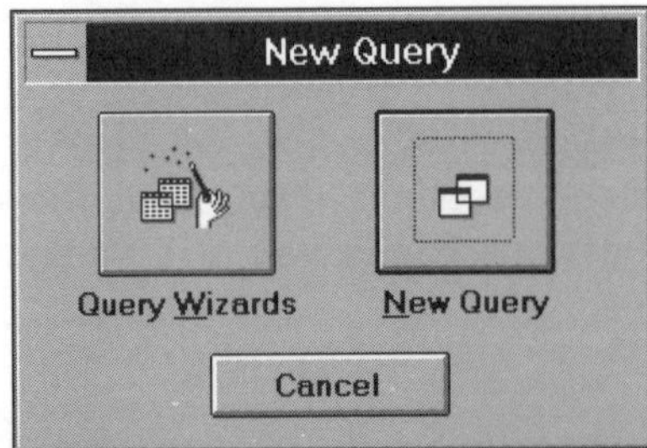

Select the New Query button to manually produce the template. We will look at the Query Wizard later on. You are now one stage away from the basic query template.

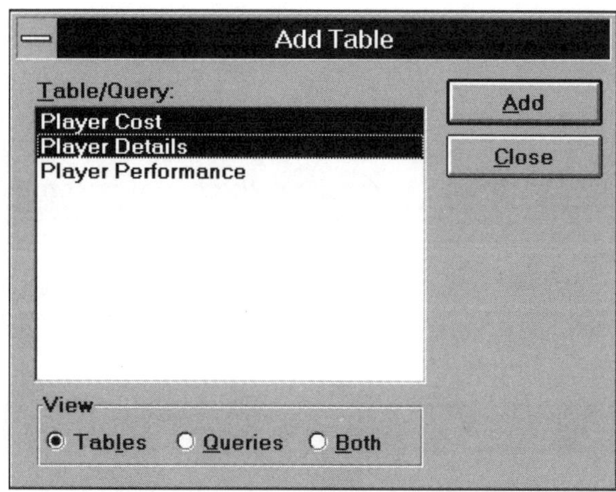

Select the tables that you want to use as the source for your query. You can use the *Shift* and *Ctrl* keys for multiple selection here. Press the Add button when you have made your choice, and Access 2.0 will place copies of your tables into the basic query template as shown below:

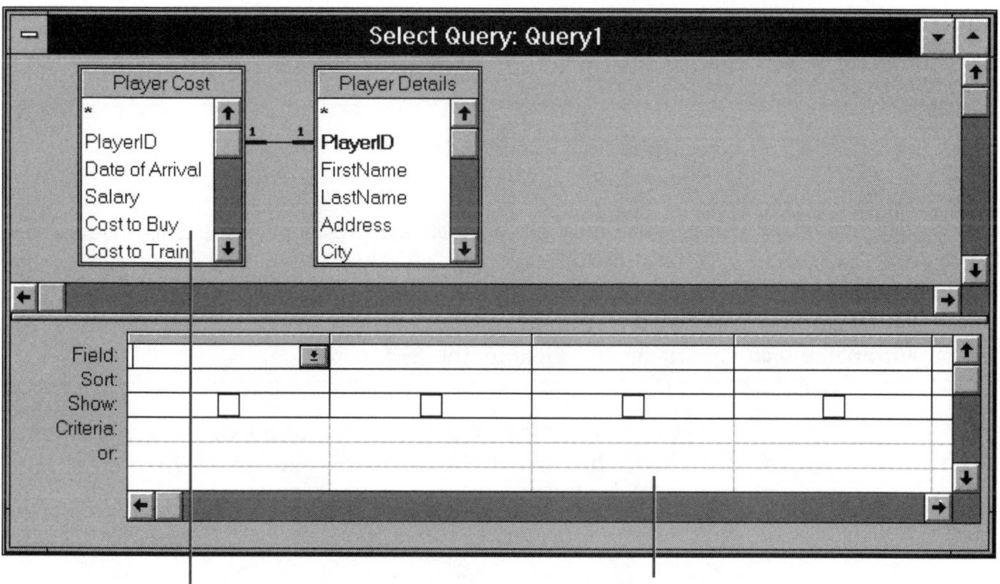

Here are the copies of your tables and the relationships that have already been defined between them.

This is called the QBE or Query By Example grid. This is where you tell *Access* the rules by which it will question your database. The answer will be a dynaset of records created from the ones contained in the tables that appear above.

Saving Your Query Design

While you are creating the query, it is not consigned to the computer's memory, however, as soon as you try to close the query, Access 2.0 will prompt you to save the design.

> *Access 2.0* only saves the query design and not the dynaset. Remember that the dynaset is a temporary table, and to that end *Access 2.0* calculates it every time you request to see it. If the query is complex and the tables are large, this recalculation can become tiresome, so we suggest you keep this to a minimum.

When Access 2.0 prompts you to save the query design, you will see the following series of windows:

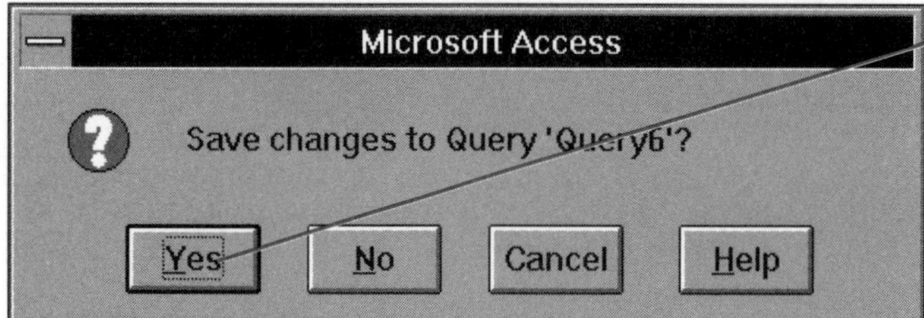

Select this button to save your query design.

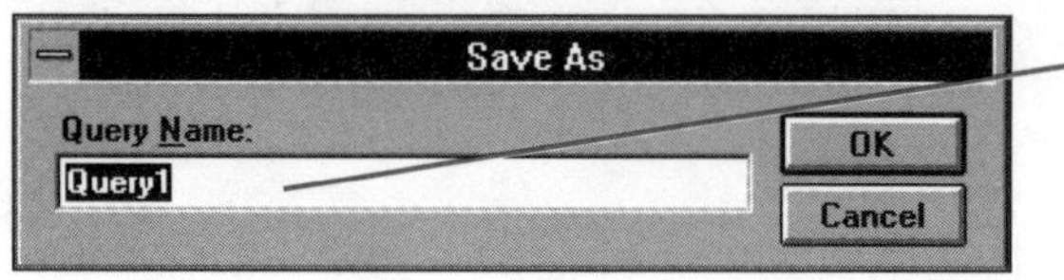

Press *BkSp* and re-type your required name here, then click on the OK button

This method works, not only when you are designing the basic query template, but also at any other times in the design's life when you close the query.

> You can save the query design at any time by selecting Save or Save As from the File menu, or by clicking the icon.

You have now successfully completed the preparation of the query template. Now you need to learn how to define the rules in the QBE grid, so the query can produce its resulting dynaset.

What is a Sort Query?

A sort query sorts the records in your selected tables using some rules attached to certain fields. As an example of its use, let's take the problem of printing out the salaries of the Surfers' players. You need to:

- Consult two tables. You need the name of the player from the Player Details table and their salary from the Player Cost table.
- Sort the players out alphabetically. This will make it a lot easier to find each player on the list.

A Guide to Designing a Sort Query

Let's look at how to create this sort query for the Surfers' database. Practise the methods using your own new database or inventing a new query for the supplied NWind database.

Create a basic query template. Select the Player Details table and the Player Cost table. The basic query template should look something like this:

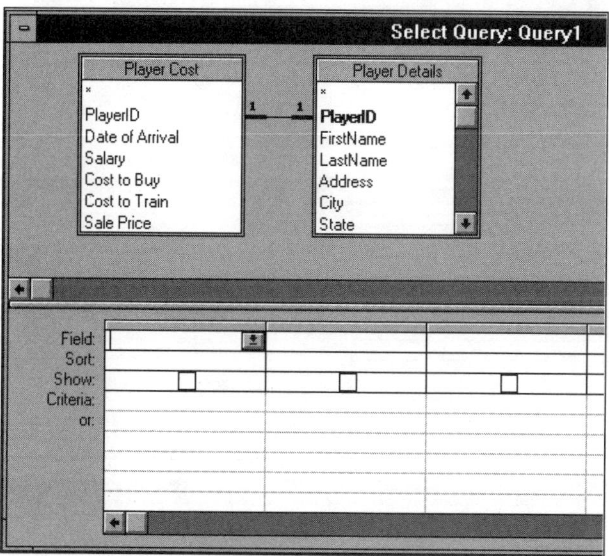

Now you have to choose the field that will make up the body of the dynaset. In this example, you want FirstName and LastName from the Player Details table and Salary from the Player Cost table. To inform Access 2.0 that you want these three fields as the body of your dynaset, you must place the field names into the QBE grid:

Put the name of the field into the cells in this row by:

- Dragging and dropping the field into the cell.
- Or, by selecting the field from the drop-down menu that's in the cell.
- Or, by double-clicking on the name of the field you require in the copies of the tables above the QBE grid. Access 2.0 automatically places that field into the next available column.

Each of the columns of the QBE grid deals with one field from the tables you have selected.

This row is used to inform Access *2.0* of the types of sort you want applied to the resulting dynaset.

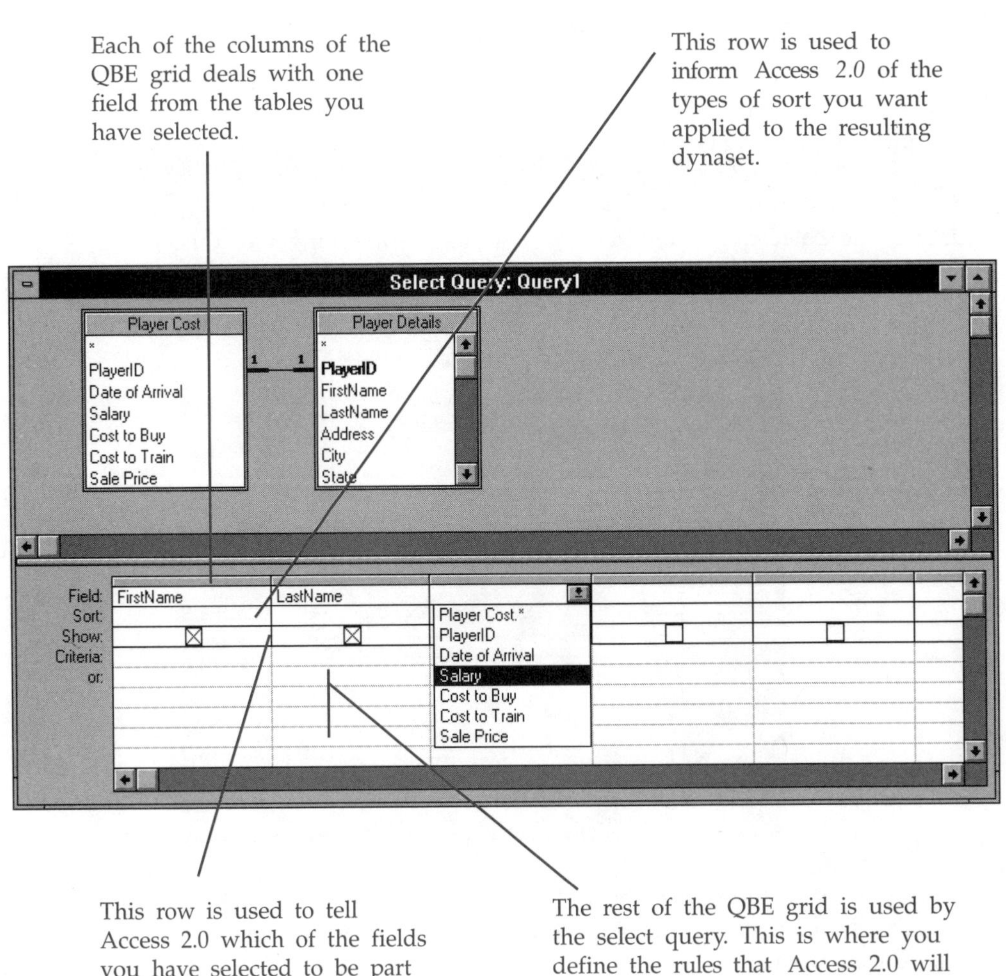

This row is used to tell Access 2.0 which of the fields you have selected to be part of the dynaset are the ones you actually want to see.

The rest of the QBE grid is used by the select query. This is where you define the rules that Access 2.0 will follow when deciding which records to select for its dynaset.

When you have selected all the fields that you want to appear in your own query dynaset, you need to apply the sorting instruction to these fields. Move the cursor to the sort row of the appropriate cell in the QBE grid. A tab will appear at the end of the cell. By selecting this tab you will get a list of all the available sorting methods:

- Ascending: this will order the entries in this field from A to Z, lowest to highest.
- Descending: this orders the entries Z to A, highest to lowest.
- (not sorted): three guesses!!

Highlight the sort that you require and it will be placed into the cell for you. In the example, you want the players sorted by name. So, in the column LastName, in the sort cell, select the Ascending sort method.

Field:	FirstName	LastName
Sort:		Ascending / Descending / (not sorted)
Show:	☒	
Criteria:		
or:		

You have now completed a basic design for this type of query. Let's look at the results, the dynaset.

The Dynaset

The dynaset is where you can see the results of all your query designs. The dynaset is a temporary table that contains all the selected records in the order that you have specified for them. This temporary table is what you use as the source of information for your forms and reports if you want them to include data from more than one table.

At any stage of your query's design you can see the results that your creation would produce by changing to the query's Datasheet View. You can do this by either:

- Selecting the icon.
- Or by choosing Datasheet from the View menu.

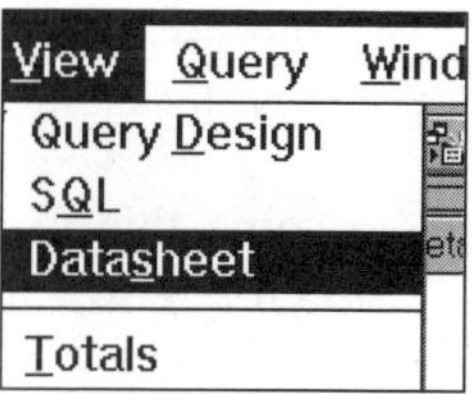

You can also see your results by clicking on the [!] Run Query icon.

Changing to the Datasheet View lets you look at the dynaset that is produced from your query design. Below you can see the way the dynaset appears using the example of the Player/Salary query.

Select Query: Query1

Last Name	First Name	Salary
Jackson	Marcus	$225.00
Jackson	Barney	$220.00
Santana	Alf	$176.00
Smith	Freddy	$150.00

As you can see, the dynaset of this query looks very similar to a table's datasheet, with the field names appearing as the column headings and each record appearing on individual rows of the datasheet. Each time you change to this view, Access 2.0 recalculates the dynaset, taking into account any changes that have been made to the query's design. This means that as you design the query you can look at the dynaset periodically and see the results of any new features that you include in the QBE grid.

Let's try a simple variant on this with the NWind.mdb sample database supplied with Access 2.0:

- Open the NWind database.
- Select a new query and choose Customers and Orders from the offered tables.
- Select Company Name as your first queried field.
- Select Ship City as your second queried field.
- Select Ascending for the Company Name sort.
- Look at the Datasheet View for the results.

Sorting on More Than One Field in the QBE Grid

One of the things you may have noticed on the dynaset of the Player/Salary query is that the names have been sorted based upon the LastName field. This causes a problem when two players have the same last name, because they are not necessarily sorted as you would expect, i.e Marcus Jackson comes before Barney Jackson.

To solve this problem Access 2.0 allows you to sort on more than one field in the QBE grid. Simply repeat the sort assign procedure to all the fields that you wish Access 2.0 to sort by.

The order that the fields appear in is important in this case. *Access 2.0* sorts the records based upon the field that appears closest to the left side of the QBE grid first. If there are any duplications in this field, it then moves to the next field in the QBE grid that has a sort definition and re-orders the duplicates following that definition. It continues along the QBE grid until all of the sort definitions have been accomplished before outputting the dynaset to your screen.

To see an example of this multiple-field sorting in action, let's return to the Player/Salary example. At the moment, with this QBE grid, the dynaset looks like this:

Field:	FirstName	LastName	Salary
Sort:		Ascending	
Show:	☒	☒	☒
Criteria:			
or:			

First Name	Last Name	Salary
Marcus	Jackson	£225.00
Barney	Jackson	£220.00
Alf	Santana	£176.00
Freddy	Smith	£150.00

If you now select the sort on the FirstName field, leaving the fields *in this order* in the QBE grid, Access 2.0 sorts on the FirstName field first *and then* on the LastName field to give the result shown below:

Field:	FirstName	LastName	Salary
Sort:	Ascending	Ascending	
Show:	☒	☒	☒
Criteria:			
or:			

First Name	Last Name	Salary
Alf	Santana	£176.00
Barney	Jackson	£220.00
Freddy	Smith	£150.00
Marcus	Jackson	£225.00

As you can see, the FirstName field has been sorted alphabetically. The LastName field is *not* sorted alphabetically any more because the FirstName field *appears on the left edge* of the QBE grid and so is calculated first. The LastName field has no duplicates so the LastName sort doesn't apply.

To get the result you really want you have to rearrange the order of the fields in the QBE grid. You do this by using the same method that you used to move columns in the table Datasheet View:

- Highlight the field's heading.
- Hold the left mouse button down.
- Drag the field to its new location.
- Release the mouse button.

Moving a Field

To move a field, first highlight it.

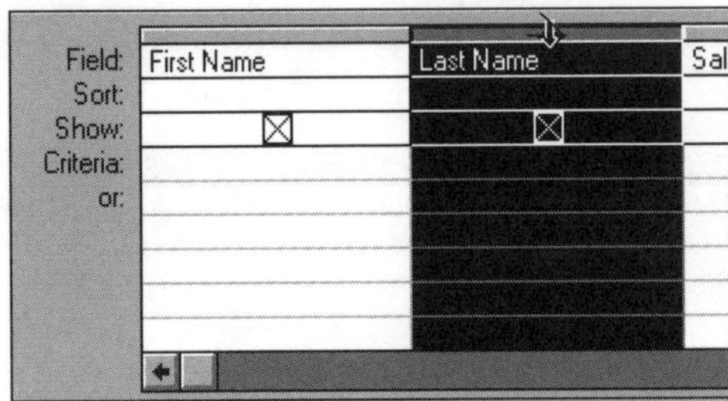

Then drag it to a new location.

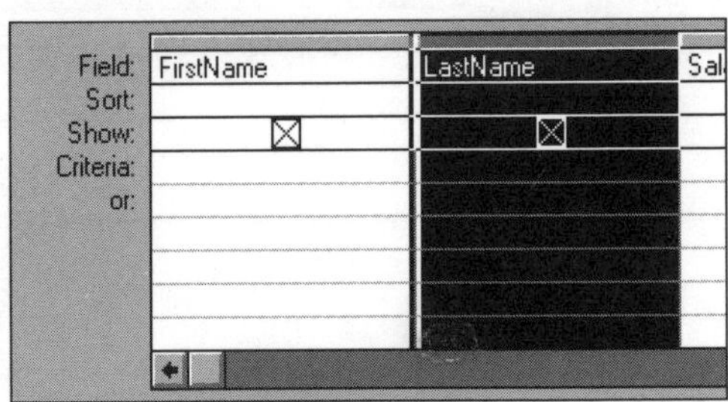

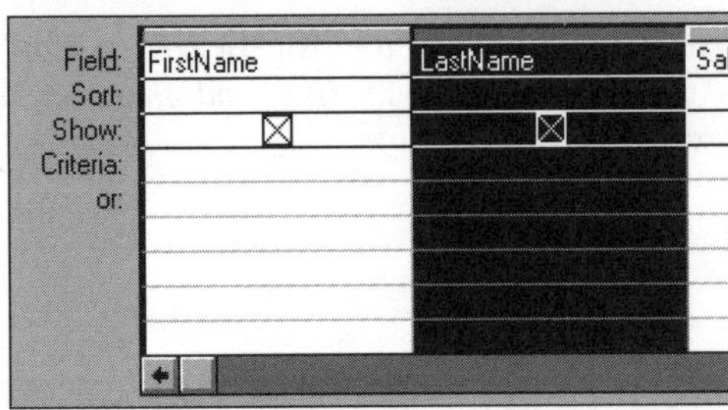

Continue dragging.

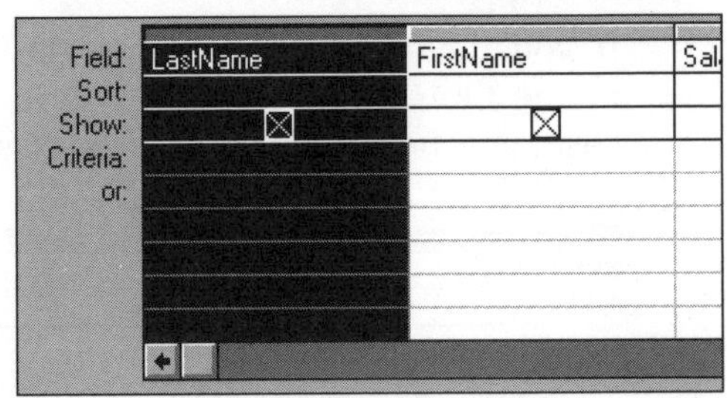

Finally, release the mouse button.

The following QBE grid shows the results of this re-positioning, while the dynaset shows the results of the new QBE grid:

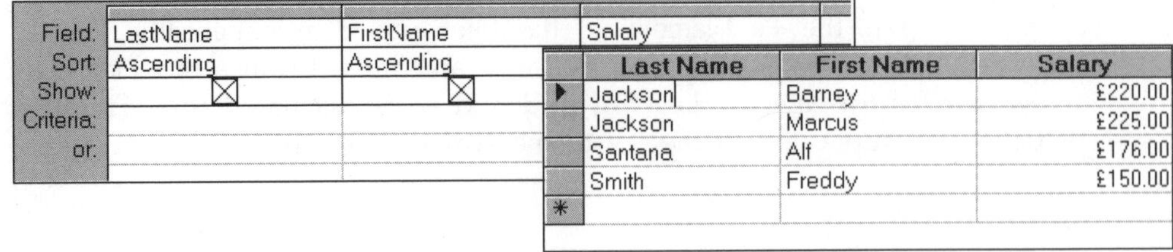

Last Name	First Name	Salary
Jackson	Barney	£220.00
Jackson	Marcus	£225.00
Santana	Alf	£176.00
Smith	Freddy	£150.00

Player	Salary
Barney Jackson	£220.00
Marcus Jackson	£225.00
Alf Santana	£176.00
Freddy Smith	£150.00

It is also possible to produce this dynaset (but you'll learn how to do that later).

Try some re-positioning of the previous query which you made in NWind.mdb.

What is a Selection Query?

A selection query selects a set of records from those contained in your selected tables, depending on some rules that you have placed into the QBE grid.

For example, in the Surfers' database, you might want to compare the performance of the linebackers, or perhaps you want to see the players that are paid more than $200. Let's look at the first of these scenarios.

You want to select all of the players that play in a given position: Linebacker.

First, let's produce the basic query template with the required tables:

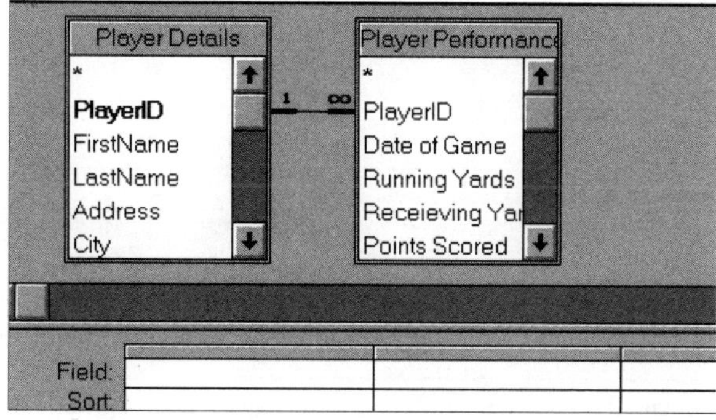

You can see how the relationship has been set - unique field to unique field, using PlayerID number.

Now, we'll add in the fields that we want to see on the dynaset. The resulting dynaset is:

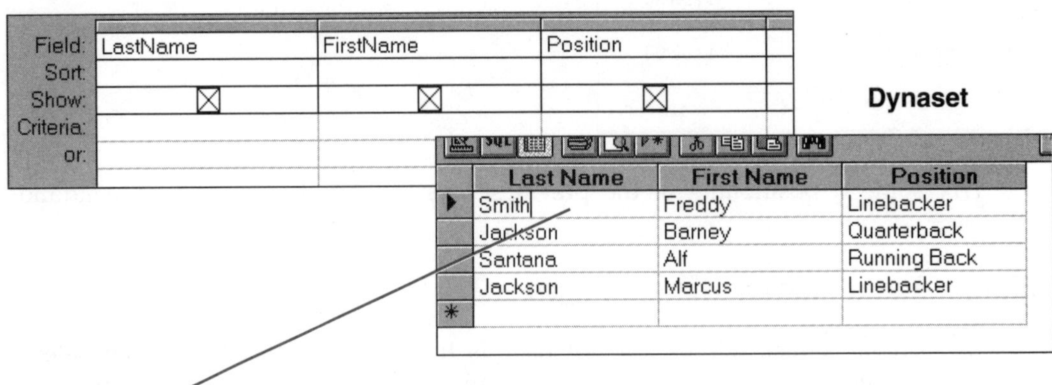

You can see that the names appear in the example in order of a PlayerID number which we invented for them. Remember that this is the **default** ordering that Access 2.0 uses if there are no alternative sort commands from the user.

Now you can limit the records that appear in a dynaset by adding some rules to the **criteria** cells of the QBE grid. In the Surfers example, you only want to see the players that are Linebackers. To do this, you need to instruct Access to only show the records of players who are Linebackers.

Use the instruction Like, giving the following dynaset:

Field:	LastName	FirstName	Position
Sort:			
Show:	☒	☒	☒
Criteria:			Like "Linebacker"
or:			

Last Name	First Name	Position
Smith	Freddy	Linebacker
Jackson	Marcus	Linebacker

This is a typical way to define the criteria for a Text field. In the next section of this chapter, you will see some of the other syntax to be used with other data types.

Using the Criteria Section of the QBE Grid

In the last example, you saw how to select a group of records with one common characteristic. Usually, you will want to select a group of records with many common characteristics. To accomplish this, you need to understand exactly how the QBE grid works.

Access 2.0 evaluates where you have put the criteria in the QBE grid using the logical operators AND and OR. Each row of the QBE grid is read with an AND between each criteria. The whole criteria is built up by reading each row in the QBE grid with an OR between them.

Look at the following QBE grid design:

Field:	LastName	FirstName	Position
Sort:			
Show:	☒	☒	☒
Criteria:	"Jackson"		"quarterback"
or:			

It you do not place an operator into the criteria, *Access 2.0* defaults to the Like operator.

You will see that the criteria is not case-sensitive.

This can be read as: "Select all the players with Jackson for a last name *and* whose position is Quarterback".

Another example, is the following QBE grid:

Field:	LastName	FirstName	Position
Sort:			
Show:	☒	☒	☒
Criteria:	"Jackson"		
or:	" Smith"		

This can be read as: "Select all the players that have Jackson as a last name *or* Smith as a last name".

We can combine AND and OR together to get quite complex results. For this question: "Select all the players that have 'Alf' as a FirstName *or* have 'Jackson' as a LastName *and* whose position is Linebacker", the QBE grid would look like this:

Field:	LastName	FirstName	Position
Sort:			
Show:	☒	☒	☒
Criteria:		"alf"	
or:	"jackson"		"linebacker"

The easiest way to become expert in the use of the QBE grid is through practice. When the design of the QBE grid is second nature to you, the creation of a fully functioning database will be transformed from a quagmire of terms and special cases to a simple, easy task that flows from your finger tips.

Using the Criteria Row of the QBE Grid With Sorts

From the way the QBE grid is laid out, you may expect that you can use both the sort and the select features of a query together. You are right! Simply place all the information for the results that you require into the QBE grid and Access 2.0 will provide you with the resulting dynaset. Access 2.0 calculates the records that you want from the criteria row, **and then** applies any sorting instructions that you have given.

An example of this co-operation between the two features is shown below:

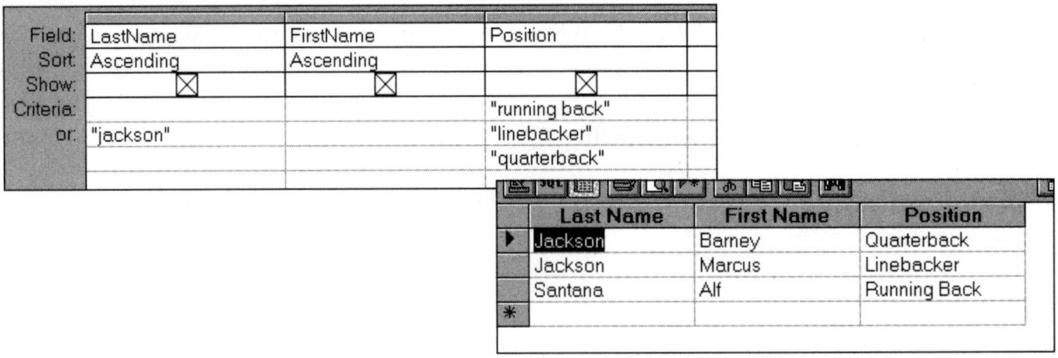

Field:	LastName	FirstName	Position
Sort:	Ascending	Ascending	
Show:	☒	☒	☒
Criteria:			"running back"
or:	"jackson"		"linebacker"
			"quarterback"

Last Name	First Name	Position
Jackson	Barney	Quarterback
Jackson	Marcus	Linebacker
Santana	Alf	Running Back

What Operators Can I Use in the QBE Grid?

An operator is usually a word or symbol that you can use to tell Access 2.0 exactly what rules you want the selection to be based upon. There are many such symbols, some to use with particular data types, all that do a specific job in conveying the exact meaning of your English request.

Below are the tables of operators that you can use in the QBE grid, as well as an example of their use:

Comparison Operators

Operator	Meaning	Example	Interpretation
=	Equals	=France	Same as France
>	Greater than	>123	Greater than 123
<	Less than	<P	Before P, alphabetically
>=	Greater than or equal to	>=1/1/90	On or after January 1st 1990
<=	Less than or equal to	<=122	Equal to 122 or less
<>	Not equal to	<>3/1/95	All dates except March 1st, 1995
Between	Between two values inclusive	Between M and S	All letters between M and S inclusive
In	Including	In (A B C)	A, B or C
Is Null	An empty field	Is null	Records with no entry in that field
Is Not Null	A non empty field	Is not null	Records that do have an entry in that field
Like	Pattern match	Like 9Z?4	Looks for entries of four characters, the first two being 9Z, and the last one 4

Logical Operator

Operator	Meaning	Example	Interpretation
AND	Both are true	>1 AND <6	2,3,4 or 5
OR	One or the other is true	1 OR 2	Either 1 or 2
NOT	Not true	NOT 1	Anything except 1

Wildcard Operators

Operator	Meaning	Example	Interpretation
?	Any character	CN-01?	Returns all entries that begin CN-01 and are 5 characters long
*	Any characters	CN-01*	Returns all entries that begin CN-01, and are any length
[...]	Some other field	=[age]	Results in the QBE grid records that have the same value in this field as in the age field

Mathematical Operators

Operator	Meaning	Example	Interpretation
+	Addition	>[a]+[b]	Greater than the addition of fields a and b
-	Subtraction	=[a]-[b]	Equal to the subtraction of field b from a
*	Multiplication	<[a]*[b]	Less than the multiplication of fields a and b
/	Division	>=[a]/[b]	Greater than or equal to field a divided by field b
\	Integer division	5\2	Results in 2 (The remainder is not kept)
^	Exponent	4^3	Results in 4*4*4 = 64
Mod	Remainder of division (modulo)	Mod 5/2[i.e. 5=(2*2)+1]	Results in 1
&	Join two strings	"go"&"od"	Results in "good"

It is also possible to use these various operators in conjunction with Access 2.0 functions.

Querying With Functions

Access 2.0 functions are built-in operations that you can take advantage of when trying to produce some complex criteria. Examples of these functions include Date (), which allows you to reference the current time and date, and UCase which converts text of both cases to upper-case.

Below are some examples of the use of the Access 2.0 Date () function:

Example	Gives
Date ()	The current date
<=Date () - 30	Dates less than or equal to 30 days ago
Between Date () And Date () + 7	Dates from now until seven days from now

A listing of all the available built-in functions of Access 2.0's repertoire can be found in the help facility. Select Help from the menu bar, and Search functions: reference to obtain a full listing.

> You can use all of these commands in your query design. As you would expect, things can get very convoluted, so a solid table structure will always help. We will use some of these commands in later chapters. In the meantime, try inventing some new queries with the NWind.mdb database to see how the results can be customized. Much of the hard work of queries can be removed with a Query Wizard, but be careful. You must have a legal question for your data, otherwise the wizard can't help you.

Let's look at some more routines that can produce highly detailed results as you 'drill down' into your data.

Summary Calculations

So far, you have looked at two of the main uses for a query: sorting and selecting records with customizable criteria. One of the other uses that a query can be put to is the production of **summary calculations**.

A summary calculation is a kind of computation or selection of records that are requested by the criteria you have set up in the QBE grid.

For a good example of these kinds of calculations, let's return to the Surfers database. The Surfers coach enters each player's performance into the database after every match. After a few matches, a player's running yards over the season becomes harder and harder to track, as the number of records relating to each player grows.

It would be much simpler to see the maximum, minimum and average running yards of each player all on one record. All you need to do is use the summary calculation to instruct Access 2.0 to supply the maximum and minimum values, and calculate the average per game. You can see how to do this using this example as a model.

Using Summary Calculations

In this example, we need information from the Player Details table and the Player Performance table. We need the player's FirstName and LastName, as well as 3 copies of the Running Yards field. So far, the query design and datasheet look like this:

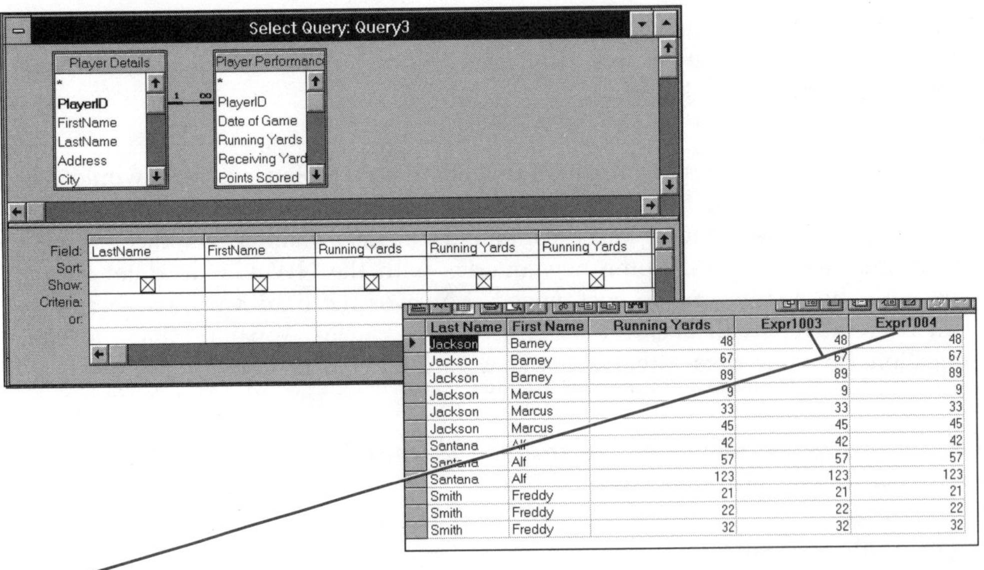

Last Name	First Name	Running Yards	Expr1003	Expr1004
Jackson	Barney	48	48	48
Jackson	Barney	67	67	67
Jackson	Barney	89	89	89
Jackson	Marcus	9	9	9
Jackson	Marcus	33	33	33
Jackson	Marcus	45	45	45
Santana	Alf	42	42	42
Santana	Alf	57	57	57
Santana	Alf	123	123	123
Smith	Freddy	21	21	21
Smith	Freddy	22	22	22
Smith	Freddy	32	32	32

When you have multiple copies of the same field in the QBE grid, *Access 2.0* renames all apart from the first, so that field names remain unique.

To call up the Summary Calculations function select the Σ icon. This icon adds another new row to the QBE grid entitled Total:

- The default setting for this cell is Group By. (We leave this entry in both FirstName and LastName cells).
- Our information will be grouped by the last/first name.
- By clicking the tab at the end of the cell we choose Max, Min and Avg from the available summary calculations for each of the three Running Yards respectively.

This produces the following QBE grid and the resulting datasheet:

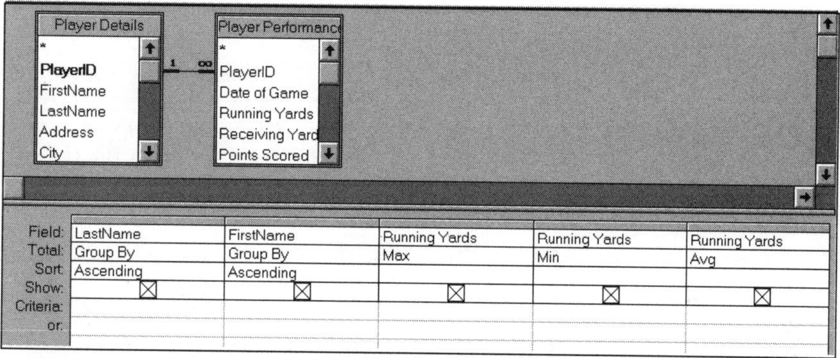

Last Name	First Name	MaxOfRunning Yards	MinOfRunning Yards	AvgOfRunning Yards
Jackson	Barney	89	48	68
Jackson	Marcus	45	9	29
Santana	Alf	123	42	74
Smith	Freddy	32	21	25

Resulting Dynaset From a Summary Calculation

This shows how you can quickly and easily summarize your data using these kinds of calculations. This is a great tool for producing effective and concise reports.

Below is a complete listing of all the summary calculations that are available, along with what you can use them for:

Summary Calculation	Use
Group By	The default setting for the fields, that groups by single records.
Sum	Totals all the values in a given field for single groupings of records.
Avg	Calculates the average of all the values of a given group.
Min	Gives the smallest value in a given group.
Max	Gives the largest value in a given group.
Count	Counts the number of records in a given group.
StDev	Calculates the standard deviation of the range of values in a given grouping of records.
Var	Calculates the variation of the same range of values.
First	Gives the value of the first record in a grouping.
Last	Gives the last value in the same grouping.
Expression	This denotes a user-defined expression.
Where	Use this summary calculation to force a search to occur *before* the calculation is completed.

Let's have one more example of a summary calculation in action using Where.

Returning to the Surfers database, suppose that you only want to look at the player's performance over the first two matches of the season. To do this you need to include a Date Of Game field in the QBE grid. This means that the grouping of the records by player disintegrates. The records concerning games are now distinct, that is, all of the fields with the Group By setting (FirstName, LastName and Date Of Match) make each record, for each game, unique.

In order to calculate this selection of games *before* the grouping, we add Where plus a range of dates to the sort:

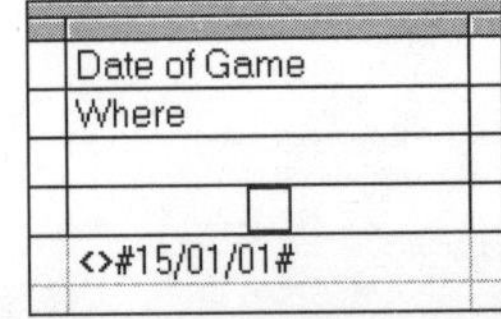

This then solves the problem and gives the correct summary calculation for each player as shown below:

Last Name	First Name	MaxOfRunning Yards	MinOfRunning Yards	AvgOfRunning Yards
Jackson	Barney	89	48	68.5
Jackson	Marcus	33	9	21
Santana	Alf	57	42	49.5
Smith	Freddy	22	21	21.5

Using this summary calculation along with the others on offer, you can produce all the statistics that you may want on a report. You now have another tool to add to your armory when fighting disorderly data and ill-prepared information.

Looking at Unrelated Tables

So far, when you have looked at queries based on more than one table, the relationships between them have already been declared. However, sometimes you might want to look at two or more **unrelated tables** in the same query. If you simply place the two unrelated tables in your query design, Access 2.0 will assume that you require the **Cartesian product** of the records stored in those tables (not a good idea!).

The Cartesian Product

The Cartesian product of the records in two tables can produce quite amusing results. We will look at it here just to illustrate an inherent pitfall when dealing with unrelated table queries.

Suppose we look at the two following tables from the Surfers database:

Player Details

PlayerID	First Name	Last Name
1	Freddy	Smith
2	Barney	Jackson
3	Alf	Santana
4	Marcus	Jackson
(Counter)		

Player Salary

PlayerID	Salary
1	£150.00
2	£220.00
3	£176.00
4	£225.00
0	£0.00

Firstly, you must realize that these are daily rates of pay!

If you assume that the tables have **not** got a relationship linking them on the PlayerID field, and you add both of the tables into a query design, the results are quite unexpected:

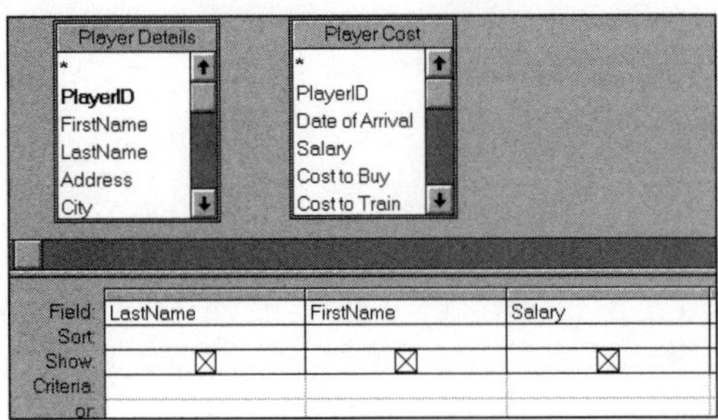

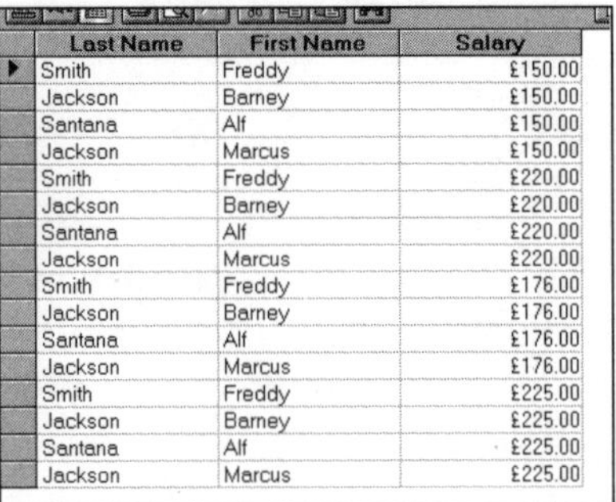

Last Name	First Name	Salary
Smith	Freddy	£150.00
Jackson	Barney	£150.00
Santana	Alf	£150.00
Jackson	Marcus	£150.00
Smith	Freddy	£220.00
Jackson	Barney	£220.00
Santana	Alf	£220.00
Jackson	Marcus	£220.00
Smith	Freddy	£176.00
Jackson	Barney	£176.00
Santana	Alf	£176.00
Jackson	Marcus	£176.00
Smith	Freddy	£225.00
Jackson	Barney	£225.00
Santana	Alf	£225.00
Jackson	Marcus	£225.00

Access 2.0 takes all the records from the first table, Player Details and applies the first record in the second table, Player Salary. It then moves onto the second record in the second table and repeats the process. There is no guidance to the query to relate records, so as each player is scanned **all** salaries are included. This means that with two tables, each with four records, the resulting dynaset has sixteen entries. This multiplying of records can be useful when you want to assign all the elements of one table to all the elements of another, but usually it should be **avoided.**

Why Would the Tables in My Database Be Unrelated?

There are several reasons why tables that you place into a query's design may not already be related. Some of the reasons include:

- You want to temporarily alter the relationship between the tables to get other information.
- You want to produce a special type of **join** between two tables that normal relationships cannot produce.
- You may have deliberately decided not to relate the tables together for design purposes or because you don't want them to be related in your database structure.

Whatever the reason, it is possible to temporarily join two tables together using joins.

Joins

Joins are simply relationships between two tables that exist only inside the query environment. Joins allow you to produce results which the rigid database structure may prohibit, as well as allowing the production of a special construction called a **self-join**. We will discuss these self-joins in more detail in a few moments, but for now, let's look at how to create a join between two tables.

Using a join essentially gives you access to the dormant and unrevealed aspects of the data. You may well use a query that defines what orders your customers are waiting for, but sometimes you may also want the other data to be shown in the results. For example, you may want to include in the results all the customers that you regularly trade with, but happen to have **no** orders with you at the moment.

Preparing to Create a Join

Before you can join two tables together, there are several things that you need to know:

- How you wish to join the two tables together, that is, which field to which field.
- Whether or not Access 2.0 will allow the join. The two fields you want to join together need to have **related data types.**
- What kind of join you want to produce: an equi-join, a left or right outer join or a self-join.

> Most data types only relate to themselves. However, the counter type also relates to number data type if it has the long integer size defined.

How you want to join the two tables together differs from design to design and depends on what the designer wishes to accomplish. Usually the fields that are joined are copies of each other, just as when a normal relationship is created. This means that the information that will appear in the fields can be similar and therefore Access 2.0 will be able to make the link between related records.

The type of join that you want to use between the tables depends on what information you want in your dynaset:

Join	Use
equi-join	This is the default setting and shows all the records that appear in either table, relating any together if the joined field entries are related. When you open most normal queries, the equi-join is already defined. It is the normal join between cross table fields (for instance, Customer ID).
left outer join	This would show all the records in a table, if they have a corresponding entry in the table to the right.
right outer join	This would show all the records in a table, if they have corresponding entries in the table to the left.
self-join	This is a special type of join, that basically involves making multiple copies of the table in the QBE grid and joining fields.

Once you have decided on all of these characteristics, you are ready to produce the query design.

Creating a Join

To create any of the three basic types of join follow these steps:

1. Produce the basic query template, placing all the tables in the query that you want to take information from, including the unrelated ones.
2. Highlight one of the fields that is to be part of the join. It isn't important which of the fields is chosen.
3. By holding down the left mouse button, drag the now changed pointer to the other field in the soon-to-be-related table.
4. Release the left mouse button when you are over the field and the temporary join will be made. By default, an equi-join will be the type of join that is assigned between the tables.
5. To alter the type of join between the tables, highlight the join with the mouse pointer. The join should become slightly thicker and the head of the join will show an arrow to denote the direction of the join. If a window entitled Query Properties appears, you did not hit the line. Close the window and try again.

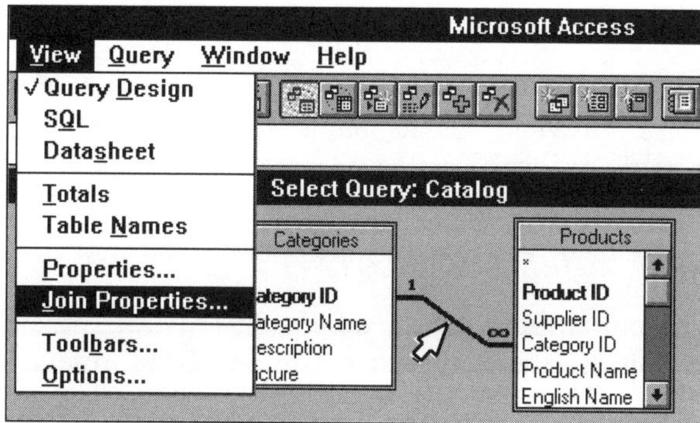

- Now select View and Join Properties... from the menu bar, to get the following window appearing on screen:

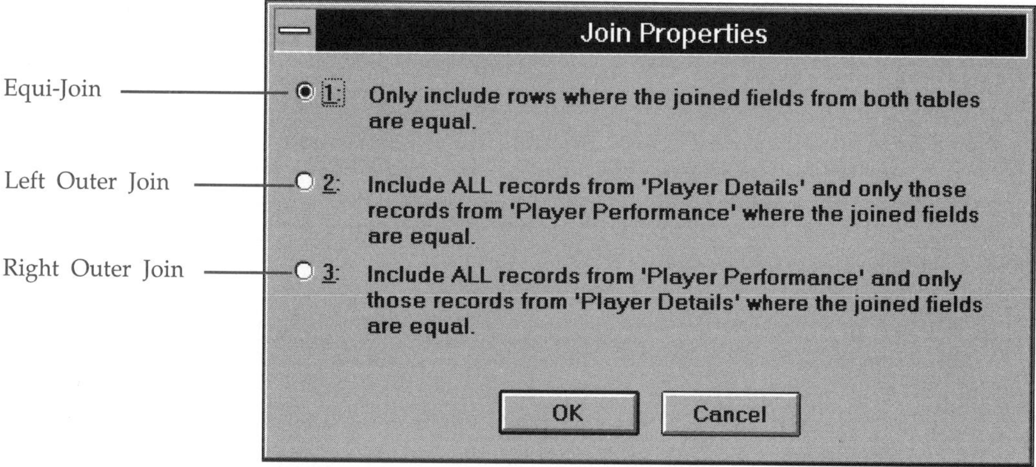

- Select the type of join that you want to appear between the two tables: equi-join, left outer and right outer join respectively.
- Select the OK button when you have made you choice and that join will be placed between the tables.

You can now continue with your query design, filling in the QBE grid as normal. The results you get in the resulting dynaset will depend on the type of join that you have selected, but rest assured that the Cartesian product is a thing of the past.

A Special Kind of Join - The Self-Join

All of the different types of join that have so far been covered relate to joining two different tables. However, as its name suggests, there is another type of join that joins a table to itself, called the self-join.

Why Would You Join a Table to Itself?

In reality, the self-join doesn't join a table to itself but rather joins a table and a copy of itself. This means that you can refer to information that may be hidden inside the actual table structure.

For example, suppose you wanted to compile a database of all of your relatives both past and present in order to produce a family tree. On each person's record there would need to be a listing of their mother, father, brothers and sisters. As long as the information was available, this would mean that on each record there would be references to other records in the same table, usually by an ID number.

As you know, ID numbers are very unfriendly, particularly when you probably know the person by name and not as "147". In order to produce a dynaset containing the names of the people rather than their ID numbers you would need to have several copies of the relevant table, and link them together with self-joins.

Let's say that your father has the general ID number 47 in your imaginary tree table. The field on *your* record that lists who your father is will be 47. This means that by connecting a General ID field to the FatherID field in another copy of the table, using a self-join, you will be able to reference the **name** of your father from the copy of the table.

Let's look at an example of this self-join in action.

How to Create a Self-Join

Let's suppose, that in our family tree database you only list fathers and the sons. Your table design could look like this:

Table: Relatives

General ID	FatherID	FirstName	LastName
1	2	Fred	Matersonn
2	5	Jeff	Callaghan
3	5	Hobey	Carmicheal
4	5	Jackson	Solmustard
5	6	Archibald	Lemming

To produce the self-join query, you need a second copy of the table to get the father names from. To do this, add the table to the QBE grid twice. Access 2.0 will automatically rename the second copy with the addition of "_1" to its title.

- Place the self-join between the ID field and the FatherID field in just the same manner that you would place a normal equi-join between two related fields.

- The creation process is complete. To see the name of each father and son, select FirstName and LastName from both tables and run the query. You will get the following results:

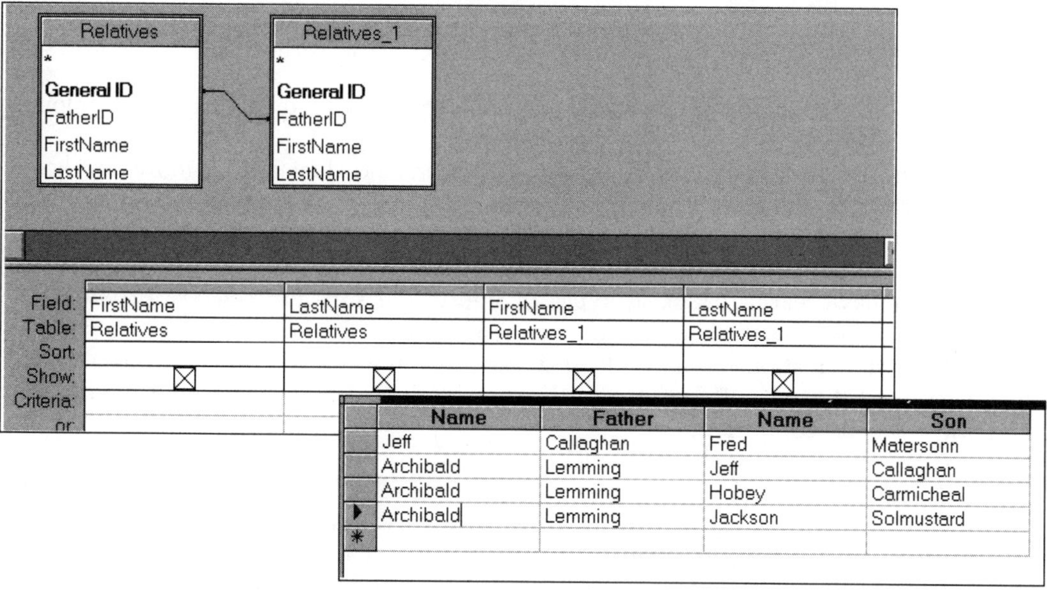

Really, the self-join is not special at all. It's just like an equi-join between two specially constructed tables that happen to be copies of the same table. Access 2.0's ability to handle this type of situation allows more innovative table design, saving time, space and energy.

Nesting Queries

So far, in this chapter you have learnt all about the basic types of query, both what they are and how to create them. You have seen how the basic types can work together to produce clean, readable results, and you should even grasp the whys and wherefores of unrelated tables in a query. You've also seen some of the built-in mathematical functions that Access 2.0 has to offer in terms of the summary calculations, but all the while the query has drawn its set of records straight from the base tables that you created in order to store your data.

Now it shouldn't surprise you that, as forms and reports can use queries as the source of their data, so can another query. This practice of using a query as the data source for another query is called **nesting**, and, used in the correct way, it can become one of the most powerful tools you could ever create.

Why Use Nesting?

You would usually use nested queries to:

- Either break down a complicated QBE grid into smaller, more manageable chunks that can be easily solved.
- Or, perform some tasks that a single non-nested query cannot do alone.

The first of these points is very easy to understand. Just as the individual parts of your database plan are easier to solve than the idea in its entirety, so the same idea can be applied to a large, highly complex QBE grid.

As you have learnt, the basic types of query (the sort and select) can work well together. Once the other features from Access 2.0 begin to creep into the design, the creation of the QBE grid may feel more like climbing Everest than a stroll in the park. If you break the task up into smaller steps, the mountain will soon be conquered.

The second use of nested queries can be difficult to understand, as up until now it has been suggested that the correct query design would be able to produce any result you could ever invent. This idea is true, in general, but only if nesting is included as part of your tool kit.

Take, for example, the summary calculations that we produced a few sections ago. It was easy to calculate the average number of running yards that each player had accumulated over a given number of games, but how would you go about comparing each player's average against the average performance for his position? This would give a fairer yard stick of each player's performance because it isn't right to expect your Linebacker to have the same average as your Running Backs.

Let's take a step back and look at what we need. We require the **average** yards running for each player. That's easy enough, as you've already seen how to produce those figures. You also need to produce figures for the average yards running **by each position**. Use the following QBE grid to produce these results:

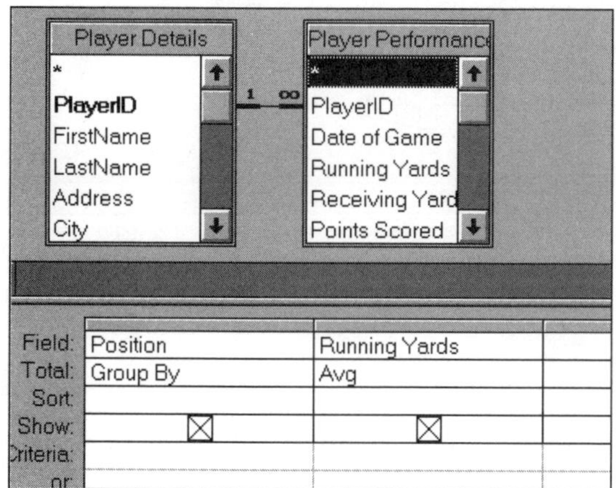

Position	AvgOfRunning Yards
Linebacker	27
Quarterback	68
Running Back	74

As you can see, all that has been done is that the records have been grouped on position and then the average running yards have been worked out (we chose 3 games). Now, by nesting the 2 dynasets that you have just seen created, we can produce the following QBE grid and the resulting dynaset (shown on the next page):

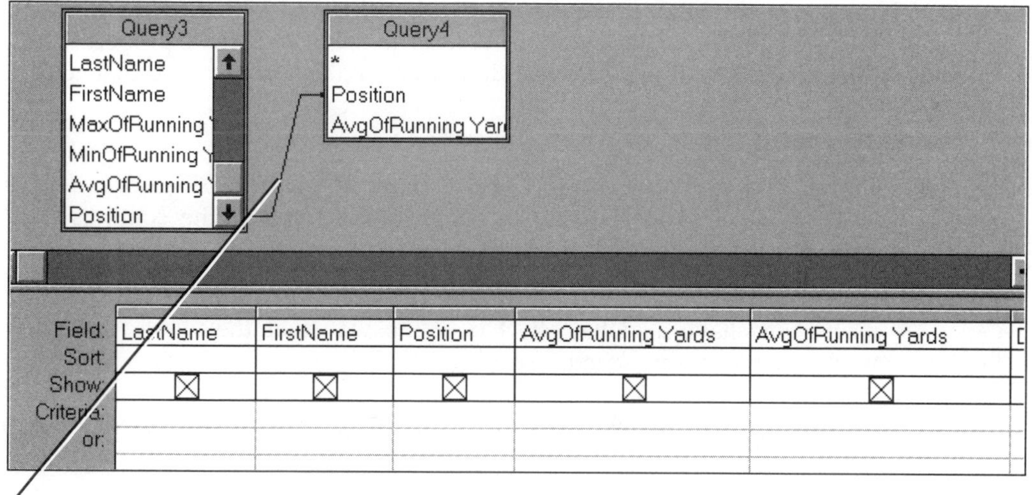

Note that the queries have been linked by their common field, Position, to stop *Access 2.0* producing the Cartesian product.

This is the custom field showing the difference between the two figures. You will see how to create this effect shortly.

Last Name	First Name	Position	Player's Avg	Position Avg	Difference
Jackson	Barney	Quarterback	68	68	0
Jackson	Marcus	Linebacker	29	27	2
Santana	Alf	Running Back	74	74	0
Smith	Freddy	Linebacker	25	27	-2

You will see that the field names are more understandable. This is done by making use of the QBE grid properties covered in the next section of this chapter.

As there is only one quarterback and one running back entered into the database, the player average is the same as the position average.

You may find that nested queries are not very easy to understand on a conceptual basis. They come into their own, however, when you have a real live problem to solve, easily lending their flexibility to the solution of any complex request. As with all queries **practice makes perfect**.

Query Properties

One of the improvements that Microsoft made to Access 2.0 was the inclusion of **query properties**. These properties allow you to take more control over what happens in the QBE grid, and so provide a cheap and efficient service when dealing with data manipulation. Just as in table and field properties, query properties allow more detailed definition of the activity at cell level.

These properties come in two basic types:

1. Query field properties - each of the columns in the QBE grid can have its own set of properties defined to regulate some of the comings and goings through the QBE grid.

2. Query proper properties - these are properties assigned to the query itself. They have a global effect over the way that the whole query works in the grand scheme of things.

Let's take a closer look at the properties that Microsoft have provided for your query.

Query Properties

Type of Property	Meaning
Description	Use this field to describe what is happening in this query (useful for database management).
Output All Fields	Use this property to determine whether or not the query has passed only the fields in the QBE grid (No) or all the fields in the underlying tables (Yes).
Top Values	Access 2.0 will either give you the top n values or the top n% of values depending on whether you enter a number (n) or a number and a % sign (n%).
Unique Values	If this property is set to yes, it will only pass records with unique values in each field. If Access 2.0 encounters duplicate entries, it allows the first occurrence to appear and bars the rest.
Unique Record	This property is similar to unique values, except that now the entire record has to be duplicated before it is barred from appearing in the dynaset.
Run Permissions	This query property enables you to restrict Access to the query with Access 2.0's built-in security features. The default value here is the user, the lowest of the low.
Source Database	The name of the database that this query will be using, in which all the data is stored.
Source ConnectStr	The name of the application that created the database given above.
Record Locks	This property is used to allow the records to be locked (or unlocked) while the query is running.
ODBC Time-out	This is the length of time that Access 2.0 will wait while it attempts to get hold of the server. This is only important if you are on a network. If you are, see your network administrator for more details.

Query Field Properties

Type of Property	Meaning
Description	Use this property to describe what is happening in this field. The description may appear on the status bar during data entry if the form is based upon this query.
Format	This property is similar to the format property associated with field definitions. This is the format that all the data which is entered into this field will appear in.
Decimal Places	This is to control the number of decimal places that any calculation can use while trying to maintain accuracy.
Input Mask	This is the screen that all data entry is made through. When you define a mask, you also define the framework that the user will see when they move the cursor into the field. It is used to help them in the decision of what information to place in this field.
Caption	This property is one of the most versatile properties that the fields in a query could have. In this cell, enter the text that you wish to use as the column heading instead of the potentially unreadable headings that Access 2.0 sometimes generates.

You should be aware that although the query properties are available in all cases (except Output All Fields which is only available when selecting Make Table and Append, see Chapter 9), the number of properties that a field can have depends upon its data type. For example, the Number data type gets all five properties, the Text type, not being interested in decimal places gets four, while the OLE Object field only has two properties: Description and Caption.

By using these properties in much the same way that the field properties were used, you can keep a tight eye on the goings on in your query. In the end it will make life simpler for you, as the database designer, having less problems to sort out. It will also be more simple for the user, who is guided through the use of the database with lots of useful hints and tips.

Filters

A filter is a basic query that Access 2.0 can quickly create and apply to the data in one single table. You can use it to sort your data into any order, and even hide some records, depending on the criteria that you supply to it. One important feature of a filter, is that it is based upon one table and one table alone. This means that it doesn't matter whatever joins you use, or whether you are going to get a Cartesian product or not, because the records can't get confused when there is only one table in the grid.

Below is the basic query template for a filter being created for the Player Details table. You create it by simply opening the table in Datasheet View and selecting the icon:

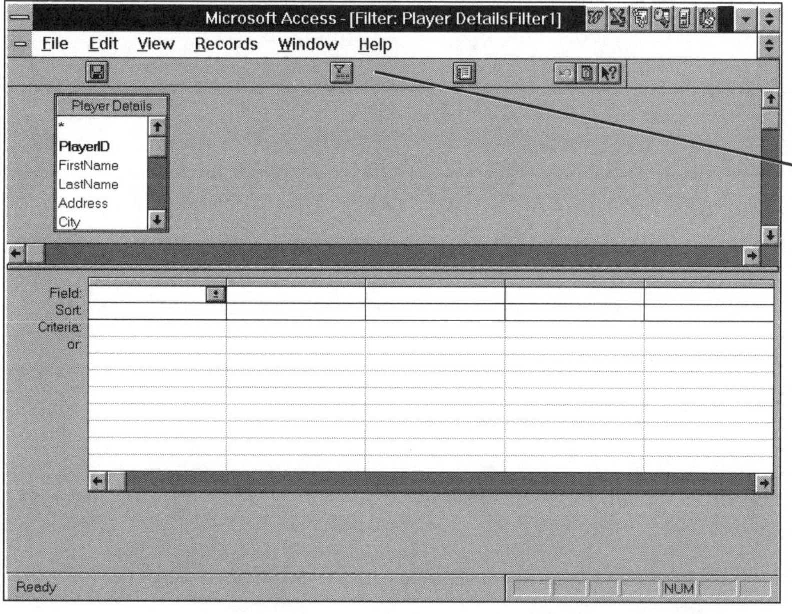

As there is only one table in the filter query, you will see that there is a reduction in icons/facilities.

As you can see, the options that you have compared to a normal QBE grid are few and far between, but the good news is, you don't need them! All you have to do is fill in the QBE grid. It stands, awaiting your instruction before you apply the finished filter using the icon.

> You can now save your filters as queries, so that you can call them up at a later date. Simply select the save icon, select Save As Query from the File menu, give the filter a name and select the OK button. To recall the filter select Load As Query from the File menu, and your filter will be returned to you, ready for you to reapply it and continue with your work.

Filters are quick, easy to create and simple to store until you really need them. They can then be recalled and applied very quickly. Making good use of your query knowledge to produce solid filter designs will make your life as a database designer much simpler.

Troubleshooting

Q&A What does this icon do?

This icon is called Table Names, because when it is selected a new row appears in the QBE grid detailing the tables from which the fields are drawn. This could be particularly useful, especially if you think that seven tables in a database could have a field called LastName. In short this feature allows you to uniquely identify each of the fields that appear in the QBE grid.

Q&A What is a custom field?

A custom field is simply a field that you have customized. A classic example of a custom field is FullName. As you would expect, FullName is a composite of FirstName and LastName. A custom field allows you to reduce the number of entries in the QBE grid, while also allowing you to rename potentially confusing fields. The syntax for a custom field is very simple. Below you can see the whole function, together with all the syntax required, to produce the FullName field:

```
FullName: [FirstName]&" "& [LastName]
```

You can see that:

- The name of the custom field is not surrounded by the square brackets and is followed by a colon (:).
- Each of the fields involved in the custom field is surrounded by square brackets.
- The &" "& syntax places a space between the data from FirstName and LastName. & is the equivalent of addition, while " " denotes a list of characters, in this case a space. So our result is, of course, FirstName space LastName.

It is also possible to carry out mathematical calculations in your QBE grid using this method. The following example calculates the total sale price of a customer's shopping basket if a 10% sales tax is applied at the counter:

```
Net Total: Sum ([Shopping List])*1.1
```

The Sum function must have a field over which to complete its task.

Custom fields can make life a lot easier, especially when you take into account that the Build button is again available to help you create the exact custom field to fulfill your requirements. In this case the Build button allows you access to the Expression Builder. This is explained in more detail in Chapter 7.

Q&A What does the SQL icon do?

This icon allows you to see the SQL (Structured Query Language) version of what's happening behind the QBE grid. As you already know, Microsoft created the QBE grid to make direct SQL programming redundant. Unfortunately, SQL can provide more functions that the QBE grid, and so you can always resort to SQL. You will need to study a specialist SQL Programming Guide if you want to move deeper in this direction.

Below is a typical result from the NWind.mdb using the Employee List query:

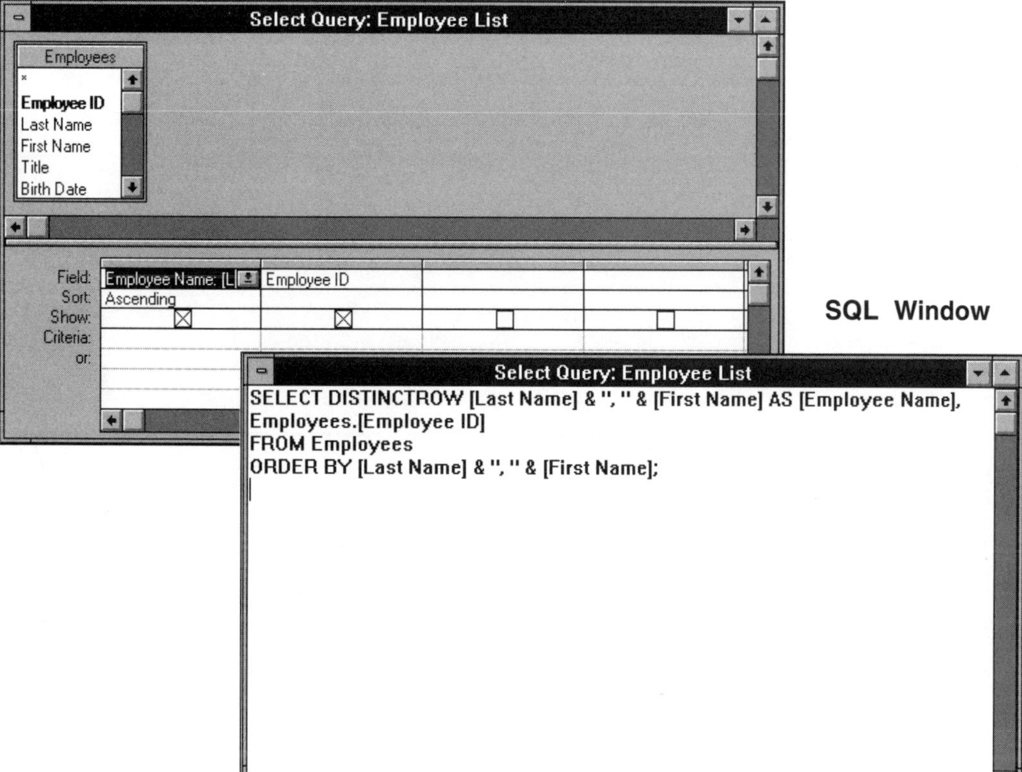

Forms

In previous chapters, you learnt how Access 2.0 stores your information and how you can instruct it to do some basic manipulation of that information. However, all this work is really a foundation for what is to come in the next few chapters. These will deal with the input and output of your data to and from the database.

In the early chapters, you saw an overview of what goes into the make up of a database. It was here that you were first introduced to forms. In essence, a form is a visually pleasing method for entering any information into your database. In addition, entering data through a form gives you more control over the information *before* it is entered. For example, the way the data is collected may be influenced by your form design. This happens so that the whole system of data collection and data entry flows from one stage to the next, without say, problems between the way the data appears on the questionnaire, and the layout of the data entry form.

Form design isn't complex because Microsoft has provided a flexible environment for you to work in. In order to give you an understanding of the subject as a whole, this chapter introduces you to Form Wizards, showing how to get working results with their help. It will then demonstrate some basic methods of customizing these results. This chapter provides you with the ability to produce reasonable form designs, and gives you the necessary foundations to customize these results or even start from scratch. See Chapter 10 for more information on how to customize the results to a greater degree.

This chapter includes:

- Form Wizards
- Form Basics
- Graphing Forms
- Customization

What is a Form?

As you learnt in Chapter 2: Planning a Database, a form can be seen as the 'front door' to a database structure. You can use it to enter information into a database in a more friendly way than typing directly into the table. The form can also be used as a tool for viewing the records in the database, either one at a time, as a list, or in a Datasheet format.

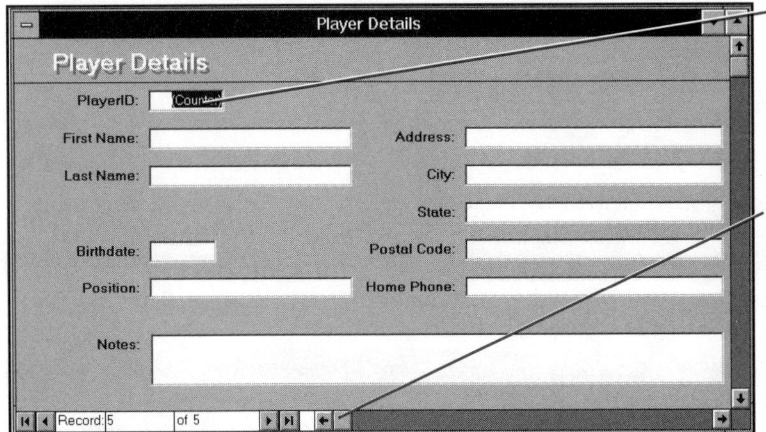

A Form Awaiting Your Data Entry

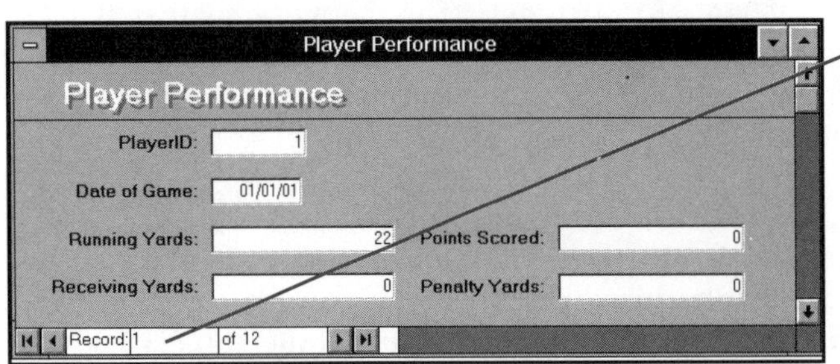

Using a Form to View Your Data

Each form design must be based upon either a table or a query. The form must have somewhere to look for, or insert information. This will depend on how you are utilizing the form.

> Note that queries are used as the basis for forms when fields from more than one table are required to make your form complete. The query is used to temporarily bring together the tables, making those fields available to the form's final design.

The Form Wizards

Using one of the Form Wizards is the fastest way to create a form design. They can remove a large amount of the legwork required to produce a form, but because the number of stock form designs is limited, the Form Wizards will probably not be able to give you the exact design you want. As you will see, you can customize a wizard's form design using some simple techniques.

Let's look at how to create a form using a wizard's help and see what stock form designs are on offer before the customizing tools are introduced.

How Do I Create a Form?

When creating a form using a wizard, you will soon realize how important it is to have a good database plan. Access 2.0, through one of the Form Wizards, will ask many questions relating to your form design, but with a good database plan you will be able to answer all of these quite easily. It is vital that you set up a logical and legal system of tables and queries so that the Form Wizard can work correctly. It has to gather the correct information for you to view so it fills in the correct tables with the information you entered.

Now, let's move on to look at each of the steps you need to take to produce a form with the help of a wizard.

Using the Form Wizards: The Opening Moves

- Select the Form tab on the initial database window.
- Select the New button. You will then be presented with the following screen:

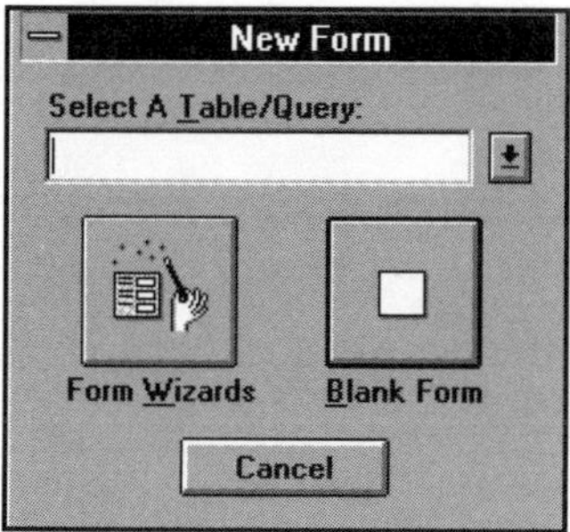

- Now we must choose the table or query that the form is to be based on. Type the name of the table or query into this window. If you are unsure of the spelling, click on the tab at the end of the cell to get a full listing of the tables and queries that you could use.

Select the Form Wizards icon to wake the Form Wizard taskmaster. This will call the right Form Wizard depending on the form design that you select. Clicking on the icon leads you to the screen shown below:

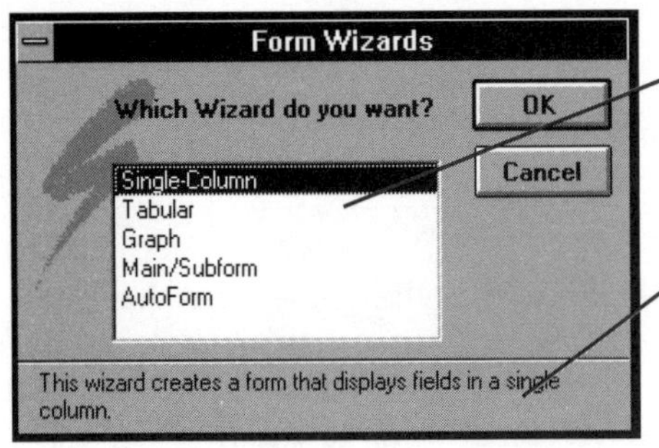

The basic stock form designs that the Form Wizards have to offer. Highlight the one you require.

In this window you'll see a short description of the form design that is highlighted.

By the time you get to this stage, the Form Wizard wants to know which of its wizards you want help from. Before you can answer its question you need to know more about each type of form design.

Using a Form Wizard: Choosing a Form Design

Before you make your choice of basic form design, let's look at each one in turn.

Single Column Forms

Single column forms are organized, as their name suggests, in a column format. This is the most common choice of format for data entry forms. All the data can be seen in a clear and easily customizable fashion. This allows common fields to be grouped together. Below is an example of the single column format:

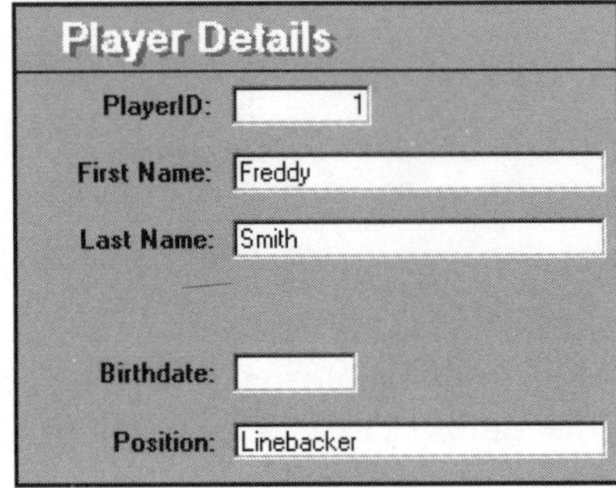

Tabular Forms

Tabular forms are organized into a table format. This format is used to simulate a spreadsheet-type display, or to provide a display similar to that of a Datasheet. This allows a fairly standard print output to be developed. The printed form will now be similar to the Datasheet View of a table. This may be a good format if data entry is going to take place from spreadsheet print-outs. Below is an example of this tabular format:

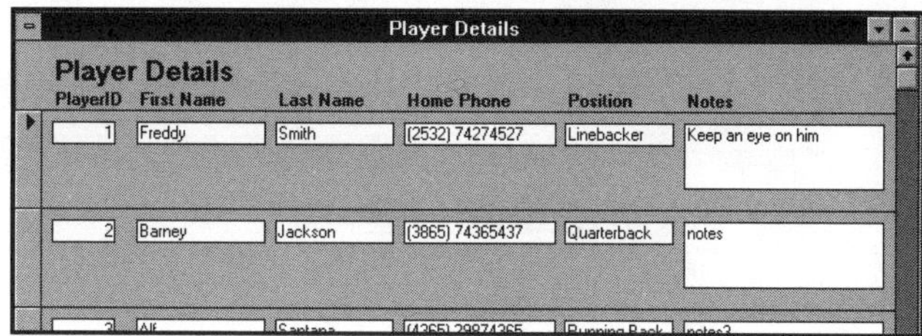

Graph Forms

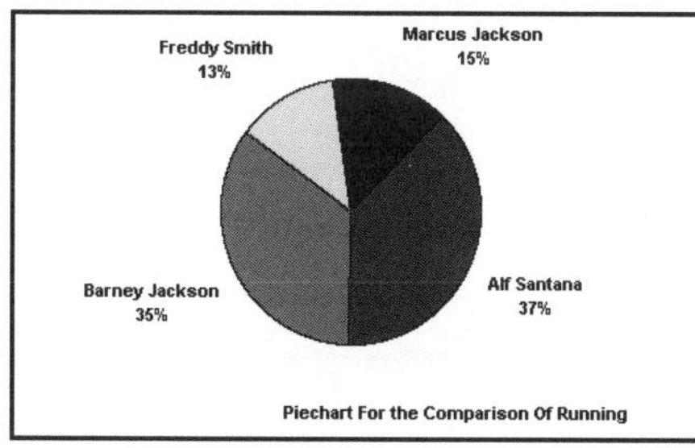

Graph forms are used for organizing the data into a more visually presentable format. This type of form is dealt with in more detail in Chapter 7: Calculations and Graphs. This is an important method of data presentation so has been given its own chapter, in order that each step can be well illustrated and easily understood.

Main/Subform

The main/subform format is used when you want to see information from two or more related tables at the same time. This multiple table form is usually used between tables that have a one-to-many relationship. All the information can be seen at a glance: both the 'one' and 'many' related records. This main/subform format is an advanced choice of form design and can be tricky to manipulate. You will cover these details in Chapter 11.

Basically, this type of form is built using two or more of the form designs seen in this chapter. So if you require the main/subform type of display, you need to know about the forms discussed here. Below is a typical main/subform:

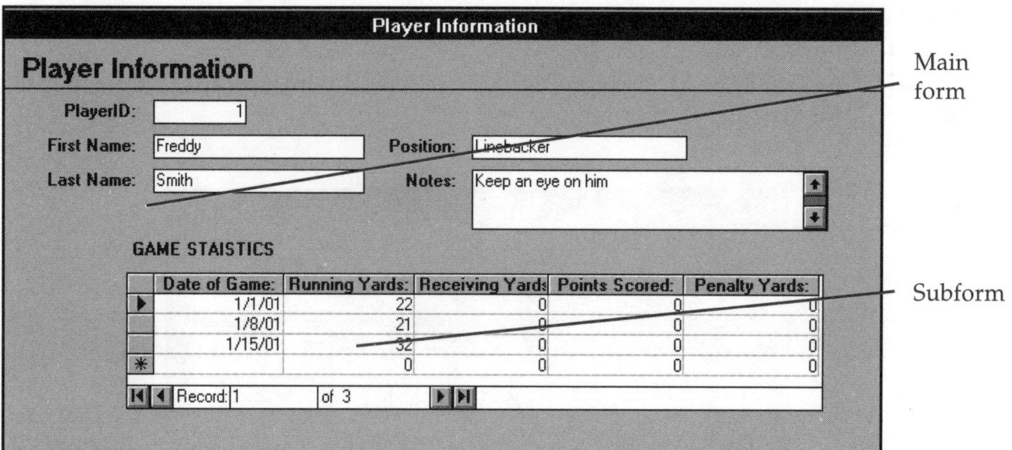

AutoForm

This new member of the Form Wizard gang uses the default responses to all the Single Column Wizard's questions and quickly produces a form for you. You can use this wizard to produce a data entry form when you want to quickly test your underlying table structure with some sample data.

> Note that it is Auto Form that you are offered in the final screens of Table Wizard.

Hopefully, during the planning stage, you will have developed an idea of how you want the layout of your form to be. You should then be able to make your design selection quickly. For now, let's use the Single Column Form Wizard as a vehicle to learn more about the basics of form design. After this you will see how to make use of the other two Form Wizards: Graph Wizard and the Main/Subform Wizard.

> Note that the Tabular Wizard uses exactly the same screens as the Single Column Wizard and that the Auto Form Wizard presents no screens at all. Remember that the Auto Form Wizard takes the default settings to the Single Column Wizard's questions to produce a form quickly for you.

Create a new table from the results of a query with a make-table query

1 Create a query, selecting the tables or queries that contain the records you want to put in the new table.

How?

2 In query Design view, click the arrow next to the **Query Type** button on the toolbar, and then click **Make Table**. The **Make Table** dialog box appears.

3 In the **Table Name** box, enter the name of the table you want to create or replace.

4 Click **Current Database** to put the new table in the currently open database. Or click **Another Database** and type the name of the database you want to put the new table in. Type the path if necessary.

5 Click **OK**.

6 Drag from the field list to the query design grid the fields you want in the new table.

7 In the **Criteria** cell for the fields that you've dragged to the grid, type the criteria.

For information on specifying criteria, click .

8 To preview the new table before you create it, click the **View** button on the toolbar. To return to query Design view and make changes or run the query, click the **View** button on the toolbar.

9 To create the new table, click **Run** on the toolbar.

Notes

- To stop a query after you start it, press CTRL+BREAK.
- The data in the new table you create does not inherit the field properties or the primary key setting from the original table.

Using the Form Wizard: Your First Design

In order to design a form you need a real working database structure to experiment with. So, for your first attempt at designing a form with one of the Wizards, let's use the Microsoft supplied sample database, NWind.mdb. You can find this in your Access 2.0 subdirectory called Sampapps.

- Close down any database you have open.
- Open NWind.mdb.
- To begin your first form design follow the steps given in Using A Form Wizard: The Opening Moves. Select the Customers table as the source for your form to get you back to the following window:

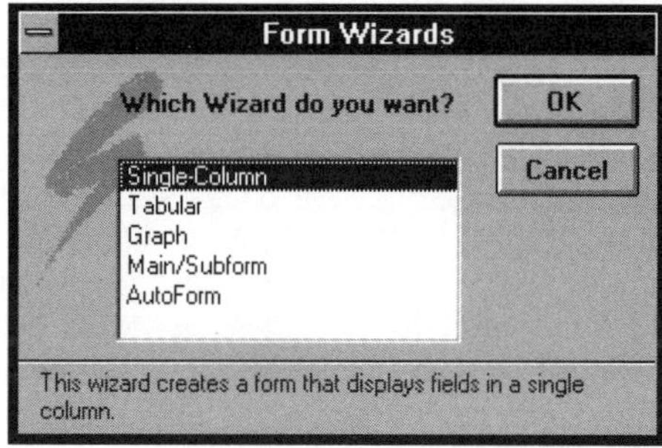

- Click on the OK button to call up the Single Column Form Wizard and the following field selection window:

All the fields that you can include in your form design are in this window. The fields that appear here are those included in the table or query you have chosen to base this form upon.

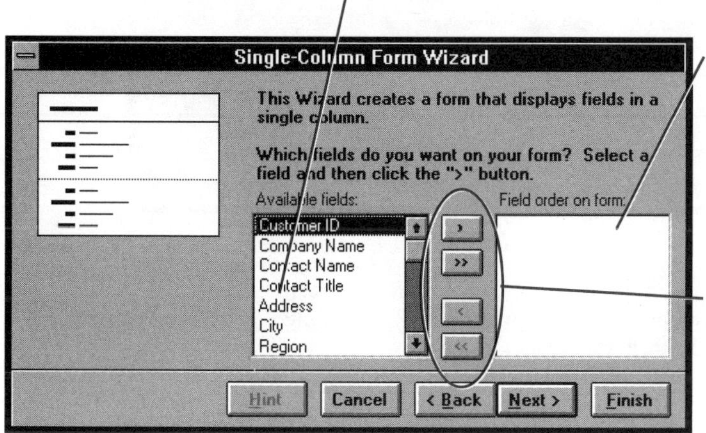

All the fields you have selected for your form design will appear in this window. The order they appear in is the order that the Form Wizard will present them on the form.

These buttons are used to select or de-select the fields that are to appear on your form. Single arrows are used to select single fields, double arrows to select all fields.

- In this case, select all the fields and click on the Next > button to move to the following window:

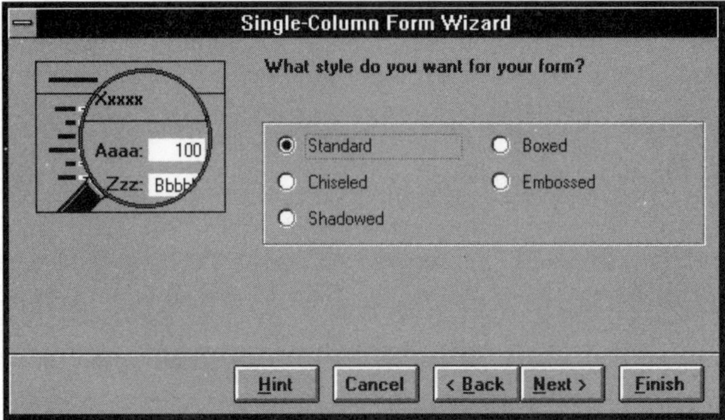

- Choose the style you want for your form. When you make a selection, an example of the style will appear 'under the lens'. In this case, select Standard for clarity, and press the Next > button.

In this box, you can inform Access 2.0 of the title you wish to appear at the top of your form. Simply press *BkSp* and re-type your required name.

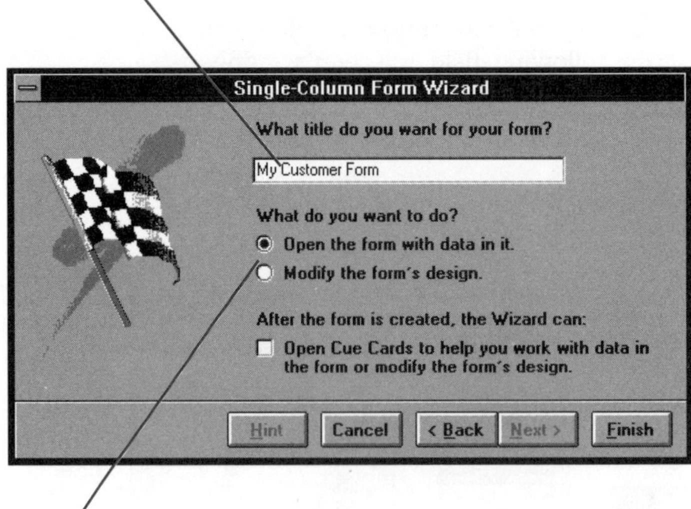

Select the appropriate radio button to inform Access 2.0 of which view of the form you want to be abandoned in. When you have selected, click the Finish button.

- On this final window, entitle the form My Customer Form.
- Select the Open the form with data in it option.
- Finally, click the Finish button to see the results of the Form Wizard's hard work.

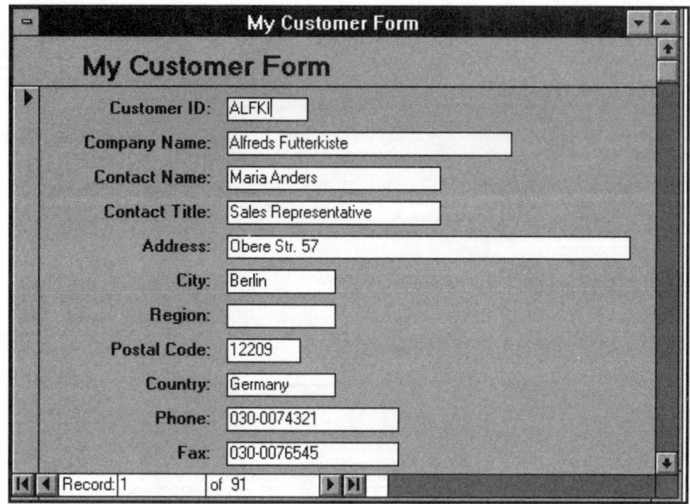

The datasheet view of the above form is as follows:

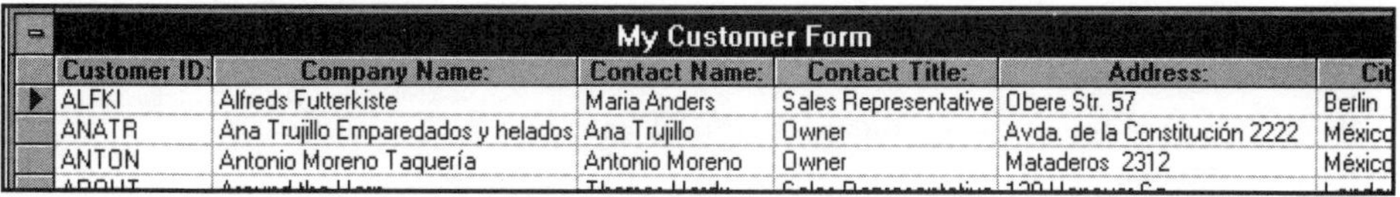

Customer ID:	Company Name:	Contact Name:	Contact Title:	Address:	Cit
ALFKI	Alfreds Futterkiste	Maria Anders	Sales Representative	Obere Str. 57	Berlin
ANATR	Ana Trujillo Emparedados y helados	Ana Trujillo	Owner	Avda. de la Constitución 2222	Méxic
ANTON	Antonio Moreno Taquería	Antonio Moreno	Owner	Mataderos 2312	Méxic

You have now completed your first form design using a Form Wizard. As you can see, the Single Column Wizard has naturally produced a single column format. Let's look at the Microsoft version of this form for comparison.

- Close down your form.
- Before closing the form down, Access 2.0 will prompt you to save it. Click the Yes button, and entitle the form My Customers Form.

> Note that you must not call this form Customers as it will overwrite NWind's version.

- Highlight the form called Customers in the initial database window, and then click on the Open button to see Microsoft's version of this form.

You will see how this field is adjacent to the others as opposed to in a column.

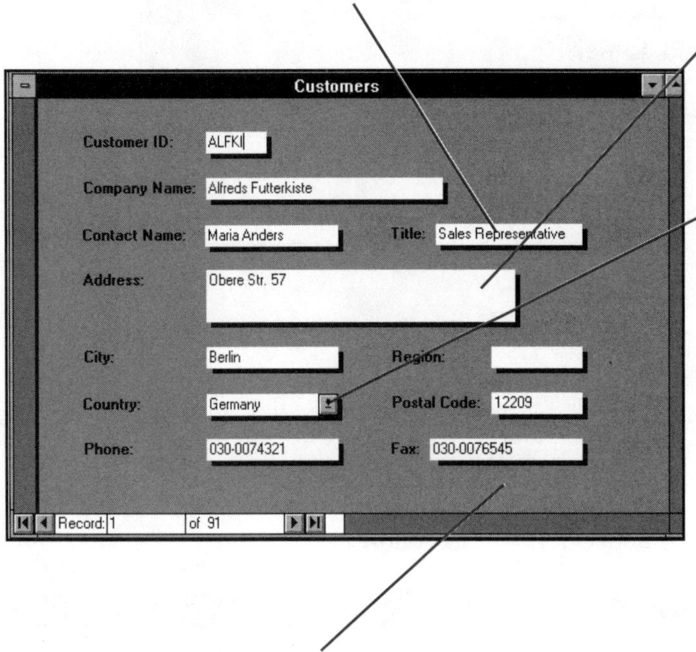

Notice how this field is twice the size of all the rest. This is because a person's address is likely to be longer than their name.

Look at this tab. It signifies a special feature: that a form may use a **combo box**. By clicking on this tab you can get a list of all the usual entries to this field. These entries can then be highlighted and Access 2.0 will automatically place them into the field. This saves a lot of time and helps to reduce spelling mistakes. We'll look at this feature in more detail in Chapter 10.

Notice that the color of the background can be changed.

As you can see, this format is slightly more exciting than the version created by your wizard. However, help is at hand in the shape of a few basic customization techniques. You can apply these techniques to the results of any wizard in order to jazz-up the look and feel of a form.

Customizing a Form Wizard's Results

Let's look at some of the basic techniques you can use to customize any results that any Form Wizard may produce for you. All the techniques covered here will enable you to produce a form that will include all but one (combo box) of the features appearing on Microsoft's Customers form.

> Chapter 10 deals with producing a form design from scratch. It covers all the techniques that Access 2.0 makes available to you, so that you can produce stunning forms.

Viewing the Form

Access 2.0 provides you with three possible views for any form you produce.

The first of these views is called the Form Design View. An example of a typical form design is shown below:

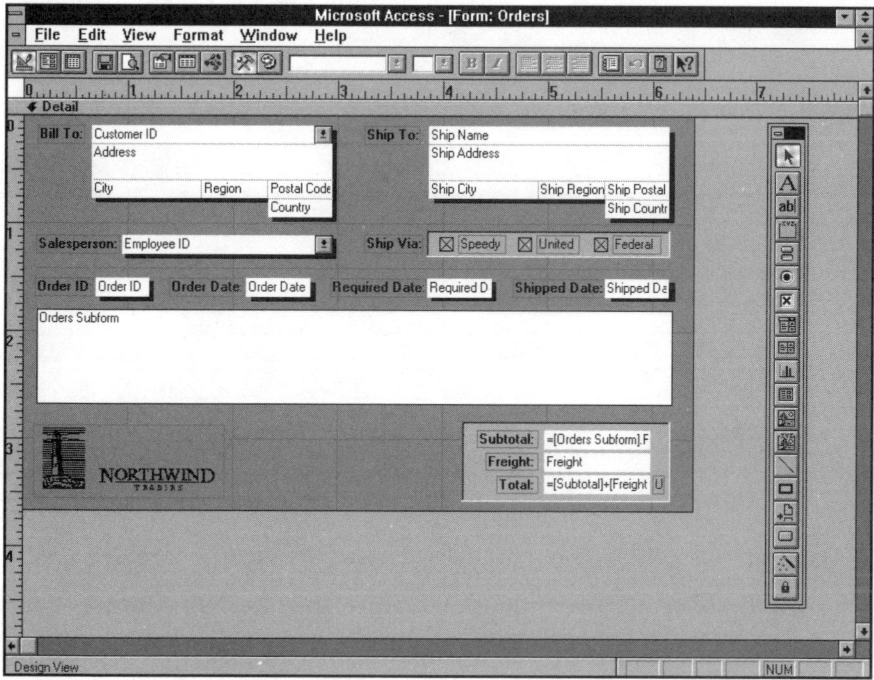

This view is where the design of new forms or customizing of current forms is done. There are three commonly used ways to get to the Design View of any form:

- By selecting the form you require and then the Design button on the initial database window.
- When the form is open, by selecting Form Design from the View menu.
- By clicking on the icon on the icon bar.
  Design View

The second of these views is called Form View. It is here that the user will spend most of their time entering or viewing the data in the database. This makes the design of the form even more important, as a user will think much more of your database if the forms are visually pleasant. Below is an example of such a form:

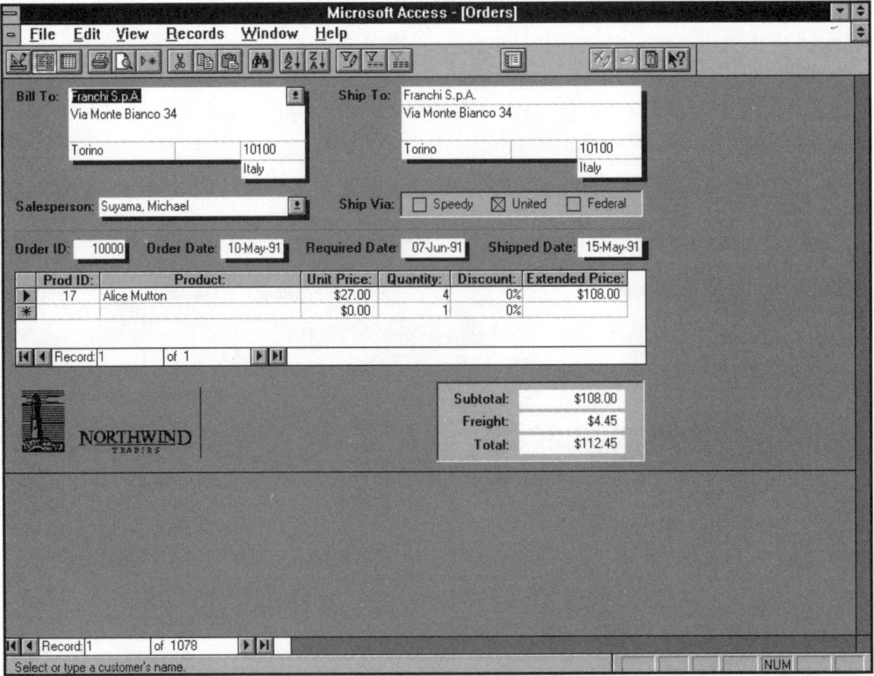

There are also three commonly used ways to view a form:

- By selecting the form you require and then the Open button on the initial database window.
- When the form is open, by selecting Form from the View menu.
- Or finally, by clicking on the icon on the icon bar.

Form View

The third and final view of your form is called Datasheet View. This view, not surprisingly, is similar to that of a table's datasheet. Below is an example of this view:

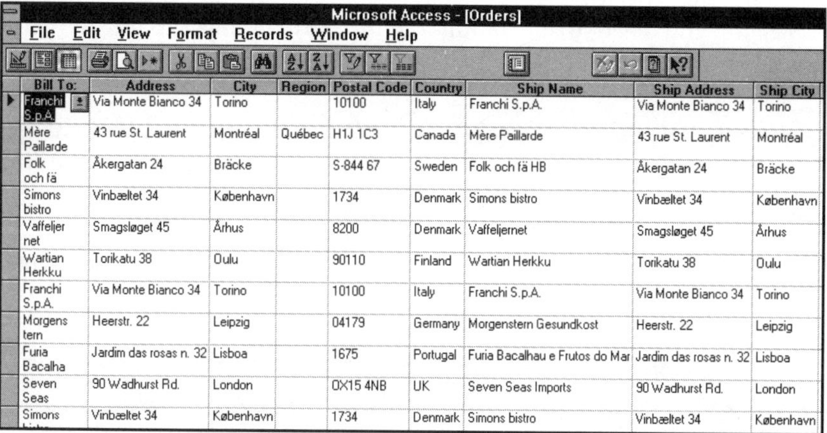

Bill To:	Address	City	Region	Postal Code	Country	Ship Name	Ship Address	Ship City
Franchi S.p.A.	Via Monte Bianco 34	Torino		10100	Italy	Franchi S.p.A.	Via Monte Bianco 34	Torino
Mère Paillarde	43 rue St. Laurent	Montréal	Québec	H1J 1C3	Canada	Mère Paillarde	43 rue St. Laurent	Montréal
Folk och fä	Åkergatan 24	Bräcke		S-844 67	Sweden	Folk och fä HB	Åkergatan 24	Bräcke
Simons bistro	Vinbæltet 34	København		1734	Denmark	Simons bistro	Vinbæltet 34	København
Vaffeljer net	Smagsløget 45	Århus		8200	Denmark	Vaffeljernet	Smagsløget 45	Århus
Wartian Herkku	Torikatu 38	Oulu		90110	Finland	Wartian Herkku	Torikatu 38	Oulu
Franchi S.p.A.	Via Monte Bianco 34	Torino		10100	Italy	Franchi S.p.A.	Via Monte Bianco 34	Torino
Morgens tern	Heerstr. 22	Leipzig		04179	Germany	Morgenstern Gesundkost	Heerstr. 22	Leipzig
Furia Bacalha	Jardim das rosas n. 32	Lisboa		1675	Portugal	Furia Bacalhau e Frutos do Mar	Jardim das rosas n. 32	Lisboa
Seven Seas	90 Wadhurst Rd.	London		OX15 4NB	UK	Seven Seas Imports	90 Wadhurst Rd.	London
Simons	Vinbæltet 34	København		1734	Denmark	Simons bistro	Vinbæltet 34	København

There are two advantages to having a form datasheet. Firstly, you can view all the records that will eventually pass through your form design much quicker than scrolling through them by hand. The second advantage, and possibly the most useful, becomes apparent when the form is based upon a query. With a query, the datasheet contains **all** the data from **all** the tables appearing in that query, thus acting like a super-datasheet for **all** the records. There are two ways to get to this super-datasheet:

- When the form is open, by selecting Datasheet from the View menu.
- Or, by clicking on the icon on the icon bar.

Datasheet View

The Design View: Your First Introduction

Before you can get down to any customization of a form design, you need to understand a little more about the environment you will be working in: Form Design View. This is where you can alter the position, shape, or color of any component that appears on the form. The number of methods available for designing forms is too large to be covered here. You will learn as much as you need to produce a reasonable form design.

The Form Worksheet

The form worksheet is the name given to the resident parts of a form design. These include the various sections of a form, the paper that makes up each section, and the grid that appears on the paper. To understand the basics of form design, you need to be familiar with each of these parts and how to control them to get the results that you want.

This is the Form Header Bar. When you select the paper that is part of the Form Header, this bar will deepen in color to indicate that your selection has been recorded. This also works for the Details Bar and the Form Footer Bar.

The Details Bar

The Form Footer Bar

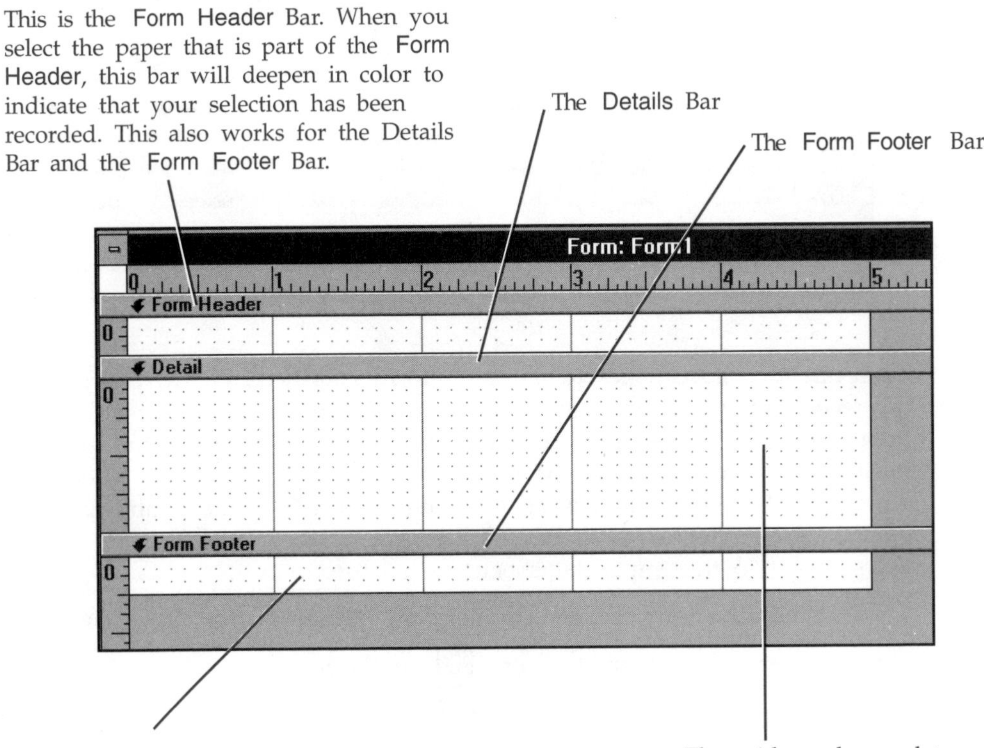

To re-size any part of the paper in any section of the form, move the pointer to the bottom or the right edge of that section's paper. The pointer will change shape to indicate that Access 2.0 is ready to re-size the paper. Hold the left mouse button down and drag the edge of the paper to its new size. You will see that as you hold down the mouse button, part of the ruler will deepen in color. This indicates, using the ruler's measurement, the size of the paper.

The grid can be used to automatically align the components that appear on the form design.

Finally, it is important that you understand two more terms used in form design. You will usually get two components for each field that you include on your form. These are the **label** and the **control.**

Labels

Labels are used, as you might expect, to label the other components on the form. These effectively make up the text that you see on a blank questionnaire. They denote where information should be given and hint at the kind of information required. To this end, you will usually have at least one label for each control, or at least one label for each group of controls. The label is usually the same color as the background paper that the form is drawn upon. This means that it will not stand out and overpower the information that it is supposed to be labeling.

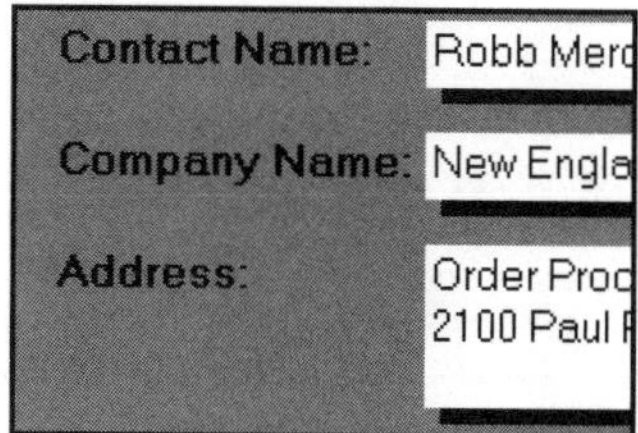

Controls

Controls are the temporary store for your information. On a form, when you are entering data, a given record is only saved when you **move from it**. This saving process takes the information stored in the controls, rearranges it into a record format and deposits it in the relevant table for more long-term storage. When you are viewing data the controls remove the data from the table and only return it when you move on to another record. This is important when you are using an Access 2.0 database on a network, because while the information from a record is in the controls on your form, no-one else can access that record. Each field in your table must have a related control on your form. Otherwise that field can never have data entered into it, nor will a user be able to see it using this form.

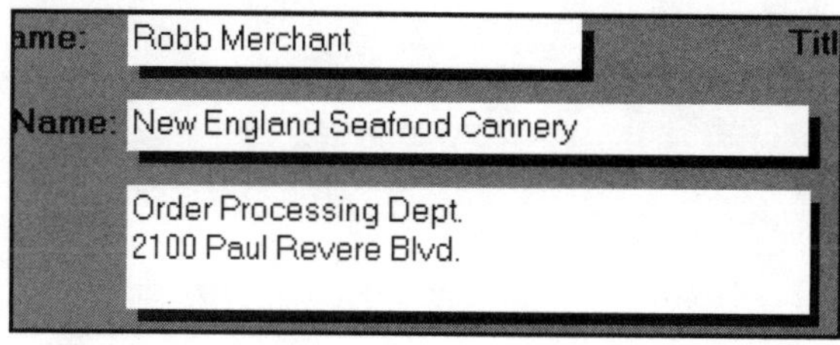

Returning to the Example

Now that you understand a little more about some of the components of a form, let's look more closely at a typical Form Design View, or more specifically, at the results of the Form Wizard that you were using. By selecting the Design View icon from the icon bar you can see the results of the Single Column Wizard's hard work.

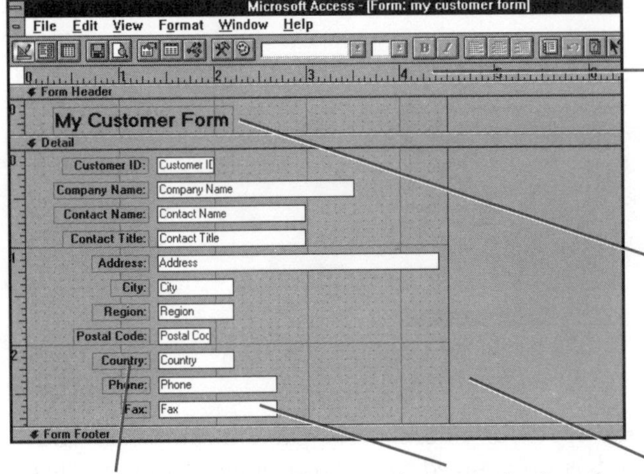

You will see that there is a ruler around the sides of the form. You can use this to align the controls or to measure the size of any components when you re-size them.

Notice the use of a label in the Form Header. The Form Header appears just at the top of each form. This means that using a label is a good method of entitling your form pages.

Look at the edge of the paper. The size of the paper that the form is drawn upon can be altered very easily, allowing you more space to move the labels and controls around in.

These components are called labels.

Here are the controls that the data appears in when you look at the form in Form view.

Remember the Microsoft version? Let's look more closely at the Design view:

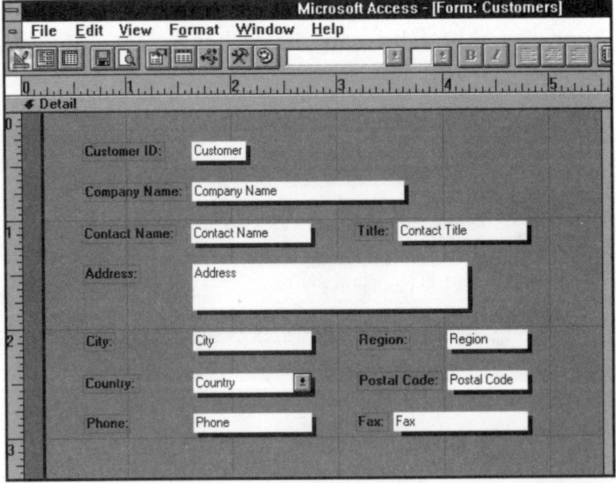

Some points of interest:

- The components aren't laid out in columns; the components are movable.
- The Address control is a large size; the components are re-sizeable.
- The background color is different to the wizard's default; all the components on a form can be re-colored using any of the available colors in the **palette**.
- The tab at the end of the Country control. This control denotes the use of a **Combo Box**, which is covered in more detail in Chapter 10.

Let's now go on to look at the individual customization techniques you can use to produce results similar to these.

Customizing Techniques

The form design techniques you will be introduced to here include:

- Selecting components that appear on a form design
- Moving the controls and labels that appear in the form design
- Re-sizing these controls and labels
- Aligning controls and labels on a form
- Changing the font of some text
- Adding color to your form

Selecting Labels and/or Controls in the Form Design View

To select a control or label, click on it to produce the boxing effect shown below:

If you select a component that has an associated partner, the partner will also get a small box in the top left of its suround.

This is the component that has the focus, i.e. is active.

If you want to select multiple components using the point-and-click method, simply use the *Shift* key in the usual way. There are also two other ways to select multiple components on your form design:

If you want to select all the components in a strip across the screen:

- Place the mouse pointer onto the ruler on the left of the screen.
- While holding down the left mouse button, sweep out the required strip.

You will see that:

- A line appears across the page denoting the top of the strip.
- A line appears (moving with the ➡ pointer), denoting the bottom of the strip.
- The section of the ruler between the two lines deepens in color.

All three of these features allow you to select exactly which components you require.

If you want to select all the components in a block on the screen:

- Place the mouse pointer onto the screen near to the top left component of the block.
- Hold down the left mouse button.
- Drag out a box to surround the components you want to select and release the mouse button.

All the components contained in this box will be selected.

You will see that as you drag the box to the required shape, the size of the box is represented on both rulers with the customary deeper color sections.

You may also notice that you don't have to surround all of a component to select it. If any part of a component falls inside the box you have dragged out, Access 2.0 will include it in the selection. It is also possible to use the *Shift* key in combination with this method to select non-continuous blocks of components in your form design.

> Note that both of these methods can be used to select both components in a partnership. This can have interesting results when applying resizing or alignment techniques to the selected components on your form design.

Moving a Component

To move a component (and its associated partner):

- Select the component you want to move.
- Place the mouse pointer over the surround of the component that has the focus.

Note that you should place the pointer on the line and not on one of the boxes that appear on the surround.

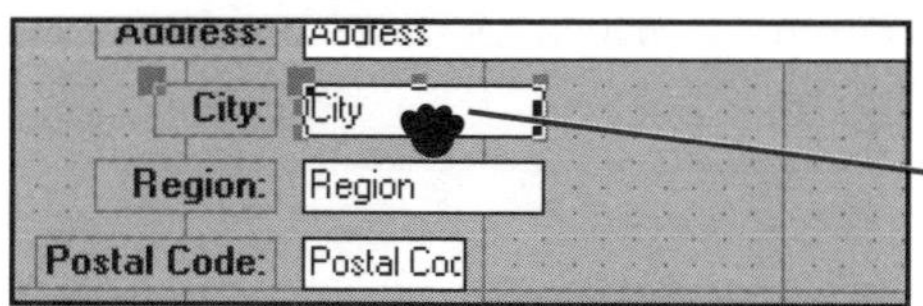

You will notice that the mouse pointer has changed shape.

Hold down the left mouse button and drag the component(s) to their new position as shown below:

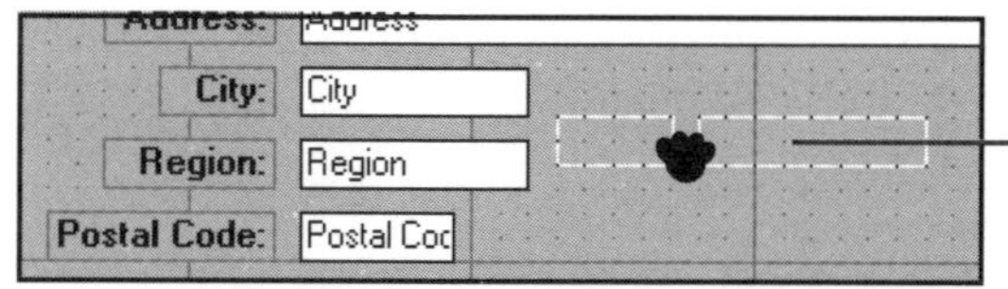

Notice the dotted lines. This is where the components will be moved to when you release the mouse button.

As you are moving the component(s) around the screen, you may notice two shaded areas on the rulers around the edge of the screen. These shadings show you the exact size of the components you are moving, as well as showing you where they will appear when you release the mouse button.

If you want to move just one of the components in a selected partnership, move the pointer onto its top left box rather than the surround of the focused component. The mouse pointer will change as shown, and while the left mouse button is held down, Access 2.0 will move that component only:

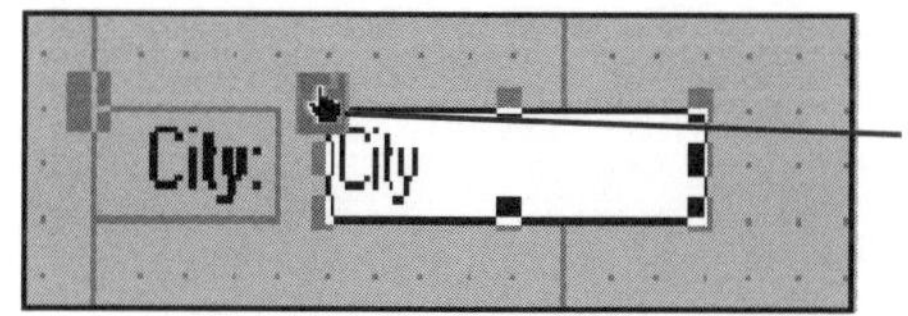

To move just the City control, place the mouse pointer on this box and drag the component.

It is also possible to get Access 2.0 to perform the movement of your components for you. Access 2.0 allows you to select several components and then ask for them to be spaced in one of three different ways.

Spacing Option	Result
Make Equal	This makes the space between the components the same. Access 2.0 does this by fixing the position of the outer components and moving the inner ones to accomplish equal spacing.
Increase	This increases the spacing between components by one grid point. Access 2.0 automatically applies the Make Equal function before increasing the space.
Decrease	This decreases the spacing between components by one grid point. Again, Access 2.0 applies the Make Equal function before increasing the space

Access 2.0 requires you to have selected at least three components before it can apply the make equal fuction

To get Access 2.0 to automatically space your components:

- Select the components that you want to auto-space.
- Select either Vertical Spacing or Horizontal Spacing from the Format menu.
- Select the type of auto-space that you want Access 2.0 to perform.

Re-sizing a Component

To re-size a component:

- Focus on the component you want to re-size.
- Place the mouse pointer onto one of the boxes that appear on the surround:

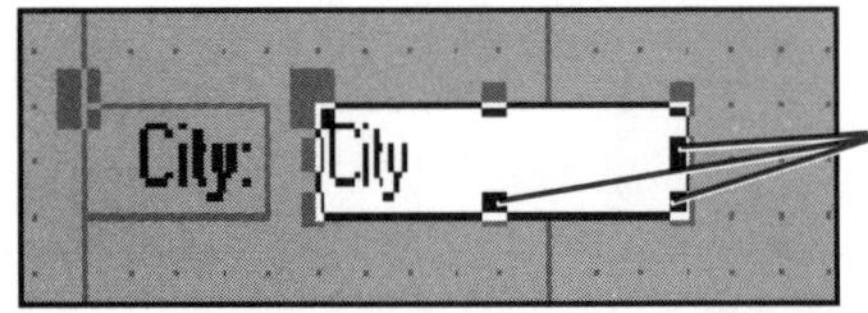

Depending on which box you place the pointer on, you can stretch the component in one of three ways; by height, by width or both.

It is also possible to get Access 2.0 to automatically re-size the components on your form. Using similar techniques to the autospace functions, you can instruct Access 2.0 to change the size of the selected components, either corresponding to one of the components, the size of the grid, or simply to fit.

The selection available includes:

Sizing Option	Result
to Grid	This re-sizes the selected components based on the surrounding grid points. Access 2.0 moves the corners of each component to the closest grid point and can therefore produce some interesting effects.
to Tallest	This re-sizes all the selected components so that they all have the same height: the tallest.
to Shortest	This does the same as 'to Tallest', but based on the height of the smallest component.
to Narrowest	This re-sizes all the selected components so that they all have the same width: the narrowest.
to Widest	This does the same as 'to Narrowest', but based upon the width of the widest component.
to Fit	This choice changes the size of the selected components so that the text can only just fit into the component size.

Note that to Fit does not work fully on all controls. For more details see Chapter 10.

To get Access 2.0 to perform any of these tasks:

- Select all of the components you wish to affect.
- Select the appropriate command from the menu given under Size on the Format menu.

Aligning Components on a Form

To align a set of components:

- Select the set of components you wish to align along one line.
- Choose Align from the Format menu on the menu bar. This gives you the choice of four different ways to align the selected components: Left, Right, Top and Bottom.

If you select the Left Align method, all of the selected components will move to a line drawn down the left side of the component that is closest to the left side of the page. This idea can be applied to each of the other three methods of alignment.

Highlight the method you require, and Access 2.0 will carry out your request. Below is a before and after sequence of the Left Align method:

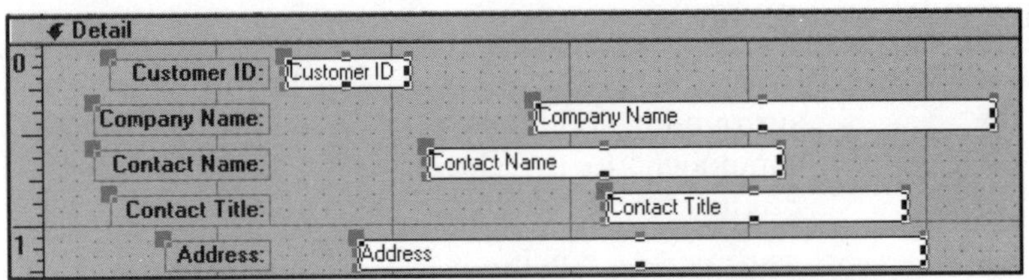

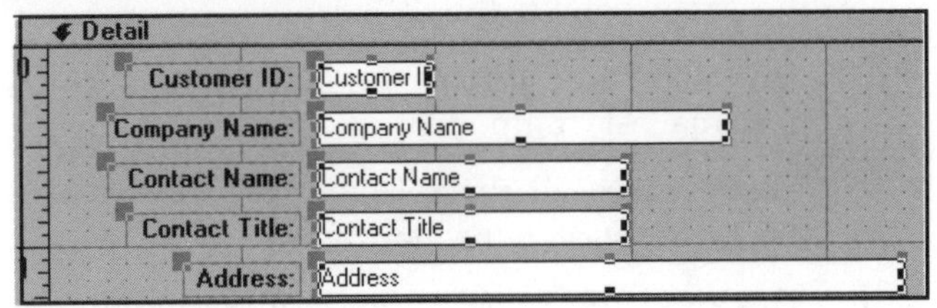

> Only the selected components move and not their associated partners. To move the partners, you need to repeat the alignment, this time selecting the partners that didn't move.

Changing the Font

Each component on your form can have a different font. To change the font of a given component:

- Focus on the relevant component.
- Select the appropriate tool to change the style you wish to alter:

Apply a justification to the text in the selected component using these buttons.

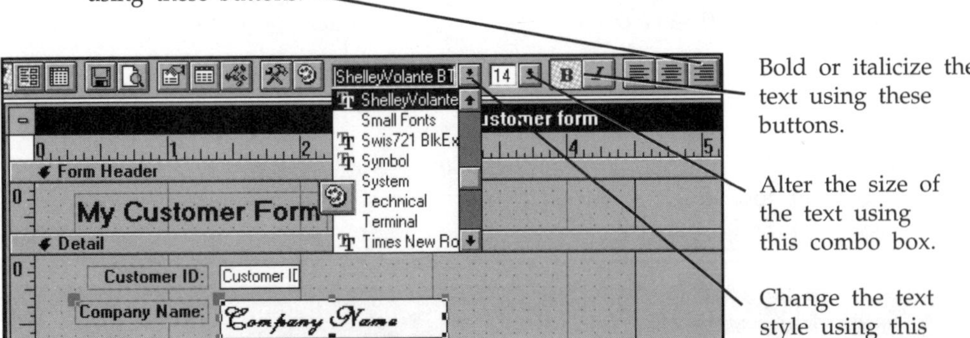

Adding More Color to Your Form

You can add color to not only the components that appear on your form, but also to the paper the components are drawn on. To add color to any part of your form:

- Select the component or the paper you wish to color.
- Click on the icon to open the palette.

Using the Palette

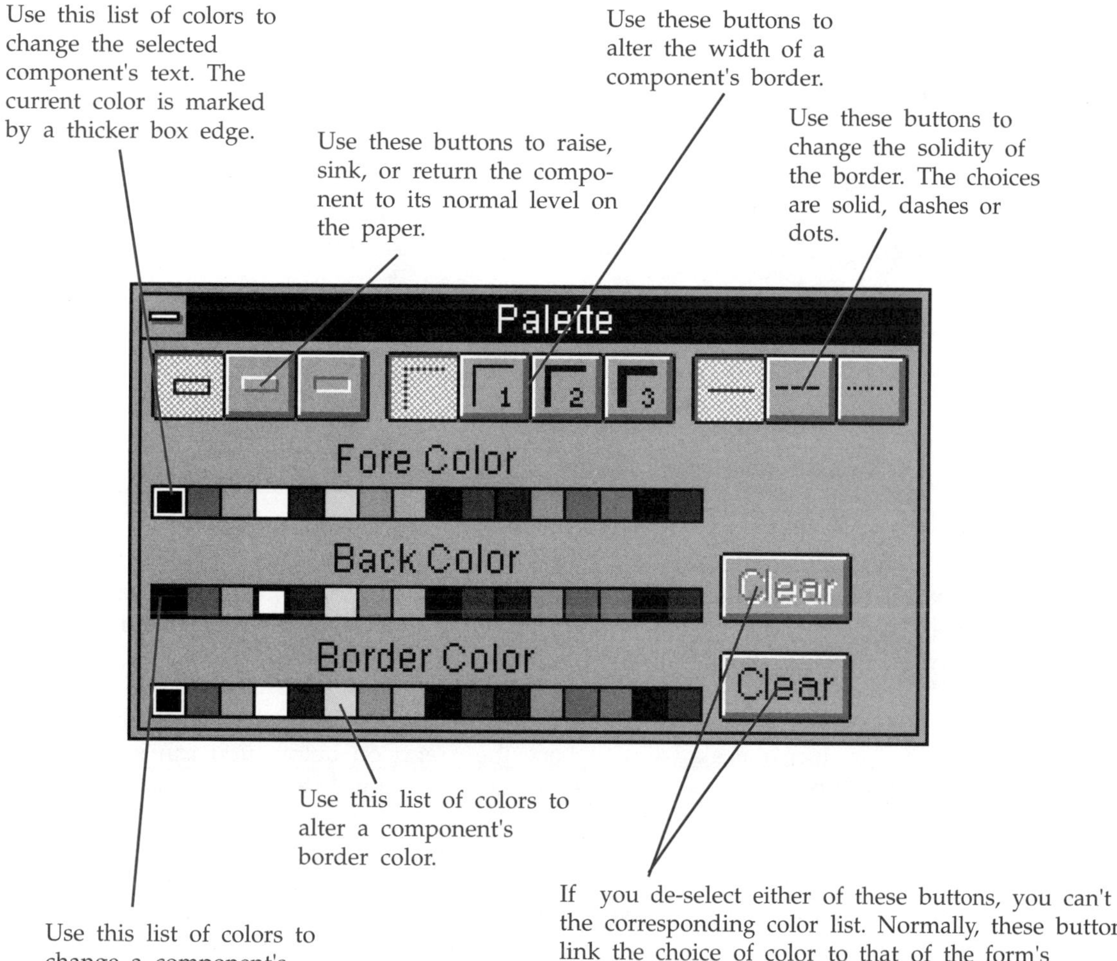

Use this list of colors to change the selected component's text. The current color is marked by a thicker box edge.
Use these buttons to raise, sink, or return the component to its normal level on the paper.
Use these buttons to alter the width of a component's border.
Use these buttons to change the solidity of the border. The choices are solid, dashes or dots.
Palette
Fore Color
Back Color
Clear
Border Color
Clear
Use this list of colors to alter a component's border color.
Use this list of colors to change a component's paper color.
If you de-select either of these buttons, you can't use the corresponding color list. Normally, these buttons link the choice of color to that of the form's paper.You will see that Back Color Clear is only available when the focused component is a label.

You can then use any of the features of the palette to add color and texture to your form design.

> If you de-select a component while the palette is open, the options that the palette offers will change. To get the options back, re-select the component. You can use this feature to quickly move between the components on your form design, leaving color changes as you go.

Saving Your Form Design

When you are happy with the form design, you will have to save the form so that you can move on to produce some other part of the database structure.

To save the form, either:

- In Form Design view, click on the icon.
- In Form view, select Save Form from the File menu.
- In Datasheet View, select Save Form from the File menu.

Then, give the main form a name using the following screen:

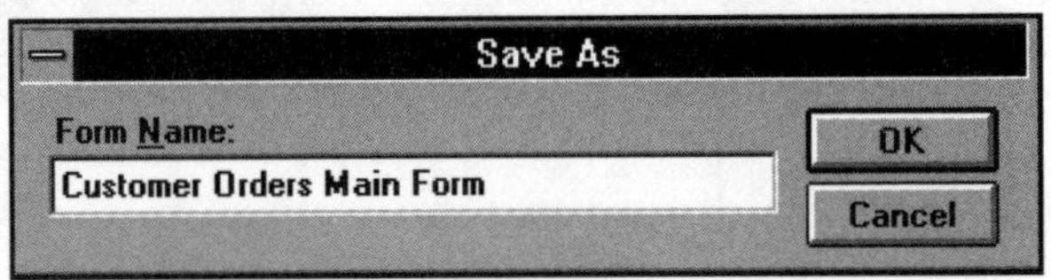

Returning to the Form Wizard - Graph

To produce a decent graph you need a fair amount of data manipulation. This is because you don't normally want to see the raw data in another format. You want your graph to be the results of several conclusions, as well as a new starting point for further interrogation.

This means, unfortunately, that good graphs can be difficult to produce, as you need to produce the statistics to base the graph on before you can start. Chapter 7 shows you how to use Access 2.0 to produce these statistics and create such figures. More importantly it tells you where this should be done.

For now we'll use one of the queries that comes with NWind.mdb, Microsoft's sample database called Category Sales for 1993. This calculates all the sales of each of the different categories that the Northwind Traders deal in, as made in 1993.

Let's begin the graphing process:

- Run through the section "Using The Form Wizards: The Opening Moves" using the Category Sales for 1993 as the source for your form.

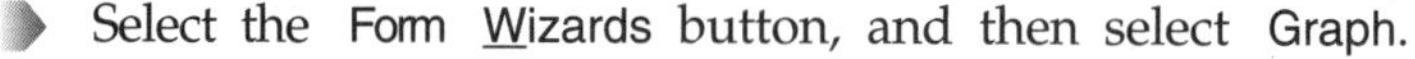

Select the Form Wizards button, and then select Graph.

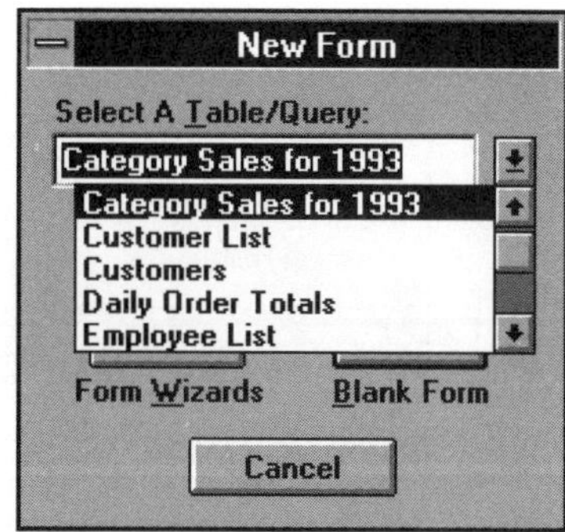

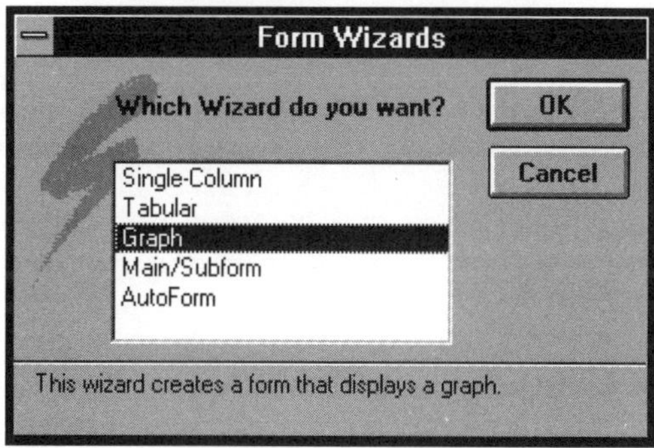

When you make this selection you get the Form Wizard taskmaster to call the Graph Wizard to your aid. It presents you with its first screen:

Use these buttons in the usual way to move one or all of the fields into and out of the wizard's grasp.

All of the fields you want the wizard to use while it is producing the graph should appear here before you leave this screen.

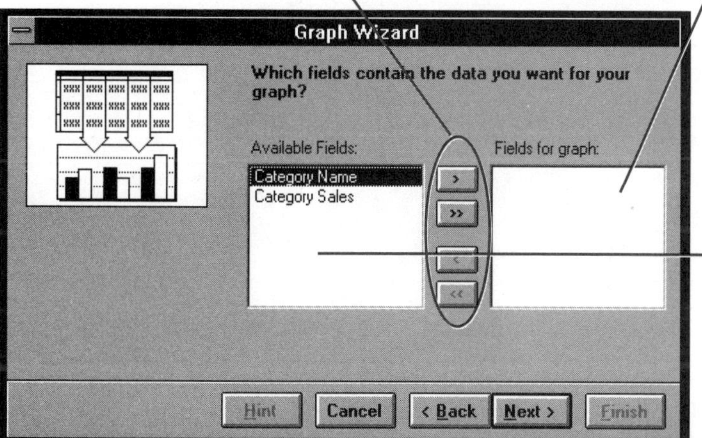

Here are the fields that make up the query that the form is based on. The fields that contain the data for your graph must appear in this listing. If they don't, you need to say 'Good-bye' to the wizard and repeat the steps so far, this time using the correct table or query.

Select all the fields that have data you wish to graph, (both in this case) and then click on the Next > button to move to the next screen:

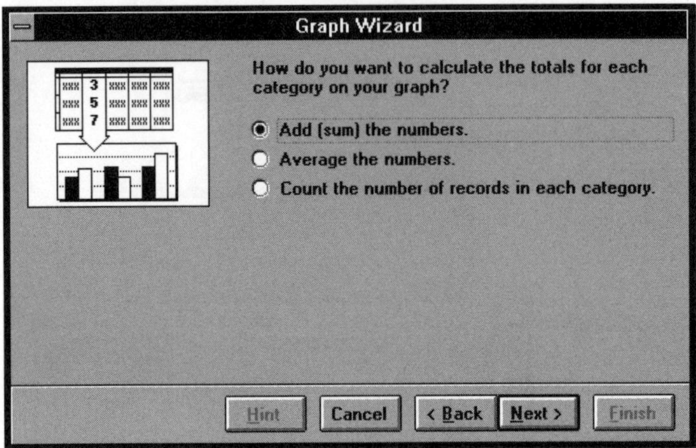

If you have data that has several common entries, Access 2.0 can, at this point, temporarily alter the data in order to produce a cleaner graph.

Let's suppose you are using your database to record information about players in your local American Football team. You want to record which player scored how many points and on what date. By passing the player name and the number of points scored to the Graph Wizard, it can produce a graph of the total number of points scored by each player, even though each player has several records. Access 2.0 temporarily adds up all of the points scored by each player and graphs them, to give the required results. It doesn't have to produce a query to do this. Access 2.0 also has the ability to average the points, or even count the number of games in which a player scored points, and then produce a graph based upon these figures.

The three choices are Sum, Average and Count respectively, from top to bottom.

- Make your choice (accept the default sum setting) and select the Next > button to continue.

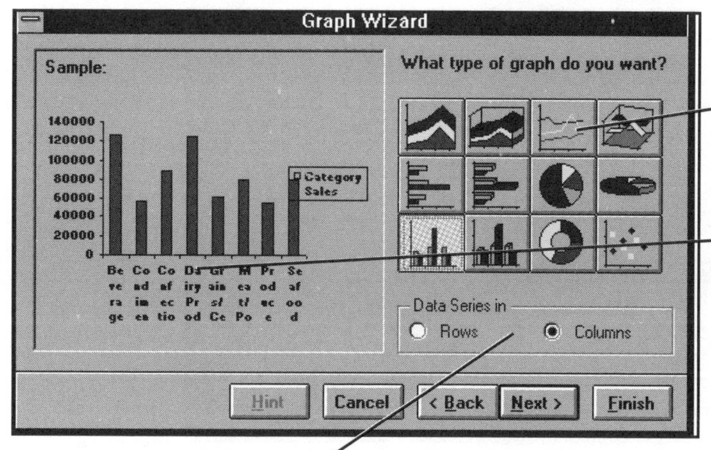

Select the type of graph you require here.

A sample of your graph will appear here, the exact appearance will depend on the data and the type of graph you have selected.

Make your choice of Data Series orientation here. By default, Access 2.0 organizes the data into the column format. For more information about this facility see Chapter 7.

- In this window you can choose the type of graph you want the wizard to produce. Make your selections (accept the default setting) and click on the Next > button to continue to the penultimate stage:

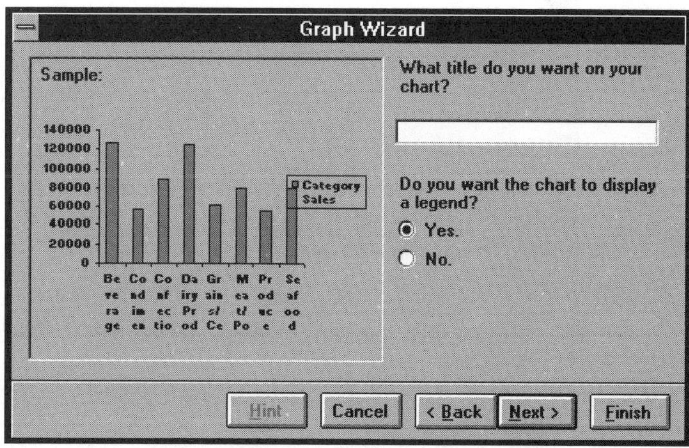

- Type in the title of your graph in this window (Category Sales in 1993) and decide whether to have the legend on the graph or not (not). Then move on to the final screen.

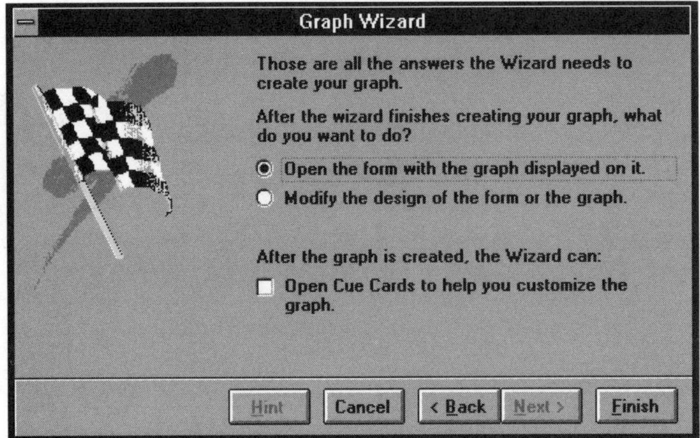

- On this final screen, all you do is inform the Graph Wizard which view of the graph you wish to be abandoned in. Select the Finish button to see the results of one of the most hard working wizards. (Again, accept the Default View, View graph with data in it).

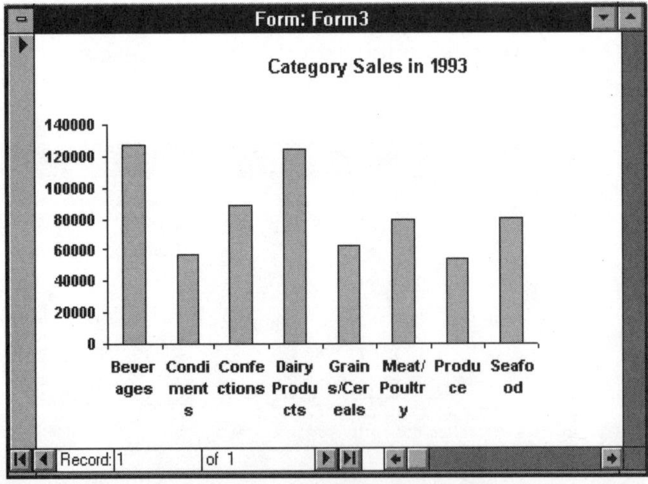

When you have finished customizing the results of the wizard, don't forget to save it!

You have now seen how to use the Graph Wizard to produce graphs of your data. To make more use of this feature, and for more information on calculations and expressions to produce better data to graph, see Chapter 7.

Returning to the Form Wizard - Main/Subform

You can use the main/subform structure to view data in many different tables without using a query to pull all the required fields into one 'super-table'. This has certain advantages, including the ability to combine single form, tabular form and datasheet type displays in the same form, as well as reducing the amount of work that Access 2.0 has to do to provide that form.

> The larger the number and the more complex the queries that Access 2.0 has to run to produce your results, the longer the delays will be between screens. You may notice this when you run certain wizards, as they are very complex indeed.

As you will see when you produce this style of form by hand, you have to create two or more separate form designs before you can relate them together into the required main/subform format. However, when you use a wizard to produce this style of form, life is much simpler:

- Run through the 'Using The Form Wizards: The Opening Moves' section using the NWind table Customers as the source for your main form.

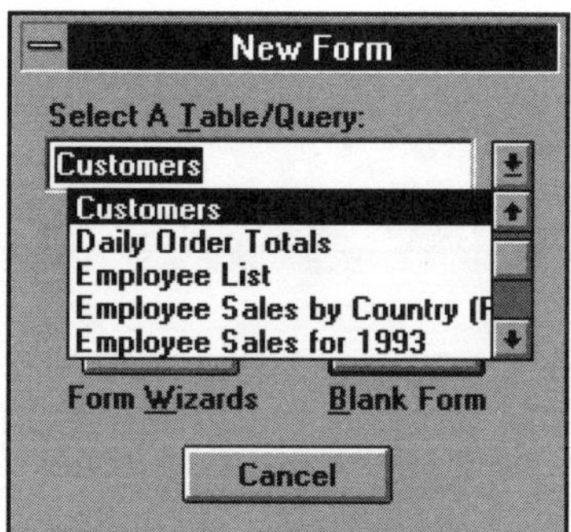

- Select the Form Wizards button, and then select Main/Subform from the following window:

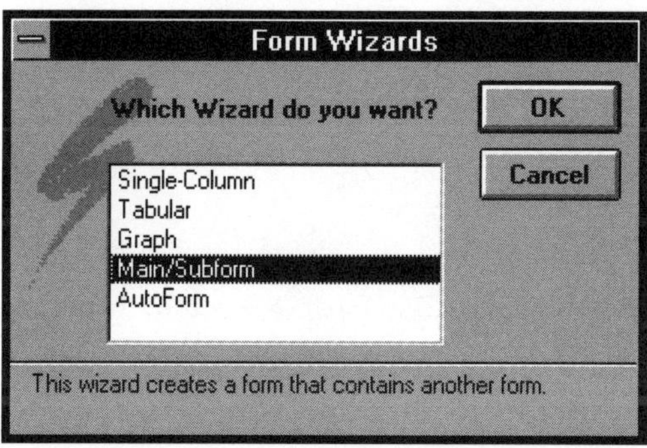

Making this selection gets the Form Wizard taskmaster to call the Main/Subform Wizard to your aid. It presents you with its first screen:

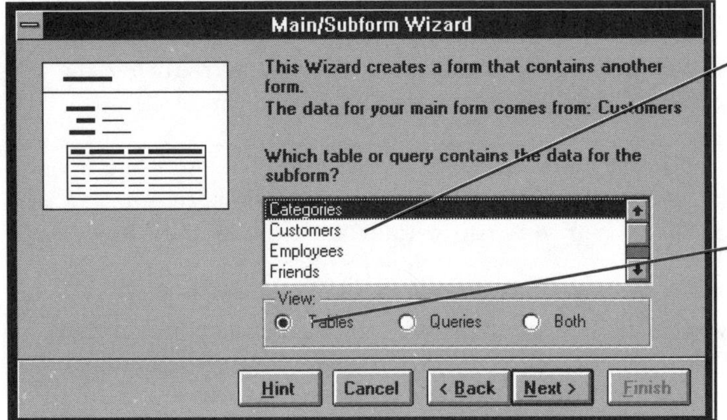

Select the composition of the listing shown above.

From the opening Form Wizard screen, you instructed the wizard which table or query to use for the main form. It is here that it asks which table or query to use for the subform. The default listing shows tables.

- Following the example, select the NWind query QuarterlyOrders by Product (Crosstab) in the queries listing, and then click on the Next > button:

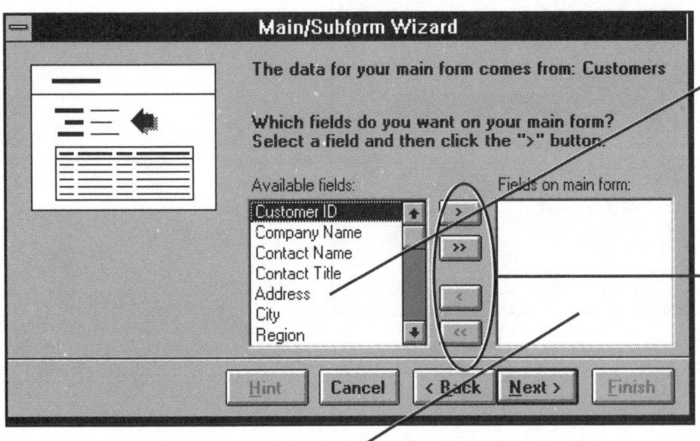

This window contains all the fields that make up the table or query you selected as the basis for the main form.

Use these buttons in the usual way to select or de-select the fields you want the wizard to use on the main form. Remember to use single arrows for single fields and double arrows for all the fields.

In this window you should see all the fields you want the wizard to use on the main form before you move to the next design stage.

- Select the following fields for the main form design and then press the Next > button:

Customer ID; Company Name; Contact Name; Phone

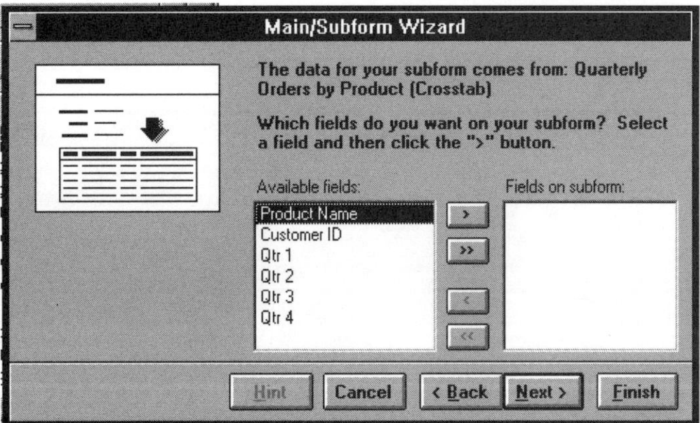

- This screen does the same thing as the last one, except now you are dealing with the fields to include on the subform. Select the following fields and click on the Next > button:

  Product Name; Customer ID; Qtr 1; Qtr 2; Qtr 3; Qtr 4

This screen deals with the styling that is applied to your form design. You can see that as you flick through the different stylings available, the description of the styling changes in the small window in the top left corner.

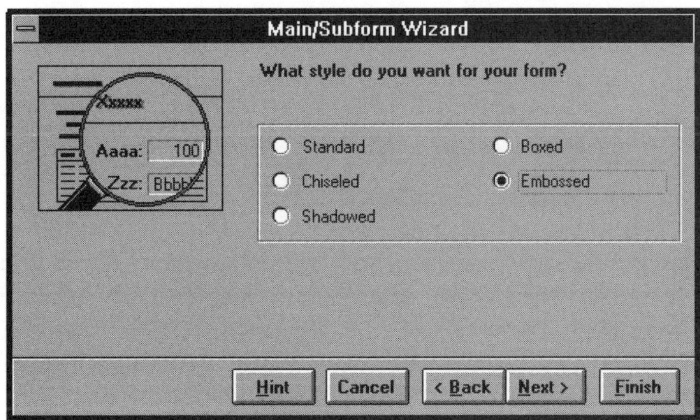

- Select the styling you want and click on the Next > button for the last time to give the final window:

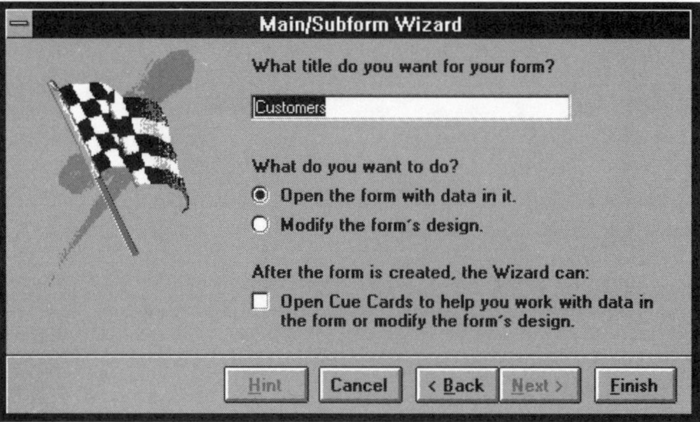

- In this final screen, give your form a name. This name will appear at the top of the form.
- Now select the view of your form that you want the Main/Subform Wizard to abandon you in, and finally, select the Finish button.
- The wizard will now tell you that you need to save the subform. Click on the OK button.

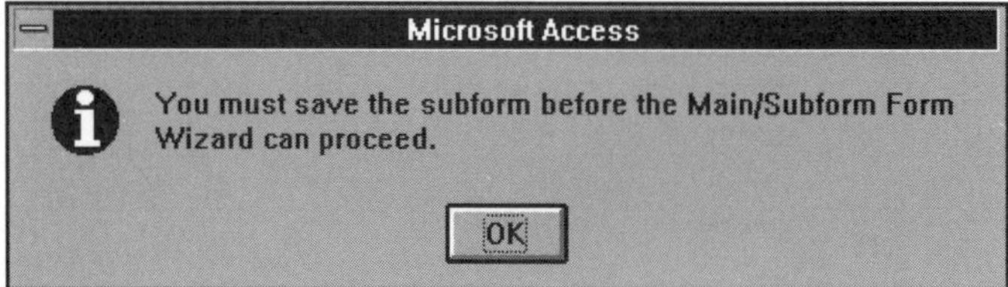

- Access 2.0 will now prompt you for a name for the subform. The name you give the subform should be related to the name of the main form. You could give the subform the same name as the main form with the addition of the word subform. This will reduce confusion on the initial database window when the number of forms grows.

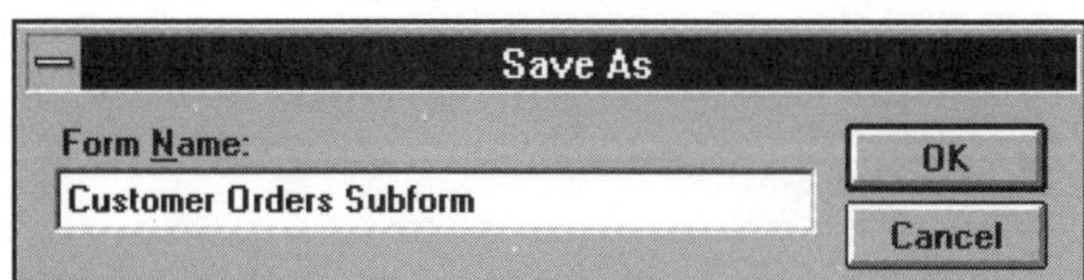

- Access 2.0 now completes the design of your main/subform and returns you to whichever view you request, before returning home.

This is the title you gave to the wizard to place at the top of the form.

Here are the fields you selected to be included on the main form.

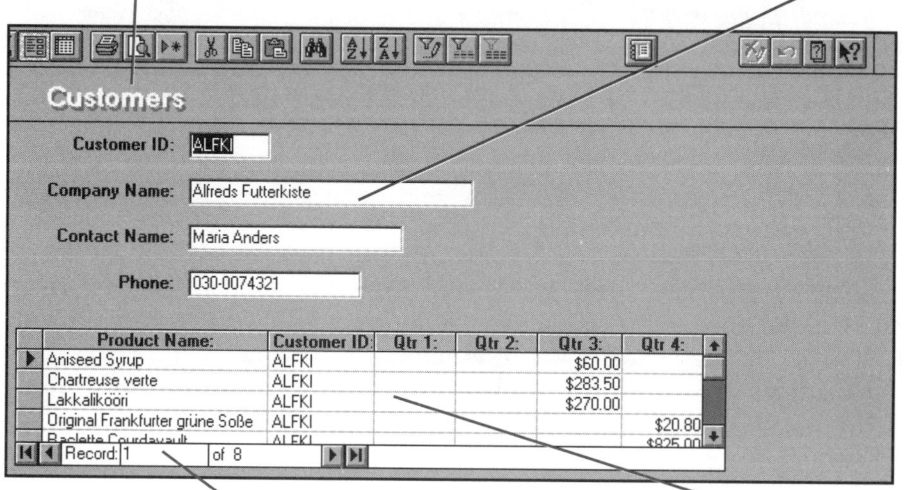

Notice the record selectors on the subform. These selectors allow you to scroll through the records that relate to this customer. Also note the current record number and the total count of records.

This is the subform, showing a tabular form of the orders that this customer has placed. As you can see, it needs re-sizing so that you can see the whole of the form. You do this in Design View by selecting the control entitled Customer Orders Subform (the name you used to save the subform), and using a combination of the re-size techniques covered earlier. Switch to Form View to note your progress.

When you have finished customizing the results of the wizard, don't forget to save it!

A Clever Form - Auto Look-Up

One use that forms are put to all over the business world is that of an Auto Look-Up. When you phone up a business which you have an account with, they need to identify you in context of the business you have done with them. More importantly they need to identify you fast as you don't want to be left hanging on the other end of a phone, while they go off to find your record.

The Auto Look-Up works on a very simple principle. You type some information into a control, and Access 2.0 sorts through the records stored in your database. It returns with the first matching record, thus filling in all the other controls on the form with the relevant record entries.

> The only disadvantage of using an Auto Look-Up Form is that it can only be applied to a multiple table structure.

Fortunately, even though an Auto Look-Up Form is very useful, it is also very easy to create. The form must be based on a query so that you can incorporate the fields from all the tables. It is also very important that you include the field that appears at the 'many' end of the relationship. It is this field that will be used as the look-up.

Now produce a form based upon this query. When you wish to look up a reference, type the appropriate entry into the look-up field, and Access 2.0 will perform the look-up for you. Below are examples of the underlying tables, the look-up query, and the resulting form. Underneath, is a typical example, taken from Orders in NWind.mdb (discussed further in Mastering Forms: Chapter 10).

Query Design

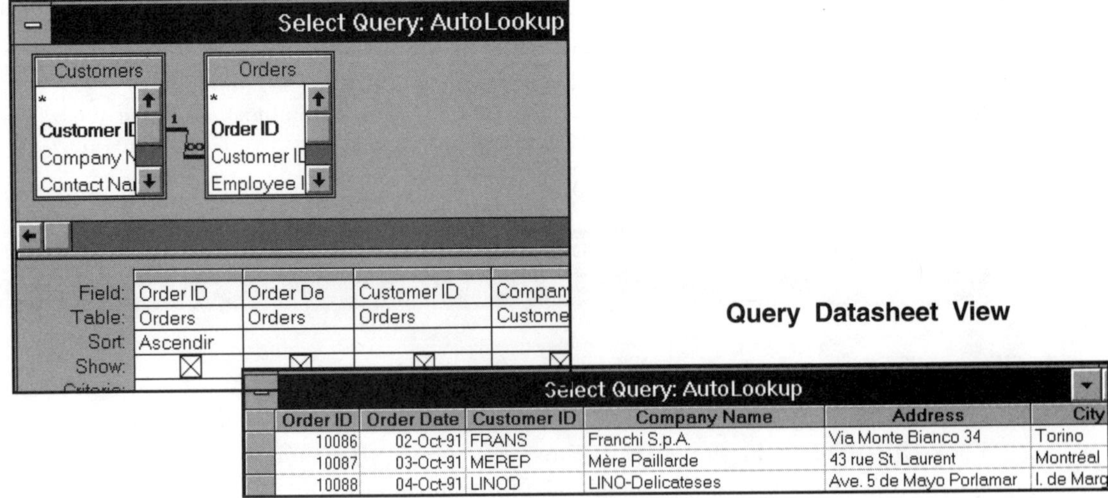

Query Datasheet View

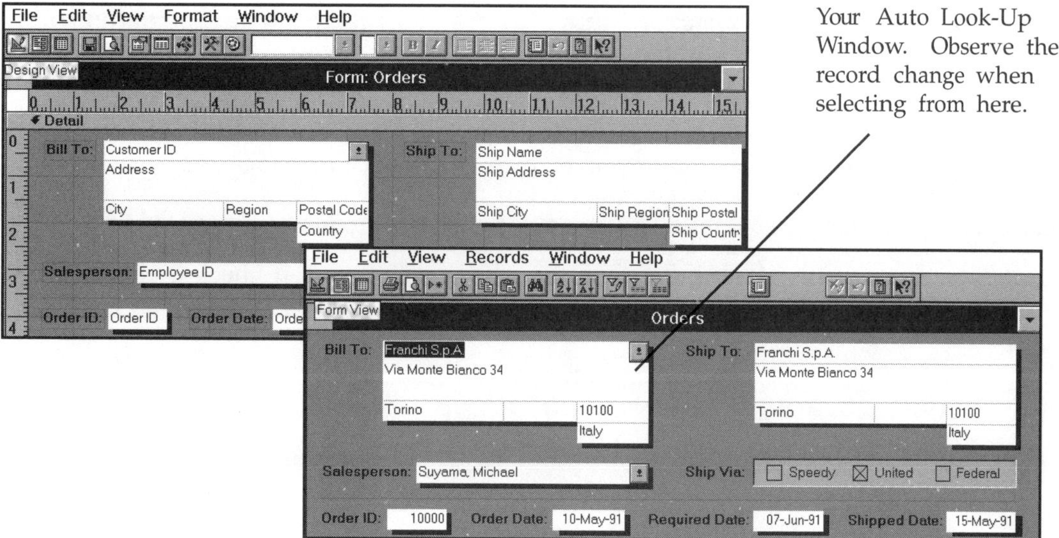

Your Auto Look-Up Window. Observe the record change when selecting from here.

A simple query can give us Auto Look-Up throughout our form document, but it will take longer!

Troubleshooting

Q&A What else can I use the grid for?

As you have seen, the form's worksheet has a regular grid-like pattern of dots appearing on the paper. This grid can be used to help align your components when moving them.

If you have the Snap to Grid function active on the Format menu, a tick appears next to Snap to Grid. Your components will appear to move in fits and starts. This is because the components will be automatically aligned with the next grid mark when you begin to move them. To activate or deactivate this function, simply select this feature from the Format menu.

You can also use the grid to re-size the components on your form. If you select the components that you wish to re-size, and then choose Size from the Format menu, and then choose to Grid, Access 2.0 will now move each corner of each component to the nearest grid point. Note that this method of re-sizing will probably result in irregular shaped components.

Q&A With large control spaces, I move to the next field instead of getting a new line. What am I doing wrong?

Remember that *Enter* is one of the methods you can use to move around in Form View. To allow you to move to the second line of a memo field for instance, Access 2.0 requires you to press *Ctrl* and *Enter* together.

Q&A I want customizable buttons on my form. How can I get them?

See Chapter 10: Mastering Forms for advice on radio and check box usage via the ToolBox facility.

CHAPTER 6

Reports With Wizards

Access allows you to alter the layout of any of the information in your database and present a clear and concise report. The facility is used to refine data down to its most important key features and groups. Reports convey the information contained in your database to other people in a tight and easily understandable form, either as network information or printed matter.

Reports are possibly one of the most useful components of any database. Producing a good report requires quite a lot of background planning to get the correct data for the report to package. If no thought is put into the requirements of the report, then the design of the database may stop you from producing the goods.

The subject of report design is as complex as that of form design, if not more so. To prepare you for Chapter 11 (which covers designing reports from scratch) this chapter will deal with reports through the use of the wizards that Access 2.0 provides. This will help you get to grips with the basics of customization.

In this chapter you will learn about:

- Single-Column and Group/Totals reports
- Mailing labels
- Summary, tabular and auto reports
- Mail merge
- Design basics
- Troubleshooting

What is a Report?

In essence, a report is a tool that Access gives you to produce the style of data presentation your boss would prefer to see.

Your raw data from the Nwind Database

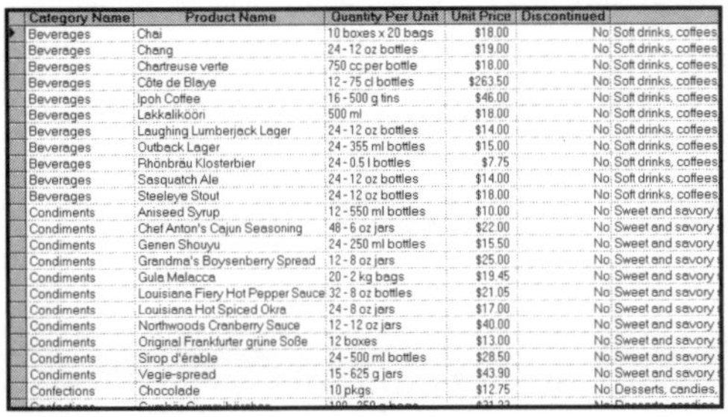

Category Name	Product Name	Quantity Per Unit	Unit Price	Discontinued	
Beverages	Chai	10 boxes x 20 bags	$18.00	No	Soft drinks, coffees
Beverages	Chang	24 - 12 oz bottles	$19.00	No	Soft drinks, coffees
Beverages	Chartreuse verte	750 cc per bottle	$18.00	No	Soft drinks, coffees
Beverages	Côte de Blaye	12 - 75 cl bottles	$263.50	No	Soft drinks, coffees
Beverages	Ipoh Coffee	16 - 500 g tins	$46.00	No	Soft drinks, coffees
Beverages	Lakkalikööri	500 ml	$18.00	No	Soft drinks, coffees
Beverages	Laughing Lumberjack Lager	24 - 12 oz bottles	$14.00	No	Soft drinks, coffees
Beverages	Outback Lager	24 - 355 ml bottles	$15.00	No	Soft drinks, coffees
Beverages	Rhönbräu Klosterbier	24 - 0.5 l bottles	$7.75	No	Soft drinks, coffees
Beverages	Sasquatch Ale	24 - 12 oz bottles	$14.00	No	Soft drinks, coffees
Beverages	Steeleye Stout	24 - 12 oz bottles	$18.00	No	Soft drinks, coffees
Condiments	Aniseed Syrup	12 - 550 ml bottles	$10.00	No	Sweet and savory
Condiments	Chef Anton's Cajun Seasoning	48 - 6 oz jars	$22.00	No	Sweet and savory
Condiments	Genen Shouyu	24 - 250 ml bottles	$15.50	No	Sweet and savory
Condiments	Grandma's Boysenberry Spread	12 - 8 oz jars	$25.00	No	Sweet and savory
Condiments	Gula Malacca	20 - 2 kg bags	$19.45	No	Sweet and savory
Condiments	Louisiana Fiery Hot Pepper Sauce	32 - 8 oz bottles	$21.05	No	Sweet and savory
Condiments	Louisiana Hot Spiced Okra	24 - 8 oz jars	$17.00	No	Sweet and savory
Condiments	Northwoods Cranberry Sauce	12 - 12 oz jars	$40.00	No	Sweet and savory
Condiments	Original Frankfurter grüne Soße	12 boxes	$13.00	No	Sweet and savory
Condiments	Sirop d'érable	24 - 500 ml bottles	$28.50	No	Sweet and savory
Condiments	Vegie-spread	15 - 625 g jars	$43.90	No	Sweet and savory
Confections	Chocolade	10 pkgs.	$12.75	No	Desserts, candies,

Now, in a friendly report format

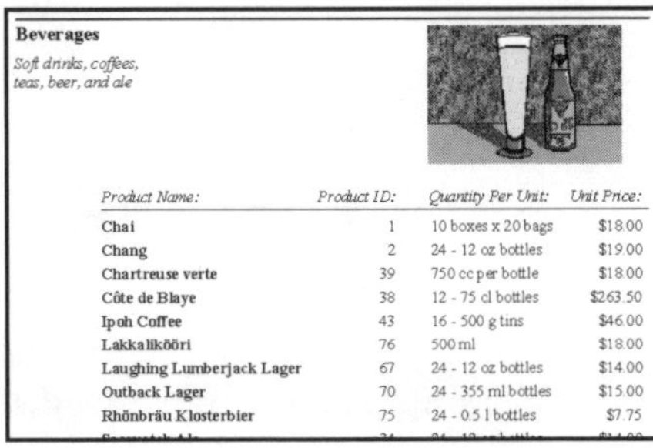

Beverages

Soft drinks, coffees, teas, beer, and ale

Product Name:	*Product ID:*	*Quantity Per Unit:*	*Unit Price:*
Chai	1	10 boxes x 20 bags	$18.00
Chang	2	24 - 12 oz bottles	$19.00
Chartreuse verte	39	750 cc per bottle	$18.00
Côte de Blaye	38	12 - 75 cl bottles	$263.50
Ipoh Coffee	43	16 - 500 g tins	$46.00
Lakkalikööri	76	500 ml	$18.00
Laughing Lumberjack Lager	67	24 - 12 oz bottles	$14.00
Outback Lager	70	24 - 355 ml bottles	$15.00
Rhönbräu Klosterbier	75	24 - 0.5 l bottles	$7.75

In Access terms, a report is a clear and concise representation of the data that is used as source. Access has many different types of report to offer, and in this chapter we will discuss each in turn. As you will see, each report specializes in the use of one feature, for example, a group/total style of report is used to group the records into a logical order and give totals to figures involved in the report.

Like forms, reports can be based on either tables or queries. A table should be used as the source of data for a report if the report is being used to display raw information in a more ordered format. A query should be used if any analysis of the data is required before it is presented.

To lay the necessary foundations, you need to manipulate the information in your database so that the report is not simply based on raw data, but has had some degree of filtering. To produce these kind of manipulations you should automatically think of queries. Their facilities, which include summary calculations and selection of records (so that summary calculations affect the correct grouping) are vital when attempting a task. Throughout this chapter, as you are introduced to the different types of report pay particular attention to the queries that the reports use for their source of information.

Let's look at the different Report Wizards Access 2.0 has to offer you, as the database designer, and see some examples of them, using NWind.

Presentation Using Report Wizards

As with all the wizards that Microsoft included with this package, the Report Wizards make the creation process easy. Each of the 7 wizards produces a different report style, and in order to finish each stage the questions you are asked by the wizard may differ quite a bit in content.

Let's just take a quick overview of each available report style.

Single-Column Report

Single Column is mainly used to display individual records, usually sorted following some criteria to make retrieval of the records easier.
A good example of the use of single column, single page reports, is when you

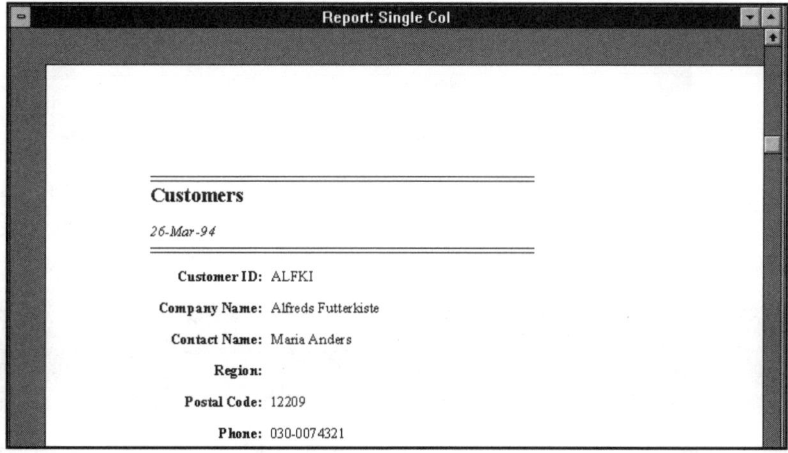

need to print some customer records showing the amount they owe your company. When each customer is being pressured to pay their bill, the telephonist/debt chaser may get confused if details of more than one customer appear on the same page.

Groups/Totals Report

Groups/Totals is mainly used for grouping records together under a series of umbrella headings or for producing subtotals of figures on the report.

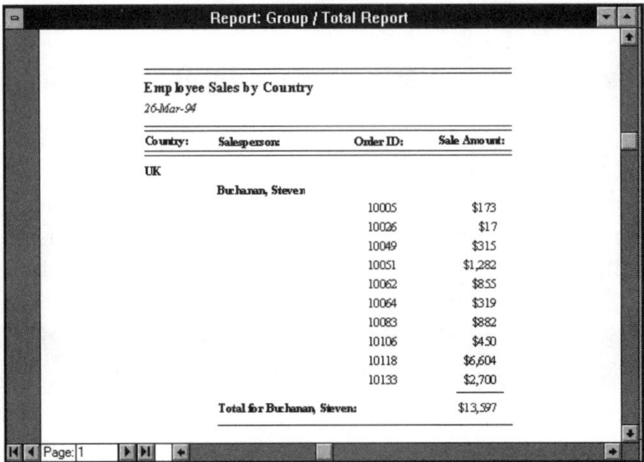

One example of the use of this type of report is an itemized phone bill. Each of the various levels of call need to have their own total, while the bill also requires a grand total to appear at the bottom of the report.

This style of report design can be a little confusing to create when using the Report Wizard, because the Report Wizard asks a lot of similar questions. Take care when you follow this procedure the first few times.

There is one final point to mention when working on this style of report, and this concerns totaling fields. Access does not ask you for the field you require totaling, but assumes it from your answers to other questions. This can be confusing, but by using the working example shown later in this chapter and by experimenting on your own, you should be able to achieve the results you want.

Mailing Label Report

Another style that the Access Report Wizard offers the user is the mailing label. This is used for printing addresses held in the database on to sticky labels. Access holds a wide range of formats for organizing the layout of addresses. They are all based on the Avery No. of the label sheet.

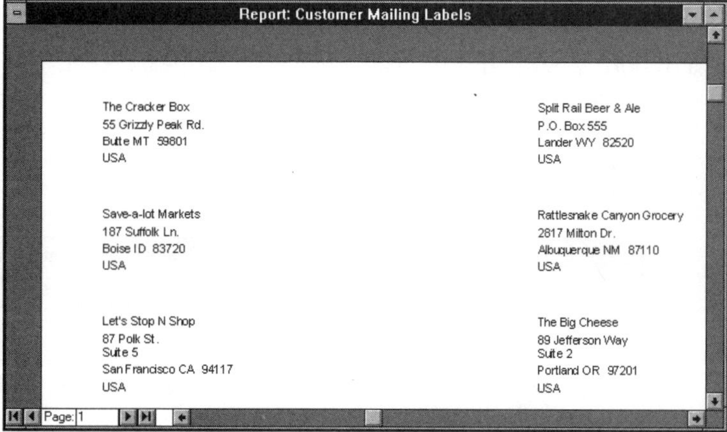

If you can't find the Avery No. of the labels you want to use, or if you aren't using one of these standard sizes then Access also provides you with the sizes of the labels and the ability to customize the basic design.

Summary Report

A Summary report is similar to the Group/Totals report in style, but a degree of detail is omitted in order to achieve concise layout. This avoids some of the clutter that the Group/Totals report usually includes. Below you can see the difference between a Group/Totals report and a Summary report:

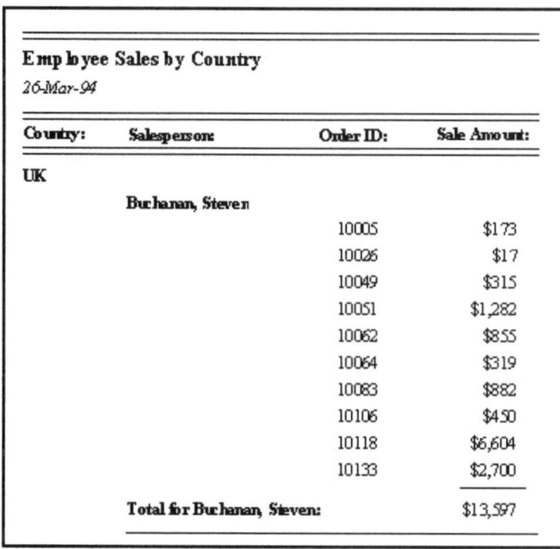

Employee Sales by Country

26-Mar-94

Country:	Salesperson:	Order ID:	Sale Amount:
UK			
	Buchanan, Steven		
		10005	$173
		10026	$17
		10049	$315
		10051	$1,282
		10062	$855
		10064	$319
		10083	$882
		10106	$450
		10118	$6,604
		10133	$2,700
	Total for Buchanan, Steven:		$13,597

Summary Report (Summary)

20-May-94

Country	Salesperson		Sale Amount
UK			
	Buchanan, Steven		$83,359.01 5.53%
	Dodsworth, Anne		$85,879.34 5.69%
	King, Robert		$145,781.69 9.66%
	Suyama, Michael		$85,581.74 5.67%
		UK	$400,601.78 26.56%

Tabular Report

A Tabular report is similar to a spreadsheet in appearance in that the fields appear as column headings and the records appear across the sheet of paper. This is useful when you want to compile a spreadsheet-like appearance with calculated figures passed from the base query. You will notice how similar this is to the datasheet formats used by both tables and queries.

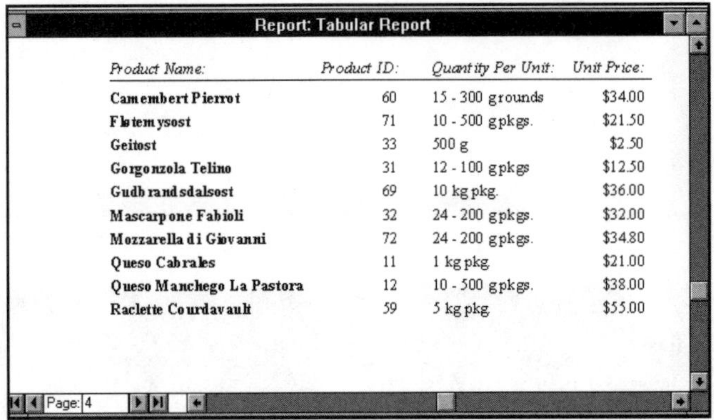
Report: Tabular Report

Product Name:	Product ID:	Quantity Per Unit:	Unit Price:
Camembert Pierrot	60	15 - 300 g rounds	$34.00
Fløtemysost	71	10 - 500 g pkgs.	$21.50
Geitost	33	500 g	$2.50
Gorgonzola Telino	31	12 - 100 g pkgs	$12.50
Gudbrandsdalsost	69	10 kg pkg.	$36.00
Mascarpone Fabioli	32	24 - 200 g pkgs.	$32.00
Mozzarella di Giovanni	72	24 - 200 g pkgs.	$34.80
Queso Cabrales	11	1 kg pkg.	$21.00
Queso Manchego La Pastora	12	10 - 500 g pkgs.	$38.00
Raclette Courdavault	59	5 kg pkg.	$55.00

Page: 4

Auto Report

This report is not really a style, but rather a quick way of producing a report. You can use this feature to produce a report for any number of reasons, but it is also useful to simply work out the amount of space required for each record. The Auto Report Wizard uses the default answers to the Single Column Report Wizard's questions, and also uses all the fields that make up the table or query source information. This helps you decide which fields to include in a mature report and where to put them.

Microsoft Mail Merge Wizard

This wizard allows you to produce personalized letters and address labels using Microsoft Word. This is another route to the facility Merge it to Word, which is supplied as an icon. In essence, this wizard helps you produce a stock letter or address label, and then feed copies of that template using the data contained in the database. Because you aren't using Access as the publisher, you have more control over the appearance of the report, especially with personalized letters.

Access 2.0's ability to produce address labels is a lot better than Word's if you use the Avery standard sized labels.

The type of report you require obviously depends on what you are going to use it for. Figure-based information naturally falls into the Tabular report style. Single Column reports are useful to display records separately, while the summary style can be useful when you want a cursory view of the information stored in the underlying table or query. Finally, with the help of the Microsoft Mail Merge Wizard and the Mailing Label Wizard the days of typing hundreds of personalized letters are over. Just press the button, sit back, and watch Access and your printer do all the hard work.

Now is the time to start worrying about the design of your tables and the quality of the queries. Reports are a sure way of revealing anomalies in design. The best thing to do is try a few initial reports on the Microsoft NWind database before styling your own data. When you are ready to commit to a style, Access 2.0 supplies a taskmaster screen to assist you.

Report Wizard Taskmaster

To enlist the help of the taskmaster and his gang of Report Wizards:

- Select the Report tab from the initial database window, and then the New button to take the first step involved in calling the taskmaster.

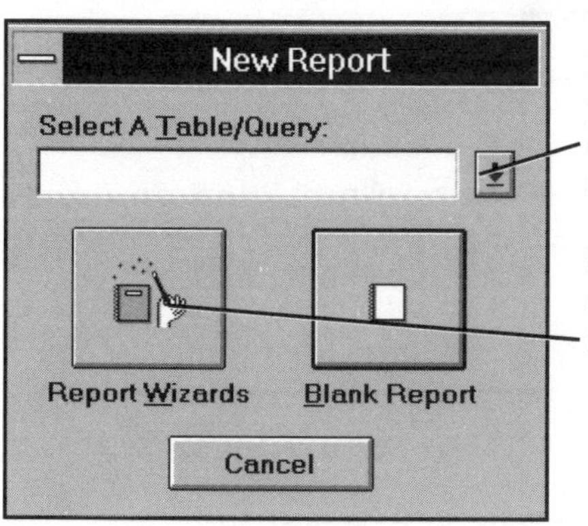

Pull the menu down and select the table or query you wish to use as the source data. If you have no data to play with then use tables or queries from the supplied sample database NWind.

Select this button to use the Report Wizards. Use the other button when you want to design your reports from scratch. This subject is covered in Chapter 11.

This calls the taskmaster, who appears with the following screen.

Highlight the style of report you want assistance with in this window.

As you flick through the different styles of report the taskmaster has on offer, an appropriate description of each style appears here.

- Once you've chosen, click on the OK button. The taskmaster will now go away and call up your selected Report Wizard, before retiring to wait until you need its services again.

Single Column Wizard

Follow this example using Catalog in Reports in the NWind database. When the taskmaster calls this wizard, it races to your assistance with the first of its questions as shown below.

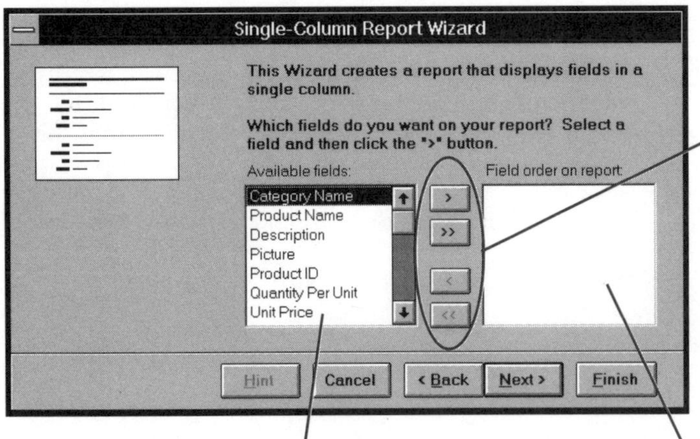

Use these buttons in the usual way to select or de-select the fields you want the wizard to incorporate into the report's design. Remember that single arrows affect single highlighted fields and double arrows affect all the fields.

All the fields that make up the table or query you use as the source for the wizard will appear in this window. If the fields you require aren't here, select the Cancel button and choose the correct table or query, or create a new query that does have the correct fields.

The fields you wish the wizard to incorporate into the report design should appear in this window before you move on to the next stage.

The order you select the fields in, and therefore the order they appear in the right-hand window, determines the order they appear in on the report.

- Select the fields you want included in your report design, and click on the Next > button to move to the next question.

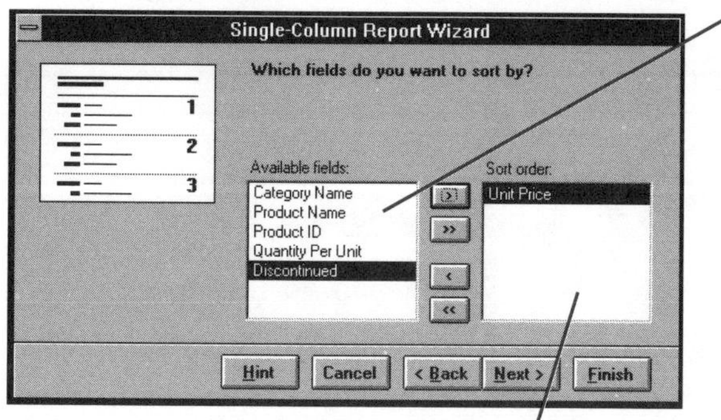

All the fields that you can ask Access to sort the records on will appear in this window. This means that instead of having them appear in order of their code number, you could have them appear alphabetically in name terms or, as in this example, highest to lowest in terms of their cost, using the field Unit Cost.

The order that your selected fields appear in the window is significant. If you select two or more, Access treats the selection in exactly the same way as it would in a query. Access sorts the records upon the first field given in the list, and if any duplication appears, it uses the second field in the list to order those. It continues down the list until it reaches the end or until there are no duplicate records.

You cannot sort records based upon fields with OLE Object or Memo data types.

- Make your selection of fields, in the order you want them. Select the Next > button to move to the next stage of the report design.

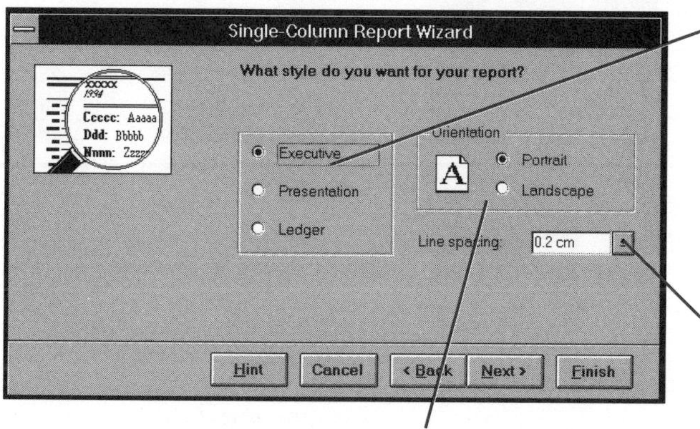

The three stock styles you can apply to your report will appear in this window. As you flick through the available styles, a graphical representation of the style appears under the lens.

This window gives you the chance to alter the amount of space left between the fields on the report. The default setting is 0.2 cms, but you can change this, either by re-typing the figure you require, or by selecting from the pull-down menu.

In this window you can select the orientation your report will appear in.

- Choose the style you wish to apply to the report, together with your choice of paper orientation and space between the fields. Then select the Next > button to move on to the final screen that the Single Column Wizard uses:

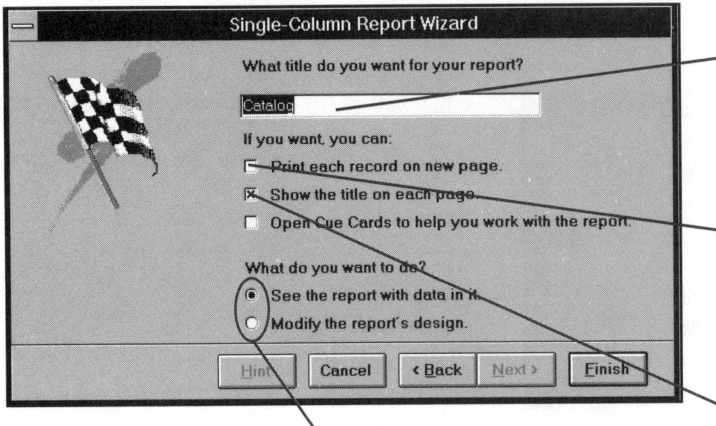

Type into this box the title you want to appear at the **top** of the first page of your report.

Select this check box, if you want each record to appear on a single page. This is a more useful feature when producing a single column report, rather than a tabular report, for example.

Select this check box, if you want the title of your report to appear at the top of each page.

Select the view you want the wizard to abandon you in. This will be either Report View or Design View.

> The default name for your report is the name of the query that you base the report upon. In this case, the NWind Query called Catalog was used to produce the report.

Click on the Finish button to see the results of the wizard's hard work.

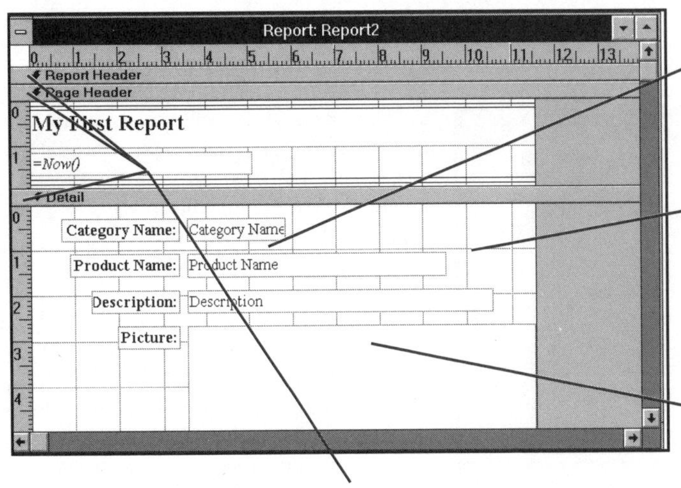

Look at the spacing between the fields. This depends on the value you selected.

This the report grid. As you will see in the section entitled Customizing These Results, it is used in much the same way as the form version.

Notice the large area that has been used here. This field has the data type OLE Object. Access 2.0 recognized this as needing more space than the average text field.

Notice the different sections of the report. We will look at these in further detail in the section entitled Customizing These Results.

You can customize these results using some of the techniques that will be discussed later.

Group/Totals Wizard

Follow this example using Products in Reports in the NWind Database. When the taskmaster calls this wizard it appears with the following screen.

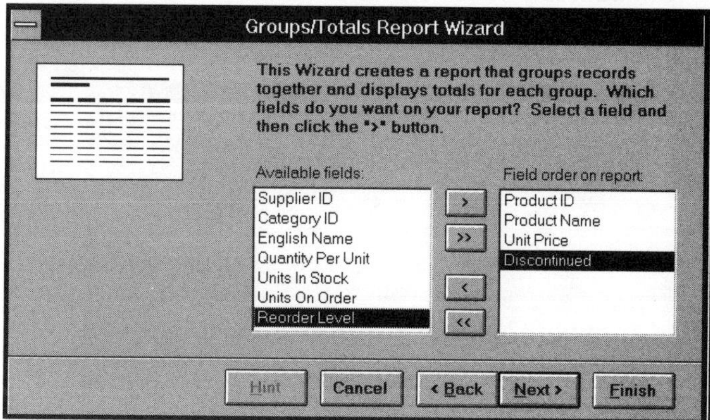

- Select the fields you wish to appear on your report and click on the Next > button to move to the next stage.

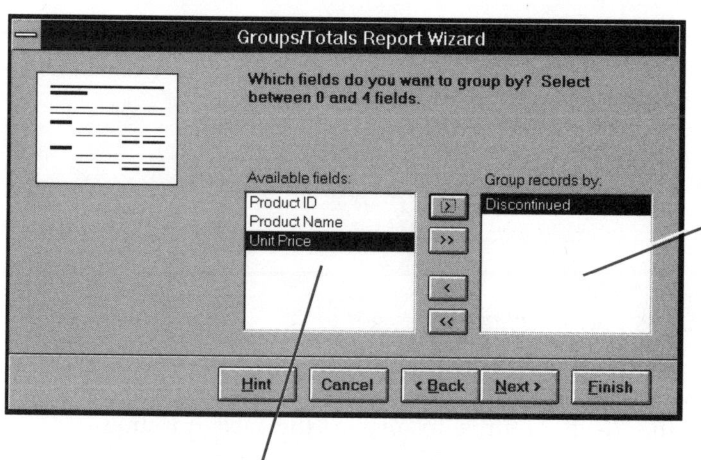

The fields you are using for grouping your records will appear in this window. Access will group records based on the first field that appears here and, in a similar way to sorting, will group the records involved by the first field, the second field, and so on, until the available fields are exhausted. You will see that you must choose between zero and four fields in this window.

All the fields you selected for your report are in this window. You can group the records that appear in your data source, either a table or a query, using the values that appear in any of these fields.

This wizard will total any fields that contain numbers, if they are not used as a method of grouping the records. If you don't want the fields to be totaled, either select that field for grouping and choose a larger band width (the next stage), or delete the control that does the calculation (see Customizing Wizard Results).

- Select the fields you want for the basis for the grouping of the records in your report (in this case the discontinued field name), and then click on the Next > button to continue.

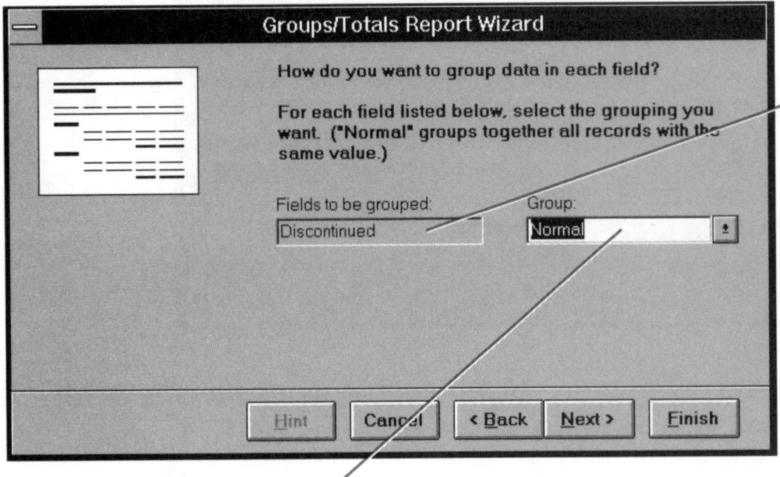

Here is the field (or fields) you selected as the basis for any grouping of records in your report. If you chose 4 fields, then 4 separate boxes appear.

Depending on the **data type** of the field you selected, the type of grouping you can use changes. Text fields use a number of characters as the basis for the grouping. For example, the first 4 characters of 2 words need to be the same before they are grouped together. Number fields use numerical band widths, so if 2 numbers are within the same hundred (123 and 145) then they are grouped together. These numerical band widths range from normal (the same number) to 500000 (within the same half million). Date fields use a set period. If two dates are within the same month they are grouped together. These date band widths range from normal (the same second) to year (in the same year).

- Select the band width you want for each of the fields you selected, before clicking on the Next > button to answer the next question.

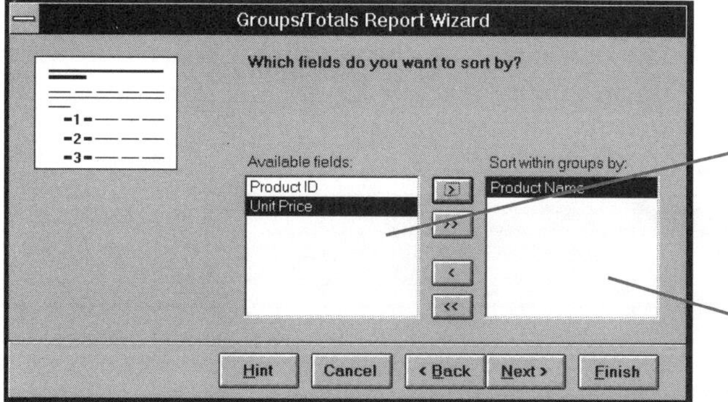

Notice that the fields you select for the grouping do **not** appear in this list.

Your selection here determines how the grouping will be sorted. In this case, grouping is under Discontinued and the sorting is by Product Name.

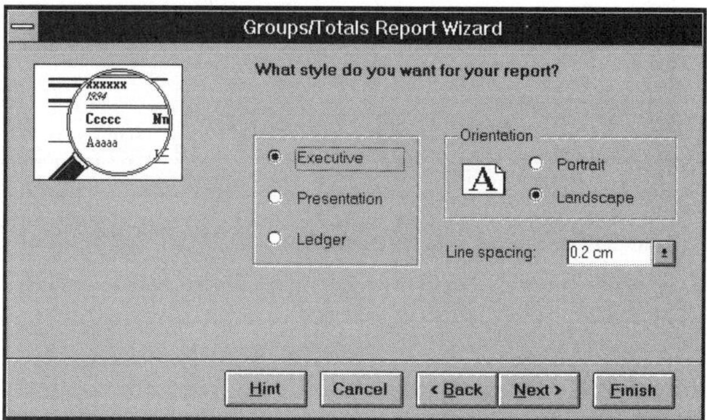

- As before, use this window to alter the default selection of appearance controls. Click on the Next > button to move to the final screen:

Select this check box if you want Access to calculate the percentages that the group subtotals make in relation to the total for the report. For example, if the employees with a last name beginning with S earned $1234, and the total for all the employees was $12340, the S group would get a percentage of 10%.

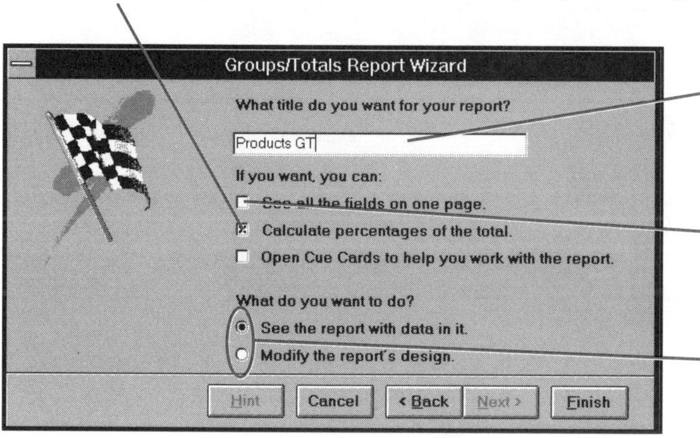

In this box type the name you want to give to your report. It will then appear at the top of the first page.

Select this check box if you want each record to appear on one page. You can only do this if Access can squeeze it all in.

Choose the view you wish to be abandoned in when the wizard has finished producing your report.

- Make the final decisions that will affect the wizard's design on your report and click on the Finish button to see the results of the wizard's hard work. It should be similar to that shown below.

Design View - Group/Totals Wizard

Mailing Label Wizard

Follow this example using Customers in reports in the NWind Database. When you select Mailing Labels in the Report Style window, you will be presented with the following screen. Access uses this to find out exactly how the mailing addresses should be organized.

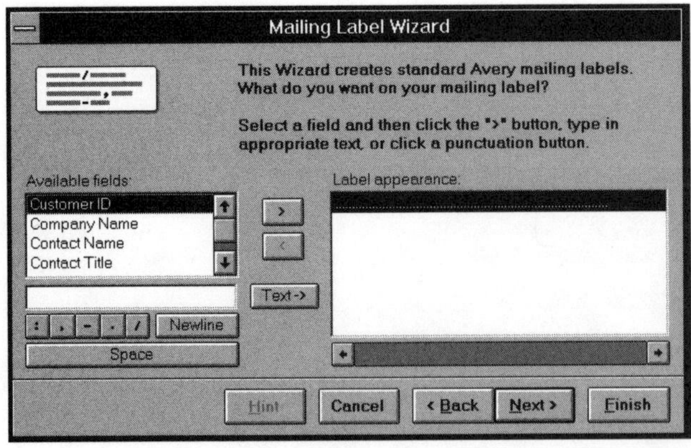

With this screen, you build up the format of the address from a combination of fields and punctuation, allowing you to customize the address to your liking.

Putting an Address Block Together: An Example

Below is a sample address label format which you may want to reproduce using this wizard:

```
Owner Manuel Pereira,
GROSELLA-Restaurante,
5ª Ave. Los Palos Grandes,
Caracas, DF,
1081, Venezuela.
```

Let's look at the steps needed to produce this label format:

- Move the first field over to the right-hand window entitled Label Appearance by highlighting the required field and then selecting the Move > button.

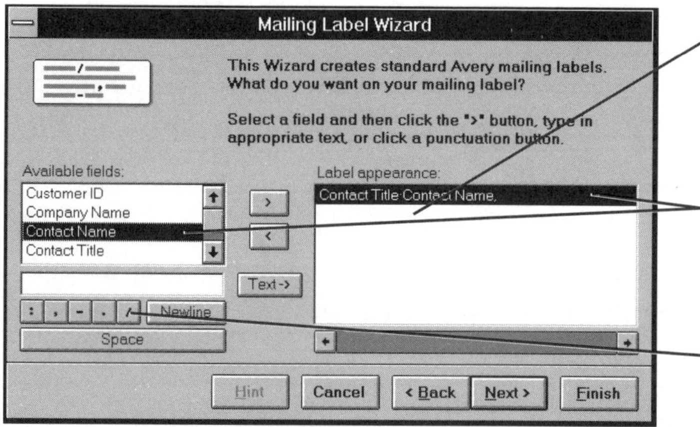

Here is your address, made up of the selected fields.

Highlight the first field (in this case use Contact Title, i.e. Mr/Mrs) and click > to move it over to the label. Add any punctuation as you go.

Carry on selecting fields and punctuation via the mini keyboard.

- Repeat this process until you have completed your address label.

- If you make any mistakes press the Remove < button to remove the offending addition.

- Follow the same steps until you have finished the design of your address label. It should be similar to the one shown below.

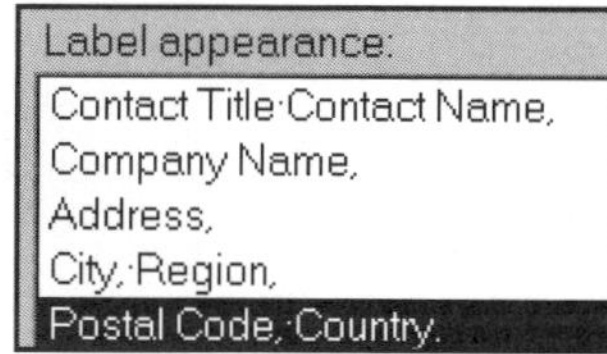

If the entries on any line of your address label are too long to fit inside the window, Access will attach any more entries to the end of the line out of your sight. To see the results of your work, you can use the arrows under the box to move to the left or right. Clicking once on either of the arrows moves the focus of the window 10 characters in the direction of the arrow.

Placing Fixed Text in Address Labels

It is possible to place fixed text into the address label. Fixed text is any constant text that will appear in the address label no matter what data Access uses to fill in the major part of the address label. Click on the white box under the available Fields box and type the text you wish to appear. Possible examples of fixed text are CONFIDENTIAL or F.A.O.

To place fixed text into the address label:

- When you have arrived at the point in the address label that the text should appear, place the cursor into the box next to the Text > button.

- Type in the text you want to appear on each of the address labels.
- Click on the Text -> button, and Access will place the text you have typed into the box at the current position of the cursor in the address label.

The text will stay in the box until it is deleted or is placed in the label as required. Also, if you use the Remove < button the text is lost.

When the address label has been created to your own specifications, click on the Next > button to move on to the following screen:

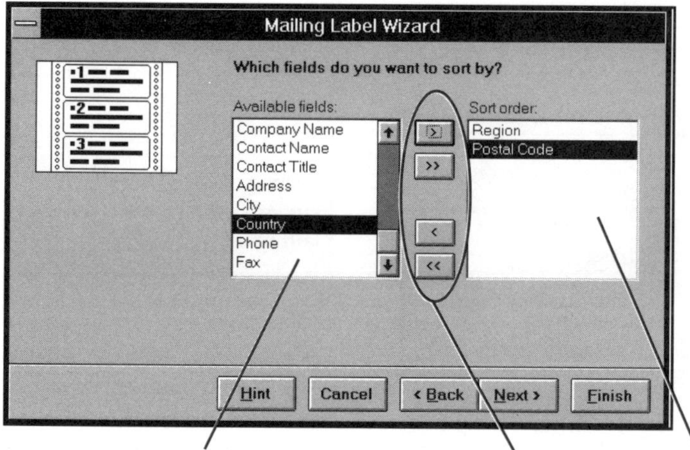

The contents of this window will be used as the basis for a sort of the records that go to make up the address labels. The order they appear in this window affects the order in which the records appear. The first field in the list is used as the basis for the sort, and then any duplication is sorted out using the second field, and so on until all duplication is eliminated, or the fields in this list are exhausted. Here, for example, all the labels will be printed in state order and postal code sequence.

Here are all the fields that appear in the table or query you gave to the wizard to use as the basis of the address. Any of these fields can be used to organize the addresses into an order for printing out.

Use these buttons in the normal way to select or de-select the highlighted field. Remember that single arrows affect single fields and double arrows affect all fields.

When you have selected the fields to be involved in the record sort, click on the Next > button to see this next screen:

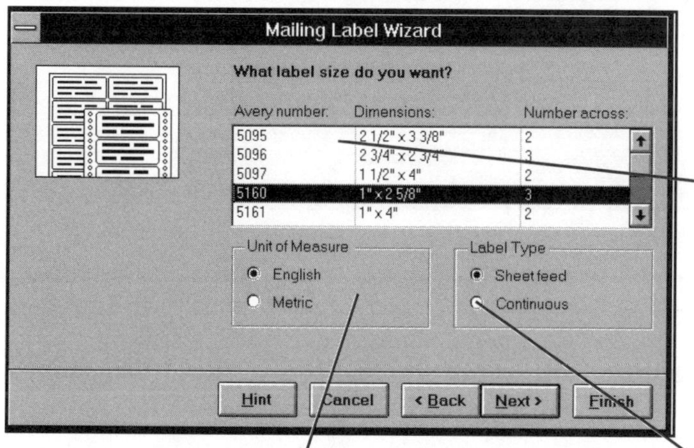

This window contains information about the type of label that the addresses will be printed on. If you are using a standard Avery sized label, you will probably be able to find the Avery No. of your labels on this list. If not, use the Dimensions and Number Across columns to find the label size and position to suit your labels.

Select the most appropriate type of feed for your labels. Sheet feed is for labels that arrive on single pieces of paper, while continuous feed is for labels that come in perforated runs.

Choose the unit of measure that is most appropriate to your labels. Each type of measure has a different listing of labels, so if you can't find your labels on one listing, try changing the unit of measure and looking through this new list.

When you have made the appropriate selections from this screen, click on the Next > button to move on to the next screen:

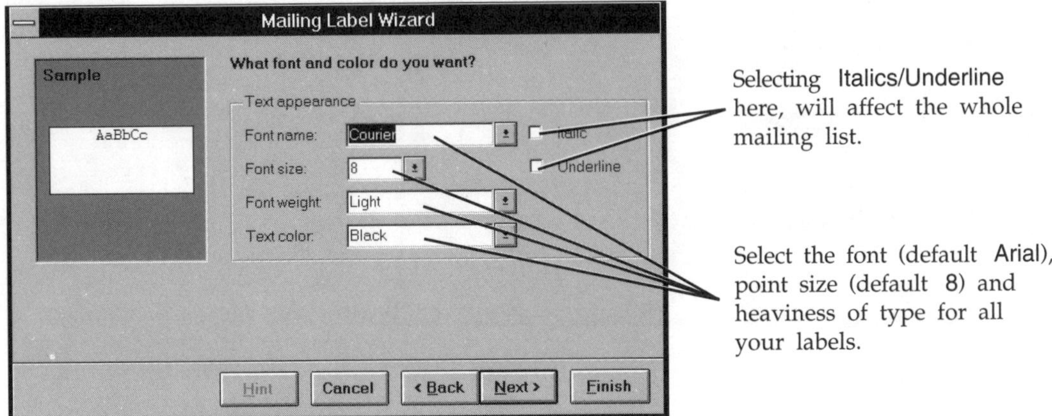

- Select the style and color you wish the text in your address labels to have and click on the Next > button to see the final stage:

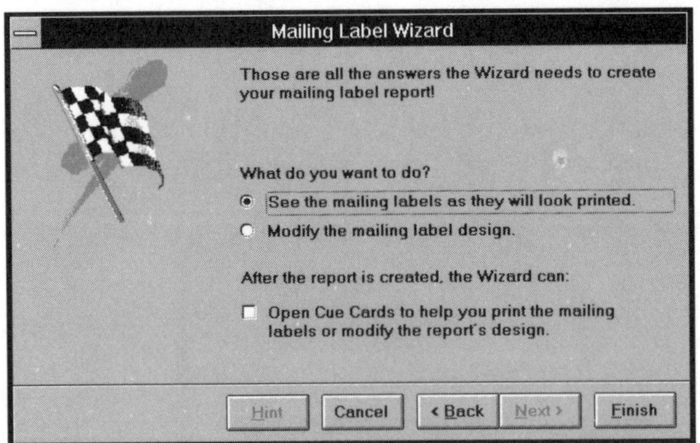

- Select the view that the wizard will abandon you in. Do a Print Preview to see how the labels will appear when you print them out, or Design View, so that you can alter the presentation of the labels. Click on the Finish button to see the results of the wizard's hard work. It will look something like this:

```
Sales Associate Patricia McKenna,
Hungry Owl All-Night Grocers,
8 Johnstown Road,
Cork, Co. Cork,
, Ireland.
```

You will see that the Post Code field of this particular address label is blank, but the punctuation has remained.

If any record has not got an entry in any of the fields that appear as part of the address label, Access will leave a blank in that part of the label.

Summary Report Wizard

Follow this example using Catalog in reports in the NWind database.

When you select this wizard, the taskmaster hurries it along so that it can produce the following screen:

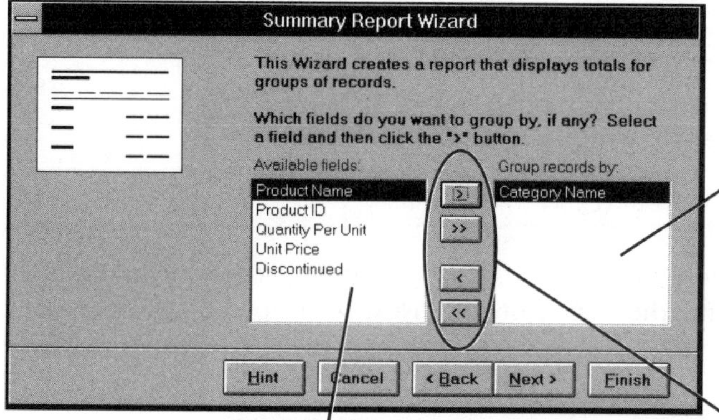

The fields that appear in this window will be used by the wizard to group the records that appear in your report. The first field is used for the first grouping, while the second field is used to sub-divide those groups still further, until all of the fields in this window have been applied to the records in your report.

Use these buttons as usual to select or de-select the highlighted field.

The fields that make up the table or query that the report is based upon will appear in this window.

- Select the fields for grouping and click on the Next > button to move to the next stage:

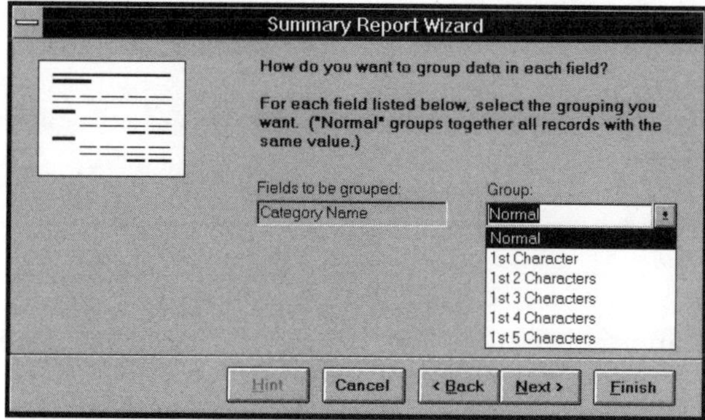

- In this screen you can refine the grouping of your records. Choose the appropriate band width for each of the fields you have selected and move on to the next stage of the report design by clicking the Next > button.

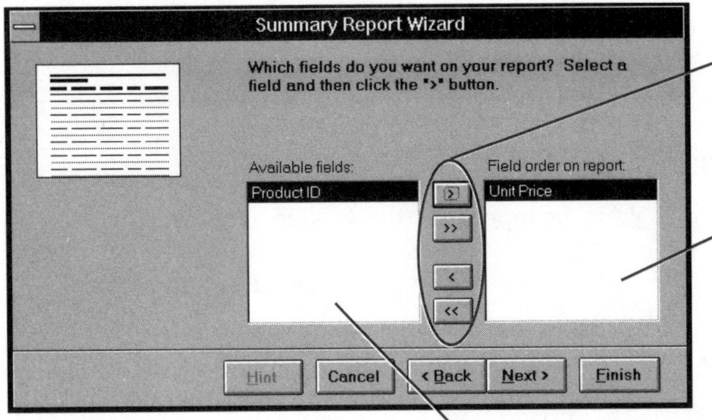

Use these buttons in the usual way to select or de-select the highlighted fields.

Access will use the fields that appear in this window to calculate the totals for the records in each different grouping.

The fields that appear in this window are the fields that were **not** selected for the grouping process and **are** of a number based field, i.e Date/Time, Currency, Counter etc. This means that all the extra information available in each record is left out, hence the summary report.

Select the appropriate fields for Access to use as the basis for its calculations when producing the totals, and then click on the Next > button to define the style of the report.

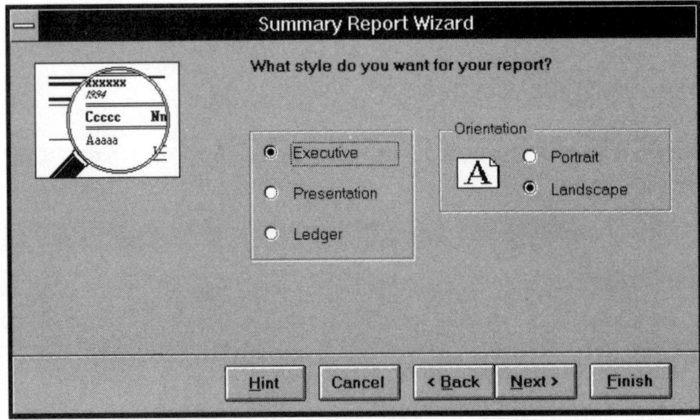

Select the appropriate style for this report, based on the stock styles of the report and the orientation of the paper. Then click on the Next > button for the final time.

Use this box to give Access the name you wish to appear at the top of your report. You will see that the default choice is the name of the table or query that the report is based upon.

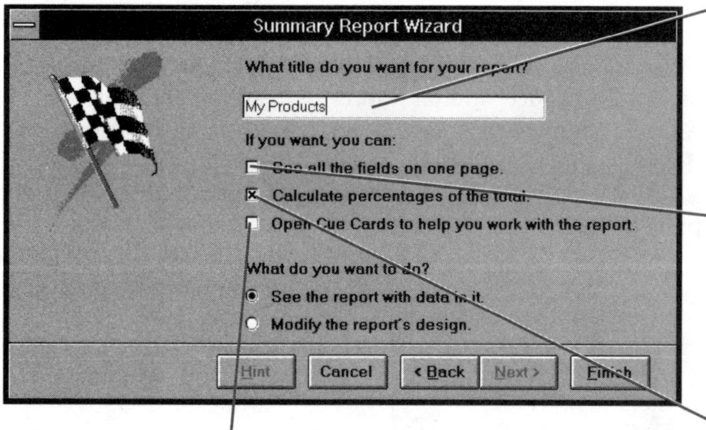

Select this check box if you require all the fields to appear on one page. Access may alter the orientation of the paper in order to carry out your request.

Select this check box if you want Access to provide the percentage equivalent of each grouping total out of the report's grand total which is found at the end of the report.

Select the view you wish the wizard to abandon you in when its work is over.

Answer these final questions and then click on the Finish button to see the results of the wizard's hard work. These will be similar to what is shown below:

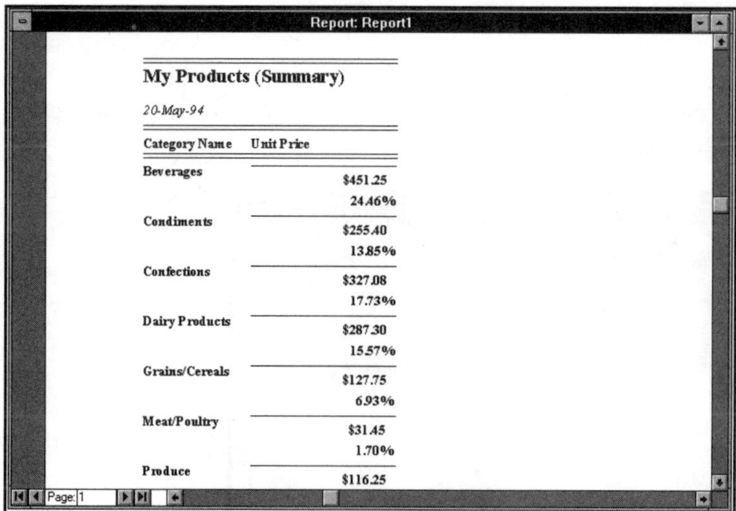

Tabular Report Wizard

Follow this example using Employees table in Reports in the NWind database.

This Report Wizard can give you a style of report similar to the layout of a table's datasheet. In this respect the Report Wizard is closely related to the Single Column Wizard, as both produce similar kinds of results. The only difference is that the Single Column Wizard labels each field of each record, while the Tabular Wizard labels the top of each column with the field name. To gain access to this facility, when you ask the taskmaster to call the appropriate wizard, it appears bearing this screen:

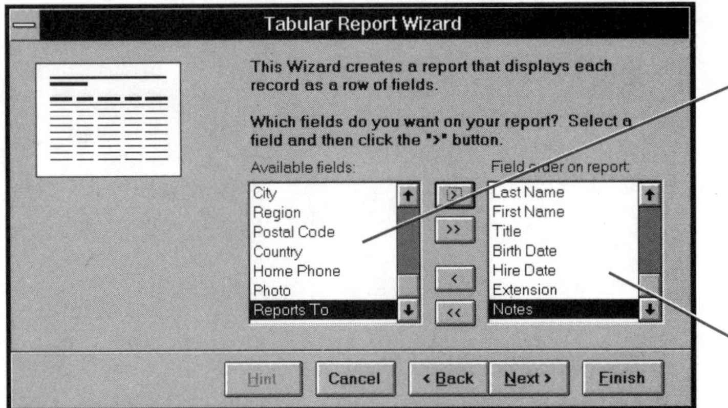

All the fields that you can include on your report are available in the listing in this window. This listing of fields will be composed from the table or query that the report is based upon.

The fields that appear in this window are the ones the wizard will use to create the report. These field names will also become the column headings as in the table datasheet's layout.

Select the fields you wish to appear in your report, and then click on the Next > button to continue.

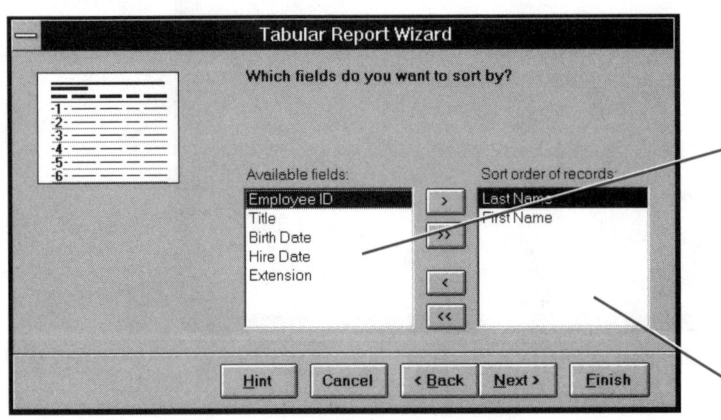

These are all the fields you can select as the basis of your sort. You will notice that one of our original selections is not available here. The Notes field cannot be used as a sort just as you cannot sort on a Memo field.

You have chosen these fields as the basis for the sort.

Select the fields you want the wizard to use as the basis for ordering, before clicking on the Next > button

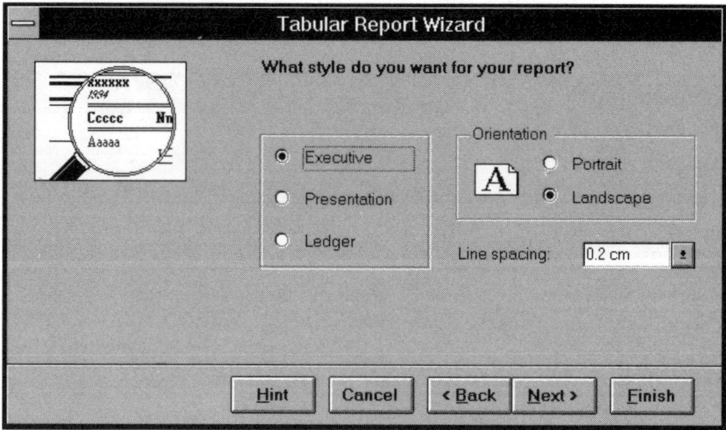

Select the style you require the wizard to apply to this report, and then move on.

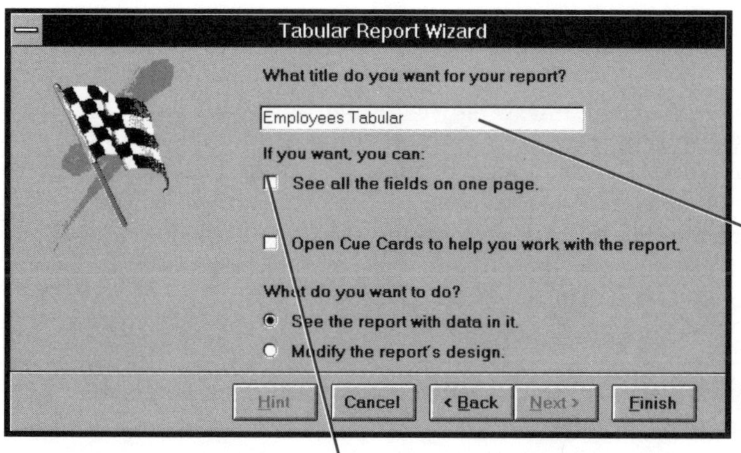

Type in the name you wish to appear at the top of this report. In this case, Employees Tabular has been entered. You will see that the default name for the report is the name of the table or query that the report is based upon.

Select this check box if you want the wizard to try to keep the fields all on one page. The wizard may alter the orientation of the paper in order to fulfill your request.

Give your report a heading, and then select the view that you want the wizard to abandon you in when its job is over. Finally, click on the Finish button. The wizard will complete the design of this tabular style report and leave you in your selected view. Below is an example of a tabular report Design View:

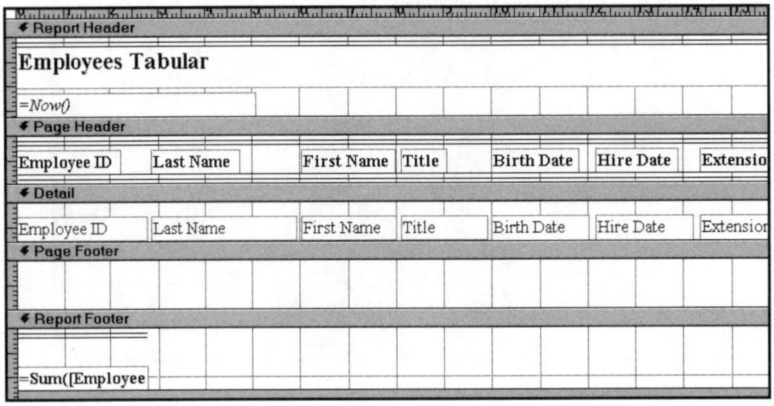

Report Header
Employees Tabular
=Now()
Page Header
Employee ID | Last Name | First Name | Title | Birth Date | Hire Date | Extensio
Detail
Employee ID | Last Name | First Name | Title | Birth Date | Hire Date | Extensior
Page Footer
Report Footer
=Sum([Employee

Now you have produced a tabular style report, see the section entitled Customizing Wizard Results to improve on the finished design.

Auto Report Wizard

This wizard takes the default answers to all of the Single Column Report Wizard's questions and quickly produces a report for you to view records supplied by the underlying table or query. Because this wizard takes the default answers to another wizard's questions, this is the simplest of the Report Wizards to operate. Simply ask the taskmaster to call up this wizard, and Auto Report will produce the report from the comfort of its own bed and post the results to you when it has finished.

> Unlike the normal postal service, the one that the wizard uses takes less than three days to produce results.

Microsoft Mail Merge Wizard

This wizard is used as a short cut to producing personalized letters or addresses. It uses the data in your Access 2.0 database and the word processing package, Microsoft Word 6.0, and allows you to take advantage of the wordprocessor's text control features.

The only screen this wizard has to use is the following one.

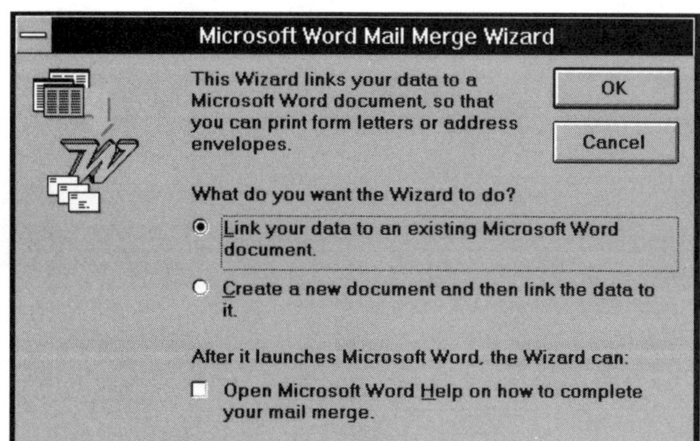

On this screen you are asked this very simple question: "Have you already produced a document that is going to be used as the body of the text for your personalized letter, or do you want to create a new one?" Simply select the option relevant to your situation and click on the OK button.

If you select the New Document option, Access 2.0 will boot up Microsoft Word 6.0, and open up a new document together with the necessary tool bar packed full of icons to help you create the new personalized letter or address label. However, if you select the already produced template, Access 2.0 will give you a normal Windows dialog box for you to select your pre-written file.

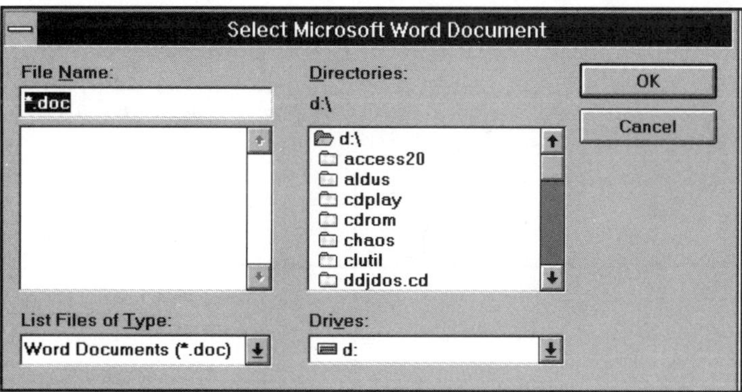

When Word is booted up it will have all the standard tool bars that appear by default, plus a database tool bar.

This database toolbar differs slightly from the regular Word database tool bar.

Using this tool bar you can create or continue to develop a personalized letter for all the people or companies you hold on your database. Each of the buttons control a different aspect of the co-operation that occurs between Access 2.0 and Microsoft Word 6.0.

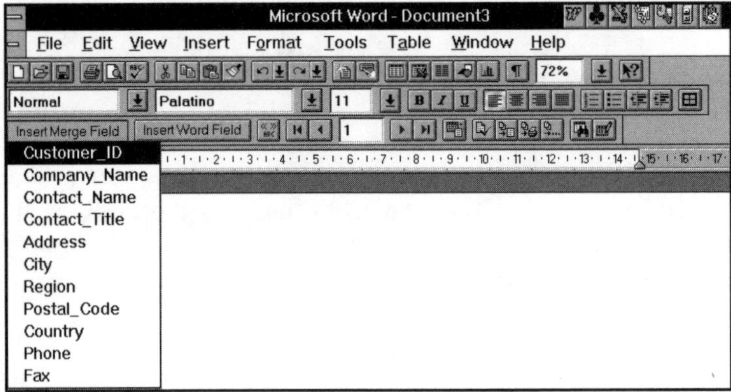

The Insert Merge Field button enables you to place the field that appears as part of the underlying table or query into the text, generated by Word. This field is called to release its information, record by record to the letter. Each letter will be personalized based on the record Access currently has in focus For example, look at the two screens below. The first shows the field, in place, in the text. The second is the data appearing in the text when the personalization has taken place.

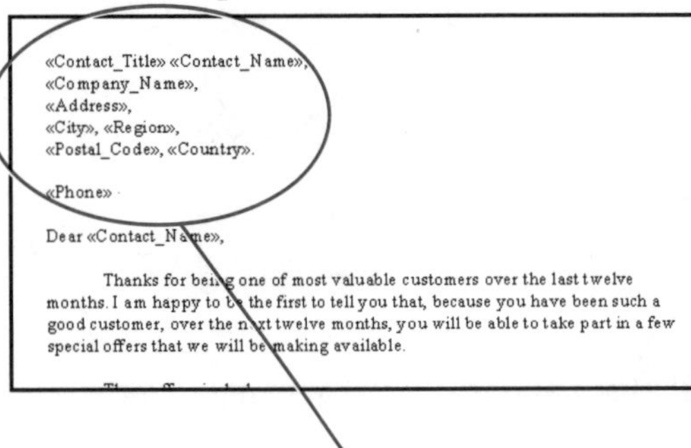

«Contact_Title» «Contact_Name»,
«Company_Name»,
«Address»,
«City», «Region»,
«Postal_Code», «Country».

«Phone»

Dear «Contact_Name»,

Thanks for being one of most valuable customers over the last twelve months. I am happy to be the first to tell you that, because you have been such a good customer, over the next twelve months, you will be able to take part in a few special offers that we will be making available.

This is how the fields will appear in the template.

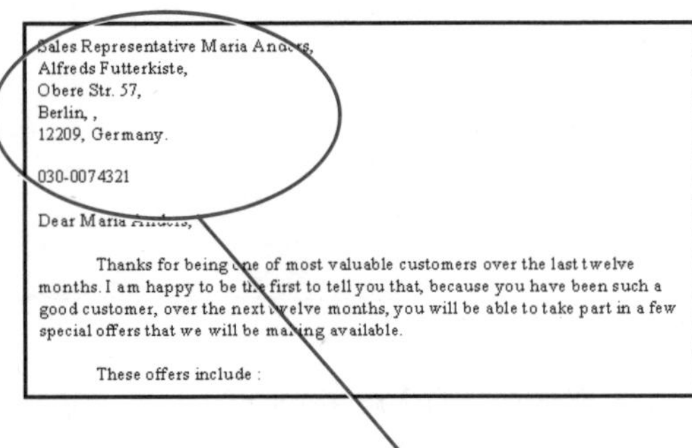

Sales Representative Maria Anders,
Alfreds Futterkiste,
Obere Str. 57,
Berlin, ,
12209, Germany.

030-0074321

Dear Maria Anders,

Thanks for being one of most valuable customers over the last twelve months. I am happy to be the first to tell you that, because you have been such a good customer, over the next twelve months, you will be able to take part in a few special offers that we will be making available.

These offers include :

This is the data supplied by the database for the field(s).

The Insert Word Field button lets you use some special features of Word merge. You may wish to ask a user for extra input or skip records automatically. See the Help screens and manuals to Word for detailed use of these features.

This button can be used to quickly swap between the field names in the text and actual data.

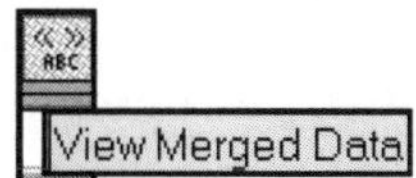

This assembly of buttons is used to identify the record the current data is being obtained from, and also to alter the record the data is drawn from.

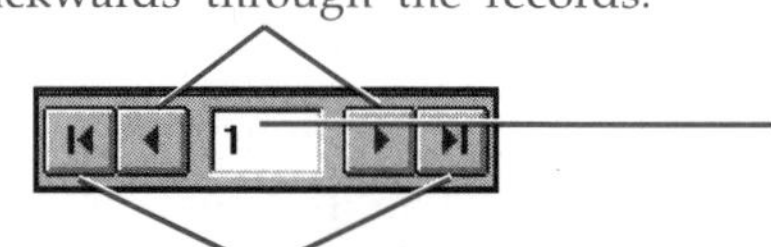

Use these buttons to move forwards or backwards through the records.
1
This number represents the current record being used as the source for the data in the letter or address.
Use these buttons to jump to the first/last records.

This button activates the Mail Merge Helper as shown below.

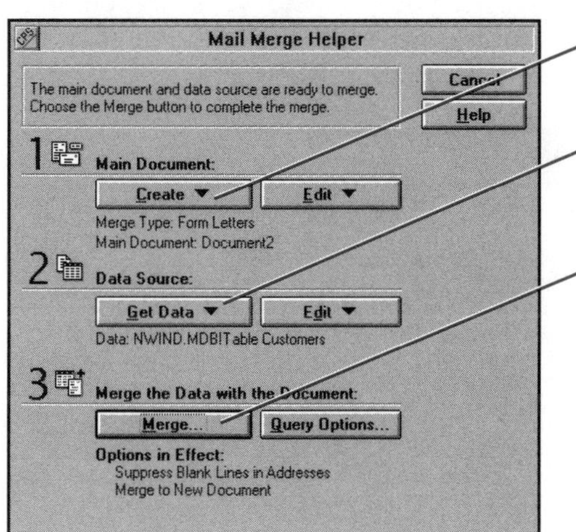

You can use this facility to alter the source of the data for this template.

This button gives you more control over how the personalized letters are finally produced. When you select this button you will see the following screen:

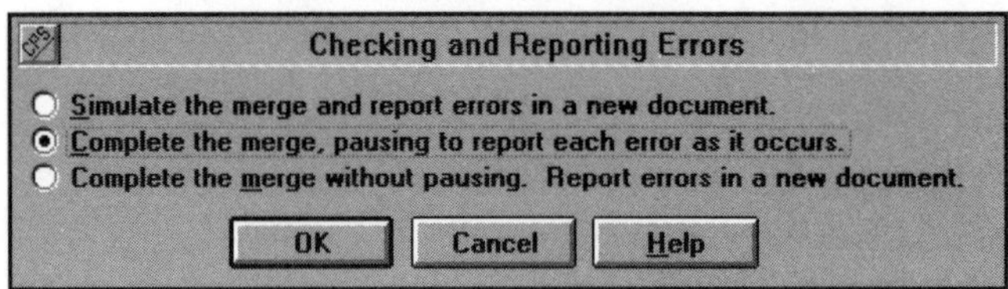

These three options allow you to select when and if Access will inform you of any errors it encounters during a merge. Select the option you are most comfortable with, and then select the OK button.

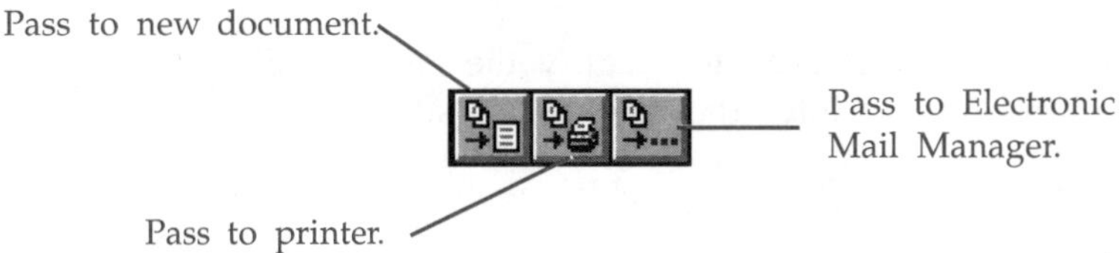

Pass to new document.
Pass to Electronic Mail Manager.
Pass to printer.

These three buttons allow you to control where the document is merged to. You have three choices; all of the newly personalized letters can be passed to a new document, passed to the printer, or to electronic mail. For more information on electronic mailing of your letters, see the Word Help screens in the section Mail Merge: Advanced Techniques.

This button allows you to specify the record you want to view, depending on the field you have highlighted and the value you enter into the box that appears, similar to that shown below:

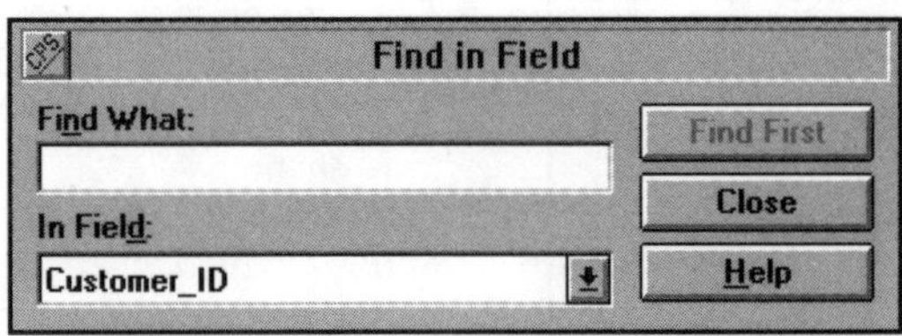

This button opens the underlying table or query that the wizard is drawing records from. This allows you to see the records available and the fields that they are composed of.

Saving These Results

When any of the wizards has finished its job and left you in your desired view, you will either want to scrap the report and start again, or save it and perhaps go back and customize it at a later date. Whatever you decide:

- Select File and Close from the menu bar.
- Access will prompt you to save the report design. Selecting **no** will scrap the report, while choosing **yes** will give you the following screen:
- Type in your report name and OK to save it.

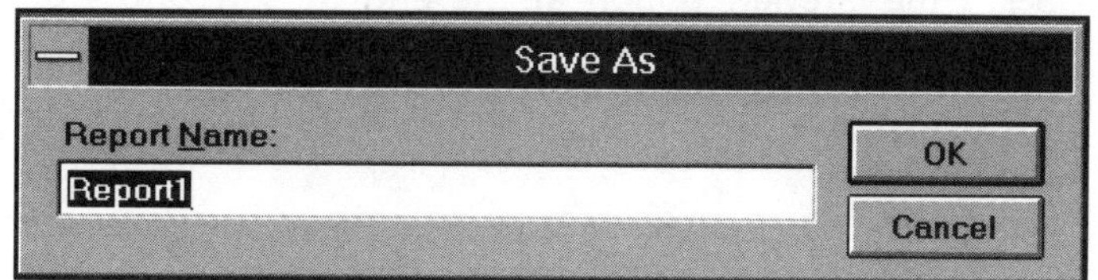

You should now be aware of the features that Microsoft have provided in terms of the Report Wizards, and with a little experimentation you should be able to produce quite good results. However, if you want to make an original you need to know how to customize.

Customizing Wizard Results

No matter which wizard you enlist to help you with the design of your reports, it certainly will not be able to produce *exactly* what you want. Microsoft have provided you with the tools to customize your reports for that tailored look.

Viewing the Reports

There are two views you can have of your generated reports: Design View, where all the down-to-earth organization occurs, and Preview which is ostensibly Print Preview.

Design View

There are 3 main ways to get to this view of a report:

1. From the initial database window, highlight the report you wish to view and then select the Design button.
2. Select the Design View option at the end of a wizard's questioning.
3. Click on the Preview icon when in Preview.

Preview

There are also 3 main ways of getting to this view of a report:

1. From the initial database window, highlight the report you wish to view and then select the Preview button.
2. Select the Preview option at the end of a wizard's questioning.
3. Click on the Design icon when in Design View.

Techniques Useful When Customizing Your Reports

The techniques for customizing are similar to those in form design.

The topics you should cover are:

- Selecting components that appear on a report design
- Moving the controls and labels that appear in the report design
- Resizing controls and labels
- Aligning controls and labels on a report
- Changing the font on some text
- Adding color to your report

Let's look at each of these techniques in turn, starting with selecting controls.

Selecting Labels And/Or Controls in the Report Design View

To select a control or a label click on it to produce the boxing effect shown below:

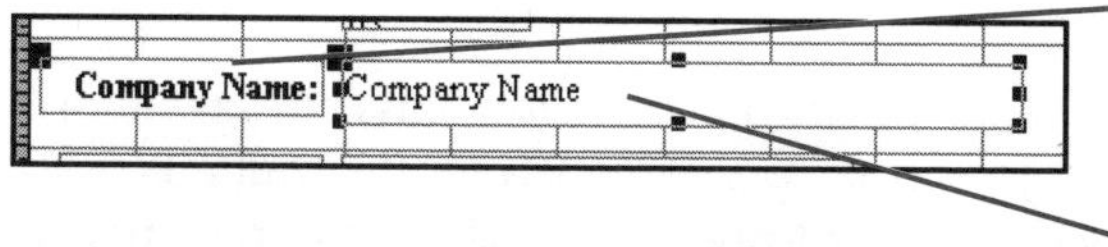

If you select a component that has an associated partner, the partner will also get a small box in the top left of its surround.

This is the component that has the focus which means it is active.

Using the point-and-click method, if you want to select multiple components, use the *Shift* key in the usual way. There are also two other ways to select multiple components on your form design:

If you want to select all the components in a strip across the screen:

- Place the mouse pointer onto the ruler on the left of the screen.
- While holding down the left mouse button, sweep out the required strip.

You will see that:

- A line appears across the page denoting the top of the strip.
- A line, moving with the pointer, appears, denoting the bottom of the strip.
- The section of the ruler between the two lines deepens in color.

All these features allow you to select exactly which components you require:

- If you want to select all the components in a block on the screen:
- Place the mouse pointer onto the screen near the top left component of the block.
- Hold down the left mouse button.
- Drag out a box to surround the components you want to select and release the mouse button.

All the components contained in this box will be selected.

Notice that as you drag the box to the required shape, the size of the box is represented on both rulers with the customary deeper color sections.

You may also notice that you don't have to surround all of a component to select it. If any part of a component falls inside the box you have dragged out, Access will include it in the selection. It is also possible to use the *Shift* key in combination with this method to select non-continuous blocks of components in your form design.

> Both of these methods can be used to select both components in a partnership. This can have interesting results when applying re-sizing or alignment techniques to the selected components on your report design.

Moving a Component

To move a component (and its associated partner):

- Select the component to move.
- Place the mouse pointer over the surround of the component that has the focus.

> You should place the pointer on the line and not on one of the boxes that appear on the surround.

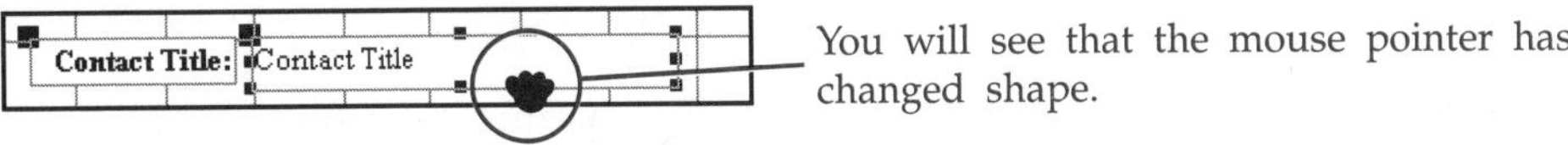

You will see that the mouse pointer has changed shape.

- Hold down the left mouse button and drag the components to their new position as seen below:

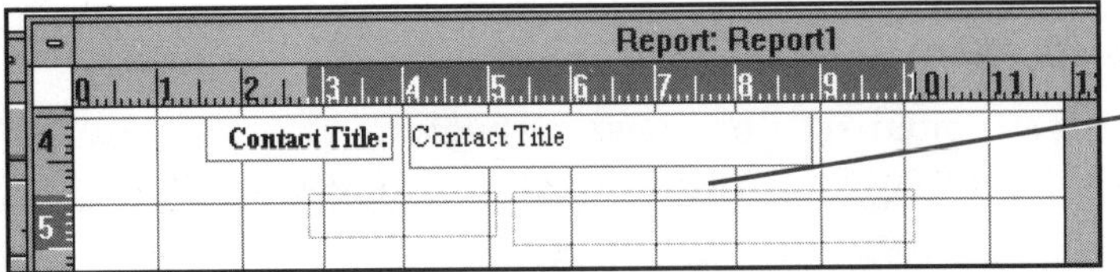

Notice the dotted lines. This is where the components will be moved to when you release the mouse button.

As you are moving any components around the screen, you may notice two shaded areas on the rulers around the edge of the screen. This shading shows you the exact size of the components you are moving, as well as showing you where they will appear when you release the mouse button.

If you want to move just one of the components in a selected partnership, move the pointer onto its top left box rather than the surround of the focused component. The mouse pointer will change as shown, and while the left mouse button is held down, Access will only move that component.

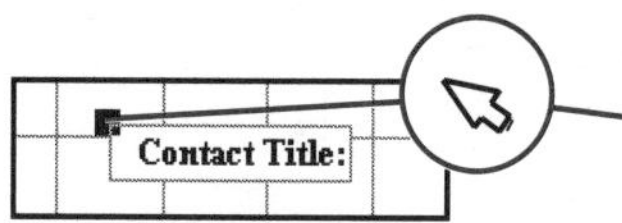

To move just the Contact Title control, place the mouse pointer on this box, and drag.

It is also possible to get Access to perform the movement of your components for you. Access allows you to select several components and then ask for them to be spaced in one of three different ways.

Spacing Option	Result
Make Equal	This makes the space between the components the same. Access does this by fixing the position of the outer components and moving the inner ones to accomplish this equal spacing.
Increase	This increases the spacing between components by one grid point. Access automatically applies the Make Equal function before increasing the space.
Decrease	This decreases the spacing between components by one grid point. Again, Access applies the Make Equal function before increasing the space.

Access 2.0 requires you to have selected at least three components before it can apply the Make Equal function.

To get Access to auto-space your components:

- Select the components that you want to auto-space.
- Select either Vertical Spacing or Horizontal Spacing from the Format menu.
- Select the type of auto-space that you want Access to perform.

Re-sizing a Component

To re-size a component:

- Focus on the component you want to re-size.
- Place the mouse pointer onto one of the boxes that appear on the surround:

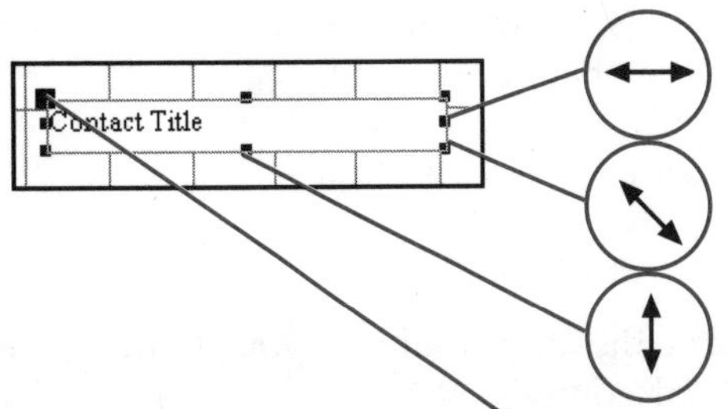

Depending on which box you place the pointer, the component can be stretched in one of three ways; by height, by width or by both.

The diagonal stretch is not available from this box. It is only used for single component moving as already shown.

It is also possible to get Access to auto-resize the components on your form. Using similar techniques to the auto-space functions, you can instruct Access to change the size of the selected components, corresponding to one of the components, the size of the grid, or simply to fit.

The selection available includes:

Sizing Option	Result
to Grid	This re-sizes the selected components based on the surrounding grid points. Access moves the corners of each component to the closest grid point, and therefore can produce some interesting effects.
to Tallest	This re-sizes all the selected components, so they all have the same height; that of the tallest.
to Shortest	This does the same as to Tallest, but based on the height of the smallest component.
to Narrowest	This re-sizes all the selected components, so they all have the same width; that of the narrowest.
to Widest	This does the same as to Narrowest, but based on the width of the widest component.
to Fit	This choice changes the size of the selected components so that the text can only just fit in the component size.

To get Access to perform any of these tasks:

- Select all the components you wish to affect.
- Select the appropriate command from the menu given under Size on the Format menu.

Aligning Components on a Report

To align a set of components:

- Select the set of components you wish to align along one line.
- Choose Align from the Format menu on the menu bar. This gives you the choice of four different ways to align the selected components: Left, Right, Top and Bottom.

If you select the Left-Align method, all the selected components will move to a line drawn down the left side of the component that is closest to the left side of the page. This idea can be applied to each of the other three methods of alignment.

- Highlight the method you require, and Access will perform your request. Below is a before and after sequence of the Left-Align method:

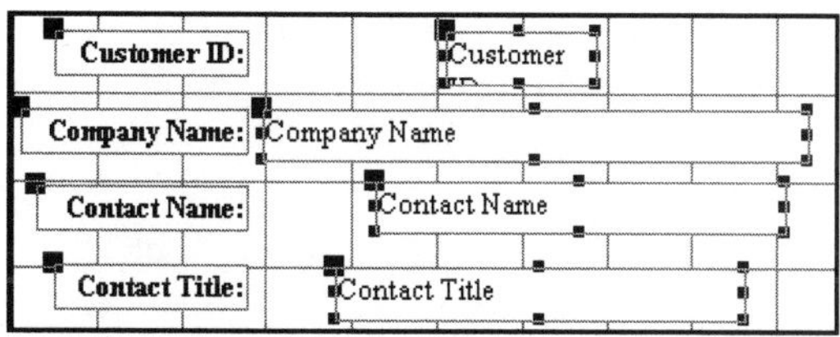

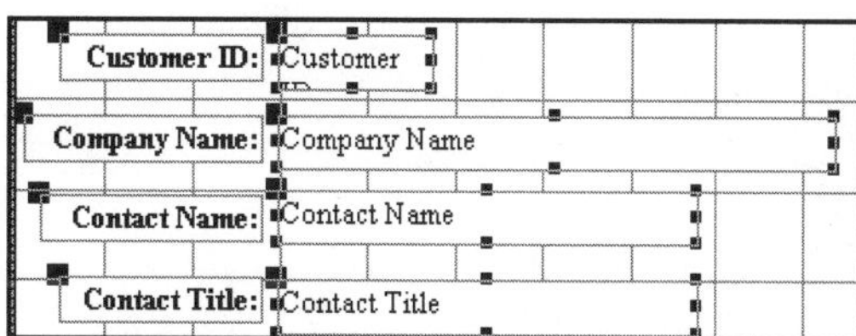

Only the selected components move and not their associated partners. To move the partners, you need to repeat the aligning, this time moving the partners that didn't move.

Changing the Font

Each component on your report can have a different font. To change the font of a given component:

- Focus on the relevant component.
- Select the appropriate tool to change the style you wish to alter, as shown below:

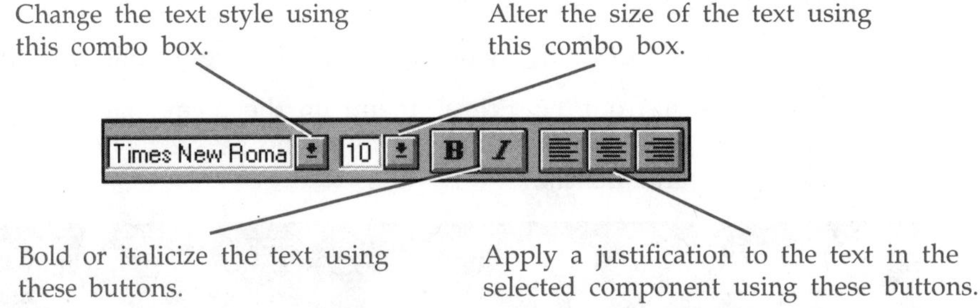

Change the text style using this combo box.
Alter the size of the text using this combo box.

Bold or italicize the text using these buttons.

Adding More Color to Your Report

It is possible to add color to not only the components that appear on your report, but also to the paper the components are drawn on. To add color to any part of your report:

- Select the component or the paper you wish to color.
- Click on the icon to open the palette.

Using The Palette

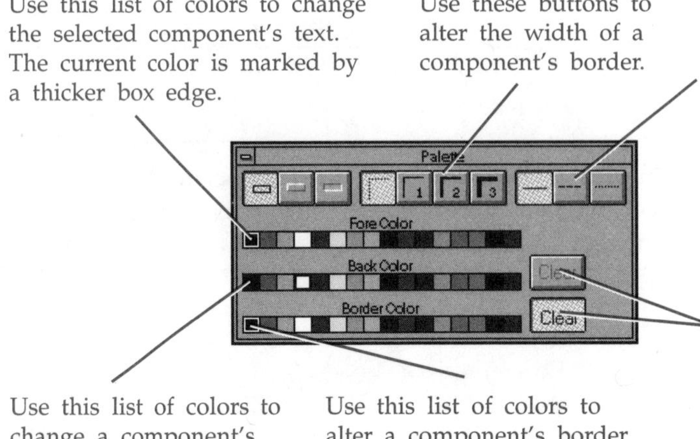

Use this list of colors to change the selected component's text. The current color is marked by a thicker box edge.
Use these buttons to alter the width of a component's border.
Use these buttons to change the solidity of the border; the choices are solid, dashes or dots.
Palette
1
2
3
Fore Color
Back Color
Border Color
Clear
Clear
If either of these buttons are de-selected, you cannot use the corresponding color list. Normally, these buttons link the choice of color to that of the report's paper. Back Color Clear is only available when the focused component is a label.
Use this list of colors to change a component's paper color.
Use this list of colors to alter a component's border color.

You can then use any of the features of the palette to add color and texture to your report design.

> If you de-select a component while the palette is open, the options the palette offers will change. To return the options, re-select the component. You can use this feature to quickly move between the components on your form design, leaving color changes as you go.

We have now dealt with all the basic features you can use to alter the results that the Report Wizard produces. Go on to advanced report generation with the chapter on calculations and graphs.

Troubleshooting

Q&A Can I improvise calculations within the report?

Yes, using Text Box with a custom expression. See Chapter 7 on calculations and graphs.

Q&A Can I embed a graph into my report?

Yes, by using a calculation to create a graph in situ with Graph Wizard, or by importing graphs from other OLE capable packages such as Excel in MS Office. See Chapters 7 and 8 on calculations and Import/Export.

CHAPTER 7

Calculations and Graphs

This is the first chapter that doesn't deal with an individual part of the database structure itself. Calculations can be used in queries, forms and reports, while the graphical outputs can be seen in both forms and reports.

Calculations are an integral part of creating useful graphs. There may be a number of excellent graphs you can produce using plain queries. Ultimately, however, you will need crafted calculations to make poignant visual representations.

If you are transferring any amount of your workload from spreadsheets, you will be familiar with a number of the calculation rules. You will be pleased with Access' ability to update graphing dynamically, just like major state-of-the-art spreadsheet software.

Microsoft Graph is on call to Access at any time, and you will find it a powerful partner in you quest for the definitive presentation.

In this chapter you will learn more about:

- Query calculations
- Uniquely identifying fields
- Operators and expressions
- The Expression Builder
- Microsoft Graph

Why Should I Use Calculations in My Database?

One of the major problems experienced by database users is that when data is entered into the package, the data doesn't always conform to the fields you designed in the first place. The source of information (the world as we know it) has given responses that didn't seem possible at the database planning stage, and so you (as the database designer) made no provision for them. This is due to a basic problem of data collection.

You can, of course, plan for flexibility. You can alter tables to handle disparate data until you review the structure or have room for rogue data in your present plan.

For example, suppose that you, along with 15 million other people, took a vacation in Florida last year, and you were asked to fill out a questionnaire that contained the following question: "Where did you go on vacation last year?" If Florida didn't appear in the list of possible answers then you and 15 million others would need to specify 'Other'. This category was added by the developer of the questionnaire to catch the small percentage of people on vacation who didn't go to the most popular destinations around the world. It wasn't really designed to catch all those who had taken a vacation in Florida itself.

Admittedly, this is a badly designed question, because everyone knows that a lot of people go on vacation in Florida every year. However, the topic is usually more abstract than 'vacation destinations', and the questions are therefore more complex to design. This means answers are more likely to be forgotten. The question may be designed by a questionnaire theorist who knows all about the ways and means of structuring questionnaires, but little about the subject matter itself. The people who are asked to fill in the questionnaire may not be very knowledgeable either. They are most likely to make a guess, based on the choices they are restricted to, rather than give an absolutely true answer.

Problems experienced in data collection could be fixed at the planning stage of the database. Data can come into the database scattered across a wide band of possibilities, even if questions are very specific. It's as important to get the structure of input correct, as it is to get the content right.

This is where calculations and graphical displays come into their own. With calculations, the data can be pushed to manipulate its information. For example, instead of simply 'hours worked' the information is given as 'normal hours' and 'overtime'. With a few set constraints on the calculation required you could produce 'pay outstanding', 'required tax' or even 'holiday remaining'.

Once you have decent calculations these results can then be collected together and presented in a form or report as a graphical representation of the data.

Before you see some results from the Access Graph Wizard, you must realize it usually bases its work on the results of calculations, and not raw data. You must know how to ask Access to perform calculations.

Calculations

Calculations can be defined at any stage of the database design after the table structure has been set up. Like a spreadsheet, Access can take entries and perform mathematical operations upon them. However, instead of working on individual cells as spreadsheets do, Access works on the entries found in a field, and produces a corresponding field of outputs.

For example, suppose in your database you have four fields called PayWeek1 to PayWeek4, each designed to hold the weekly pay for each employee. You can ask Access to add these four fields together to give PayMonth, a field that holds the monthly pay of each employee.

The calculation will produce the required information for *each* employee, and place it in the relevant cell in the PayMonth field. The entries in this new field will be used as the basis for your graph.

There are two ways of asking Access to perform a calculation - the first involving a query, the second involving forms and reports.

Query Calculations

The method for creating a custom calculation in a query is simple:

- Open the query that has the correct underlying tables containing fields you wish to work on.
- Move into a new column of the QBE grid.

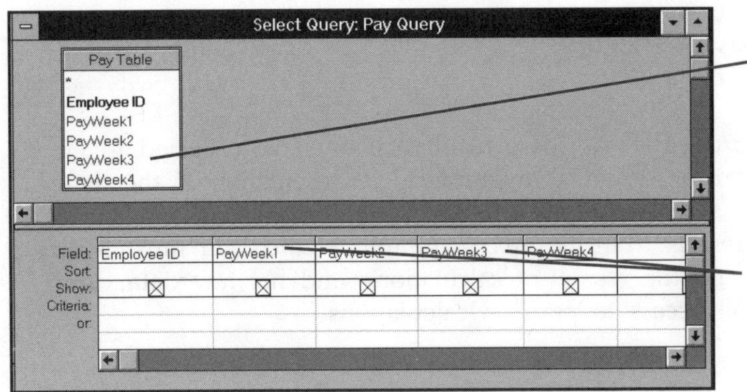

This is the table that contains all the fields you need to create the required calculation.

These fields have been placed in the QBE grid to illustrate it. They are not required for the calculation to work.

- Type the name you will use to refer to the calculation, and place a colon after it.

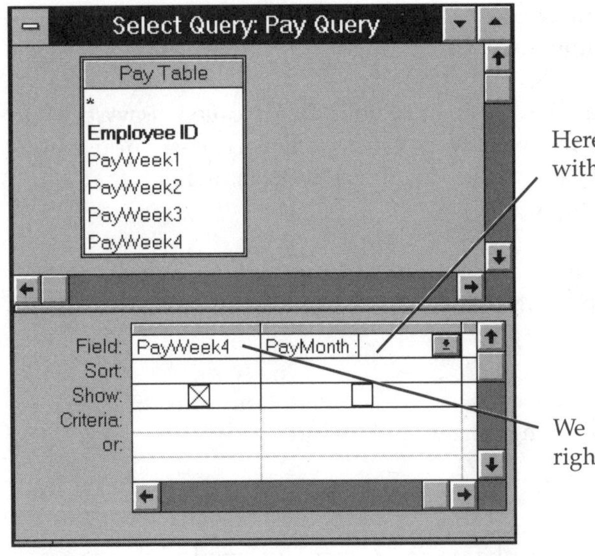

Here is the start of our custom calculation, with its colon.

We have moved the QBE grid along to the right to work on the calculation space.

- After the colon, type the required expression ('4 weeks of pay'). The expression can refer to other fields contained in the underlying table or query by typing in the name of the field surrounded by square brackets ([ ]). These field names are used just like set constraints. For example, [PayWeek1/5] is the value of Pay Week1 divided by 5 to give a daily wage.

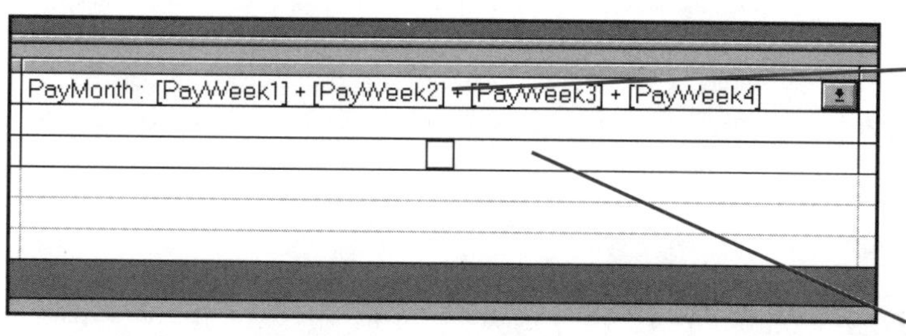

You need to use square brackets around the field names.. The syntax for the expression is very similar to a normal mathematical version.

This calculation happens all in one section of the QBE grid.

The query can now be run by selecting the Run button. When you select this option, Access checks the Show box for this custom calculation, and then produces a query dynaset something like this:

Select Query: Pay Query

Employee ID	PayWeek1	PayWeek2	PayWeek3	PayWeek4	PayMonth
1	£23.65	£432.56	£352.45	£56.32	£864.98
2	£435.23	£345.87	£345.50	£1,746.45	£2,873.05
3	£456.77	£345.65	£1,242.46	£456.75	£2,501.63
4	£987.45	£435.50	£46.57	£408.47	£1,877.98

You can see the title of the calculation is used by Access for the column heading.

This column shows the sum of each employee's pay over the four weeks that make up this month.

There are three ways to alter the contents of the column headings that appear in the dynaset:

- Change the field name back in the table (not recommended).
- Use the Caption property found in the Query Properties box.
- Use the custom calculation syntax:

```
NewName : [OldName]
```

A custom calculation column heading cannot be changed using the Caption property.

Sample Calculations

Some examples of calculations with the correct syntax that can be used in a QBE grid are:

```
PayMonth: [PayWeek1]+[PayWeek2]+[ PayWeek3]+[ PayWeek4]
```

This calculation adds up the pay for each employee over the four weeks of the month and places it in the PayMonth calculated field. You may now refer to this field name as if it were a true field, filled with data entered by the user of the database.

```
AveWeekPay: [PayMonth]/4
```

This calculation takes the calculated data in PayMonth and divides it by 4 to give the average weekly pay for each employee, and places this information in the AveWeekPay calculated field.

```
FullName: [FirstName]&" "&[LastName]
```

This calculation brings together the first and last names of your employees into one field. Note a space is placed between the contents of the two entries. This is important as Access doesn't recognize a space is required unless you state you want one.

```
Length Of Employment: DateDiff ("d", [Date of Employment], Now())
```

This calculation works out how many days each employee has worked at the company, based on today's date, given by the Now () function, and the field Date Of Employment, which contains the date that appears on their initial contract.

Using Calculations in Forms and Reports

The second method for using calculations in your database involves forms and reports. You may have noticed when in the design view of a form or report the control component of each field contains some text.

This text shows you where the information Access will place in this component comes from. For example, the screen below shows the text in the control component of a field from the Orders form in the Access 2.0 sample database, NWind:

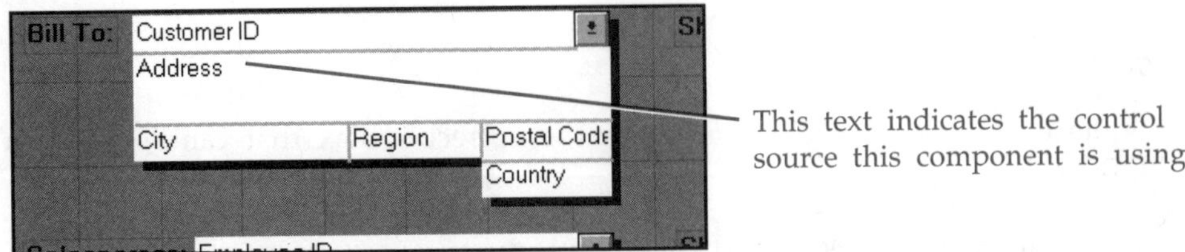

As you can see the control contains the text Address which informs Access that the information that must appear here should come from the field called Address. If the form or report is based upon a query that has the custom calculation included, then the name of the custom calculation will be given here. However, the mathematical expression you have used in the query cannot be viewed here using this method. Only the name you gave to the expression can be viewed (such as PayMonth or AveWeekPay).

To avoid this problem and the need for a query, Access allows the custom calculation to be defined at the form or report design stage. This means the need for a query is removed, so saving memory space. You will lose the advantages of using a query (in other words the sorting and the selection that is also available when using a query). However it does mean the calculation Access will perform is visible on the form or report design view, and therefore can also be edited.

The method for placing components onto the form or report is dealt with in Chapters 10 and 11. However, the method required to produce the whole custom calculation is dealt with in this chapter.

Creating Custom Calculations in Forms and Reports

To create custom calculations in your forms and reports follow the steps given below:

- Open the toolbox by selecting the icon from the tool bar.
- Select the Text Box button in the toolbox as shown below:

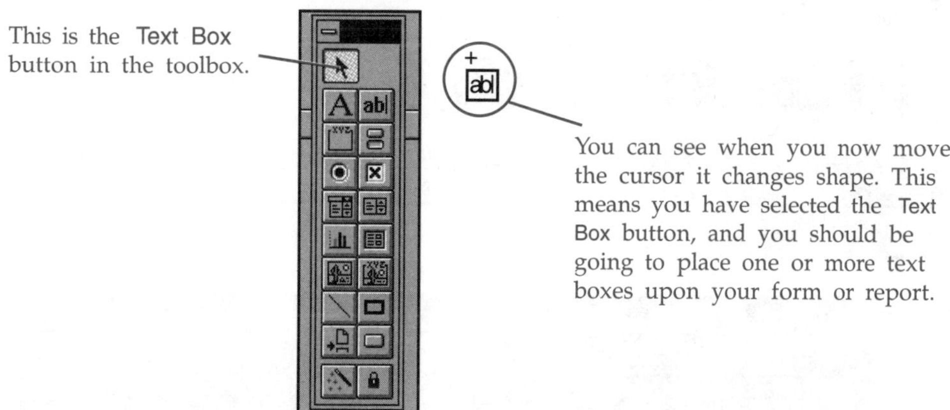

This is the Text Box button in the toolbox.
You can see when you now move the cursor it changes shape. This means you have selected the Text Box button, and you should be going to place one or more text boxes upon your form or report.

- Place the pointer onto the paper of your form or report, at the place you want the top left of the text box to appear.
- While holding down the left mouse button, drag out the shape of the text box you require so it looks something like the one shown below:

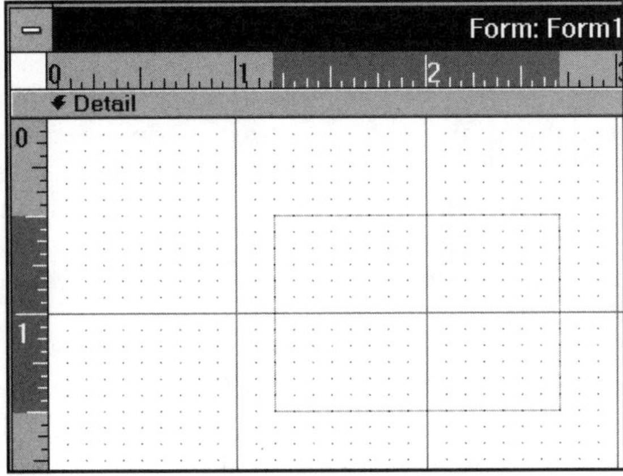

- Highlight this unbound control (the one you have just made) with the pointer and its Properties box to see the Control Source property.
- In that property type is the expression you wish Access to calculate. All expressions should begin with an equals sign. This tells Access the control source with this component will use the following expression:

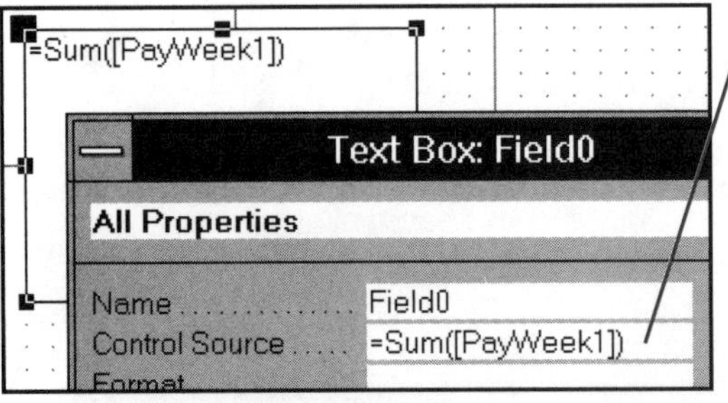

The control source entry and the text that appears in the component are the same.

> The correct choice of the operator or expression is important in terms of the field type the operator or expression is going to act upon. Some maths operators will only work on number fields, and some text operators will only work on text or memo fields. These restrictions are given in the guide in Appendix II or in the Access Help screens.

- Remember to place square brackets ([ ]) around any names of fields you wish operators or expressions to act upon. This tells Access which words definitely refer to field names. Access may insert them itself if it recognizes any field names in the text you type.

Uniquely Identifying Fields

All these rules are the same as when a custom calculation is defined by a query. The only difference between the two processes is that you may have to give the path of any fields you wish to use in your calculations. Computer language users will already be familiar with the idea of the path of the field. It's this method that Access uses to uniquely define the fields that are included in the database (that is, a guide to their position in storage).

Access uses identifiers to connect the names of the various components of the database together to produce the required path. There are two identifiers that Access recognizes: the exclamation mark, (!), and the dot, (.). Access also recognizes the words form, report and screen. Form and report clearly refer to the forms and reports included in the database, while screen refers to what is appearing on screen. This, together with a combination of other commands, can be used to refer to other forms and reports that may be active on screen. Access will also recognize the names of the parts of the database you have named if you place square brackets ([ ]) around them when you refer to them in the path.

Two examples of the full path names of parts of the sample database are:

Path	Explanation
[Pay Table]![PayWeek1]	The PayWeek1 field in the Pay Table table
Report.[Pay Report]![Employee ID].Visible	The Employee ID field's Visible property in 'Pay Report' report

You can see the path begins with the most general part of the database, and becomes more specific as the path is read from left to right. Using these definite paths for the various parts of the database, you can unambiguously define the calculations you require Access to work out in forms and reports.

Note that the exclamation mark (!) denotes that the following term is user-defined, while the dot (.) denotes the following term should be an Access 2.0 key-word, such as Table or Visible.

Operators and Expressions

In these calculations there are several types of operations Access allows the user to employ to produce the required effects. These include:

- Maths operators (add, subtract, tan etc.)
- Constant values and value comparisons
- Logic operators (Not, And, Or, etc.)

There are more complex operators that deal with more specific problems such as definite object naming and text manipulation.

> There is a difference between an operator and an expression. An operator is a simple symbol (usually mathematical) used to signify an operation; for example, (+) means add together. An expression is a more complex instruction for Access which combines several operations; for example, Sum means add up all the contents of this group.

For a guide to the operators and expressions you can use in any calculation in Access see Appendix II (or look in the Access Help screens).

You can now produce custom calculations in all parts of the database allowed by Access 2.0. You are on your way to being able to produce impressive results from your raw data through a combination of queries and calculations.

One feature that you may find particularly useful in your database design (and especially in expression creation) is the Build function, which we will now discuss.

Building With Access 2.0

Microsoft took to heart requests from database designers to include something like builders in the new Access. In Access 2.0 terms, a builder is a tool designed to help you create a given part of your database. Unlike a wizard, the builder doesn't produce large database components such as tables or reports. It concentrates instead on lesser problems such as the choice of color for your paper, or the macro for an event property of a component.

Some of the builders you may come across when you select the Ellipse button, [...] , include:

The Field Builder in Table Design

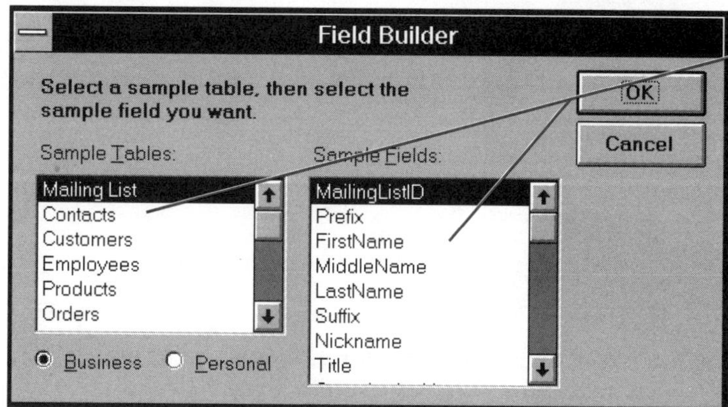

Select any of the fields the Table Wizard can use to create a table and it will be added into the table design from which you called the builder. Highlighting the different tables will give you a different list of fields to choose from.

The Color Builder in the Properties Box

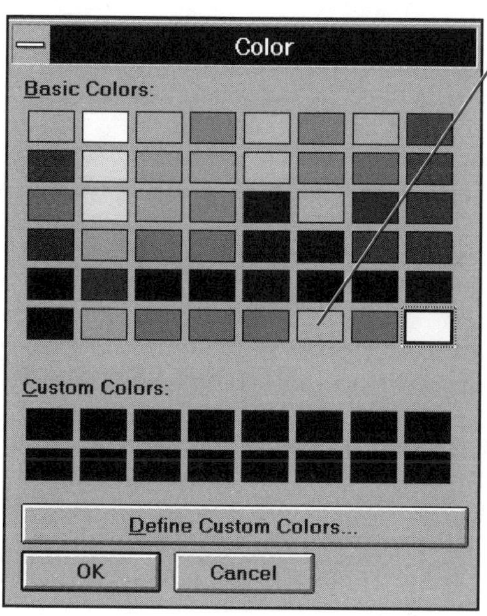

To select the color you want for the property (selected by the Build button) click the left mouse button when the pointer is over the color you require.

The Choose Builder in the Properties Box

To select a method code behind event properties you use the Choose Builder from the Properties Box.

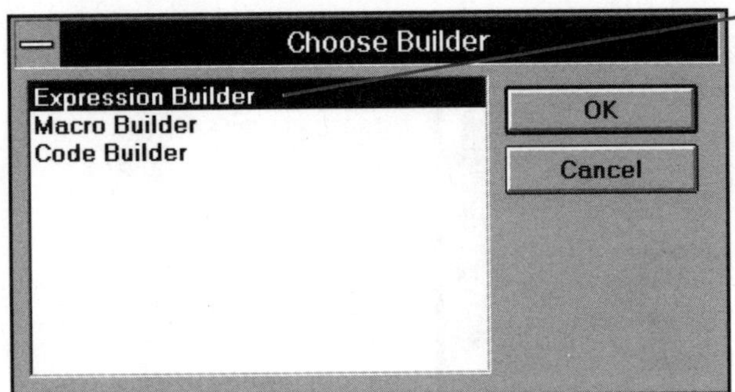

Select the method you want to use to create the code. The code will be triggered when the event from which you called the builder occurs.

There are many other builders you may stumble across in your journey through database design which help you with your input masks (including the Input Mask Builder). One is the query builder which helps you transform a basic table query into one that generates reports and forms. However, the most important builder, and the one that crops up the most, is the Expression Builder.

The Expression Builder

The Expression Builder was the number one builder requested by database designers when Microsoft asked for suggestions. One of the most common errors that occurs when producing any expression or calculation in the database is that the appropriate syntax goes adrift and makes the expression or calculation do inappropriate things.

Essentially the Expression Builder is a simple tool working on a clever principle. The user selects each individual term or symbol and Access fills in the appropriate syntax.

When you select the Build button which calls the Expression Builder (select it from nearly anywhere in the database design including property boxes and conditions in macros) you will be presented with the screen opposite.

The Expression Builder Screen

This window contains the expression you are building. If the entry from which you called the Expression Builder has any contents in it, when you open the Expression Builder it will be displayed here.

You can click on these buttons to quickly select the appropriate operator instead of going through the screens below.

When you have highlighted the property of the component in the given database object you can place it into the Expression Builder window (and therefore the entry from which you called the Expression Builder) by double-clicking on it or by selecting Paste.

This folder represents the place where the Expression Builder was called from, in this case Form1.

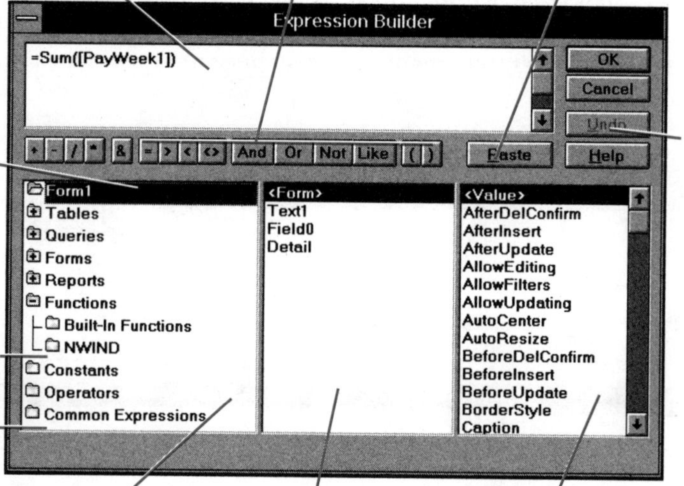

Select this button to reverse the last action you performed.

These folders contain all the common expressions (Sum), operators, (+) and constants (Date()) Access 2.0 has to offer.

Here are all the components of your database, stored in folders, just like Windows File Manager. If the file contains a plus sign it shows it contains subfiles. You can view these subfiles by double-clicking on the file. This gives a breakdown of which subfiles it contains. A minus sign in a file shows it's already open.

In this window you will find the contents of the folder you have highlighted. In this case it's the names of all the components that appear on Form1, as well as the name of the object itself. Through this object name you can get to all the properties of that object.

This window contains all the properties associated with the component you selected in the previous window. <Value> is used to get the contents of the component, while the rest of the entries in the list are the properties that would appear in the Properties box for that component.

To see some of the interesting features of the Expression Builder let's look at each step involved in creating an expression with it.

Using Date Diff (): An Example

The following steps give the stages you will have to complete to create a DateDiff () expression. They also illustrate some of the points that can help you with your inventions. DateDiff is a function that calculates the difference between two dates using a given unit of counting; that is minutes, days, months and so on.

- From the appropriate part of your database design call up the Expression Builder. In this example the query design, Pay Query, is being used. The DateDiff function is being used to calculate the term of employment of each employee by finding the difference between the start of their employment and the present time. The Expression Builder looks like this:

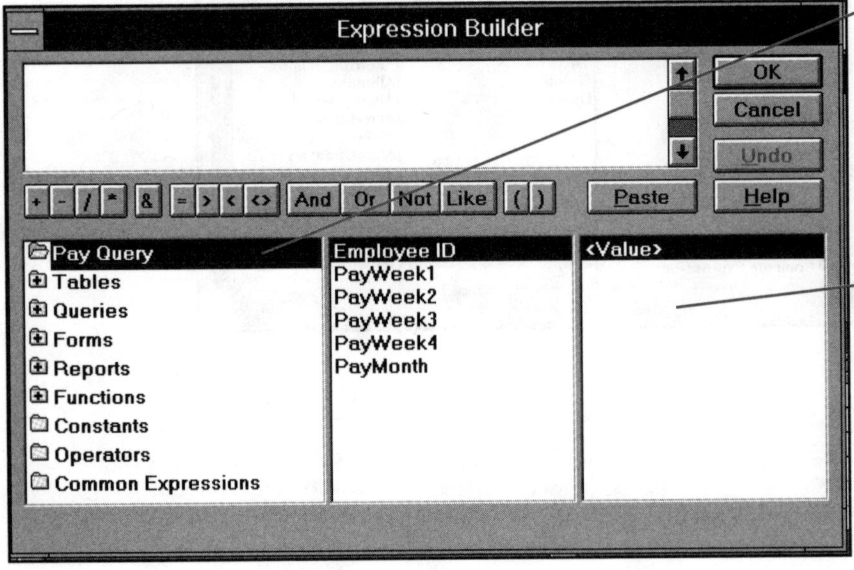

Pay Query appears as the source object.

This window is blank. This shows there is currently no entry in the column that has been selected for the DateDiff calculation in the QBE grid.

- Select Built-in Functions
- Highlight the DateDiff function as shown below, and press the Paste button.

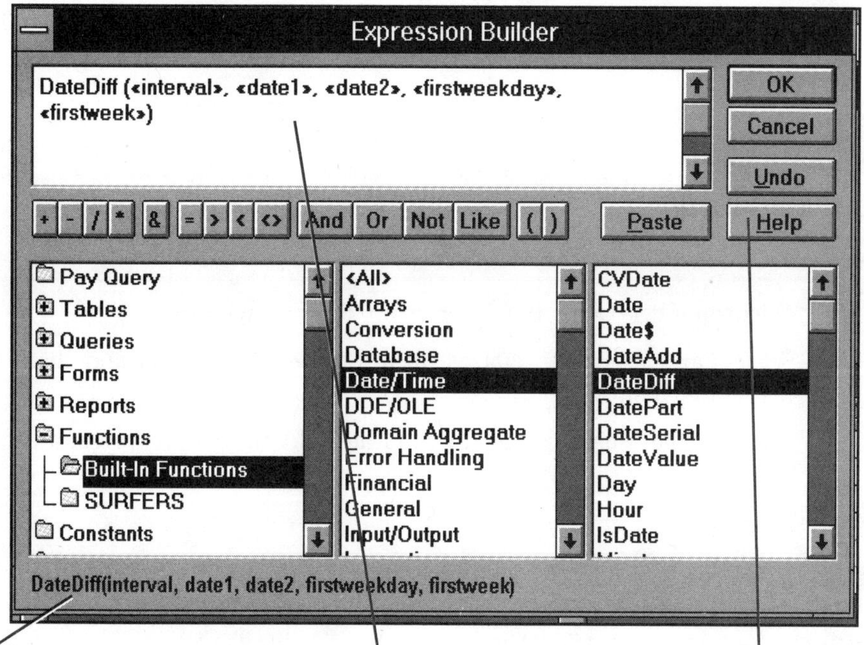

Access gives you an example of the syntax it expects from the function you highlight.

You can see when you press Paste Access puts a copy of your highlighted selection into this window. You must now customize this general template to get the exact results you require.

Select the Help button if you don't understand any of the syntax. The symbol << >> means it's asking for an entry.

- You now need to customize the DateDiff function that has been placed into the Expression Builder window. If you don't understand any of the syntax given with the general template, select the Help button while the function is still highlighted. The terms you should be interested in are:

Term	Explanation
Interval	The unit of count the function uses to work out the difference between the two dates.
Date1	The beginning date of the interval.
Date2	The end date of the interval.
Firstweekday	One of the reference points Access may use depending on the selected interval. You can select any day of the week.
Firstweek	This deals with the first week of the year defaulting to 1st January and is the one reference point Access may use. You can choose the first full week or the first with four working days.

- Click on the word 'interval' in the Expression Builder window. The whole word should be highlighted. Type 'ww' as shown below:

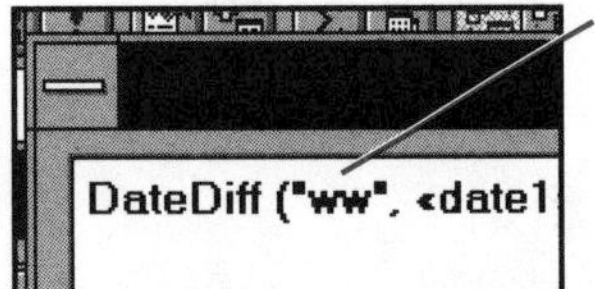

The interval ww is understood as 'count using weeks as your units'. The Help button gives you more information on the different available intervals (it shows you the DateDiff screen).

- Click on <date1> in the Expression Builder window.
- Select Pay Table under Tables, then Start of Employment and then <Value> (as shown below).
- Click on the Paste button to put the field into the expression.

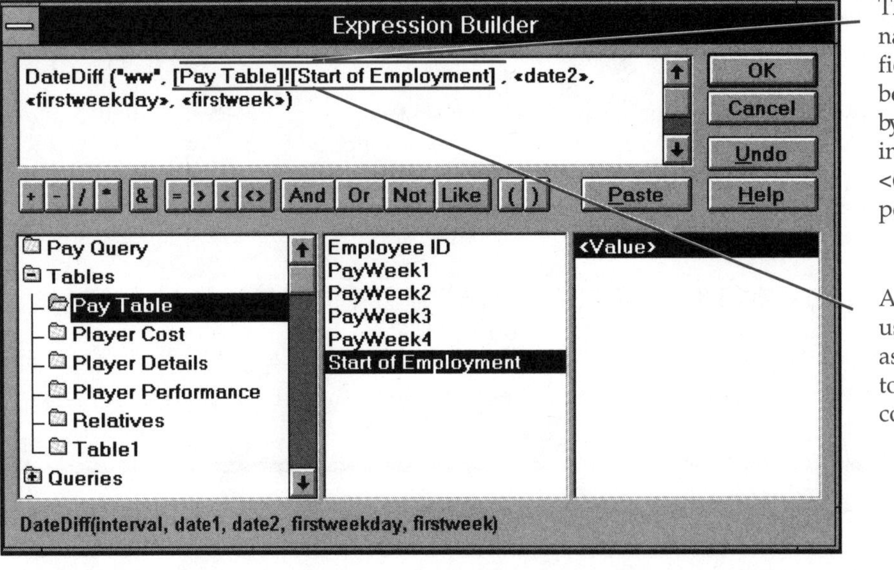

The full path name for the field has been inserted by Access into the <date1> position.

Access will use this date as the place to start the count from.

- Click on <date2> in the Expression Builder window. Select Common Expressions, Current Date and Date () as shown below. Put this field into the <date2> position using the Paste button:

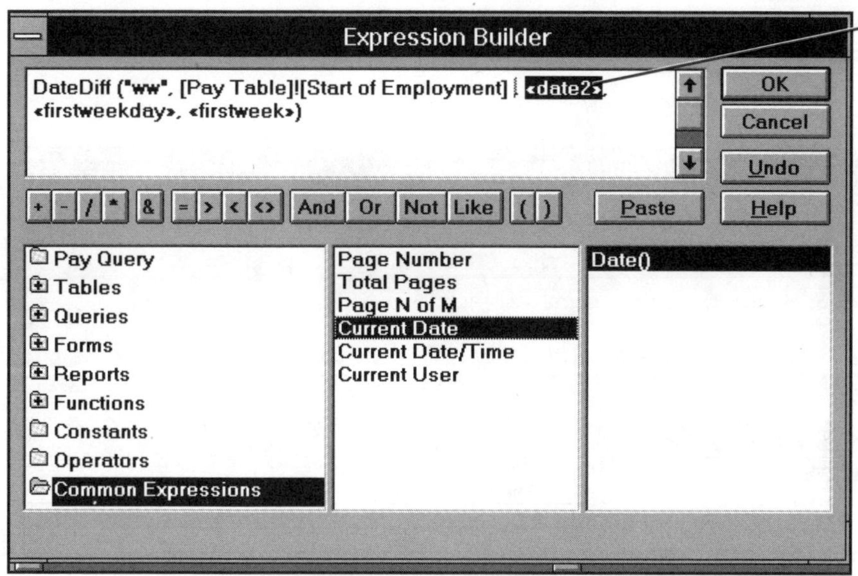

Access will use this date as the finishing point for its count; that is, today's day automatically defined by the term Date(). Access is finding the length of time between each employee's first day at work and the current day.

- You can accept the default values in a function by leaving them blank. In this situation the defaults are acceptable, therefore highlight the rest of the function syntax as shown below and delete it.

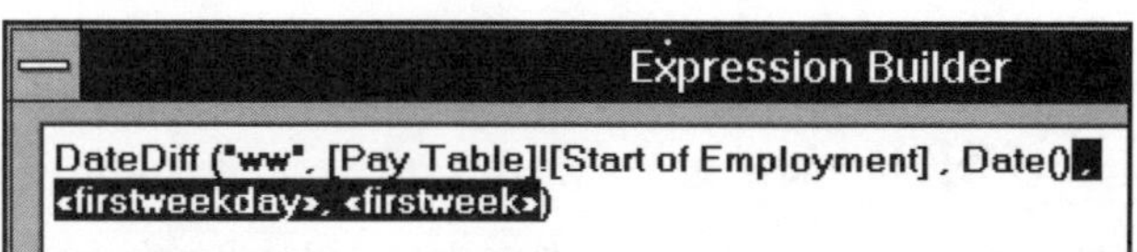

- Because this expression is going into a QBE grid, you need to attach a descriptive name to the front of the expression. This is the usual practice with custom calculations. Doing so will give you the final results.

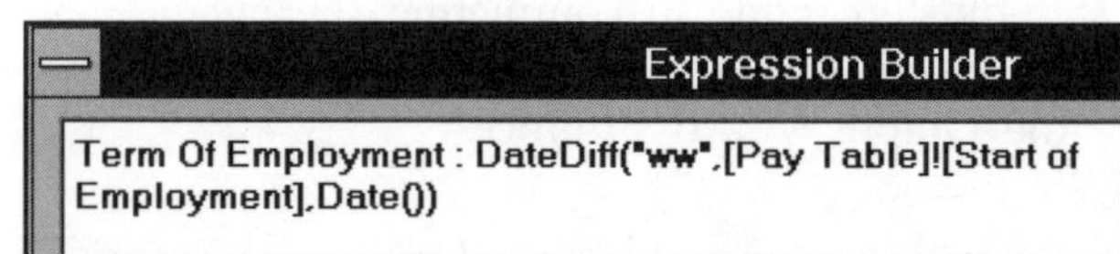

If you are producing a custom calculation for a form or report instead of a descriptive name use an equals sign (=) in front of the expression.

Now select the OK button, and Access will transfer the contents of the Expression Builder window into the appropriate column in the QBE grid.

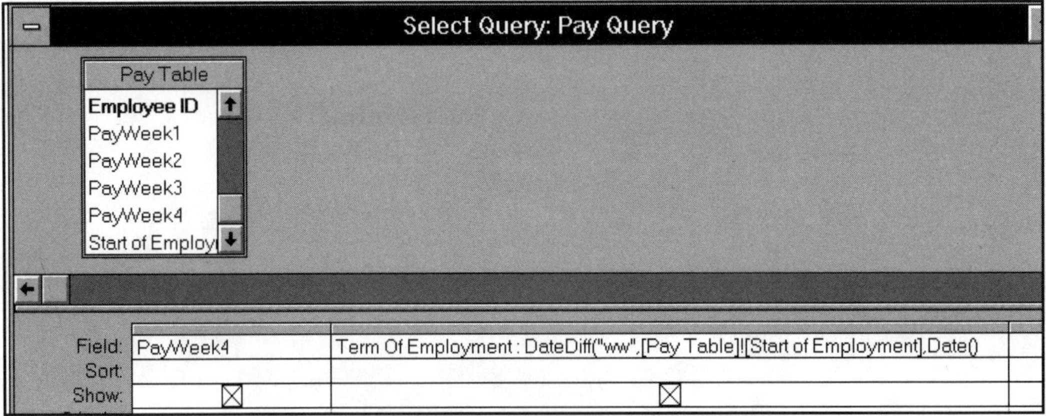

This example shows how you can use the Build button and the Expression Builder to produce custom calculations anywhere in your database design. All you need are the help screens on the various function syntax and a good database plan.

Microsoft Graph

Microsoft has included a Graph Wizard to help Access with the creation of the graphs and other visual presentations of the information in the database. The Graph Wizard can be called from the Form or Report windows and the graph you create can be placed in the form or report. Follow the procedure for placing all other new components as given in chapters 5, 6 and 10.

Here is a step-by-step guide to completing the creation of a graph with the aid of the Graph Wizard, showing how to provide the correct data, and the default results that the Graph Wizard produces.

The Graph Wizard

The Graph Wizard can be used to create two general types of graph: the embedded type (included in the body of a form or report) or the stand-alone type used for single-page emphasis.

The stand-alone graph is produced through the form design process for a type of form (Graph being one of the choices). Requesting the Graph form calls the Graph Wizard and prompts you for the information it needs to construct the graph, as we will then show you.

To call up the Graph Wizard for the construction of an embedded graph you must be in either Form or Report Design View, with the underlying table or query in view.

The Graph Wizard is currently asleep, and to wake it you must call it from the toolbox.

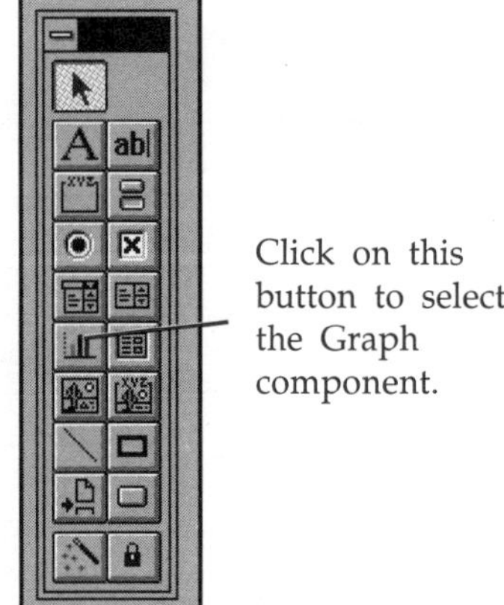

Click on this button to select the Graph component.

Place the mouse pointer onto the form or report's paper, and holding down the left mouse button drag out the size and shape of the control that will hold the graph.

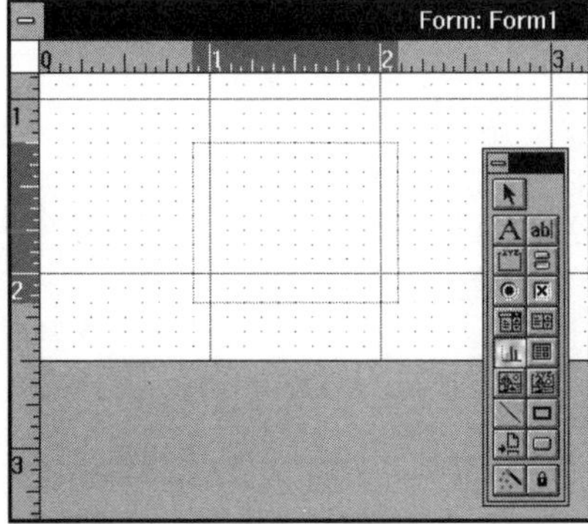

Release the mouse button when you have the size and shape of the control approximately correct. This causes the Graph Wizard to appear with its first screen. The taskmaster noted that you selected the button in the toolbox and prepared the Graph Wizard for your call. Follow the directions given on this screen and the following screen to produce your graph (a more detailed explanation of this procedure is given in Chapter 5).

There are different types of graph you can produce with the Graph Wizard.

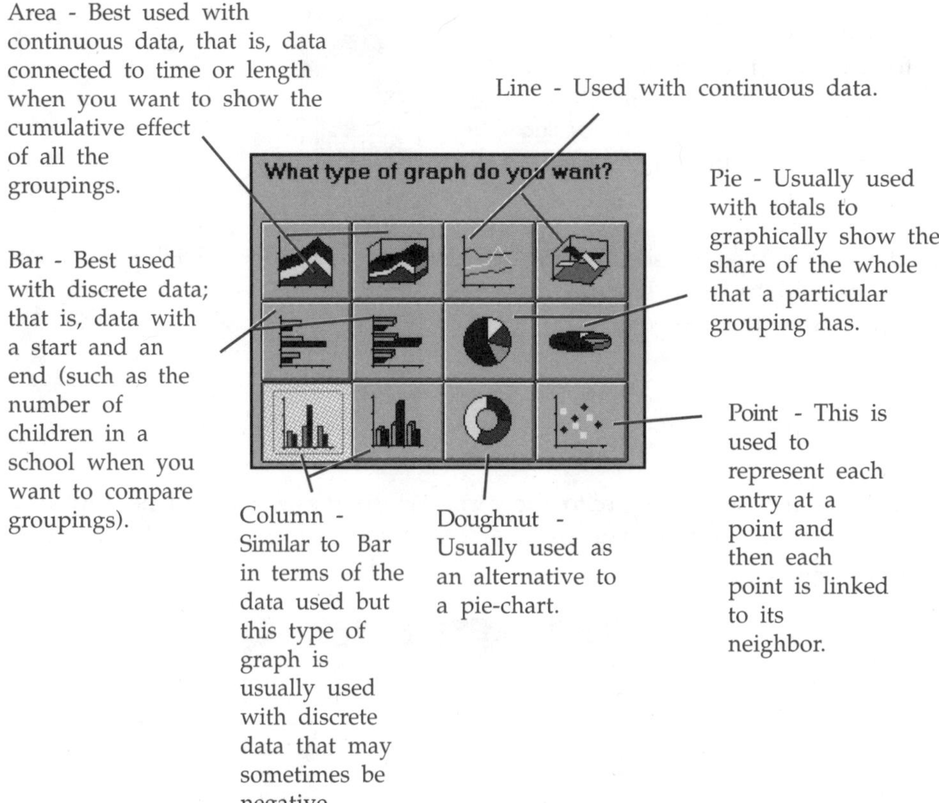

Area - Best used with continuous data, that is, data connected to time or length when you want to show the cumulative effect of all the groupings.
Line - Used with continuous data.
What type of graph do you want?
Pie - Usually used with totals to graphically show the share of the whole that a particular grouping has.
Bar - Best used with discrete data; that is, data with a start and an end (such as the number of children in a school when you want to compare groupings).
Point - This is used to represent each entry at a point and then each point is linked to its neighbor.
Column - Similar to Bar in terms of the data used but this type of graph is usually used with discrete data that may sometimes be negative.
Doughnut - Usually used as an alternative to a pie-chart.

The choice of graph you make really depends on the way you want the data presented. There are some forms of data that naturally fit with some kinds of graph; for example, distinct numbers work well with column or bar charts, while continuous numbers work better with pie-charts or line graphs.

> Distinct numbers are individual whole numbers like 1, 2 and 3, whereas a continuous range would be 1 to 3 and includes fractions (1.1, 2½ and so on).

Microsoft Graph

When you have answered the questions posed by the Graph Wizard you will be given a graph, either in a form or report. It probably won't look like this:

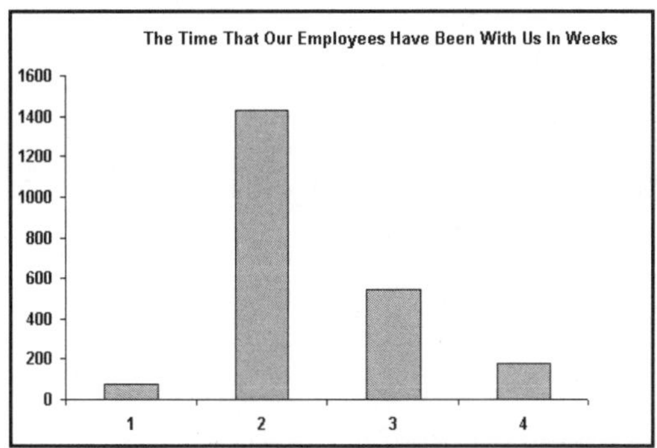

The Graph Wizard is quite limiting and some of the questions it asks are ambiguous at times. This is because the Graph Wizard only has access to a small amount of the power contained in Microsoft Graph. Fortunately, Access 2.0 allows you to go straight to Microsoft Graph once you have completed your question and answer section with the Graph Wizard. This enables you to use the power of the true Graph Designer.

To get to Microsoft Graph double-click on the control that contains the graph in your form or report. Access will open Microsoft Graph and pass through your graph's details.

This is the table of data Access has provided for Microsoft Graph to work on.

This is the graph Microsoft Graph has produced based on the data Access 2.0 has provided.

All the alterations you can make to the graph are controlled by the icons and menus given here.

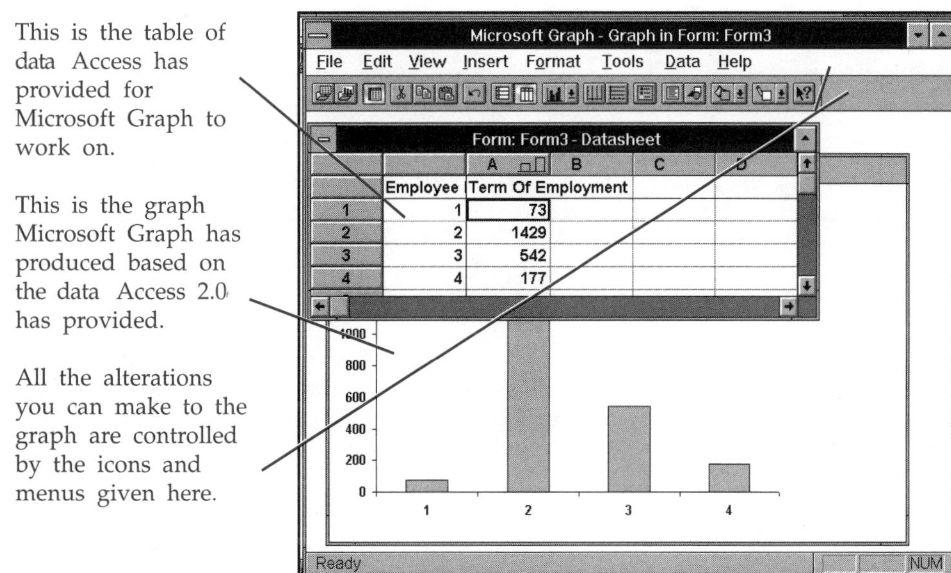

Let's look at each of these three important sections of Microsoft Graph in turn. This will give us an idea of what Microsoft Graph can do. You can then see an example of the alterations that can be made to some Graph Wizard results.

The Table of Data

The table of data Access passes to Microsoft Graph will look something like this.

		A	B	C	D
	Employee	Term Of Employment			
1	1	73			
2	2	1429			
3	3	542			
4	4	177			
5					
6					

The columns of data under relevant headings.

Rows hold data from individual records.

It is these rows and columns the Graph Wizard is concerned with when it asks you if the data is organized in rows or columns.

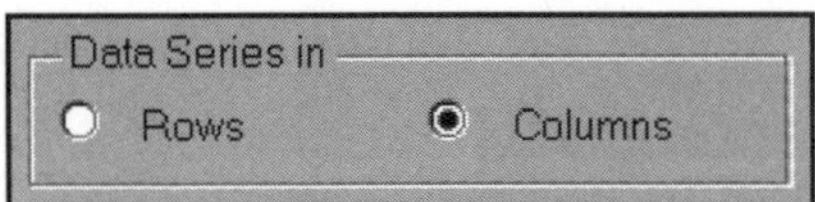

By default Access 2.0 will provide the data in a columnar pattern (as shown above). In some cases you want the data to be taken by row so you should therefore:

- Select Row option in the Graph Wizard screen
- Select Series In Rows from the Data menu
- Click on the icon in Microsoft Graph

It's in this window that any changes to the data should be made. These changes can only be seen in either the graph in Microsoft Graph or the graph control while in Design View. As soon as you change to the proper view of the form or report, Access goes back to the underlying table for data to create a graph from. You should alter the data in the table to make permanent changes to a graph's contents.

The Graph

When you enter the graph into Microsoft Graph the end result produced from the table data looks a little like this:

The title of the graph can be changed to anything you want. The default is usually the setting given by the table or query on which the graph is based.

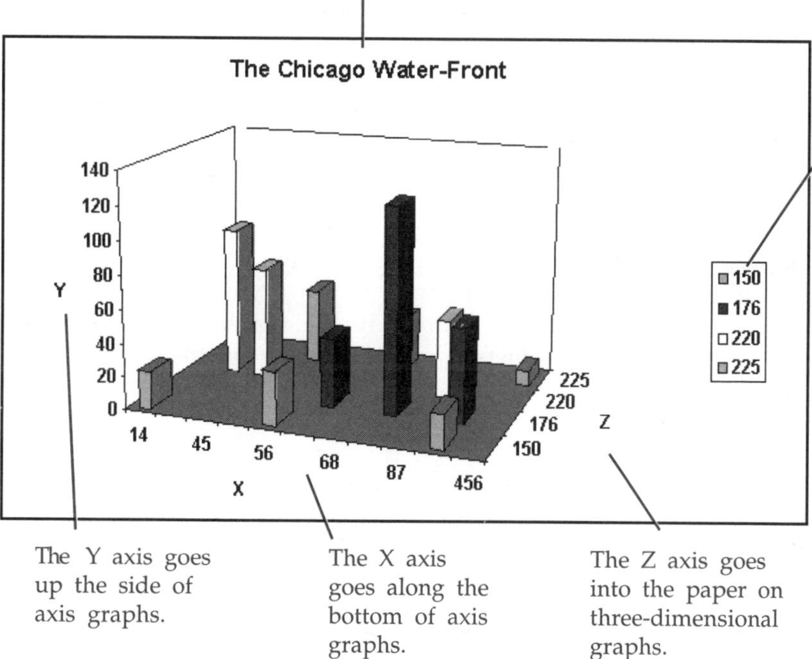

The legend for the graph is mainly used on graphs like pie-charts to distinguish between the different subjects that appear on it. Usually a pie-chart is multi-colored or multi-shaded, each color or shading representing a different subject contained in the data table.

The Y axis goes up the side of axis graphs.

The X axis goes along the bottom of axis graphs.

The Z axis goes into the paper on three-dimensional graphs.

This screen is useful for selecting the part of the graph you want to alter. In the same way as selecting components on a form or a report just click on the part you are interested in and it will be surrounded by boxes to indicate it's ready for alteration.

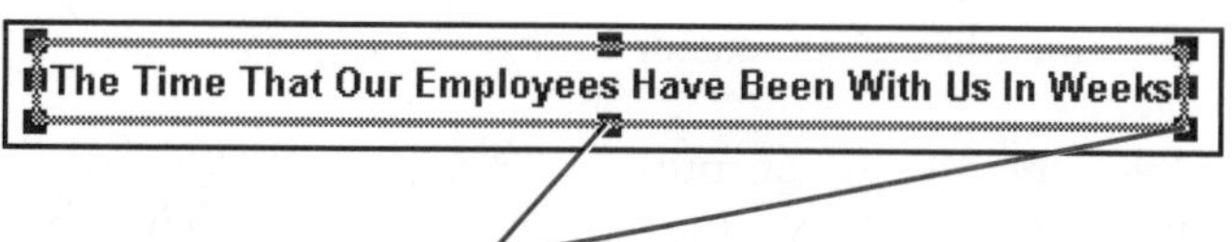

These are the boxes that appear around the selected part of your graph. Any of the commands you issue from the menu or icon bars will now affect this highlighted section of the graph rather than the graph in general.

To re-type any of the headings change them in the data table. If you want to change any of the labels that appear in the graph double-click on them. A cursor will appear at the end of the text and you will be able to delete and re-type the contents of the label.

The Menu and the Icons

These icons and menus (like all the others in Access 2.0) are where you get control over the shape, look and overall presentation of your graph.

Rather than describe all the facilities that appear on the icon and menu bars, let's go through an example of translating results from Graph Wizard into a really impressive graphical display of data.

Microsoft Graph: An Example

Let's use the Graph Wizard to create a free-standing graph in a form. Microsoft has produced a query in NWind (upon which a graph can easily be based) called Orders Details Extended. You can produce a graph of all the orders the company has received from customers by plotting them on the Y axis. You will then be able to see the spread of total order costs over a fairly long period of time.

The directors of the company would be able to use this to forecast the growth of the company, while the accountants could pull lots of interesting figures from this graph (for example, the amount of money available to be spent in eighteen months time).

You can get this free-standing graph by going through the normal procedure to create a new form, based upon the Order Details Extended query, and then choosing the Graph Wizard option to produce the graph:

- Select the Order ID and Extended Price fields to be included in the graph. Order ID identifies each order. Extended Price is the custom calculation it will produce by multiplying Unit Price by Quantity Ordered.
- Select the Order ID to appear on the X axis.
- Select a 2D column chart. This is best suited to the data because it's discrete and allows an easier comparison between values.

Now as you click on the Finish button the Graph Wizard will return you to the form's design view. To access Microsoft Graph double-click on the control that holds the graph. It will look something like the screen opposite.

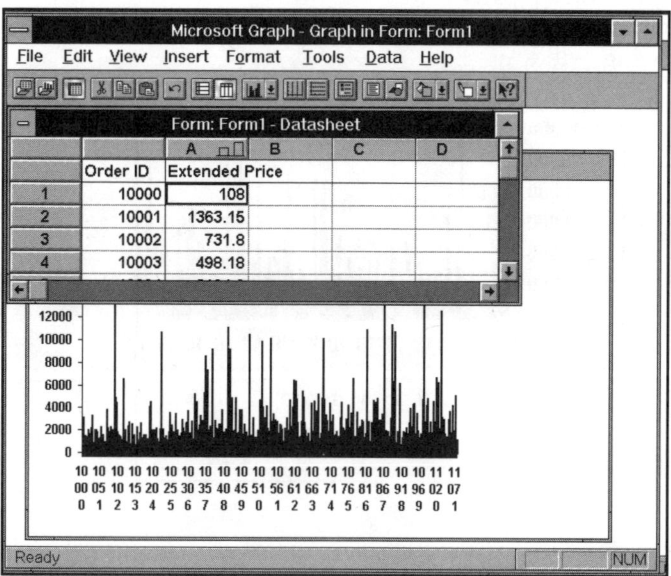

Double-click on the title of the graph, delete the old contents and re-type in the proper title; for example: Graph To Show the Total Order Price of the Last 1078 Orders.

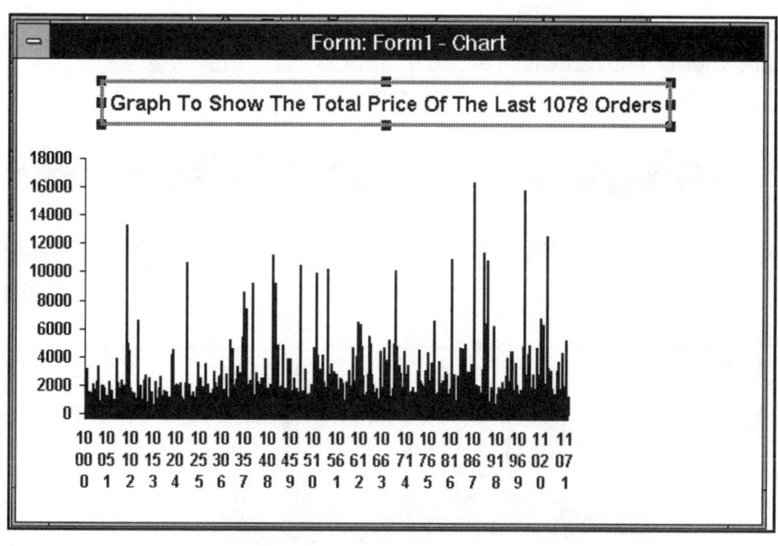

Now you need axis labels on the graph. Select Titles from the Insert menu to get the following window:

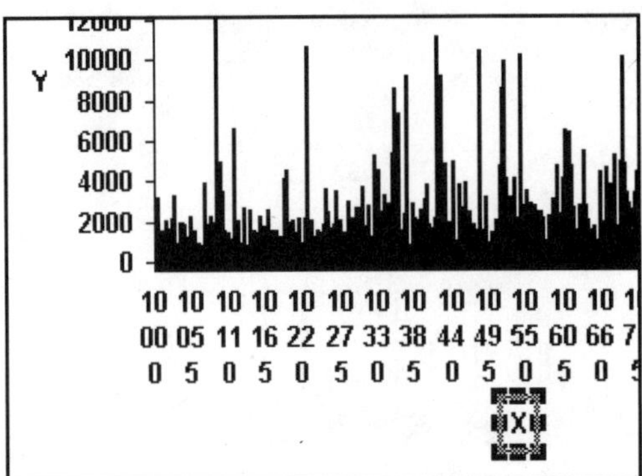

Select both of the options for the X and Y axes, and two letters (X and Y) will appear on the graph letters as the axis labels. Change the contents of these labels in the same way you changed the graph title text.

As you can see the Y axis label still appears in a horizontal format. You can change the orientation of the text by selecting: Format / Selected Chart Title... / Alignment and then Orientation. Also apply this to the Order ID numbers that appear on the X axis by clicking on them and following the same menu choice to rotate them. The graph will now appear like this:

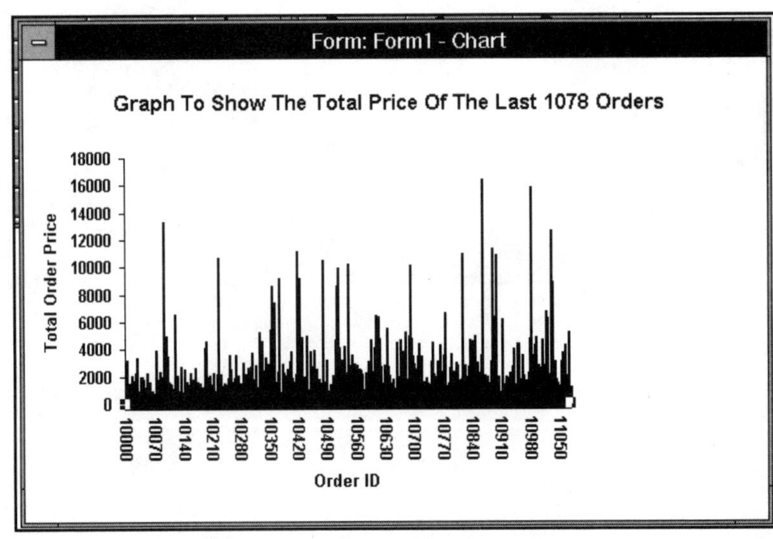

Now add in some Major Gridlines on the Value (Y) Axis to make the values of the orders easier to compare. Do this by selecting Insert / Gridlines... / Major Gridlines on the Value (Y) Axis .

The final thing to do is to update Access to the new graph, and leave Microsoft Graph. You can do this by selecting:

- Update from the File menu, then
- Exit & Return To Access, also from the File menu.

If you now change to Form View you will be able to see the results of the work that you and the Graph Wizard have done together.

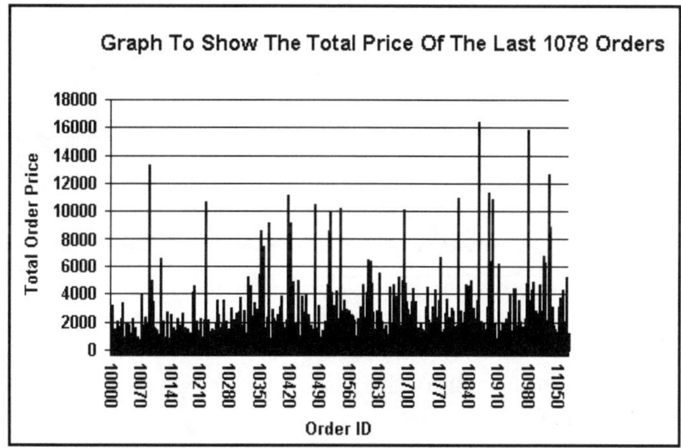

Using the techniques covered here, together with some of the techniques given in Chapter 5, you should now be able to produce impressive graphs which your boss will be delighted with in those boardroom presentations.

Troubleshooting

Q&A My cell is too small to show all of my calculation. What should I do?

Place the cursor in the cell and press *Shift+F2*. This activates the Zoom box which appears something like this:

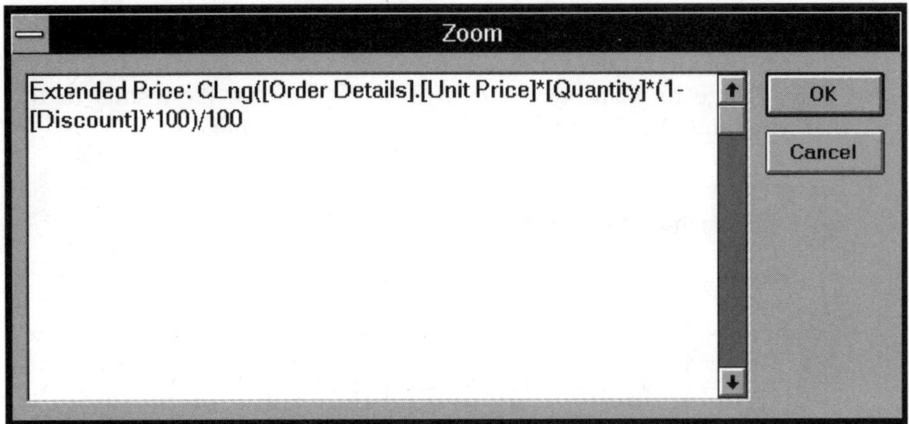

You can edit or simply view the contents of a cell using the Zoom box. When you have finished with that cell choose the OK button. Access 2.0 will place the contents of the Zoom box into the cell from which it was called and then close down the box itself.

Q&A I've got a collection of records I want to group by certain criteria. Must I use a query to do this?

Access has the ability to sum or average values or even count the number of any multiple records that fall into a given category. These categories are given as the values in the field assigned to the X axis. In the example of using Microsoft Graph in the above section this property was used to sum the costs of the individual product costs for each order. This saved a query, and therefore both memory and time.

CHAPTER

8

Import, Export and Attachment

There will come a time when you will have to think about working outside Access' parameters. You may well have come to Access from dBase usage, or from another Windows-based database package. Either way, Access can accept or send data from the other leading database, spreadsheet or wordprocessor packages. This means that the heavy investment you have already put into active data isn't wasted when you transfer it to Access or when you work in tandem with Access.

In this chapter you will cover:

- Connections with other database types
- ODBC
- Talking with spreadsheets
- Importing or exporting text
- Connecting one Access database to another
- Mail merge

Working Outside Access

The two ways Access exchanges information with other information centers are import/export and attaching.

Import is the process of copying data from another package into the Access environment. Importing is similar to the process of grabbing material from another Windows program. The data will be saved to the Access system and is kept as Access home-grown information. Export involves copying data to a foreign environment.

Attaching is the dynamic linking of Access to another package. The host-package continues to work on files as normal, allowing Access to come in and attach to certain data. It then behaves as if it were the host package itself - even to the point of working on the same file as the host (if allowed).

When to Attach?

Importation can be a more effective process than attaching, as you get a quicker response from your data (the data behaves like native Access). You will also be able to customize structures. Your colleague's data will also be free from corruption by your actions.

The advantages of attaching include the saving of disk space (someone else will have to worry about the storage of 10,000 dBase files) and the presence of up-to-the-minute information from the host data. The main drawback is the regular demand for attaching to index and memo files as well as data. Access can import more types than it can attach. This is because importing complete chunks of data requires less interaction between packages.

Other Databases

An Import Example

The main method for executing any form of exchange is via File on the main menu bar. Let's take an easy method to deal with a typical scenario - importing work from a Paradox 4.5 database to Access. First, select File, and Import... This gives you the Access import/export initial dialog screen.

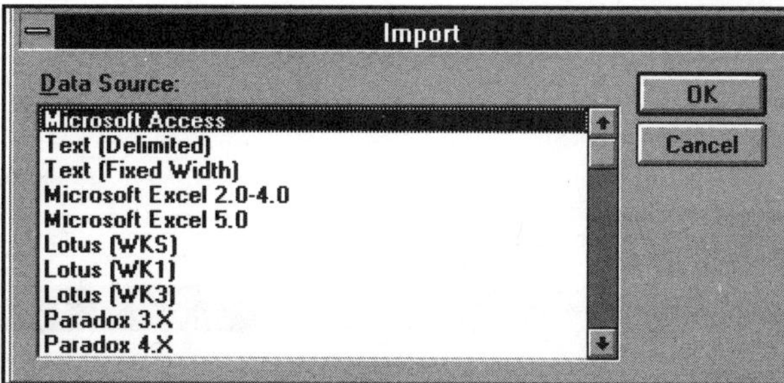

- Select the package type you want to import from (here it's Paradox 4.X).

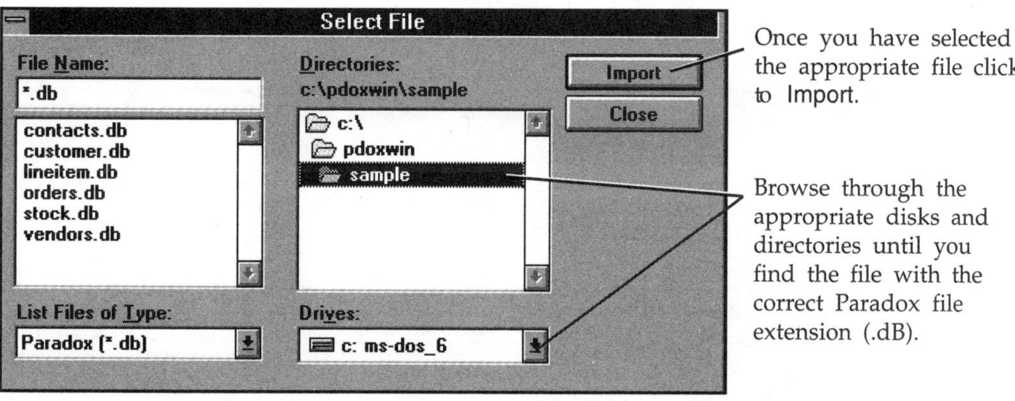

If the settings in your internal Windows files set up by Access are still at their default, then the following message appears:

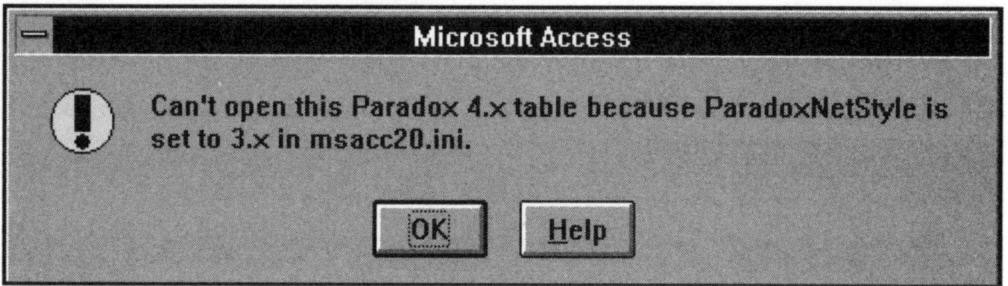

We have included the above screen in this chapter to show from the outset that import/export and attaching demands some patience and work on your behalf. To move in the world outside Access, settings in the host package and in your own computer are highly relevant, especially when connecting across networks.

Let's have a look at the settings in Windows to see if we can change the Paradox set-up. Start up any Windows text viewer (Notepad or Write will do) and search the Windows directory for the msacc20.ini file.

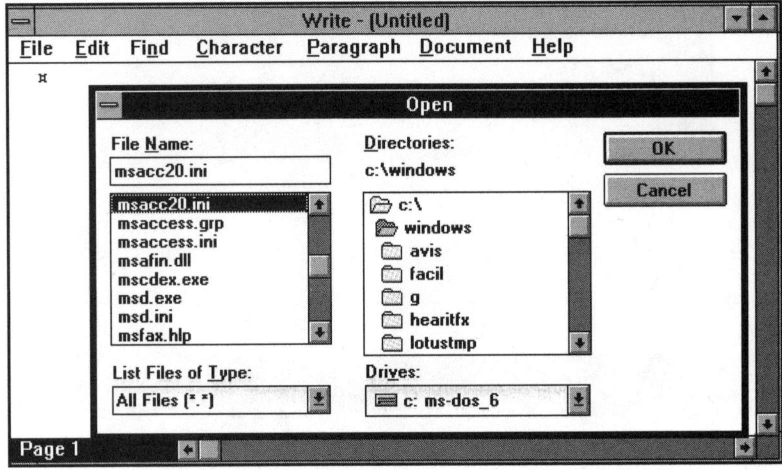

When you select the file you are presented with the information Access gave to Windows on initial set-up.

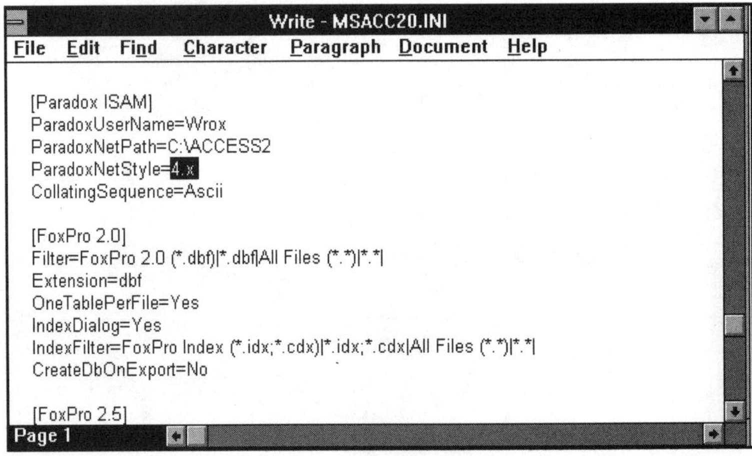

The many settings for the various packages Access can talk to are in this file. We want the [Paradox ISAM] listing. Access defaults to 3.X as a setting in ParadoxNetStyle. We must change it to 4.X to use it. We then save the msacc20.ini file (as altered). When you re-start Access this will be the setting used and we can progress with our experiment.

Let's import a typical Paradox for Windows 4.5 table using the above method. This time importation is allowed. We must select our .dB file in the normal way, click Import, and our path opens.

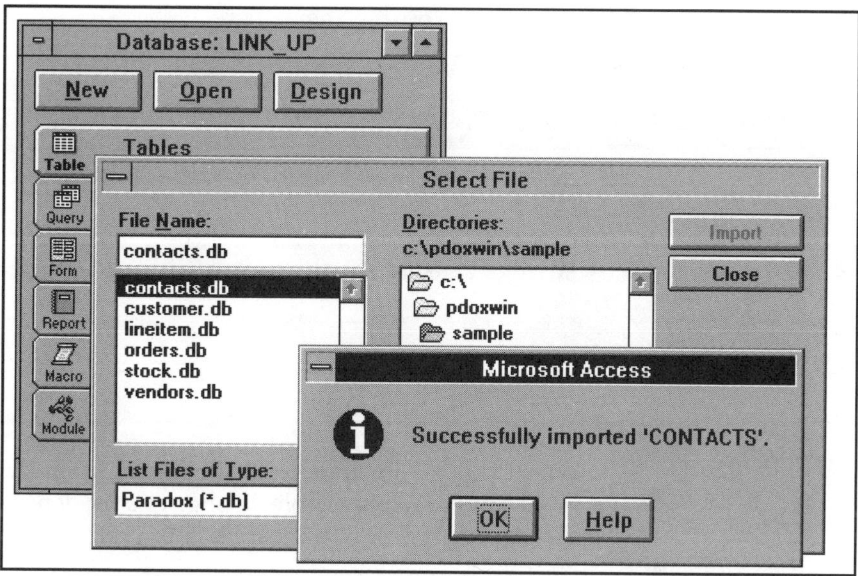

Select OK and Access will import a table into your normal table listing (it also waits to see if you want to do some more imports). Open up the table in design view to see the Paradox table in native Access form.

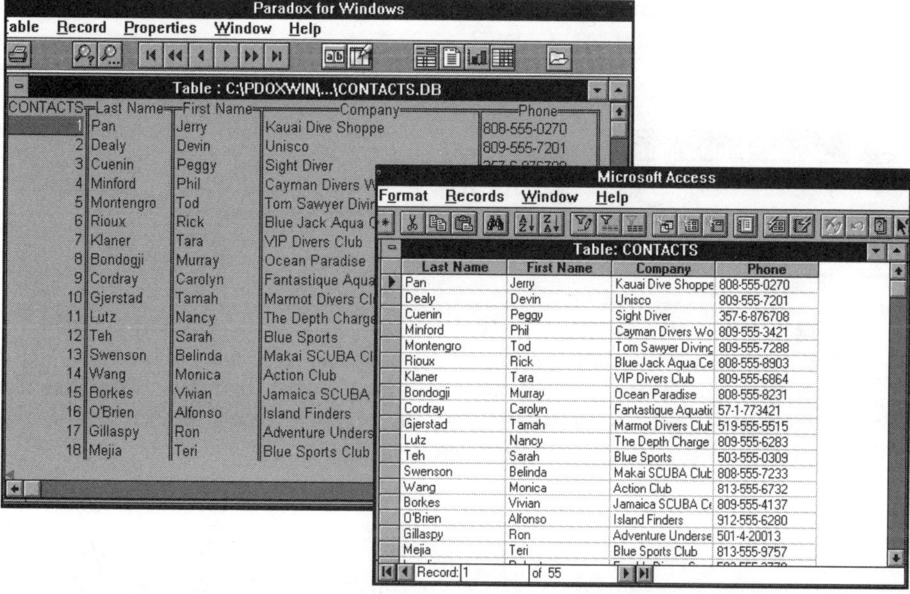

An Example of Attaching

As you can see, the imported Paradox table now has a normal Access table icon in the listing. Let's attach a similar table.

- Select Attach Table... from File on the menu bar.
- Select the chosen attached file type (Paradox 4.X in this case).
- Select the file from the appropriate disk/directory and click Attach.

Now you will see the welcome message.

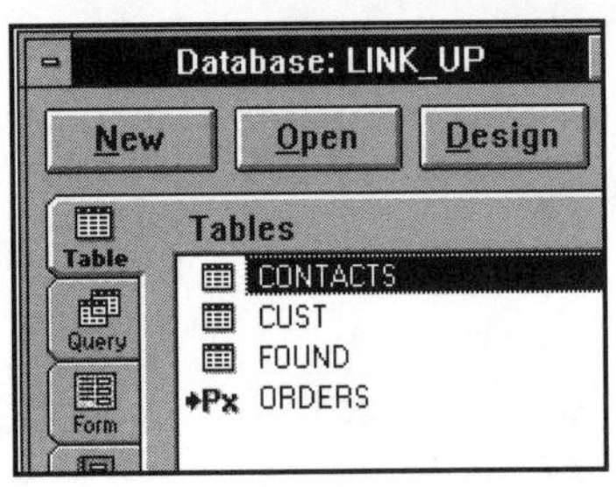

When you accept this you will find the Paradox table is on your database table listing, and is denoted by a special symbol. It's marked as attached.

> If you import a table and already have a table/database of the same name Access will re-name the file. For example, if you already have Orders1 Access will re-name the import Orders2.

Now we are attached. You can view and edit data in the attached table as if you were in the package (which of course you are). If there was a password set in the original Paradox database, then you are prompted to quote it.

You can automate the process (if you find you are connecting regularly) by using macros (see Chapter 12) and the Imp/Exp Setup... techniques. Appendix III shows you the special macro actions that control Transfer Database/Text and the like. These actions simulate the File Import.../Export.../Attach Table... menu commands (see also the macro Help screens).

> Access can't proceed if another user moves the files you are attatched to. You will have to close down and re-attach to the new address. It's also sensible to set a Primary Key if you are connected to a table that doesn't already have one.

The above example is true for all the available Import/Export/Attach files and packages in the Access dialog box. Special conditions and obstacles exist in each of the foreign applications and these are discussed later in the chapter. If you operate across a network, it's worthwhile gaining some familiarity with the protocols and conventions your network administrator has set up. This will stop most of the connection problems before they begin.

ODBC

The inclusion of Open DataBase Connectivity (ODBC) in Access lets you connect to a Structured Query Language (SQL) Server (for example, Oracle). The standard way packages communicated (SQL) had become abused and was in danger of becoming non-standard. The agreement of many software vendors to stick by ODBC as a communications conduit to SQL-based sources means that Access has a route through to the most powerful database systems.

You already have connections set up for the common packages via the import/ export and attach lists. Access with ODBC operative is another way to connect to the wider world.

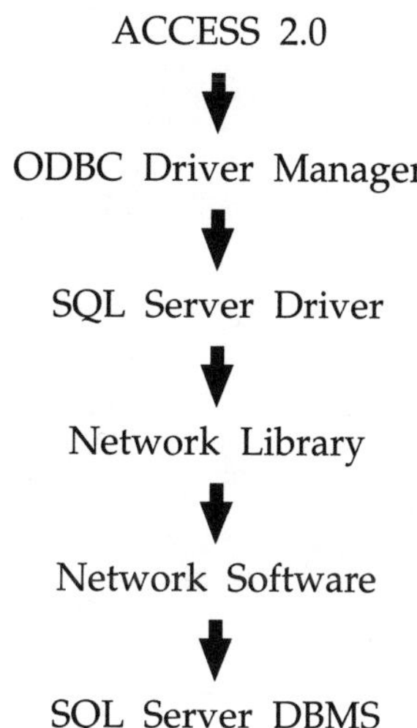

You can take advantage of the SQL system by arranging an ODBC driver. These drivers take charge of all the movements of data between Access and SQL pathways in the outside world. You can install a driver by utilizing the disks that are part of your Access package. You will find assorted ODBC manager/help/drivers/administrator files on the disks.

- You must run Access 2.0. Setup to make use of the ODBC drivers.
- Move through the set-up screens and select Add/Remove.

This screen will appear:

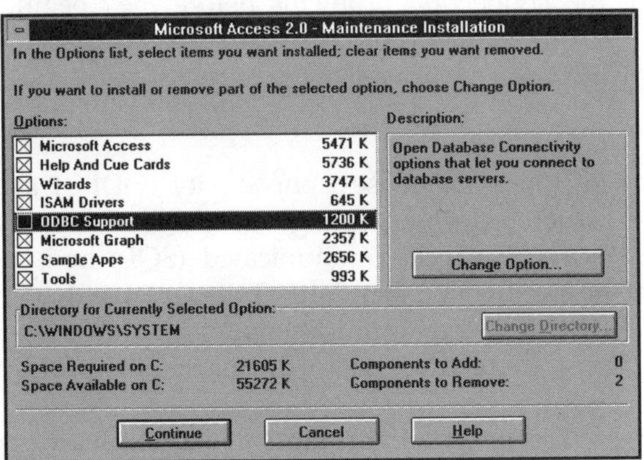

- Check the ODBC selection.
- Select Change Option... for your installed drivers.

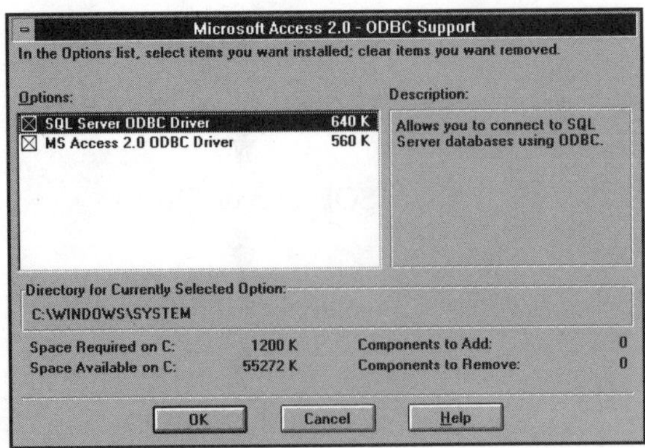

If you want to add a particular driver there are now many vendors offering ODBC connection to their packages. Access has drivers for Microsoft SQL Server, Sybase SQL Server already included.

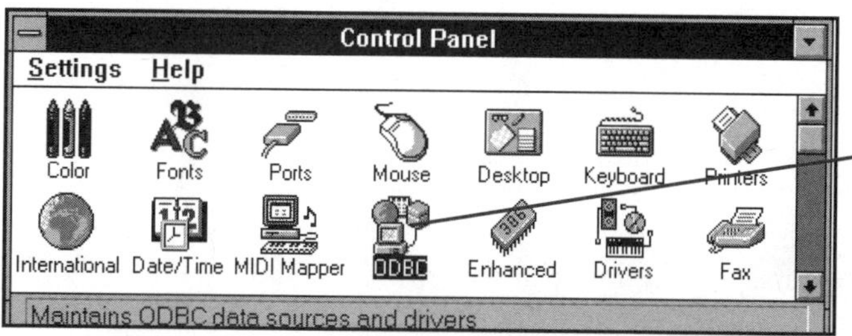

Now you are installed you will find a new addition to your Windows Control Panel.

Double-click on your new facility and you will see the ODBC drivers and set-ups that are at your disposal.

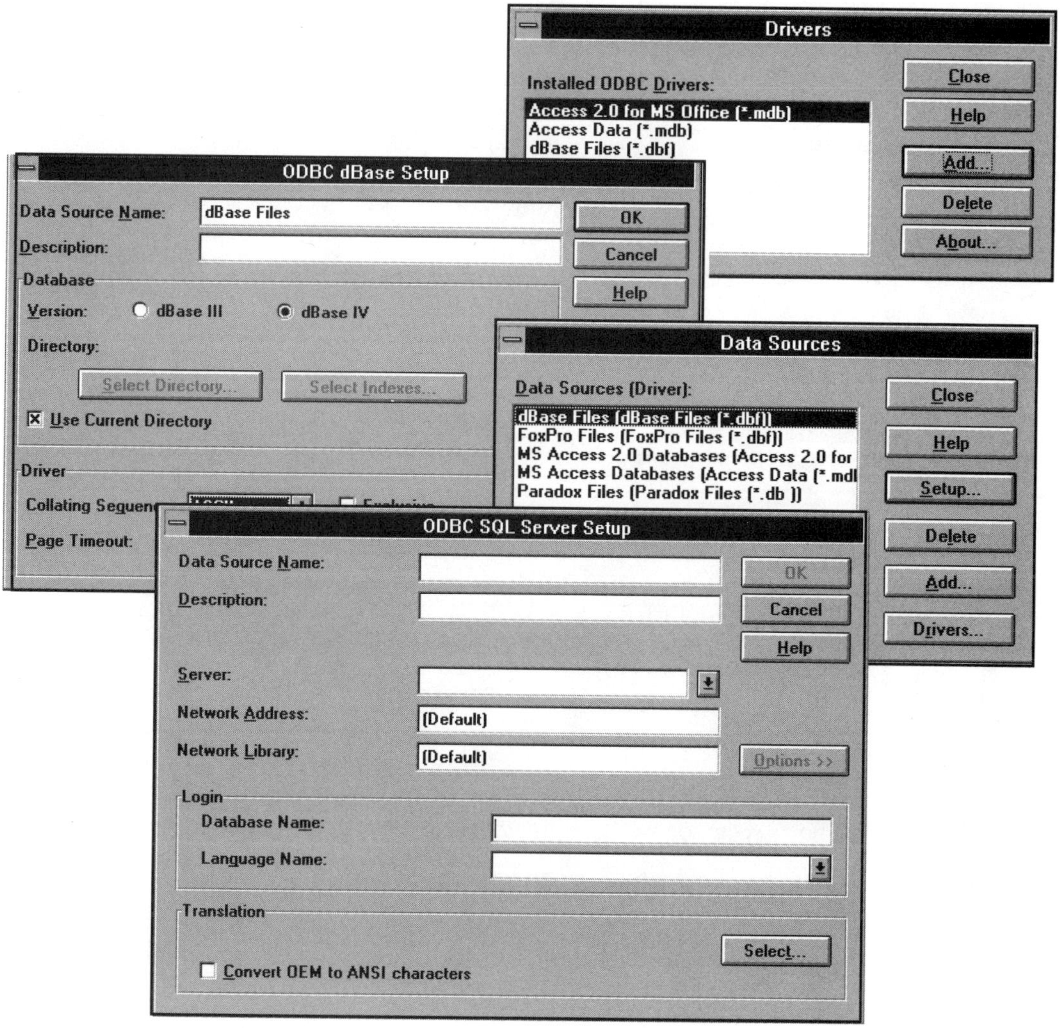

You may have to tune your connection to SQL Servers using the ODBC setup for each server type.

You can set up any new ODBC drivers using these screens (as well as selected network connections and protocols). These screens also set up custom connections to your Btrieve, dBase or Paradox servers. Talk things over with your network administrator to get the complete system or type information.

It's now possible to connect to an SQL Server via the <SQL Database> option in File, Import.../Export.../Attach Table... You must select the SQL data source from the Data Sources dialog box. This displays the list of objects you can choose your SQL tables from.

Remember that when you are attached you may be talking to a very large database. Even though you are in attached mode, Access may be creating large temporary indexes on your hard disk!

Data Sources

We said in our example that the method for connecting outside is similar for most external packages. If you open the appropriate Import/Export or Attachment dialog and select from the list, there will be an easy link. You can check the msaccess20.ini file for any special connection information involving Paradox, dBase, FoxPro, Btrieve, Lotus and SQL systems.

Let's look at the connection details you may need for each of the major packages. We will then look at text and spreadsheet movement.

dBase Files

With Access you can connect to dBase III and IV. You need to select files with the .DBF extension. You can also attach to index files (.ndx/.mdx). Names of files in transit don't usually change.

Import

To import files:

1. Open the Access database you want to import the files to.
2. Select File on the menu bar, and choose Import...
3. Select either of the dBase versions from the dialog box. The Select File dialog box appears. Find the .DBF file that you want from the various disk/directories.
4. Click the Import button

Attach

Attaching files is a similar to importing them (described above). Open the Access database you want to attach the files to and then select File/Attach... Do the same as point 3 above and at point 4 click the Attach button instead of Import.

You will be presented with the Select Index Files dialog box.

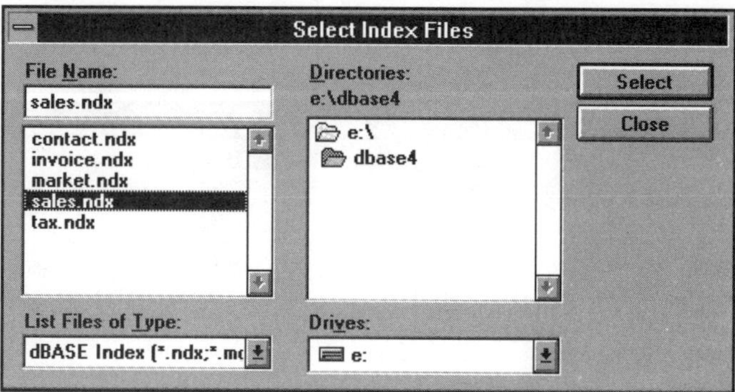

Select the various indexes you need and say if you want updates in joins.

Export

To export files you again open the Access database you want to export the files to and then select File/Export... Point 3 is the same as for importing. At point 4 when you select the dBase type you are presented with the Select Access Objects screen.

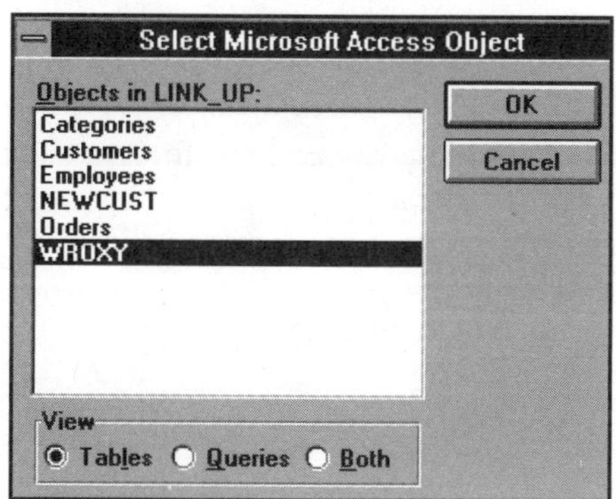

Here you must use View to select the Tables or Queries list. Chose the appropriate file.

When you click it you are presented with the Export to File dialog box. Here you specify the filename for the export file storage place.

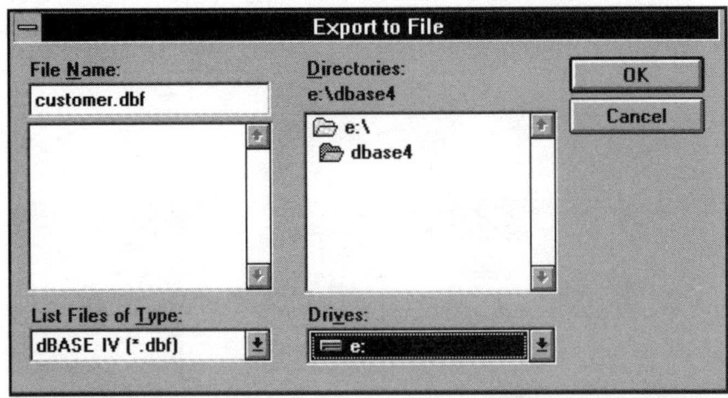

Click OK to complete the task.

Notes for Exporting dBase III & IV

When working internally Access allows long names for its table. When you export to dBase you will sometimes find that Access will suggest a shortened name to create a file that dBase can handle more easily.

Access uses variable length text fields. Because Access arranges this value dynamically it makes for great savings in storage. Unfortunately dBase sets a fixed length for text fields - whatever they are. Therefore, if you have left the default length (50) in your Access work, *that* is what will be transported and used by dBase. dBase also only allows field names of 10 characters - Access field names longer than this will be truncated. You could alter the FieldSize property in Access before connection to ensure an unadulterated transfer.

> Remember that Access 2.0 does not apply DOS naming restrictions to its objects. For instance, field names can be up to 64 characters long.

Access will not export to dBase with a file name which already exists in the receiving dBase.

FoxPro Files

Notes for Importing, Attaching, and Exporting FoxPro

You can import, attach and export FoxPro files with the same procedure as you used for dBase. Access behaves in the same way with FoxPro as it does for dBase so you can use the same rules.

Remember:

- FoxPro files have the extension DBF.
- FoxPro keeps index data in separate files with the IDX and CDX extensions.
- FoxPro 2.5 DOS & Windows have common file formats.

Paradox Files

Notes for Importing, Attaching, and Exporting Paradox

You can import, attach, and export Paradox with the same procedure as you used for dBase. Access behaves in the same way with Paradox as it does for dBase so you can use the same rules.

Remember:

- Paradox files usually have the extension DB.
- Paradox 4.0 for DOS and 4.5 for Windows can be treated as the same for communication purposes.
- Paradox 1.0 for Windows can be addressed using 4 rules:

    1. If Paradox has a primary key set it will be in a separate file (.PX).
    2. If Paradox has a Memo field set, it will be in a separate file (.MB).
    3. Both .MB and .PX files must be read by Access before it can open .DB files.
    4. If the Paradox table has some OLE Objects in it, Access won't be able to open them.

Btrieve Files

Notes for Importing, Attaching, and Exporting Btrieve

You can import, attach, and export Btrieve files with the same procedure as you used for dBase files. However, after selecting Btrieve in the initial list box, you must select File.DDF in the consequent Select Files dialog box. Access then gives you a route to the listing file from where all the Btrieve tables can be chosen.

Remember:

- Access needs the Dynamic Link Library (DLL) called wbtrcall.dll.
- You will have to get a copy of the Btrieve DLL and add it to your Windows directory.
- Access talks to Btrieve versions 5.0x & 6.0.
- Access needs to have both the .DDF and Field.DDF files made available to it from Btrieve to discern the structure of the tables it will be connecting to.

SQL Source Files

Notes for Importing, Exporting and Attaching SQL

You can import, attach, and export with the same procedure as with dBase files. However, to proceed beyond the list of packages you need to have installed the appropriate ODBC Drivers. When you select <SQL Database>, you will be presented with a special screen.

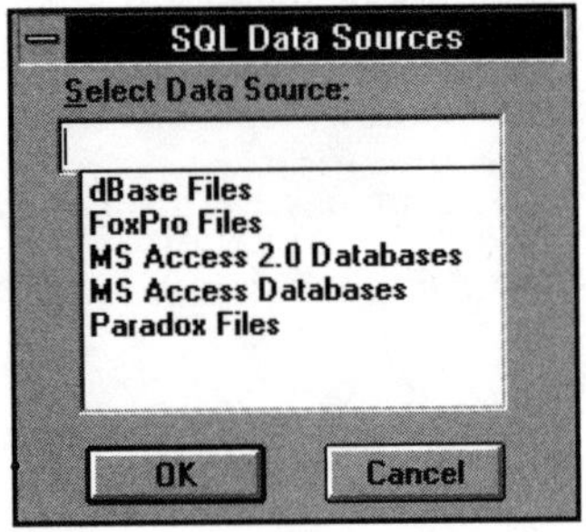

When you have selected the SQL source you want to connect with, Access will offer you an Object listing transmitted from the SQL Server. Choose the table you want to import or attach from this listing. Satisfy any password or log-in procedure and proceed with your work.

SQL Data Types

Access, like all other database packages, has a unique way of referring to the various data types in its tables (such as text, number and so on). If you are planning to connect with other packages (especially when attaching and querying) you should be aware of the differences between packages. In most cases connection will be transparent, but if you plan to integrate on any serious level you will have to compare data types beforehand.

Access	Paradox	dBase/FoxPro	Btrieve
Text	Alphanumeric	Character	String, Istring, zstring
Double Number	Number	Numeric/Float	Float, bfloat
Integer Number	Short Number		Int/Autoincrement
Date/Time	Date/Time	Date/Time	Date/Time
Memo	Memo	Memo	Note
OLE Object	BLOB/Graphic	General	Lvar
Currency			Money

Engaging With Spreadsheets and Text

Many Access users will have experienced data in a grid through their use of spreadsheets. The easy use and efficiency of spreadsheets leads people to force data types into their spreadsheets which are too complex. In truth, much of the activity in spreadsheet work is better suited to the database environment.

Because powerful Windows-based databases are available for the desktop and the local network, there should be a re-assessment of which is the right tool for the job. The ability to work with text, delimited or otherwise, is still demanded by database users. We shouldn't forget the weight of text-based data which at some time will need to be brought under the database umbrella. We also need to remember that not everyone has access to up-to-date Windows-capable machines. Text-based data will continue to accumulate. If you are transferring data to Access or vice versa you will want a smooth transition for all your hard-won data listings.

Spreadsheets

Access can import and export successfully with Excel (2.0 - 4.0 and 5.0) and Lotus formats (WKS and WK1). Use the Lotus formats for a Quattro Pro transfer. The process is easy, providing you do some preparation. You might want to choose to set the limits of the spreadsheet data (using range for example) before you attempt an import. You might also want to edit Access field types before you export.

To Import

Make sure there are no cells in your spreadsheet that contain formulas before you import, and that the format matches that of Access.

- Open a database ready for receiving.
- Choose File/Import...
- Select the package type from the listing (make sure the sheet is not protected with a password).
- Choose the file you want in the Select Files dialog box, and click Import.

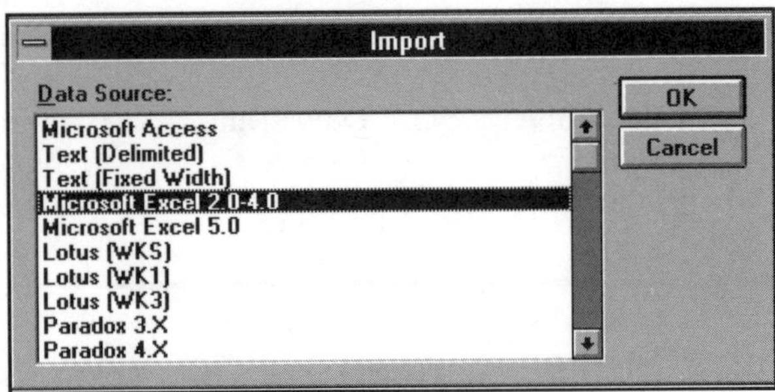

Access opens the Import Spreadsheet Options box once you have selected the location of your file.

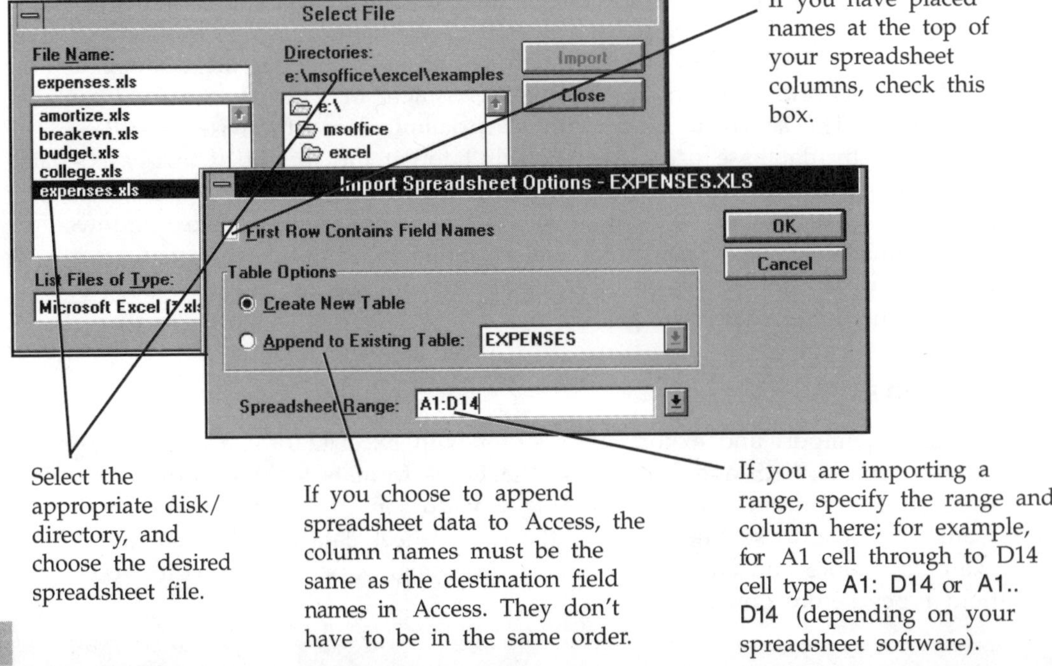

Select File
File Name:
expenses.xls
amortize.xls
breakevn.xls
budget.xls
college.xls
expenses.xls
Directories:
e:\msoffice\excel\examples
e:\
msoffice
excel
Import
Close
List Files of Type:
Import Spreadsheet Options - EXPENSES.XLS
First Row Contains Field Names
Table Options
Create New Table
Append to Existing Table:
EXPENSES
Spreadsheet Range:
A1:D14
OK
Cancel
If you have placed names at the top of your spreadsheet columns, check this box.
Select the appropriate disk/ directory, and choose the desired spreadsheet file.
If you choose to append spreadsheet data to Access, the column names must be the same as the destination field names in Access. They don't have to be in the same order.
If you are importing a range, specify the range and column here; for example, for A1 cell through to D14 cell type A1: D14 or A1.. D14 (depending on your spreadsheet software).

After clicking OK you should receive the welcome message:

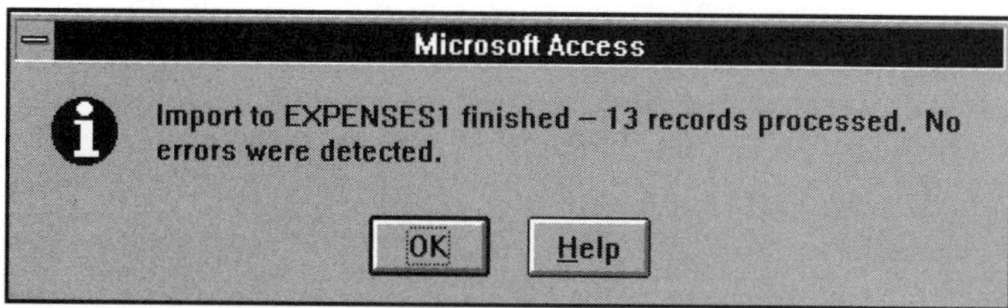

You now have a new table in your database. If the spreadsheet you imported had a name that already existed in your database, Access will re-name it, but with a figure attached; for example, EXPENSES becomes EXPENSES1. Here are the typical before and after screens of an Excel to Access connection:

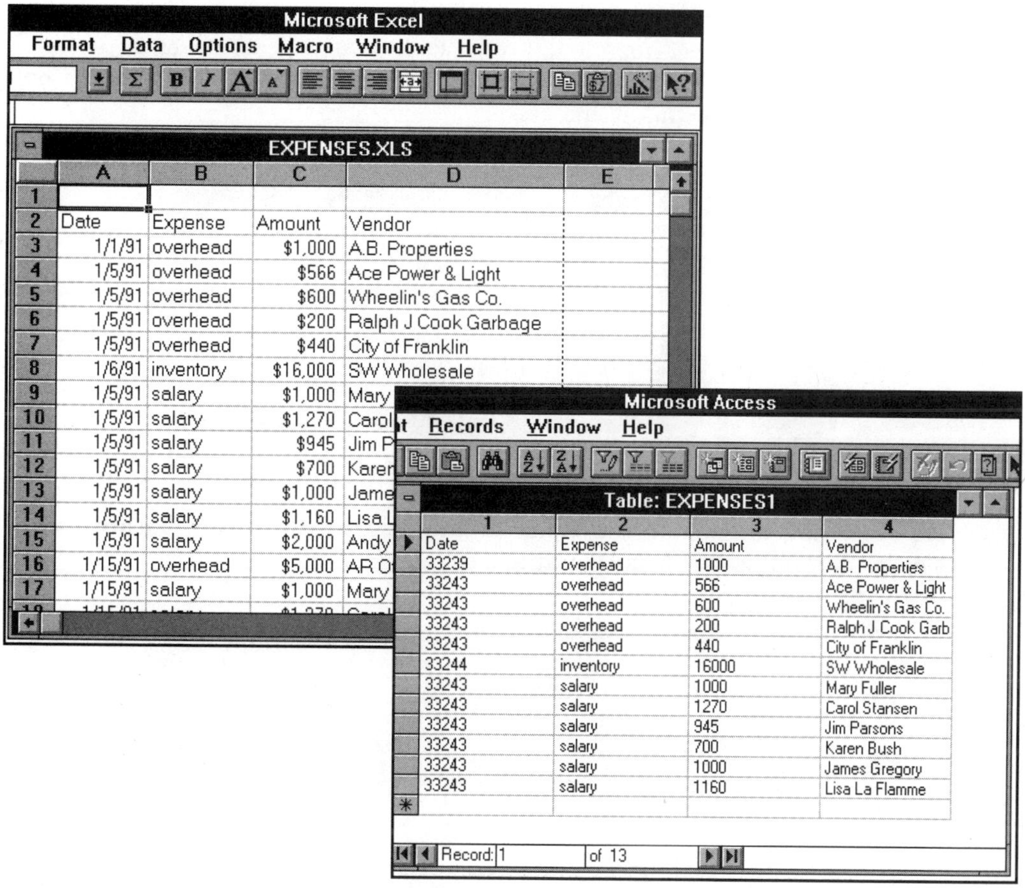

Microsoft Excel

Format Data Options Macro Window Help

EXPENSES.XLS

	A	B	C	D	E
1					
2	Date	Expense	Amount	Vendor	
3	1/1/91	overhead	$1,000	A.B. Properties	
4	1/5/91	overhead	$566	Ace Power & Light	
5	1/5/91	overhead	$600	Wheelin's Gas Co.	
6	1/5/91	overhead	$200	Ralph J Cook Garbage	
7	1/5/91	overhead	$440	City of Franklin	
8	1/6/91	inventory	$16,000	SW Wholesale	
9	1/5/91	salary	$1,000	Mary	
10	1/5/91	salary	$1,270	Carol	
11	1/5/91	salary	$945	Jim P	
12	1/5/91	salary	$700	Karen	
13	1/5/91	salary	$1,000	Jame	
14	1/5/91	salary	$1,160	Lisa L	
15	1/5/91	salary	$2,000	Andy	
16	1/15/91	overhead	$5,000	AR O	
17	1/15/91	salary	$1,000	Mary	

Microsoft Access

Records Window Help

Table: EXPENSES1

1	2	3	4
Date	Expense	Amount	Vendor
33239	overhead	1000	A.B. Properties
33243	overhead	566	Ace Power & Light
33243	overhead	600	Wheelin's Gas Co.
33243	overhead	200	Ralph J Cook Garb
33243	overhead	440	City of Franklin
33244	inventory	16000	SW Wholesale
33243	salary	1000	Mary Fuller
33243	salary	1270	Carol Stansen
33243	salary	945	Jim Parsons
33243	salary	700	Karen Bush
33243	salary	1000	James Gregory
33243	salary	1160	Lisa La Flamme

Record: 1 of 13

Notes for Importing Spreadsheets

If you try to import a spreadsheet which has conflicting field information to the type established by Access (for example, when a first fax number in a series of plain numbers have the following ones are a mixture of brackets and dashes with numbers in them), then you *will* be able to build a table. However, it will be called Import Errors - <user name>. In this table you will be able to find some clue to the error in conversion that Access detected.

When Access has to import a spreadsheet, it must work out what kind of fields it's going to create in response to the data coming in. These field data types will be invented by Access and based on the *first* row of data it receives from the spreadsheet.

An Example Error

Let's change the above conditions and try to append more information onto our already spreadsheet-imported Access table (we will set an entry to be required in salary). When we try to import spreadsheet data that has no entry into our Access table this is the result:

EXPENSES.XLS

	A	B	C	D
26	2/5/91	overhead		Ralph J Cook Garbage
27	2/5/91	overhead	$440	City of Franklin
28	2/5/91	overhead	$500	City of Franklin
29	2/5/91	salary		Mary Fuller
30	2/5/91	salary		Carol Stansen
31	2/5/91	salary	$1,890	Jim Parsons
32	2/5/91	salary	$1,400	Karen Bush

We are trying to append some data to an Access table which already has similar data imported from the spreadsheet.

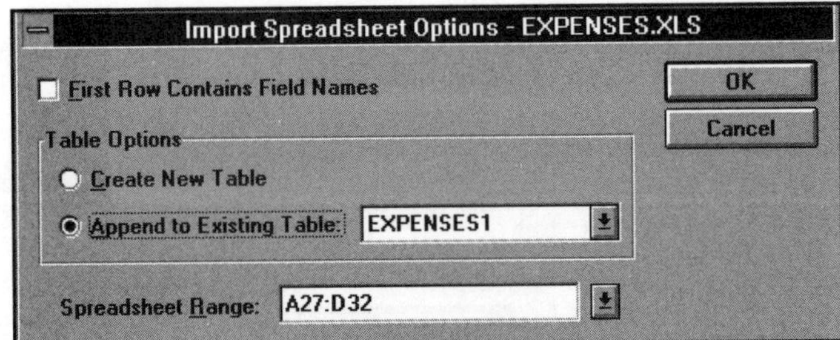

Because we have designed a conflict, Access gives us a standard warning of the error. It also tells us where we can find more information about it.

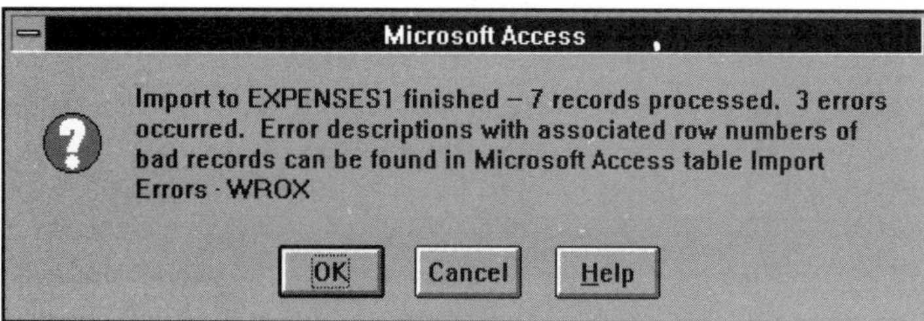

Now look at the resultant error table that Access has created. Detailed clues have been left for us. We can therefore check the field properties for the Access table and decide on the best repair before re-importing the spreadsheet data.

Table: Import Errors - WROX

Error	Field	Row
Null in Required Field		27
Null in Required Field		30
Null in Required Field		31

Record: 1 of 3

Errors in transfer can be difficult to work out. Experiment with a few records from the spreadsheet. Remember that it can be worthwhile simply altering the layout/properties in a new imported table if the data has been cleanly transferred, but just misplaced in appearance.

Notes for Exporting Spreadsheets

You can export spreadsheets with the same procedure as you used to import to dBase. You should note that a change occurs when you are defining the data elements before you export. You must inform Access of what you are sending.

Select Microsoft Access Object

Objects in NWIND:
Categories
Customers
Employees
EXPENSES
EXPENSES1
Order Details
Orders
Paradox
Products
Shippers
Suppliers

OK
Cancel

View
Tables Queries Both

Select the appropriate data and click OK to send it to your chosen spreadsheet package.

MSOffice Users

You can make a quick export to Excel via the Analyze It with MSExcel button  or you can select File/Output To... on the toolbar.

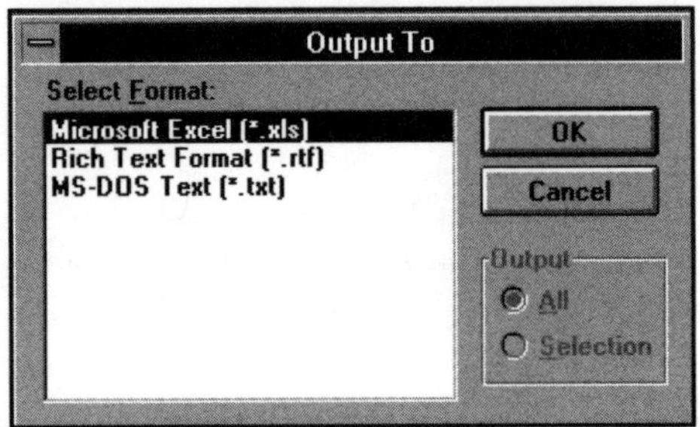

Access prompts you if the file name you choose for the exported data is already present in the Excel spreadsheet.

Importing and Exporting Text

You can transfer text so you are able to communicate with a host computer that prints in text format. You can also send information to Access via a wordprocessor. Importing may be coming from paper-data that has been placed on disk; or there may be people in the field with only text-based computing power (you can't take a large PC on an expedition to the rainforest to database insect families.

In each case Access communicates textually in one of two ways:

1. Delimited
2. Fixed width

Delimited

This is where the text has also been given a certain amount of column definition. This time the text must be distinguished by an Access-recognizable separator - either a comma, *Tab* marker or *Space*. The actual data must be surrounded by double or single quotation marks.

“ResearchID”,”Organization”,”ContactTitle”,”Name”,”Town”,”Extension”
“025678”,”French Industries Consolidated “,”Mr”,”Cheese”,”Paris”,”657"
“027585”,”Japanese Import Commission”,”Mr”,”Rice”,”Tokyo”,”01"
“042983”,”British Banking Group”,”Mr”,”Tea”,”London”,”7402"
“034884”,”Australian Group”,”Mr”,”Lager”,”Perth”,”943"

Things get complex if, for instance, you wish to have double quotation marks actually *in* your text. If this is the case you can use single quotation marks as the delimiter. Remember that you can't have a mixture - it's either consistently single or consistently double.

Fixed Width

This document has a set number of columns of entry as layout, and each column has exactly the same start and finish point. You *can* allow shortened records *if* they retain the same fixed length format and *if* you finish with a carriage return. Here is an example of fixed length text entry:

025678.... French.Industries.Consolidated... Mr..... Cheese...... Paris............ 657
027585.... Japanese.Import.Commission...... Mr..... Rice........... Tokyo........... 01
042983.... British.Banking.Group................. Mr..... Tea............ London........ 7402
034884.... Australian.Group......................... Mr..... Lager......... Perth............943

Delimited Text Transfer in Operation

Access defaults to the convention we have just demonstrated. If your data is lengthy (and you will be carrying out several importations over the following months and years) you will have to enter the specialized screen that Access provides for text connection. To do this you should prepare for importation by selecting Import/Text [Delimited].

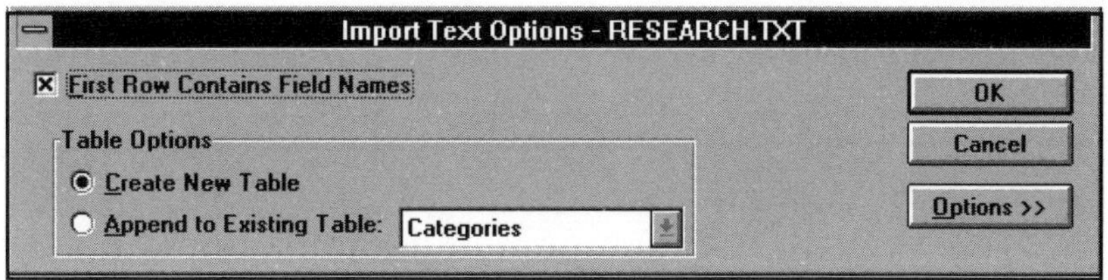

If your text is guaranteed, you should set up then click OK and fill out the path to the file. If you don't do this, you will have to select Options >> and give Access a detailed breakdown of the data it will be receiving.

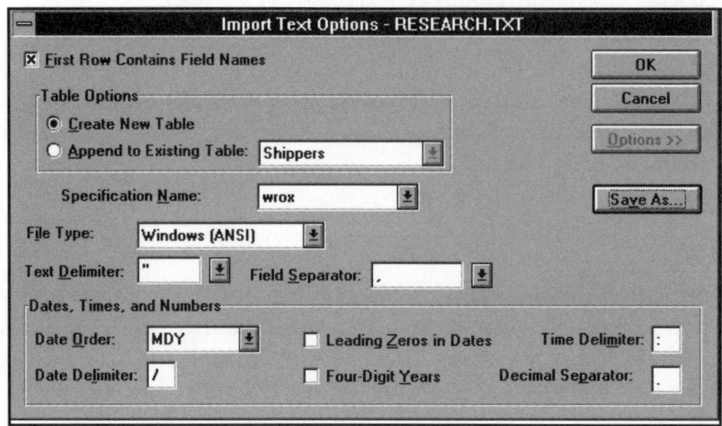

Select the template conditions you want to set as your standard. Access will then ask for a name to give to these parameters. Access will use this name as the template whenever you want to process this kind of text in the future. Once your delimited template is set up, press OK to create your table.

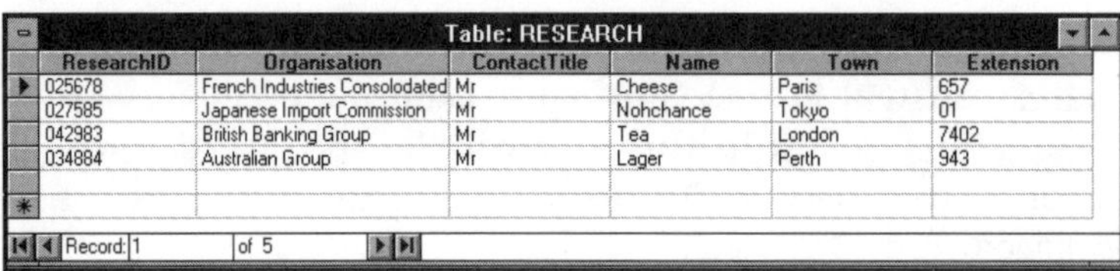

Table: RESEARCH

ResearchID	Organisation	ContactTitle	Name	Town	Extension
025678	French Industries Consolodated	Mr	Cheese	Paris	657
027585	Japanese Import Commission	Mr	Nohchance	Tokyo	01
042983	British Banking Group	Mr	Tea	London	7402
034884	Australian Group	Mr	Lager	Perth	943

Record: 1 of 5

Fixed Width Text Transfer in Operation

Things are more difficult with fixed length text transfer. You must tell Access the location of each column so that it can make a field from it. Select the import procedure and Text [FixedWidth]. This brings up a set-up screen.

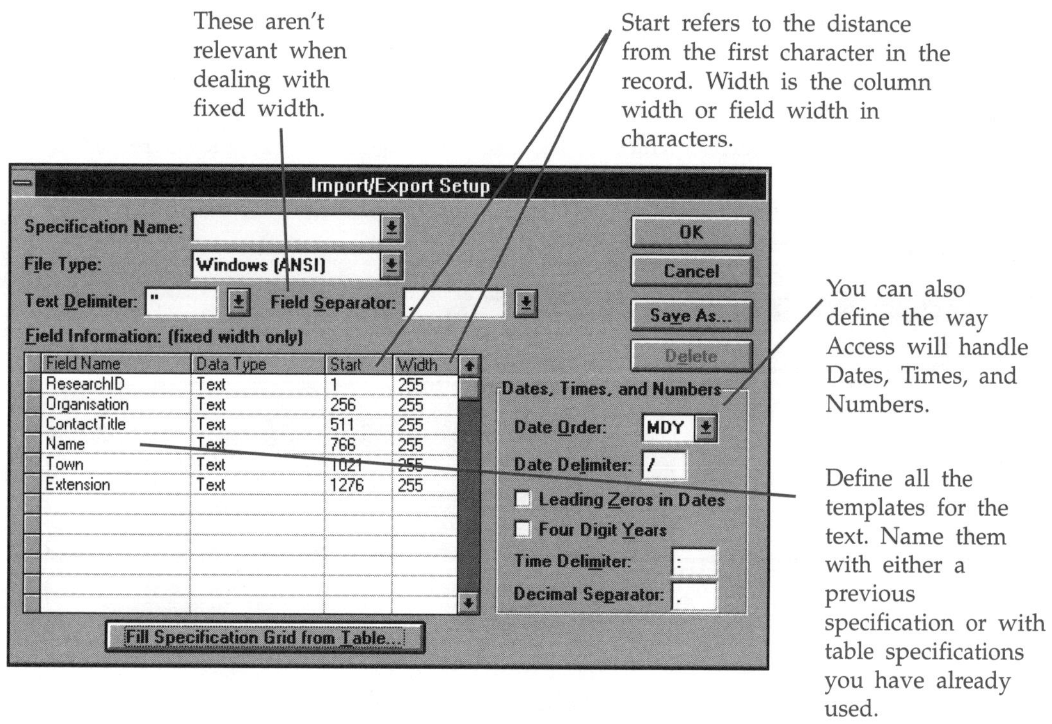

> Remember that the import will fail if your text file is still active, that is, if it has been left open for work by its package

Connecting With Access

You can attach, import and export to other versions of Access, and you can convert these versions for use with Access 2.0.

To Convert to Access 2.0.

You can look at previous versions of Access, but you can't do much with them unless you convert the older version. You may encounter problems with validation rules as the parameters for Access 2.0 have changed completely.

Select File/Convert Database... (only when all other databases are closed down on your system).

To Attach, Export, and Import

When importing or exporting to another Access database system, you follow the normal procedure, as given earlier in the chapter. However, Access will offer you an extra screen which is the Access Objects screen and is relevant to either process. Here you can choose the specific object and whether or not to import or export the structure (that is, a table's definition information) or the data *and* the structure. Here are two typical screens:

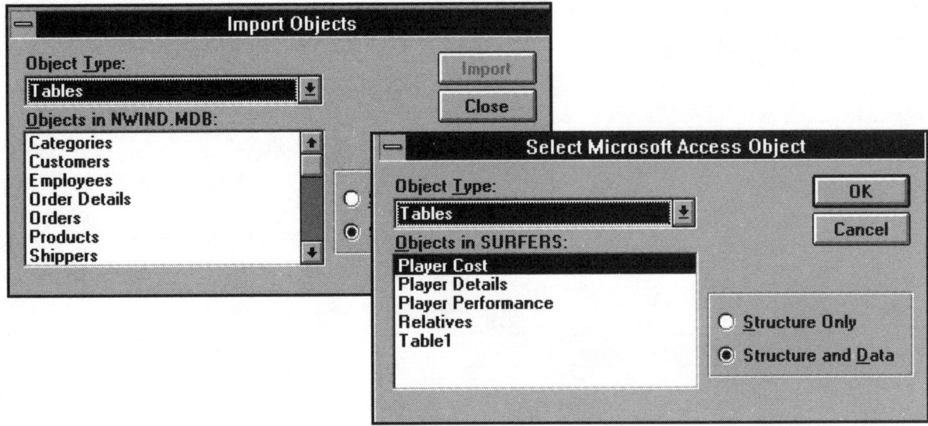

To attach, you can use the normal attach command in File. You will then be given the opportunity to choose which tables in the partner Access database you wish to attach to. Remember that Access will add a figure to the attached table if it finds a duplicate. Also, to show the fact that Access is attached to another Access table, the normal arrow will appear by that table symbol in your listing.

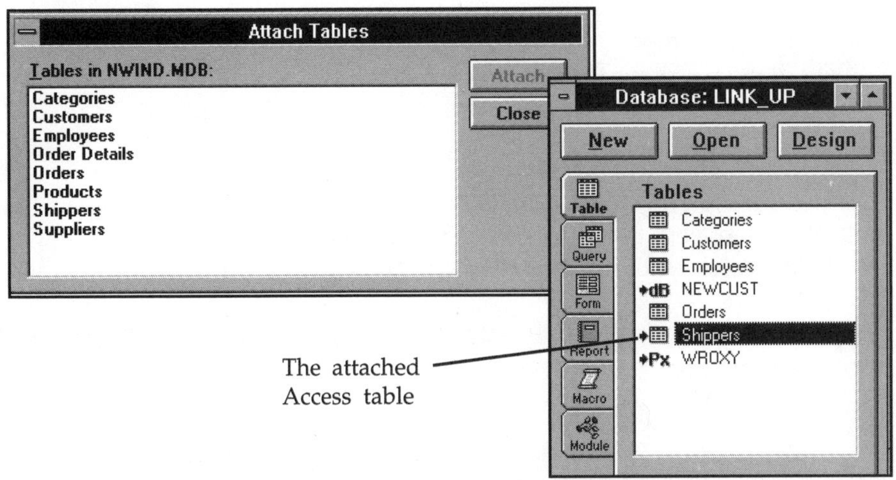

Grabbing The Whole Access System

Using the Add-ins menu you can import a complete Access database. You can import every object in that database and use it as your own (providing you have set up the ownership properly [see the Microsoft Access manual 'Building Applications').

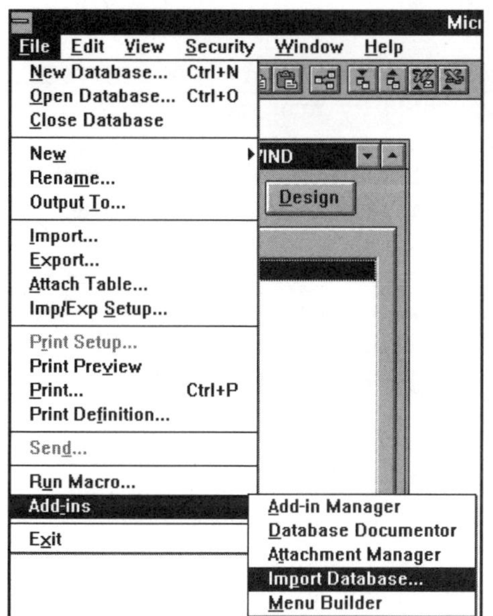

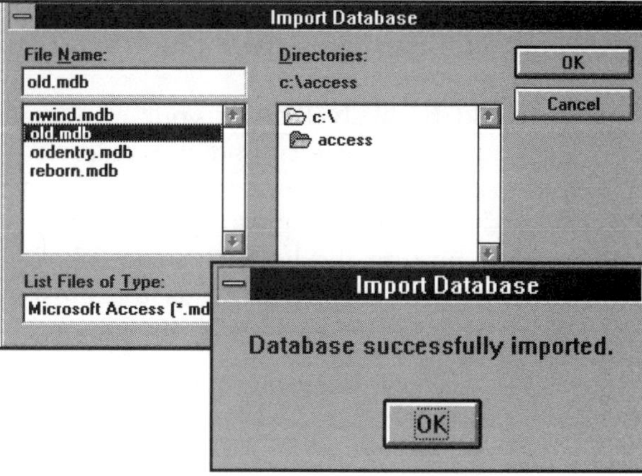

Keeping Track of Attachments

You can select File/Add-ins/Attachment Manager to see a complete run-down of your present attachment status. This facility enables you to check any attachments that you think may have changed. Access will open up the appropriate Select File dialog box for you to regain connections that may have strayed.

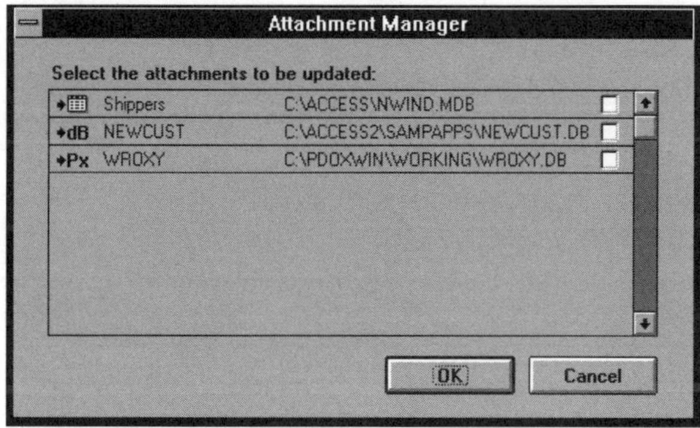

> Remember to de-attach from any system. Highlight the attachment on your database list and delete by pressing the *Del* Key or Delete from Edit on the menu bar.

Access With Word Mail Merge

You are able to embed from Access 2.0 directly into the Word for Windows environment. This is most powerfully demonstrated by mail merge.

It would be likely that all your customer/contact information would be kept on your database files and it would be a great advantage to merge with a powerful wordprocessor to accomplish a large mail-shot. Mail merge has been very difficult in the past, with all sorts of inappropriate macros and template screens making the best of a bad job. Microsoft has come to our aid with what many people may consider as the most welcome wizard of all - the Mail Merge Wizard. Here is how to manifest it.

- Open a database.
- Select the table/query you wish to embed in Word.
- Click on the Merge It button in the Access toolbar.

The wizard starts by offering a new document for you to merge with Access data or to embed into an already prepared Word template.

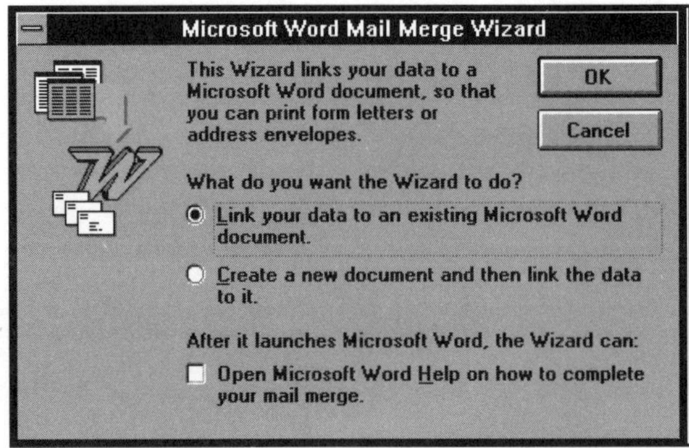

- Word is booted up for you with a new toolbar.

- Select the Mail Merge Helper icon on your Word toolbar.
- This will give you the composition screens for your document or label maker.

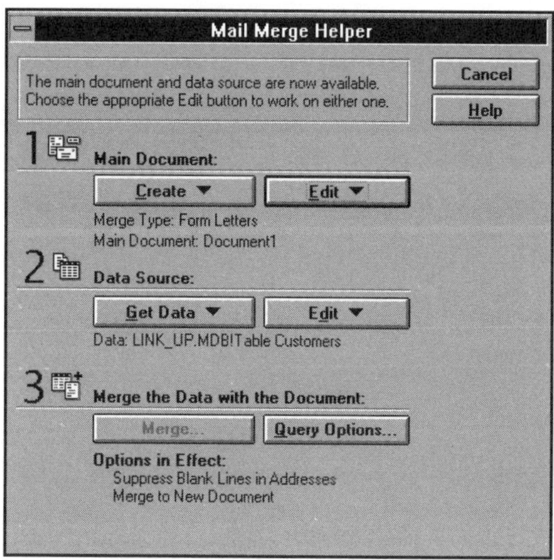

- If you select 1 Create, you will get an opportunity to start a fresh or prepared mail label/document. In this case we chose Label Maker.
- Choose 2 Get Data. The wizard serves up a Select File screen for you where you can choose the required table as source.
- Choose Avery sizes and Printer type to suit the equipment. In this case we chose Mailing Label to utilize the Customer table in NWind database as the source material.

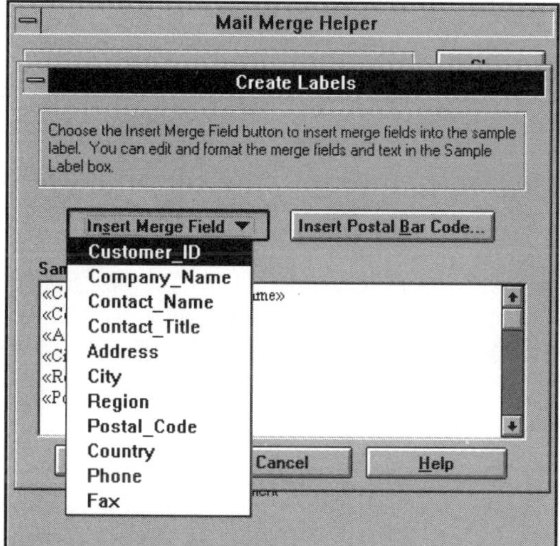

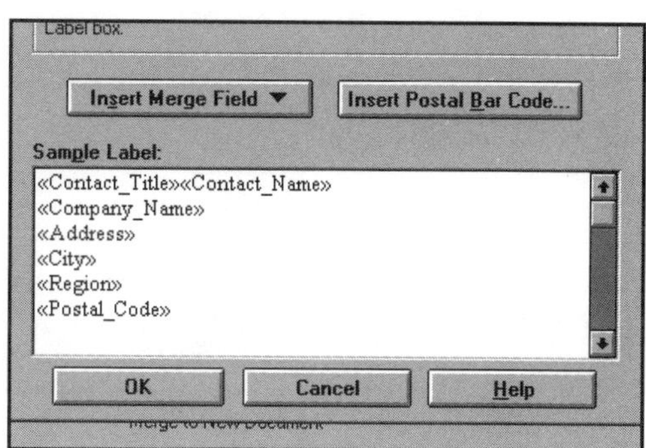

- Select the data from Access one field at a time.
- Choose 3 Merge to complete the process.
- Select OK and see the resulting document which is ready to print.

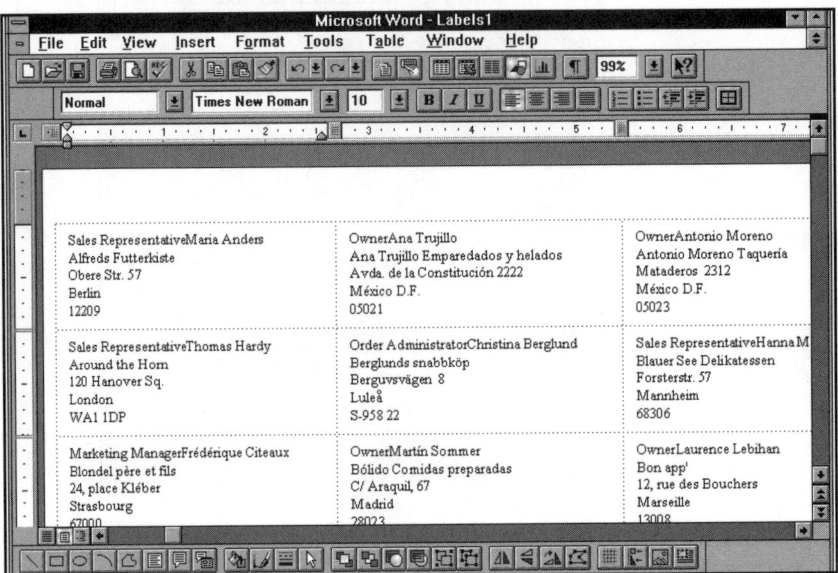

There are many different screens and facilities, and their use depends on the different kinds of form letters and labels you want to generate. You can experiment to become familiar with them, or you can consult the Word Help screens or manuals.

Conclusion

Communicating with other software is becoming easier but remember that traveling among specialist networks with your data requires specialist protocols. It's worth investigating the rules and regulations of common networking routes, so as to help you pre-empt any potential problems.

The methods described here, together with those in Chapters 1 to 7, will help you construct a reliable and flexible initial database. Read Chapters 9 to 13 to discover how to customize your basic database structure to make it a professional application.

CHAPTER 9

More On Queries

Whether you come from an SQL background or have mastered the QBE grid, the vagaries of complex interrogation always require concentrated effort. With solid design underneath your database, advanced queries can really make the data dance to your tune. It will make all that time and money you invested in data entry seem worthwhile. It is important that you have a good understanding of the ideas brought to you in Chapter 4: Basic Queries. The techniques included here are built on the basics you covered.

As you know, queries are powerful tools for manipulating your data. Up until now queries have been limited to sorting and selecting records from your tables. However, queries aren't just limited to this task. With a little adaptation they can be made to alter records, move them around your tables, delete them, and much more. These are referred to as action queries, simply because they are more dynamic than the ordinary select queries and enable you to get even more from your data. As ever Microsoft have provided a wizard to help you with this, as it can be a complicated operation.

In this chapter you will learn about:

- Action queries
- Crosstab, Update, Delete, Append and Make-Table queries
- Pass-Through and Data Definition queries
- Query Wizards
- Parameter query
- Find Duplicates/Unmatched query
- Archive query

Action Queries

We have shown you how queries can be made to sort or select the records that appear in the underlying table or nested query. It is possible to get even more power from these data manipulation tools by the position of the records in your tables. To get this new power, you have to translate your current select queries into what are called action queries. Action queries can do a variety of jobs: moving records around your database structure, deleting selected records on-mass, and altering data.

To get a better idea of what specific action queries have to offer, let's look at them in turn.

The Different Types of Action Query

There are seven different action queries you can make use of as a database designer:

1. Crosstab query
2. Make-Table query
3. Update query
4. Append query
5. Delete query
6. Pass-Through query
7. Data Definition query

The Crosstab Query

The Crosstab query doesn't affect the structure of your database or the positioning of your records in that structure, but rather the way the data appears. The word Crosstab is an abbreviation of the title Across The Table meaning that the data is displayed in tabular format, and can be very useful for answering questions such as "Who sold how many, of what, this week?" A sample of the results of a Crosstab query appears below:

Employee ID	Row Summary	Jan	Feb	Mar	Apr
1	£10,450.91	£1,054.17	£877.84	£914.81	£392.18
2	£10,694.25	£890.61	£1,692.66	£2,096.34	£563.28
3	£13,347.13	£1,512.86	£1,274.85	£1,453.40	£2,192.94
4	£14,046.90	£1,423.41	£626.31	£1,828.95	£421.46
5	£4,352.02	£86.70	£124.42	£112.24	£189.01
6	£4,344.71	£162.20	£516.49	£884.07	£272.90
7	£7,967.62	£506.65	£808.85	£1,603.12	£90.66
8	£10,084.86	£507.63	£1,967.00	£994.46	£646.78
9	£3,918.26	£387.44	£192.72	£855.51	£261.84

Here are the sales reps.

Here are the totals of the freight charges that each sales rep ran up in each month.

Here are the months.

The Make-Table Query

This dynamic query is used to make a copy of selected records and then to place them into a new table. It is a query first and foremost so you can run it to see if all the records etc. in the dynaset are as you want to see them, before accepting the result. Of course, you also have the opportunity to select a new name for your new table.

A Make-Table is of great use, if you find you are running the same query continuously. This may be due to an oversight at database planning stage, or if you need a history table containing out-of-date information. This is helpful if you are not vigilant in saving all information from an associated table. It would be a little difficult retrieving the sales reps' results from 5 years back, if some of your people no longer exist on the present sales personnel listing!

When Access 2.0 performs a query upon a table, every record must be looked at to see if it fulfills the criteria for selection, or to see whether it's in the right order when sorting is in operation. As the number of records in a table grows, so does the time required for the queries to do their job. Making a library of records, using Make-Table, will produce significant time savings on medium to large databases (see also Database Compacting in the Introduction).

Another good use for the Make-Table query is as a method for isolating some records into their own table, so that summary calculations can be applied to just that particular group. This can be another useful time saver, as a dynaset of those records may normally take several nested queries to create.

Dynasets are only temporary, so if you want to see the calculations on several occasions, the time required multiplies. If calculations were performed and then the results were passed into a new table, they would be instantly accessible - and this is to your advantage. The calculation queries don't have to be run again until your data changes and your new Make-Table table needs refreshing.

Update Query

To change one entry in your database you have to:

- Open the appropriate table or related form.
- Scroll to the appropriate record.
- Select the appropriate entry cell.
- Delete the contents, and re-type.

This method can become a little cumbersome if a large number of records need to be changed. Fortunately, Access provides the Update query. Updates allow you to change the contents of a field over a number of records, **if** the changes follow a common theme.

For example, suppose that at the end of the financial year, you decide that the price of all your aluminum ladders has to rise by 6.75%. Now, as one of the leading ladder manufacturers, you don't produce just one type of ladder - you've got short, long and various other miscellaneous sizes in-between!

To go through and change all the prices of each type by hand is prohibitive - each ladder has a different price, scattered around your Products table. A much better idea would be to get Access to select all the ladders from your Products table and then multiply the cost of each by 1.0675 before returning the records back to the original table. An Update query allows you to do just that, and not only for mathematical returns. You can also alter text, when, for example, the name of the metal that your ladders are made from changes from aluminum to aluminum/titanium alloy; or you can delete the contents of a field altogether.

Below is a typical Update query QBE grid:

Field:	Product ID	Unit Price	
Update To:		[Unit Price]*1.0675	
Criteria:	Like 12 Or 34 Or 35		
or:			

The Append Query

The Append query is very useful for moving your records from table to table. You can use this facility to, say, move records to a table created by a Make-Table query - in other words, regular archiving. You wouldn't want to create a separate history table for these records, so use an Append query to simply add them.

The Delete Query

The Delete query is used for similar types of job as the Append query, but instead of adding, it's used to delete records that you no longer require. Of course, it's easy to delete records in the Datasheet View of a table, but to delete a large number of records that share a common theme (and are the only records that share that common theme!) the Delete query is the tool for you.

The Pass-Through Query

This action query lets you communicate directly with the tables stored on a remote ODBC Server. Instead of attaching the tables to your database, you can run your queries in Pass Through and Access will attempt to see the data that is held outside your local Access environment.

The disadvantage is that you can no longer use the QBE grid. Instead, you must often use raw SQL statements as the communication medium, as all the contact is performed at an SQL level.

Data Definition Query

This type of action query is similar to the Pass-Through, in that it allows you to communicate directly with a remote ODBC Server. It is significantly more powerful; Pass-Through acts like an SQL snapshot. Data Definition queries can act **dynamically** like any of the Access 2.0 Action queries. In other words, with this you can create, alter or delete a table, as well as do something that the Access 2.0 equivalents cannot do - create or delete an index. This gives you control over the structure of a database held on a remote server, and is the obvious tool to use when re-designing systems around the new Access environment.

> Remember that you can save your action queries. They will appear on your query listing with the appropriate icon and an exclamation mark (!) beside them. Look on the NWind database to see several examples.

Now that you have an idea of the things you can get these powerful action queries to do, let's see how you can go about creating them.

Creating Action Queries

The first five of the seven action queries (Crosstab, Make-Table, Update, Append and Delete) are all produced the same way. First, produce a Select query to decide on the group of records that you want to affect, and then translate it into the appropriate action query style.

A Word of Warning

Any of the action queries that affect the structure and content of your database can generate irreversible and unwanted effects if run indiscriminately. Back-up your database regularily, and if you use an action query do a Select query first.

Database Back-up

This essentially means that you take a copy of your database and store it where the actions you are about to take cannot affect it (also good practice if any data is lost as a result of hard disk malfunction).

We would suggest that you back up your database onto floppy disks if your database is small enough, otherwise onto another computer's hard disk.

Running the Select Query

One of the reasons that an action query may go rogue is because it affected the wrong records. In order to eliminate this possibility, look at the select records by running a Select query before you convert it to action. It is easier to alter records at the query stage, where criteria can be tuned and data sources can be refined, rather than working after the event.

> Queries can be stopped from running, for any reason, by pressing *Ctrl* and *Break* together. This only works during calculation by Access. Remember though, once Access has completed the query, then the results are set in stone and cannot be changed. Also, don't forget what is both the advantage and the problem with action queries - they're fast!

You have been warned! Action queries can seriously affect your database.

Action Queries Within the Walls of Access

The steps you need to follow to produce any of the first 5 action query styles are:

- Produce the Select query that affects only the records that are required.
- Choose the action query style that you want to translate your Select query to, from the following table:

Type	Description	Icon	New line in QBE grid
Select	The default, when selecting: 'New Query'.		
Crosstab	Similar to a spread-sheet result.		 Crosstab:
Make-Table	A new table created from a dynaset - with the selected records copied into it.		 Query Properties Make New Table Table Name: Current Database Another Database: File Name: OK Cancel
Update	Alter some entries in records with a com-mon theme.		 Update To:
Append	Add a selected group of records to another table.		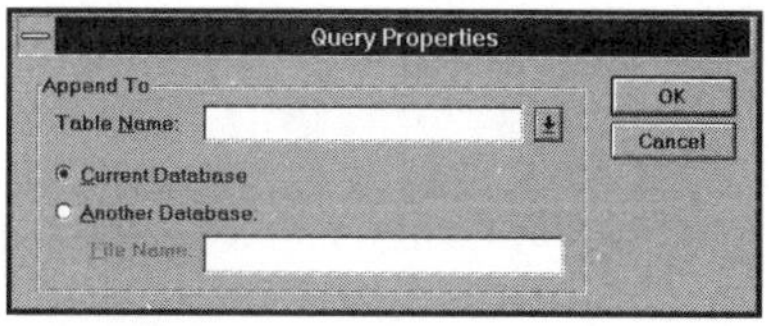 Query Properties Append To Table Name: Current Database Another Database: File Name: OK Cancel
Delete	Delete records from a table that have a common theme.		 Delete: Where

Depending on the type of action query you choose, either enter the relevant information for each field into the new line that appears in the QBE or fill in the window that is given. The choices are shown next.

The Crosstab Newline

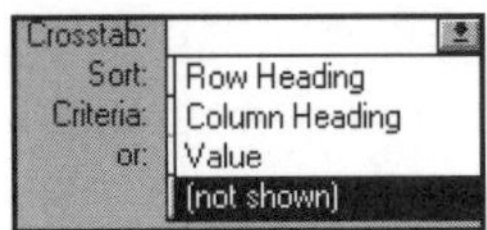

For each field in a Crosstab query you get the following choices.

Field	Use
Row Heading	This field will be used as a row heading.
Column Heading	This field will be used as a column heading. *All* the unique entries that appear in this cell across *all* the records, will appear as column headings.
Value	This field will be used to fill in the tabular structure produced using the row and column titles.
(not shown)	This field will not appear in the dynaset. This field would be used to further refine the group of records that went into the tabular structure.

You can have more than one row heading. If you do, Access sorts the records by the first field and then by the next, and so on.

As you are essentially creating a spreadsheet-like appearance, you must choose one field to be a Row Heading, one to be a Column Heading and one with a Value. Also, Row and Column must have a Group By in Total. Without these conditions, Crosstab will not operate.

With this in place you can select an expression for your Value to be based upon and then filter the results using other fields and Sort fields. You can also determine the order of Column Headings by entering them directly into the Query Properties box. (Click in the upper portion of the QBE grid and then click the Properties icon).

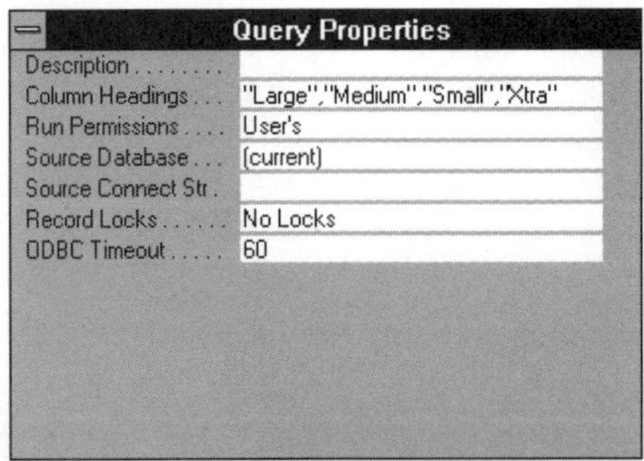

The Make-Table Window

When you select the Make-Table icon, you will be presented with the following window:

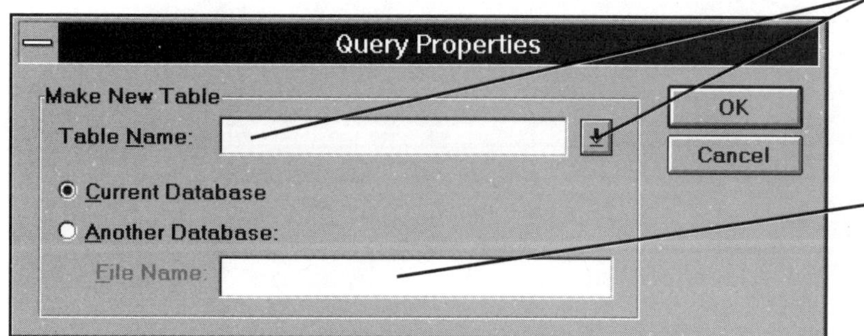

Type the name of the new table you want to create, or select the table you want to overwrite in this box.

Select the database you want to add the table to. If you select Another Database, you must also state the database's file name.

Fill in this window and click on the OK button. Access will now produce the table with the name you gave, when the query is run. If your new table is to be an amalgamation of one table by updating it with associated information from another, then on completion of the query you will be informed of the new rows created in the process.

Update Newline

This cell is the easiest to fill in. Simply enter the expression or new value that you want Access to use for that field in all the selected records. If you want the field to be left blank, enter the special expression Null into the cell. When the query is run, Access will update your records as you have requested. When the query has been completed Access will let you know how many rows have been updated.

Access allows you to update several fields at a time. Simply add them to the QBE grid as you go.

Remember also, that Access updates by using a Copy table. Your amendments to data are carried out on a copy of the table in question, and after completion the results are posted to the original. This can be handy when updating using data in the same table. You can specify updates on some fields by simply including other fields (in square brackets) in the QBE Update cell.

Append Window

When you select the Append icon, the following window appears:

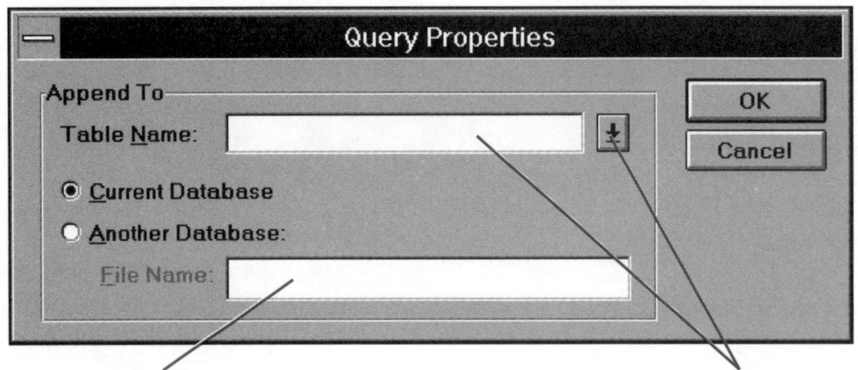

Select the database that the table is part of. If you select Another Database, you must also state the database's file name.

Type the name of the table you want to append the selected records to, or select it from the list revealed, by clicking on the tab at the end of the cell.

Fill in this window, and click on the OK button. Access 2.0 will now append the records to the table with the name you gave, when the query is run. This is fine if you are appending fields of the same name, such as Name, Address or Phone. However, if you are appending similar information that is held under different field names, remember to alter those names in the Append To cell in the QBE grid. For example, LastName is the other table's equivalent of your field called Contact Name. Simply add Contact Name in the Append To cell. If you place a field that has an exact match in the appended table, the entry is made automatically as you place the cursor in the Append To cell.

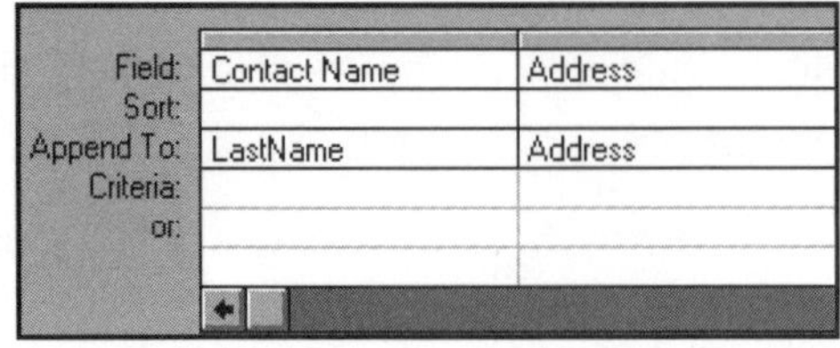

Delete Newline

This powerful query is irreversible - so be extremely careful before running it. Use a Select query first if you feel unsure and take special notice of the referential integrity. Deleting some fields here may lead to deletion of related fields over there! When you select this query's icon, the Delete row will appear already filled in with either of the two entries that are available: Where or From.

The Where entry is applied to the field you are operating on; you may set its criteria. The From entry applies to whole tables from which records will be deleted (see Asterisk and Cascading below).

Using the Asterisk in the QBE grid

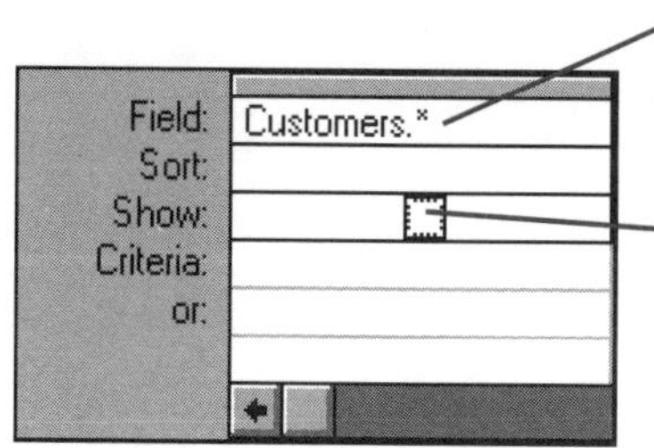

If you wish to include *all* the fields from a table in the QBE, then use the asterisk that appears at the top of the field listing in any table.

If you wish to use any of those fields for some kind of sort or select, add those fields into the QBE grid as normal and de-select the Show box so that only one occurrence of that field appears in the dynaset. The Delete query uses the **asterisk field** as a marker to choose which tables to delete records from. (This is in a multi-table query).

Cascading Updates and Deletes

When you defined relationships between tables in your database structure, you may have enforced referential integrity. If so, you also had the option to allow cascading updates and cascading deletes. These options really come into their own when using Update or Delete. If these options were *not* selected, it is possible you may break the rules of referential integrity when adding records to child tables or deleting records from parent tables. If you violate this set-up, Access will display the following screen:

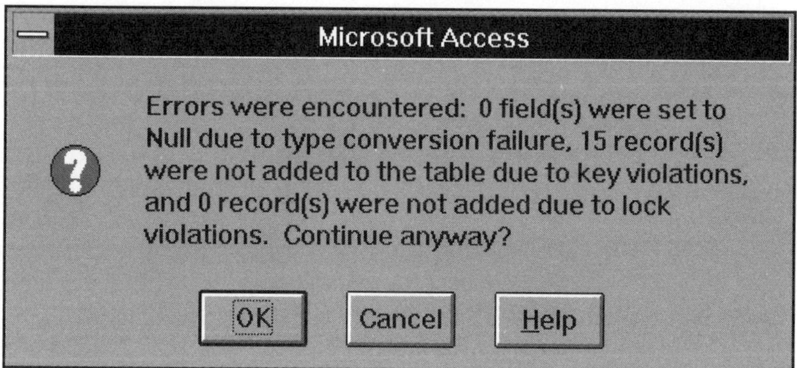

By **enabling** the cascading features of a relationship, Access takes care of all the rule breaking. Access will update the associated parent records in the case of Update and delete all associated child records in the case of Delete.

Combining Action Queries

You can combine some of the different Action queries together. For example, you can combine a Crosstab and a Make-Table to produce a new table (made up of the records displayed in the Crosstab) or you can combine an Update and an Append to add updated versions of your current records to another table. This way you get the benefits associated with both types of Action query.

Action Queries Outside of Access

Pass-Through Query

To create a Pass-Through query:

- Select the Query tab from the initial database window and click on the New button.
- Select the New Query button.
- Click on the Close button on the Add Table window. Don't add any tables to the QBE grid.
- From the menu bar select Query/SQL Specific and then Pass-Through. Access displays the following window:

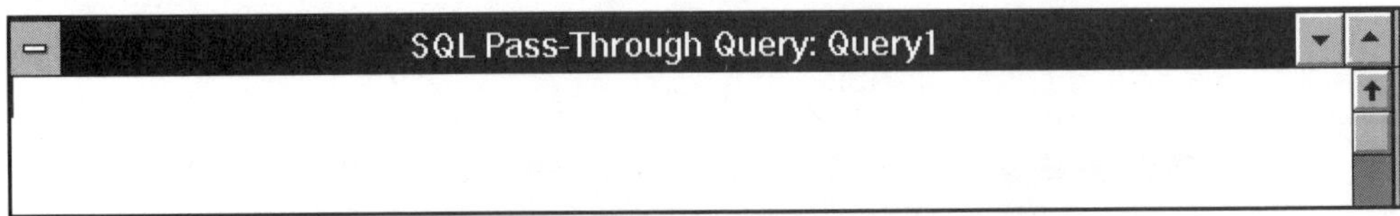

Open the Query Properties box with the icon.

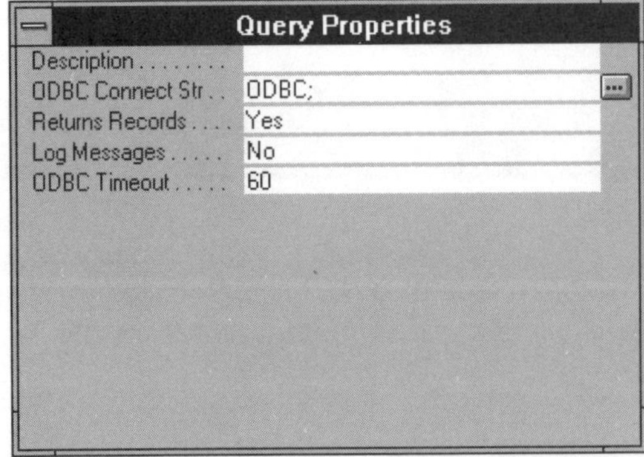

- Fill in the ODBC ConnectStr property to give Access the information it needs concerning the database you want to connect with. You may use the ODBCConnectStr Builder (the drop-down list at the end of the cell) to auto-create the correct link-up string.
- Fill in the Returns Record property as appropriate (setting to yes allows you to use the results from the Pass Through in queries, reports and forms etc.).
- Close the Query Properties box, and type your query into the SQL window.
- Click on the Run icon to run the query. If the query returns any records you can view them by selecting Datasheet View.

For more information on this type of query, see the Access 2.0 Help screens under Pass-Through and Pass-Through query.

Data Definition Query

To create a Data Definition query:

- Select the Query tab from the initial database window and click on the New button.
- Select the New Query button.
- Click on the Close button on the Add Table window. Don't add any tables to the QBE grid.
- From the menu bar select Query/SQL Specific and then Data Definition.

Open the Query Properties box with the icon.

Follow the same procedure as for Pass-Through query in the Query Properties box. For more information on this type of query, see the Access 2.0 Help screens under Data Definition and Data Definition query.

The Query Wizards

Unlike the other wizards, the Query Wizard isn't designed for you to be able to produce any of the basic queries quickly. Instead, Microsoft have used it to allow you to produce complex queries, tailored to special tasks. These special tasks include:

Query	Use
Find Duplicates query	This query will find all the duplicate records in one table or query.
Find Unmatched query	This query will find all the records in one table that have no matching records in another table.
Archive query	This query allows you to make copies of records to a history table - and on completion asks if you want the originals deleted.

Microsoft have also provided a wizard to help you with Crosstab queries.

Creating a Query Using a Wizard

As with the other wizards that appear in Access 2.0, you must first call up the Query taskmaster, which will enlist the help of the correct wizard for your problem.

1. Select the Query tab from the initial database window, and then click on the New button.
2. Select the Query Wizards button, and the Query taskmaster will present you with the following screen:

Choose the specialized Query Wizard to produce the type of query you require. Let's look at each of these wizards in turn to get an understanding of what they require in terms of answers to their questions.

Crosstab Query Wizard

The first thing the wizard needs to know is which table or query you wish to draw your data from. To this end, you are presented with the following:

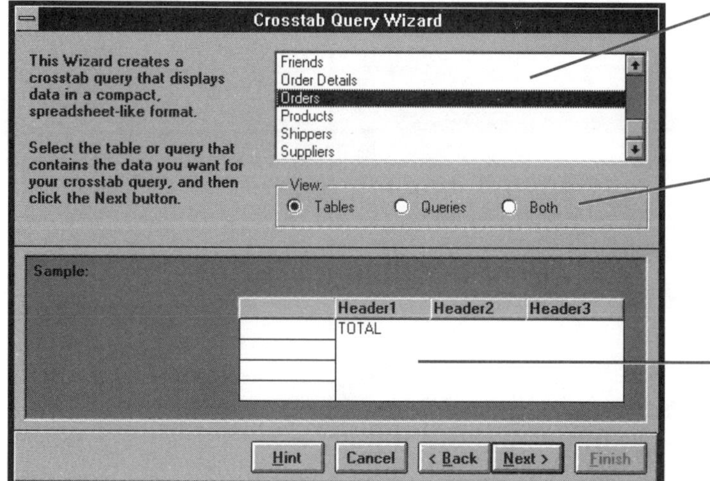

All the tables and queries contained in your database will appear in this window.

Use this area to select the contents of the above window.

In this window Access 2.0 will show you the query dynaset slowly building up as you go through the wizard's questions.

Select the table or query that you want the wizard to use. In this example, the table called Orders was selected. Click on the Next > button to continue.

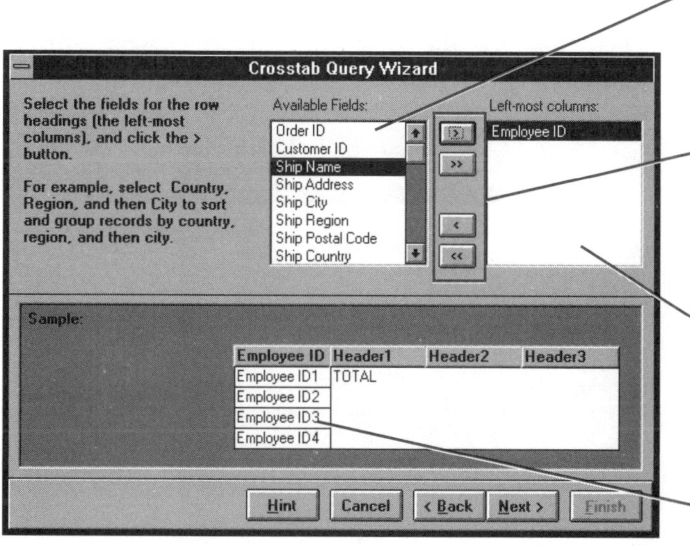

In this window you will see all the fields that make up the table or query that you selected on the previous screen.

Use these buttons in the usual way to select or de-select the highlighted field. Remember that single arrows affect single fields and double arrows affect all fields.

All the fields that appear in this window will be used by the wizard as row headings, as explained before in the Crosstab query description.

In this column there is a listing of all the employee IDs from the records in the underlying table.

Select the fields you want to use as the row headings (in this case Employee ID was selected) and then select the Next > button to choose the column headings.

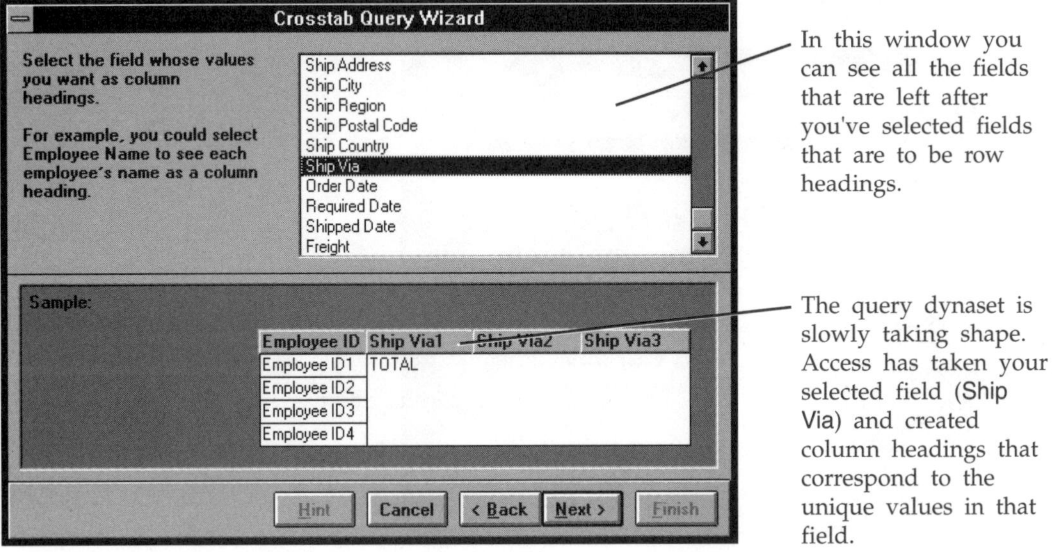

In this window you can see all the fields that are left after you've selected fields that are to be row headings.

The query dynaset is slowly taking shape. Access has taken your selected field (Ship Via) and created column headings that correspond to the unique values in that field.

Select the field whose unique entries you want to appear as the column headings. In this case, Ship Via was selected. Now choose the Next > button to continue.

If, at any point, you select a field that has the Date/Time data type, you will be presented with the following screen:

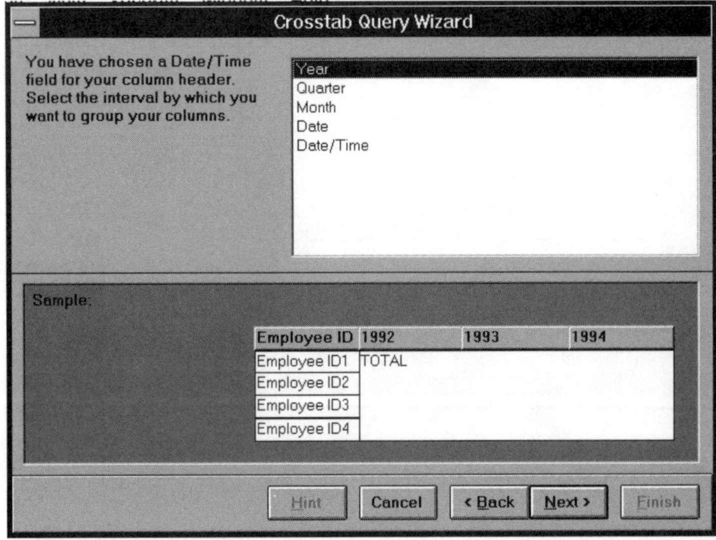

Simply select the band width you want to group the dates and times together with, and click on the Next > button to continue.

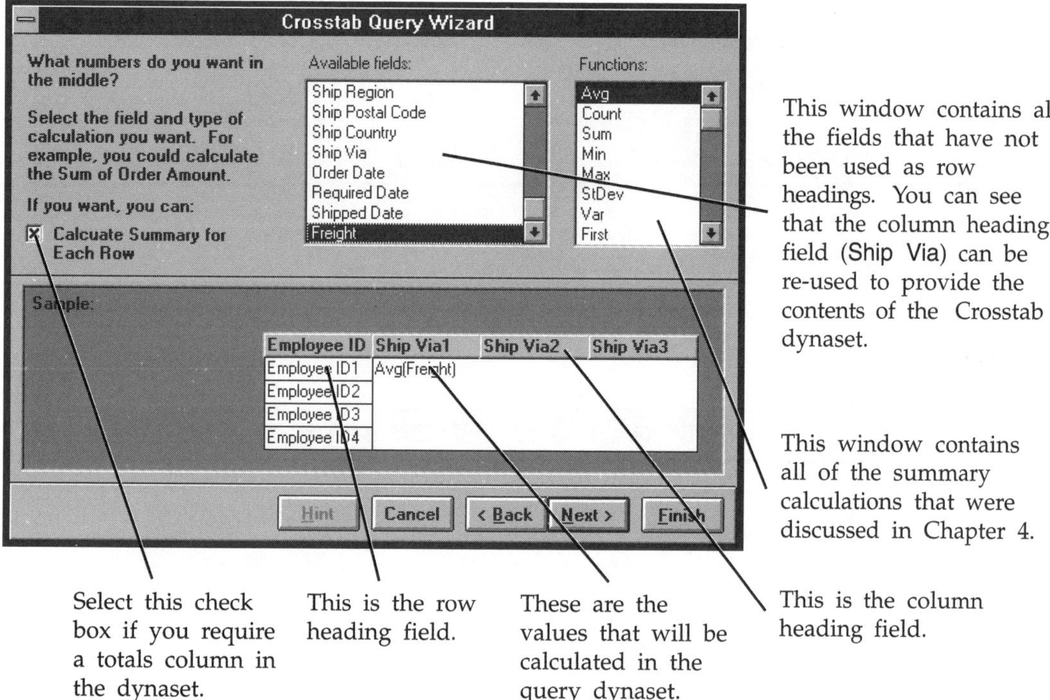

This window contains all the fields that have not been used as row headings. You can see that the column heading field (Ship Via) can be re-used to provide the contents of the Crosstab dynaset.

This window contains all of the summary calculations that were discussed in Chapter 4.

Select this check box if you require a totals column in the dynaset.

This is the row heading field.

These are the values that will be calculated in the query dynaset.

This is the column heading field.

Select the field that will provide the contents of the Crosstab dynaset, and also select the function you wish to apply if many values fall into the same cell. For example, in the above crosstab we chose to average the freight cost that each employee ran up for each method of shipping. Now move to the final stage:

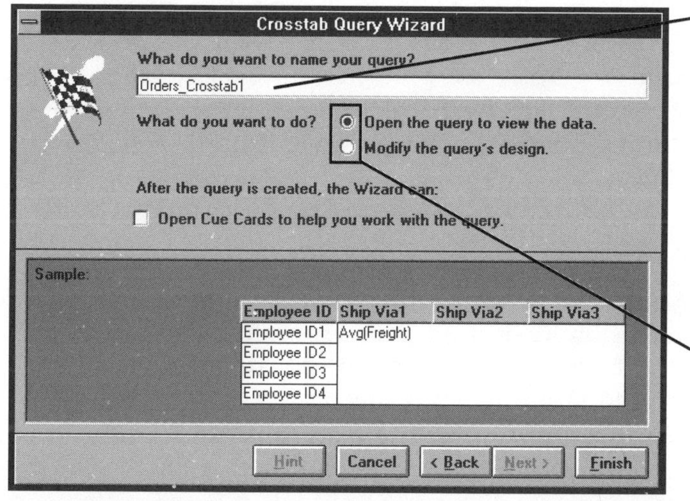

Enter into this box the name you wish to appear in the initial database window as the name for this query. The default name is a combination of the table or query that is used as the source for the Crosstab query, together with the title crosstab followed by a number for identification purposes.

Choose the view you wish the wizard to abandon you in when it has finished its work.

When you select the Finish button, the wizard will calculate the Crosstab dynaset and present you with the Design View or the datasheet of the query.

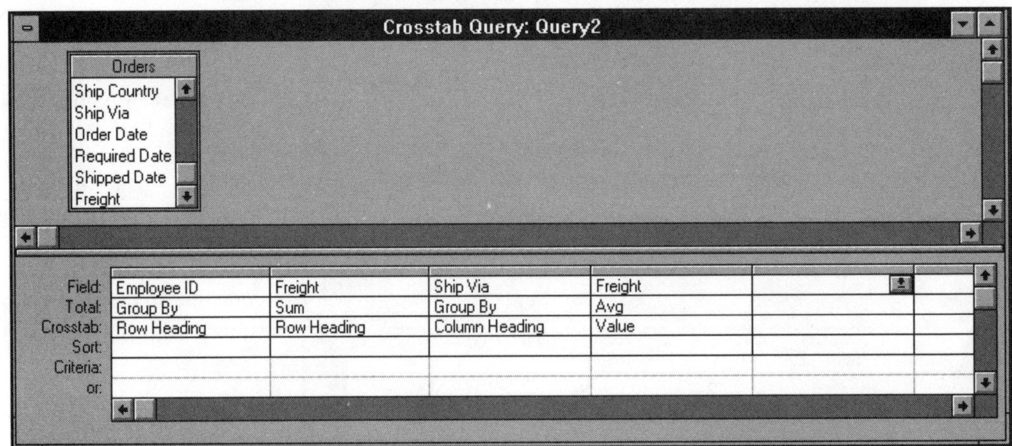

Crosstab Query: Query2

Employee ID	SumOfFreight	1	2	3
1	$10,450.91	$53.04	$72.03	$76.96
2	$10,694.25	$63.55	$108.39	$81.71
3	$13,347.13	$67.50	$84.84	$86.43
4	$14,046.90	$65.44	$64.50	$73.13
5	$4,352.02	$86.47	$100.05	$50.20
6	$4,344.71	$43.45	$45.98	$62.05
7	$7,967.62	$59.59	$119.05	$77.80
8	$10,084.86	$59.38	$78.87	$76.43
9	$3,918.26	$66.69	$82.55	$64.78

If you combine the column heading field with the function Count, it allows you to obtain the rate of occurrence of a particular event.

Using the NWind database Orders table, the above screens show the results of a Crosstab query asking: "Our employees use 3 different methods of shipping our goods. Show me the average expenditure that each employee has run up with each shipper over the last 12 months. Also, give me the total shipping expenditure for each employee."

The Find Duplicates Query Wizard

You may want to use this query for identifying errors in data entry. For example, if you had a Primary Key Code field, Access would allow you to enter the same record several times - giving each record a different identifying code. This is an obvious way to create incorrect duplicate records. Find Duplicates helps you identify these rogue records, even though they have differing codes.

The first screen this wizard presents you with deals with the table or query you want the records to be drawn from.

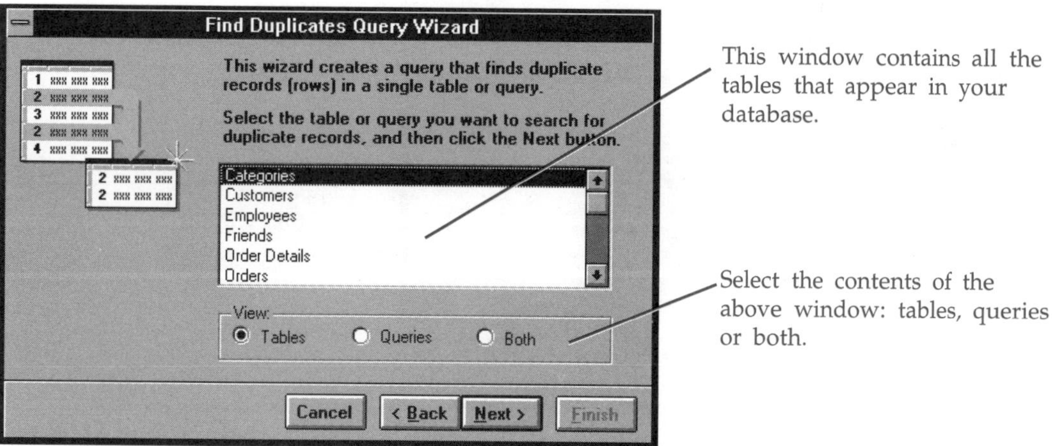

Select the table or query you want the wizard to use as the basis for this query (in this example the Customers table from NWind.mdb was selected) and click on the Next > button to continue.

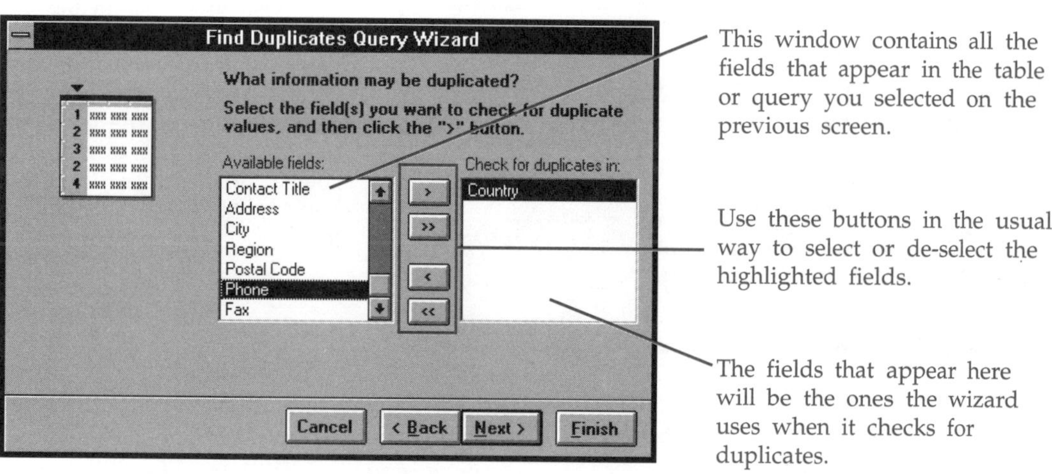

If you choose more than one field, the entries in all the selected fields must be identical so that Access will pick them up as duplicate records.

Select the fields you want to check for duplicate entries (in this case Country was selected) and move onto the next stage.

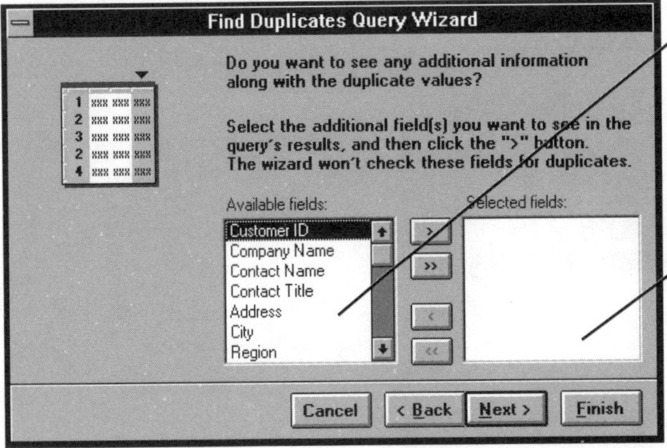

This window contains all the other fields that occur in the underlying table or query which have *not* been selected on the previous screen.

Put all the fields you want to appear in the query dynaset in this window.

Select the fields that contain the rest of the information you want to appear in the dynaset. In the example no fields were selected. Now click on the Next > button to move onto the final screen.

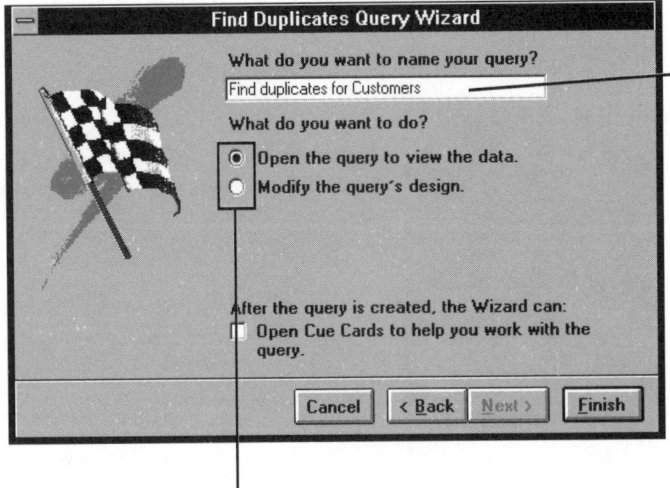

Enter into this box the name you wish to appear in the initial database window as the name for this query. The default name for this query is a combination of the table or query that is used as the source for this query together with the title Find duplicates for ....

Choose the view you wish the wizard to abandon you in when it has finished its work.

When you select the Finish button, the wizard will calculate the resulting dynaset and present you with the Design View or the datasheet of the query.

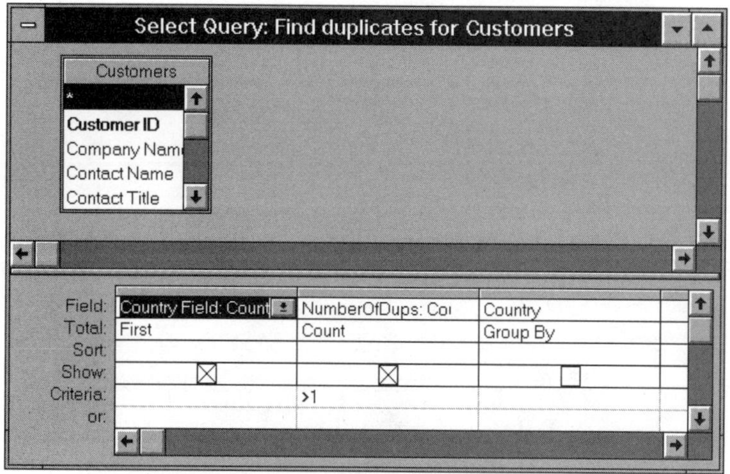

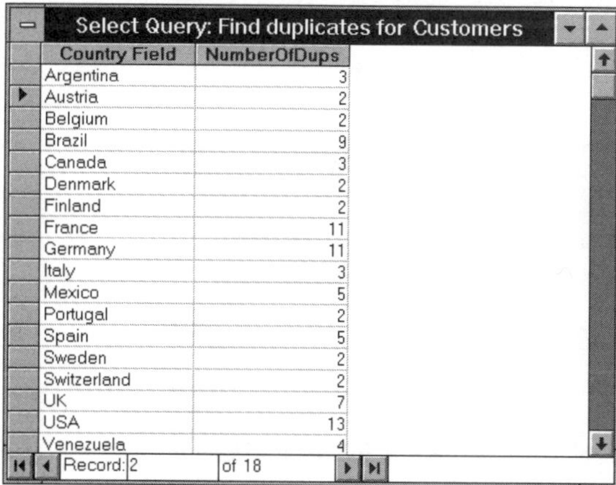

Find Unmatched Query Wizard

We can look at another example. Let's say you have an Employee Details table, that covers all the personal information on your workforce. To keep accurate records it's important for you to ensure that all the personal data is present for *all* your workforce. What you need to know is whether there are any employees that haven't as yet given over their details. In this scenario you would run a Find Unmatched query between Employee and Employee Details tables to uncover the omitted records.

The first screen this wizard produces looks like this:

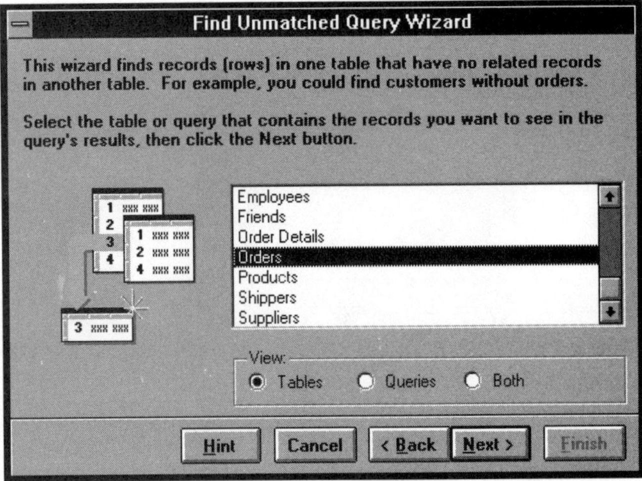

Select the first of the two tables or queries that the wizard will look through for unmatched records (in this case the Orders table from NWind.mdb was selected), before clicking on the Next > button to select the second:

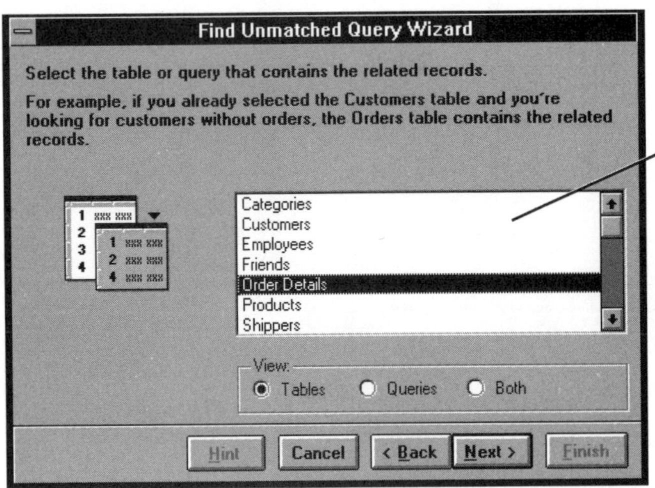

The table or query you selected in the previous screen does not appear on this list (in our case the Orders table).

When you have selected the second of the two tables or queries for the wizard to check in, move to the next stage.

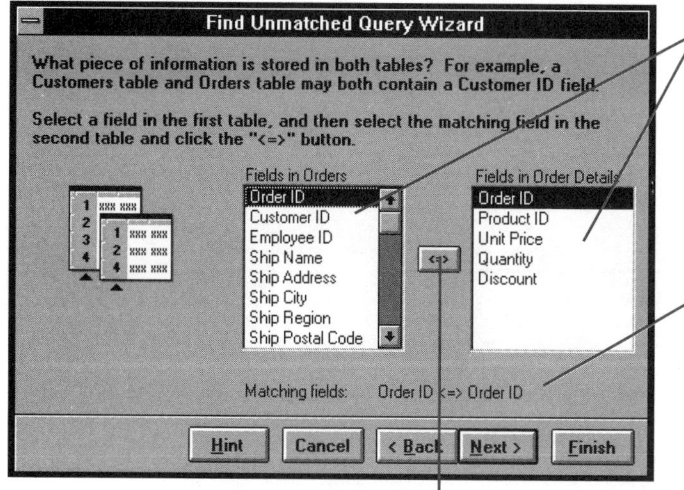

Select the common field that links the two tables or queries together from the lists in these two windows. These fields will usually be the primary and foreign key fields.

The current fields that are being used for the link are shown here.

Click on this icon to inform the wizard of the two fields that link the tables or queries together.

Select the two fields that link the tables or queries you have selected together, click the link button and move to the next stage.

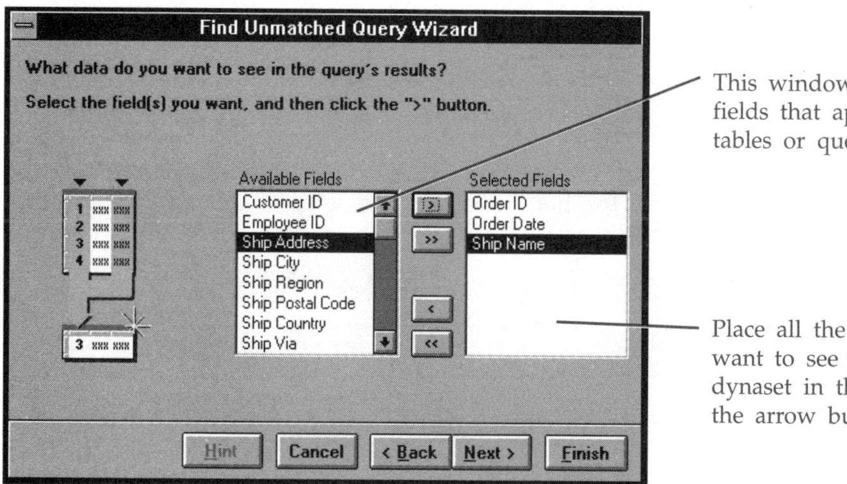

This window contains all the fields that appear in both the tables or queries you selected.

Place all the fields you also want to see in the resulting dynaset in this window using the arrow buttons as usual.

Select the fields you also want to see in the resulting dynaset and then click on the Next > button to move onto the final stage.

Type in the name you wish to appear in the initial database window that represents this query. Notice the way the default name is made up.

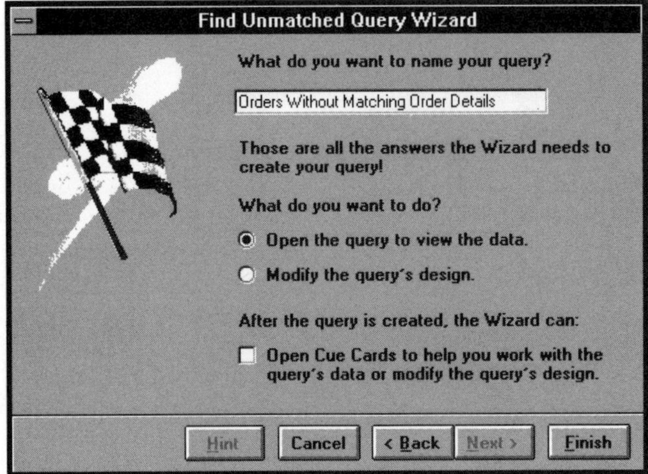

Select the view you wish the wizard to abandon you in when it finishes, and select the Finish button to see the results of all that hard work.

If you run this query you'll see that the resulting dynaset is empty. This means that no records in either of the selected tables have been orphaned and your NWind database is, as you hoped, up-to-date.

Archive Query Wizard

When you ask the taskmaster for help from this wizard, it calls the wizard up and produces this first screen:

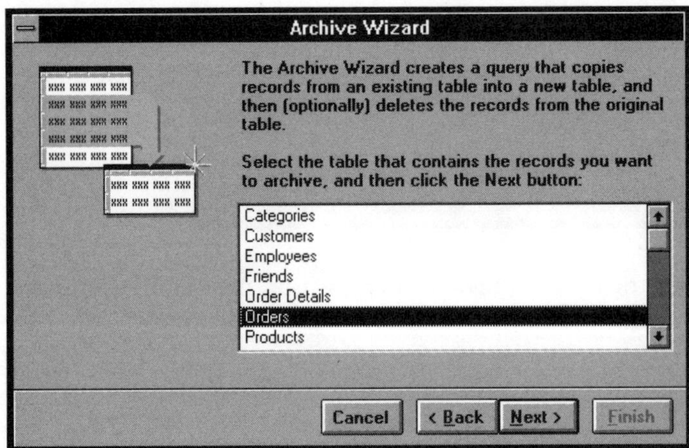

Select the table you want the wizard to take records from for archiving. Click the Next > button to move to the following screen.

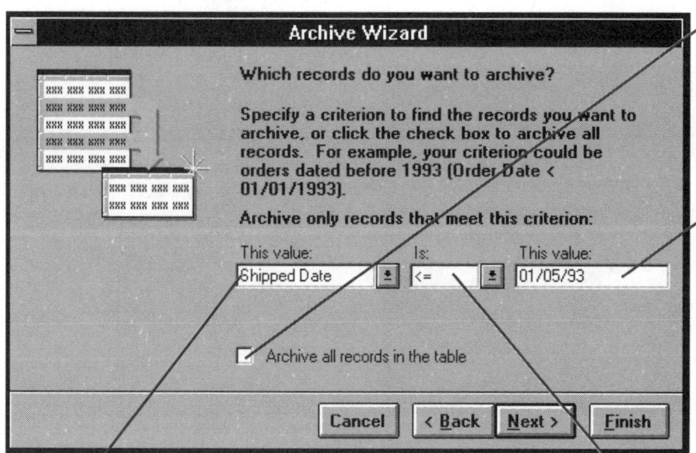

Check this box if you wish to archive all the records in this table.

In this window, the wizard is expecting you to enter a fixed reference point that the operator can be used with. In our example Access would archive all records that have a Shipped Date less than or equal to 01/05/93.

This window contains all the fields that make up the selected table (use the pull-down tab to see them all). Select the field the wizard will use when deciding which records to archive. In this case we are using the Shipped Date Field.

This window contains a number of mathematical operators. Choose the one that is most appropriate to your needs. These operators and the ways to use them are covered in more detail in Chapter 7.

Enter the criteria you want the wizard to use when deciding on a group of records. Remember that the reference point value should be of the same data type as the field being used in the criteria setting. Select the Next > button to continue:

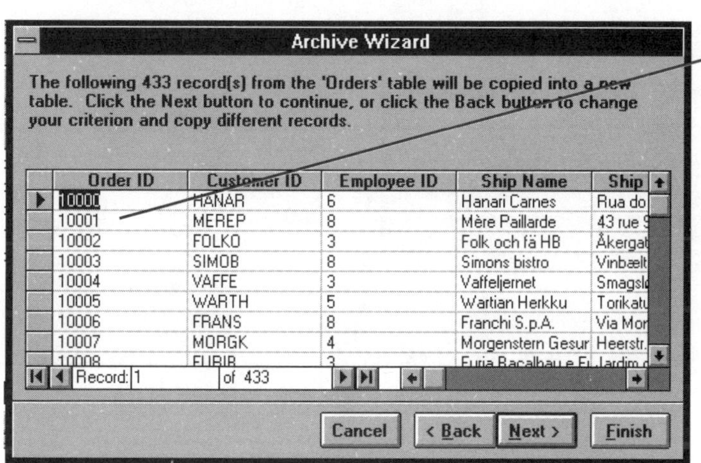

Here you will see all the records that conform to the criteria you have just selected.

Check the records to see if they all need archiving, and then click on the Next > button if they are alright, or the < Back button if there are records that don't need archiving. By selecting the < Back button, the wizard allows you to return to the previous screen to change the criteria. The following screen looks like this:

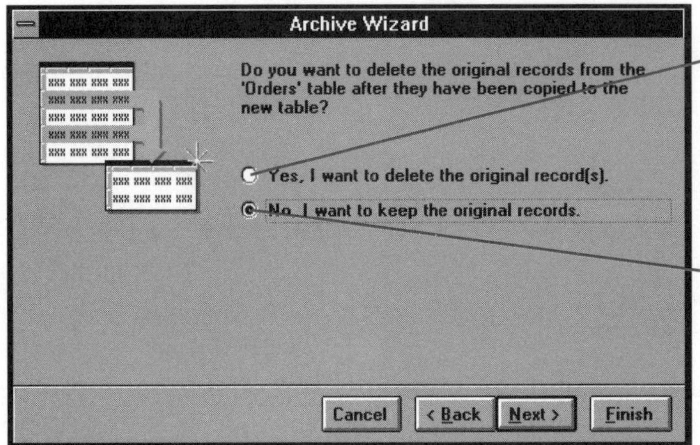

Select this option if you want a true archiving to take place (i.e. records are essentially **moved** from one table to a new history table).

Select this option if you want a Make-Table type of action (i.e. the records are **copied** to another table).

Choose the type of archiving you need and click on the Next > button to see the final screen:

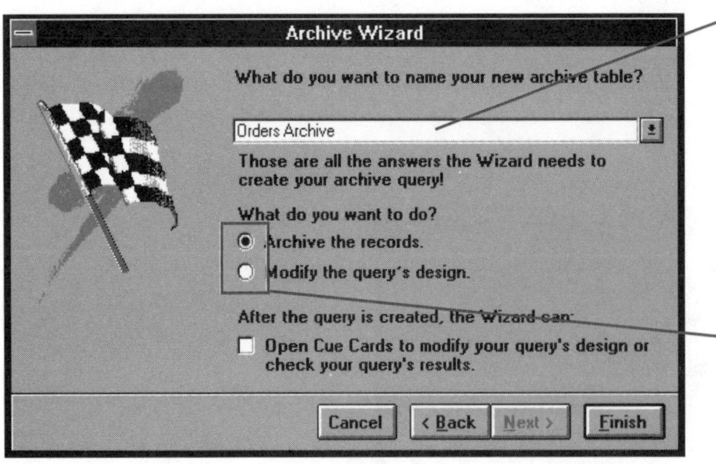

Choose the name for the table that the archive records will be stored in. It is possible to select from a list of the current tables, but if this is done the old table will be lost as the new archive table **overwrites** it.

Select the last action of the wizard, either to run the query and archive the records or look at the design view of the query to perhaps modify it.

Make your final choices on this screen and click on the Finish button to see the results of the wizard's hard work. When you run this query, Access will ask you a question similar to the following one.

This is the final check before the archiving proceeds. Select No to abandon the process, Yes to see the final acknowledgment screen:

When you click the OK button, Access selects the records and places them in a new table with the name that you gave the wizard previously. You can see this if you select the Table tab after running the query to see the new table listed on the initial database window.

You have now covered all four of the wizards that Microsoft has provided for your convenience. However, before this chapter and the topic of queries is finally closed (for this book anyway) we must look at a completely different but useful query called the Parameter query.

The Parameter Query

As a database designer, the queries you have designed so far are set in stone in so much as the records they can affect. The only records that will be affected will be the records that happen to fall within the criteria you set, usually before any records were entered. This can be a pain when you want to provide the user with the ability to view just a selection of the records in a table, without requiring them to return to a QBE grid to alter any criteria themselves.

Well, Microsoft thought of this problem, and evolved the Parameter query to solve it. In essence, the Parameter query, when run, will ask the user a series of questions about the data they want to view, and then go away and use these entries as criteria for the selection. Essentially, you are creating user-friendly criteria settings.

To Create a Parameter Query

Create the query as normal, basing it on tables and queries as required and choosing the fields to be included in the query.

Instead of the specific criteria, place the question you wish to ask the user in the appropriate field criteria cell, surrounded by square brackets. For example, suppose you were posing a question for the sales team, to provide the criteria for a sales query. The QBE grid entry, under the Sale Date field, would look something like this:

[Beginning Date]

The contents of the square brackets must not be a field name, as this is the convention for referring to a field name as well as a general parameter request. (You may find that this overload of one technique may be the reason why a normal query isn't producing the required effects.) Check the spelling of any text included inside square brackets:

Select Query from the menu bar and Parameters from the resulting drop-down menu to produce the following screen:

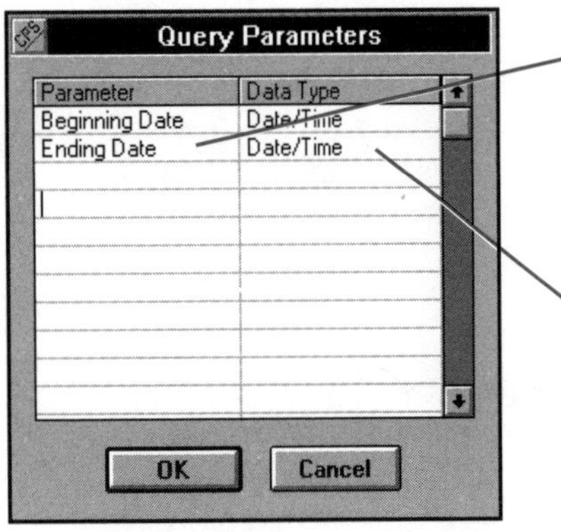

Type the question you placed in the criteria section of the QBE grid (*without* the brackets) into this half of the window.

Select the data type of the answer you will be expecting from the user. This should be the same as the data type of the field where the question appears.

This window is used to tell Access what order to ask for the parameters (more than one parameter may be assigned to one query), and what data type the answer should be. It is important to spell the parameters exactly as they are spelt in the criteria row of the QBE grid, otherwise Access will believe that you want to define two parameters, one in the grid and one in the parameters box. If this happens, Access will ask both questions which should alert you to the problem.

Enter the parameters and their data types into the window and then select OK to complete the design of the Parameter query.

When the Parameter query is run, a screen similar to the one shown below will be given to the user to complete. The entry in here will be used by Access as the criteria in the field where the parameter was defined and the resulting dynaset will be displayed.

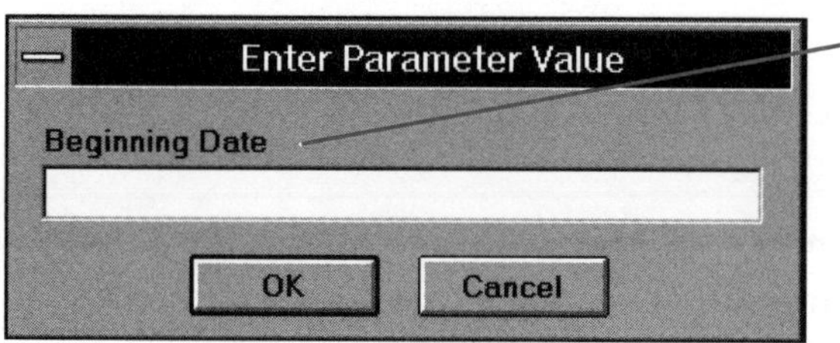

The question that is placed in the QBE grid and the Parameters Box appears here. It is therefore a good idea to make the question as simple and direct as possible.

The Parameter query is a very simple tool to create, and a great tool for transferring some power from you to the user. This means they will have more control over what they see and therefore will be happier with your database design.

Troubleshooting

Q&A I've decided that the QBE grid has gone horribly wrong. Can I delete everything to start again?

You can simply highlight all of the columns and select the Delete button, or you can select Clear Grid from the Edit menu.

Q&A What is the difference between [Datasheet icon] and [!] ?

Changing to the Datasheet View when you are creating an action query allows you to see the records that are selected by the query without applying the action. By clicking on the Run icon, you are asking Access 2.0 to select the records and then apply the action.

Q&A When would I use SQL?

SQL has been refined by the leading software companies to retain parity across packages. It is still IBM's standard for databases to talk to each other. As previously discussed, all the operations in the QBE grid are converted into SQL - your QBE grid is simply a mask for its activity. Consequently, SQL would be the language that you would most often use when outside the safety of the Access 2.0 environment. Structured Query Language is a whole subject on its own - you will need to study SQL syntax, as if you were studying any programming language. Some of the simple actions can be observed if you just look at the SQL statements generated by your Access QBE entries. Press the SQL button on your icon bar, or select SQL from the View menu.

Q&A I am getting error messages with my initial experiments in action queries?

Action queries have behind them an error trapping system. There are 4 basic flags:

Error	Meaning
Data Conversion Errors	These occur when you are trying to append data to a table or query, and the field that you are appending to has a different data type to that of the data. For example, you're trying to append text to an integer field.
Locked records	This happens when Access is trying to update or delete a record that another user has open in your database.
Duplicate Primary Key	This occurs if a duplicate Primary key or unique index exists on your appended data. For example, Product ID 46 already exists and therefore you can't append another 46 to your table.
Validation Rule	This means that records being inserted or updated violate a field or table validation ruling.

CHAPTER 10

Mastering Forms

In this chapter and also in Chapter 11: Refining Reports and Forms, you will see the improvements Access lets you make to the presentation of your database; what the software companies call front-end design. You will be able to create customized visual presentations for other users of the database to interact with. This means you don't have to use the overpowering, jam-packed Access screens that are utilized to create the database itself. To this end, Access provides you with the ability to rearrange the look of your forms, add color and, if you have the appropriate hardware, add sound and video.

Most of the aspects of form design are assisted by Microsoft's wizards, but you can also manipulate components by hand for true customization. There are simple methods for designing, using the wizards for the spade work while you progress with the fine tuning. In the basic chapter on forms, you saw how to create a form and then alter it using a set of basic tools. Now we will look at the more advanced features of forms so you can produce a really great and easy-to-use database.

In this chapter, you will learn about:

- Creating a form from scratch
- Customizing your paper and components
- Using the toolbox
- Overviewing properties
- Option groups, list and combo boxes, command buttons
- Adding pictures and sound
- Switchboards

Creating a Form From Nothing

When you are designing a form, instead of using a Form Wizard, Access allows you to start from a completely clean piece of paper. You can place the fields and alter the custom features in whichever way you want and you can make as many changes to the form design as you like before you put the form to bed.

Some of the screens and techniques you will be using will already be familiar, but the following guide is meant to be complete. It lists all the stages you will have to go through to produce your own custom form. First of all, you will need to absorb the basic starting point, a blank sheet. You can then place very powerful buttons onto the form with a toolbox (you can specialize the buttons and the presentation by changing their properties).

Getting to the Blank Paper

In the planning stage of the database design, work out the basic design of the form. Also decide where the data that the form uses is stored (i.e. which table or query the form should be based on). When these decisions have been made you need a blank page to create your form.

- From the initial database window, select the Form tab, and then the New button to bring up the next screen.

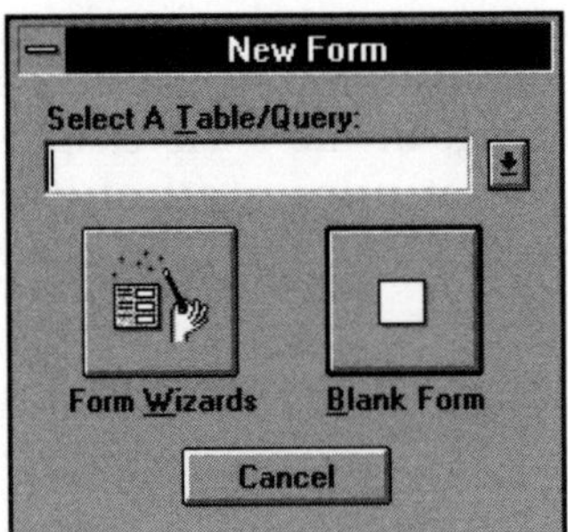

- Select the table or query you want to base the form on either by pulling on the tab to get a full listing or by typing in the name of the table or query you want to use.
- Now select the Blank Form button. Access will create a basic blank form linked to your selected table or query. A typical example of what Access will present you with is given opposite.

A Blank Form

This is the details section of your form. This is where most of the labels and controls will appear. There are no other sections of your form design defined yet.

Look at the depressed icons. They are, from the left, Properties, Field List and Toolbox. Clicking on these icons allows you to open or close these facilities quickly and cleanly.

Look at the grid on the paper. This is made out of a regular pattern of dots and can be used to align labels on the paper, or size the controls.

This is the Field List box. This contains a list of all the fields that make up the underlying table or query. You can use this box to pick up a field and drag and drop it into the form. The field will default to the basic Label or Text Box set.

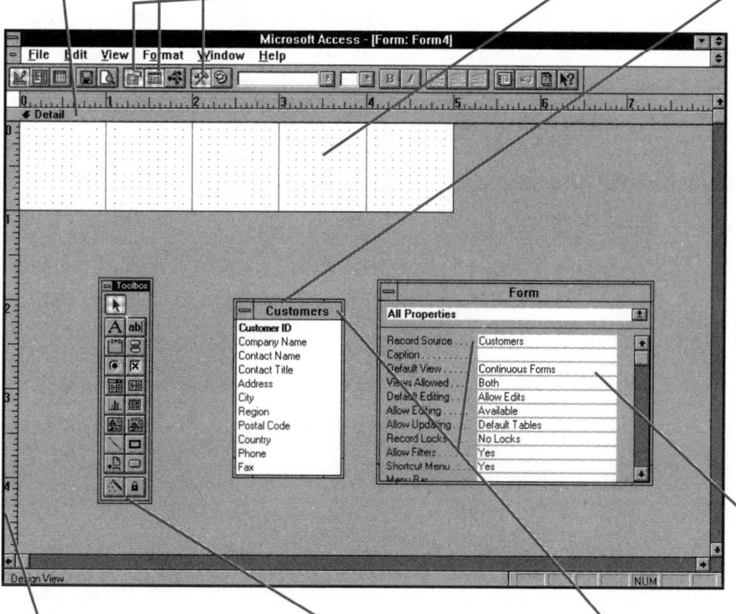

This is the ruler that surrounds your paper. You can use this to measure the size of labels or to select a group of controls. The largest size that this section can cover is 22 inches square.

This is the toolbox. It contains all the different types of labels or controls that Access 2.0 has to offer the advanced form designer.

There are two ways to find out the name of the underlying table or query. Check at the top of the Field List box, or look under the Record Source property in the Form Properties box.

This is the Form Properties box. It holds more specialized information on the properties of the selected label, form or control form section in a similar style to the Table Properties box or the Query Properties box.

Once you have reached this stage you are ready to begin designing the form itself.

Customizing Your Paper

First, you need to prepare the foundations of the form. This means:

- Deciding on the size and shape of the paper.
- Chosing which sections of the form you are going to use.
- Removing any of the facilities you don't need.

You can see that the window has been maximized. Combine a maximized window and a tidy screen by clearing away all the unnecessary boxes, windows, tools and controls. You will soon see results as the form begins to take shape and take on a new complexity. For instance, try opening the NWind form called Orders. If you open it with a small window and all the facilities active it's a nightmare!

Re-sizing the Paper

The first thing to do is re-size the paper. This is currently the white rectangle with regularly spaced dots on it, measuring about 5 inches by 1 inch.

- To re-size the paper move the mouse pointer to the edge of the paper. Depending on where you move to, the pointer will change shape as you pass over the edge, as shown below:

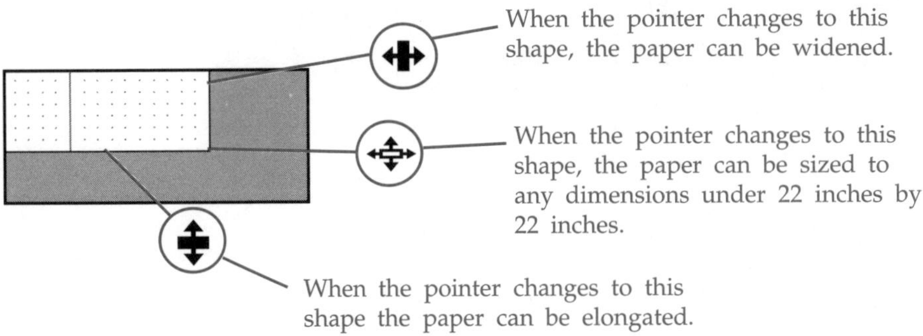

When the pointer changes to this shape, the paper can be widened.
When the pointer changes to this shape, the paper can be sized to any dimensions under 22 inches by 22 inches.
When the pointer changes to this shape the paper can be elongated.

- When the pointer has changed to the shape that you want, hold down the left mouse button and drag the paper out to the size that you require. Then let go of the button.

The Grid and the Ruler

The on/off switches for both the grid and the ruler can be found in the View menu. If the tool that you are interested in has a tick mark next to it, then the tool is active. To alter the state of either the grid or the ruler, simply select the appropriate name in the list.

The scale of measurement that the ruler uses is based on the selection made in your Windows Control Panel International setting, either metric (centimeters) or English (inches).

You can alter the spacing between the dots of the grid, using the Form Properties box.

- Make sure that the title at the top of the box reads Form.
- If it doesn't, click on any part of the gray table top that appears behind the paper and Access 2.0 will change the focus of the box back to the form as a whole.
- Scroll down in the box until you find the top properties called Grid X and Grid Y.
- By default these settings are 10 and 12 respectively. You can change these numbers to anything up to 16 and retain the grid on screen. Any higher than that results in the dots disappearing, although the grid lines remain.
- When you have changed these values, move out of the properties to see the effects of your changes

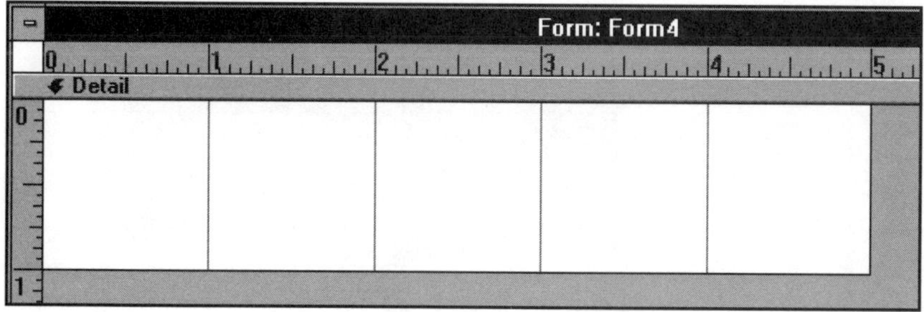

Paper With Grid Lines Only

The Boxed Facilities

You can quickly open and close the Toolbox, the Field List Box and the Form Properties Box by selecting the appropriate icon on the icon bar. These icons are shown below:

Adding Field Components to the Form Design

Now the paper has been prepared, both in terms of size and tidiness, let's look at the different ways of placing the labels and controls that make up the fields on to the form.

There are two main ways of placing labels and controls onto the form. The first is based on the method that the Form Wizards use and the other uses the contents of the Toolbox that Access 2.0 provides for the more advanced form designer.

Copying the Form Wizards

This method of getting the required labels and controls onto the form is the easiest, but, as is usually the case, it is also the most restrictive.

- Select the Field List Box icon for the list of available fields. This list is the same as the one given to you by any of the Form Wizards when you are asked for the fields that you wish to include.

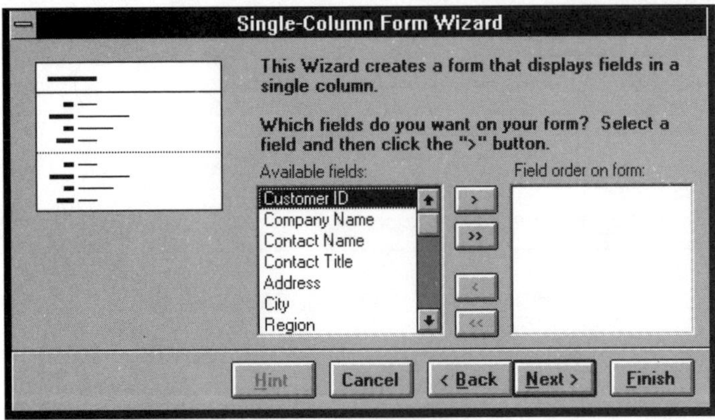

- Highlight the fields you want to place onto the form. You can select multiple fields using the normal *Shift* and *Ctrl* methods.
- Holding down the left mouse button, drag the field (now represented by a small rectangle) to the position on the form you require. This doesn't need to be accurate as the field can be moved later using the techniques given in the basic form design chapter.

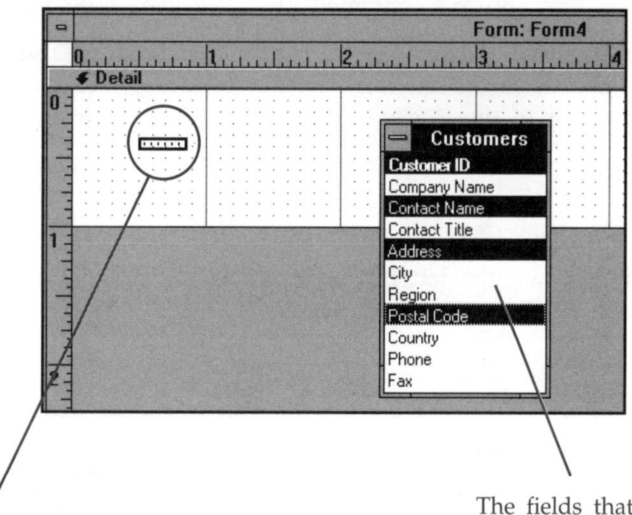

The mouse pointer has changed shape to inform you that it is transporting fields to the form paper.

The fields that have been selected don't appear consecutively. This was done using the *Ctrl* method of selection.

- Release the mouse button when the rectangle is in approximately the right position and Access will place the label and control belonging to the selected fields onto the form. Remember, wherever you release the mouse button, the top left corner of your label will be set at that position.

By following these steps you have started on the long and rocky trail to producing your first complete custom designed form.

Using the Toolbox

The second method of placing fields onto the form is more constructive, and therefore slightly more time consuming, but it does give you the freedom to produce the exact results you require. This method uses the basic building blocks of fields themselves, the label and the control.

To place labels and controls contained in the Toolbox onto your form:

- Click on the tool you wish to use in the Toolbox. (The uses for all these tools will be discussed later, when you are given a more detailed guided tour of the Toolbox itself.)
- Move the pointer to the position on the paper where you want the top left of the label or control to appear. You can see that the pointer changes shape depending on the tool you've selected.
- Holding down the left mouse button, drag out the shape of the component to the required size.
- Release the mouse button and Access will fix that component to the paper at the selected position and at the given size.

> When you select tools from the Toolbox and place them on the form, the tools only have basic properties. These properties are assigned by Access, based on the default template. Altering this template is discussed in detail later in the chapter.

When you first place these labels and controls onto the form, they are described as being unbound. This means they have no connection either to information held in or to the actual structure of the database. By using these unbound field components, you can produce any results you can think of, simply by binding them to one part or another of the database structure and letting them draw from your reservoir of data.

To achieve results, you will have to constrain these unbound labels and controls (more than when you used Form Wizard), but fortunately this is a simple task.

Looking at the Toolbox in Detail

All the field components that are available to the custom form designer can be found in the Access 2.0 Toobox. The Toolbox is shown opposite.

The Toolbox

The **Pointer** can be used if you have finished using a tool and want to manipulate the labels and controls you have placed on the form.

The **Label** is used as a tag for the controls on your form design or as a way of placing permanent text onto your form.

The **Option Group** is used in conjunction with the Toggle Buttons, Option Buttons and Check Box controls to group related mutually exclusive options.

The **Option button** is used to graphically represent Yes/No data types.

The **Combo Box** is a type of control used to give the user a choice of ready-typed entries in a pull-down menu format.

Graph is described in Chapter 7. It allows you to embed graphs in your forms and uses MS Graph Wizard.

The **Unbound Object Frame** is used to display an independent graphic on the form.

Line is used to improve the presentation of your form through the use of lines.

Page Break is used to artificially end the page. This is mainly used to split a multi-page form over more than one page at the point you want, rather than the natural full page mark.

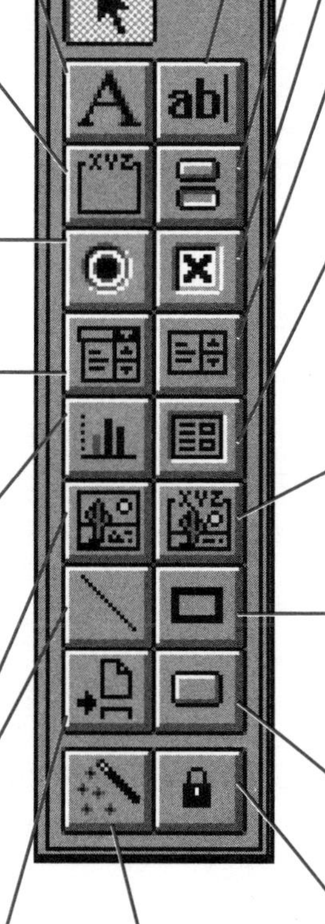

The **Text Box** is used to show the results of a calculated control or the contents of a field (the default control type).

The **Toggle Button** is used to graphically represent Yes/No data types.

The **Check Box** is used to graphically represent Yes/No data types

The **List Box** is used to give the user a choice of ready-typed entries, by presenting a listing in a special window.

Subform/Subreport is used to place one form inside another or one report inside another. This is mainly used to see the one-to-many relationship that exists between records in separate tables.

The **Bound Object Frame** is used to display a graphic contained in a database file.

Rectangle is the second tool for you to refine the presentation of the form.

The **Command Button** is used to create your own buttons for automating the database, i.e. with switchboards.

Tool Lock is used to lock your tool selection to the pointer.

If you select **Control Wizards** when you place an Option Group, Combo Box, a List Box or a Command Button on your form design, Access will call a wizard to help you with the design.

When you select the tool you require and then place the label or control on the form, Access reverts back to the normal pointer. This can be annoying when you wish to place a number of labels or controls of the same type on to a form. You can solve this by selecting a tool and then selecting tool lock. The pointer will stay active upon that tool until you de-select. You can then place multiple labels or controls with ease.

All of the tools given here are the building blocks required for a fully functioning form. To produce the results you want, you need to customize the properties of all or some of the components in your form design. You use the Form Properties box (introduced earlier) to achieve this.

Using the Form Properties Box

As with table properties and query properties, the form has a list of detailed information about itself which you may alter. The properties are relevant to the part of the form you are in. For instance, if you click on the gray background, the listing relates to the properties of the form body itself. If you clicked on a control, then the focus will change to that component and its properties will be displayed.

Let's look at it in more detail to see exactly what it can be used for. There are three different groups of properties that this box can be used to view:

1. The properties of the form itself
2. The properties of the various sections in the form (Details, form/page headers/footers)
3. The properties of the numerous labels and controls that appear on your form

To call up a property box, if one isn't already open, click on the icon to activate it.

Before you look at the properties available in the box associated with each of these groups, let's look more closely at the structure of the box itself. A typical Form Properties box is shown opposite.

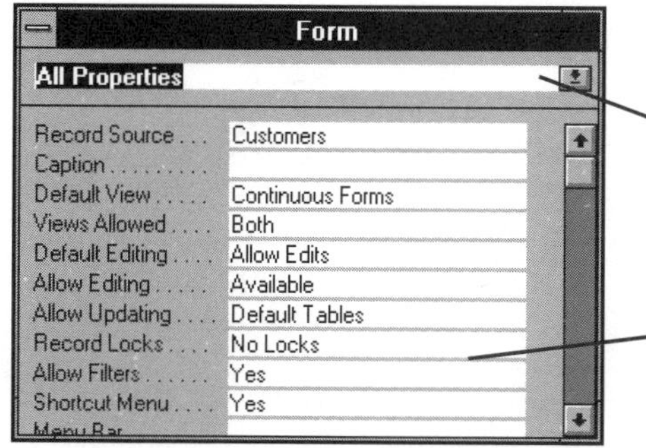

The entry here determines which family of properties is listed and appears below.

You are given a list of properties dependent on the box heading.

In the top part of the box you can select different groupings of properties to appear in the bottom section of the box. You can see the selection of groupings you can choose from below.

This selection is the default setting and shows you all of the properties of the selected part of your form.

This grouping deals with the data that will appear in your form, as well as such properties as whether you can edit it, or whether an input mask will be used.

This grouping deals with the layout of the form. For example, you have properties that deal with the dimensions of your controls, or whether scroll bars are present.

All Properties
All Properties
Data Properties
Layout Properties
Event Properties
Other Properties

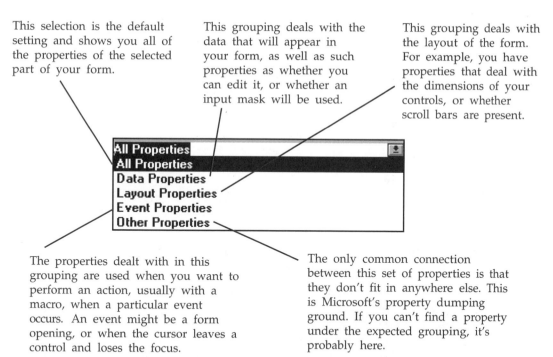

The properties dealt with in this grouping are used when you want to perform an action, usually with a macro, when a particular event occurs. An event might be a form opening, or when the cursor leaves a control and loses the focus.

The only common connection between this set of properties is that they don't fit in anywhere else. This is Microsoft's property dumping ground. If you can't find a property under the expected grouping, it's probably here.

To alter properties, place the cursor in their cell in the listing and click. There are often more choices available once you're in the cell, via Builder buttons and drop-down menus. To close the properties box, simply double-click in the top left corner as usual, or re-press the icon.

Changing the Focus of the Form Properties Box

The Form Properties box can only show the unique properties of one part of your form at any one time, and so when it's showing the properties of a particular part of the form, that part is said to be in focus. Access shows the part of form that's in focus by highlighting it in some way. Labels and controls have boxes that appear on their edges, while a form section has its title bar highlighted.

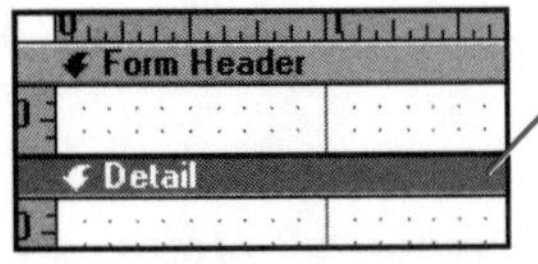

The details section of this form has the focus.

Access defaults the focus to the form itself if none of the other parts of the form are selected.

To change the focus to a specific part of the form:

- To focus on the form itself click on the background table (the gray background that appears under the paper), or click on the ruler. If you click on the ruler you may select any labels or controls that appear below or to the right of your pointer.
- To focus on any of the form sections, click on the section title or click on any part of the paper in that section (other than that covered by labels or controls).

To select a label or control there are three methods:

1. Click on it with the mouse pointer. Remember that *Shift* can be used to selected multiple components.
2. Place the mouse pointer to the top left of a group of components and while holding down the left mouse button drag out a box. This light gray box will encompass components on your form. As long as it has just a part of that component within it, then the components are focused. This is a great method for fast group selection.
3. Place the pointer onto the ruler. Holding down the left mouse button, sweep out a length of form you wish to select. This length is translated into a shaded column across the form, and all components that partly fall into that column will be selected when the mouse button is released

A new feature of Access 2.0 means that when you select multiple components on a form, only the properties shared by all the selected components will appear in the box. This can be very useful when you wish to assign the same properties to several components, because the entries you make in this shared properties box will be copied into all of the individual components' properties boxes.

Now that you know how to look at the properties of each part of your form, let's look more closely at those properties and what power they give to the designer.

Using the Properties Box

Each of the different components you can place on your form have a different set of properties. To give you an idea of what the most commonly used properties for all the components do, let's examine Text Box properties in detail. Most of these properties appear in other components' properties, therefore looking at this example will also lay the foundations for those components.

A full listing and explanation of all the properties and their special features appears in Appendix I.

The next page is an excursion through typical properties that are illustrated with a Text Properties box. We have marked any entries with the words 'menu' or 'build'. This means that the entry will also have a drop-down menu available (menu) or a builder button available (build).

The Text Properties Box

Lets you define text or figure display. Defaults to the format of the control source data type, e.g. currency format displays a leading $ (menu).

The name that the control will be known by.

The source for the contents of this control. Comes from a choice of fields contained in the underlying table or query (menu and build).

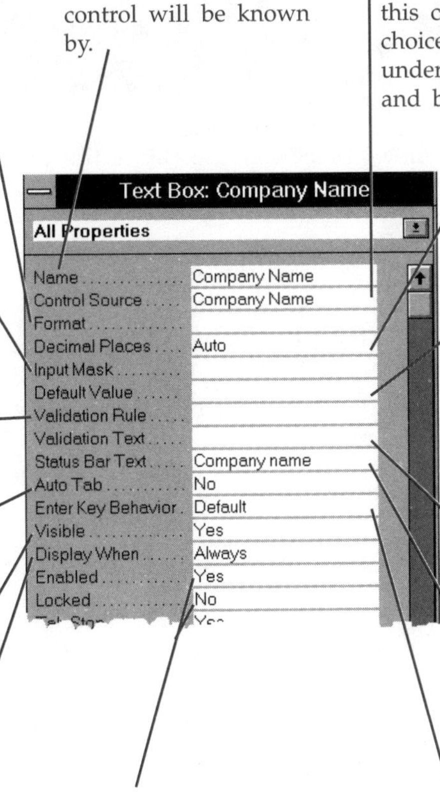

See Chapter 3. If you don't set Format the display defaults to the Input Mask setting (build).

A rule that polices a user's data entry (build).

Moves the focus automatically. Yes or No choice.

Informs Access if the control should be made visible on the form. Yes or No choice.

Sets the control to Visible. Options are: Always, Only When Printing or Only On The Screen (menu).

Deals with the user's ability to alter the data in the underlying table or query. Yes or No choice.

Sets the limit of decimal places that are displayed. Usual default is 2.

Lets you set a default value for this control; normal setting is blank. Exceptions: OLE, Counter and Memo (build).

This is a warning given if the user breaks the validation rule.

The text that appears on the status bar. Used to help the user on the type of entry the control is waiting for.

Sets what happens after *Enter* is pressed: e.g. to jump to a new control or start a new line (menu).

Allows the user to move the focus by pressing *Tab*. Yes or No choice.

If data is too large to fit in the control, scroll bars allow you to view (menu).

Deal with the position and size of label or control (where it appears in relation to the ruler). Use Left and Top for top left corner, Width and Height for the size.

Sets special effects applicable to label or control. FX include normal, raised and sunken (menu).

These five properties deal with changes to the font of the text that's included in the label or control. Yes or No choice.

Used to add a custom Help screen to the label or control. Needs a copy of the Windows Help Compiler and a wordprocessor that supports rich text format (RTF) to create the custom help file. (Not covered in this book.)

Tab Stop	Yes
Tab Index	1
Scroll Bars	None
Can Grow	No
Can Shrink	No
Left	1.625 in
Top	0.6563 in
Width	2 in
Height	0.1667 in
Back Color	16777215
Special Effect	Normal
Border Style	Normal
Border Color	16777215
Border Width	Hairline
Border Line Style	Solid
Fore Color	1
Font Name	MS Sans Serif
Font Size	8
Font Weight	Normal
Font Italic	No
Font Underline	No
Text Align	General
Help Context Id	0
Tag	
Before Update	
After Update	
On Change	
On Enter	

The rest of the properties form here down are used with attached macro or Access Basic procedure which will run when the conditions of these properties are met. This is known as event programming.

Shows the position control has in the Tab Order. Defaults to the order you designed them in. 0 = the first, 1 = the second etc.

Sets whether control can change size if the data is too large to fit. Only affects the printed form and not the screen form. Yes or No choice.

Sets paper color inside the control. Use to emphasize text (build).

These four properties deal with changes you can make to the border that surrounds the control.

This sets the color of the text in the control (build).

This deals with alignment of text in the control, either Left, Center, Right or General. General is numbers on the right and text on the left (menu).

A marker for this control that macros and Access Basic can use to refer to it.

If you look at the properties given above that apply to a Text Box you should get some understanding of the opportunities open to you to customize your form design. The other components you can use as part of your form design also use most of these properties, as well as special ones of their own. For more details on the properties that other components use, see Appendix I. However, the sheer weight of numbers involved can sometimes be overpowering, especially if this is your first time, so let's look at some of the forms in NWind and the properties that have been assigned to their controls.

Form Control Properties: Examples of Their Use

Open the NWind Products form in Design Vew as shown below.

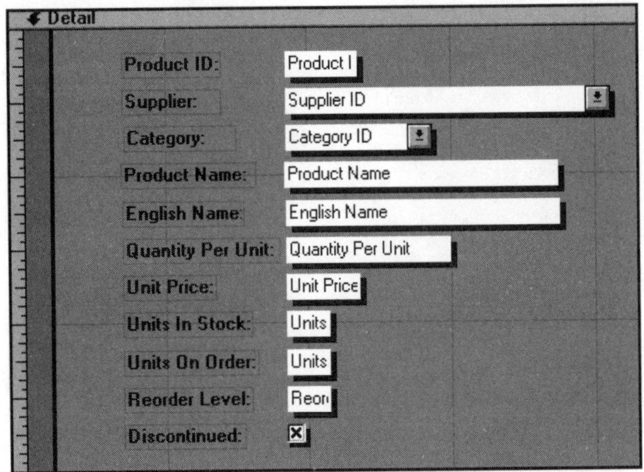

Open the Form Properties box. Check out some of the entries that have been made. Move the focus to a few different controls or labels. Can you see what each property setting does? Change to the Form view. What do you think makes that control operate like that? Which property makes it do that?

Some of the interesting points are:

- Text from the status bar has been used in the Product ID control. Remember that this is used as a 'what to do' prompt to the user.
- Look at the format used for the Unit Price control. You can use this property to alter the way the data appears after you have entered it in.
- The Tab Index figure in the Quantity Per Unit control is 5. Therefore, this will be the 6th control to take the focus

Now open the Products And Suppliers form as shown below:

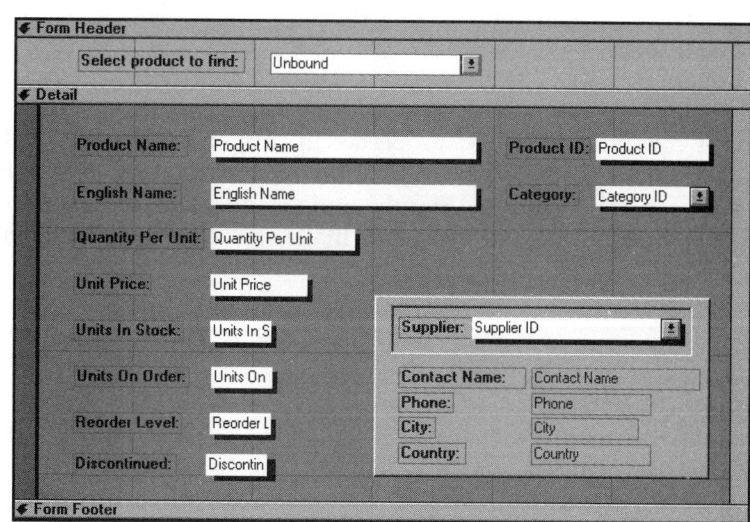

- Look how the raised and sunken rectangles have been put to good use to provide a visually impressive result
- Look at the Discontinued control. Notice how a Text Box with the Yes/No format can do the same job as a Check Box.

Finally open the Suppliers form as shown below:

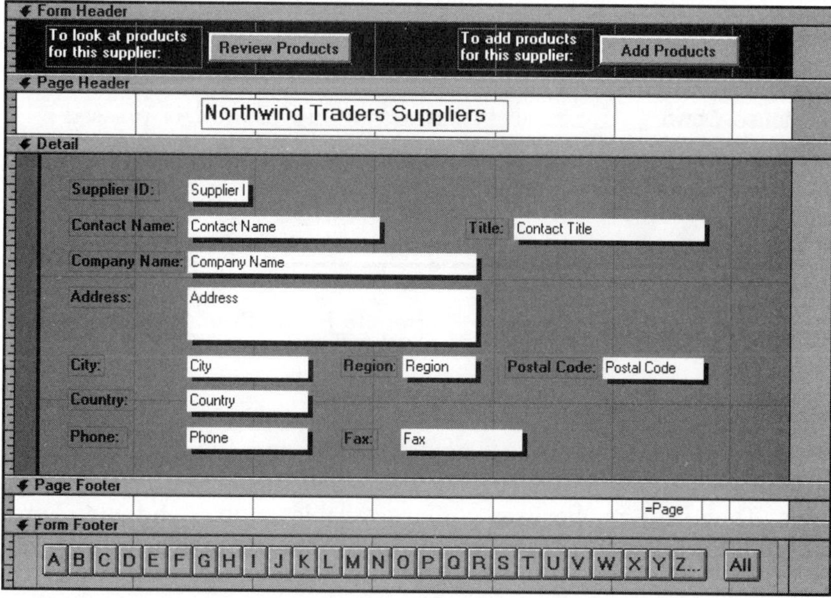

- Look at the use of color across the form design.
- Notice the Command Buttons in the form header and footer. See the macro that's attached to the On Click property of the Review Products button.

By using a combination of the properties in Appendix I, looking at the properties used in NWind, and by a little experimentation, you should be able to produce impressive results. Simply understanding which property controls what and what kind of entry you can make will help you with your design.

Event Programming

When people use your database they will cause events to occur. Events are happenings, triggered by some action that the user performs such as opening a form, or altering the data in a record. These events are used by Access 2.0 to link together the various objects that make up your database, such as your tables, queries and reports. You can also make use of them through the Event Properties that are attached to all controls as well as your forms and reports.

You can attach macros and Access Basic to your database so that when different events are triggered by the user storming through the database, your macros or Access Basic code is also triggered.

Some of the Event Properties you may encounter are show below:

Event Property	**Triggered**
On Open	When the form or report is opened, before the first record is displayed
On Mouse Down	When any mouse button is pressed
After Update	After the changes you have made to the data have been updated
On Got Focus	When a form control receives the focus

For more information about the different Event Properties that are available see Appendix I.

One of the most effective uses these events can be put to is when switchboards (which will be discussed later) and Command Buttons are used together. Switchboards are special forms that are generally made up of Text Boxes. These inform the user of the available options and the Command Buttons they should select to gain entry to these options. All the command buttons need macros or Access Basic code to run when they are pressed. Otherwise, the buttons are reduced to being redundant visual effects. These command buttons make use of the On Click property that notes when a button is pressed and runs any code that is attached to that button's property.

Form Properties and Section Properties

The properties that are associated with the form itself and each of the sections that go towards its make-up are very similar in style to the component properties. Each is laid out in its own order and each has its own special properties to perform certain tasks. For example, the form has two properties that allow you to remove the max and min buttons from the window (so you can't alter the size of the window with them), whereas the sections have a property that makes Access put that section on a new page.

Each of the properties in both the general Form Properties box and the sectional equivalents are explained in detail in Appendix I, but we suggest you whizz through the forms in NWind just to see how the various properties are put to use and what results they produce.

Specializing Controls

Up until now it has been assumed that all the controls are created in much the same way. You place the control onto the form and customize the properties. To some extent this is true, but some controls need more work than others. The simpler controls to produce include the Label, the Text Box, the Option Button, Toggle Button, the Check Box and the Line and Rectangle. The rest of the controls need slightly more work and therefore are dealt with in more detail here. Remember that there is yet another set of wizards to help you here. They assist in building List, Combo, option groups and Command Buttons.

Some of the more specialized topics included here are:

- Using an Option Group
- Creating a List Box
- Creating a Combo Box
- Adding Command Buttons to your form
- Adding pictures and sound to your form
- Adding graphs to your form
- Making a form within a form

For the first four of these tasks, Microsoft have provided help in the form of wizards to help you through the design. So that you can understand what properties you need to concentrate on when designing them by hand, let's first look at the wizards for each case.

Page Break

This is not a wizard. The page break is very simple to use and it only has four properties. To produce the required results simply place it on the form in the position you want. Normally, you don't need any customization as the only properties the control has to offer are Name, Left, Top and Tag.

Property	Use
Name	This is its name in your design (i.e. page break 1).
Left	The break starts at the default (0 inches on the left).
Top	This is distance from the top of the page that the break starts.
Tag	This gives a flag to a macro or Access Basic routine, for example to set page breaks automatically.

Option Groups

An option group is a group of option buttons, toggle buttons or check boxes that stand for the options a user can choose from, and is used when only one of the options can be selected for each record. In other words we restrict the entry to only one choice

For example, with the question "Are you American, British, French or from somewhere else?" on your form, you may only choose one response, even though you could answer Yes or No to all the individual questions: "Are you American?", "Are you British?" etc. In this case, you could use four option buttons, one for each of the answers, and place them in an option group so that the user would then only be able to select one. With the Option Group we can use the Control Wizard to help us complete the process.

Option Group With a Wizard

- Select the button in the Toolbox to enable the Control Wizard.
- Also select the button in the Toolbox to prepare to place the option group onto the form design.
- Place the option group onto the form, allowing enough room to get all the buttons or boxes and their associated labels into it. You will enter the number in the following wizard.

- Release the mouse button to fix the size of the option group and the Option Group Wizard comes to your aid with the following screen. Remember to drag out a box size big enough for the type and number of components you plan to have.

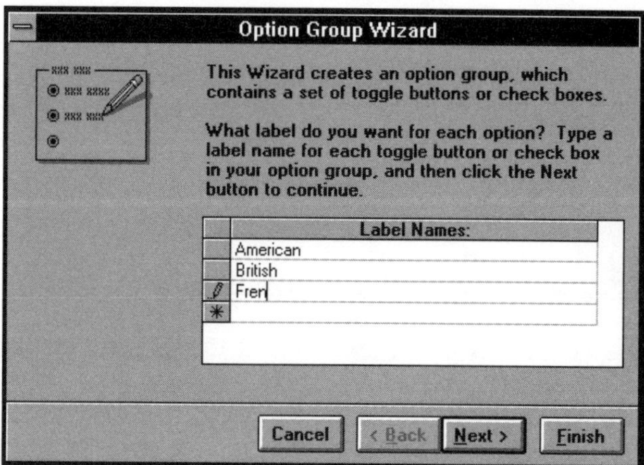

- Type in the labels you want to attach to the buttons or boxes that will be inside the option group before clicking on the Next > button.

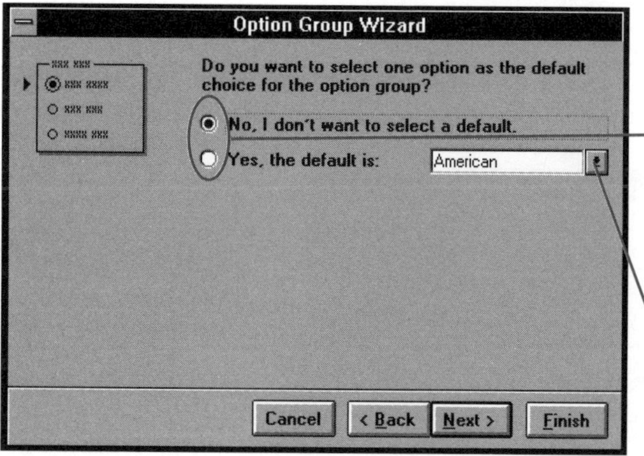

Select the appropriate option button to chose whether or not to have a default entry. A value will be entered if none are chosen. For example, in our short example above, choice may default to "from elsewhere".

If you do choose to have a default entry, select the option you want from the list obtained by pulling on this tab.

Decide whether you want a default entry, and if you do, which of the options it will be. Then move onto the next stage.

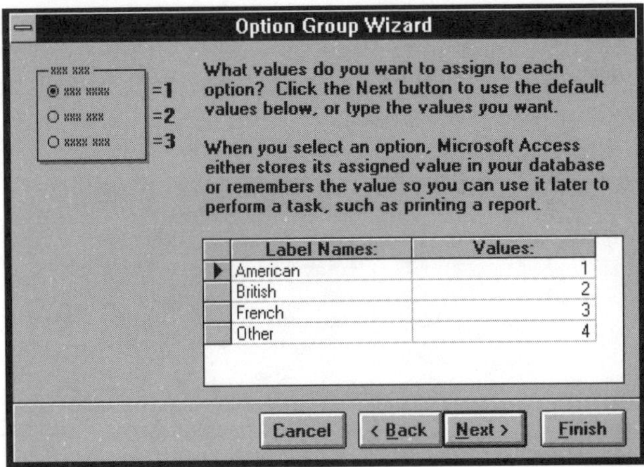

When you use an option group, Access 2.0 doesn't place the actual answer into the field in the table, it places a number. If you want to have the actual answer in your records, you will need to design a look-up table with two fields: Value and Response. Place the information you see on this screen into the table and link the Value fields together. This will allow you to use a query to produce the response with the rest of the record. The look-up table will have two fields: the value and the actual (American, French etc.). You must tie the original table where you are entering data to the look-up table via a query. This will give a dynaset comprising all the original information with proper responses included.

- Accept the default entries in this table or alter them to any custom numbers you may require. Now click on the Next > button to continue.

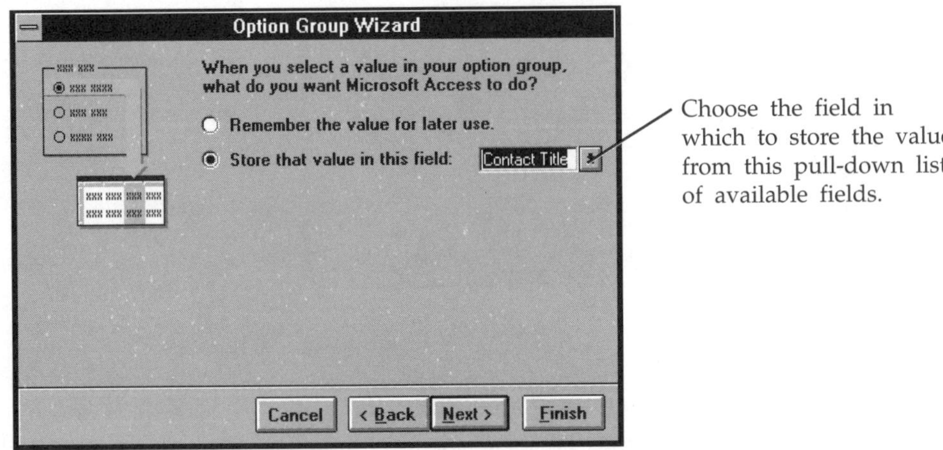

Choose the field in which to store the value from this pull-down list of available fields.

- Access can remember the selection for later use. For example, if the option group was used to decide on where to go to in the database structure next (the opening screen or the weekly report). Or it can store the value in a field in the table that underlies the form (if the value was "French" for example). Make the appropriate choice and if it's storage then select the field in which Access should place the value.

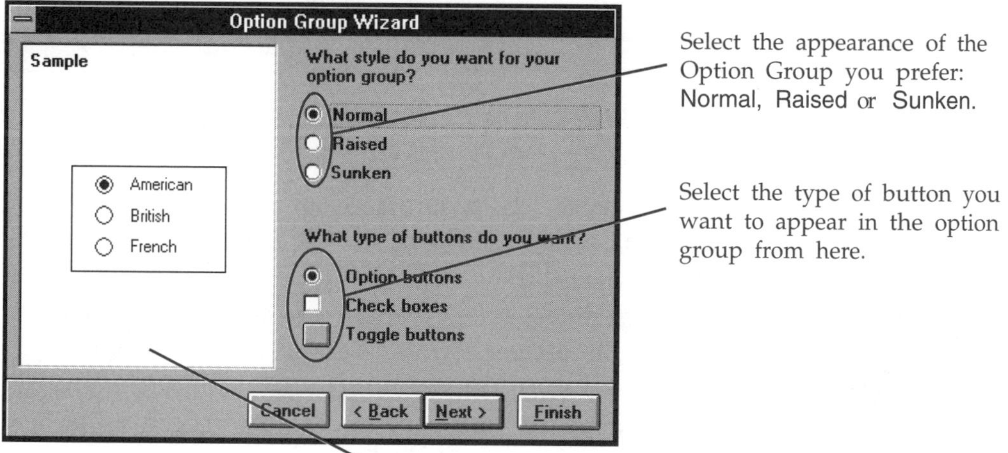

Select the appearance of the Option Group you prefer: Normal, Raised or Sunken.

Select the type of button you want to appear in the option group from here.

Notice that the sample changes depending on the choices you make.

- Choose the style and appearance of the option group and click on the Next > button to move onto the final screen.

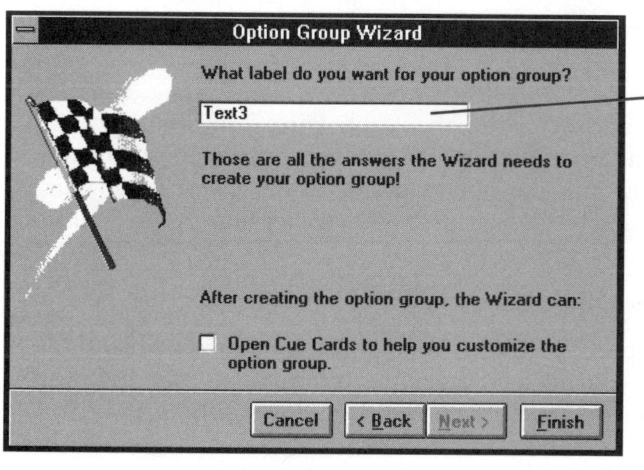

Type in the text you want to appear on the label for this option group here. For example, 'Selection A' or 'Nationality'.

- Select the Finish button and the wizard will create your completed option group, as shown below.

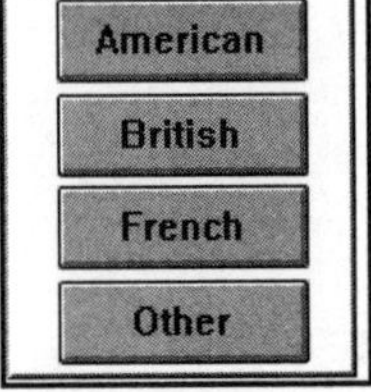

Option Group by Hand

To produce this option group by hand, you need to complete the following steps:

- With the Control Wizard button *deselected*, place the option group onto your form, remembering to leave enough room to get all the buttons or boxes inside it.
- Now select the type of button or box you want to include in your option group and lock the pointer to that selection with the Tool Lock button
- Place as many boxes or buttons into the option group as is required. Notice that when the pointer is over the option group, the group changes to a black background. This means that you are about to create an option grouped button.
- Re-size and shape the buttons you have placed in the option group using the usual methods.
- De-select the tool by removing the tool lock and returning to the pointer.

At this point, you have the necessary components on your form, but they aren't linked to any of the underlying tables. To get your option permanently saved into a table you need to link the option group to the table. To do this, you need to open the Properties box associated with the option group you are designing:

- Highlight or focus the option group, and call up the Properties box.
- The Control Source property of the option group is at present blank. Select the field where you need to store the information your buttons will generate, from those obtainable on the drop-down list.

So that the user knows exactly which button does what, you need to add captions to the buttons.

- Open up the Form Properties box with the focus on the first button.
- Type in the appropriate text in the caption property.
- Repeat this for all the buttons.

Whether you have connected the option group to the database structure, or if you only wanted Access to remember the value for later, you now need to alter the presentation of the option group so that the buttons will produce the effects you want.

- Select the option group, and call up the Palette.
- Use the facilities in the Palette to alter the presentation of the Group in terms of the size of the edging, the attitude and the colors of the various components.
- Repeat this process for all of the buttons.

When you have completed this presentation stage you will now have a fully functional option group of buttons.

List Boxes

A List Box is used to give the user a selection of predefined entries in order to save time and eliminate spelling errors. This form of display is undynamic, in other words it doesn't change shape (which of course is dependent on the contents of the list) and the amount of space required for the List Box depends on the number of entries it contains. An example List Box is shown below:

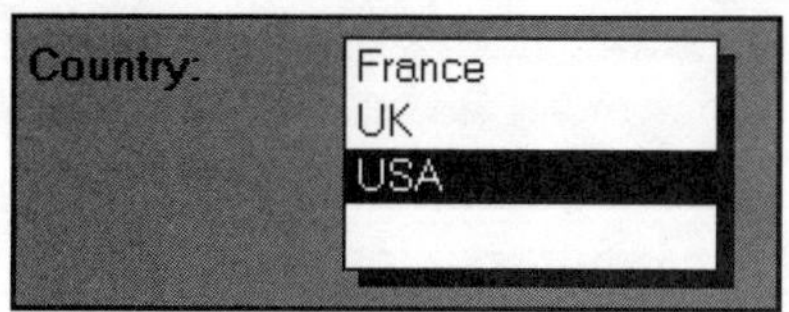

Let's look at how you can use the List Box Wizard to help you with this task.

A List Box With a Wizard

The window below deals with the source of the alternative entries you offer the user. You can either type in a list, or give the wizard a table in which to look for the entries.

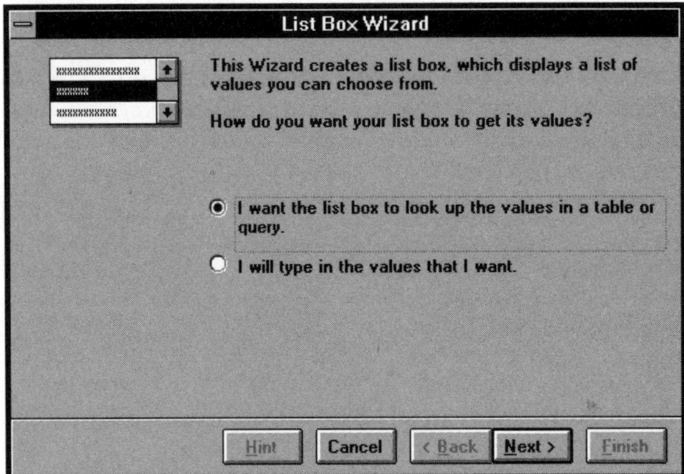

Clearly, the fields you inform the wizard to use will make the basis for a list. This is done to help people make decisions. Even though the user can only select the contents of one column in the List Box, the associated columns are helpful in context. In this example, we've chosen CustomerID and Company Name - the ID as the user choice, and company name as the reminder.

So, making the table or query choice gives you the following screen:

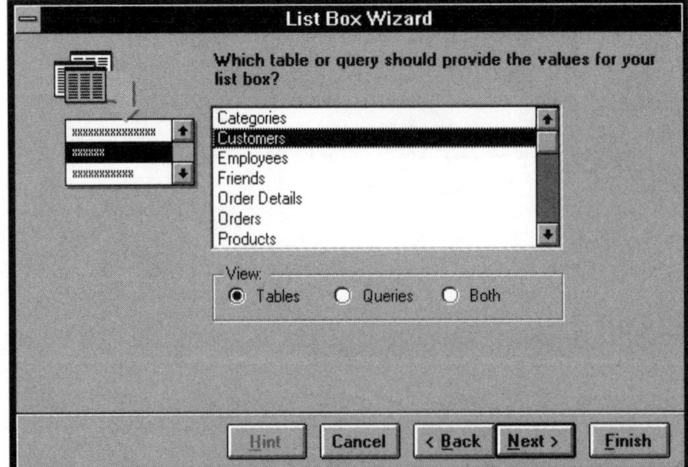

- Select the table or query in which the wizard will look up the information and then move on.

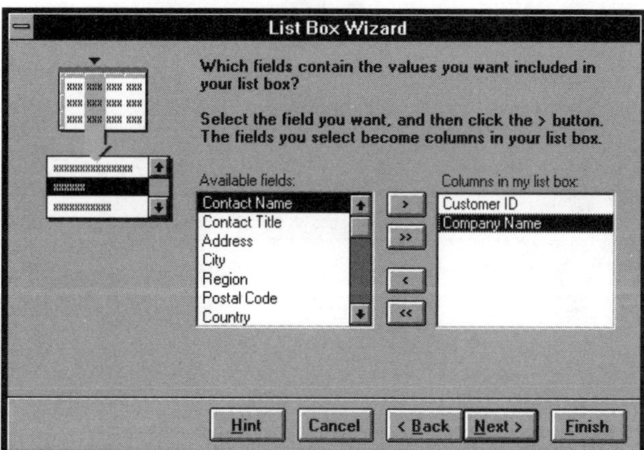

Select the fields you want to appear in the List Box. You may choose more than one; the selections will become separate column headings. Press the Next > button to continue.

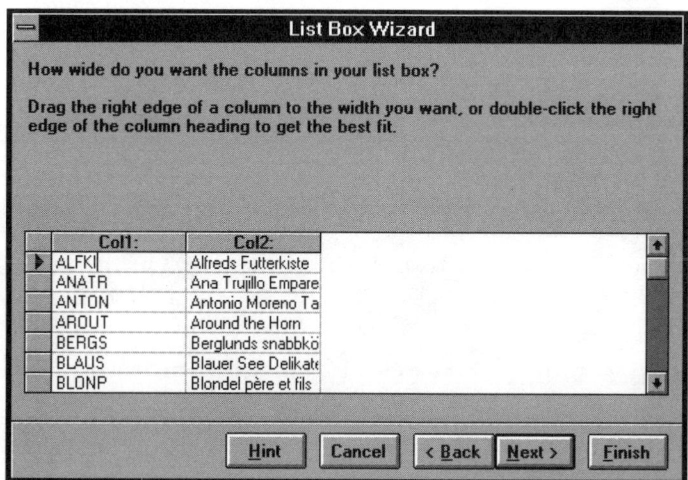

- Use this screen to re-size the columns containing your data. A list of 20 choices will be too much to display on a simple form. You can squash them a little to get them all on without recourse to using scroll bars. Move to the next stage.

If you select the Type alternative, you are presented with the screen that follows.

A List Box Typed In

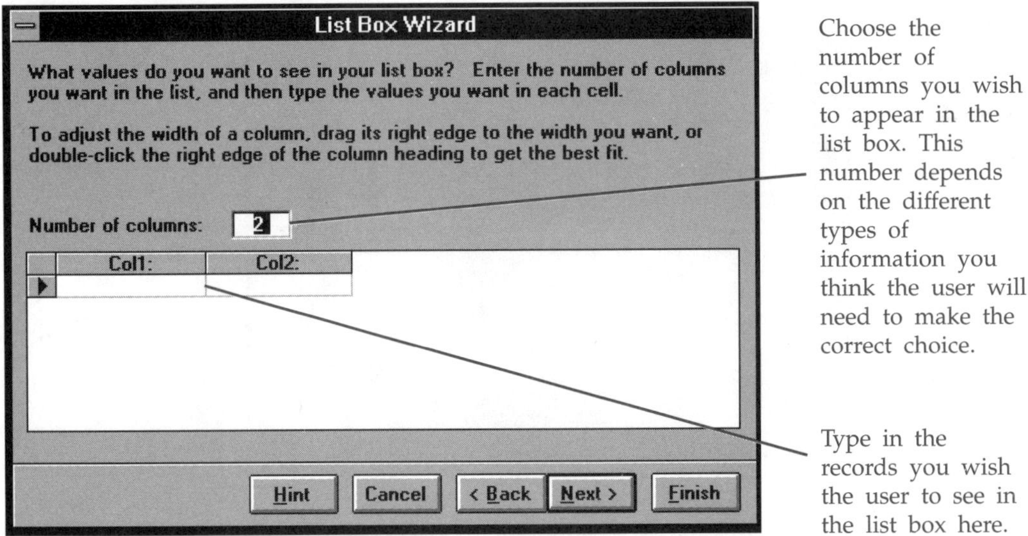

- Enter into this grid the information you want to appear in the list box and click on the Next > button to continue.

To complete the creation of a list box, the wizard now uses exactly the same screens procedure for either selecting from a table/query list or typing that list in.

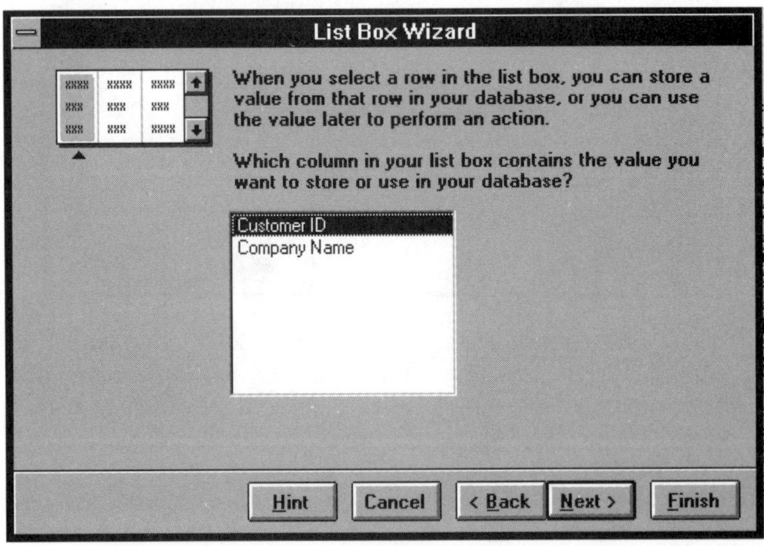

- Select the column which has the data in it that you want to store or use in your database. In our example we chose ID as the information to be saved. This is pretty true to reality, as an ID field would be a typical choice for storage if you make a table from form-generated data.

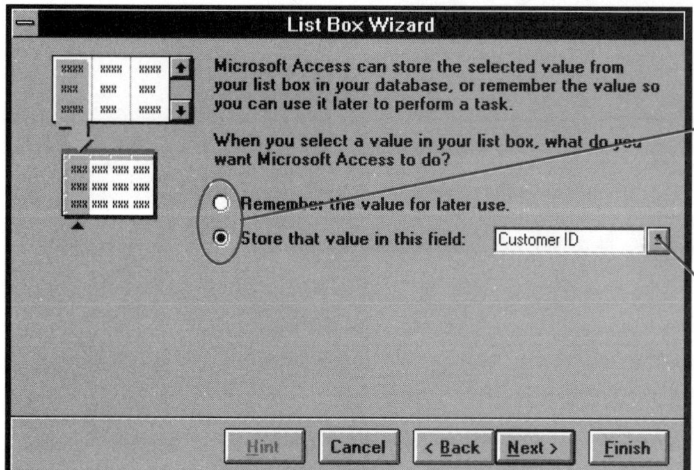

Use these option buttons to choose whether you want to store the data in the database or just have Access remember it for later on.

If you select the store data option, select the field in which you want to store it from this list.

- Choose what happens to the data and select the Next > button to move to the final screen. In our case, we'll be storing the value of CustomerID in a table for this form's data.

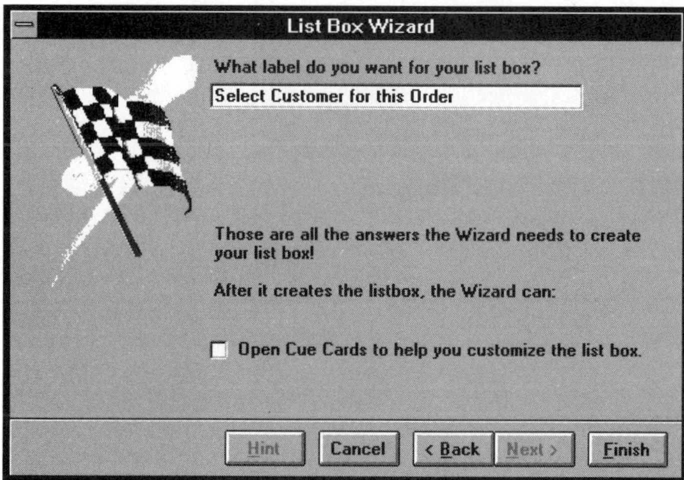

- Type in the text you want to appear in the associated label and click on the finish screen to see what the wizard has produced after all its efforts. It will be similar to the screen below.

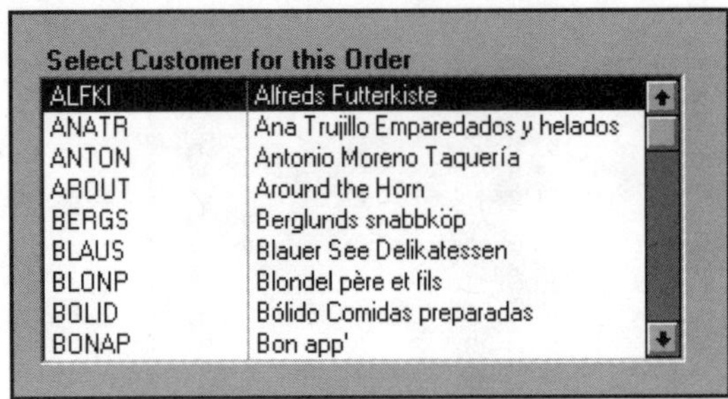

A List Box By Hand

If you want to reproduce the wizard's handy work using the basic building blocks then you will have to complete the following steps:

- Making sure that the Control Wizard button is deactivated, place the list box onto your form, approximating the size that will be required. A best guess will do, as the shape and size can be altered later.
- Now move to the form's associated Properties box to see a screen something like this:

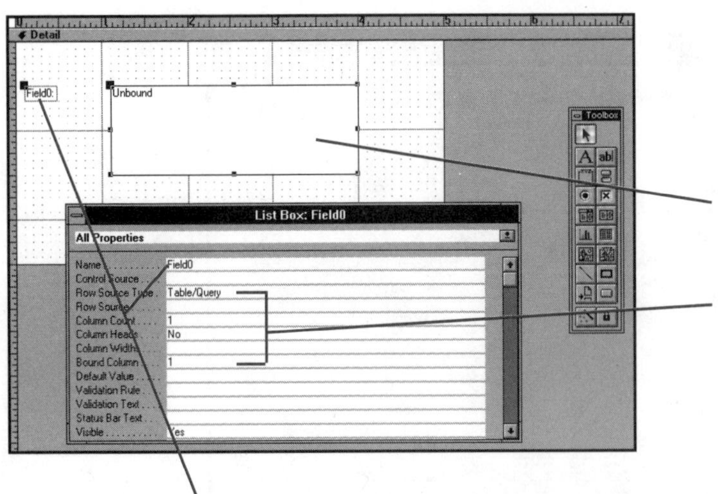

This is the Unbound list box that you placed upon the form.

These are the new properties that you will relate to your hand design.

Notice that the name of the control and the text of the label are the same. This allows you to group associated labels and controls together quickly.

- First of all, you need to bind the list box to the database structure if you want to store the user's selection in your underlying table or query. Select the field you wish to store the data in from the drop-down list available under the Control Source property.
- Now you must choose where the list box will get its information from. To do this you use the Row Source Type and Row Source properties, keeping an eye on Column Count.

The Row Source Type property gives you three options to choose between:

Option	Result
Table/Query	The list box will go to a table or query and take the first X columns of data (the number X is given shortly).
Value List	The list box takes its information from a list of data that you enter in now.
Field List	The list box goes to a table or a query and takes the names of the fields for its contents.

The Row Source works in tandem with Row Source Type:

1. If you select Table/Query, the list of available tables or queries is presented as a drop-down list in Row Source.
2. If you select Value List, you must type in your own list of contents in Row Source.
3. If you select Field List, the list of available tables or queries is presented in a drop-down list in Row Source.

Remember the choice you made in Row Source Type (either the first or last option) will affect the way the wizard will use the table or query you select in Row Source (either the first or last option). Choosing Table/Query means the wizard will use the entries in the selected table. Choosing Field List means the wizard will use the field names.

You use Column Count to enter the number of columns you want in your list box (this will be value X mentioned above). When you select Table/Query in Row Source Type, the value set in Column Count is also used by the wizard as the number of fields to take from the table.

The wizard takes the first field definition from the chosen table or query and all the field definitions that follow, up to the limit set in Column Count. Use a query to push the fields you want selected into the first position.

Open the NWind Employee form and look at the Country control for an example of a Value List in use.

ALFKI	Alfreds Futterkiste
ANATR	Ana Trujillo Emparedados y helados
ANTON	Antonio Moreno Taquería
AROUT	Around the Horn
BERGS	Berglunds snabbköp
BLAUS	Blauer See Delikatessen
BLONP	Blondel père et fils
BOLID	Bólido Comidas preparadas

Column Heads and Widths

Next you come to Column Heads. This simply tells Access whether or not you want the columns in your list box to have headings. The contents of the heading differs depending on your Row Source Type entry, but are usually the field names that the data is drawn from.

Penultimately, you now alter the Column Widths. Simply type in the widths as you see the columns in the list box and Access will apply that width to each column respectively.

You don't need to place in the type of measurement (inches or centimeters) or place semi-colons between the entries, as Access will automatically format these entries as required.

Finally, you need to tell Access which column you want to take the data from to store in the underlying table or query, or even to remember for later. To do this, simply type the number of the column (counting from the left and starting at one) into the Bound Column property.

When you have completed this final task, all you need to do is improve the presentation of your functioning list box using Palette.

The Combo Box

The combo box is similar to the list box in that it's used for the same purpose: to provide a selection of entries for the user to choose from, saving time and spelling errors. However, the difference between the two is that a combo box takes up less space on your form design, as the list of entries is pulled down when it's required, as opposed to being on show at all times.

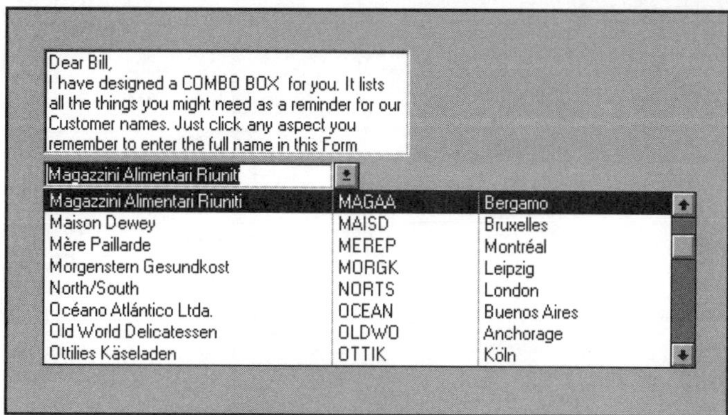

You can pack more information onto one form by only sacrificing a small amount of the user's time in pulling down a list.

A Combo Box With a Wizard

Let's look at how the Combo Box Wizard can help you with the construction of this feature, starting with this first screen.

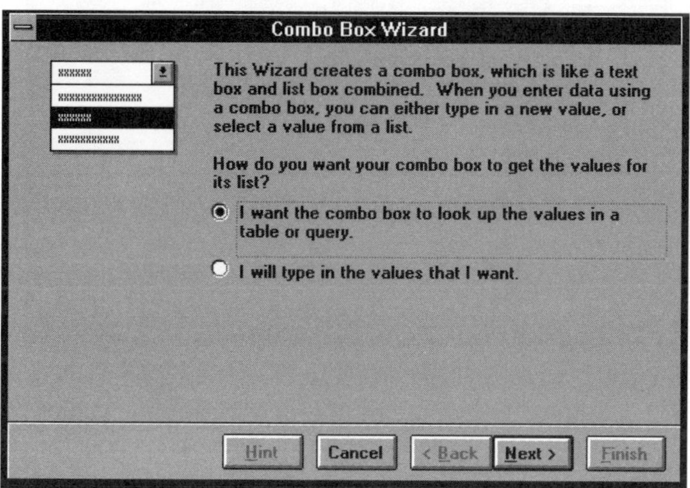

- Select whether or not you want to type in values of your own, or whether you want the Combo Box to contain information from a table or query. For now, suppose that you opt for typing in your own values. The next screen appears like this:

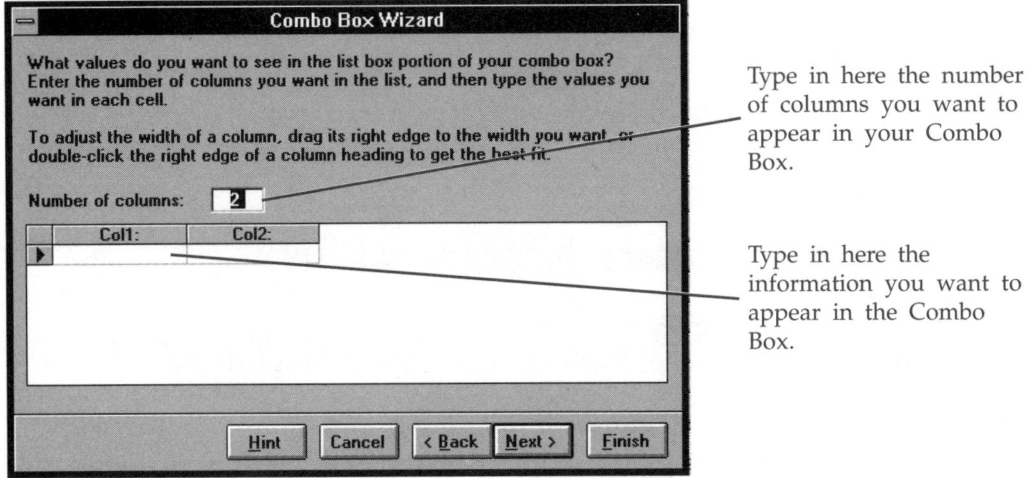

- Fill in the information that this screen requests and click on the Next > button to continue.

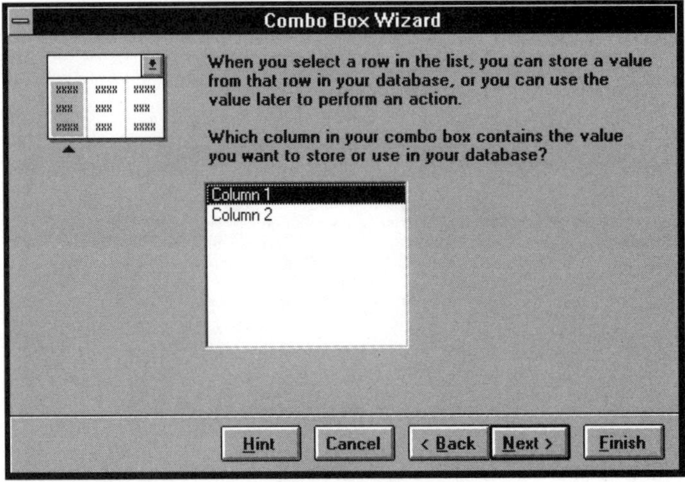

- Select the column that contains the important information, i.e. the data that is to be stored or remembered for later screens.

If you select the look in a table/query option on the first screen, you will then be presented with the following screen.

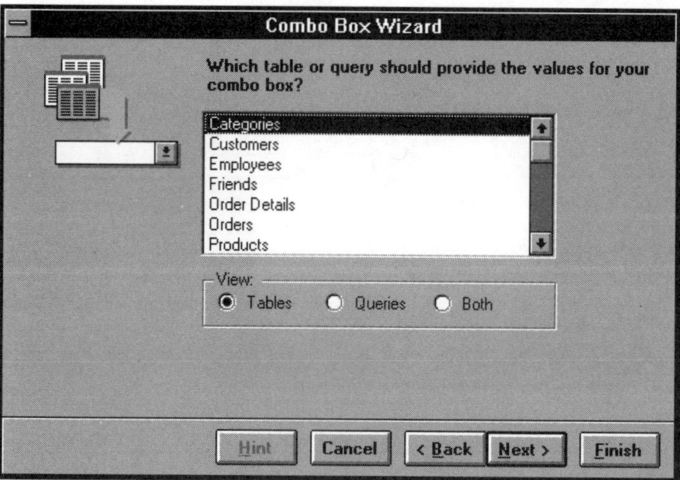

- Select the table or query that you want to use as the source for the data for the Combo Box, and click on the Next > button to continue.

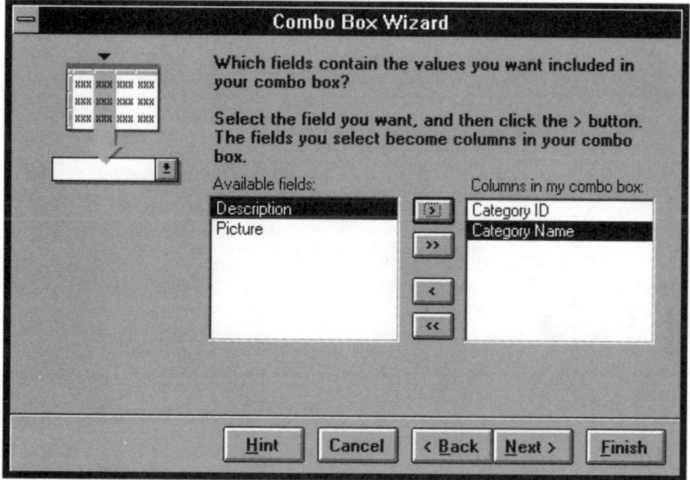

- Using the usual methods select the fields you want to appear in the Combo Box. The order that they appear in the right window determines how they appear in the Combo Box. The field at the top of the window will be the left-most in the finished Combo Box.

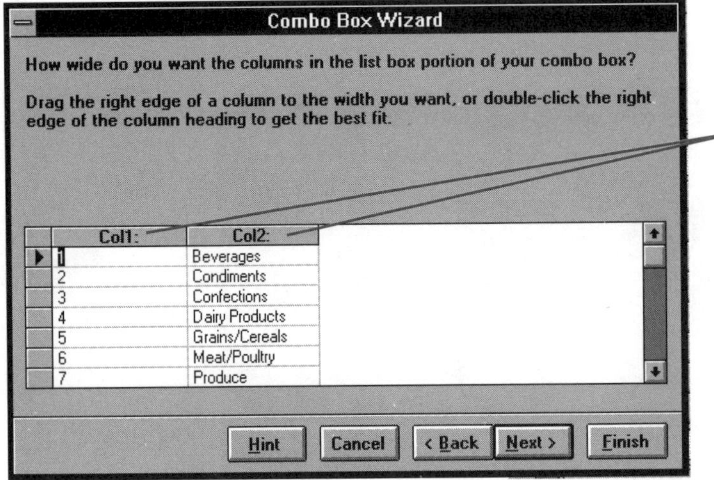

These are the two fields that were selected on the previous screen.

- Alter the widths of the columns, taking notice of the width that's required so that all the data can be seen. Click on the Next > button when you are satisfied with the columns.

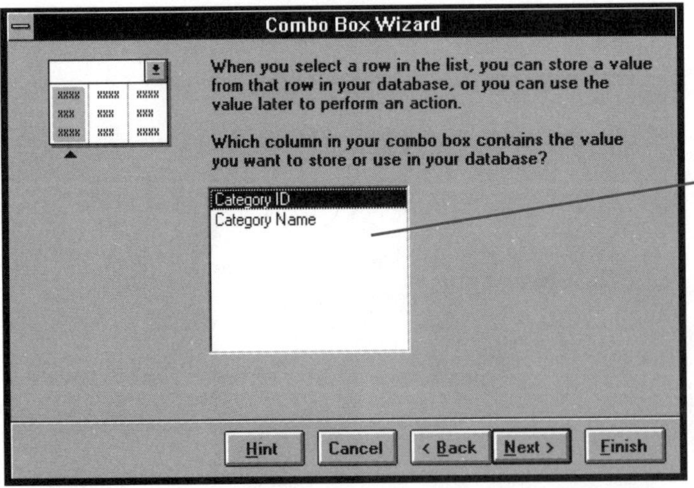

On this screen you select the abstract column (i.e. the actual chosen data that may be difficult to fathom), as the other data fields are usually provided to help the user choose a correct abstract entry.

- Select the column you want Access to use as the important information column, that is, the column that contains the data it will store in the underlying table or query, or remember for later use.

To complete the creation, the wizard now uses exactly the same screen procedure for either method.

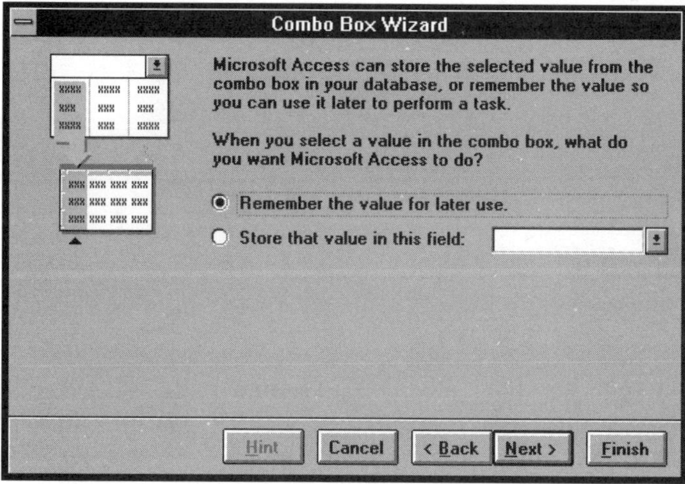

- Inform the Combo Box Wizard what you want to do with the user's selection: remember it for later or save it to the underlying table. If you choose the latter, you must also tell it which field to save the data to. Click on the Next > button for the final time to see the last screen.

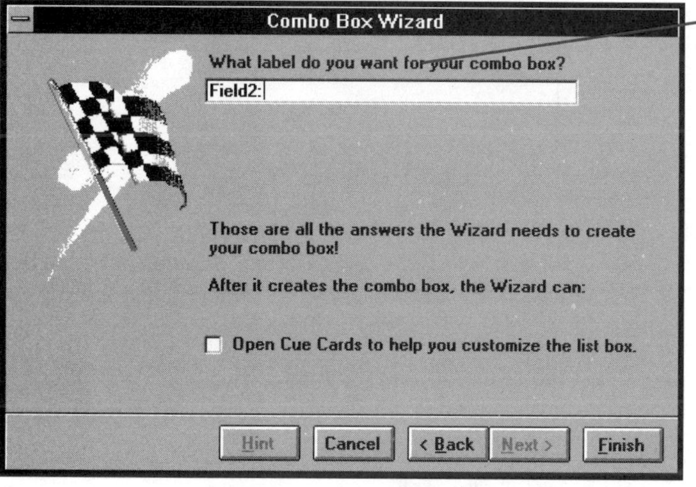

Type into this box the text you want the associated label to use.

- Fill in this last screen and click the Finish button to see the culmination of all that effort. It will be similar to the one shown below.

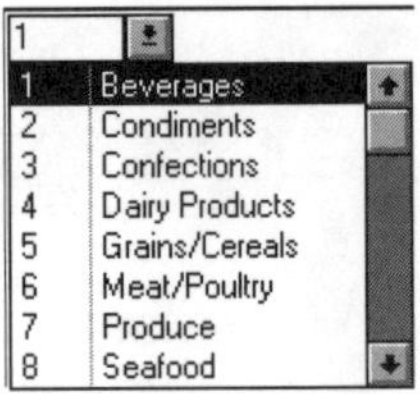

A Combo Box By Hand

To create the Combo Box seen above by hand, you have to follow the following steps:

- Making sure that the Control Wizard button is de-selected, place the Combo Box onto your form. Remember that you only have to make it one line of text high, as most of the time you won't see all of the listing.
- To customize this unbound feature, open the properties box with the focus upon the Combo Box.

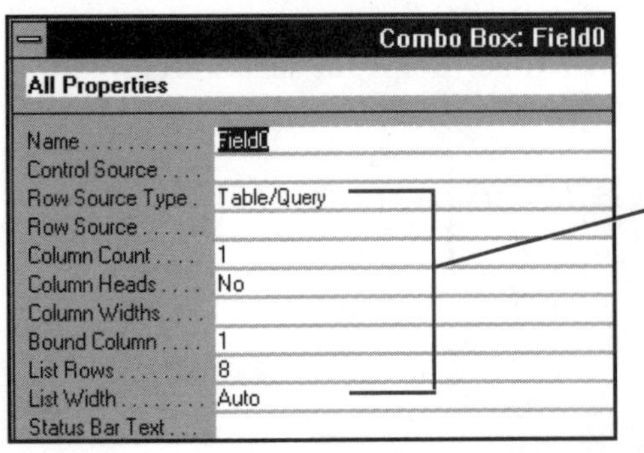

These are the properties you will be using to customize your combo box.

- Starting with the first property on your list, Control Source, type in the name of the field in which you want to store the user's selection.
- Next, just like in a list box, inform Access of the type of list you want to use in the Combo Box: Table/Query, Value List or Field List. Then tell Access exactly what information you need.
- Now you can alter the properties that deal with the columns: Column Count, Column Heads, and Column Width.

> Remember that Column Count should show the number of columns you want in the Combo Box, Column Heading informs Access whether you want them or not, and Column Width can be used to alter the widths of each column.

- Next is the Bound Column property. Use this to tell Access which column in your Combo Box is the one with the important information, i.e. the data you want it to store in the table or remember for later use.
- The next property you should be concerned with is called List Rows. This property deals with the number of rows that will appear in the drop-down list when you click on the tab at the end of the Combo Box cell. This means you can reduce the amount of screen that is lost behind the drop-down menu when it's selected, by keeping this number as low as possible.
- The final property you need to be concerned with is called List Width. This is similar to Column Width in that it allows you to alter the width of the columns in the drop-down list, as opposed to the widths in the Combo Box itself.

When you have completed this final property assignment, you have completed the customization and binding of the Combo Box. All you have to do now is improve the presentation using Palette, and you will have created a functional Combo Box for your form.

Command Buttons

Command buttons are used to fire up macros or Access Basic code in order to produce some kind of effect, such as opening a new form or putting a message box on the screen to inform the user of some important information. This means that simply putting a command button on the form is not enough. You also have to produce the macro or the Access Basic code for the command button to run when the user clicks on the button. This topic is covered in Chapters 12 and 13.

Fortunately, Microsoft has provided a wizard that not only supplies a well-organized command button, but also provides the code for the button to actually affect the database. Let's look more closely at this wizard and the different buttons it can produce.

Command Button With a Wizard

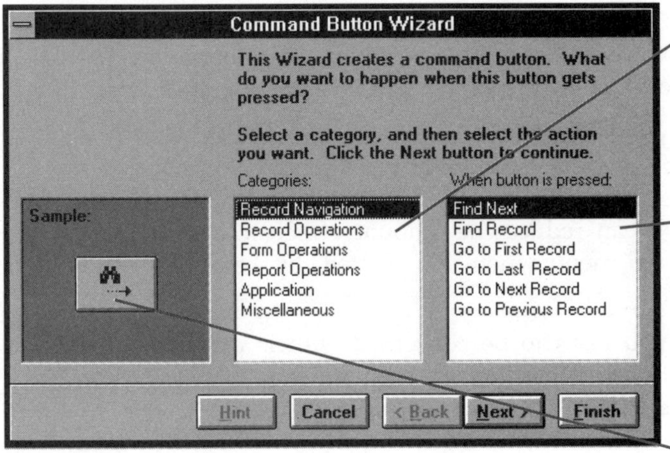

This window contains all the categories of action you can use for code. This will run when you press the command button.

This window contains all the specific operations that the buttons can be used for. The list of operations are dependent on your selection in the other window.

Notice this button and the symbols that appear on it. This updates depending on the operation that you select.

- Choose the operation you want the button to execute when pressed and click on the Next > button to continue.

Command Button Wizard
What do you want on the command button?
Either select Text and type the text you want, or select Picture and choose the picture you want. Click Browse to select a custom picture.
Sample:
Text: Find Next
Picture: Find Next
Browse...
Show All Pictures
Hint
Cancel
< Back
Next >
Finish

Choose whether you want text or a picture to appear on the button.

Type in here the text you want to appear on the button.

Click on this button if you want to use a picture you created somewhere else. The picture must be of the .bmp or .ico file extension types. This shows they are either a bitmap or an icon.

Select the picture you want to appear on the button. To see all the Access 2.0 pictures available, check the box entitled Show All Pictures.

- Select the contents for the front of your button and continue to the final screen.

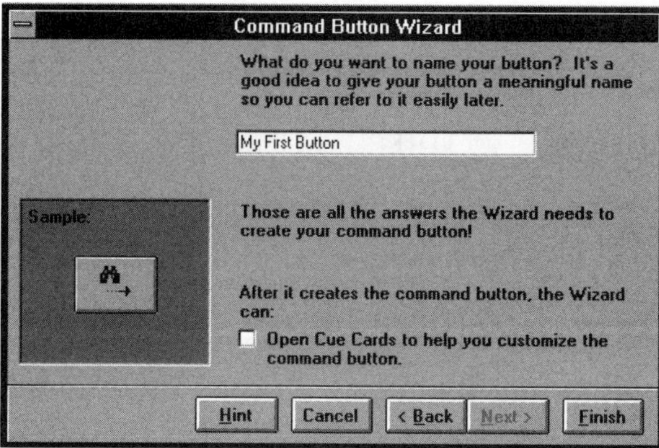

- Type in the name you want your button to be known by and select the Finish button to see the result. Remember, behind the scenes the wizard has done a lot of hard work to also include all the code to make the command button actually do something!

All you have to do now is re-shape your button to the size that you require and press it whenever you want that facility.

The Code

If you open the associated Properties box you will be able to see a prime example of both the use of event properties and the code that Access 2.0 can generate. The Properties box will look something like this.

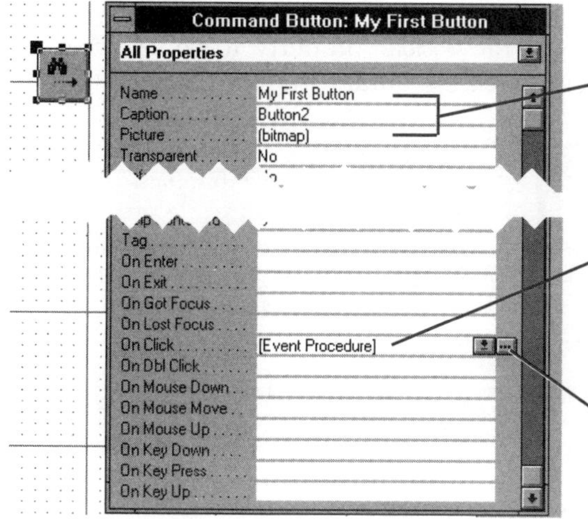

Notice that some of the information that was given to the wizard now appears in the Properties box, i.e. its name and the fact that it has a bitmap picture.

The code that Access 2.0 produced has been attached to the On Click property. This means that when the button is clicked or pressed the code given here will be executed.

If you click this Build button, you can see the Access Basic code that was generated to power the button (see the screen opposite).

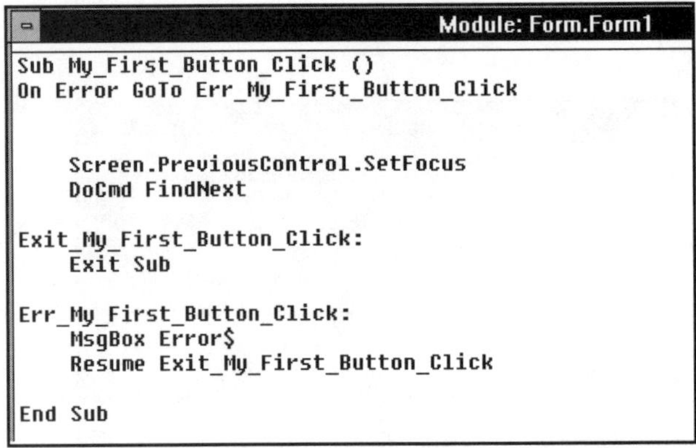

The Code Behind the Command Button Wizard's Results

Don't worry about Access Basic. The subject is touched upon in later chapters, and most of the time you can use a macro to do the same job. Access Basic is a powerful language for Access developers. Its potential is best discussed in partnership with Visual Basic and general office development techniques. Professional programming is outside the scope of this book. But you may wish to get a taster from our Chapter 13. Macros are much easier to use than Access Basic and are covered in Chapter 12.

Command Button By Hand

It is easy to produce a command button by hand, simply:

- Make sure that the Control Wizard button is deactivated. Select the Command Button icon and place the command button onto your form, approximately at the size you require.
- Type in the text you want to appear on the button in Caption Property or select the Build button at the end of the Picture property to choose the bitmap or icon you want from Access 2.0's library, shown below:

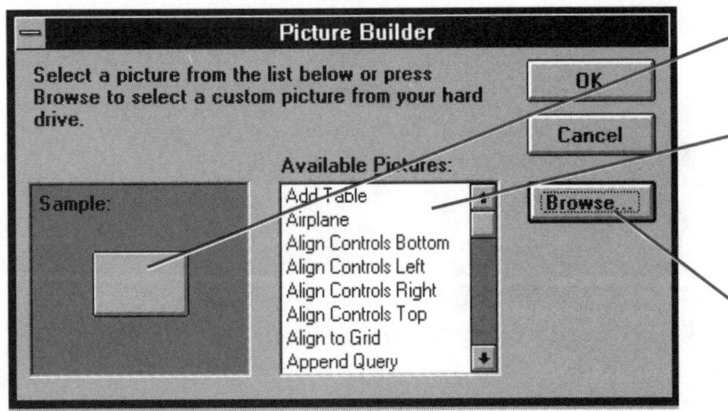

This is how the button will look with your chosen bitmap in place.

Here is a list of available bitmaps. When you highlight each one in turn, it appears in the window to the left.

Select this button to use one of your own bitmaps or icons stored on file.

You have now completed the design of a command button. However, to make this process any use at all, you need to attach some code to one of the event properties of this button. If you already know Access Basic, then carry on.

You have now seen the four different controls that have a wizard attached to help you design features. As you can see, especially in the case of the command button, the wizards can dramatically reduce the amount of work you have to do as a form designer. As with all wizards, the range of results they can produce is limited, and therefore to produce completely customized results you will have to dive into the Properties box on more than one occasion. As a means of producing the main, advanced features on your design, wizards are the way to go.

Now let's look at two more refinements, but without the wizard's help: adding sound and pictures to your form and adding a graph to your form.

Adding Pictures and Sound to Your Form

It is possible to add pictures and sound to your form, to give it much more punch. Below is an example (if you put your ear to this page you may hear the sound file included):

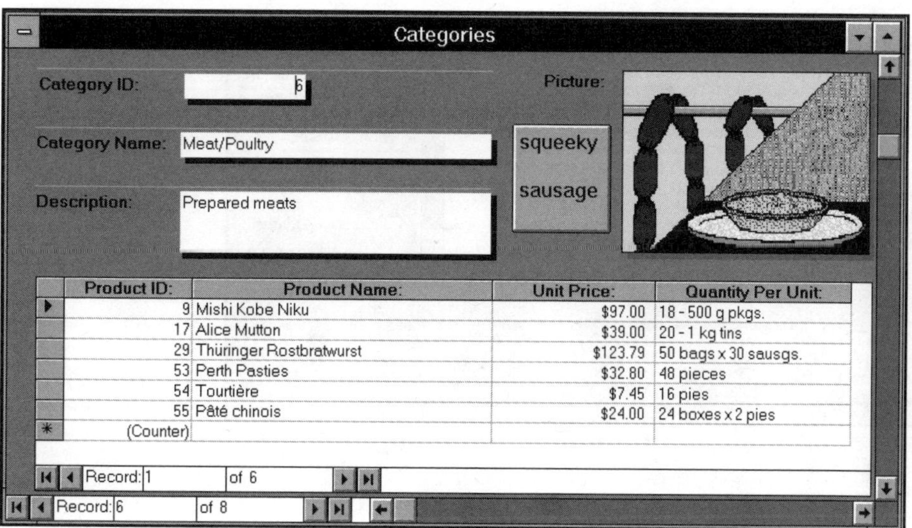

These pictures and sounds are stored in files in your computer, and Access 2.0 refers to them as objects. To add these objects to your form you have to place one of the object-dependent controls onto it, and then tell Access where to get the source file for that control. With graphs, still pictures and graphics, Access will display them when asked. However, with sound and other multimedia sources, Access places the source inside the object control. To see the object, you have to select and run it. There are two types of object-dependent controls: bound and unbound.

Unbound Object Controls

The unbound object controls are used to show graphics or hold sound that isn't included in any of the underlying tables in your database. Suppose you wished to include a company graphic in the header of your form. This graphic would be universal, or in other words would not be attached to any one specific record. Therefore, it would make sense to include it on the form header using an unbound object control, by completing the following steps:

- Select the unbound object control from the Toolbox and place the control in the required position. When the control is placed the following window appears.

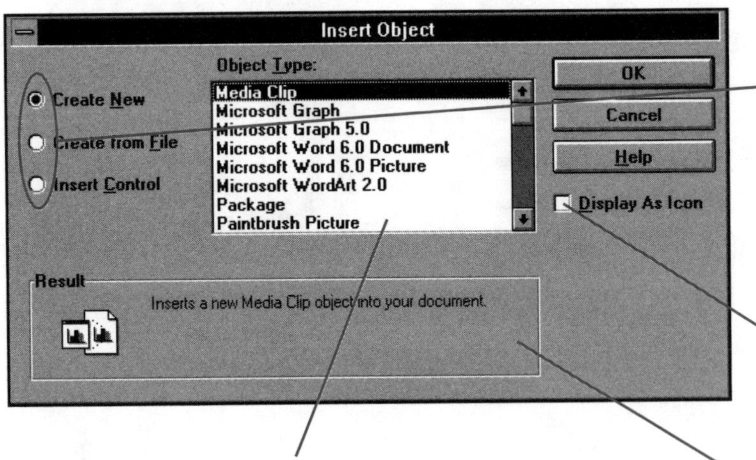

Choose which source you want to get the object from: create a new one, get one from a file, or import an OCX / DLL / EXE (specialist program from libraries or often built with Visual Basic).

Check this if you want to display an icon of the facility, like a small microphone icon for a sound (.wav) file.

This is the list of object types your computer can produce. This ability relies on your computer having the software to produce each kind of object, for example Windows Paintbrush to produce a Paintbrush Picture.

Your current choice is shown in this Result box.

- Depending on your choices here, Access will either fire up the appropriate package to allow you to create the object, or it will take you to a further screen where you can select the appropriate file containing the object you want to appear. You can link the object stored in Access to its original, which allows the copy to be automatically updated when the original is changed
- After you have finished your creation or selection process, when you return to Access you will find the file placed in the control. You can check this visually in design mode. If you have made the transfer successfully there will be a graphic or a picture placed in your object control: a small microphone if it's a sound file, a small film reel if it's a multimedia clip.

Clearly, the visual files work all the time in the unbound object controls, but to see the multimedia clips or hear the sound file, the user has to inform Access of their request. There are two ways to run these files:

- In Form Design View select Edit from the menu bar, and then [your selected object] Object and Play from the resulting drop-down menus. Your object or application is added to the drop-down listing of Edit.
- If you are not in Form Design view, double-click on the control itself.

Now you can use any sound or graphics file in your forms either before or during your database design, providing you have the appropriate software to create and run the required files.

Bound Object Controls

The bound object controls are used to show graphics or hold sound that is included in any of the underlying tables in your database.

Suppose that you want a copy of each employee speaking their own name to appear on their record. This is a useful feature if they have unusual names that may be difficult to pronounce from written text. In the table dealing with employee details you would set up an OLE field and in each employees record you would record each persons monologue into this field.

In the form you can access this field using a Bound Object Control, obtained from the Toolbox, and simply by changing the control source to the field that contains the sound file, the control will be ready for action.

Specializing Form Features

So far, you have seen how to produce forms from nothing and how to customize the components that you have placed in the form, whether they are simple text boxes or complex option groups. However, you can take your forms to new heights, using more of the Form Properties box.

Read Only Forms

One feature you may find very useful is the Read-Only form. This allows you to stop the user from being able to alter any data laid out before them. This can be useful when Access is used in a multi-user environment, where most of the users only need to see the data and should not be allowed to alter it.

> It is possible, using the security systems integral to Access, to limit data entry facilities to individual named users.

To make individual fields read only involves two properties that can be found in all controls: Enabled and Locked.

The Enabled Property

The Enabled property deals with the focus of the database. The focus is the active part of the database and can be likened to the part of the database that has your attention at any one moment.

If the Enabled property is set to YES, the field on the form can receive and pass on the focus, whereas if the property is set to NO, then the focus will pass over the field.

The Locked Property

The Locked property deals with whether the field can be changed or not. If the property is set to NO, the field is not locked and the data can be changed. With a YES setting the field is locked and the data cannot be changed.

Using these two properties together you can get any type of field lock you may ever require. The various combinations are shown below.

Settings	Meanings
Locked - No Enabled - Yes	This is the default setting that Access gives to all controls. The field can have the focus and it can also be edited.
Locked - No Enabled - No	This means the field cannot have the focus, and so it can't be changed or copied. However, the field is not locked, and to represent this the text is dimmed.
Locked - Yes Enabled - Yes	This means the field can have the focus, so the field contents can be copied to the clipboard. However, because the field is locked the field contents can't be altered.
Locked - Yes Enabled - No	This means the field can't have the focus and is locked. You can't be more protective than this!

You should also be aware that there are certain types of fields that are always read only. These field types include:

- Fields that are contained in a table on the one side of a one-to-many relationship.
- Any calculated control or the results of a calculated field in a query.
- Any field that holds the results from a summary or crosstab query, or has the Unique Values property set in the underlying query.

Customized Form Presentation

It is possible to create your own custom appearance for the form, by combining several of the components that Access 2.0 provides. The number of combinations that are credible is large, but, as an illustration, one of the combinations is given below:

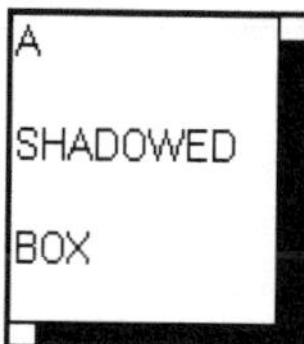

This illusion of a shadow is simple to construct by placing a solid dark rectangle under the control, slightly off center.

To accomplish this:

- Place the rectangle onto the form first, the dimensions matching the required size of the control.
- Change the border and fill in with the required color, to provide a solid color rectangle.
- Now place the control over the rectangle exactly. Using the cross hairs and the change of border color when the lines overlap you can get an exact size match. The grid and the option of Snap To Grid under Format may also help.
- Now select the control and move it slightly off center to achieve the final result.

> The layering that you produce now will always be enforced. This means that if you place the rectangle on top of the control, no matter how you move the controls around, the rectangle will always remain on top. To alter this layering, use the commands under the Format menu called Bring To Front and Send To Back to shuffle the controls as you like.

Form Templates

When you create a form straight onto a blank sheet of paper, Access uses default settings for the characteristics of the blank paper. These characteristics are called the template for the form design.

Access allows you to change these default settings to create your own custom template. This is particularly useful if you are going to create a lot of forms all with the same general characteristics. The characteristics on the template that you can change include:

- Default settings for the Toolbox
- Form properties, as given in the Form Properties box
- The coloring of the form
- Details of the form's headers and footers and details sections, including size and shape

To produce a template for future form designs, you first have to set up the basic template you want to use. This is done by simply taking a new form and altering the characteristics of that form to produce the template. You can then customize the template. This means that you can even use a form design you have already created as the template for some of your future form designs. Now you have to inform Access that you wish this template to be used in future. You can do this by:

- Closing down the form and giving it a name that shows it to be the base template, for example, "Form Design Template 1/2/94"
- Select View from the menu bar and then Options from the resulting drop-down menu to give you the following screen:

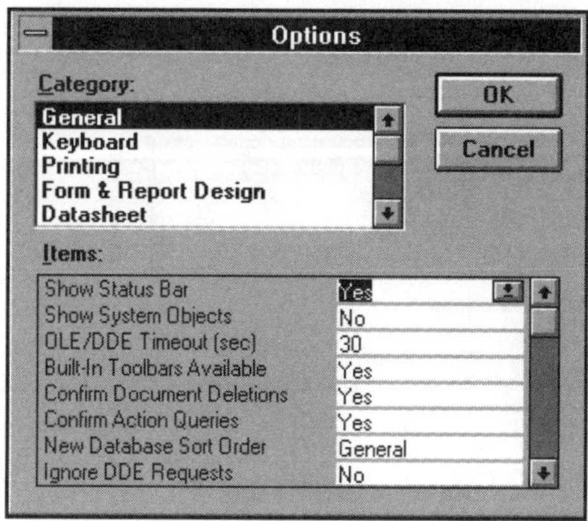

- Select Form & Report Design from the window and the items section of the window changes to this:

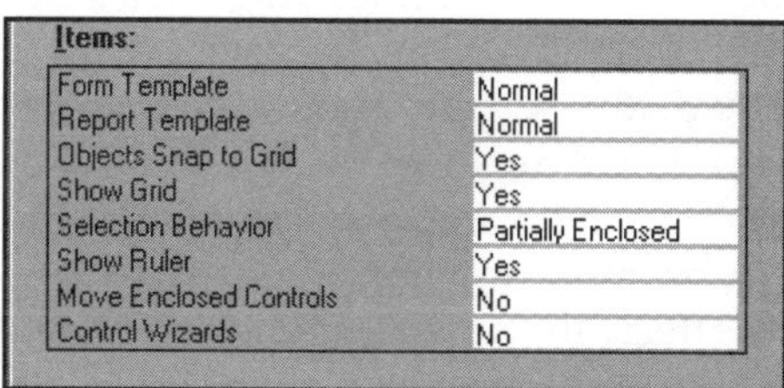

- Select the Form Template option, delete Normal, and enter the name of the form you wish to use as the form template. Select OK to accept this entry and Access will now create all new forms using this basic template.

To reverse the process, repeat the steps above, but instead of deleting Normal and re-typing the name of the form you want to use, delete the name and replace it with Normal.

Switchboards - Unbound Forms

Switchboards are used to get the user around your database automatically, restricting the choices that are available. This means the user quickly gets to know the database due to the small number of choices required to obtain results, and also gives more stringent error trapping. This occurs because you, as the database designer, can prepare for the entries the user will make more carefully, as there are less places where things can go wrong.

Below is an example of a switchboard from the NWind database:

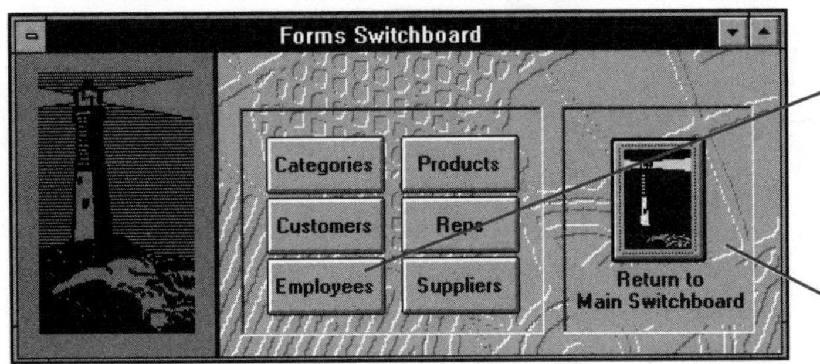

Notice the command buttons on the switchboard that take you to further screens, where more detailed information may be found.

Also, notice the visual impact this form design has upon a user, compared to the normal initial database windows.

The switchboards are created using **Unbound Forms**. These are forms that are not based on any of the possible underlying tables or queries. By definition, the switchboards give information to the user on the choices they make from that screen. To that end, the screens should contain text boxes as well as command buttons; the latter are used with attached macros to move the user around the database, providing the results that text boxes promise. Switchboards tend to be more inviting than the usual Access design screens, and to produce that effect, they make use of color and object controls, while appearing as simple to use as possible.

To create a switchboard, you have to create an unbound form, onto which you place the required custom controls. The methods for placing and customizing the custom controls are given above, but to create an unbound form see below.

- From the initial database screen, select Form and the New button to begin the creation process.
- Leaving the table/query selection window empty, press the blank form button. Access will take you to the usual blank Form Design screen shown opposite.

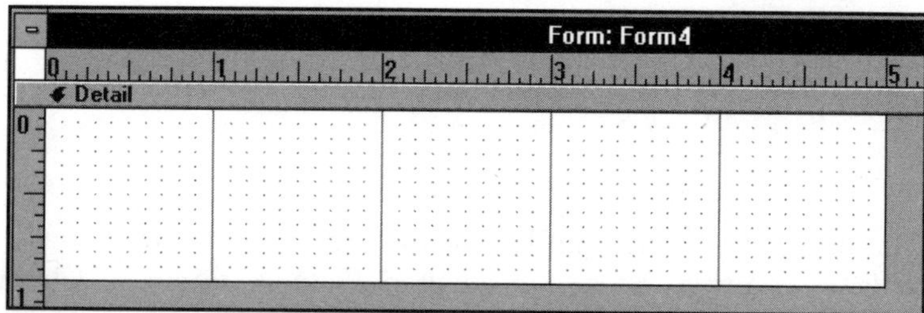

Now you can use the methods that have already been discussed to create your own custom switchboard screen.

- Place controls where you require them.
- Create command buttons ready for macros to be attached to their On Click property.
- Generally produce a welcoming and friendly screen for users to interact with.
- We would also suggest that if you feel unsure about macros or Access Basic you use the Command Button Wizard.

For more details on the macros you could use with the switchboard and how to create them, see Chapter 12.

Troubleshooting

Q&A I only want a section header. Can I delete the footer?

You can't have a header or a footer on its own without its partner. If you only require one of them, you select both and then make the one that you don't want invisible. You can do this by selecting the Visible property in the appropriate section and change the choice to No.

Q&A I've got a comprehensive listing in my Combo Box. Can I stop the user from adding their own entries?

Another useful feature that Access makes available to the designer is the ability to restrict the user to making a selection from the given list, and not allow free-hand entries.

Each of the enhanced data entry controls handles this differently:

- List Boxes - by default this list cannot be edited, so the user can't enter extra data.

- Combo Boxes - change the Limit to List property to Yes. This means that the user can still type in the box, but the entry they make must match one from the list.

Q&A How do I produce calculations on my form?

You can produce calculations similar to the ones in the Orders form in NWind using calculated controls. These are covered in more depth in Chapter 7, but briefly, they are text boxes that you customize to take figures from elsewhere. They follow some kind of ruling given as the Control Source property of the text box, and then output the final calculated figure in the control. Below is an example using the Orders form:

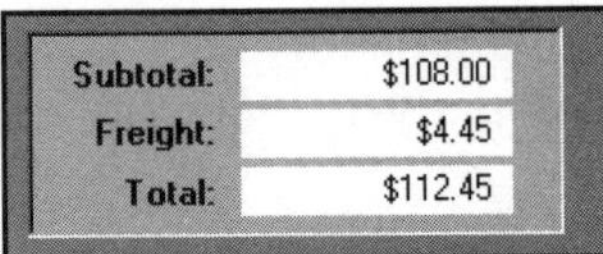

Q&A I want to dictate the way the user is pushed around the entry form. Can I do this?

Yes, you can stipulate the place where the cursor will jump to when the user presses *Tab*. This is very useful for emphasizing entry sequence, i.e. Address first, then Phone Number. You can do this by using the Tab Order.

If it's not already present call up the Tab Order Command icon. Then:

- Select View and then Toolbars... from the menu bar
- Select Customize...from the given toolbar selection window
- Choose Form Design from the list as shown below

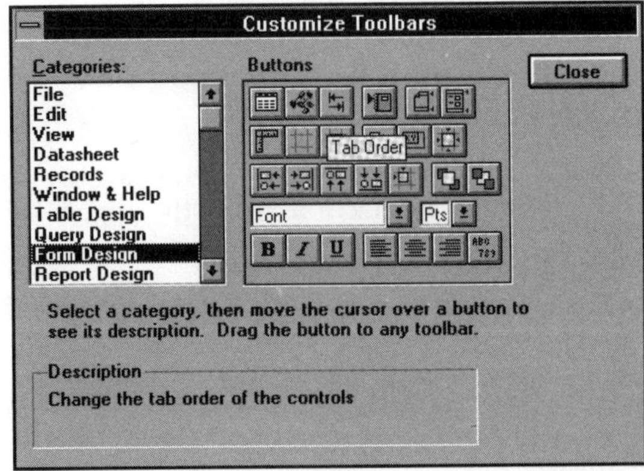

Drag and drop the Tab Order icon to your toolbar. Now you can press it in Form Design View to see the screen below:

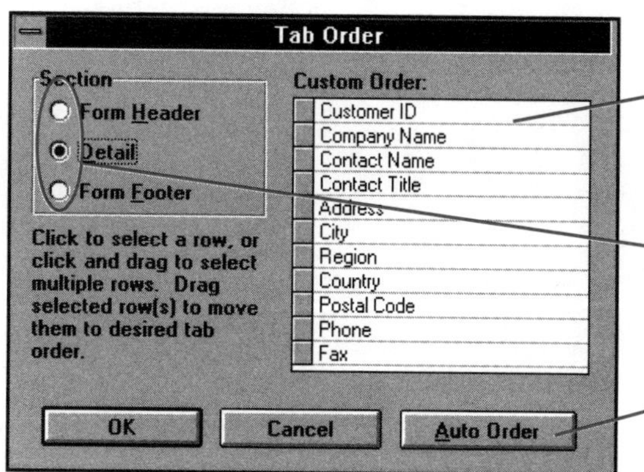

Shown here are your form components in order of their creation. Highlight and drag components in the normal way to get a new order sequence.

You can dictate the order of the Header and Footer components, as well as details.

Click to revert back to the original setting for the sequence (top left to bottom right) if your user is starting to feel sick!

See also Tab Index, Tab Stop and Auto Tab in the Properties box, detailed in Appendix I.

CHAPTER 11

Refining Reports And Forms

In this chapter you will see the facilities that Access has available for the database designer who doesn't want to be constrained by the Report Wizard.

Do you want to produce your own customized reports? Have you been under pressure to produce a business letter - maybe using the addresses stored in your database in conjunction with a wordprocessor? Or maybe you have had to give a boardroom presentation, perhaps using data that you have imported from your spreadsheet. You may have wanted to organize other business paperwork such as invoices, pay slips, or receipts? You may also want to create specially organised reports such as those with multi-columns.

To produce these kinds of reports read on. The general methods of report design are discussed initially, while at the end of the chapter there is a selection of the most commonly required reports. You will see how to produce reports within reports, allowing you to view data from a variety of sources in one document. The ability to produce sub reports is fundamental. This method of viewing the one-to-many relationship is carried forward in the coverage of subforms in the chapter. The sample database NWind is full of examples of the main/sub in action - not surprisingly, as it's such a powerful viewing tool.

In this chapter, you will look at the following points in detail:

- Creating a report from scratch
- The different views for reports
- Adding components to reports
- Report properties
- Grouping and sorting
- Main/subforms reports and forms
- Making a composite report

Creating a Report From Scratch

Just as with form design, Access 2.0 allows you to create a report starting from a blank page. The techniques are much the same as for form design, and therefore if you understood the basics of the previous chapter, you will find creating reports quite simple. However, reports are different to forms, and because of this there are some interesting features that allow you to control the output of your report much more tightly, thus giving professional results.

These features include a report's ability to group and sort records before presenting them, as well as the ability to do mathematical calculations 'on the fly'. The printed, finished document is of paramount importance in reports. The central purpose of many databases is the production of hard copy reports on a daily basis. Before you see how to include all these features in your report design, let's look at designing a basic report, starting with a blank page.

The Blank Report Page

To get to a blank report page:

- From the initial database screen, select the Report tab and click on the New button.
- Select the table or query you wish to base the report on and then click on the Blank Report button. Access will provide you with a screen similar to that seen below:

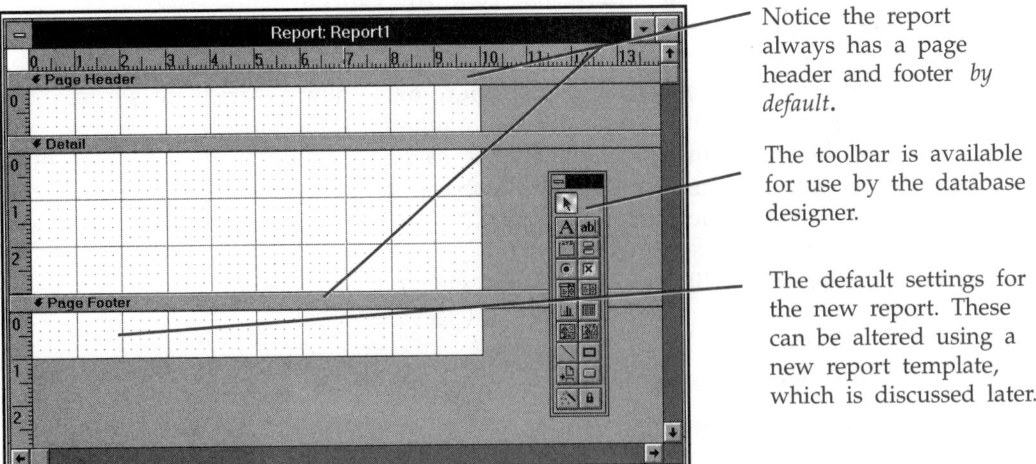

Report: Report1
Page Header
Detail
Page Footer
Notice the report always has a page header and footer *by default.*
The toolbar is available for use by the database designer.
The default settings for the new report. These can be altered using a new report template, which is discussed later.

All the usual techniques employed in altering the blank page that were covered in form design are also available here. Try altering the layout of the page. Prepare the area where you will be designing your report.

- Alter the size of the paper by putting the pointer on the edge that you want to move. When the pointer changes shape, hold down the left mouse button and drag it to the new position.
- Add or remove any of the boxes such as toolbox or properties box by selecting their icons on the icon bar.
- Add page breaks into the various sections of your report in order to emphasize the data.

> Notice that the maximum size of any section of your report is 24 ins by 24 ins (60 cms by 60 cms).

You can also alter the properties of the grid and the ruler. The regularity of the grid dots can be altered using the two properties called Grid X and Grid Y found in the properties box associated with the report itself. The unit of measurement used by the ruler can be changed between metric centimeters and imperial inches in the windows control panel, under the International Settings - measurement property.

> Remember that the grid will lose its dots if you alter the figures in the two grid properties to over 16, leaving just the grid lines.

Viewing Your Report

There are four ways to view your report:

View	Use
Design View	This is used when you wish to alter the report structure.
Print Preview	This is used to see what the report will look like when printed out. This view has all the data in the report in finished layout style.
Sample Preview	This view takes a sample of the data that will appear in your report, and applies it to your design. This allows you to see the general structure of your report, without having to wait for Access to compile the entire report (possibly a lengthy task if many records are involved).
Print Out	This is your report on the page.

There are three main ways of getting to most of these views of your data. Let's look at the individual methods for each view.

Design View

To get to the Design View:

- From either of the Preview screens, click on the icon. This will take you back to the Design view if you came from it, or back to the initial Database window if you came from there.
- From the initial Database window, select the report you wish to view, and click on the Design button.
- From the final question of any of the Report Wizards, select the Design View option.

Print Preview

To get to Print Preview:

- From the Design View, click on the icon.
- From the initial database window, select the report you want to see and click on the Preview button.
- From any of Report Wizard's final questions, select data inclusive and view the option.

Sample Preview

To get to the sample preview:

- From the Design view, click on the icon.

Print Out

To print out the report:

- From the initial database window, select the report you wish to print out, and click on the icon.
- From either of the previews, click on the icon.
- From the Design View, select Print... from the File menu.

Now you can move swiftly between the different views of your report that Access 2.0 has to offer. Let's look to build on the report by adding components.

Adding Components to Your Report

Just as with forms, there are two main ways to get the components you want onto your report paper: the Field List box, and the toolbox. The Field List box method is similar to that used by Report Wizard in getting components onto the report. The toolbox method is pure customization.

The Field List Box

Open the Field List box using the  icon to see the following:

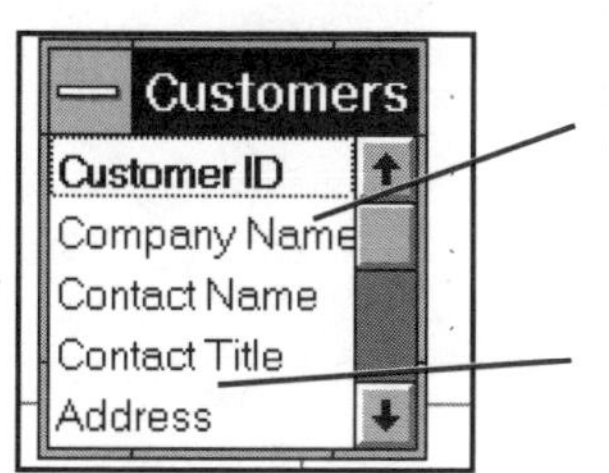

This is the name of the underlying table that was chosen for this report.

In this list you'll find all the fields that make up the underlying table or query for your report

In order to place any of the fields onto your report:

- Highlight the fields you wish to place on the report. Remember that to select multiple fields in this box, you can use either *Shift* to highlight a continuous list of fields or *Ctrl* to highlight a non-continuous one.
- Place the pointer over any of the fields that you have highlighted and, while holding down the left mouse button, drag the newly shaped pointer to the position on your report where you want the top left of the first field component to appear.
- Release the mouse button to place the field components onto your report.

You can now utilize the usual techniques to re-size and align the components that you have placed on the report:

- Select the component that you wish to re-size and, placing the pointer onto any of the edge boxes that appear, hold down the left mouse button and drag the component to the required size.
- Select the group of components that you wish to align and select the Align option from the Format menu. Choose the type of alignment that you require, and Access will perform the operation for you.

> Remember that if you have the Snap To Grid option active (i.e. ticked) they will spring to the nearest grid dot. If this option is not active, selecting it from the menu will rectify this.

The Toolbox

The toolbox is discussed in great detail in the previous chapter. In short, it allows you to place any component anywhere on your report.

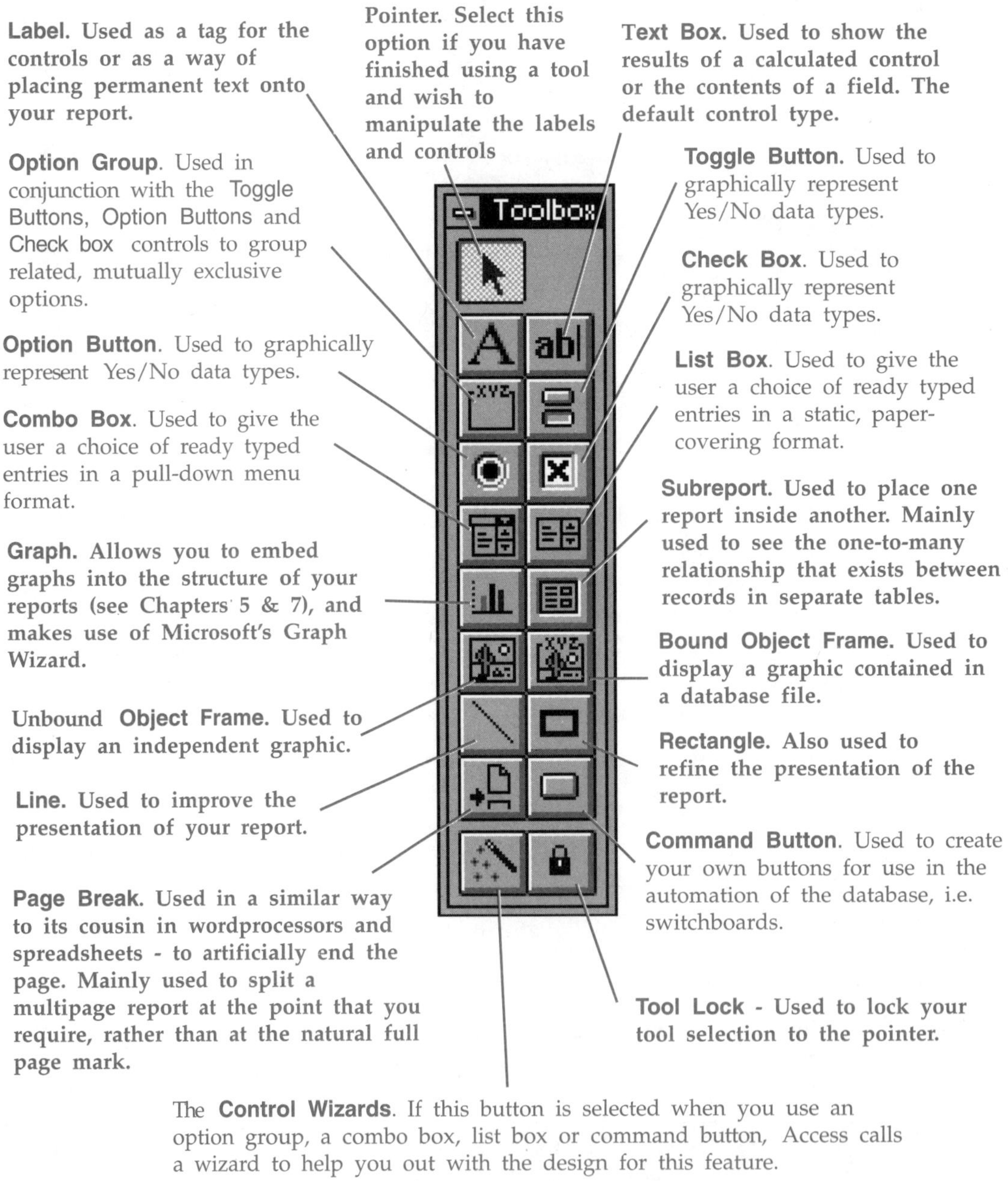

Label. Used as a tag for the controls or as a way of placing permanent text onto your report.

Pointer. Select this option if you have finished using a tool and wish to manipulate the labels and controls

Text Box. Used to show the results of a calculated control or the contents of a field. The default control type.

Option Group. Used in conjunction with the Toggle Buttons, Option Buttons and Check box controls to group related, mutually exclusive options.

Toggle Button. Used to graphically represent Yes/No data types.

Check Box. Used to graphically represent Yes/No data types.

Option Button. Used to graphically represent Yes/No data types.

List Box. Used to give the user a choice of ready typed entries in a static, paper-covering format.

Combo Box. Used to give the user a choice of ready typed entries in a pull-down menu format.

Subreport. Used to place one report inside another. Mainly used to see the one-to-many relationship that exists between records in separate tables.

Graph. Allows you to embed graphs into the structure of your reports (see Chapters 5 & 7), and makes use of Microsoft's Graph Wizard.

Bound Object Frame. Used to display a graphic contained in a database file.

Unbound **Object Frame.** Used to display an independent graphic.

Rectangle. Also used to refine the presentation of the report.

Line. Used to improve the presentation of your report.

Command Button. Used to create your own buttons for use in the automation of the database, i.e. switchboards.

Page Break. Used in a similar way to its cousin in wordprocessors and spreadsheets - to artificially end the page. Mainly used to split a multipage report at the point that you require, rather than at the natural full page mark.

Tool Lock - Used to lock your tool selection to the pointer.

The **Control Wizards**. If this button is selected when you use an option group, a combo box, list box or command button, Access calls a wizard to help you out with the design for this feature.

Some of the tools given in this toolbox are not usually used on reports, as they are primarily used for record or entry selection, a task not usually available in reports. Those not directly relevant include list and combo boxes and the command and toggle button.

The check box and the option button are sometimes used because they can represent Yes/No data quite well or, in conjunction with an option group, they can represent a mutually exclusive choice that is given on a form using the same device.

In the main, text boxes, lines, rectangles and page breaks are the fundamental tools used on a report, the latter three being solely concerned with the appearance of the report. Text boxes shoulder most of the weight of data display, either directly from the table or query, or as a container for calculations as shown in Chapter 7.

Take a look at the reports in the NWind sample database supplied with Access. In any of the reports you open in Design View you will see that most of the components fall into one of the four groups.

To place the components onto the paper:

- Making sure that the Control Wizard button is de-selected, click onto the button in the toolbox that represents the component you want.
- Click on the Tool Lock button if you want to place more than one copy of the selected component onto the paper.
- Move the pointer to a position on the paper where you wish the top left-hand corner of the component to appear, and press the left mouse button.
- When you have finished placing all the components of that type onto the paper, return to the toolbox, de-select the tool lock if you used it, and click on the pointer button to return to normal operation.

You can now place other types of component into the paper, before you re-size and align the complete collection, using the usual techniques.

The Object Controls

The object controls come into their own (especially the unbound type) when you use them on reports. As you've seen in Chapter 10, the object controls are used to display the output from other software packages, such as hand-drawn pictures from Windows Paintbrush, spreadsheets from Microsoft Excel; or documents from Microsoft Word. They can also be used to give sound, display video clips and most other graphical display formats.

The visual impact of a report can be the deciding factor in whether or not it is acceptable. Because of this, knowledge of a drawing package may come in useful to produce exciting report headers, company logos and the like. These can be placed into the object controls in order to produce a stunning, complete package.

To place the unbound type of control (the type that doesn't refer to a particular record) onto the paper, follow the normal method of selecting the correct tool from the toolbox and place it on the paper. Access will then provide you with the following screen:

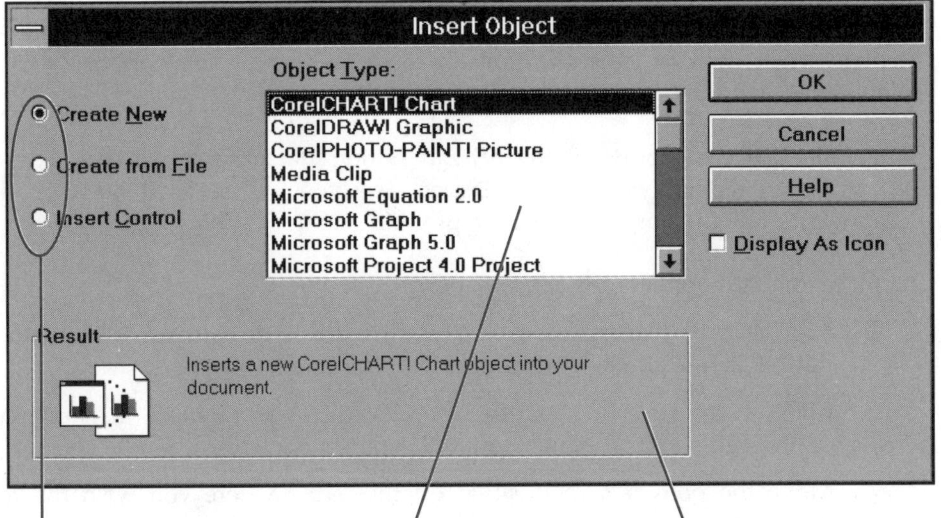

Choose the source from which you want to get the object: create a new one, get one from a file, or import an OCX/DLL/EXE file (specialist program features from libraries or built with Visual Basic).

This is the list of object types that your computer can produce. This ability relies on your computer having the software to produce each kind of object, e.g. Windows Paintbrush to produce a Paintbrush Picture.

Your current choice is shown in this Result box:

Depending on your choices here, Access will either fire up the appropriate package to allow you to create the object, or it will take you to a further screen upon which you can select the appropriate file that contains the object you want to appear on your report. Notice that you can link the object stored in Access to its original which allows the copy to be automatically updated when the original is changed.

When you have finished your creation or selection process, if you go back to Access you will find the file placed in the control. You can check this visually in design mode. If you have made the transfer successfully there will be a graphic or a picture: a small microphone if it's a sound file, a small film reel if it's a multimedia clip, in your object control.

> Note that it is advisable not to use objects that need outside stimulus in order to work, as it's not possible for the user to execute them while looking at the report itself, only while in Design View.

You will only need to place one of the bound controls onto your report if each record possesses the kind of data that requires an object control (in order to see it). In the case of a report, these are only useful for seeing visually static images such as photographs, pictures or mathematical graphs.

Follow the usual methods for putting the component onto your report. You will then need to customize that control, and bind it to the field in question, for the picture to appear. This is dealt with in the next section which covers the Report Properties box.

The Report Properties Box

The Report Properties box is exactly the same as the Form Properties box, except that it applies to report design. It's also used in exactly the same way to customize the components that you place.

Some of the commonly used properties are given below:

Property	**Use**
Name	This is the name of the component, used within the Report Design view to identify that component.
Control Source	This property identifies the field in the underlying table or query to which the control is bound. It's this field that the control looks into, or passes the required information to.
Top/Left/Width/Height	These four properties define the position of the component on the page.
On	These properties are called event properties. They are used to attach macros or Access Basic code to your database, and will be executed when the condition shown by the property is fulfilled.

For a listing of all of the properties that are available here, see Appendix I.

One example of the way to use the Report Properties box would be with a bound object control. When you place the bound object control onto the paper, it's not bound to any particular field in the underlying table or query. This means that no data will be displayed in it when you look at the report itself. In order to see the data stored in the base table, you need to set several properties:

- Set the Control Source property to the field in the base table that contains the data.
- Set the Size Mode property to either Clip, Stretch or Zoom. Clip takes the data at full size and only lets you see part of it, as if the control was a window. Stretch twists and bends the data to fit the control. Zoom takes the shortest side of the data, and stretches it to the length of the shortest side of the control. It keeps the data in proportion, so a gap may appear between the edge of the data and the control - or some of the data may be lost - just as with Clip.

When you have set these properties, you will be able to see the objects on your report which relate to the record that is being viewed.

Grouping and Sorting

One of the major uses of a report is to convey the information to a large group of people in such a way that it will be quickly understood. In order to do this, the layout of the information becomes vitally important and although queries can be used to filter out unwanted data, something more is required. The major feature that Access 2.0 reports have to offer a database designer is the internal report grouping and sorting facility.

With this facility you can group the data into umbrella headings, carry out internal sorts upon those groups, and quickly produce summary calculations on the contents of each grouping.

For an idea of what a good group and sort can make on a report, open the Employee Sales By Country report, in Design View (see opposite):

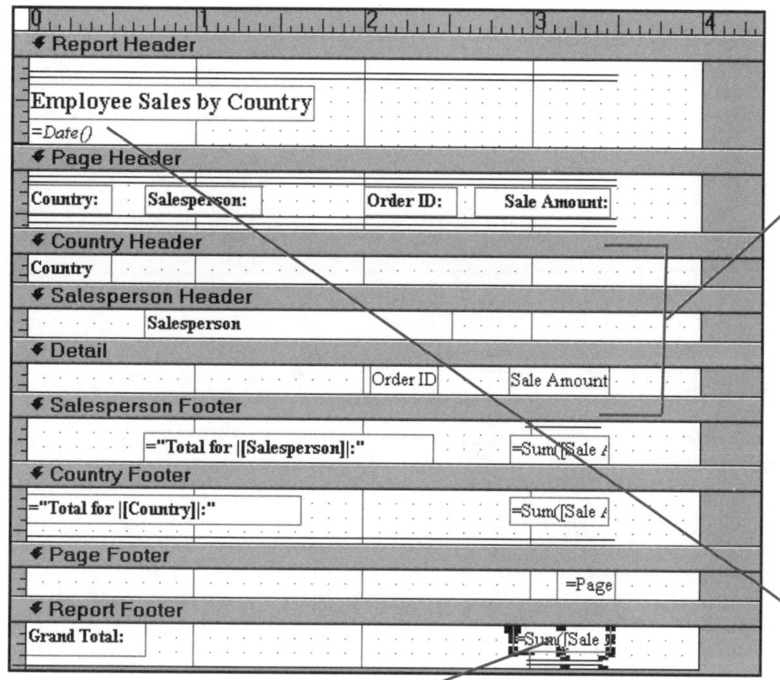

Notice the different headers that are now available to the report designer. Each group that you create will have its own header and footer in which to place information.

This is a custom field (i.e. a text box not bound to a particular field), but takes its contents from a combination of fields, or from Access itself. In this case it's the latter, as this control shows today's date.

This is also a custom field. It's being used in the group footer to sum the contents of each of the field entries that appear in that grouping. This is a quick and easy way of producing summary statistics of a group of records without having to first split them with a query, and then run summary calculations on those results.

We suggest you experiment with different section headers and footers to find out where to place your custom fields. To tell you in words might only confuse matters. We suggest you have a go at placing the text boxes around the work and see what results you get.

Pay close attention to the reports in NWind. Some of the suggested reports to look at include:

Catalog	A good use of the report header and footer.
Sales By Category	A good use of the group header.
Employee Sales By Country	A good use of the sum operator in custom fields.

However, before you can place the custom fields into your report, you need to be able to produce the different headers and footers that you require. For this you need to learn about the Sorting And Grouping box.

The Sorting and Grouping Box

Open a new report (non-wizard) from, say, the NWind Customers table. Open the Sorting And Grouping box by either:

- Clicking on the icon.
- Or by selecting the Sorting And Grouping... option under the View menu.

You will be presented with the following box:

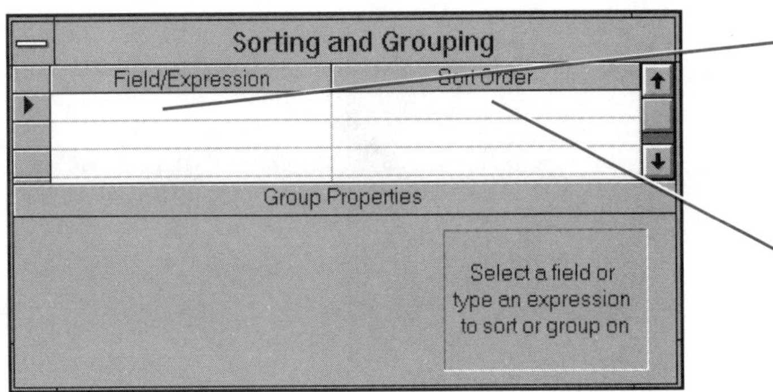

In this column (via drop-down lists) appear all the fields of the table/query you can choose to base the report on - Access will use them to sort the records.

This column shows the type of sort that will be carried out using this particular field.

When you choose a field to sort by, for example, Postal Code, the box changes slightly to appear like this:

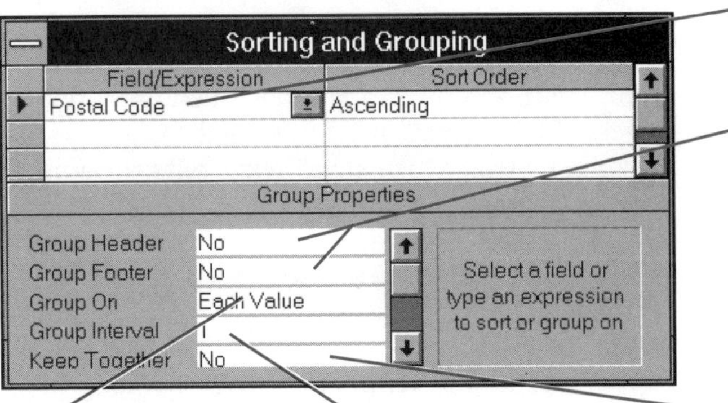

The selected field on which to sort the records in your report.

Choose a group header or footer. Selecting either of these properties means that grouping by the associated field will occur. Note that this is the only time that a header can exist without a partner, and vice versa.

Select the way that you want the grouping to occur: with identical values, or by a range. For example if your field is a date, you may choose to group by months (works in tandem with group interval).

Select the range upon which you wish the grouping to occur, the ranges depending on the data type of the field. This works in tandem with Group On. For example if you are grouping on months, you may choose an interval of 4 to create a specious quarter performance.

Section print commands. No option means no restrictions are set due to grouping. Whole Group option means it prints, if the group can fit on the page. First Detail option means the group only begins if group header/first record fits on the same page. If the groupings are larger than one page, the settings are ignored.

If you wish to continue and group using this field, you must follow these steps:

- Decide on whether you want a group header and/or a group footer and change the properties to indicate these choices.

> Note that when you select either of these properties to be active, Access places a [symbol] symbol in the pointer column next to the appropriate field to indicate that it is being used as a source of grouping.

- Decide on the type of grouping that you require and then decide on the grouping interval (if required).
- Finally, decide if you want any restrictions on how the grouping appears on the printed page.

Now close the Sorting And Grouping box, using the icon or the menu methods, and you'll see that your report design has changed to include all the alterations that you've just given Access via the Sorting And Grouping box. An example of the type of changes you might expect to see is shown below:

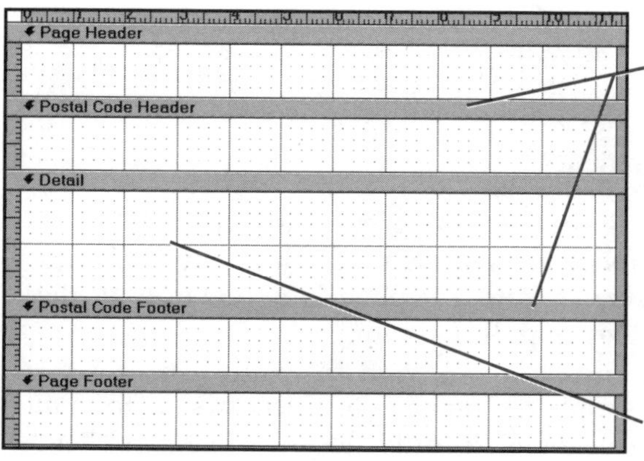

Notice that the report design now has a Postal Code header and footer. Remember that the headers and footers that appear in your report will appear at the top and bottom of the appropriate section; that is, the report header will appear at the top of the report, while the Postal Code footer will appear at the bottom of every Postal Code grouping.

Also note that any components you put into the details section before you added the Postal Code grouping will now be affected by the grouping, as that section appears between the group header and footer.

You can see that the order the fields appear in the Sorting And Grouping box is important to the appearance of your report.

Look at the Design View of the report with the following field ordering:

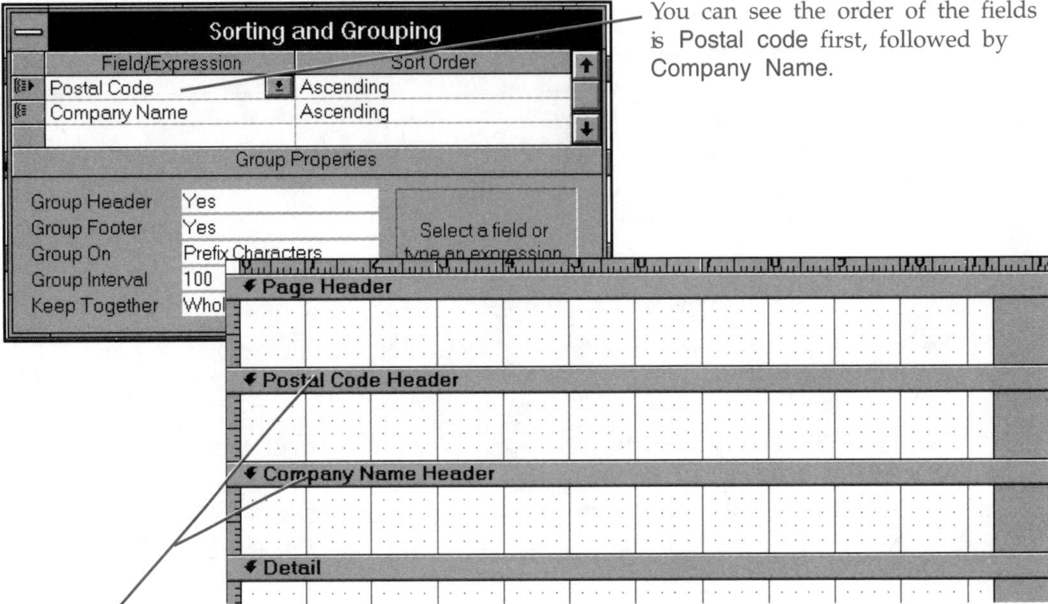

You can see the order of the fields is Postal code first, followed by Company Name.

Here, the Postal Code Header appears before the Company Name Header. This means the Company section will appear inside the Postal section and the records that appear in the Company section will be affected by the Postal grouping.

An Example of Grouping and Sorting

Taking the NWind sample database as the working ground, suppose you wanted a report that answered the following question: Which of my suppliers have the highest profile in each category? Rate a supplier's importance by the sum of the unit prices of products they supply us with.

Clearly, you will need to group by supplier company, in order to sum the unit costs. You'll also need to group by categories, in order to see which supplier is most important in each.

Already, things are starting to get a bit complex. Let's take a step back from the problem and reassess the situation.

If you group by supplier company, and then by category, all the categories will appear under each company name. This won't help, because you want to compare supplier to supplier under each particular category (for example, the performance of a list of companies who supply simply my confectionery items).

This can be solved by using category, followed by supplier company in the Sort and Grouping box.

You should also ask yourself what information you want and where it should go. You'll need as raw data the supplier company name, category name, product name and unit price.

Also, it would be helpful to have cost totals at the end of each list of products from a supplier, and a percentage figure (that is, each supplier's unit cost as a whole) for the entire category. This would help to identify the major players in each of the categories. To obtain this figure, and also give more information on the report, let's add in a total figure for all suppliers in each category.

Where exactly the data should appear depends on what type of data it is. Clearly, the supplier company name and the category name need to appear in the corresponding headers. This means they'll appear at the top of their grouping, either as products or supplier's respectively. The product names and unit prices need to appear in the details sections because they are affected by all groupings. The supplier total needs to appear in the supplier company footer, so that it appears at the bottom of the listing of products. The category total needs to appear in the category footer for the same reasons.

Let's look at the stages you need to follow in order to get this report:

- Create a query that contains all the fields you require. You'll use this to base your report on.

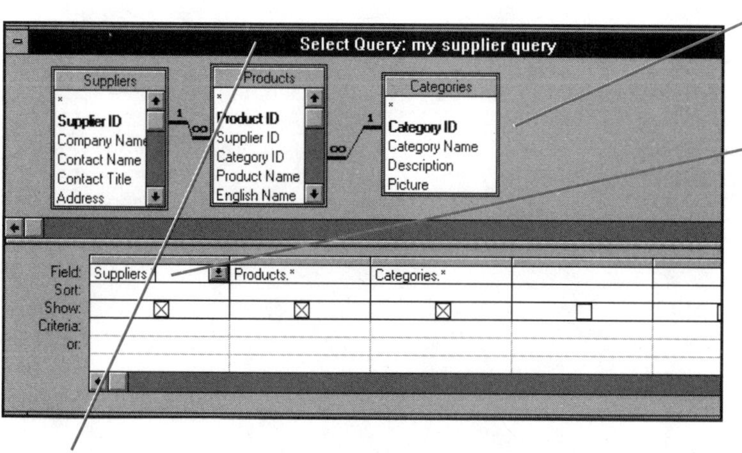

These tables contain the raw information that you will use in the report.

For simplicity, the asterisk method has been used to select the fields from the underlying tables.

Notice that this query has been saved with the name "my supplier query".

- Create a blank report based upon this query.

Click this button to create a blank report based upon the selected query (without the help of one of the many Report Wizards).

- Open the Sorting And Grouping box and add Category Name and Supplier Company Name to the list, giving both of them group headers and footers.

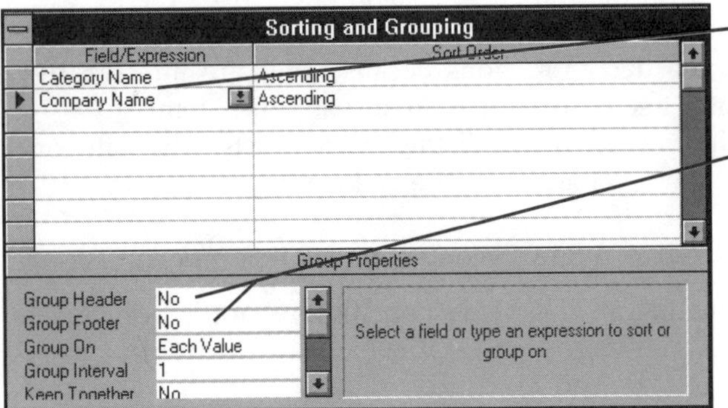

Make sure the order of these fields is correct, otherwise the report will break down.

Give the report the required headers using these two properties, when the field pointer is on Category Name and Supplier Company Name respectively.

- Constrain the category group to appear on a page only, if it will fit. This gives the report some backbone, and makes it easier to read, rather than flicking between pages to see different supplier companies.

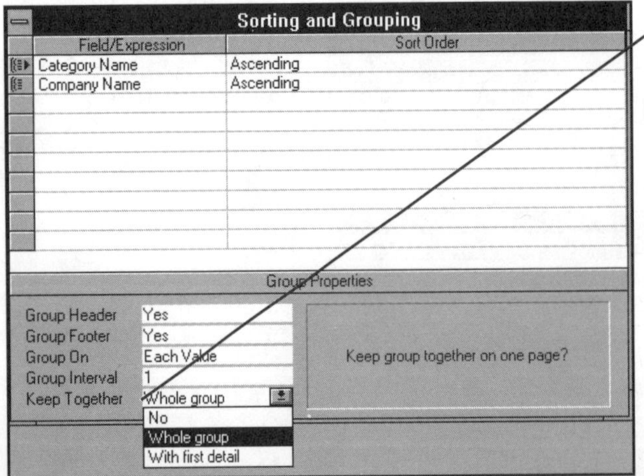

Choose the Whole Group option for the Category Name property. They will Keep Together to get the required print out effect.

- Place the Category Name field, and the Supplier Company Name field into the respective headers.

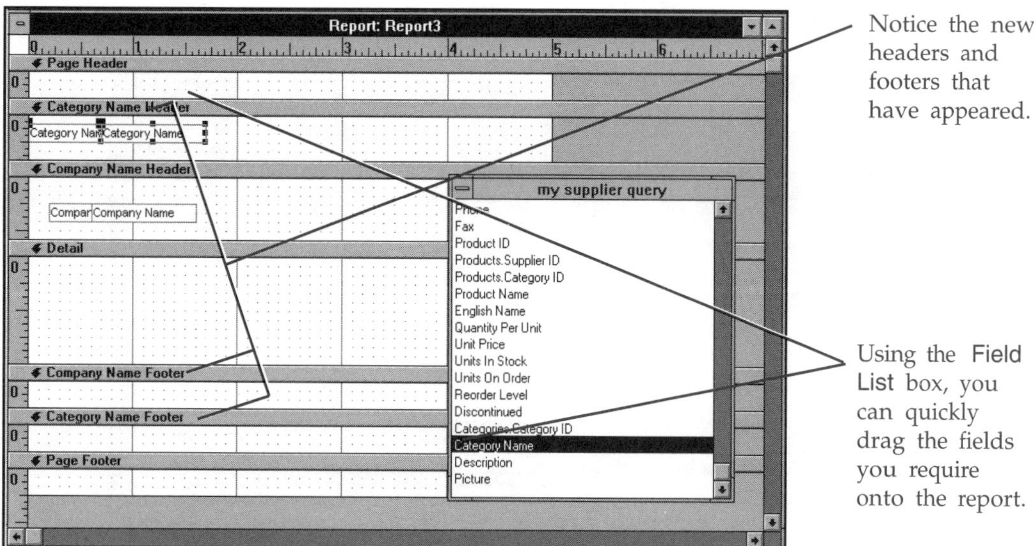

- Improve the presentation of your report by altering the labels and reducing the free space around the components. This means that the report will take up just enough room to fit in all the detail required.

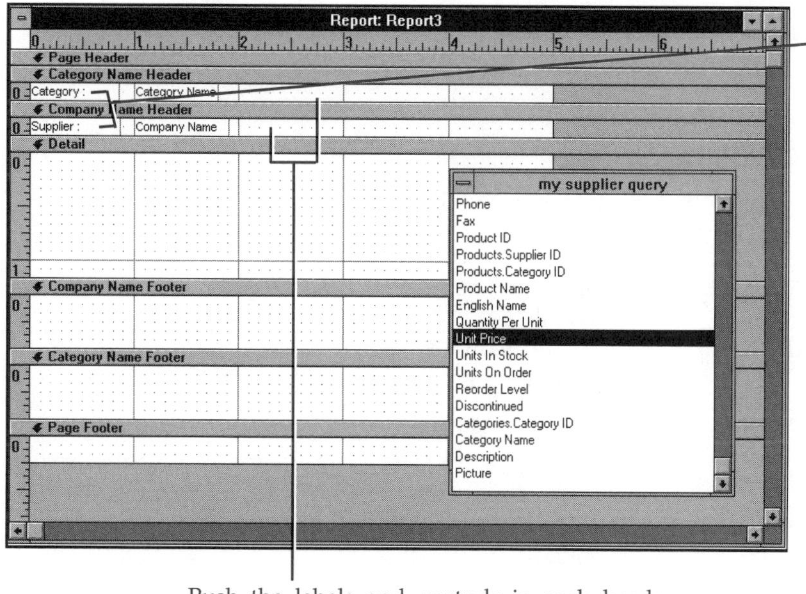

- Place the Product Name and the Unit Price fields into the details section of your report, realign the labels and controls, rename the labels and reduce the white space.

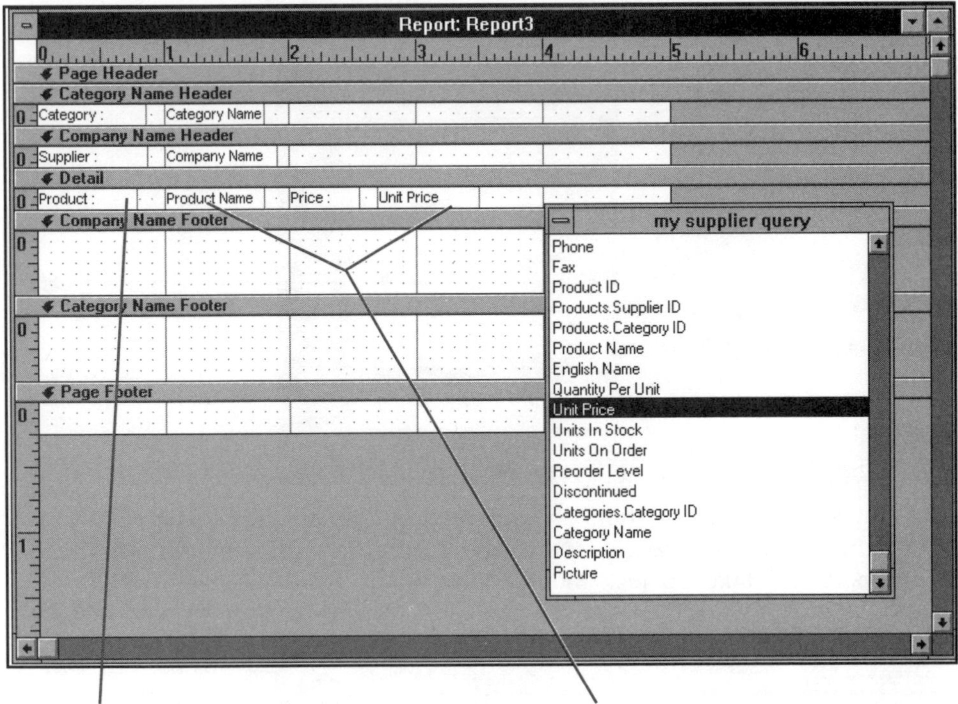

Notice the tidied up appearance of the components in the details section. This reduces the amount of white space while giving the report your own personal style.

The Product Name and the Unit Price appear side by side, so that they appear on the same line in the report.

Next, place a text box onto the report to contain a custom field. This field will be used to work out and display the sum of the unit prices for each supplier. This, of course, appears in the company name footer. Use the expression builder to create your custom calculation in the Control source of the new custom field's text box.

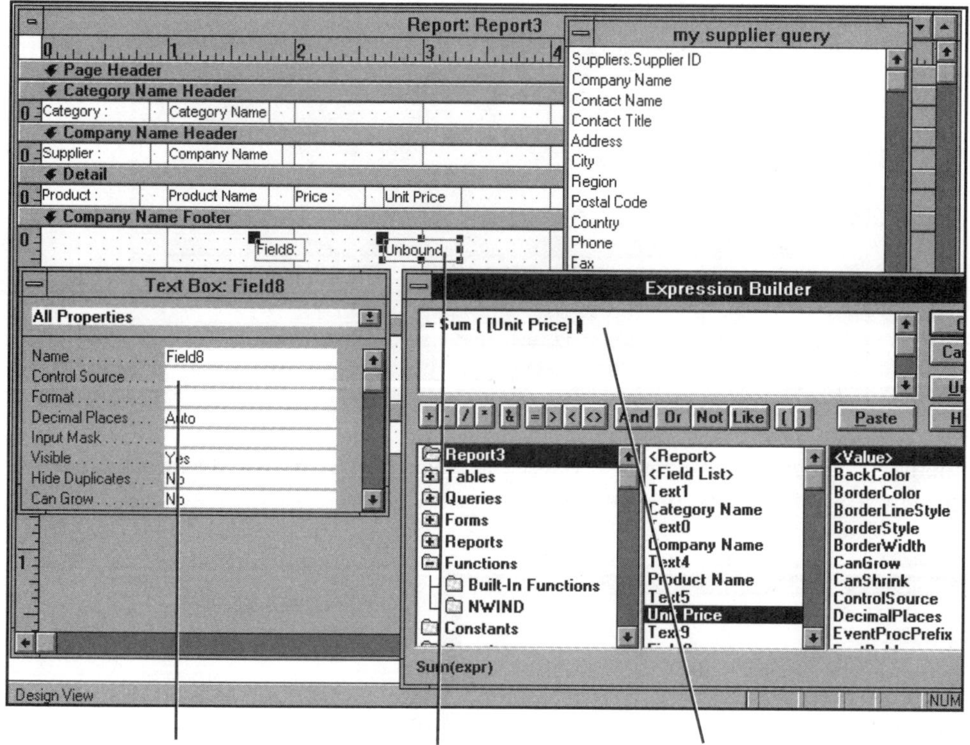

You can see that the control source of the text box is empty, showing the component is Unbound.

The unbound text control will become the custom field containing a sum of the unit prices.

The Control Source property is using the expression builder to produce the calculation =Sum ([Unit Price]).

Change the format property of the custom text box to Currency. This will provide the correct number of decimal places and currency symbols in front of the numbers. You can also alter the label for this control to read Supplier Total. Repeat the process to create a custom field to calculate the sum of the unit prices for each category. The text box should appear in the category footer, but the calculation is the same.

The calculation is the same for both custom fields because:

1. The custom fields sum all the unit prices that fall within their groupings, i.e. the supplier custom field sums each supplier's unit prices, while the category custom field sums all the supplier's unit prices as they all fall between the category header and footer.

2. The sum of the supplier grouping subtotals is the same as the sum of the individual unit prices.

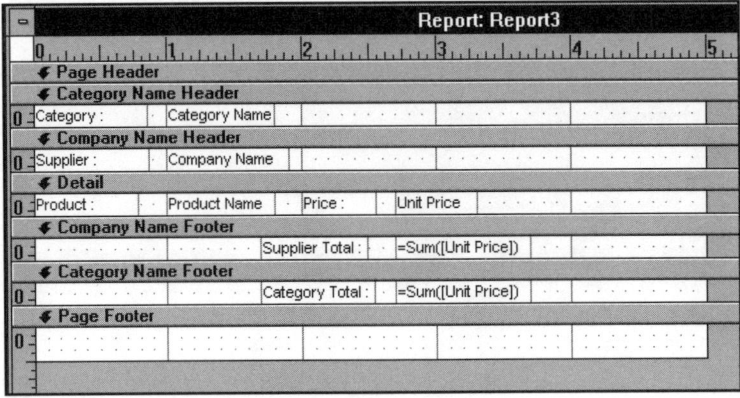

With that final entry, you have broken the back of the report design. Let's have a look at a sample page of your report:

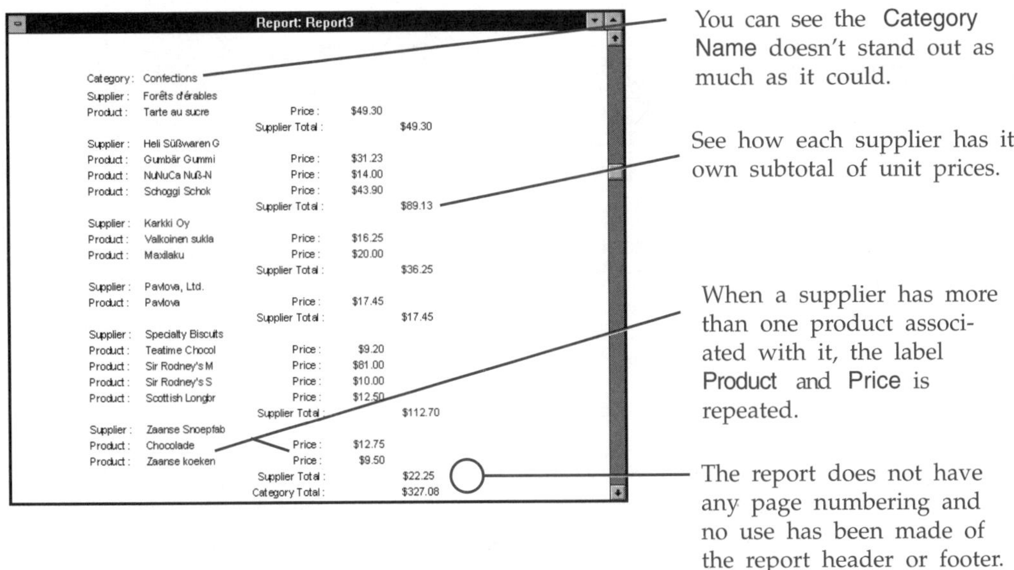

So what is left that would improve the overall presentation of the report?

- The inclusion of a report header
- The addition of page numbers
- The amendment of the fonts in several cases, for emphasis
- Producing list headings
- Additional custom controls

Including a Report Header

To include a report header into your creation:

- Select the Report Header/Footer option in the Format menu and Access will place the appropriate sections into your report design.
- Now you must import an impressive work of art to both stun your boss and convey the contents of the report. Place an unbound object control into your report header, and import the header from a graphics package. Alternatively, simply use a label with large font.

See below for an example of the type of results that you can produce:

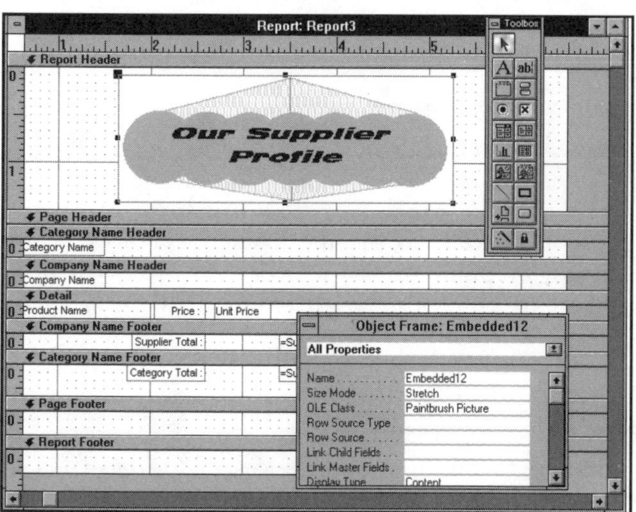

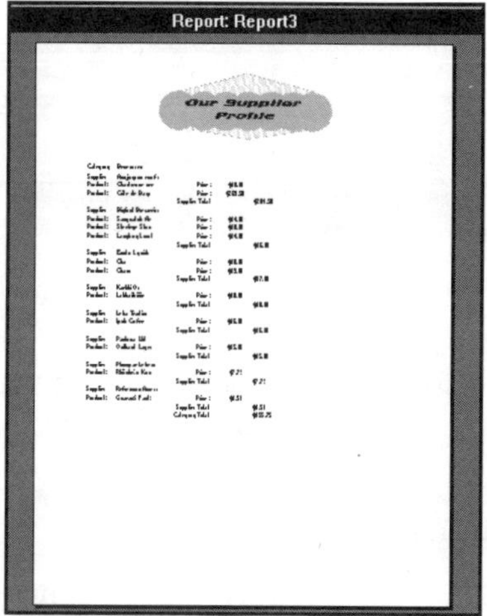

Including Page Numbers

To add page numbers to your report, place a text box somewhere in either the page header or footer, depending on where you want the numbering to appear.

- Use the Expression Builder to produce the expression that is required for page numbering, or type it directly into the control source property of the text box.

Access has several options for the appearance of the page numbers including the following:

=Page	Results in 1, 2, 3 etc.
="Page " & Page	Results in Page 1, Page 2, Page 3 etc.
=Page & " of " & Pages & " Pages"	Results in 1 of 10 Pages, 2 of 10 Pages etc.

For more examples of the type of expressions that you can use, see the Access Help screens, under Adding Page Numbers to a Form or Report: Examples.

Using Fonts for Emphasis

To make the category and supplier names stand out on the printed output, you can use different fonts and larger point sizes for emphasis of the headings.

To alter the font or point size of any label or control:

- Focus the appropriate component and go to the icon bar, where the current font and point size are shown, as below:

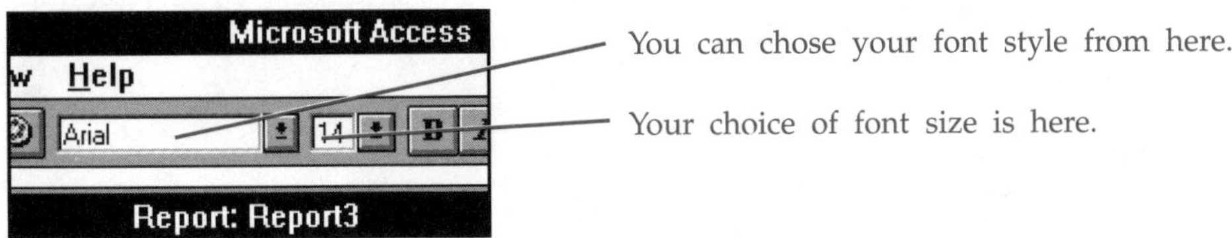
Microsoft Access
w Help
Arial
14
Report: Report3
You can chose your font style from here.
Your choice of font size is here.

- Select the tabs at the ends of the cells to see the available choices, highlighting the required font or point size as it's located. Access will automatically apply that font or point size to all entries that the label or control supports.

Moving Labels to Produce Listing Headings

To produce list headings as opposed to multiple occurrences of the label (as in the case of the Products or Prices in the NWind example) place the label in the section directly above the associated control. For example, place the product name label in the company name header, and move the product name control underneath the label. See the finished report design at the end of this section for an example of this.

The Extra Custom Controls - Percentages

As with the other custom controls, to produce the percentages for each supplier based upon the total for each category, place a text box next to the Supplier Total control.

Using the expression builder, or simply by typing straight into the control source property of the text box, produce the following expression:

=[Name of the Supplier Total Control]/[Name of the Category Total Control].

where the Name of the Supplier control and the Name of the Category control are given in the Control Name property of the respective components.

The Completed Report

By following all of the steps given you should be able to create a Sort and Group styled report similar to the one shown below:

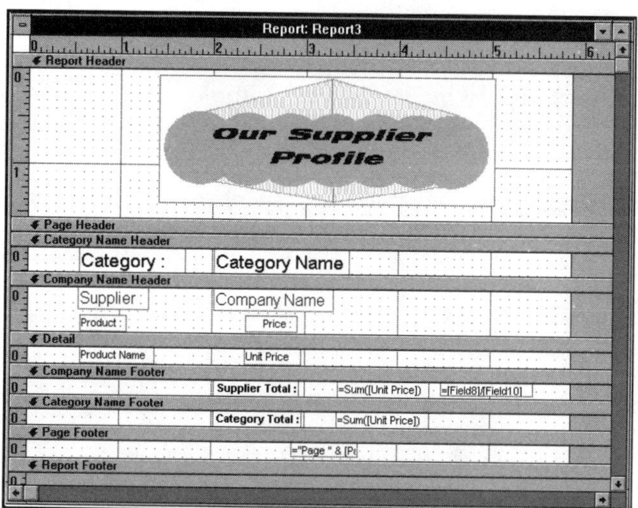

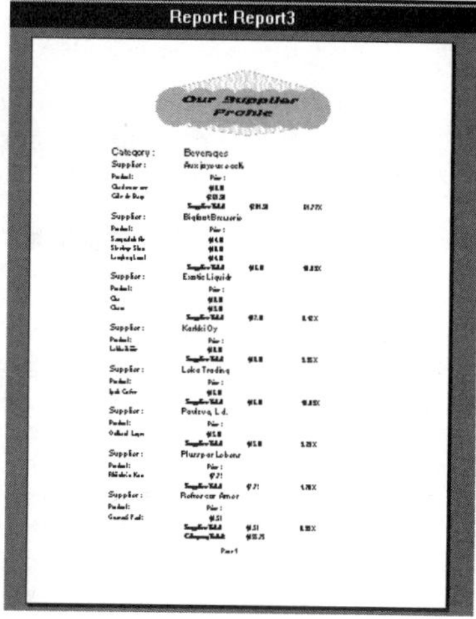

Notice all the features that have been discussed are shown in this report, from percentages to highlighted headings, grouped products to unit price sums. All these features should allow you to create the exact report and to answer any question that is posed (if you have the required information in your Access database).

Now let's go on to look at a tool that applies not only to reports but also to forms and which allows you to incorporate other forms and reports into your creation.

Main/Subforms and Reports

Quite simply, a main/subreport is a structure you can apply to any report you create. It allows you to include other forms or reports into your main report. These additions to your main report are called subforms or subreports depending on where you acquired them.

This structure lets you create more complex reports by creating a master report out of two or more minor ones. The minor ones might cover a different aspect or focus of the master, or perhaps you want to include a summary of the results found in a master report. Simply create a summary report of the subject covered and place it in the report or page header.

This process of building up your finished report means you can tackle small and simple chunks of the task - making the overall project easier to handle. You could also go beyond the limits of a single report in terms of the content and position of the information you required in your report.

Example

Take a look at the Sales By Category report in the NWind sample database. It looks something like this:

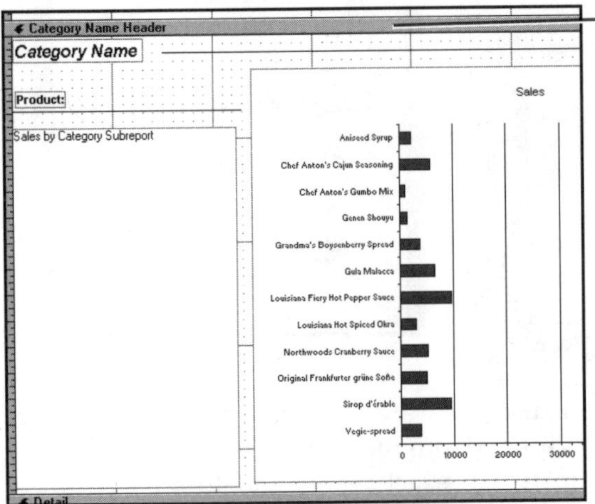

Note that the focus of this report is based in the Category Name Header, and the details section is empty. This is because the graph, created in this section using the help of the Graph Wizard and Microsoft Graph (see Chapters 5 and 7 respectively) is required to have all the products contained in one category upon it. The subreport is then used to show the details of the graph next to it, as opposed to below it. This means all the data will be together rather than being spread over several pages, as the number of products grows larger.

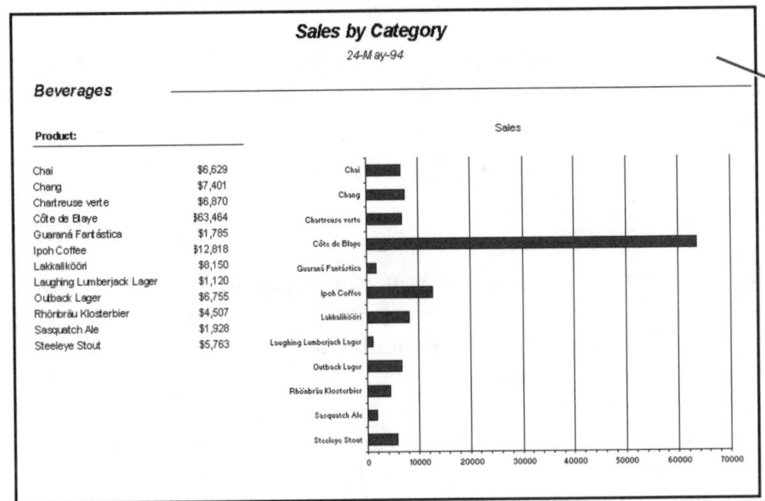
Sales by Category

24-May-94

Beverages

Product:	
Chai	$6,629
Chang	$7,401
Chartreuse verte	$6,870
Côte de Blaye	$63,464
Guaraná Fantástica	$1,785
Ipoh Coffee	$12,818
Lakkalikööri	$8,150
Laughing Lumberjack Lager	$1,120
Outback Lager	$6,755
Rhönbräu Klosterbier	$4,507
Sasquatch Ale	$1,928
Steeleye Stout	$5,763

You can see this report uses a subreport to show the detailed figures associated with the graph. Also note that if you flick through the pages of the report, the contents of the subreport change to keep track of the contents of the graph.

This report is a classic example of the use of a subreport to give summary information to the reader. But what about a composite report? A good example of this type of report can be easily produced using the NWind database. Let's look at the idea behind this type of report and then look at how to produce it, while learning how to manipulate the nuts and bolts of main/sub report design.

A Composite Report

A composite report is a report built using two or more self-contained reports in order to produce a finished comprehensive document. Let's look at the NWind database for some ideas on this type of report.

Example

The report called Summary Sales by Quarter gives you a listing of the total sales the company has made, broken down into yearly quarters; a particularly good component for a board meeting (it shows a healthy growth in sales!).

The second report you should look at is called Freight Charges and details the cost of transporting the products to the customers, broken down into the 3 freight handlers the company use. This is a good report to include as it shows the amounts of cash being used to ship goods around the country, and will be useful for comparisons between shipper and amount of goods shipped as shown in the other report.

At the moment, Freight Charges is running off a query of the same name that restricts the orders shown to a given week in March 1993. If you replace the criteria with the following `Between #1/1/93# And #12/31/93#`, the reports will be of more use when comparing figures, and you won't have to keep typing these figures into the parameter dialog boxes. Make a note of the criteria, so you can replace it after this report design has been completed, allowing the NWind database to run in the way it was meant to, at the expense of the new report.

With a combination of these reports, and the alterations to one of the underlying queries, it's possible to create a report from both of these by following these steps:

- Open an new unbound report. You can do this by *not* providing the opening report screen, shown on the next page, with a table or query from which to draw information.

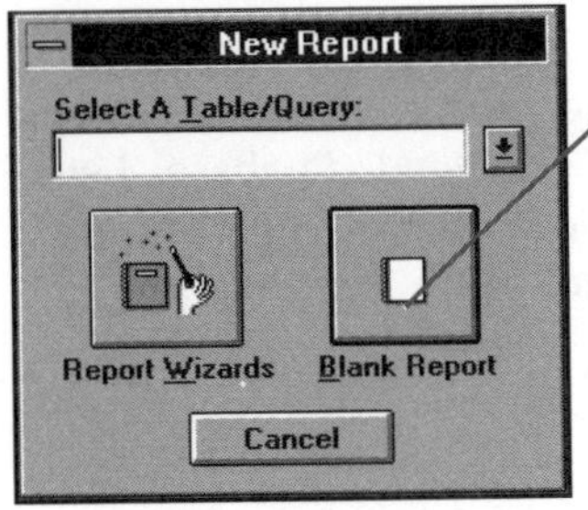

Just select this button without filling in the window above to obtain an unbounded report.

- Open the tool box using the toolbox icon, and select the Subform/Subreport button
- Place two unbound subreport controls, together with their associated labels, into the details section of the report, as shown below:

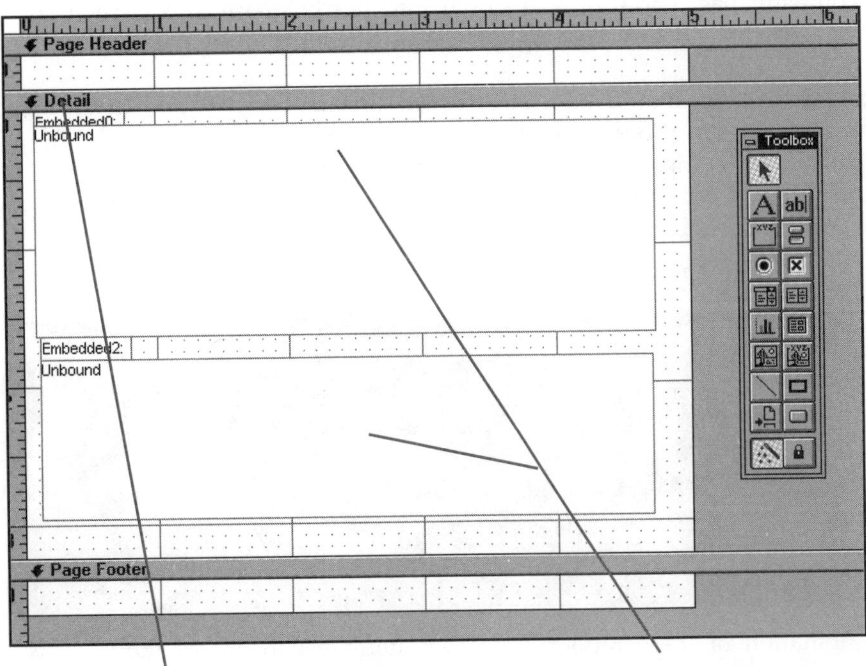

Remember that the only constraint that you have in the details section is the size: 24 ins by 24 ins. If your reports are longer than 12 ins, you can use the report header and footer to hold the subreports, remembering that these sections appear before and after the details section when it's printed out.

Place the subreport controls where you want the different reports to appear. Remember that in this section of your main report, all of the first report will be shown before the second report is begun, if you place them as here. If the reports are thin enough, you can place them side by side.

- Select one of the controls. When you open the Report Properties box, you will find the Source Object property. In this property the name of the report that you want to be present in this control should appear. Either type in the name of the report or select it from the drop-down menu that appears when you select the tab at the end of the cell.

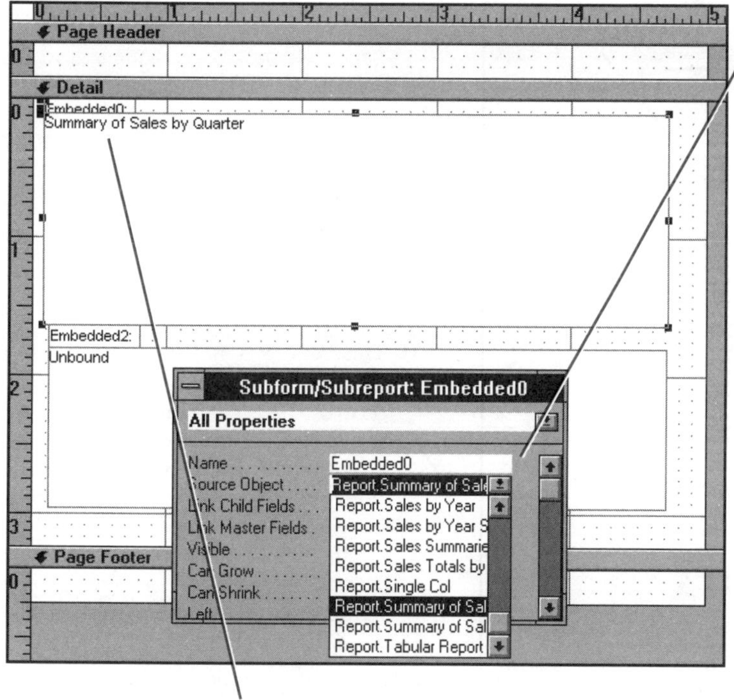

You can see how Access refers to a report when other objects such as forms or tables are around. It uses the syntax Report.Report Name. You will use this method when you cover macros and Access Basic in the following chapters.

You can see that the report you have selected for this control has appeared here.

As you can see from the contents of the drop-down menu, you can also include forms in your reports. This allows you to present individual records in a report, and is covered shortly.

- Repeat the process for the second report.
- Let's view the report and see what has been produced. Select the Print Preview icon from the icon bar to see the report, which has a similar layout to the one shown opposite.

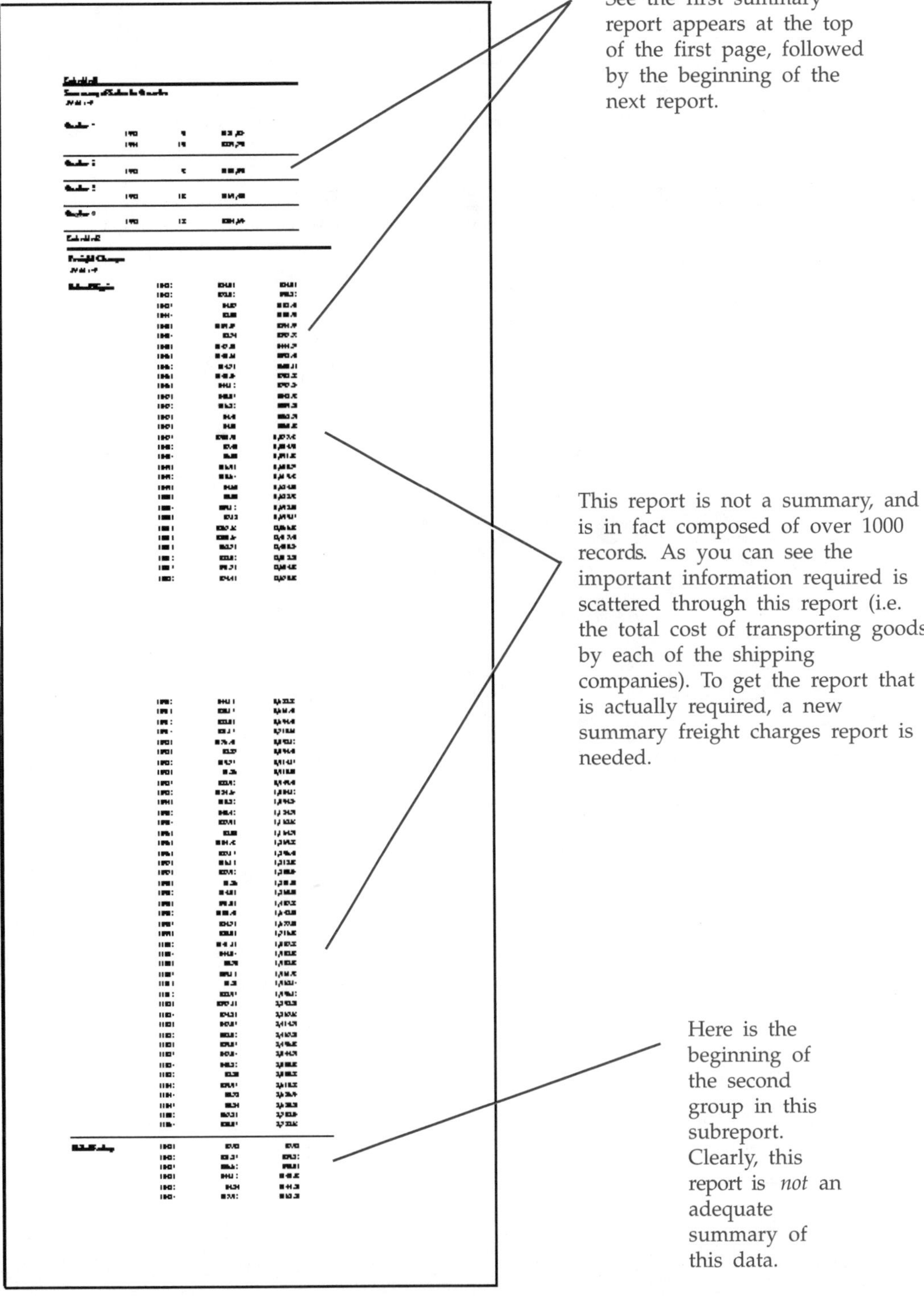
See the first summary report appears at the top of the first page, followed by the beginning of the next report.
This report is not a summary, and is in fact composed of over 1000 records. As you can see the important information required is scattered through this report (i.e. the total cost of transporting goods by each of the shipping companies). To get the report that is actually required, a new summary freight charges report is needed.
Here is the beginning of the second group in this subreport. Clearly, this report is *not* an adequate summary of this data.

The New Freight Charges Report

Produce (using the methods already covered in this chapter) a report design that looks something like this:

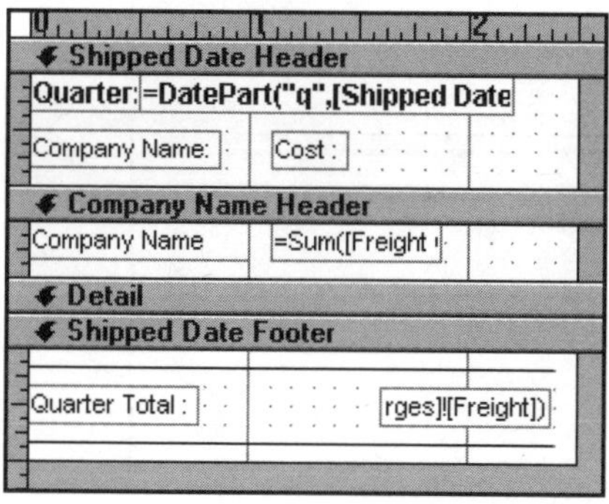

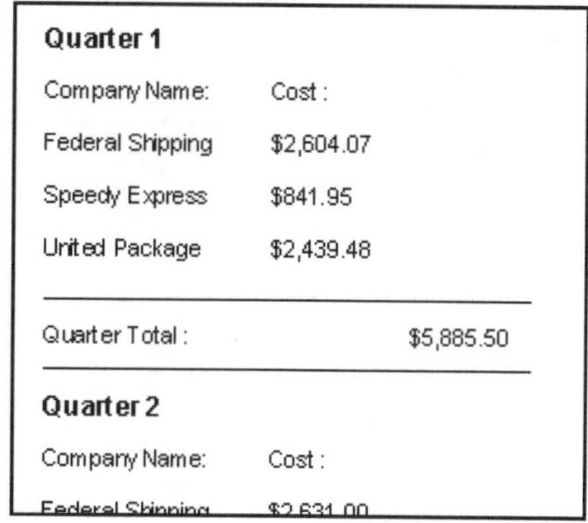

Points Of Interest:

- Custom control for Quarter .... =DatePart("q",[Shipped Date]).
- Custom control for Company name sum .... =Sum ([Freight Charges]![Freight]).
- Custom control for Quarter Total sum .... =Sum ([Freight Charges]![Freight]).
- Format property on all controls that hold a cost, is set to Currency.
- Quarter and Number are Bold 9pt.
- Lines placed on paper with Snap To Grid (on) - to align them more easily.

With this new freight report you can now produce a sensible composite report simply by changing the Object Source property of the second subreport control to the name of the new freight report. Running the composite report produces the output shown on the next page.

Notice that the headings for the columns in the first report are missing. If you look back to the source report, you will immediately see why - they appear in the page header, and this subreport hasn't got any pages, so it doesn't appear.

Quick note to remember - subreports cannot use page headers or footers!

Summary of Sales by Quarter
24-May-94

Quarter: 1			
	1993	95	$121,824
Quarter: 2			
	1993	93	$150,596
Quarter: 3			
	1993	107	$169,458
Quarter: 4			
	1993	137	$204,694

Quarter 1

Company Name:	Cost :	
Federal Shipping	$2,604.07	
Speedy Express	$841.95	
United Package	$2,439.48	
Quarter Total :		$5,885.50

Quarter 2

Company Name: Cost :

A Composite Report: Tabular and Groups/Total

Using the Main/Sub Technique on Forms

As you may have already realized you can also use this technique of 'object within object' solely based on forms. Why would you want a form within a form?

There are two main reasons why you would want to include subforms in a main form:

1. It gives you the ability to enter data into several tables at once using one form, and without the need for a query.
2. It enables you to show all the records involved in a one-to-one or one-to-many relationship in one form: i.e. one Hollywood actor and all the houses that he/she owns could be shown on one form.

Remember, the one-to-many relationship use of main/subform cannot be done easily on a normal form design. Continuing the analogy, the number of houses that each actor owns may vary dramatically. To produce one single form that could cope with this situation, you would have to include into the design one set of controls for each house owned. This becomes uneconomical when the number of houses grows greater than two. It also ruins the purpose of a relational database, as you will also have to repeat the fields required in order to store the extra house data; i.e. house1 details and house2 details etc.

To identify which house belongs to who, it's more efficient to divide the table into two: the first part with the person's details and the second part with the house details, linking them together with a code field. Then use a main/subform to fill in the details of the one-to-many relationship.

Example

Let's look at a main/subform in action in the NWind sample database. Two good examples in this database that you can open are called Orders and Quarterly Orders. Quarterly Orders is discussed below.

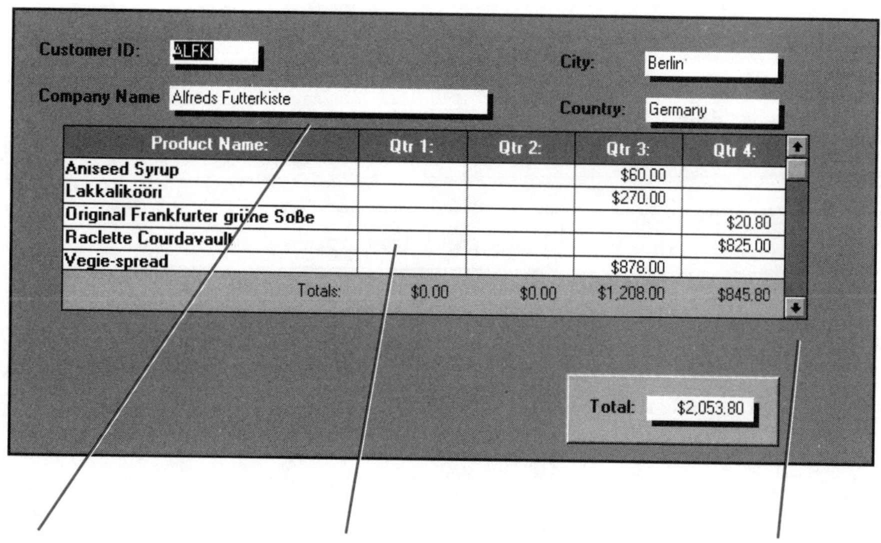

Here you're given the name of the first customer who has ordered some of your goods over the last twelve months.

Here you're given a tabular form to show the total costs of the different products the customer has ordered over the last twelve months. Note there is more than one record in this tabular form for this customer.

Notice the scroll bars on the edge of the subform. These allow you to have many records listed, while only taking up a small amount of space on the actual paper.

How to Create a Main/Subform

The steps involved in the creation of a main/subform are very similar to the corresponding steps for a main/subreport:

- Create the subform, including all the fields contained in the underlying many-sided table, just as if it were a normal form.
- Create a main form as usual, including all the components to allow you access to the one side of a relationship.
- From the toolbox, select the Subform/Subreport control and place it upon the form in the approximate position required, with the appropriate size and shape to accommodate the subform.
- Place the focus upon the Subform control, and opening the Form Properties box locate the Source Object property.
- Type in, or select from the drop-down menu, the name of the subform you have just created. This means the subform will appear in this control when you have informed Access of the links between the main form and its subform.

Linking the Two Forms Together

Before Access will show you the appropriate subform for the main form record that is showing, you must inform it of the common field that links the two forms together.

> This field is usually the **code field** that appears in the many-sided table.

Access uses the code field entry in the main form to identify the records that should appear in the subform. It does this by looking for the same code field entry in the many-sided table which appeared in the main form record. It then restricts the contents of the subform to these related records, thus providing the full one-to-many record listing.

To link the two forms together, you need to focus on the subform and open the Form Properties box. The two properties you are interested in are called Link Child Fields and Link Master Fields.

Fill in the Link Child Fields property with the name of the field in the subform that is part of the link between the two forms, and fill in the Link Master Fields property with the corresponding field name, which appears in the main form.

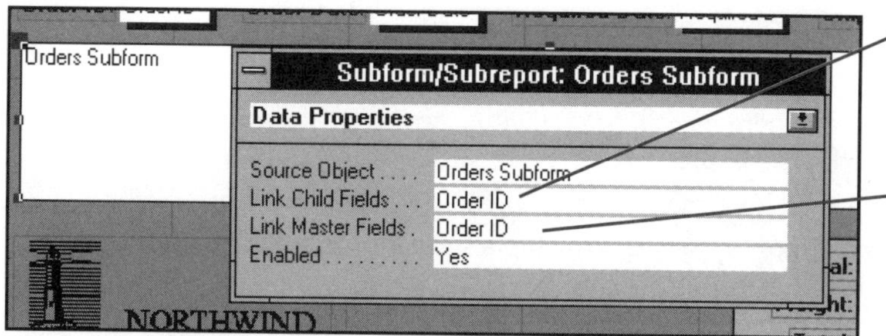

Field in subform that is part of the link between the two forms.

Field in main form that is part of the link between the two forms.

When you have linked together the two forms you will be able to enter and view data in the single form from the underlying tables or queries covered by both the form and the subform.

Troubleshooting

Q&A I want to print out a copy of the form or report design that I have been working on. Can I do this?

You can, but only up to a point. You can't print out what you see on screen, but you can get a wordy description of what you have done. Select Print Definition.... from the File menu, and follow the instructions given in the screens that follow. If you choose to have a complete listing of all the features in your form or report, you will get a print out something like that shown below:

C:\ACCESS2\SAMPAPPS\NWIND.MDB — Tuesday, May 24, 1994
Report: Freight Charges — Page: 1

Properties

Count:	22	Date Created:	3/17/94 3:02:29 PM
Date Grouping:	US Defaults	Fast Laser Printing:	Yes
Grid X:	10	Grid Y:	12
Help Context Id:	0	Last Updated:	3/17/94 3:04:03 PM
Layout For Print:	Yes	Owner:	admin
Page Footer:	All Pages	Page Header:	All Pages
Palette Source:	(Default)	Record Locks:	No Locks
Record Source:	Freight Charges	Visible:	Yes
Width:	7200	Window Height:	5535
Window Width:	9705		

Objects

Group Level 0

Control Source:	Company Name	Group Footer:	Yes
Group Header:	No	Group Interval:	1
Group On:	Each Value	Keep Together:	No
Sort Order:	Ascending		

Group Level 1

Control Source:	Order ID	Group Footer:	No
Group Header:	No	Group Interval:	1
Group On:	Each Value	Keep Together:	No
Sort Order:	Ascending		

Q&A I want to export the complete report: images, text and records to Word. Can I do that?

Yes, with reservations, as there is no easy facility to 'grab' a complex report and throw it into Word. There are extensive facilities for transferring the textual heart of the report. You may simply press [W] (the Publish It With MSWord icon). This will boot up your Word package automatically and transfer the text, and sometimes the graphics, quite well (depending on which other package created the original graphic, and whether it is OLE compatible etc.). You will find that Picture Objects seem to lose themselves in the process. Ultimately, you could transfer the text and link Word to the separate objects one by one, as if it was simply calling up contained images (from file) into a document (you're limited to the normal Word filters). Remember, you can't link or embed Access objects into another OLE application.

You could take a snapshot of the whole thing, page by page, using Print Screen on your keyboard. You would Snap the screen and place it into a drawing package to tidy it up. Then you could save as, say, a Bitmap (.bmp) file and import into your Word document using Insert and Picture on the menu bar. See your Access Help screens for detailed rulings on links, embedding and OLE/DDE.

CHAPTER 12

Macros

You may have used macros before with other applications. Most, if not all Windows programs include some kind of macro facility. If you are using Access 2.0 as part of Microsoft Office, then both Word 6.0 and Excel 4.0 have macros. There are differences between these packages, but the idea behind macros is the same in both cases - to make tasks easier.

In this chapter we are going to show you how to write your own macros. Write is probably a strong word to use with macros, as the amount of actual typing required is minimal. Macros can speed up a whole range of your package functions. If you are confident enough to master macros, the savings in finger strain and process planning are there for free. Macros are the friendliest way to surreptitiously manipulate Access, without having to use a programming language.

In this chapter you will cover:

- What a macro is
- The design window for macros
- Message boxes
- Macro actions
- Adding macros to the database
- Adding conditions to macros
- Macro groups

What is a Macro?

Put simply, a macro is a list of instructions that Access carries out for you. These instructions are not at all like a true programming language. Instead they are words which represent actions you would normally perform with either the keyboard or mouse.

These actions are generally things like opening tables, causing a report to be printed, or automating key sequences. You may have noticed that all of these actions can be done from the menus, and that's just the point. Macros allow the user to use any menu action, without actually using the menus!

In Access, macros go a little further than that. Some of the words you can use don't have any equivalent in the menus. They are there to allow you to do special things that will make you look like a really clever person. Examples include things like turning the pointer into an hourglass, or displaying a message on the screen.

Automating Tedious Tasks

This is all very well, but it doesn't explain why you would want to use a macro instead of the menu in the first place. The answer is that you are letting the computer do something instead of the user. This can relieve the tedium of repeating processes, whilst at the same time allowing the programming of repetitions.

Let's say you have a large customer database, which is so important to your company that you keep a print-out of every customer's details.

You could do a print-out on every customer once a week, but some customer's details won't change, and therefore won't need to be reprinted. You could print the customer's details only when they were updated by the users. However, if you tried this, then it's obvious a mistake would happen sooner or later. Either the user would forget to print or would print the wrong thing.

Macros get around this problem completely. You can easily set up a macro that will print the customers details every time one of the customers gets updated. It would never forget, and never print the wrong report. Macros could save your business!

The Macro Design Window

By now you will have decided that macros are wonderful things which should be part of every database, so just how do you go about writing one?

Starting a New Macro

As with all other features of Access, in order to create a macro you first need to click on the Macro tab of the database window, and then the New button. This opens the Macro Design window.

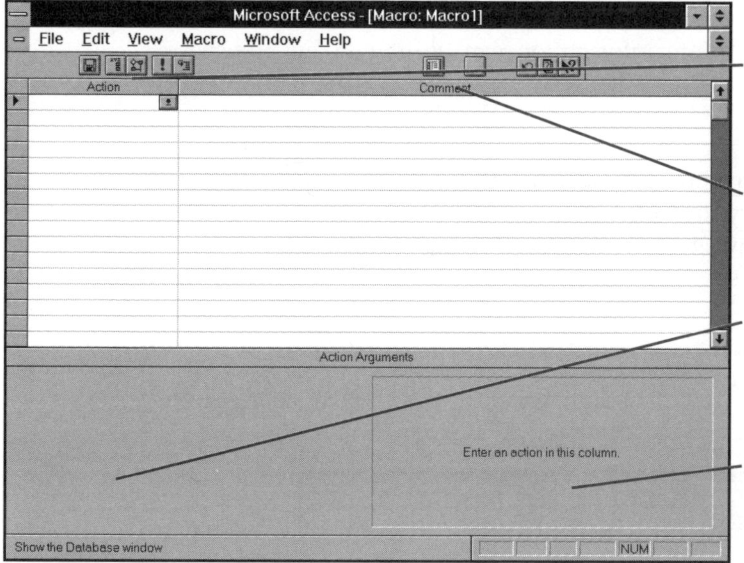

Action. This is where you define what your macro actually does.

Comment. Use comments to make notes about the macro for future reference.

Help Box. These are little notes to help you design your macro.

Refinement. Lets you define what an action does more precisely.

Action

This area of the Macro Design window is where you specify the actions you want your macro to perform. Most of the time a single action is not enough, which is why there are several lines available in this region. A macro always starts at the first line, and keeps going until there are no more actions to perform, or until it is told to stop by a special action.

You don't have to remember the action names, as Access 2.0 provides you with a drop-down list of possible actions when you click on a line.

Comment

Comments are very useful. The idea behind a comment is to tell you what the macro does. Access 2.0 doesn't fill this in itself, it's up to you. You may think this is a tedious thing to do, and in some cases this may be true. However, not all macros are obvious in what they do, and if you need to change a macro six months after you wrote it, will you remember how it works? And what if someone else has written the macro?

This is why it's good practice to put comments in your macros. Access 2.0 lets you put a comment against each action, so you can either have a detailed blow-by-blow account of the macro, or just an overview.

Help Box

The Help box is the first line of help that Access 2.0 provides for you. Whatever has the focus (highlighted on the window) is accompanied by a relevant help message below. More information can be gained by pressing *F1*.

Refinement

This is where you specify exactly what the action is to be. You may wonder why this is necessary, but consider a macro that opens a form. The problem is which form? You have to tell the macro which form you want to open and the view you want to use.

New Toolbar Buttons

When you open the Macro Design window the toolbar changes and new buttons appear on it.

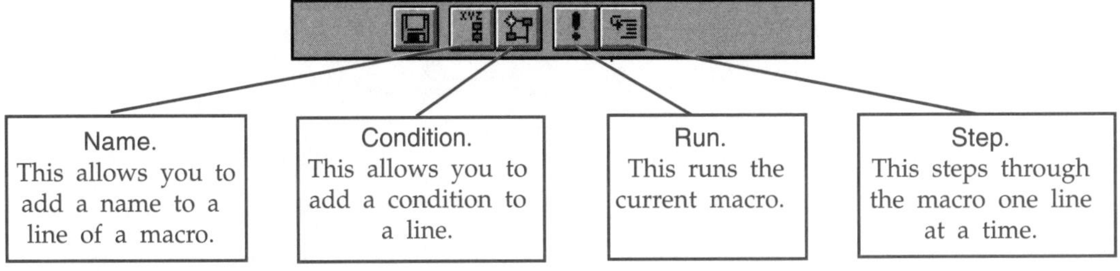

Name.
This allows you to add a name to a line of a macro.
Condition.
This allows you to add a condition to a line.
Run.
This runs the current macro.
Step.
This steps through the macro one line at a time.

Three of the buttons are completely new and one has a slightly different meaning.

Run

This button is similar to the Run Query button and allows you to run the current macro you are working on. This is not the normal way of running macros and is really there to allow you to check the sequence and make sure the macro works.

The usual way to run macros is to assign them to events that happen in other parts of the database, like on forms.

Step

Step is almost the same as Run, except that it runs the macro one line at a time. The reason for doing this is quite simple. If you have made a mistake in your macro, it's not always obvious where that mistake occurs. By using Step, you can normally pinpoint exactly where the error is.

The Step button is a toggle button, so you have to remember to click it again once you have finished. When you are using Step, click Run to start the macro. A Dialog box appears giving details of the action, and allows you to Step to the next action, Halt running the macro, or Continue running the macro without stepping.

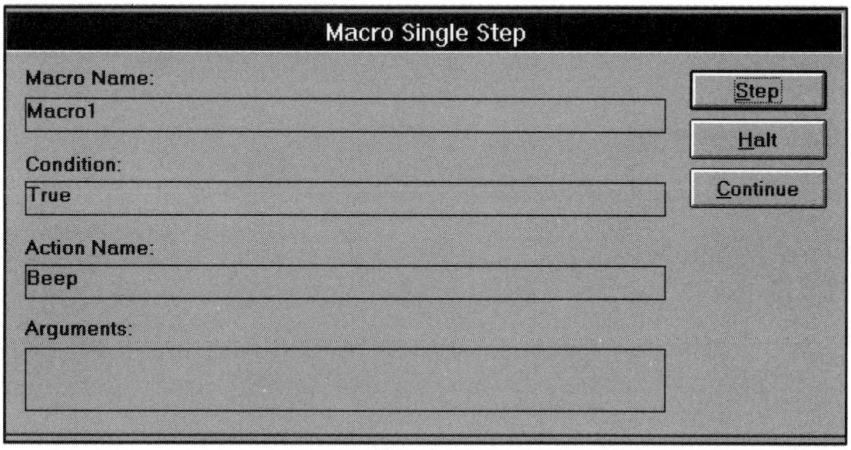

Macro Single Step

Macro Name:
Macro1

Condition:
True

Action Name:
Beep

Arguments:

Step
Halt
Continue

Name

When you click this button, a new column appears on the Macro Design window called Macro Name. Macro name allows you to add a name to a particular line of the macro.

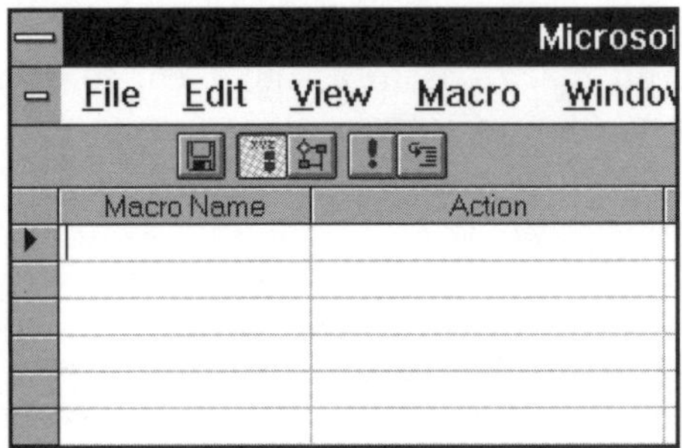

There are two reasons why you would want to do this:

- It allows you to group several macros together. For instance, you could have a print report macro group that contains macros to print three different report styles or contents.
- It allows you to jump to a different part of the macro.

Condition

This simply allows your macro to do different things depending on certain conditions. When you click on the button another column is added called Condition.

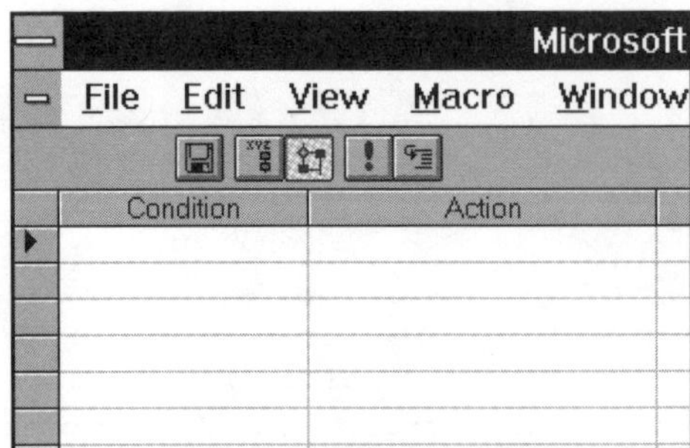

You can use conditions in conjunction with names, but this is not compulsory. We will add details to all of these subjects throughout the chapter. Let's have a go at creating a macro straight away.

Your First Macro

Now we are ready to start writing our first macro. So what is it going to do?

Let's do something to make our database look slick by displaying a message on the screen. You may think this is difficult to do and requires programming experience, but in fact it doesn't; you can do it in one line.

Attaching an Action

Access 2.0 has 47 different actions to choose from, but the one we are interested in is called MsgBox. You have two ways of entering this action:

- Type MsgBox in the top line of the Action column.
- Click on the top line of the Action column, then click on the List Button, scroll down the list of actions until you get to the MsgBox action and then click on it.

Most of the time it's better to use the drop-down list and select the action from there. This avoids the embarrassment of mis-typing the action name. It also means you don't have to remember them all.

Either way, once you have the action name in there, click on Save (accept the default name - Macro1), then hit the Run button. There you have it, a message on the screen!

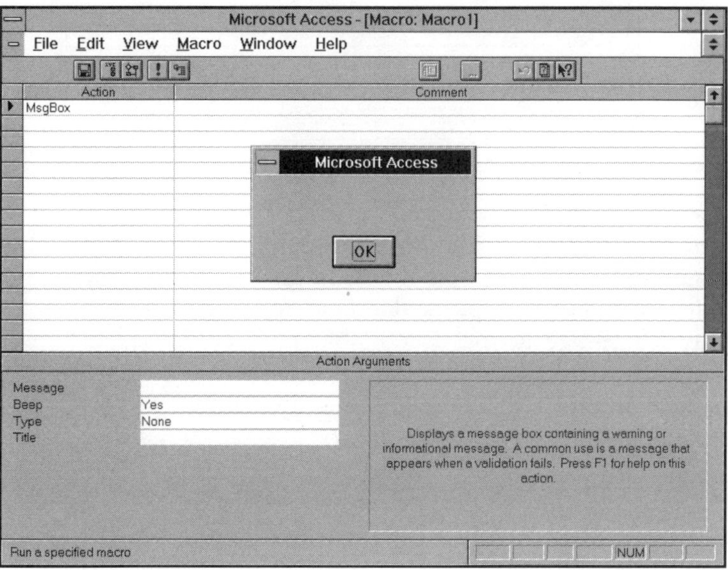

Refining the Action

You will probably be asking where the message is. After all, only the Message box appears on the screen when you run this macro. However, this shows the power of using macros with Access 2.0. With one simple action you are able to get Access 2.0 to draw a box on the screen and make the computer beep.

If you have tried this macro, you may have also noticed that you can't do anything else with Access 2.0 until you have clicked the OK button on the Message box.

Obviously, having a Message box without a message isn't really a lot of use. This is a problem with most of the actions. If you don't specify what the action does, it isn't really very useful.

You can put meat on the bones by using the refinement area of the Macro Design window. In the case of our action, MsgBox, there are four option boxes you can use.

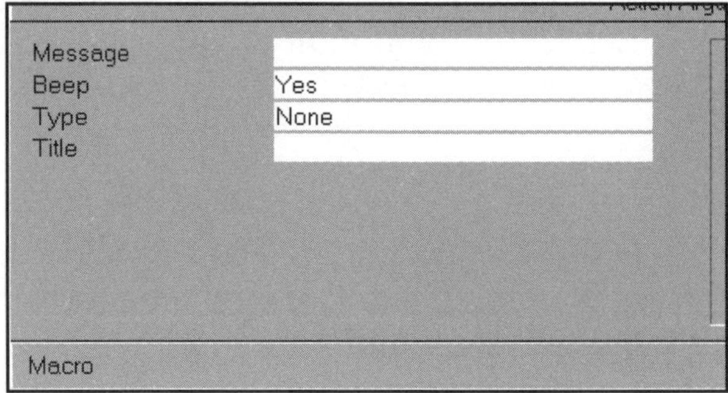

Message

The Message option is where you can type the message you want to appear in the Message box. This can be any message you want. Normally, you would use a Message box to indicate something important to the user. For example, if your database required a particular field to contain data, then you may want to display a message to the user if that field is blank.

The message should tell the user something useful. So, for our example let's type in, 'I'm going to open a form.'

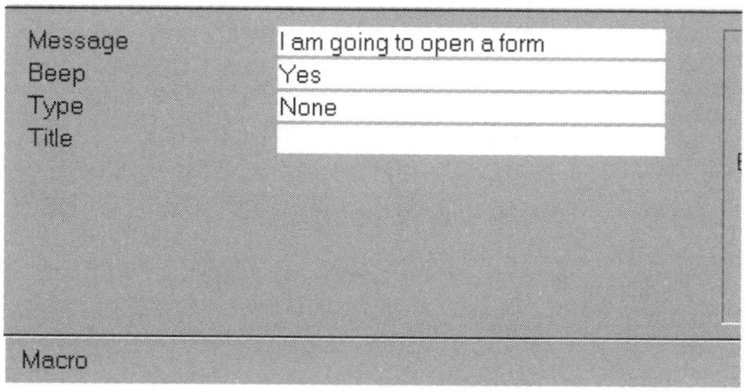

Message	I am going to open a form
Beep	Yes
Type	None
Title	

Macro

Whatever the message is, this box is where you put it.

Beep

This option can be either Yes or No, and is fairly self-explanatory. We will use No, as the beep can become a little annoying.

Type

The Type option governs how the Message box appears on the screen. There are five options: None, Critical, Warning?, Warning! and Information. This option only actually changes the icon that appears in the Message box.

Type	**Appearance**
Critical	 STOP
Warning?	 ?
Warning!	 !
Information	 i

We will leave this as the default, None.

Title

This option allows you to give the Message box a title. Again, this can be anything you want, but should relate to the purpose of the message you are displaying. For our example we will give it a title of Open Form.
As with the message, make this title useful.

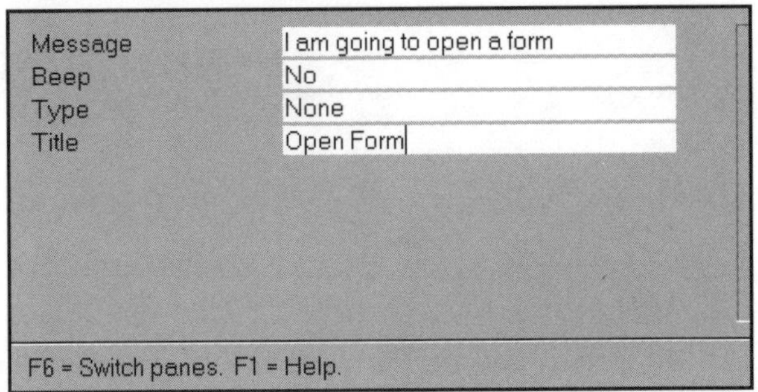

The Complete Message Box

If you run the macro now, you will get a Message box on the screen which is a lot more useful to the user. However, this is only a message, and Access 2.0 doesn't actually respond to just messages. In order to move on we are going to have to add more actions to the macro.

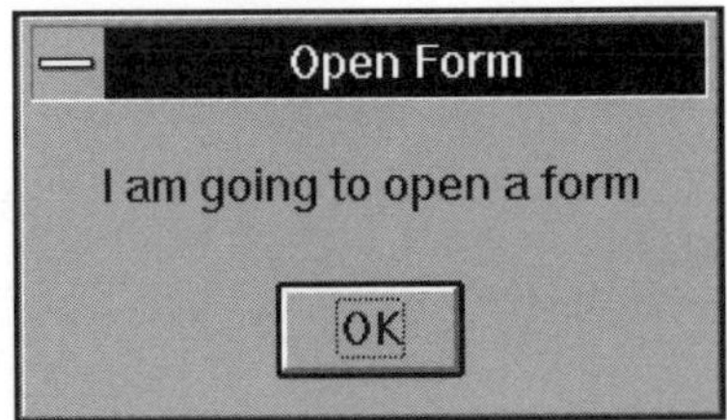

Active Actions for Macros

Access 2.0 gives you 47 different actions to choose from. We won't bore you with the complete list here, but will just describe those actions that are useful in order to grasp the examples.

A complete list of actions is given in Appendix III.

Open Form

This action allows you to open a form. Several more options are offered when using this action:

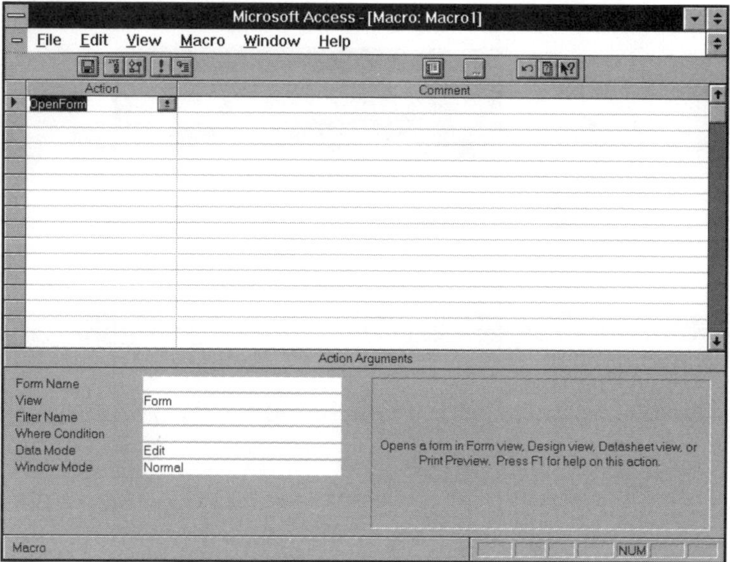

Form Name. This is the name of the form as you have saved it in the database. A drop-down list of forms is available.

View. There are four different views available from the drop-down list: Form, Design, Print Preview and Datasheet. The default is Form, and this is generally the view used.

Filter Name. If it's helpful to you, you can apply a filter to the form you open to get the information you want, in the order you want it.

Where Condition. This is an SQL statement which opens the form on the record that meets the criteria you specify in the statement. This is useful when you are searching for a particular record.

Data Mode. There are three different modes you can open the form in: Add, Edit and Read Only. This option can be seen from a drop-down list. This is used to specify what you can and can't do to the records connected to the form.

Window Mode. This specifies how the window looks when Access 2.0 opens it. There are four options accessible from a drop-down list. They are windows in Normal, Hidden, Icon and Dialog mode.

DoMenuItem

This action, as the name suggests, allows you to accomplish any command from the normal menus with a macro. There are four options, all of which are used to specify which command on the menu bar you wish to control.

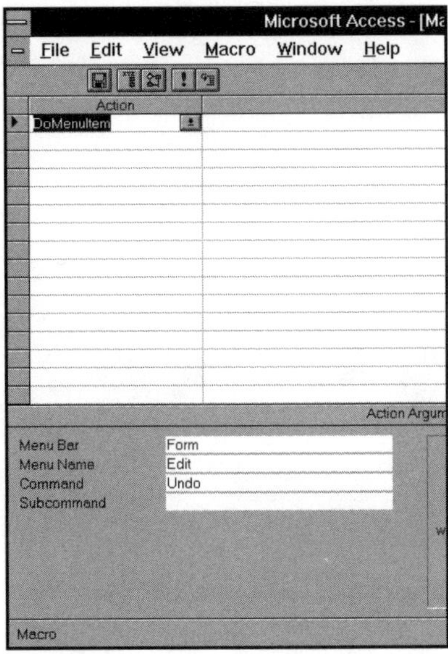

One word of caution about this action. Some of the menu commands in Access don't actually do anything immediately, but instead bring up a Dialog box. They then wait for the user to do something. This can make life a little difficult for macro writers.

We won't go into detail about the commands available, as there are hundreds in Access, most of which you have already used. The easiest way to find out how to program this task is to go through the motions yourself, noting which selections that you make. The selections on your list will be the entries that you make into the refinements associated with the DoMenuItem task. In the previous shot, the task of selecting the Form menu bar, and then selecting the Undo subcommand from the Edit menu is illustrated.

SendKeys

The SendKeys action allows you to automatically have something typed into Access each time the macro is run.

There are two options. The first, Keystrokes, emulates the actual text you want to enter. This can be any text at all, and includes keys like *Enter*, etc. If you attempt to type these keys in, however, you will find it doesn't work. Access 2.0 uses a special way of describing these keys. Generally, it is the name of the key surrounded by braces {}. A list of the most useful of these is shown below.

Key	Access 2.0 code
Enter	{enter}
cursor down	{down}
cursor up	{up}
cursor left	{left}
cursor right	{right}
Tab	{tab}
Del	{del} or {delete}
BkSp	{bksp}, {bs} or {backspace}

If you want to send more than one press of any key, then you can do this by enclosing the key to be pressed, followed by a *Space* then the number of times in braces. For example:

Keystroke	Equivalent to:
{H 5}	HHHHH
{down 2}	{down}{down}

The second option, Wait, allows you to halt the macro. If you are using SendKeys to type something into a record, then it's usually a good idea to wait, otherwise the record may not have been updated before the macro performs another action on it. However, if you don't wait, then the keys are stored in the computer until Access 2.0 requires something to be typed in.

SendKeys can be used to input into the computer at any point, even via Dialog boxes. This is very useful indeed.

Maximize

This action has no options and simply maximizes the window which is currently active.

RunMacro

This is a useful action as it allows you to run another macro. It comes with 3 refinements:

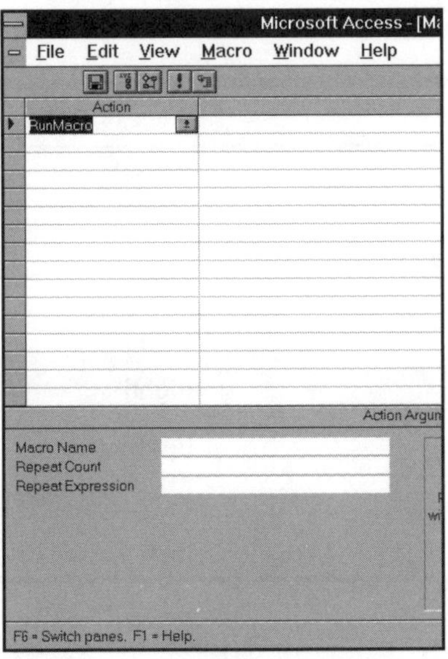

Option	Use
Macro Name	This is the name of the macro you want to run. The names are available from a drop-down list, but you have to save the macro before it will appear on the list.
Repeat Count	RunMacro allows you to run the macro more than once. You can specify the number of times you want it to run in this option. If you leave it blank, then Access 2.0 assumes you want to run the macro only once.
Repeat Expression	Instead of specifying a fixed number of times you want the macro to run, you can use an expression. Every time the macro is repeated, Access 2.0 evaluates the expression, and if the result is false, the macro is stopped from repeating. This allows you, for instance, to change all the records of a customer database that have smith as the surname to Smith.

You can specify both a Repeat Count and a Repeat Expression. If you do this, the macro is repeated until *either* the macro has been repeated the number of times specified in Repeat, *or* the expression becomes false.

StopMacro

This action halts the macro that is currently running, and doesn't require any options.

OpenReport

This is very similar to OpenForm, although there are only four options:

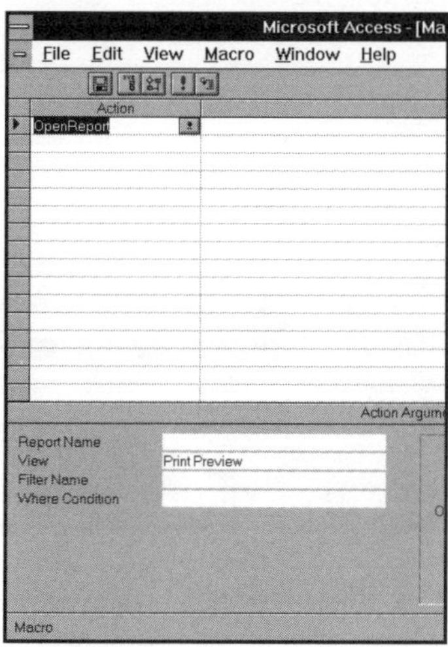

Report Name. This is the name of the report, as you have saved it in the Report Design window. All report names are available from the drop-down list.

View. There are only three possible views with reports. Design and Print Preview are the same as for OpenForm, but Print allows you to print the report without intervention from the user. This is useful if you don't want the user to cancel printing.

Filter Name and Where Condition are the same as for OpenForm.

Multiple Lines

Macros of only one line are not that useful. Most of the time you will want to do several things in Access 2.0 before you return the control of the computer back to the user.

Adding more actions to your macro is easy. You simply add the action onto the next line down the list. So, to improve the macro we're working on, add the OpenForm action to the line below MsgBox.

We will use the defaults for most of the options, so all we need to do is tell the action which form to open. The best way to do this is to click on the Form Option box, click on the drop-down list, and select a form from it.

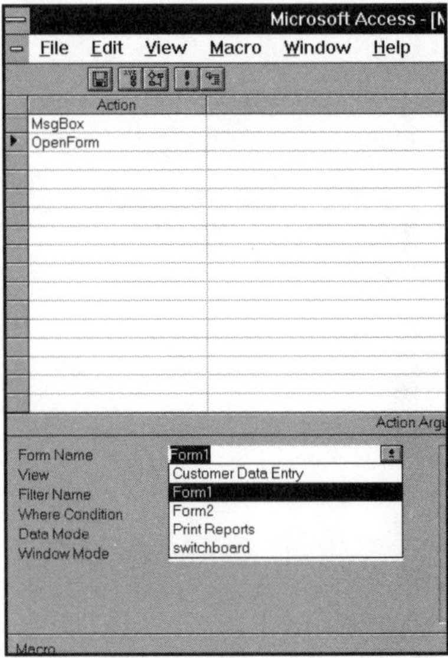

If you run this macro, the Message box appears first, then once you've clicked the OK button, the form you specified is opened.

Inserting a new line

If you want to insert a new line into an existing macro, select where you want to insert it and choose Insert Row from the Edit menu.

You can select the row by clicking on the Row button to the left of the Action column in the same way you would for a table.

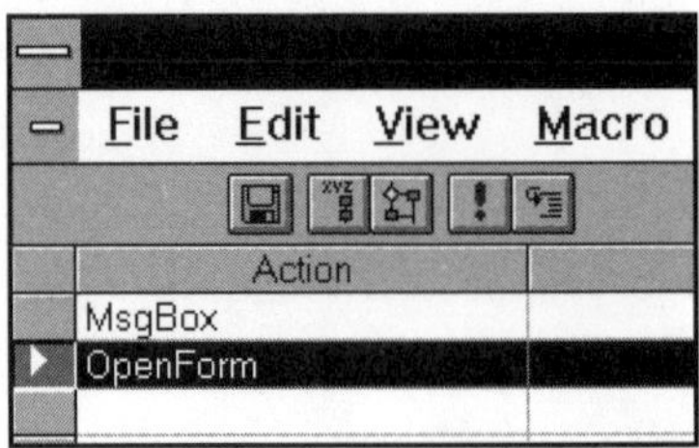

Deleting a line

Similarly, to delete a line, select the line and then choose Delete Row from the Edit menu.

Dragging and Dropping

You can automate some of the typing-in by using the normal drag and drop methods used in Access and Windows. For example, let's start off a simple open form macro action:

- Open a new macro by selecting the Macro tab and clicking New.
- Alter the size of the window by pulling the borders.
- Click on forms, tables, queries or reports in the Database window.
- Drag them over to the Action column in the Macro window.

See below:

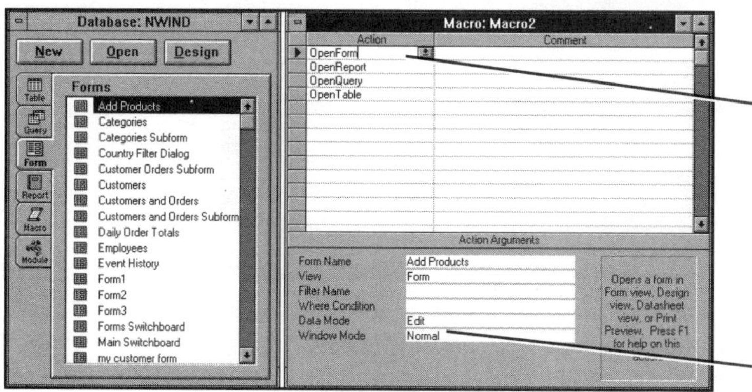

By dragging the Add Products form from the initial database window and dropping it into the Action column of the Macro Design screen, Access places this action into the design.

Notice that Access also automatically inserts the appropriate form name, and applies the default entries to the other refinements.

Adding Macros to Your Database

Okay, so we now have a macro that opens a form. This is quite useful, but do you really want to have to go into the Database window, select Macro, then the macro you want to run and finally click the Run button?

Of course not. Fortunately, Access lets you use macros that respond to events. When you spend 8 continuous hours on your computer, you trigger an argument with your partner - you have caused an event. Access has its own events, and it lets you interrupt these by addressing the Property box.

Events

Events are occurrences of an action. When you select a menu option, you are causing a menu event. When you change a record, you cause an update event.

Access 2.0 lets you decide what to do about these events, as well as handling the event itself.

When we told you how to create forms and reports you saw that most, if not all the controls and sections etc. had an associated selection of properties that can be accessed by the Properties Dialog box.

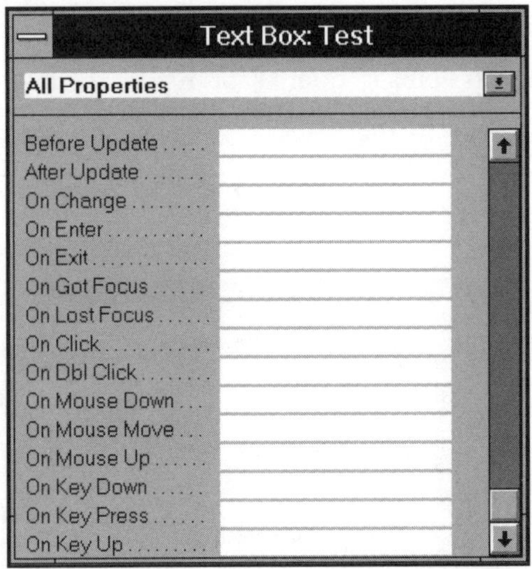

You have already covered these properties and the events that are associated with them, so we'll try to avoid repetition here. Properties have events associated with them, so we will take advantage of these to build powerful macro sequences.

A Quick Example

Let's make a form. We won't worry about attaching a table or query to it, as this form is just going to act as a container for a button. By now you will be familiar with starting a new form, so take this first step and create a blank form.

Add a button to this form (any button will do for now). Make sure the Wizard function is turned off. If you open the Property box for the button and scroll down the list of properties, you'll come to the On Click property.

Click on the cell and then on the drop-down list button. This will give you all the macros you can attach to the event. Select the macro we have written above, save the form then view it.

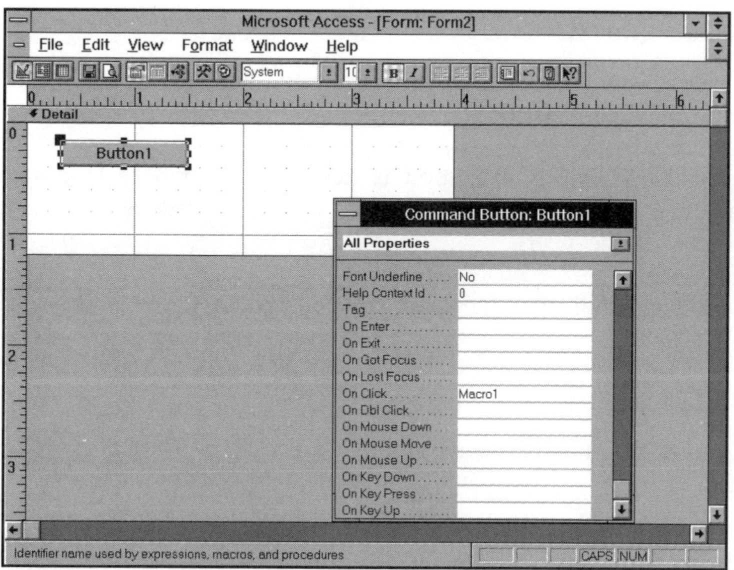

Click on the button, and, hey presto, our Message box appears. Click OK, and the form appears.

Obviously a form that opens another form isn't much use. However, by adding several buttons, each opening a different form or report, we could generate a very useful form. These actions on a form are used extensively in Access databases, and are known as a **switchboard**.

The Control Wizard

Access 2.0 actually makes doing this kind of thing almost automatic by using the Control Wizard. When you add a button to a form with the Wizard button on, you can select how Access 2.0 handles the event.

This does the same job as your macro, but the Wizard actually generates Access Basic and not a macro. This makes it difficult to change what happens when you press the button.

Also, for performing a simple task like opening a form, the macro is only one line, while the code generated by the Wizard is 17 lines long! So, if you want more control over what happens, it's not always wise to rely on the Wizards to do it for you.

The AutoExec Macro

There is a special macro that your finished database shouldn't be without. This macro is called the **AutoExec** macro.

It is special because its execution is tied to the database loading into Access. This makes it very powerful, allowing you to completely hide the underlying database from the users.

You would generally get the AutoExec macro to perform the following actions:

1. Hide the button bar, possibly showing your custom-made one
2. Hide the Database window
3. Hide the menus, again possibly showing a Custom menu
4. Open a switchboard form

This then completely isolates the user from Access, so you don't have the task of teaching all your users how to use Access, only how to use your database.

To make the AutoExec macro work as it is designed, i.e. to run when the database is first fired up, you must follow two important rules. Firstly, the name of the macro should be exactly "AutoExec", together with capital letters and no spaces. Secondly, this macro cannot be included in a macro grouping (this is explained later). The macro should be alone in its design window.

Hiding the Built-in Toolbar

You can hide individual toolbars with the ShowToolbar action. The problem with this is that it only hides one toolbar. To hide all the toolbars that are built into Access would take quite a few lines.

If you want to turn off the built-in toolbars using the mouse, select Options... from the View menu, and set No in the appropriate cell.

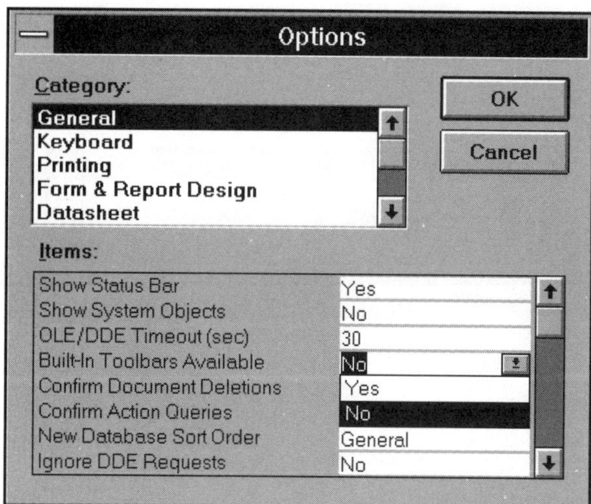

So how do we do this with a macro? Well, we've already discussed the DoMenuItem action, and this is what we need to use. Add this action to the AutoExec macro, and then select Database for the Menu Bar, View for the Menu Name and Options for Command.

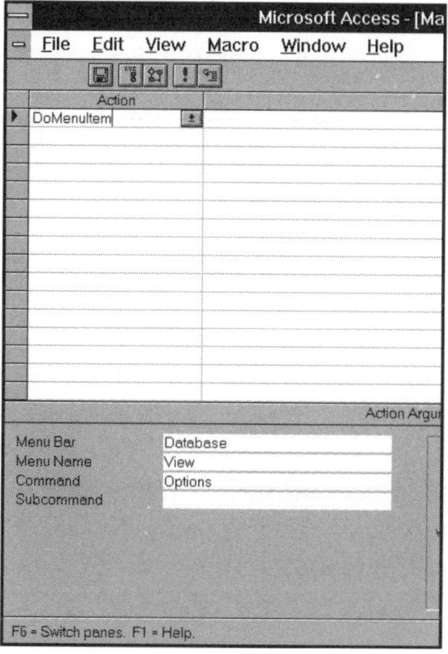

If we run this macro we find that the Options... dialog box is open, but to actually turn off the toolbars we have to use the mouse again. This isn't very satisfactory.

We can get around this by using the SendKeys action. To turn off the toolbars, you would move three options down the list, type no, then press *Enter.* All we have to do is tell SendKeys to do this. So in the Keystrokes Option box we type {down 3}no{enter}.

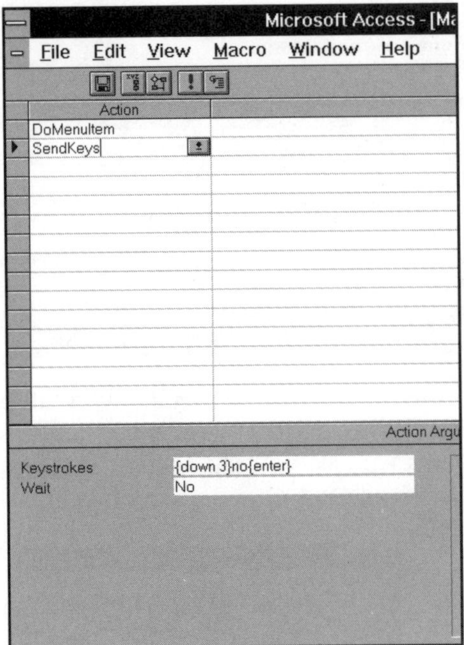

You will see that putting this after the DoMenuItem didn't work. The problem is that the Options dialog box is expecting input, but the action to provide that input hasn't happened yet. To get around this problem you must put the SendKeys action before the DoMenuItem action. This way the input that the dialog expects is already waiting to happen.

Adding a Custom Toolbar

Once you have removed the built-in toolbar, you may want to supply your users with your own toolbar. This is easy to do. Simply use the ShowToolBar action, and specify your custom toolbar as the one you want to show.

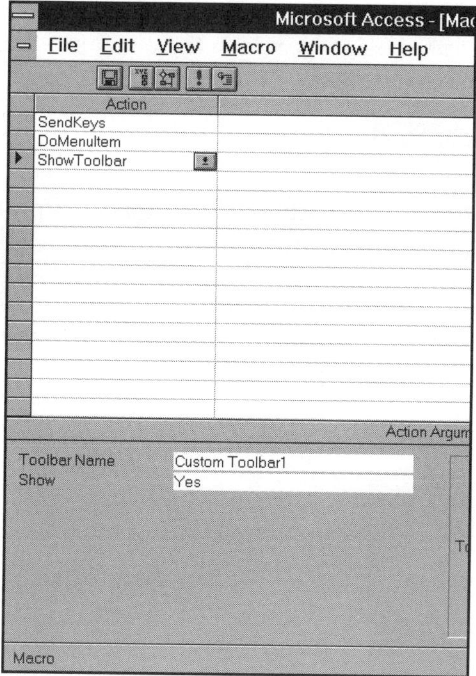

There are a few points you need to remember about using this:

1. You may not actually want to show your custom toolbar when you start up the database, but rather wait until a relevant form has been opened. It really depends on what is on your custom toolbar.

2. Once you have turned off the built-in toolbars, you no longer have the option of turning them on or off with ShowToolBar action.

3. Any ShowToolBar actions that do reference the built-in toolbars are simply ignored by Access.

Switchboard - Hiding the Database Window

At some time you will probably want to hide the Database window so that your users don't have a route to all the different parts of your design. If your users can get to your design and they don't know that much about Access 2.0, you could easily end up having bits of your work disappearing mysteriously from the database.

If you're going to provide a switchboard, then all parts of the database should be accessible through that switchboard. The user shouldn't need to use the Database window at all.

The easiest way of doing this is to use the DoMenuItem action. If you run the macro from the Macro Design window there's a problem, as then the Macro Design window is the one that's hidden!

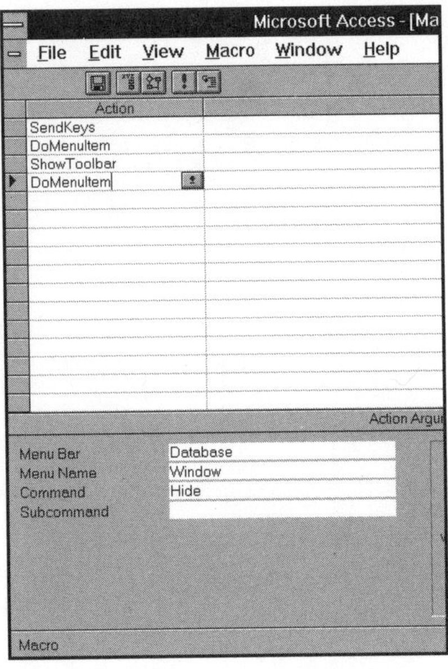

Fortunately, this isn't a problem when you run the AutoExec macro when loading in the database. The only window open at the time is the Database window. So the Database window is hidden, which is exactly what we want.

Opening the Switchboard

Finally, you need to open up the switchboard. Use the OpenForm action.

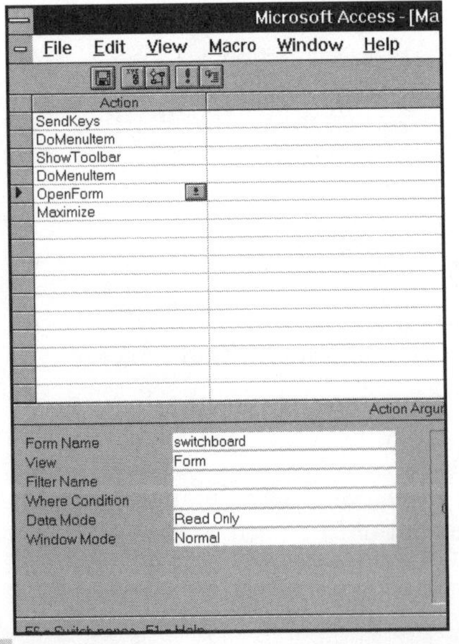

The only other possible action you might want to perform is to maximize the switchboard form. The Maximize action does this without asking any questions.

This is only an example of what you can do in the AutoExec macro. It's really up to you, and your database requirements.

Adding a Condition to a Macro

Sometimes you don't want your macro to repeat certain actions. An example of this might be a macro which checks to see if a required field is empty or not. You can do this with a validation rule to some extent, but there are problems when using the validation rule.

Let's suppose you have a form for entering in customer details. During data entry, you wouldn't want the surname to be blank. To stop this happening, define the field in the table as Required, and set Allow Zero Length to No.

You can also set a validation rule of Is Not Null or <> " " on the field of the form, but when you use the form, you can still leave the field blank! (Actually, you can't leave the record with the field blank, but you can move the focus to another field.) The validation rule doesn't seem to work properly. If, however, you type something then delete it, it works. If you step through the field with *Tab* or *Enter* then the validation rule is not checked. If you leave the record with the field blank, then the table rules kick in, and you get an Access generated message, telling you that you can't leave the field blank.

What we can do is write a macro that checks the field to see if it's blank, and if this is the case, tells the user and returns to the field for them to type something in.

Writing Conditions

What we are asking Access to do is check the contents of the field. We do this in a macro by adding a condition to the action we want to perform.

So let's write a macro to check to see if the surname field of the form has been left blank. Start off as usual by creating a new macro. As we want to use a condition, click on the Conditions button on the toolbar in the Macro Design window.

Let's assume that you have already designed a form called Customer Data Entry, and that there is a Surname field on this form. We now want to check the field to see whether it's blank. In Access 2.0, you need to specify the field you are checking. Do this by typing:

```
[Surname]
```

You could specify the full path of the field you are referring to by typing:

```
[Forms]![Customer Data Entry]![Surname]
```

The problem with using the full path is that you can't re-use the macro on another form. Using [Surname] only means that any form where you want to make this particular check can use this macro.

We haven't checked the actual value of the field yet. We do this by asking a question of the field. In this case, we want to know if it's blank. Access has a special way of referring to blank fields, and this is Null. So, to find out if surname is Null, type in the following to the Conditions column:

[Surname] Is Null

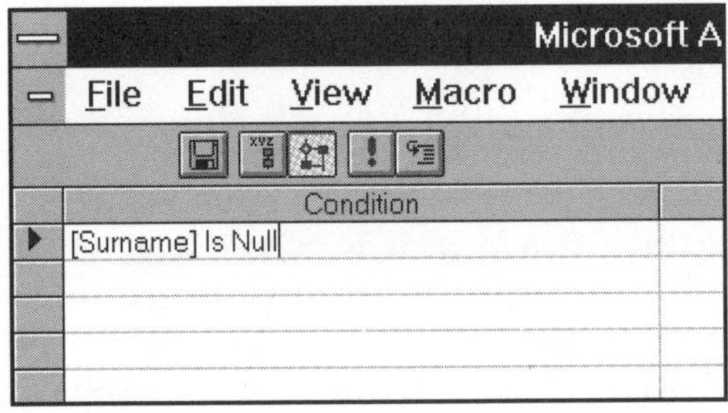

We don't need a question mark as Access understands this as a question. All that remains to do is tell the user they need to put something in the field. We do this by using our friend, the MsgBox.

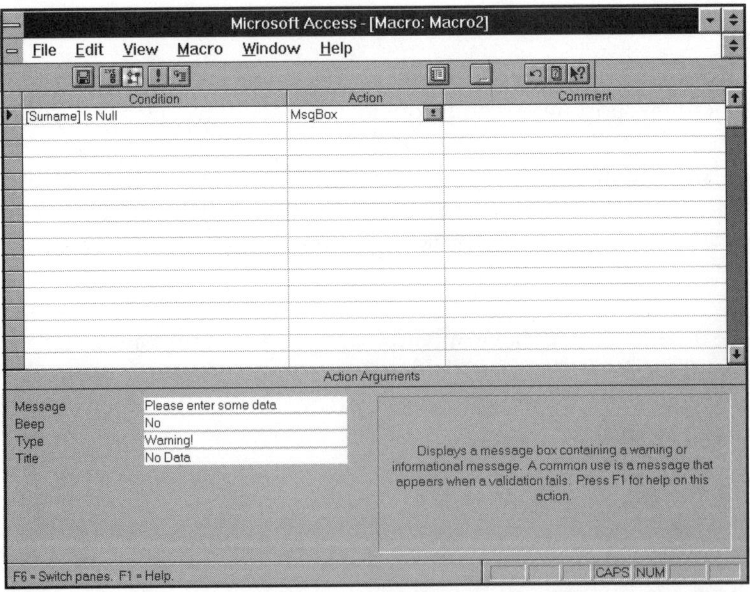

Adding Our Macro to a Form

We need to attach the macro to a form. The events we have to respond to depend on how the underlying table is set up. If we need the surname field and it is not allowed to be null, then we have to use the macro twice, once each on two separate events. If these conditions are not set, then only one event has to be handled.

Taking the latter first, the event we need to handle is simply whenever the field loses the focus. There are two events you can use for this, On Exit and On Lost Focus. The difference between these two is evident when the event occurs. The On Exit event happens *before* the field loses the focus, while On Lost Focus occurs *when* it loses the focus. We'll use the On Exit event for a reason that will become apparent later.

If on the table Required is Yes and/or Allow Zero Length is No for the Surname field, then you will still need to check for the loss of the focus. However, this is not the only event you must check. Rules you have applied to the table are enforced when you add something to the table. To stop the default error messages from occurring, you must deal with things before this.

When you enter data into a field, this does not cause the underlying table to be updated immediately. Updating occurs when the field loses the focus. However, running the macro before the field loses the focus is not good enough, because when you move the focus, Access generates more than one event, and the order these occur in is important. The two events we are interested in, Update and LoseFocus, occur in that order. To stop the default table checking you must run the macro in response to the Before Update event.

It's not enough to use the macro in the Before Update event alone. The reason for this is that Access is intelligent, and doesn't do work which is unnecessary. So, if the value of the field hasn't changed, then it doesn't update the table. You still have to handle the On Exit event as well. This means that you run the macro twice, but it's the computer that's doing the work, not you.

How Conditions Work

This leaves the question of how the condition works. It's actually quite simple. If the condition is true, then the action on the same line is executed; otherwise the line following is executed. If there is a line following, and if the condition is true, then the following line is also executed.

Condition	Action	Comment
Ask a question —True→	Action 1	
—False→	Action 2	

Situations do occur, however, when one action is not enough for the task you want when the condition is true. Access provides you with a method of running more than one action when the condition is true. Do this by using three dots (...) in the Condition column, in the lines following the condition. These three dots are called an **ellipse** and Access reads them as 'apply the last given condition to this task as well'.

Condition	Action	Comment
Ask a question —True→	Action 1	
	Action 2	
	Action 3	
—False→	Action 4	

If you try the macro leaving the field blank, the Message box pops up telling you to fill it in. However, when you return to form by clicking on OK you will still move to the next field. This is a problem. The whole point of the macro is to stop the user leaving the field if it's empty. The reason this doesn't happen is that the loose focus event is still there, waiting for Access to deal with it.

You need to kill the event. As you don't want to cancel the event if the condition is false, use ellipses in the Condition column, and the CancelEvent action.

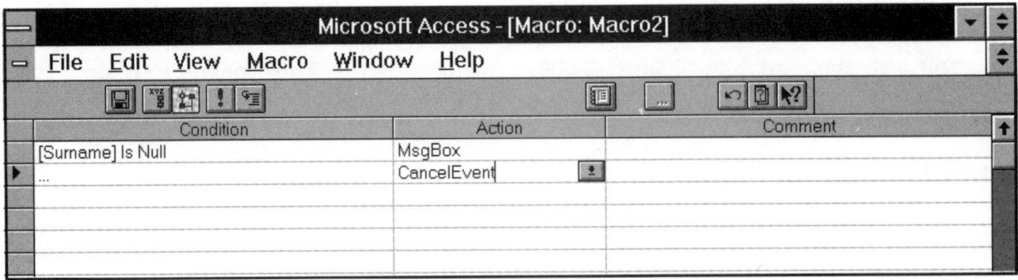

Macro Groups

You will notice that this leaves you with a slight problem. What if you want to do something completely different if the condition is false? Let's use our test for null macro. What we want to do is display a message congratulating the user if they have filled in the surname. To do this we add a MsgBox to the end of the macro.

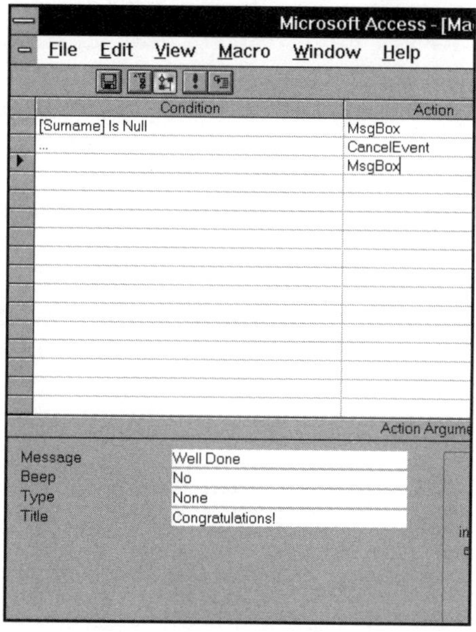

This is great if the field has some data in it - the message is displayed. However, if it is blank the user receives both messages. We can stop this from happening by putting a condition on the second message. This condition needs to be the opposite of the first condition, so type:

```
[Surname] Is Not Null
```

> If you are actually trying this out in Access you may have noticed a problem with this macro. If you are using it to handle both the Before Update and the On Exit events, you will get the message twice. If you are handling the On Exit event you will get the message when the focus is on that field and you are moving through the records. In a real situation you would have two macros, one for On Exit which checks to see if the field is blank, and a second for the Before Update event. This checks to see if the field is blank and, if not, displays the congratulations message.

This is not the only way you have of doing this. The second way uses macro names.

Grouping Macros Together

Macro names are included in Access to allow you to group macros together. It's up to you how you group the macros, but generally you would group them by one of two factors: where they are used, or what they do. For example, you could have a group called customer data entry which is a collection of all the macros you need for the customer data entry form. Or you could have a group called validation, where all the macros that check for blanks fields are kept.

The other use of names is to give you control over how the macro works, depending on the conditions you have included in your macro.

Let's change the macro again and remove the second condition from it. We have to do a bit more work this way, as you need to think carefully about what you are doing. Let's start by schematically showing what we did in the old macro.

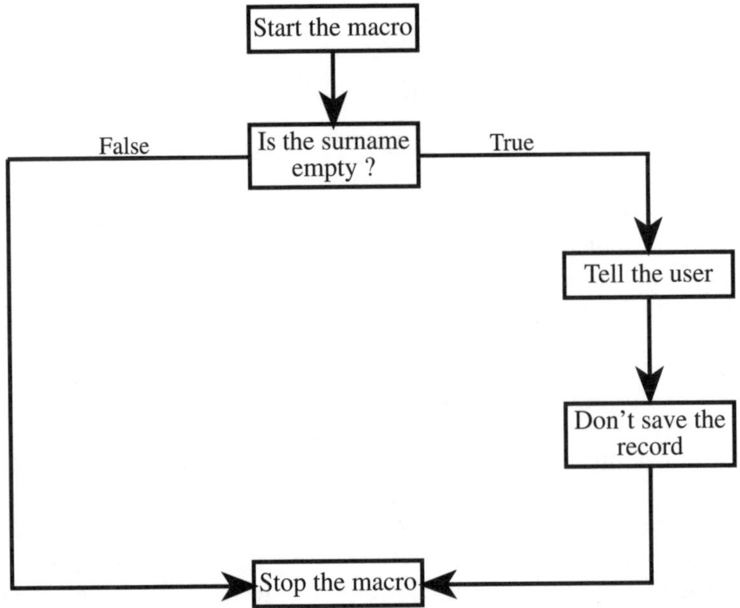

For the new version, keep the first condition and use the RunMacro action to run the appropriate actions. Place these actions, MsgBox and CancelEvent, a couple of lines below. Give it a name, by clicking on the Name button on the toolbar, then typing in No data in the Name column next to the MsgBox action.

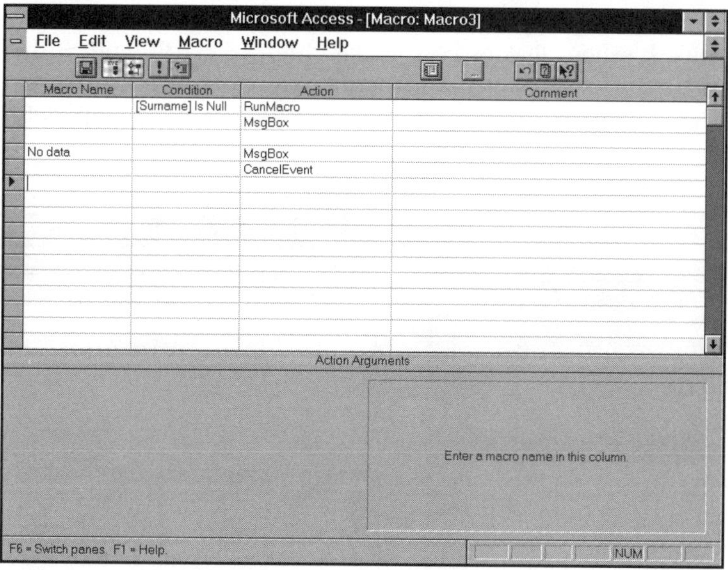

Using a Macro From a Group

Go back to the RunMacro command. We have to specify which macro we want to run in the refinement area. If you click on the Text box, then on the drop-down list button, you will be in for a shock.

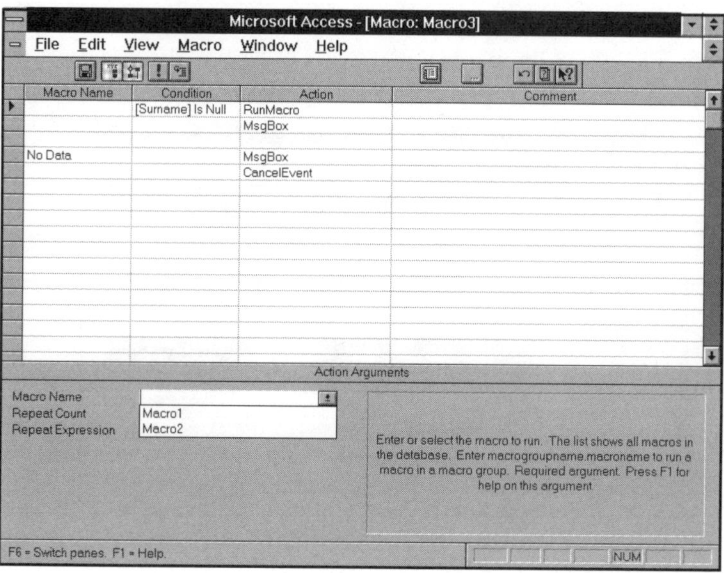

As you can see, the drop-down list does not contain the macro name or the macro group. It's here that Access makes life rather difficult with the names it uses. If you don't use any names, then you have a macro. If you use names, then you have a macro group, and each section of the group defined by the name is a macro.

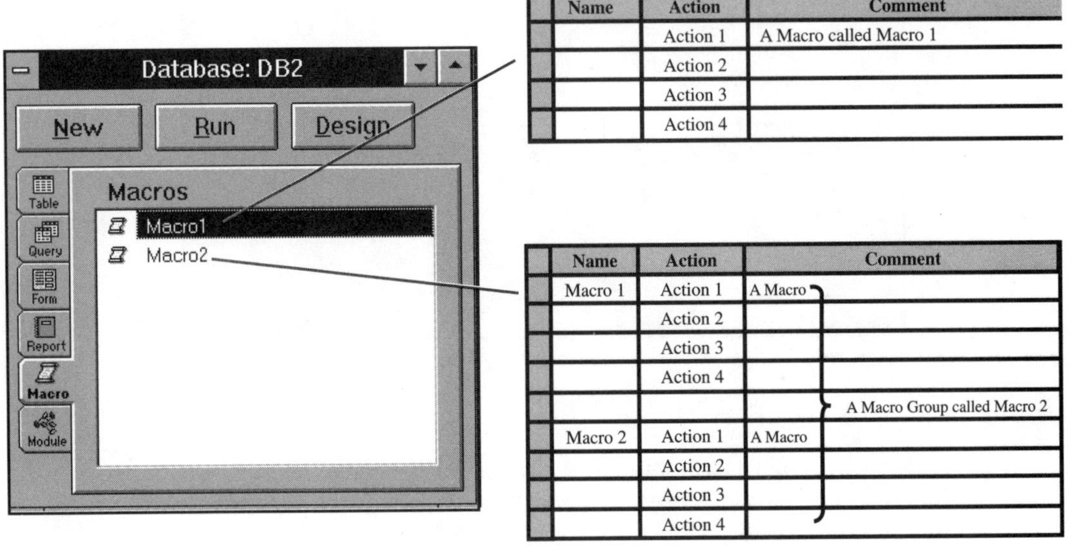

This is because Access doesn't actually know about the macro yet, as it hasn't been saved. See what happens when we now save the macro:

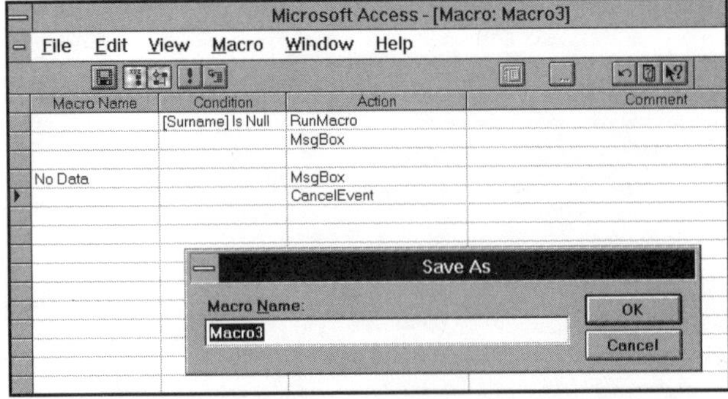

Now go back to the drop-down list. The macro group and the named parts are there.

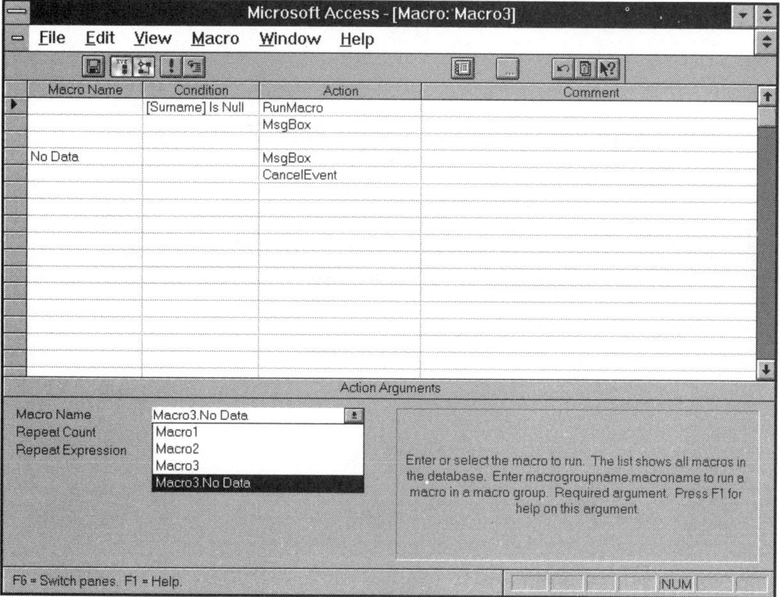

So, we can select no name as the macro to be run.

> With macro names the full-stop is used differently from tables, forms, etc. Here, user-defined parts are referenced with an exclamation. Also, with macros you have to use the name without the square braces [ ] even if there's a space in the name.

If we try this macro, then we find that when the surname field is empty, we get both messages. The reason for this is in the RunMacro action. This action causes the macro to run, but when it has finished, it then goes back to the macro that called it.

Name	Action	Comment
	RunMacro	Run Macro 2
	Action 2	
	Action 3	
	Action 4	Macro stops here
Macro 2	Action 1	
	Action 2	
	Action 3	
	Action 4	

This is frustrating and means that using names is not always a good solution. To avoid this, you can use the StopMacro action in no name. This halts the macro completely.

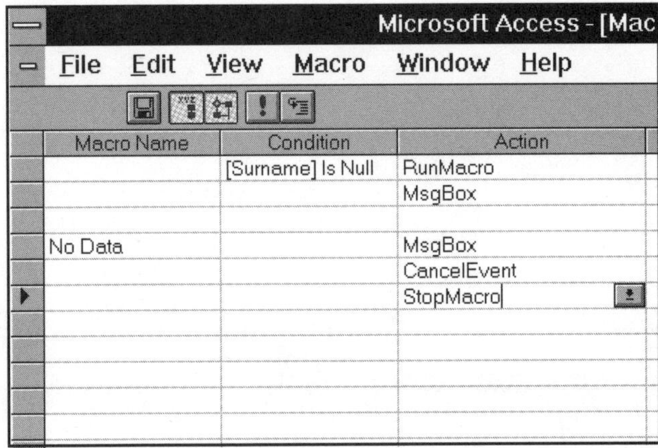

Why Use Names?

The main reason for using names is to group macros of a similar nature together, or to group macros that are used in the same form, etc.

It was probably a waste of time to have used names for our example. It would have been better to just use an ellipse in order to perform the tasks. In the original version we showed you a second condition to stop the problem of both Message boxes appearing. We could just as easily have used the StopMacro action instead:

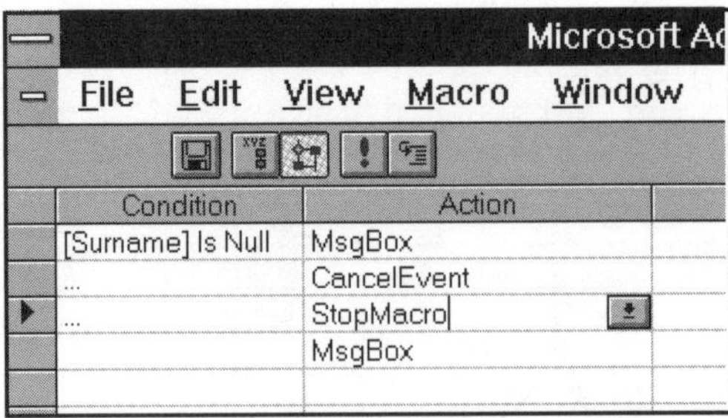

It's really a matter of taste. If the number of actions you want to perform is more than five, then put them into a named section, otherwise just use an ellipse.

A Final Exercise

All we need to do now is look at a single example that brings together all we have learnt in this chapter. Let's look at how to provide our own Print dialog box.

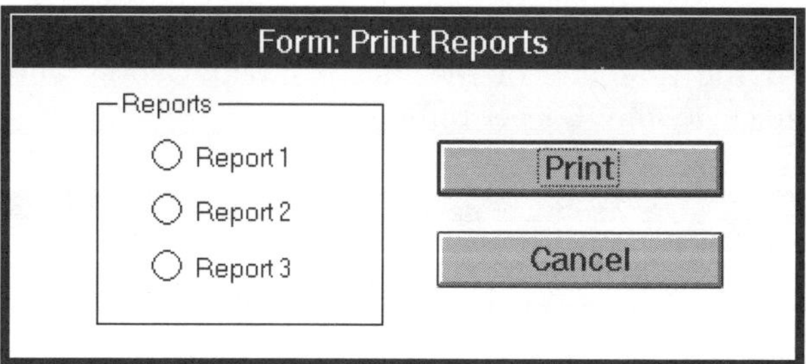

The form we are going to use is fairly simple. We have a control group containing three radio buttons. There are also two other buttons. (We have given the Control box a different name to its default name, for reasons which will become obvious).

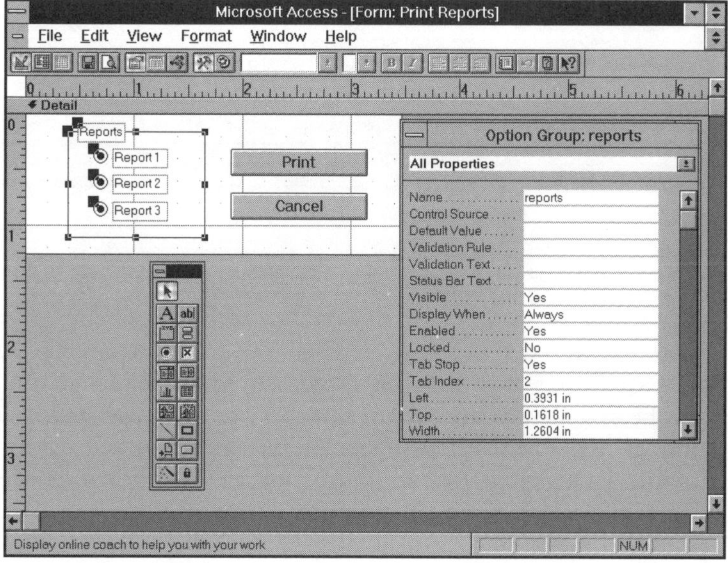

There is no data source for this form, so we have removed the scroll bars, record navigator, and also set the border style to Dialog. That is really all there is to the form. We'll get to the buttons in a moment.

The Macro

In the macro we have combined:

- Grouping macros that relate to the form
- Using names with conditions

We have named the first line of the macro group Cancel, and this is the macro that we will attach to the Cancel button.

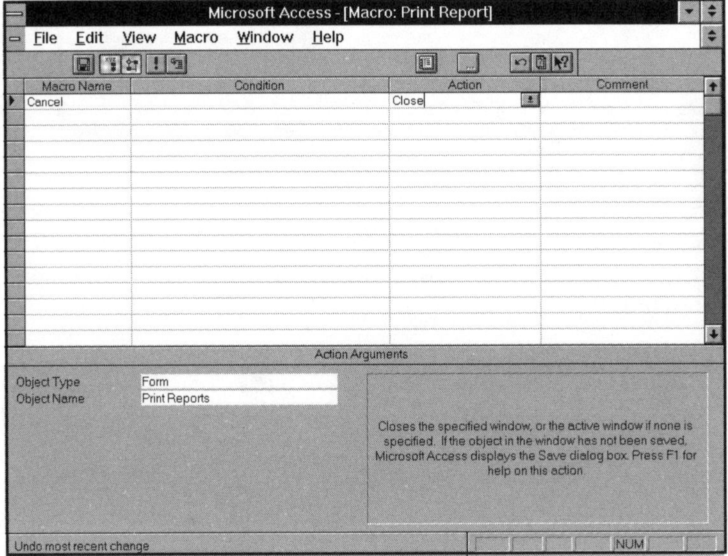

The action we want to perform is to close the form, so we use the Close action, specifying the Print Report form to be closed.

Next we want to handle the occasion when the user presses the Print Report button. The way we do this is to check to see whether any of the radio buttons have been pressed, and if so, which one. This was why we named the control group on the form. When one of the controls in the group is pressed, its control value is assigned to the control group. We therefore need to check the control group's value three times, once for each control.

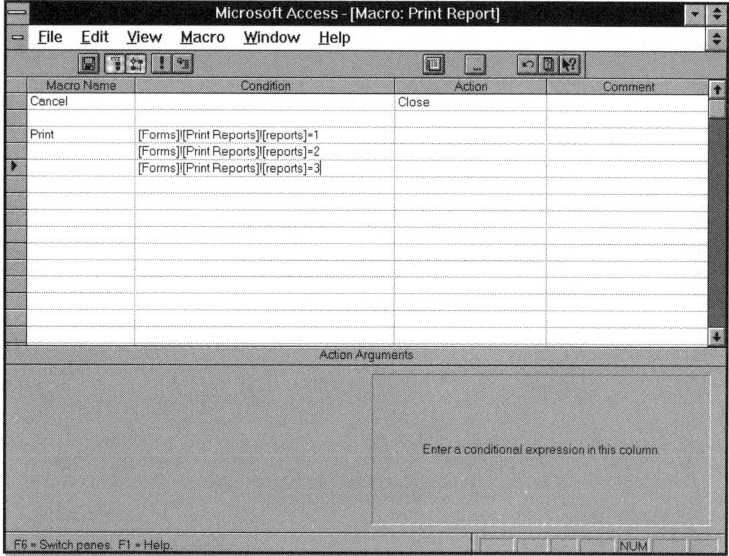

We named the first condition Print, so we can then assign these lines to the Print Report button. For each condition we then use RunMacro to call a macro to print the report.

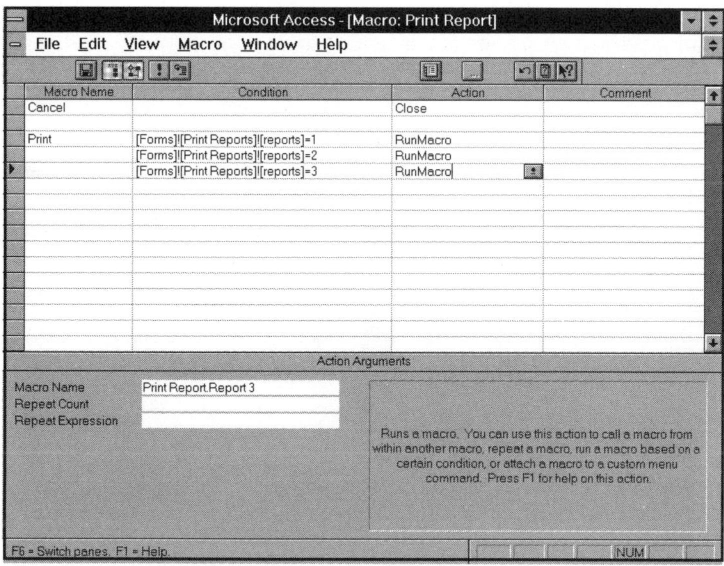

There are then three macros, each of which does a similar task of printing the relevant report. The macro uses the OpenReport action, specifying the report and also that we want to print the report immediately.

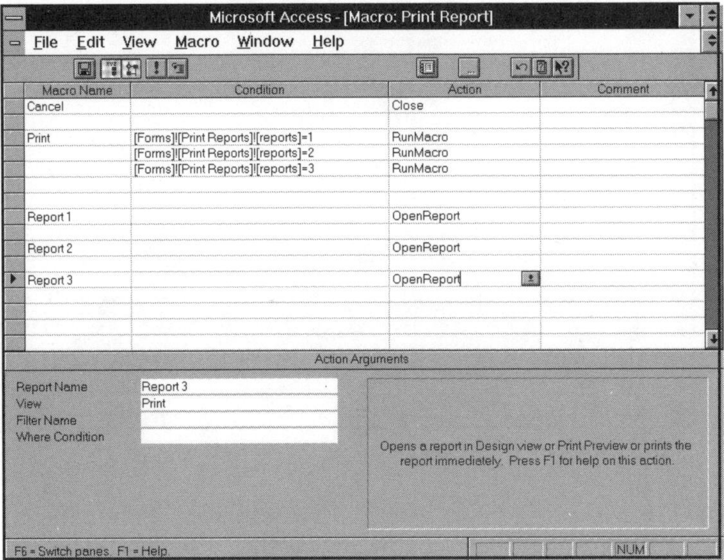

The macro group is almost complete. There are two things we need to finish. Firstly we need to stop the macro. We don't want the macro to continue after it has printed the report, but we want to return control to the user. Do this, as before, with the StopMacro action. (In the previous example we used StopMacro in the named section.)

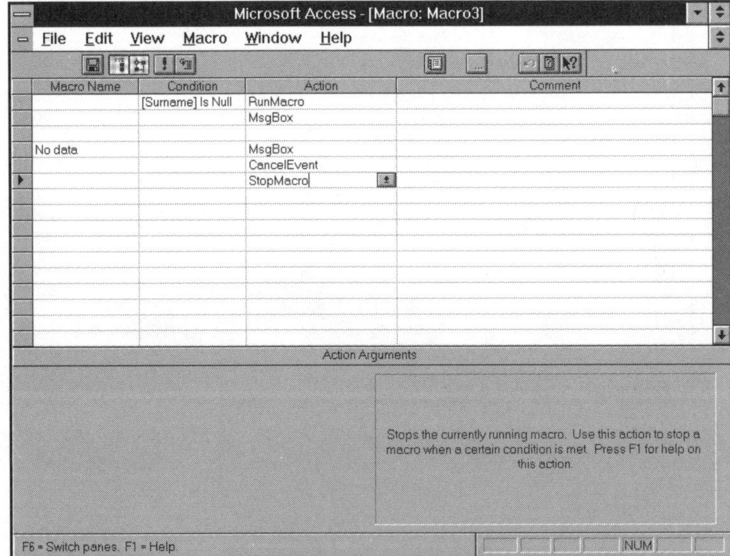

But if we try it on this macro, it doesn't work. However, this is not too much of a problem, as we can add a line below each of the conditions to halt the macro.

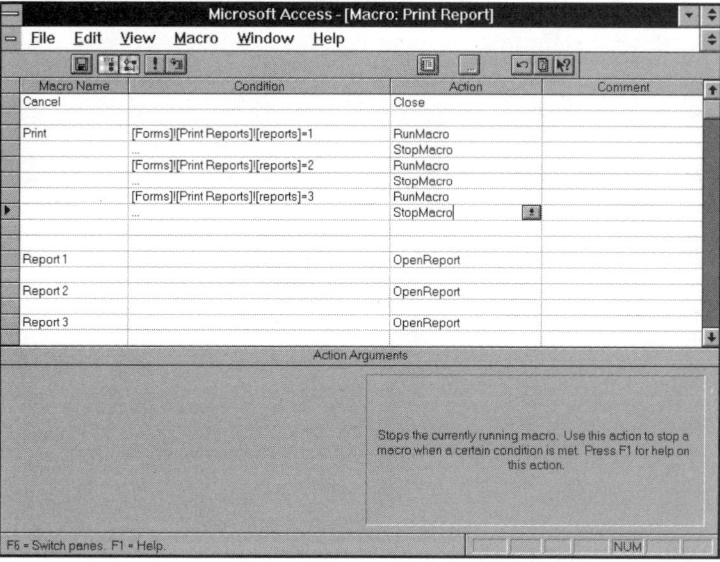

Finally, to round things off, we have added a message to the end of the conditions, informing the user that they haven't made a selection. This should never occur, but if it does, you definitely want to know about it, because something has gone wrong with your macro or form.

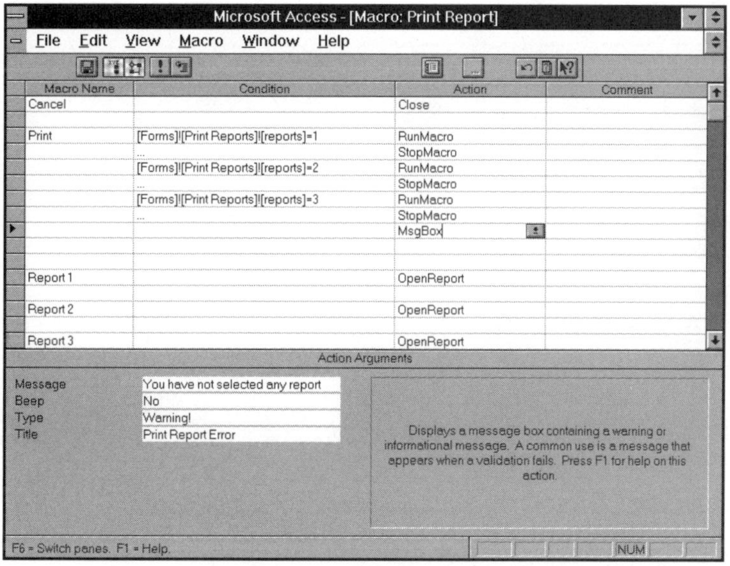

Hopefully, you now have an insight into macros. Remember, macros are there to relieve you of the tedious jobs and hand them over to the computer. If you use them properly they will be a powerful way of making your database professional and easy-to-use.

CHAPTER 13

Access Basic

This final chapter will provide an insight into the topic of Access Basic and its container which is called Modules.

Access Basic is a complete programming language and many books feature it exclusively. Its wide range of concepts and techniques need a good deal of study before they can be effectively applied. However, if you have familiarity with a basic or high-level structured language then Access Basic will be understandable. For example, Visual Basic is similar in its make-up and its techniques to Access Basic.

The coverage in this chapter is merely an appetizer for programming in Access; the advantages in learning event-driven programming will become evident as applications become more interactive.

In this chapter we will begin to learn about:

- Modules
- Using a simple function
- Using some simple statements
- Running a program
- Closing work

What is a Module?

Up to this point you have learnt how to create tables and how to link them together. You have also seen how to produce forms, reports and how to write queries. In addition to these functions Access 2.0 has also provided an option on your main database window called Module.

Module is where you house and design your Access Basic programs. You can run your programs here one step at a time or even study code generated by wizards. Modules are split into two categories: global or local. A global module is what results from your interaction with the tools that are explained in this chapter - the creation of Access Basic code that you can apply to any Access object. A local module is Access Basic code which is woven into the foundations of a form or report. A local module cannot be produced using the methods in this chapter, as it's created by the implicit actions you perform on the given form or report itself.

The Fundamentals of Access Basic

Access Basic is event-driven. This means that sections of your program can respond to events that occur in Access either normally, or as a result of command button settings. You therefore need to be familiar with events in Access (even if you know another Basic language). It also means that macros in Access are very powerful controllers and can cause very complex events to occur. You should therefore use macros and not Access Basic for automating day-to-day tasks.

Access Basic is made-up of several functions or sub-procedures which are individual specialized containers which hold the code you write. A function procedure returns real and dynamic information back to the program for it to then use. A sub-procedure completes its task without returning a value. Your Access events are essentially sub-procedures and you will find it useful to trigger them to perform regular tasks.

Statements are the detailed instructions of functions and sub-procedures. When an Access object (i.e. a form or report) calls a function, the statements you created for that function are executed.

You have already used functions in form and report designs without realizing it. For instance, the `Now()` function, returns the current date and time. With Access Basic, you can write your own functions that return values. These values could then be assigned to be default entries, for example, in the fields of a form.

We can illustrate some of the advantages using a simple example.

Using Basic Instead of Queries

Let's construct a problem that seems to be beyond the scope of a query.

Imagine we commissioned a survey to find out about database usage; we might want non-standard conclusions from the questions. If we wanted to know about four leading brands of database we could ask the question "Do you like product *x* a little or a lot?". If the answer is neither yes nor no, it's assumed they didn't own or use the product. We could then distill certain information from the responses. First we might want the total number of Access users. This should be fairly easy to answer, once a basic table for the responses has been established. A small, two-field table is set up.

The Table

This is the table:

Field Name	Data Type
Customer	Counter
Access like a little	Yes/No
Access like a lot	Yes/No
Paradox like a little	Yes/No
Paradox like a lot	Yes/No
Foxpro like a little	Yes/No
Foxpro like a lot	Yes/No
SQL like a little	Yes/No
SQL like a lot	Yes/No

You can see that each type of database is split into two fields: 'like a little' and 'like a lot'. Both of these are fields of the Yes/No format. If we wanted to, we could have a validation rule to make the two fields mutually exclusive.

From here it's a simple matter to produce a report that shows the number of customers that use a particular database. If we need to know how many customers use Access 2.0 'a lot' or 'a little', we would use the following query:

Field:	Customer	Access like a little	Access like a lot
Sort:			
Show:	☒	☒	☒
Criteria:		Yes	
or:			Yes

This query's dynaset would list the twenty customers who use Access 2.0, and either like it a lot or a little. At this point we want to know more; for example, how many people use only *one* database from *any* of the four listed types?

It's possible to ask this question using queries, but you would have to use four queries - one for each of the databases. This is the organization of those four queries:

Field:	Custome	Access li	Access li	Paradox	Paradox	Foxpro lil	Foxpro lil	SQL like	SQL like
Sort:									
Show:	☒	☒	☒	☒	☒	☒	☒	☒	☒
Criteria:		Yes		No	No	No	No	No	No
or:			Yes	No	No	No	No	No	No

The Impossible Report

Finally, we might want to know how many customers have none, one, two, three or four databases. Again, this can be done using similar queries, but we would have to have fifteen queries, which is an afternoon's work.

There are only four databases to choose from in the questionnaire. What if there were twenty? The number of queries would be 2,097,151!

There is an easier way of doing this and it's called Access Basic.

Adding a Function to a Module

When you want to write some Access Basic code, the first thing you must do is to add a new module. On the database window click on Module and then New. This provides the Module editor.

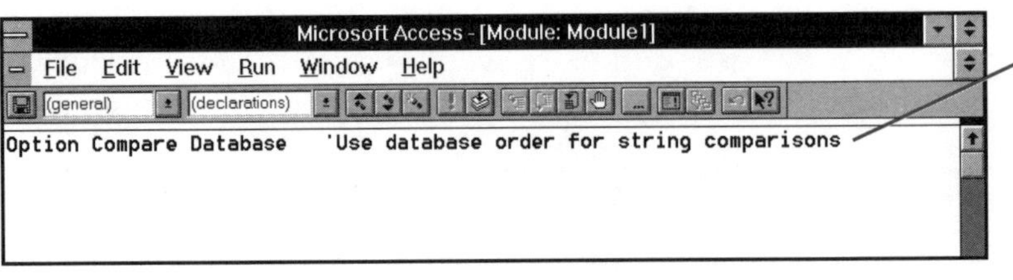

Don't worry about the first line as it's generated by Access 2.0. All the modules have this line, and unless you are an advanced Access Basic programmer you can leave it there.

The toolbar gives you access to almost all of the Access Basic editor functions, but most of them are beyond the scope of this book. The ones we will be using are:

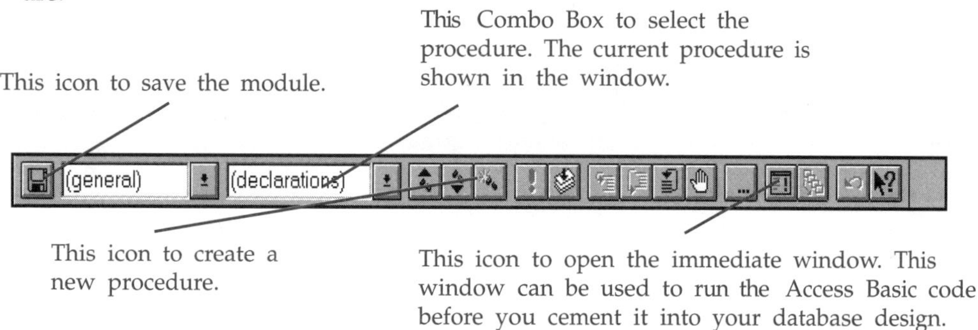
This icon to save the module.
This Combo Box to select the procedure. The current procedure is shown in the window.
(general)
(declarations)
This icon to create a new procedure.
This icon to open the immediate window. This window can be used to run the Access Basic code before you cement it into your database design.

To add a function click on the New Procedure button on the button bar. This opens a dialog box which asks you for the name of the procedure.

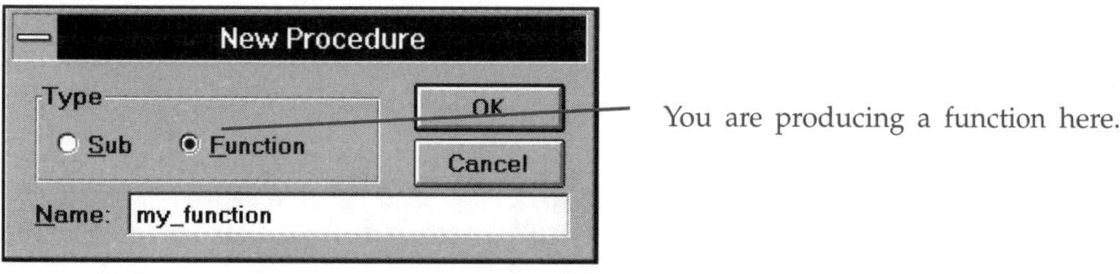
New Procedure
Type
Sub
Function
OK
Cancel
Name:
my_function
You are producing a function here.

Type in my_function and press *Return*. The window will change and a small amount of code will be created. It's simply the name of your function and the **End Function** statement. It waits for you to add the details. For this function we are going to design the return of a random number.

These are the two steps:

1. Make sure the number we get is truly random. We do this with the **Randomize** statement. This makes Access randomly choose a starting point for the random number generator from which it can begin.
2. We must get a random number using **Rnd**. The next screenshot shows this function's code:

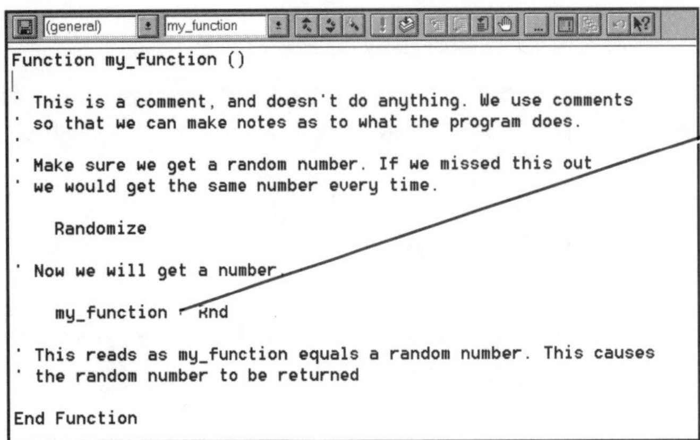

```
Function my_function ()

' This is a comment, and doesn't do anything. We use comments
' so that we can make notes as to what the program does.
'
' Make sure we get a random number. If we missed this out
' we would get the same number every time.

    Randomize

' Now we will get a number.

    my_function = Rnd

' This reads as my_function equals a random number. This causes
' the random number to be returned

End Function
```

We return the value we want by making the function name, in this case my_function, equal to the value.

Using a Function

Using the function you have written is easy. You use it in exactly the same way as the built-in functions like **Now()**. There are some restrictions to where you can use your own functions - the main one is you can't use them in the table properties. The easiest way to find out if you can use your function is to use the Expression Builder (see Chapter 7). You can use my_function in a form by using the following syntax:

```
=my_function()
```

This is entered into the default value for a field and is shown below. Because the function returns a number between 0 and 1, we give this field definition the Number data type, with the addition of Double, in the Field Size property.

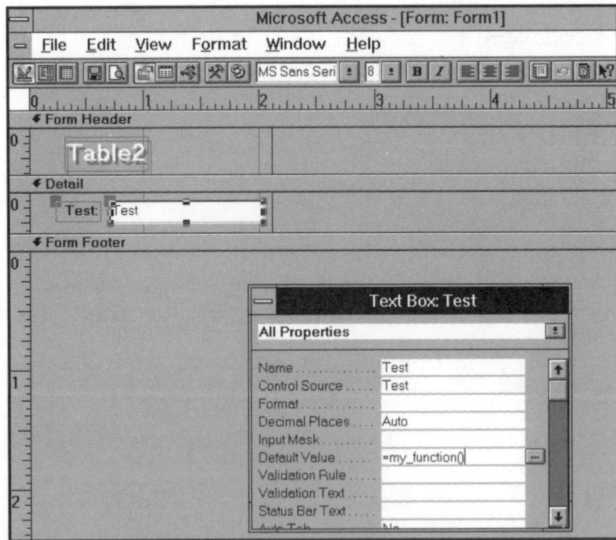

The Immediate Window

You can use your own functions almost anywhere you would use a built-in function. One of the main places is in the immediate window of the editor. You can use this window to test out your functions or sub-procedures with some test inputs.

To use the function, type print or '?', then the name of the function, then a pair of brackets.

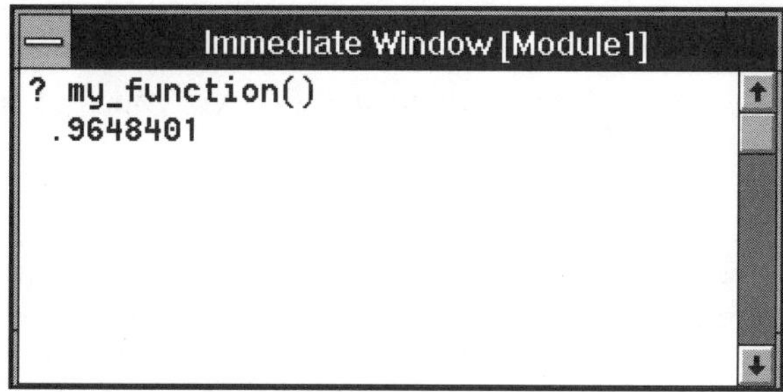

This prints the value that the function returns. If you do it several times, you will get a different answer each time.

A Simple Program

After that initial taste of Access Basic we can now return to our questionnaire and try and squeeze out a more complex report. We want to find the number of customers with none, one, two, three or four databases. It's best to save the data into a table so that we can both see the results and provide a report.

Number of Databases	Number of Customers
0	0
1	0
2	0
3	0
4	0
0	0

To fill the table we will run the function from the immediate window. It would also be possible to run the code from a macro (RunCode macro command), or assign it to the On Update property of a form.

Updating Tables

We want to look at each customer, count the number of databases they use and then increase the count in our new table. To do this we must:

- Open the two tables.
- Go through all the customers in the first table counting the number of databases used.
- Save the number in the second table.
- Close the two tables.

This will introduce a number of new things to you, but we will explain them as they come up.

The Program

Before you open the two tables you need to create a new function. To do this you can either create a new module or add a new function to the existing module.

In both cases click on the new function button, and call the function count in the dialog box.

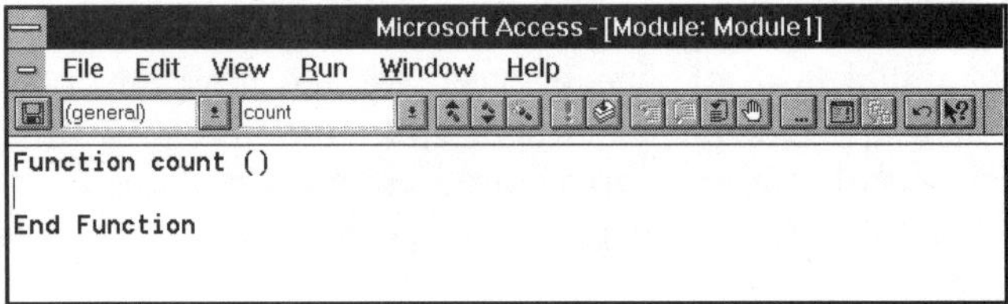

Opening a Table

Now you can open the two tables. To do this you must declare three variables. You can think of a variable as a field that you use in your code. You store data in this field, and then use it in different places within the program.

For the tables, you need special variables to store the tables in. You also need a variable to store the database in, so that the program can find the tables. You tell the program that the variables are special by using **`Dim:`**

```
Dim questionnaire As Database, customer As Table, answers As Table
```

The three variables are **`questionnaire`**, **`customer`** and **`answers`**. Now you must open the tables. To do this we must first open the database. As this module is part of the database we want to open, Access Basic has given us an easy way of doing this:

```
Set questionnaire = CurrentDB()
```

The **Set** is there to tell Access Basic that you are setting one of the special variables. Now we can open the tables. Again Access Basic helps us as the special variables have their own properties and methods, as do forms, reports, fields, and the like. We can therefore use one of the methods from the database variable to open the two tables:

```
Set customer = questionaire.OpenTable("customer")
Set answers = questionaire.OpenTable("answers")
```

You can see we have used **Set** again.

> Note that the method is part of the variable questionnaire, and not of the type Database. The reason for this is that if you had two databases open, Access Basic would not know which database you were referring to if you used Database.OpenTable(). Instead you must tell it by using the variable name.

Specify which table you want to open by using the name of the table in quotation marks, inside the parentheses. If you don't use quotation marks Access Basic thinks you are using a variable and this can cause any number of problems.

Going Through the Records

Now we have the two tables open we can begin to go through the customers.

To begin with we must make sure we are on the first customer. Again Access Basic helps us as tables have methods and properties, in a similar way to databases. We must use the method MoveFirst:

```
customer.MoveFirst
```

This ensures we are at the beginning of the table. Now we must go through all the records in the customer table. Access Basic provides us with a pair of commands which loops through each bit of code several times:

```
Do
...
Loop
```

When Access Basic meets the **Loop** command it goes back to the **Do** command, so any commands in-between these two will be repeated over and over again.

Access Basic gives you an opt-out clause so you don't have to switch off your computer to stop the running of the code. Instead of just using **Do** use **Do Until <condition>**. When the condition becomes true, Access Basic jumps to the line following the **Loop** command.

In our example, we want to stop once we have reached the end of the table. The table property that becomes true when we reach the end of the table is called End of File (EOF). Therefore in our program we use:

```
Do Until customer.EOF
...
Loop
```

We must remember to move to the next record in that table each time we go through the loop. This is another safeguard against having to switch off the computer. We move record position by using a table method called MoveNext.

Therefore to go through every customer in the table, the code is:

```
Do Until customer.EOF
  customer.MoveNext
Loop
```

Counting the Number of Databases

Just going through the customers in the table is not enough because we haven't actually counted how many databases they use. To do this we need another variable which we can call **dbcount**. We start the counting from zero for each customer and increase it by one for each database they use. We must therefore make sure **dbcount** is zero. As the loop is carried out for each customer, it's easy to set the code at the beginning of the loop. We do this with this code:

```
dbcount = 0
```

Now we must see if this customer uses Access. We can do this by checking to see whether either of the two Access fields on the table is set to Yes. This is done in a similar way to a query - if 'Access like a little' is Yes or 'Access like a lot' is Yes then we increase **dbcount** by one. We have already almost written the code for this:

```
If customer![Access like a little] = True Or customer![Access like a lot] =
↬True Then dbcount = dbcount + 1
```

If you compare the code against what we said we wanted to do, you will see it's almost the same. One difference is that Access Basic uses **True** instead of

Yes (and **False** instead of No); another is the change in the way the **dbcount** variable is increased.

All you must do now is to repeat the process for the other three databases:

```
If customer![Paradox like a little] = True Or customer![Paradox like a lot]
↳= True Then dbcount = dbcount + 1
If customer![Foxpro like a little] = True Or customer![Foxpro like a lot] =
↳True Then dbcount = dbcount + 1
If customer![SQL like a little] = True Or customer![SQL like a lot] = True
↳Then dbcount = dbcount + 1
```

Following this, **dbcount** adds up the number of databases the customer uses. All that remains to be done is to save the data in the answers table.

Saving the Results

The table we have been using has this structure:

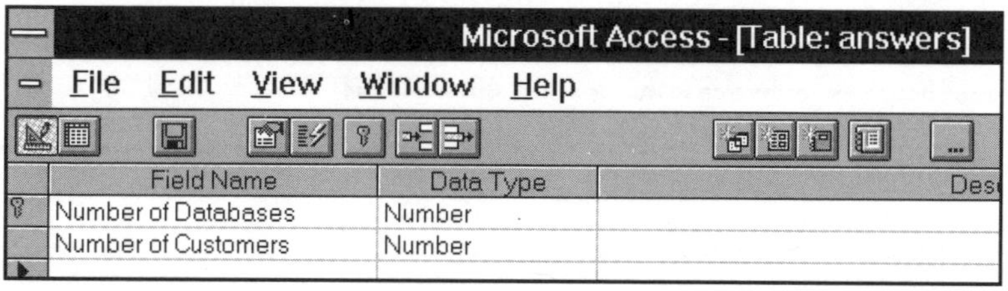

Microsoft Access - [Table: answers]

File Edit View Window Help

Field Name	Data Type	Des
Number of Databases	Number	
Number of Customers	Number	

The Number of Databases field of the table has been set as the primary key. To store data, we should search the answers table for the record in which the entry Number of Databases field equals the variable **dbcount**.

We can do this by telling Access Basic which field we are going to search on. Microsoft has provided properties for tables and the one which defines the field to search on is called the index. We can set the index of the table using:

```
answers.Index = "PrimaryKey"
```

We only have to do this once so we can put this line in immediately after we have opened the table. Now we can search on the primary key (Number of Databases). Again we use a table method to do this for us:

```
answers.MoveFirst
answers.Seek "=", dbcount
```

Use the MoveFirst method before the search to make sure we start from the first record. If **Seek** doesn't find the record we will get an error message.

The Final Stage

Now we can address the record that we want to update. First we want to discover how many customers already have *this* number of databases. Then we want to increase this total by one.

We can use another variable to store the number of customers temporarily. We receive the data from the table with this code:

```
custcount = answers![Number of Customers]
```

We then increase this by one:

```
custcount = custcount + 1
```

Now we save it back in the table:

```
answers![Number of Customers] = custcount
```

Remember that the table must be in edit mode for you to do this. Therefore, before we save the customer count back to the table we put the table into edit mode:

```
answers.Edit
```

Simply writing to the table is not enough. Access 2.0 always gives you the option of changing your mind when you do something to a record. Access makes a copy of the record so any changes you make will *only* apply to that copy. To change the original we must copy the copy back. This is called updating the table, and in Access Basic the table has an update method which we have to use after we have made the change:

```
answers.Update
```

Tidying up

If we apply our small program to all the records in the Customer table, the Answers table will have all the data it needs to answer the original question: "How many customers use 1,2,3 or 4 database products?"

Now we just have to close the tables we have used:

```
answers.Close
customer.Close
```

The complete code should look like this:

```
Function count ()
    Dim questionnaire As Database, customer As Table, answers As Table

    Set questionnaire = CurrentDB()

    Set customer = questionnaire.OpenTable("customer")
    Set answers = questionnaire.OpenTable("answers")

    answers.Index = "PrimaryKey"

    customer.MoveFirst

    Do Until customer.EOF
        dbcount = 0

        If customer![Access like a little] = True Or customer![Access like a
↳lot] = True Then dbcount = dbcount + 1
        If customer![Paradox like a little] = True Or customer![Paradox like
↳a lot] = True Then dbcount = dbcount + 1
        If customer![Foxpro like a little] = True Or customer![Foxpro like a
↳lot] = True Then dbcount = dbcount + 1
        If customer![SQL like a little] = True Or customer![SQL like a lot] =
↳True Then dbcount = dbcount + 1

        answers.MoveFirst
        answers.Seek "=", dbcount

        custcount = answers![Number of Customers]
        custcount = custcount + 1

        answers.Edit
        answers![Number of Customers] = custcount
        answers.Update

        customer.MoveNext
    Loop

    answers.Close
    customer.Close

End Function
```

If we were to use the Immediate window to run this code, and all the tables had been set up properly, we should get the following results:

Number of Databases	Number of Customers
0	1
1	7
2	6
3	5
4	1
0	0

Where Now?

This has only been a brief look at the power of Access Basic. We have introduced a number of new things which may have confused you. The main thing to remember is that Access Basic allows you to handle the data in your tables in exactly the way you want to.

If you just use tables there are many methods and properties which can give you access to the nuts and bolts of Access 2.0. If you then include forms, queries, SQL, and a whole host of other things, you will get an idea of the true size of Access Basic.

Hopefully you will have realized that using Access Basic is not too difficult. In this chapter you have been following a simple and powerful program. If you now want to learn more about Access Basic and programming in general then we have achieved our aim.

APPENDIX I

Properties

This appendix explains what all of the properties for each of the Access objects is for. There are tables covering:

- Forms and report properties
- Table properties
- Query properties
- Control properties

The function of each property is explained, and the objects it refers to are listed. There is a key to the abbreviations we have used at the end of this appendix.

Form and Report Properties

Property Name	Applies To...	Is Used To...
AfterDelConfirm	Forms	Cause a macro or associated Access BASIC event procedure to run when the AfterDelConfirm event occurs.
AfterInsert	Forms	Cause a macro or associated Access BASIC event procedure to run when the AfterInsert event occurs.
AfterUpdate	Forms	Assign a macro or some Access Basic code to this event. AfterUpdate refers to after any alterations are accepted to the data in a record.
AllowEditing	Forms	Determine whether the allow editing command on the records menu is enabled when a form is opened in Form view or Datasheet view. Possible settings are Available (default) or Unavailable.
AllowFilters	Forms	Determine whether records can be filtered. The default is to allow filtering. The property can be set with the property sheet, a macro or Access BASIC. If this is set to NO, then Edit Filter/sort, Apply Filter/sort and Show All Records are disabled.
AllowUpdating	Forms	Determine which tables you can edit when a form is in Form view or Datasheet view. The default setting is that only the default tables and their bound controls may be edited. Other settings are none and any.
AutoCenter	Forms	Determine whether a form will be automatically centered in the application window when the form is opened. Default setting is NO.
AutoResize	Forms	Determine whether a Form window opens automatically sized to display a complete record. Default setting is YES.
BackColor	Form sections, Report sections	Specify the color of the paper of the section. Use the palette or the Color Builder to assign this color.
BeforeDelConfirm	Forms	Cause a macro or associated Access BASIC event to run when the BeforeDelConfirm event occurs.
BeforeInsert	Forms	Cause a macro or associated Access BASIC event to run when the BeforeInsert event occurs.
BeforeUpdate	Forms	Assign a macro or some Access Basic code to this event. Before Update refers to before any alterations are accepted to the data in a record .

BorderStyle	Forms	Determine the type of border and border elements (title bar, Control menu, maximize and minimize buttons) to use for the form.
CanGrow	Form, Report sections	Allows Access to increase the dimensions of the control to fit the entry. This only applies to print-outs where scroll bars are useless.
CanShrink	Form, Report sections	Allows Access to decrease the dimensions of the control when printing.
Caption	Forms, Reports	Provide the text that appears in the title bar in Form view, or provide the title for the report that appears in Print Preview.
ControlBox	Forms	Specify whether a form has a control menu in Form view. Default is YES.
DateGrouping	Reports	Inform Access which settings to use when grouping dates; US options or the options given in the Options Dialog box, e.g. Sunday is the first day of the week, and the first week of the year commences on the 1st of January.
DefaultView	Forms	Specify the opening view of the form.
DisplayWhen	Form sections, Controls	Restrict when a control is displayed. You can choose to have it displayed always, only when printing or only on screen
FastLaserPrinting	Forms, Reports	Determine whether lines and rectangles are replaced by rules when you print a form or report using certain laser printers.
FontItalic	Reports	Inform Access that the text that has to be italic when the report is printed.
FontName	Reports	Inform Access of the particular font that you require the data printed out with.
FontSize	Reports	Inform Access of the size of the font that you wish to use.
FontUnderline	Reports	Inform Access of the text that should be underlined when the report is printed.
ForceNewPage	Forms, Report sections	Determine whether Access starts printing a section on the current page or at the top of a new page.

GridX	Forms and Reports	Specify the horizontal distance between the grid dots.
GridY	Forms and Reports	Specify the vertical distance between the grid dots.
Height	Form sections, Report sections	Specify the height of the sections in the form or report, i.e. the length of the paper in each section will be given in the appropriate Height property.
HelpContextID	Forms and Reports	Link the appropriate custom help file to the control.
HelpFile	Forms and Reports	Inform Access of the particular custom Help file that you wish to associate with the form or report.
KeepTogether	Form and Report sections except page header and footer	Inform Access that you require the contents of the given section printed out on the one page if possible.
LayoutForPrint	Forms and Reports	Inform Access whether to use screen fonts (No) or printer fonts (Yes). Note that both look much the same on screen, the difference occurs when printing.
Left	Reports and Report sections	Mark the gap between the edge of the paper and the current section.
MaxButton	Forms	Informs Access whether a form should have a maximize button.
MenuBar	Forms and Reports	Select the menubar which will appear at the top of the window. Use a zero length string to obtain the built-in menubar.
MinButton	Forms	Informs Access of whether a form should have a minimize button.
Modal	Form	Inform Access that as soon as this form receives the focus, do not allow it to move from the form until it is closed
Name	Forms and form sections, Reports and Report sections	Specify the name by which the object or object section is know by. The default for the objects is the object type followed by a number, while the default for the sections is the title of the section followed by a number corresponding to the number of sections above it.

NavigationButtons	Forms	Specify whether the record counter and the VCR-like navigation buttons appear on the page or not
NewRowOrCol	Forms and Report sections except page header and footer	Specify how a multiple column layout is organized. Depending on the setting given to the Item Layout in the Print Setup dialog box, this property can be used to specify whether the section is printed on a new row or column or not.
OnActivate	Forms or Reports	Assign a macro or some Access Basic code to this event. This event occurs when the form or report first receives the focus and becomes the active window.
OnClick	Forms and Form sections	Assign a macro or some Access Basic code to this event. The Click event occurs when the user presses the left mouse button when the pointer is over this control.
OnClose	Forms and Reports	Assign a macro or some Access Basic code to this event. This event occurs when the form or report is closed and removed from the screen.
OnCurrent	Forms	Assign a macro or some Access Basic code to this event. This event occurs when the focus moves onto another record.
OnDblClick	Form and Form sections	Assign a macro or some Access Basic code to this event. This event occurs when the user presses the left mouse button twice in quick succession, when the pointer is over this control.
OnDeactivate	Forms or Reports	Assign a macro or some Access Basic code to this event. This event occurs when the form or report first receives the focus and becomes the active window
OnDelete	Forms	Assign a macro or some Access Basic code to this event. This event occurs when the user performs one of the actions to cause a deletion, but before the deletion actually takes place.
OnError	Forms and Reports	Assign a macro or some Access Basic code to this event. This event occurs when a run-time error is produced by the JET database engine, as opposed to run-time errors created by Access Basic.

OnFormat	Report sections	Assign a macro or some Access Basic code to this event. This event occurs after Access has decided what information should appear in which section but before it is positioned.
OnGotFocus	Forms	Assign a macro or some Access Basic code to this event. This event occurs as the control receives the focus.
OnKeyDown	Forms	Assign a macro or some Access Basic code to this event. This event occurs when Access realizes that a key has been depressed by the user.
OnKeyPress	Forms	Assign a macro or some Access Basic code to this event. This event occurs when Access identifies that the user has pressed and released a key or key combination that relates to an ANSI code.
OnKeyUp	Forms	Assign a macro or some Access Basic code to this event. This event occurs when Access realizes that a key has been depressed by the user.
OnLoad	Forms	Assign a macro or some Access Basic code to this event. This event occurs when the form is opened and the first record is displayed.
OnLostFocus	Forms	Assign a macro or some Access Basic code to this event. This event occurs just before the focus leaves the control.
OnMouseDown	Forms and Form sections	Assign a macro or some Access Basic code to this event. This event occurs when Access registers that a mouse button has been depressed by the user.
OnMouseMove	Forms and Form sections	Assign a macro or some Access Basic code to this event. This event occurs when the user moves the mouse pointer.
OnMouseUp	Forms and Form sections	Assign a macro or some Access Basic code to this event. This event occurs when Access registers that a mouse button has been released by the user.
OnOpen	Forms and Reports	Assign a macro or some Access Basic code to this event. This event occurs when you enter Form View but before the first record is displayed, or just before the report is provided or printed.
OnPrint	Report sections	Assign a macro or some Access Basic code to this event. This event occurs when the report sections have been formatted for printing but before the printing begins.

OnResize	Forms	Assign a macro or some Access Basic code to this event. This event occurs whenever the form is opened or the size of the form changes.
OnRetreat	Report sections	Assign a macro or some Access Basic code to this event. This event occurs when Access has to back track in the report for some reason. These reasons include deciding whether a section contains all the correct components and whether or not they will all fit onto the same page (Keep Together property).
OnTimer	Forms	Assign a macro or some Access Basic code to this event. This event occurs at regular intervals depending on the setting of the TimerInterval property.
OnUnload	Forms	Assign a macro or some Access Basic code to this event. This event occurs when a form is closed but before it is removed from the screen.
Page	Form or Report	Return the number of the current page. This cannot be changed only used in expressions, a macro or an event procedure.
PageFooter	Report	Specify whether or not the page footer is printed. See the drop down list for all the available options.
PageHeader	Report	Specify whether or not the page footer is printed. See the drop down list for all the available options.
Pages	Form or Report	Return the total number of pages in the form or report. This cannot be changed only used in expressions, a macro or an event procedure.
PaletteSource	Form and Report	Informs Access of the palette that should be applied to the form or report.
PopUp	Forms	Determines whether the form will stay above the other windows until it is closed (Yes) or not (No).
RecordLocks	Forms and Reports	Determines which records are locked from other users when they are actively in use in your form or report.
RecordSelectors	Forms	Indicates whether a form displays record selectors, i.e. the boxes at the side of the records that are required to be selected before a record can be deleted for instance.

RecordSource	Forms and Reports	Specify the default table or query that the form or report takes its information from.
ScrollBars	Forms	Inform Access of your decision to include or exclude scroll bars should the data that has been entered or is to be viewed be too big for the control.
ShortcutMenu	Form and Report sections	Inform Access whether a short cut menu should be displayed when the right mouse button is de-pressed
SpecialEffect	Forms and Form sections,	Inform Access of how you wish the controls to appear; on a par with the paper, sunken or raised.
Tag	Reports and Report sections	Add any more details to the control that you wish to be remembered ad infinitum. This entry can be up to 2048 characters long and does not affect the control's ability to function, it is purely notational.
TimerInterval	Forms	Indicate the interval between the timer event occurring. This is given in milliseconds.
Top	Reports	Mark the distance between the top of the paper and the beginning of the report.
ViewsAllowed	Forms	Inform Access whether or not the user should be allowed to change the view of the form. The various options given in the drop down menu allow you to restrict the user to the views you want to allow.
Visible	Form and Form sections, Reports and Report sections	Inform Access of whether or not the control is visible. This property differs from transparent as Visible also disables the control whereas transparent controls can still be activated, i.e. the OnClick macro on a transparent button can be executed whereas the same on an invisible button cannot. Yes/No.
Width	Forms and Reports	Specify the width of the page for the form or the report

Table Properties

Property	Is Used To...
AllowZeroLength	Inform Access of whether a zero length string is a valid entry. This differs from a null entry as a zero length entry means that the information doesn't exist, where a null entry means that the information may exist but isn't known.
Caption	Notify Access of some more meaningful text that you wish to appear on the column heading in the datasheet applicable to this field. This text defaults to the name of the field.
DataType	Set the data type of the selected field. This restricts the type of data that the user can enter, but allow queries to work faster and also forces some basic structure upon both you and the user. For a complete listing of all the available data types and a detailed description of their uses see the Access Help screen under "DataType Property".
DecimalPlaces	Define the number of decimal places that are shown when displaying numbers. Auto calls the format property setting into action whereas the use of a whole number between zero and fifteen sets the number of decimal places to be used ; any numbers to the left of the decimal place come under the control of the format property setting.
DefaultValue	Set a default entry into a field in a blank record. The default value setting is usually the most common entry that the user will make. This setting is either an expression or straight text.
Description	Give extra information about the table or its fields. The maximum length of the comment is 255 characters.
FieldName	Uniquely identify the various fields in your table design.
FieldSize	Set the maximum amount of data a field can store. Even though the field stores are dynamic, i.e. the memory taken up by the field varies depending on that required to store the information contained in the field, smaller settings for this property allow the field to be processed more quickly. For more detailed explanation of the types of setting that you can use in this property, see the Access Help screens under "FieldSize Property".
Format	Specify the format used for any type of display in the appropriate table field. For a full listing of the default formats that are available see the Access Help screens under "Format Property".
FrozenColumns	Indicate the number of columns that are frozen to the left hand side of the datasheet. These columns are fixed in that position even if the uer scrolls to the right.
IgnoreNulls	Inform Access that any null values that it uncovers in its attempt to correlate an index containing this field should be ignored.

Indexed	Set up a single field index based upon this field, the settings being either No, for no indexing, Yes (with duplicates) for an index that allows the user to duplicate entries in this field, and Yes (without duplicates) for an index that disallows the entry of duplicate data in this field.
InputMask	Give the user a template to fill in when entering data. Some symbol is used to inform the user of the number of characters that is required to produce a complete entry. Note that Access provides an Input Mask Wizard to help you create the correct entry for this property.
Primary	Set the primary key for the table. In design view, use the Primary Key icon or the Set Primary Key option from the Edit menu to add the appropriate field to this property.
Required	Informs Access that an entry is required in this field, and so stops the user from progressing until an entry is made.
Unique	Allow the index to be optimised. A unique value index works faster that a multi-field index, because when this property is set to Yes, Access understands that when it finds one entry that matches the criteria there will be no more. It therefore stops the search and returns the appropriate value.
ValidationRule	Set the rule that will be applied to the data that the user enters. If the rule is broken, the data is not transferred to the appropriate field and Access will inform the user of the error.
ValidationText	Inform the user of the broken validation rule, using more friendly terms than the abrasive default message that Microsoft have provided.

Query Properties

Property	Is Used To...
Alias	Temporarily rename the tables or queries that you use as the source for the data involved in the query. Usually of use when you use a self-join to rename the second table to a more meaningful name than Table_1.
Caption	Give the column heading more interesting text than the default which is the name of the field itself.
ColumnHeadings	Select the columns that you wish to display and the order that they should be displayed in. This property only applies to Crosstab queries and is made up of the column headings that you require separated by a comma.
ColumnHidden	Inform Access if you wish the column to be visible (0) or hidden (-1).
ColumnOrder	Identify the columns position in the QBE grid. Setting 1 appears on the far left, 2 next door and so on.
ColumnWidth	Set the width of the column. This is measured in twips, of which there are 567 to the centimetre, 1440 to the inch. Give a number of twips for the column width or use one of the three given choices. (0) hides the column (-1) sizes the column to the default size, and (-2) sizes the column to the dimensions of the visible text.
DatasheetFontHeight	Specify the point size of the text that appears in the dynaset.
DatasheetFontItalic	Inform Access of which text in the dynaset should be italic.
DatasheetFontName	Specify the font used for the text that appears in the dynaset.
DatasheetFontUnderline	Inform Access of which text in the dynaset should be underlined.
DatasheetFontWeight	Define the thickness of the pencil used to draw any lines or write any text in the dynaset.
DecimalPlaces	Define the number of decimal places that are displayed when a figure appears in the dynaset field. Auto calls the format property setting into action whereas the use of a whole number between zero and fifteen sets the number of decimal places to be used; any numbers to the left of the decimal place come under the control of the format property setting.
Description	Give extra information about the query or its fields. The maximum length of the comment is 255 characters.

DestConnectStr	Give the type of database that you will be connecting to when you produce an Append or Make Table query.
DestinationDB	Inform Access of the connect string, or the message to send to open the database ready for the data.
DestinationTable	Inform Access of the new table name or the table destination for the data that is being transmitted.
Format	Specify the format used for any type of display in the query field. For a full listing of the default formats that are available see the Access Help screens under "Format Property".
InputMask	Give the user a template to fill in when entering data. Some symbol is used to inform the user of the number of characters that is required to produce a complete entry. Note that Access provides an Input Mask Wizard to help you create the correct entry for this property.
LogMessages	Inform Access when you wish to store the messages that are generated when a Pass-Through query is executed.
ODBCConnectStr	Inform Access of the required information to complete the connection between Access and another SQL database.
ODBCTimeout	Give the number of seconds that Access will wait before causing a time error to be generated.
OutputAllFields	Inform Access of your need to override the Show row in the QBE grid. If this property is set to Yes, the Show row is overridden and all fields are shown, otherwise only the fields with a checked Show box are made visible.
RecordLocks	Determines whether the records involved in a query are locked away from other users while the query is being executed.
ReturnsRecords	Inform Access whether a Pass-Through query will be returning any records. Yes means there will be a return, No means there won't.
RunPermissions	Globally alter the permissions for this query in a multi-user environment. With this property it is possible to allow all users access to the dynaset of this query even if some of them did not have the correct permissions normally.
ShowGrid	Inform Access of your need to have the ruled lines in the dynaset that appear by default. Alter this property using the Gridlines option in the Format menu.

Source	Contains the name of the source database that any imported or attached tables originate from.
SourceConnectStr	Specify the application that created the database that holds any attached data.
SourceDatabase	Specify the name of the external database that holds any attached data.
TopValues	Inform Access of the required top n or top n% of the entries in this field, together with the rest of the associated records.
UniqueRecords	Request Access to return only the unique records in the dynaset.
UniqueValues	Request Access to only return the unique values in this field. If there are any duplications, Access provides the full record from the first entry in the list of duplications.

Control Properties

Property	Associated With...	Is Used To...
AddColon	BOF, Chk Bx, Cmb Bx, Cmd Bn, L Bx, Opt Bn, Opt Gp, Sub, Txt Bx, Tog Bn	Automatically add a colon after text in new labels. Yes/No
AfterUpdate	BOF, Chk Bx, Cmb Bx, L Bx, Opt Bn, Opt Gp, Txt Bx, Tog Bn	Assign a macro or some Access Basic code to this event. AfterUpdate refers to after any alterations are accepted to the data in a record.
AutoActivate	BOF, Graph, UOF	Allow the user to activate an OLE object by double-clicking this control, or by giving it the focus. Menu.
AutoExpand	Cmb Bx	Inform Access that you wish it to attempt to identify the unique entry from the Combo Box list, that the user is beginning to type in. Yes/No.
AutoLabel	BOF, Chk Bx, Cmb Bx, Cmd Bn, L Bx, Opt Bn, Opt Gp, Sub, Txt Bx, Tog Bn	Automatically assign a label to any new controls that you create. Yes/No.
AutoRepeat	Cmd Bn	Cause Access to repeat a macro or some Access Basic code while the command button is held down. Yes/ No.
AutoTab	Txt Bx	Inform Access to automatically jump to the next control when the final character is entered into an input mask.
BackColor	Cmb Bx, Graph, Label, L Bx, Opt Gp, Rect, Txt Bx, UOF	Specify the color of the paper of the control. Use the palette or the Color Builder to assign this color.
BackStyle	Graph, Label, Opt Gp, Rect, Sub, UOF	Inform Access whether or not the BackColor property is used. If BackStyle is set to Clear then BackColor is not used and the control is made transparent. If BackStyle is set to Normal then the BackColor setting is applied to the control.
BeforeUpdate	BOF, Chk Bx, Cmb Bx, L Bx, Opt Bn, Opt Gp, Txt Bx, Tog Bn	Assign a macro or some Access Basic code to this event. Before Update refers to before any alterations are accepted to the data in a record.

BorderColor	BOF, Cmb Bx, Graph, Label, Line, Opt Gp, Rect, Txt Bx, UOF	Informs Access of the color of the controls border. Use the palette or the Color Builder to make your choice.
BorderLineStyle	BOF, Cmb Bx, Graph, Label, Line, Opt Gp, Rect, Txt Bx, UOF	Informs Access of the make-up of the border around the control. Menu.
BorderStyle	BOF, Cmb Bx, Graph, Label, Line, Opt Gp, Rect, Txt Bx, UOF	Determine whether the border is visible or transparent. Menu.
BorderWidth	BOF, Cmb Bx, Graph, Label, Line, Opt Gp, Rect, Txt Bx, UOF	Determine the width of the border around a control. Use the given menu or the palette to make your width choice.
BoundColumn	Cmb Bx, L Bx	Specify the column in the Combo Box, which Access will take data from when an entry is made by the user into the field specified in the ControlSource property.
Cancel	Cmd Bn	Inform Access which button on your form acts as the Cancel button, in other words will cancel any event that the user has called up. Note that only one button can be assigned this property. Yes/No.
CanGrow	Sub, Txt Bx	Allows Access to increase the dimensions of the control to fit the entry. This only applies to print-outs where scroll bars are useless.
CanShrink	Sub, Txt Bx	Allows Access to decrease the dimensions of the control when printing.
Caption	Cmd Bn, Label, Tog Bn	Notify Access of the text that you wish to appear on the label or button. Note that this text defaults to the name of the control.
Class	BOF, Graph, UOF	Illustrate the type of OLE Object contained in this control. This is usually filled in by Access when the control is defined.

ColumnCount	Cmb Bx, Graph, L Bx, UOF	Define the number of columns in a List or Combo Box or the number of columns, and therefore data, passed to another control such as a graph for some type of processing. Note that this entry must be a whole number between one and the maximum number of fields, in the underlying table or query.
ColumnHeads	Cmb Bx, Graph, L Bx, UOF	Inform Access of your desire to have the appropriate field names as the headings of your lists. Yes/No.
ColumnWidths	Cmb Bx, L Bx	Indicate the widths of the columns in your lists. Use semi-colons (;) to separate the numbers, one for each column, that represent your desired widths. Note that the minimum width is one inch, but if you give a column width 0 then that column will be hidden.
ControlSource	BOF, Chk Bx, L Bx, Opt Bn, Opt Gp, Txt Bx, Tog Bn	Bind that control to a field in the underlying table or query, or sets the expression to be used as the basis for a custom calculation.
DecimalPlaces	Txt Bx	Define the number of decimal places that are displayed when the text box is used to display numbers. Auto calls the format property setting into action whereas the use of a whole number between zero and fifteen sets the number of decimal places to be used ; any numbers to the left of the decimal place come under the control of the format property setting.
Default	Cmd Bn	Set one button on your form as the default choice when a new record is viewed. Yes/No.
DefaultValue	Chk Bx, Cmb Bx, L Bx, Opt Bn, Opt Gp, Txt Bx, Tog Bn	Set a default entry into a control on a blank form. The default value setting is usually the commonest entry that the user will make. This setting is either an expression or straight text.

DisplayType	BOF, Graph, UOF	Determine whether an OLE object appears as itself or its associated icon. Menu.
DisplayWhen	BOF, Chk Bx, Cmb Bx, Cmd Bn, Graph, Label, Line, L Bx, Opt Bn, Opt Gp, Rect, Sub, Txt Bx, Tog Bn, UOF	Restrict when a control is displayed. You can choose to have it displayed always, only when printing or only on screen.
Enabled	BOF, Chk Bx, Cmb Bx, Cmd Bn, Graph, L Bx, Opt Bn, Opt Gp, Sub, Txt Bx, Tog Bn, UOF	Define whether or not a control is able to receive the focus. If this property is set to No when you attempt to tab into this control the focus passes straight on to the next control in the tab index which has the enabled property set to Yes.
EnterKeyBehavior	Txt Bx	Determine what happens when the user presses the enter key. You can choose whether to accept the default option of moving to the next control or to allow this key press to begin a new line in the text box. Menu.
FontItalic	Cmb Bx, Cmd Bn, Label, L Bx, Txt Bx, Tog Bn	Set the text in any of these controls to an italic font.
FontName	Cmb Bx, Cmd Bn, Label, L Bx, Txt Bx, Tog Bn	Set the text in any of these controls to a given font.
FontSize	Cmb Bx, Cmd Bn, Label, L Bx, Txt Bx, Tog Bn	Set the size of the text.
FontUnderline	Cmb Bx, Cmd Bn, Label, L Bx, Txt Bx, Tog Bn	Underline the text in any of these controls.
FontWeight	Cmb Bx, Cmd Bn, Label, L Bx, Txt Bx, Tog Bn	Determine the thickness of the lead in the pencil that is used to write the text.
ForeColor	Cmb Bx, Cmd Bn, Label, L Bx, Txt Bx, Tog Bn	Set the color of the text, in a given control. Make your selection with help from the Color Builder.
Format	Txt Bx	Set the appearance of the data that will be shown in this control, e.g. a dollar sign before dough or the inclusion of brackets in your phone number.

Height	BOF, Chk Bx, Cmb Bx, Cmd Bn, Graph, Label, Line, L Bx, Opt Bn, Opt Gp, Rect, Sub, Txt Bx, Tog Bn, UOF	Set the height of your component.
HelpContextID	BOF, Chk Bx, Cmb Bx, Cmd Bn, Graph, L Bx, Opt Bn, Opt Gp, Txt Bx, Tog Bn, UOF	Link the appropriate custom help file to the control.
HideDuplicates	Chk Bx, Cmb Bx, L Bx, Opt Bn, Opt Gp, Txt Bx, Tog Bn	Get Access to hide a control if the data it contains in this record is the same as that contained in any preceding records.
InputMask	Txt Bx	Give the user a template to fill in when entering data. Some symbol is used to inform the user of the number of characters that is required to produce a complete entry. Note that Access provides an Input Mask Wizard to help you create the correct entry for this property.
LabelAlign	BOF, Chk Bx, Cmb Bx, Cmd Bn, Graph, L Bx, Opt Bn, Opt Gp, Sub, Txt Bx, Tog Bn	Define which part of the control LabelX uses as its zero value. Note that general and left settings are equivalent and that all settings are based upon the top edge of the control.
LabelX	BOF, Chk Bx, Cmb Bx, Cmd Bn, L Bx, Opt Bn, Opt Gp, Sub, Txt Bx, Tog Bn	Inform Access of the position of the left edge of the associated label relative to the setting of LabelAlign.
LabelY	BOF, Chk Bx, Cmb Bx, Cmd Bn, L Bx, Opt Bn, Opt Gp, Sub, Txt Bx, Tog Bn	Inform Access of the top edge of the associated label, relative to the LabelAlign setting.
Left	All	Mark the position of the top left hand corner of the component relative to the vertical ruler.
LimitToList	Cmb Bx	Restrict the user's choice of selections to the given list. Yes/No.
LineSlant	Line	Inform Access of which way the given line slants, e.g. top left to bottom right or bottom left to top right.

LinkChildFields	Graph, Sub, UOF	Set the field in the underlying table or query associated with the child component i.e. the component that relies on the rest of the form for its data, that will be used to link the two entities.
LinkMasterFields	Graph, Sub, UOF	Set the field that will work in conjunction with that set in the LinkChildFields property. This ensures that the relationship between the data shown in both objects is always related.
ListRows	Cmb Bx	Inform Access of the number of rows of information that you wish to appear when you select the tab at the end of the Combo Box control. Note that if the number of applicable rows of data is greater than the figure assigned to this property then Access will provide scroll bars in order for the user to view all the data.
ListWidths	Cmb Bx	Sets the widths of the columns that appear when you select the tab at the end of the Combo Box control.
Locked	BOF, Chk Bx, Cmb Bx, Graph, L Bx, Opt Bn, Opt Gp, Sub, Txt Bx, Tog Bn, UOF	Stop the user from altering the data that may appear in this control. This property does not affect the control's ability to gain the focus just the ability to alter any entry.
Name	All	Define the name of the control. Access provides a default entry for this property when the control is produced. This control name will appear in the tab order box therefore it is suggested that this name should be descriptive so that the tab order is easier to calculate.
OLEClass	Graph, UOF	Supplement the Class property entry thus describing in detail the OLE Object source.
OLEType	BOF, Graph, UOF	Identify if the control is being used as an OLE container and if so whether the source material is linked or embedded.

OLETypeAllowed	BOF, Graph, UOF	Specify what type of OLE can be performed upon the control.
OnChange	Cmb Bx, Txt Bx	Assign a macro or some Access Basic code to this event. The Change event occurs when any change in the data shown in the control is identified by Access.
OnClick	BOF, Chk Bx, Cmb Bx, Cmd Bn, Graph, Label, L Bx, Opt Bn, Opt Gp, Rect, Txt Bx, Tog Bn, UOF	Assign a macro or some Access Basic code to this event. The Click event occurs when the user presses the left mouse button when the pointer is over this control.
OnDblClick	BOF, Chk Bx, Cmb Bx, Cmd Bn, Graph, Label, L Bx, Opt Bn, Opt Gp, Rect, Txt Bx, Tog Bn, UOF	Assign a macro or some Access Basic code to this event. This event occurs when the user presses the left mouse button twice in quick succession, when the pointer is over this control.
OnEnter	BOF, Chk Bx, Cmb Bx, Cmd Bn, Graph, L Bx, Opt Bn, Opt Gp, Sub, Txt Bx, Tog Bn, UOF	Assign a macro or some Access Basic code to this event. This event occurs just before the control receives the focus.
OnExit	BOF, Chk Bx, Cmb Bx, Cmd Bn, Graph, L Bx, Opt Bn, Opt Gp, Sub, Txt Bx, Tog Bn, UOF	Assign a macro or some Access Basic code to this event. This event occurs just after the control loses the focus.
OnGotFocus	BOF, Chk Bx, Cmb Bx, Cmd Bn, Graph, L Bx, Opt Bn, Txt Bx, Tog Bn, UOF	Assign a macro or some Access Basic code to this event. This event occurs as the control receives the focus.
OnKeyDown	BOF, Chk Bx, Cmb Bx, Cmd Bn, L Bx, Opt Bn, Txt Bx, Tog Bn	Assign a macro or some Access Basic code to this event. This event occurs when Access realises that a key has been depressed by the user.
OnKeyPress	BOF, Chk Bx, Cmb Bx, Cmd Bn, L Bx, Opt Bn, Txt Bx, Tog Bn	Assign a macro or some Access Basic code to this event. This event occurs when Access identifies that the user has pressed and released a key or key combination that relates to an ANSI code.
OnKeyUp	BOF, Chk Bx, Cmb Bx, Cmd Bn, L Bx, Opt Bn, Txt Bx, Tog Bn	Assign a macro or some Access Basic code to this event. This event occurs when Access realises that a key has been depressed by the user.

OnLostFocus	BOF, Chk Bx, Cmb Bx, Cmd Bn, Graph, L Bx, Opt Bn, Txt Bx, Tog Bn, UOF	Assign a macro or some Access Basic code to this event. This event occurs just before the focus leaves the control.
OnMouseDown	BOF, Chk Bx, Cmb Bx, Cmd Bn, Graph, Label, L Bx, Opt Bn, Opt Gp, Rect, Txt Bx, Tog Bn, UOF	Assign a macro or some Access Basic code to this event. This event occurs when Access registers that a mouse button has been depressed by the user.
OnMouseMove	BOF, Chk Bx, Cmb Bx, Cmd Bn, Graph, Label, L Bx, Opt Bn, Opt Gp, Rect, Txt Bx, Tog Bn, UOF	Assign a macro or some Access Basic code to this event. This event occurs when the user moves the mouse pointer.
OnMouseUp	BOF, Chk Bx, Cmb Bx, Cmd Bn, Graph, Label, L Bx, Opt Bn, Opt Gp, Rect, Txt Bx, Tog Bn, UOF	Assign a macro or some Access Basic code to this event. This event occurs when Access registers that a mouse button has been released by the user.
OnNotInList	Cmb Bx	Assign a macro or some Access Basic code to this event. This event occurs when the user attempts to make an entry into a Combo Box that is not in the predefined list and the LimitToList property is set to yes.
OnUpdated	BOF, Graph, UOF	Assign a macro or some Access Basic code to this event. This event occurs when the data associated with an OLE Object is updated.
OptionValue	Chk Bx, Opt Bn, Tog Bn	Identify the mutual exclusive options represented by the boxes or buttons shown in an option group. It is these values that are passed to the field for storage, and need to be translated with a look-up table is the whole record is going to be displayed without the aid of the option group. These values must be whole numbers and cannot be composed of text.
Picture	Cmd Bn, Tog Bn	Identify the position and filename of the bitmap that you wish to appear upon the button. Note that Windows Paintbrush can be used to create bitmaps for this purpose.

RowSource	Cmb Bx, Graph, L Bx, UOF	Specifies the exact source of the data that will appear in the control. How this data is manipulated before it appears in the control depends upon the entry in the RowSourceType property.
RowSourceType	Cmb Bx, Graph, L Bx, UOF	Specify the type of source for the data that will appear in the control, and works in tandem with RowSource to produce the required effects.
RunningSum	Txt Bx	Define whether or not the text box contains the exact data relating to the record, the alternative being the production of a cumulative sum of the data. The options that you can select for this property also define the part of the report that the running sum is calculated over.
ScrollBars	Txt Bx	Inform Access of your decision on the inclusion of scroll bars should the data that has been entered or is to be viewed is too big for the control.
SizeMode	BOF, Graph, UOF	Determine whether the OLE data is clipped to fit the size of the control, or whether it is reduced in size proportional to the original data or stretched to fill the control.
SourceDoc	BOF, Graph, UOF	Specify the whole file that you wish to connect to the OLE Object control. This property applies to both linked and embedded files.
SourceItem	BOF, Graph, UOF	Specify the part of a given file that you wish to link the OLE Object control. Use in conjunction with the SourceDoc or SourceObject properties to access the correct file.
SourceObject	Graph, Sub, UOF	Specify the file that you wish to link to the OLE Object control.
SpecialEffect	BOF, Chk Bx, Cmb Bx, Graph, Label, L Bx, Opt Bn, Opt Gp, Rect, Txt Bx, UOF	Inform Access of how you wish the controls to appear; on a par with the paper, sunken or raised.

StatusBarText	BOF, Chk Bx, Cmb Bx, Cmd Bn, L Bx, Opt Bn, Opt Gp, Sub, Txt Bx, Tog Bn	Provide Access with the text that will appear in the Status Bar when the control has the focus.
TabIndex	BOF, Chk Bx, Cmb Bx, Cmd Bn, Graph, L Bx, Opt Bn, Opt Gp, Sub, Txt Bx, Tog Bn, UOF	Identify the control's position in the tab order. This defaults to the order that the controls were created, 0 marking the first.
TabStop	BOF, Chk Bx, Cmb Bx, Cmd Bn, Graph, L Bx, Opt Bn, Opt Gp, Sub, Txt Bx, Tog Bn, UOF	Informs Access whether you wish to allow the user the chance to move the focus onto the control using the tab key. Even if this property is set to No, the user can still make the control receive the focus using one of the other methods of moving the focus, i.e. the Enter key or the mouse click. Yes/No.
Tag	All	Add any more details to the control that you wish to be remembered ad infinitum. This entry can be up to 2048 characters long and does not affect the control's ability to function, it is purely notational.
TextAlign	Cmb Bx, Label, Txt Bx	Specify the alignment of the text in the control, just as in a word processed document. Note that the General setting means that text will be left aligned while figures will be right aligned.
Top	All	Specify the position of the top left corner of the component relative to the horizontal ruler.
Transparent	Cmd Bn	Identify whether or not the button is transparent.
UpdateOptions	BOF, Graph, UOF	Identify whether the data in an OLE Object control is updated manually or automatically.
ValidationRule	Chk Bx, Cmb Bx, L Bx, Opt Bn, Opt Gp, Txt Bx, Tog Bn	Set the rule that will be applied to the data that the user enters. If the rule is broken, the data is not transferred to the appropriate field and Access will inform the user of their error.

ValidationText	Chk Bx, Cmb Bx, L Bx, Opt Bn, Opt Gp, Txt Bx, Tog Bn	Inform the user of the broken validation rule, using more friendly terms than the abrasive default message that Microsoft have provided.
Verb	BOF, Graph, UOF	Force Access to perform an action on the OLE Object control. For a full listing of these Verbs see the Access Help screens under Verb Property.
Visible	All	Inform Access of whether or not the control is visible. This property differs from transparent as Visible also disables the control whereas transparent controls can still be activated, i.e. the OnClick macro on a transparent button can be executed whereas the same on an invisible button cannot. Yes/No.
Width	BOF, Chk Bx, Cmb Bx, Cmd Bn, Graph, Label, Line, L Bx, Opt Bn, Opt Gp, Rect, Sub, Txt Bx, Tog Bn, UOF	Specify the width of the component.

Key to Object Abbreviations

BOF	**Bound Object Frame**
Chk Bx	Check Box
Cmb Bx	Combo Box
Cmd Bn	Command Button
Graph	Graph
Label	Label
Line	Line
L Bx	List Box
Opt Bn	Option Button
Opt Gp	Option Group
Pg Brk	Page Break
Rect	Rectangle
Sub	Subform/Subreport
Txt Bx	Text Box
Tog Bn	Toggle Button
UOF	Unbound Object Frame

Operators For Expressions

Expressions are fundamental to specify criteria for queries and macros or Access Basic.

An expression can include a combination of operators, identifiers, literal values, contstants and functions.

Operator	Conditions	Syntax	Description
*	If value is Null or Empty result is Null or 0.	result=<value> ***** <value>	Multiplies two numbers together.
+	+ can be used to concatenate strings. For safety of concatenation use &.	result=<value> **+** <value>	Adds two numbers together.
-	If value is Null or Empty result is Null or 0.	result=<value> **-** <value> **-** <value>	Subtracts two numbers or creates a negative.
/	If value is Null or Empty result is Null or 0.	result=<value> **/** <value>	Divides two floating point numbers.
\	If value is Null or Empty result is Null or 0.	result=<value> \ <value>	Divides two integers. Result is either an Integer or a Long.
^	Multiple exponentions are carried out left to right. If either is Null result is Null.	result=<value> ^ <value>	Raises a number to the power of an exponent.
Mod	Returns only the remainder of the result as an integer. If value is Null or Empty result is Null or 0.	result=<value> **Mod** <value>	Divides two numbers, e.g. 6Mod2.3 result = 1.
And	Both values must be nonzero (true) to get True. If either is 0 then result is False.	result=expr1 **And** expr2	Logical conjunction on two expressions.
Eqv	If value is Null or Empty result is Null or 0.	result=expr1 Eqv expr2	Logical equivalence on two expressions.

Operator	Conditions	Syntax	Description
Imp	expr1 expr2 result true true true true false false true null null false true true false false true false null true null true true null false null null null null	result=expr1 **Imp** expr2	Logical implication on two expressions.
Not	exp result true false false true null null	result= Not expr	Negates a numeric expression.
&	Value that are Empty (0) treated as zero length string.	result= <value> **&** <value>	Forces string concatenation of two values.
Or	expr1 expr2 result true true true true false true true null true false true true false false false false null null null true true null false null null null null	result=<value> **Or** <value>	Logical disjunction on two expressions.
Xor	expr1 expr2 result true true false true false true false true true false false false	result=<value> **Xor** <value>	Logical exclusion on two expressions.

Operator	Conditions	Syntax	Description
Between...And	First element of syntax is the field where data is. Next two elements are expressions against which you evaluate the expression. Including [Not] gives the opposite condition, i.e. values are not within said range.	expr [Not] **Between** <value> **And** <value>	Discovers whether the value of an expression is within (or not) a specified range of values.
In	First element of syntax is the field where data is. Next two elements are expressions against which you evaluate the expression. Including [Not] gives the opposite condition, i.e. values are not in the list.	expr [Not] **In** (<value>,<value>,<value> etc.)	Discovers whether the value of an expression is equivalent (or not) to any values in a list.
Is	Can be used with [Not] to see if expression is not null.	expr **Is** [Not] Null	Discovers whether an expression is Null (or Not).
Like	Can use wild cards or a complete value in a field. Can be used with [] and & "*" to receive input from user. To search for a control, put identifier in "" and | |.	Like "pattern"	Compares two string expressions.

Comparison Operators

Operator	Conditions	Syntax	Description
<	true expr1 < expr2 false expr1 > = expr2 null 1 or 2 = null	result = expr1 < expr2	Less than.
<=	true expr1 <= expr2 false expr1 > expr2 null 1 or 2 = null	expr1 < = expr2	Less than or equal to.
>	true expr1 > expr2 false expr1 < = expr2 null 1 or 2 = null	expr1 > expr2	Greater than.
> =	true expr1 > = expr2 false expr1 < expr2 null 1 or 2 = null	expr1 > = expr2	Greater than or equal to.
=	true expr1 = expr2 false expr1 <> expr2 null 1 or 2 = null	expr = expr2	Equal to.
<>	true expr1 <> expr2 false expr1 = expr2 null 1 or 2 = null	expr1 <> expr2	Not equal to.

Identifiers For Expressions

Use identifiers to mark the the value of a field or control for an expression. Enclose the name in brackets, e.g: [Prices] will give the value of the field / control Prices to the expression.
To give more accuracy you may place the name of the Form or Report, for example, in front of the normal identifier. E.g, Reports![Foreign]![Prices].

Use ! and . as the identifier operators.

Do not use the .(dot) operator before a field name.

Conditions

Both the above operators show the relationship between fields, controls and properties. The ! operator is followed by a user defined name. The . operator is usually followed by a property name.

Constants For Expressions

Constant values cannot change. There are three kinds of constant:

- Intrinsic constants
- System constants (Yes,No,On,Off,Null)
- Access Basic constants

Intrinsic Constants

These can be used in coding in modules, when Access is started. They have to remain unchanged - you cannot re-declare them. Intrinsic constants should not have the same name as your created constants. See the list of intrinsics in Help under:

- Data access constants
- Event procedure constants
- Macro action constants
- Security constants
- Variant constants
- Miscellaneous constants

System Constants

Use these constants anywhere in Access except in a module. Use after =; e.g. Reports![Customers].Visible = No.

See Help for Access Basic constant examples.

APPENDIX III

Macros Keyword Guide

This appendix tells you all the macros that can be assigned to a special key or key combination, and explains what each macro can do.

Macro Task	Is Used To...	Refinements Include...
AddMenu	Include custom menus onto the menu bars. This Macro will create a custom menu bar and adds a drop-down menu as given by the refinements. Several of these tasks are usually grouped together in one macro, one for each of the custom menu entries that you required. See the Nwind Order Review Form and Order Review Custom Menu Macro for details of a working model.	Menu Name - used to specify the custom menu that this option will be attached to. Menu Macro Name - used to specify the macro that will be executed when this option is selected. Status Bar Text - text that will appear on the status bar when this option is highlighted on the appropriate custom menu.
ApplyFilter	Remotely apply a filter to some given data. This restricts the displayed information in a report or form by the application of a named filter to the appropriate underlying object records.	Filter Name - the name of the filter that will be applied. Where Condition - an SQL statement that you can use instead of a pre-defined filter.
Beep	Inform the user of some event. This produces a sound.	None.
CancelEvent	Controlling the action flow. This cancels the event that caused the execution of the macro that this task is part of. You cannot use this with macros that define menu actions or for the OnClose report event.	None. This task can only be used with the following events - BeforeDelConfirm, Before Insert, BeforeUpdate, DblClick, Delete, Exit, Format, KeyPress, MouseDown, Open, Print and Unload.
Close	Close either a form, query, report or a table. This can close either a specified window or the active window, i.e. the window that currently has the focus. If the Database window has the focus when you run a Close action with no window specified, then Access will close the database.	Object Type : used to identify the type of object that you wish to close. Leave this blank to close the active window. Object Name : used to specifically identify the object that you wish to close.
CopyObject	Copy any object in the current database with a new name or with any specified name to another Microsoft Access database	Destination Database - the new database that the object will be copied to. New Name - the new name that the object will be given Source Object Type - the type of object that you wish to copy. Source Object Name - the specific object that you wish copied.

DeleteObject	Delete any form, macro, module, query, report or table. If you don't specify a particular object, Access will delete the active object without a warning message.	Object Type - the type of object that you wish to delete. Object Name - the specific object that you wish to delete.
DoMenuItem	Control the action flow. This executes a command from the standard Microsoft Access menu bar. It can be used in a macro that defines a custom menu to make selected Access menu commands available on the custom menu.	Menu Bar - used to select the menu bar that holds the command that you wish to execute. Menu Name - used to specify the menu to choose the command to perform. Command - the command that you wish to use. Subcommand - used to specify any subcommands that may be necessary.
Echo	Inform Access whether or not you wish the screen to be updated while a macro is running. This allows you to hide the results of the macro's actions, but dialog boxes will still appear. Echo is automatically turned on when a macro is completed.	Echo On - select Yes if you want the screen to update, No if you don't. Status Bar Text - used to place text on the status bar to inform the user of what is going on.
FindNext	Find the next record that meets the criteria previously set by a FindRecord task or in the Find dialog box.	None.
FindRecord	Find a record that meets search criteria specified in the macro action. You can specify all the parameters available in the Find dialog box using this macro task.	Find What - the criteria for the search. Where - which part of the selected field to search in. Match Case - is the search case sensitive? Yes/No. Direction - which way does the search take place through the records, Up or Down. Search As Formatted - does the format of the entry make a difference to the search. Search In - the field that you wish to apply the search criteria to. Find First - start here (No) or at the first record (Yes).

GoToControl	Set the focus to the specified control in the current record.	Control Name - the specific control that you wish the focus to move to.
GoToPage	Move to a specified page in a report or form.	Page Number - the number of the page on the current form or report that you wish to move to. Right - this moves the top left of the Access window this distance to the right when the page is too large to fit completely into the window. Down - this moves the top left of the Access window down this distance.
GoToRecord	Move to a different record and make it current in the specified form, query or table. You can move to the first, last next or previous record. When you specify "next" or "previous" record, you can move by more than one. You can also go to a specific record number or to the new record place holder at the end of the set.	Object Type - the type of object that contains the record that you wish to move to. Object Name - the name of the object you wish to move to. Record - the manner in which you wish to move. Offset - either the number of pages that you wish to move in the given direction or the number of the record that you wish to move to.
Hourglass	Change the mouse pointer to an hourglass icon while a macro runs. Access automatically sets Hourglass On to No when the macro is completed.	Hourglass On - select Yes to change the pointer to the hourglass, No to change it back.
Maximize	Maximize the active window, i.e. the window with the focus.	None.
Minimize	Minimise the window with the focus to an icon at the bottom of the screen.	None.
MoveSize	Move and size the active window, i.e. the window that has the focus.	Right - the new horizontal position of the top left corner of the window relative to the current position. Down - the new vertical position of the top left corner of the window. Height - the new height of the window. Width - the new width of the window.

MsgBox	Display a warning or informational message to the user, and optionally to produce a sound. It is necessary to click OK to close the box and proceed.	Message - the text that will appear in the main body of the message box. Beep - does the computer make a sound when the message box appears? Yes/No. Type - the type of icon that appears in the message box - see the Help screen MsgBox Action for a listing. Title - the text that will appear in the title bar of the message box.
OpenForm	Open a form in either Datasheet, Design, Form or Print Preview. You can also apply a filter or a Where condition to a Datasheet view, Form view or Print Preview.	Form - the name of the form which you wish to open. View - the view that you wish the form to be opened in. Filter Name - the name of the filter that you want to apply to the records that the form is used to show. Where Condition - an SQL expression used as an ad hoc filter. Data Mode - marks the restrictions that are imposed on the user's ability to alter any data in this form. Window Mode - the type of window used to display the form i.e. normal/ hidden/icon/dialog.
OpenModule	Open a module in design view and display the named procedure.	Module - the name of the Access Basic container that contains the procedure you wish to view. Leave this blank to search all modules for the given procedure. Procedure - the name of the procedure you wish to view. Leave this blank to view the Declarations section of the given module
OpenQuery	Open a query in Datasheet, Design view, or Print Preview. If you specify an action query, Microsoft Access performs updates specified by the query.	Query Name - the name of the query that you wish to work with. View - the view of the query that you wish to see. This is only applicable to Select or Crosstab queries. Data Mode - marks the restrictions that are imposed on the user's ability to alter any data in this query.

OpenReport	Open a report in Print Preview (as default), prints the report, or opens the report in Design view. A filter or Where condition can also be specified for Print and Print Preview.	Report - the name of the report that you are interested in. View - the view that you wish to have of the specified report. Filter Name - the name of a predefined filter that restricts the records that are included in the report. Where Condition - an SQL expression used as an ad hoc filter.
OpenTable	Open a table in Datasheet, Design view or Print Preview.	Table Name - the name of the table that you wish to work with. View - the view of the table that you wish to see. Data Mode - marks the restrictions that are imposed on the user's ability to alter any data in this table.
OutputTo	Output the named table, query, form, report or module to a Microsoft Excel (XLS), Microsoft Word for Windows (RTF), or windows Notepad text (TXT) file and optionally start the application to edit the file. For forms, the data output is from the form's Datasheet view. For reports, Microsoft Access outputs all controls containing data (including calculated controls) except memo, OLE, and sub-form or sub-report controls. Some of the data in the new copy of the object may change when this translation takes place e.g. Yes/ No is translated to -1/0.	Object Type - the type of object that you wish to output. Object Name - the name of the object that you wish to output. Object Format - the format of the file that you will output to, i.e. Excel (.xls). Object File - the name of the file that you will output the specific object to. Auto Start - whether or not the application is booted up to allow you to edit the output.
Print	Print the active object in the open database. Can also print the active datasheet, form, or report. A range of pages can be specified, also the number of copies, print quality and collation. You must use one of the Open... tasks if you wish to restrict the records that will be printed out.	Print Range - the selection of pages from the active object you require printed. Page From - the first page to be printed when you select Pages in the Print Range refinement. Page To - the last page to be printed. Print Quality - the quality of the print out that you require. Copies - the number of copies of the object that you require printed out. Collate Copies - are the copies collated? Yes/No.

Quit	Close all windows and exit Access. Access does not run any actions that follow Quit in a macro!	Options - used to inform Access of what to do with any unsaved data that is in the open windows when Quit is requested.
Rename	Rename the specified object in the current database. The new name must follow Access standard naming conventions.	New Name - the new name you wish to apply to the given object. Object Type - the type of object that you wish to rename. Old Name - the specific object that you wish to rename.
RepaintObject	Force the repainting, i.e. updating, of the screen for the specified object. Also it forces recalculation of any of the formulas in controls on that object.	Object Type - the type of object that you wish to update. Leave this blank to update the object in the active window. Object Name - the exact object that you wish to update.
Requery	Ensure that the active object or one of its controls displays the most recent data. If no control is specified, this action requeries the source of the object itself. Controls include: list boxes, combo boxes, sub forms and OLE objects.	Control - this is the name of the control that you wish to requery. Leaving this refinement blank tells Access that you wish to requery the underlying table or query.
Restore	Reverse the last maximise or minimise that was applied to the active window.	None.
RunApp	Starts another MS-DOS or Microsoft Windows application.	Command Line - this is the full path name that you would type in at the MS-DOS C:\> prompt.
RunCode	Execute an Access Basic function procedure. Other actions following this action execute after the function is completed. (Note: to execute an Access Basic sub-procedure, call that procedure with another function.)	Function Name - this is the name of the Access Basic function that you wish to execute. Remember to follow the name of the function with two brackets, e.g; MyFunction().
RunMacro	Execute another Macro. Actions following this action execute after the other macro is completed. The macro can be part of a macro group. You can produce a similar effect on macros with this task as you can when you nest queries.	Macro Name - the name of the macro that you wish to run. Repeat Count - the number of times that you wish the macro to be executed. Repeat expression - the macro keeps repeating until the expression given here evaluates to false.

RunSQL	Execute the specified SQL INSERT, DELETE, SELECT...INTO, or UPDATE statement. You can refer to form controls in the statement to limit the affected records. If a complex query is needed (more than 256 characters long), then it will be necessary to use the Access BASIC version of RunSQL instead.	SQL Statement - the SQL code that you wish to execute.
SelectObject	Select the window for the specified object. This can be used in tandem with Restore or Maximise to open up a minimised object.	Object Type - the type of object that you wish to work upon. Object Name - the name of the specific object that you wish to work upon. In Database Window - choose Yes to select from the initial database window, No to select from objects that are already open.
SendKeys	Store keystrokes in the keyboard buffer, i.e. the list of keystrokes that Access is waiting to use. If you intend to send keystrokes to a modal form or dialog box, you must execute the SendKeys action before opening that feature.	Keystrokes - the list of keystrokes that you wish to add onto the end of the keyboard buffer. Wait - inform Access of whether or not the macro should pause until the keystrokes have been processed.
SendObject	Output a table datasheet, a query datasheet, a form datasheet, data in text boxes on a report, or a module listing to a Microsoft Excel (XLS), Microsoft Word for Windows (RTF), or windows Notepad text (TXT) file and embed the data in an electronic mail message. You must specify to whom the message is to be sent. You must have Email software installed that conforms to the MAPI (mail application software interface) standard.	Object Type - the type of object that you wish to mail. Object Name - the name of the object that you wish to mail. Output Format - the format of the file that you wish to mail the given object in, e.g. Excel (.xls). To - the names of the recipients of the mailed object. Cc - the names that will appear on the Cc line of the mail header. Bcc - the names that will appear on the Bcc line of the mail header. Subject - the text that will appear on the Subject line of the mail header. Message Text - any text that you wish to add to the database object. If you leave the Object Type and Object Name refinements blank, just the text

		given here will be sent. Edit Message - specifies whether or not the message can be edited before it is sent.
SetValue	Change the value of any control or property that it is possible for you to update manually.	Item - the name of the control that you wish to modify. Expression - the new entry for that control or the expression that will be performed upon the current contents to get the new entry.
SetWarnings	Cause an automatic Enter key response to all system warning or informational messages displayed in a dialog box. This does not halt the display of error messages. To avoid the display of the error messages this macro should be used in conjunction with the echo action set to Off. Caution must be used with regards to system messages; you may not want to continue with a macro if certain warnings are displayed.	Warnings On - select Yes to see all appropriate warnings as they are generated, No to remove the system warnings for the picture.
ShowAllRecords	Remove any previously applied filters to the active form.	None.
ShowToolbar	Hide/show any of the standard or custom toolbars.	Toolbar Name - the name of the toolbar that you wish to hide or show. Show - select Yes to make the toolbar appear on screen, No to hide it.
StopAllMacros	Stop all macros that are currently running.	None.
StopMacros	Stop the macro that contains this task.	None.
Transfer Database	Export data to or import data from another Microsoft Access, dBASE, Paradox, FoxPro, Btrieve, or SQL database. This task can also be used to attach tables or files from any of	Transfer Type - type of transfer that you wish to use, i.e. import, export or attach. Database Type - type of database that you wish to interact with. Database Name - the full path file

	those databases.	name of the database that you wish to interact with. Object Type - the type of object that you wish to pass around. Source - object that you wish to pass around. Use the object's full name, including file extensions if applicable. Destination - the new name of the object when it reaches it's destination. Structure Only - do you only want the structure of the object (Yes) or do you want the data as well (No)?
TransferSpreadsheet	Export or import data from Microsoft Excel or Lotus 1-2-3 spreadsheet files.	Transfer Type - the type of transfer you wish to use, i.e. import / export. Spreadsheet Type - the type of spreadsheet that you wish to interact with. Table Name - the name of the Access Table that the interaction with the spreadsheet will affect. File Name - the full path name of the appropriate spreadsheet file. Has Field Names - specifies whether to include the idea of field names in the import/ export. Range - the range of cells that you wish to import. Leave this blank to import the entire spreadsheet. On exporting Access ignores this refinement.
TransferText	Export or import data from text files.	Transfer Type - the type of transfer you wish to use, i.e. import / export. Specification Name - the name of the specification that describes the type and rules of this type of transfer. These are set using the Imp/Exp Setup command obtained from the File menu. Table Name - name of Access Table that interaction with the spreadsheet will affect. You can also use a Select Query name here. File Name - the full path name of the appropriate text file. Has Field Names - specifies whether to include the idea of field names in the import/export.

APPENDIX IV

The Main Access 2.0 Toolbars

The following are the standard Toolbars you will find on the major screens in Access 2.0.

- Database Toolbar
- Table Design Toolbar
- Table Datasheet Toolbar
- Query Design Toolbar
- Query Database Toolbar
- Form Design Toolbar
- Form View/Datasheet Toolbar
- Report Design Toolbar
- Print Preview Toolbar
- Macro Design Toolbar
- Module Design Toolbar
- MS Graph Standard Toolbar
- MS Graph Formatting
- MS Graph Drawing Toolbar

Over the next few pages, you will see each of these toolbars, complete with annotations.

Database Toolbar

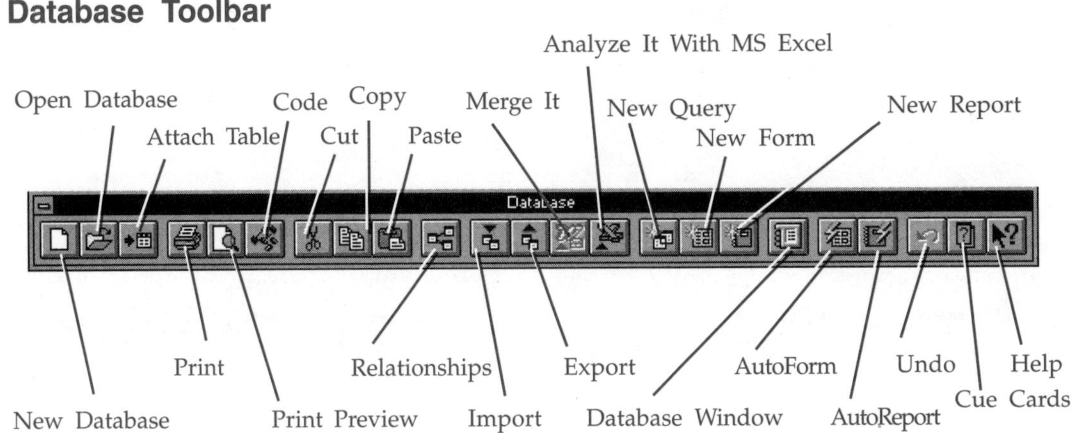

Table Design Toolbar

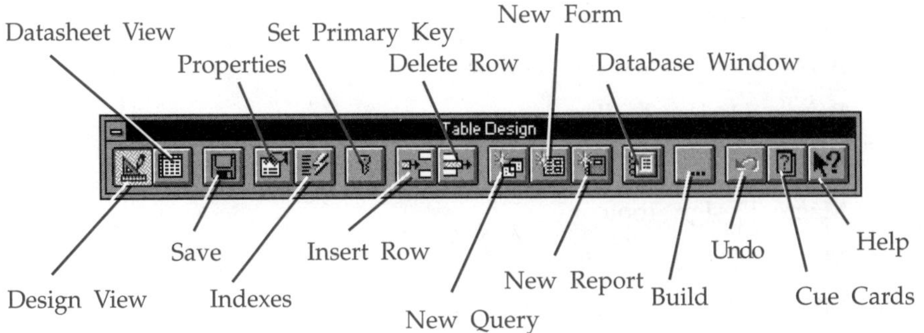

Table Datasheet Toolbar

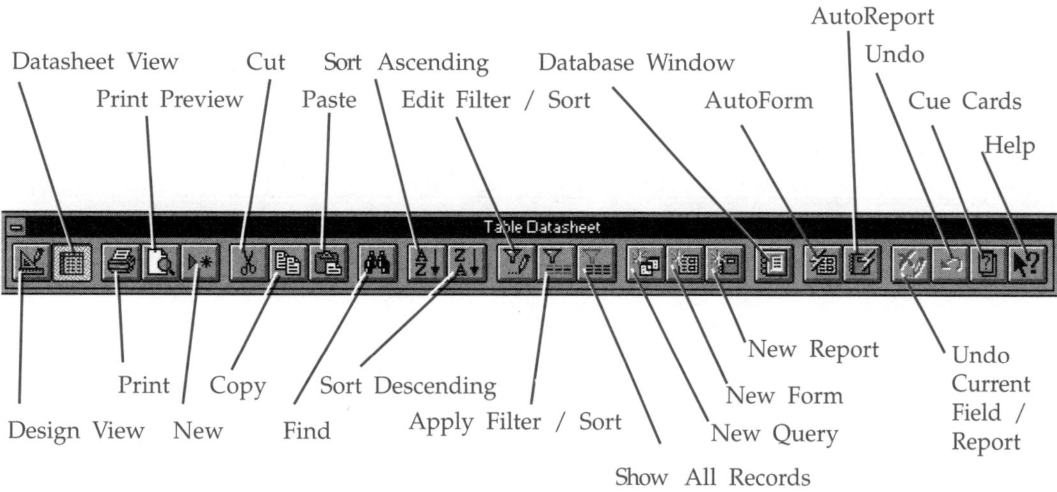

Query Design Toolbar

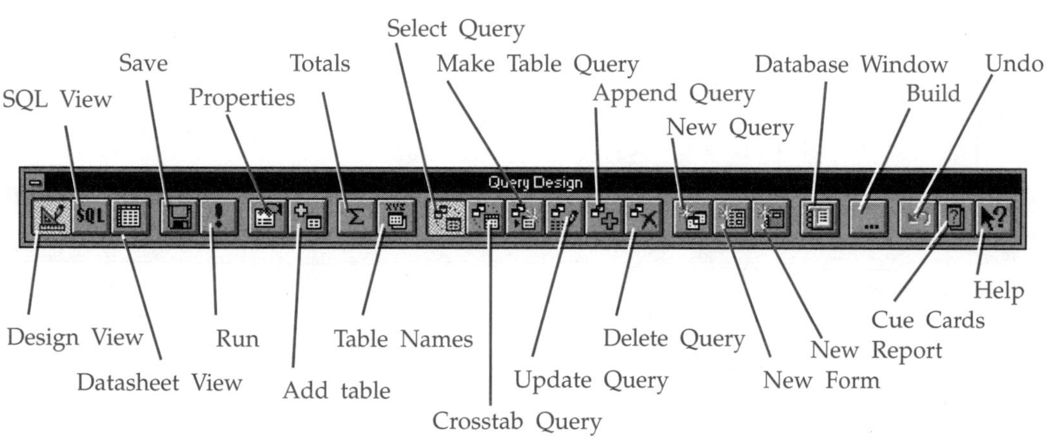

Query Datasheet Toolbar

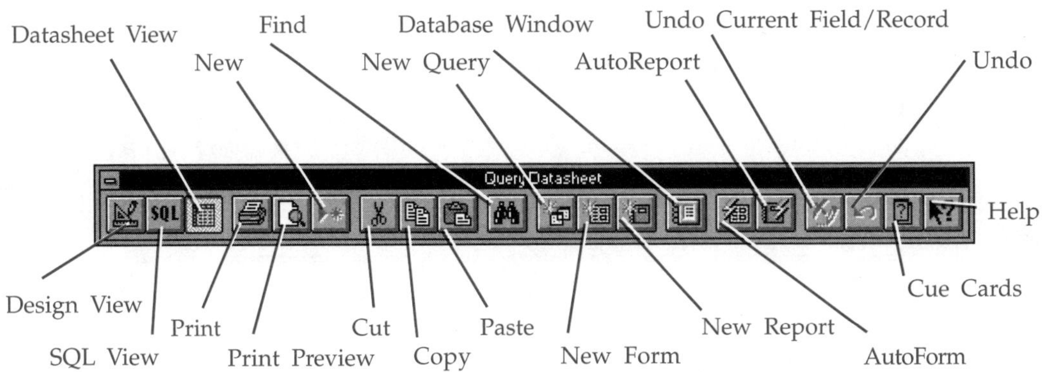

Form Design Toolbar

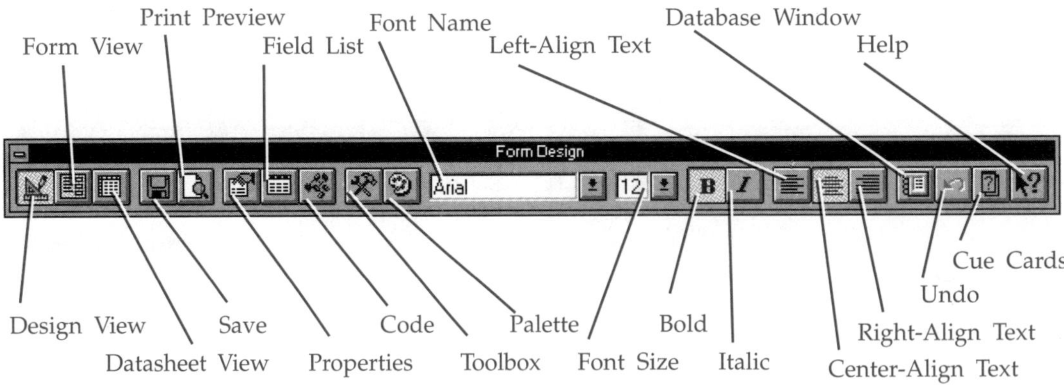

Form View / Datasheet Toolbar

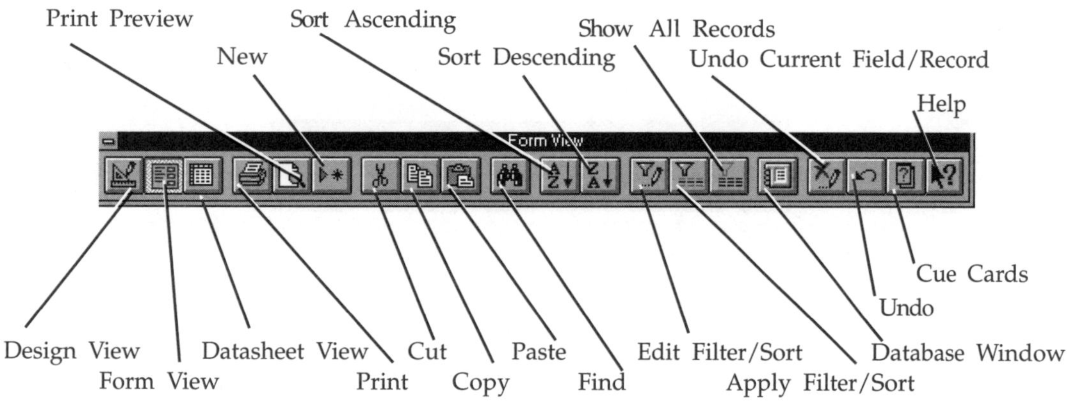

Report Design Toolbar

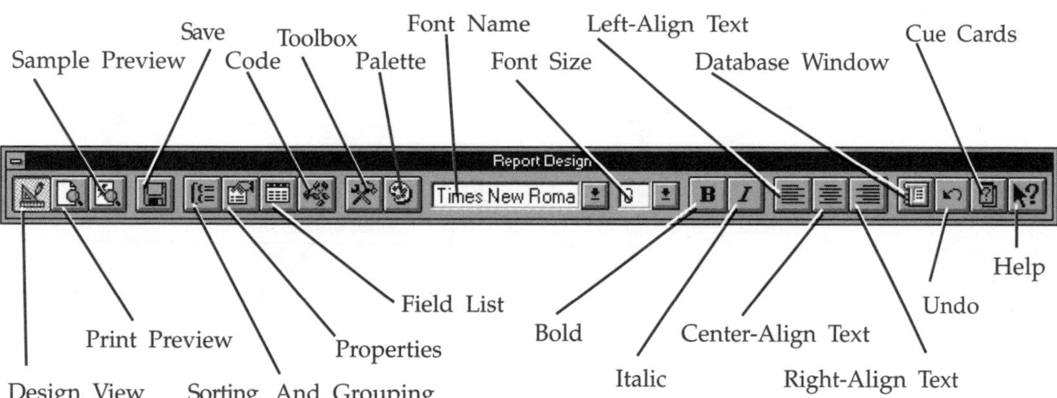

Print Preview Toolbar

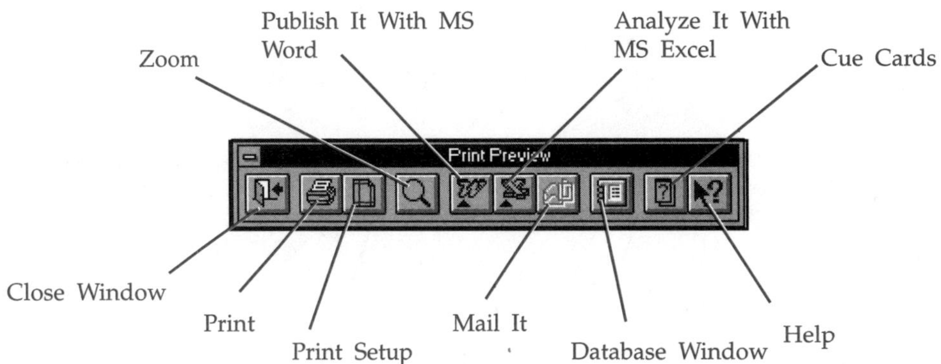

Macro Design Toolbar

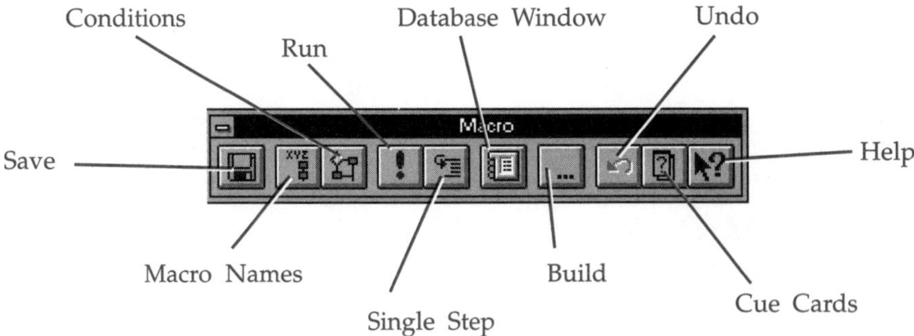

Module Design Toolbar

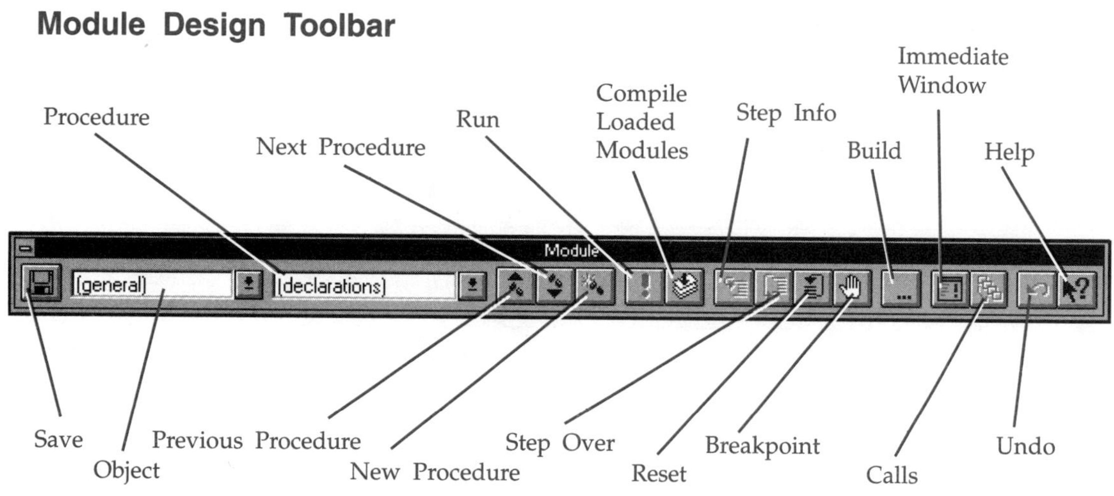

MS Graph Standard Toolbar

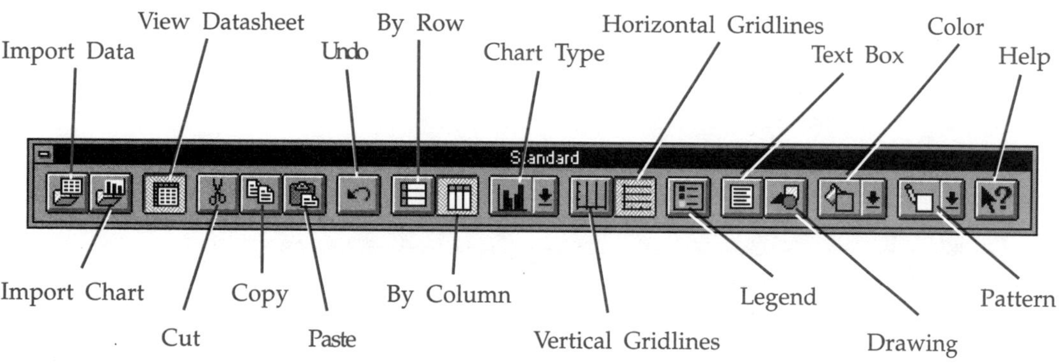

MS Graph Formatting Toolbar

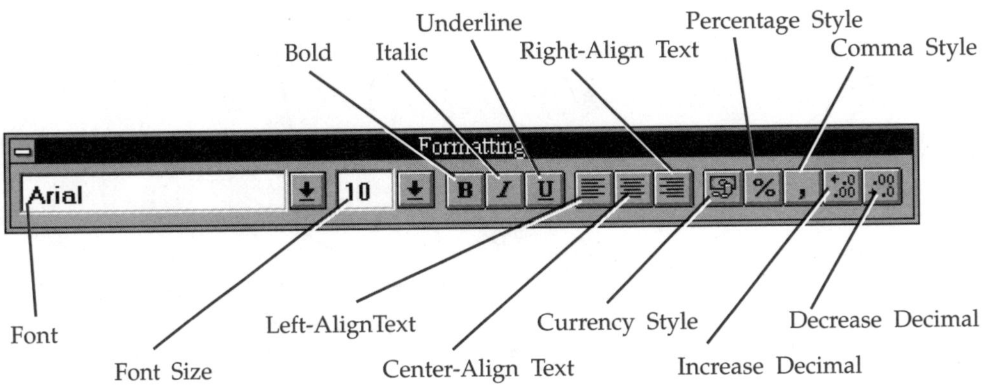

MS Graph Drawing Toolbar

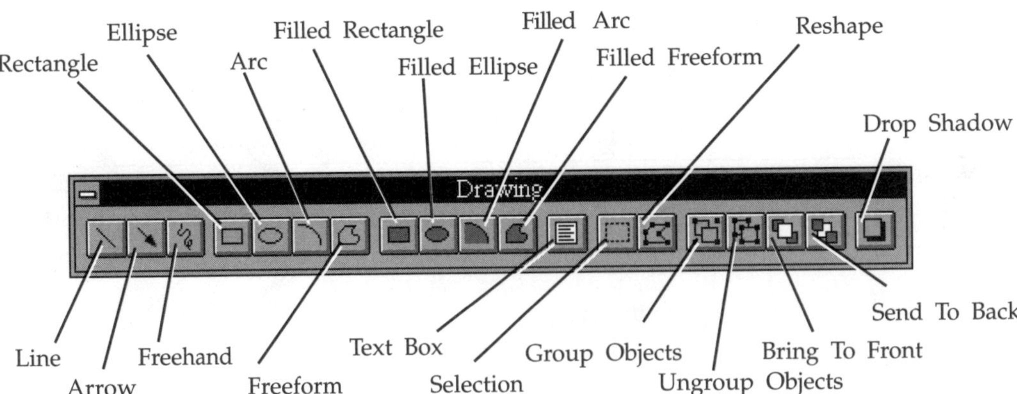

Index

G

H

N

O

S

T

The Beginner's Guide to Visual Basic

Takes a holistic approach to teaching Visual Basic, building up skills around actual tasks rather than the standard groupings of the language. The book focuses on hands-on tutorials with plenty of screen shots and example programs.

Author: Peter Wright
Includes disk
$29.95 / £27.99
ISBN 1-874416-19-2

The Beginner's Guide to Turbo Pascal

Turbo Pascal is the ideal language for the ambitious beginner in programming who wants to get into applications beyond the limitations implicit in BASIC. This book takes you on the fast track of learning, providing you with an easy and rapid route to the power of Turbo Pascal and introducing the basic concepts of the latest programming methodology - Object Oriented Programming.

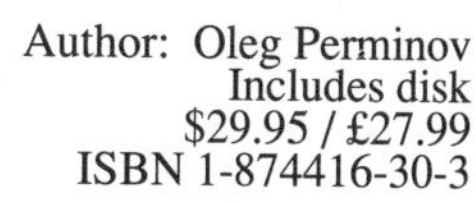

Author: Oleg Perminov
Includes disk
$29.95 / £27.99
ISBN 1-874416-30-3

The Revolutionary Guide to Visual C++

The book teaches the essentials of objects to allow the reader to write Windows programs with the MFC. Section One of the book allows the C programmer to quickly get to terms with the difference between C and C++, including the concepts involved in object oriented design and programming. Sections Two and Three are a comprehensive guide to writing complete Windows applications.

Author: Ben Ezzell
Includes disk
$39.95 / £37.49
ISBN 1-874416-22-2

The Beginner's Guide to C

This is a well-structured tutorial on application programming, not merely a language reference. The author builds a complete application with the reader, step by step, leaving them with a useful tool and a sense of achievement. The ANSI C language is given comprehensive coverage in a friendly environment.

Author: G. Kesler
$29.95 / £27.99
ISBN 1-874416-15-X

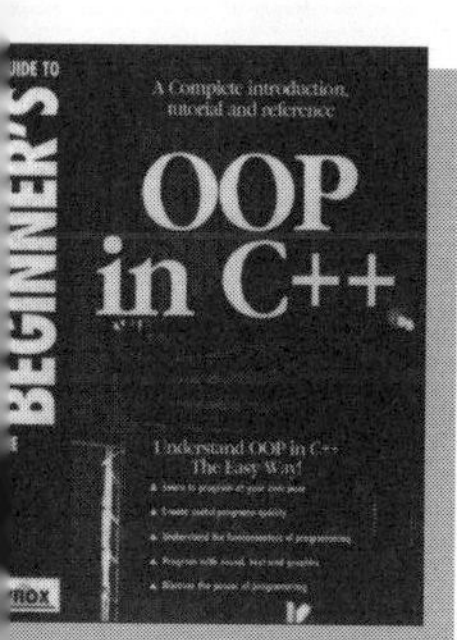

The Beginner's Guide to OOP in C++

This Beginner's Guide teaches OOP to programmers from the procedural world, assuming a small amount of programming knowledge. The information is presented in a manner which teaches aspects of the language on a need-to-know basis. This gives the reader not only the tools, but also the methodology to actually use them.

Author: L. Romanovskaya
$29.95 / £27.99
ISBN 1-874416-27-3

World Class Programming

ENTER NOW!

Fill in the card below and return it to us to receive

AN UPDATE ON ALL WROX TITLES

and enter the draw for the

5 WROX TITLES OF YOUR CHOICE

FILL THIS OUT to enter the draw for free Wrox titles

Name ______________________

Address ______________________

____

____

______________ Post code/Zip ______________

Occupation ______________________

How did you hear about this book ?

- ☐ Book review (name) ______________
- ☐ Advertisement (name) ______________
- ☐ Recommendation
- ☐ Catalog
- ☐ Other ______________

Where did you buy this book?

- ☐ Bookstore (name) ______________
- ☐ Computer Store (name) ______________
- ☐ Mail Order
- ☐ Other ______________

What influenced you in the purchase of this book?

- ☐ Cover Design
- ☐ Contents
- ☐ Use of Color
- ☐ Other (please specify)

How did you rate the overall contents of this book?

- ☐ Excellent
- ☐ Good
- ☐ Average
- ☐ Poor

____

What did you find most useful about this book? ______________

____

What did you find least useful about this book? ______________

____

Please add any additional comments? ______________

____

What other subjects will you buy a computer book on soon?

____

What is the best computer book you have used this year?

____

Please do not put me on your mailing list ☐

214

WROX PRESS INC.

Free phone from USA 1 800 814 3461
Fax (312) 462 4063

Wrox writes books for you. Any suggestions or ideas about how you want information given in a modern book will be studied by our team. Your comments are always valued at Wrox.

Compuserve 100063,2152.
UK Tel (4421) 706 6826 Fax (4421) 706 2967

Computer Book Publishers

WROX PRESS LIMITED *
FREEPOST BM6303
1334 WARWICK ROAD
BIRMINGHAM
B27 6PR
U.K.

WROX PRESS INC *
2710, W TOUHY
CHICAGO
IL 60645
U.S.A.

* Delete as appropriate